ALSO BY JEANINE BASINGER

I Do and I Don't: A History of Marriage in the Movies

The Star Machine

Silent Stars

The "It's a Wonderful Life" Book

The World War II Combat Film: Anatomy of a Genre

Anthony Mann

A Woman's View: How Hollywood Spoke to Women, 1930–1960

American Cinema: One Hundred Years of Filmmaking

The Movie Musical!

The
Movie Musical!

Jeanine Basinger

ALFRED A. KNOPF | NEW YORK | 2019

THIS IS A BORZOI BOOK
PUBLISHED BY ALFRED A. KNOPF

Copyright © 2019 by Jeanine Basinger

All rights reserved.
Published in the United States by Alfred A. Knopf,
a division of Penguin Random House LLC, New York, and
distributed in Canada by Random House of Canada, a division
of Penguin Random House Canada Limited, Toronto.

www.aaknopf.com

Knopf, Borzoi Books, and the colophon
are registered trademarks of Penguin Random House LLC.

Library of Congress Cataloging-in-Publication Data
Names: Basinger, Jeanine, author.
Title: The movie musical! / Jeanine Basinger.
Description: New York : Alfred A. Knopf, 2019. | Includes bibliographical references and index.
Identifiers: LCCN 2018046325 (print) | LCCN 2018049809 (ebook) |
ISBN 9781101874073 (e-book) | ISBN 9781101874066 (hc)
Subjects: LCSH: Musical films—United States—History and criticism.
Classification: LCC PN1995.9.M86 (ebook) | LCC PN1995.9.M86 B38 2019 (print) | DDC 791.43/6—dc23
LC record available at https://lccn.loc.gov/2018046325

Jacket image: *Singin' in the Rain*, 1952. Credit: MGM/Photofest
Jacket design by Carol Devine Carson

Manufactured in the United States of America
First Edition

For my daughter, Savannah, and my granddaughter, Kulani,
who share my love of dance

Contents

Introduction

I WAS RAISED ON MUSICALS, and I love them. I feel as if the day I first opened my eyes I was looking at the hot pop of 1940s Technicolor, and Betty Grable was singing and dancing to "Run Little Raindrop Run." Rita Hayworth was rushing down a long stairway from somewhere in heaven, her golden gown billowing out behind her. Fred Astaire was singing "My Shining Hour" to Joan Leslie, while Judy Garland and Gene Kelly stepped around lightly, "Ballin' the Jack," etc., etc., etc. Millions of people my age have the same memories, the same cultural touchstones, and they were musical, magical, and memorable . . . but "musical" is the key element. I was drawn to the adult emotions implied in the songs and dances, to which, because they were only songs and dances, a child was allowed access. In the midwestern world I grew up in during World War II, it was considered not only bad manners but downright unpatriotic to shout and scream and shove your emotions down someone else's throat. Everybody was sharing in the shortages, the sadnesses, the losses, and the suffering, so just keep it quiet, please. Go to a musical and let yourself feel it through song and dance. Zip-a-Dee-Doo-Dah.

My oldest sister took me to a revival of a movie made the year I was born, *Swing Time*, with Fred Astaire and Ginger Rogers. I already knew I liked "old" movies—this wasn't my first one. I had been introduced to Keaton and Chaplin, Harold Lloyd and Gloria Swanson, the Marx Brothers, Errol

Flynn and Olivia de Havilland, Greta Garbo and Jean Harlow and plenty more. I knew Astaire from *Holiday Inn* and Ginger Rogers as Kitty Foyle, but *Swing Time* was my first Fred-and-Ginger-together as singers/dancers, and it had everything: comedy, music, glamorous clothes, ritzy nightclubs, fur coats, and even fake snowflakes that were pretty and fluffy (as opposed to the ones I was experiencing on a daily basis, which were cold, ugly, and blowing in my face at about forty miles an hour).

I liked all the musical numbers of *Swing Time*, but there was one that allowed me to feel what it must be like to be a grown-up. It took place in a sparkly nightclub that had apparently been built on the side of a hill, because it had a steep incline. You entered at the top, walked down some stairs, and if you wanted to dance, you had to go all the way down to the bottom and find the shiny black floor. All I could think about was that I wouldn't want to have to wait tables in that place. (Children are always practical.) The nightclub had cellophane tablecloths and globular table lamps and orchids and all kinds of amazing things that I wanted to have for my own. There was a big crowd of people who seemed to be having so much fun, and they had hairdos and jewelry and tuxedos and boutonnieres, and I liked all that stuff, but what I liked best was when all of them had gone home and the nightclub was left empty . . . all except for Fred Astaire and Ginger Rogers. A lot of plot had gone down, and I knew that, as always happened in movies before it got sorted out, a real problem had come up and it meant that Fred and Ginger were never going to be together. I knew that movie moment, and it always arrived. I hated its disappointment and misunderstanding and its stopping of the film while I waited for it to get resolved and go away.

Ah, but *Swing Time* gave me "that moment" in musical terms. Faced with separation, Fred and Ginger did not weep, did not beat their breasts, did not slap one another, did not exchange desperate words, did not stop the forward motion of my viewing world. None of that. Instead, they took to the dance floor and performed a hauntingly beautiful, palpably heartbroken (yet still exhilarating) song and dance while the Silver Sandal nightclub glittered and winked behind them.

I never forget what happens. At first, Ginger tries to walk away. She and Fred have had a clumsy conversation in their attempt to say goodbye, and he's pledged that after he's danced with her, he's "never gonna dance again." She leaves him, turning and beginning to climb the inexplicably jagged black stairs. Reluctant to let her go, Astaire follows and in medium close-up begins to sing strange lyrics about "never gonna dance," and "la belle, la perfectly swell romance" and "though I'm left without a penny, the wolf was discreet" and "weird tattoos of the St. Louis Blues," none of which meant anything to me at the time. While he sings, the movie cuts to Rogers, standing against the background of the glittering nightclub, sparkling in her white dress, already set apart from him in a separate world of unattainable dreams. She sighs deeply, turns, and continues to climb, but he presses on. "All I really want is you," he sings. He vows his love, his face a triangular pucker of pain and misery. Resigned, she turns and walks past him, descending to the floor as the music changes to "The Way You Look Tonight." She takes the floor, and they walk, holding hands, not looking at each other, and then they flow forward into dancing. They weave and sway. They bend and turn, with Rogers's serpentine back undulating. When the music returns to "Never Gonna Dance," she tries again to walk away, but he grabs her, almost roughly, and spins her toward him. Then they take off. It's goodbye sex of the purest form, as the music gives us their past relationship by repeating the music they've shared while falling in love. "Waltz in Swing Time" rockets out, and they whirl and twirl, with each finally leaving the other to ascend opposite staircases, dancing upward. At the top of the stairs, the only cut after the dance begins takes place, reflecting the practiced separation they've endured to get up there and the one that will follow. After a final crescendo of rising passion and a frenzy of spins, Rogers flies out the door on her tiny slippered feet. She's gone, just gone. Astaire is left alone, his arms stretched out to her. *He's* never gonna dance, but *I* had found my movie genre.

This book, *The Movie Musical!* is an effort to tell the story of that genre "from then to now": its birth, its development, its star performers and plot strategies, and ultimately its evolution into an original American art form. Much time and energy have gone into books and articles defining the western, which is considered the quintessential American movie genre. Yet the musical, too, is an original format that grew from our earlier traditions and moved into the movies at a specific time and dominated the box office. Of course, many informative and important books on musicals have already been written, although perhaps not quite as many as on the western film. There are beautiful, lavishly illustrated picture books that evoke viewing memories of films we've enjoyed; reliable books that document the films (and their songs) for reference; highly focused books that analyze individual artists such as Fred Astaire, Gene Kelly, Judy Garland, and the

Astaire/Rogers team; well-researched histories that examine specialized eras of musical development like the transition to sound, the Depression, and World War II; books that explain changes brought by the technological developments of sound, color, widescreen, and special effects; studies of movie choreographers Charles Walters, George Balanchine, and Gower Champion; and scholarly analyses that theorize on the genre's difference from other films (and which sometimes offer thought-provoking questions: "Is Cyd Charisse a dancing penis?"). But I wanted to write a summation of all those things, the story of how the Hollywood studio system adapted to the new genre's possibility when sound liberated the musical universe. I wanted to look at the musical as it evolved over time, step by step, film by film, taking two steps forward and one step backward in the inevitable way that a commercially dominated art form would evolve. I wanted to try to see the genre emerge as the business adapted and shaped, making successes and failures, always linking the product to the reactions of an audience. I'm fascinated by the concept of Hollywood at work—the business that was the art, or the art that was the business—a system using and reusing, stealing from Broadway and Europe, yet managing to develop an original definition for the American musical. With a touch of larceny, a jolt of energy, and a lot of razzmatazz, Hollywood created "The Musical!" with all its glorious nonsense that somehow captured the heart and the mind. This book traces the birth and growth of that genre beyond the first thing I ever grasped about it when I was a child: it has music.

Musicals do have music, but nothing about them is really that simple, and I wanted to think about that. I had never forgotten the impact of "Never Gonna Dance." It was characterization, conversation, love and sex, despair, depth, a form of suicide, plot, tragedy, emotional crisis . . . and song and dance. It gave me loss, but oh, it was la belle, la perfectly swell, so much fun to watch, so very *musical*. As they used to say in those biopics about composers, "I sat down at the piano . . ." I sat down and looked at musical after musical after musical—looking for the history, looking for the definition. I found some confirmations, and I found some surprises, and I found a lot of emotions, and I had a lot of fun. Those things turned out to be what musicals, stylized as they are, are all about.

Rouben Mamoulian, who directed Broadway musicals (*Oklahoma!*) and groundbreaking movie musicals (*Love Me Tonight*), said, "Musical stylization brings people a deeper reality if it is well done than any kind of everyday kitchen-sink realism or naturalism can" ("Never gonna dance"). But

the mass moviegoing audience had to be led to both understand and accept that songs and dances could have deeper meaning, that the musical numbers could be key to the core of the film, and could dictate meaning as well as emotion. The way this was learned and executed inside a business like Hollywood over a few decades is the subject of this book.

La Belle Ginger Rogers and *La* Perfectly Swell Fred Astaire, "Never Gonna Dance" from *Swing Time*

I

About Musicals

MUSICALS ARE DECEPTIVELY HARD TO DEFINE. A film is not a musical just because someone gets up and sings a song . . . or steps up and does a little jig. No, just having a musical number in a movie does not make it a musical. Music can turn up anywhere. Sometimes gangsters go to nightclubs and a chorus line dances out, and after doing a little number to set the atmosphere they disappear or recede into the background. Street singers on the sidewalk can appear in horror films. Marching troops in a combat movie can be singing "Over There." All through the 1941 version of the western *Billy the Kid*, a character named Pedro plays his guitar and sings, and when the leading lady (Mary Howard) has a birthday party, the entire cast sings. In *Captains Courageous* (1937), in which Spencer Tracy inexplicably plays a Portuguese fisherman (and even more inexplicably wins an Oscar for it), Tracy sings. The idea is that all Portuguese fishermen would naturally sing because . . . well, because they are Portuguese. Or maybe because they're fishermen, since the whole crew sings chanties while they chop and prepare bait. Their boat is a musical universe, except that the film is not a musical, and neither is *Billy the Kid*.

These films are using songs, but are not presenting music as *performance*. The musical moments are supposed to be about natural behavior, and as such, they are additions to a level of realism or believability that an audience can recognize. If it's someone's birthday party, we sing "Happy Birthday," right? Seamen sing chanties, right? These are seemingly spontaneous musical presentations by characters. The movie is asking a viewer to accept them as real behavior, not musical-movie behavior.

"Spontaneous musical presentation" can be stretched pretty far in movies, particularly if a star associated with singing does it. Songs can appear out of the blue. Marlene Dietrich, playing a jewel thief, sits down at a piano somewhere in Spain and calmly warbles a tune designed to seduce Gary Cooper in Frank Borzage's 1936 *Desire*. (And Cooper falls for it.) Dietrich is and always was associated with her *Blue Angel* "Falling in Love Again" tactics, which could ruin an innocent man's life; so her prior films and established persona make this single song seem natural. Dietrich even manages to insert a little faux dance. She wears an off-the-shoulder black gown adorned by thin feathers sewn to "stand up" around her arms. These feathers are set in motion by her hands moving across the piano keys. The feathers do a little hula, sinuously waving at Cooper as if they were tiny fingers beckoning him near. When Dietrich shifts her mood and suddenly begins to play her song at a faster pace, turning it into a jaunty little flirtation, the feathers speed up, too. They pep up into a saucy little tap number. Dietrich sings—but also manages to "dance" through fashion—without ever getting up off the piano bench.* And the movie is not a musical, nor is she playing a musical performer.

It's easy to eliminate movies with "natural behavior" songs (even dances) from the musical genre, but there are actual musical performances all over the place in movies that aren't supposed to be musicals. In *Tarzan's Desert Mystery* (1943) a harem girl sings "Boola Boola," the Yale song, to a group of Nazis. In *After the Thin Man* (1936), Dorothy McNulty leads a hard-tapping, gyrating chorus line in song and dance, and also performs the solo "Smoke Dreams."† Dietrich performs an elaborately designed and costumed dance number in the 1944 *Kismet*, which is not the later, musical version of the story. She plays the "queen of the Household of the Grand Vizier," which means she's the queen of his harem dancers. She wears a superstructure of braids for a hairdo, and has her beautiful legs covered by gold paint. In the 1937 *She's Got Everything*, Ann Sothern plays a broke heiress working as a secretary to Gene Raymond, a wealthy "coffee tycoon." The movie is a romantic nonmusical comedy that runs a scant seventy minutes, but it has time for the two of them to visit a nightclub

---

* Dietrich could pull off musical numbers motivated by fashion excuses like no one else. In *Blonde Venus* (1932), also not a musical (although she does play a housewife forced to become a performer to support her family), she comes onstage dressed in an ape suit. To get out of it, she does a show-stopping striptease, tantalizing her onscreen audience by slowly emerging, wearing diamond bracelets, feathers, and a blonde Afro wig and singing "Hot Voodoo."

† McNulty was born as Mariana Dorothy McNulty and appeared in the 1927 Broadway show *Good News* as well as the 1930 version and several other films. After she dyed her hair blonde and changed her name to Penny Singleton, she was cast in the long-running *Blondie* movie series.

where Sothern suddenly sings "It's Sleepy Time in Hawaii" to Raymond. Sothern is not playing a singer. She has never sung before in the film, nor will she sing again. While she is crooning away ("Let me go to sleep and dream of love"), Raymond listens, but does not sing back to her, although Raymond was an established musical star, well-known as a singer. He isn't given the opportunity to sing because he's not playing a singer and the movie is not a musical. Yet out of nowhere, Sothern's character sits at her table and, accompanied expertly by the orchestra, does what can only be called a "number." When she finishes, the nightclub audience applauds. It's the world of Hollywood moviemaking where musical things can happen, do happen, but they don't make the film a musical.

There are "reasons" for all of this. A harem girl is supposed to entertain—and besides, she's a spy, and "Boola Boola" is her code recognition (what a code!). McNulty is one of Nick Charles's murder suspects, and she's a nightclub entertainer. Dietrich's job is to entertain the head potentate of the realm whenever he calls her out to do it, and "dancing" was the censors' idea of what that could mean. Taking advantage of a harem-girl character and a nightclub entertainer gives the moviemakers a chance to liven things up, fill time, and develop dubious plot complications without turning a movie into a musical. The Ann Sothern case is one of the things people who want to believe all Hollywood films are masterpieces don't want to think about. It's seventy minutes of low-budget filmmaking, a song will help things along, and Sothern is lovely and can sing, and besides, this is a little romantic comedy and the audience isn't going to care if she sings. They'll love it . . . and they did, even though the boundaries of logic had been violated by Sothern's out-of-nowhere "performance" of a musical number. The assumption was supposed to be: Don't you ever sing to your loved one? Publicly? With an orchestra? In a nightclub? No? Well, you know you'd like to, so our star will do it for you.

The Ann Sothern case—why is she singing?—is hardly the only non-musical movie that has a form of "performance." All around the western heroes of John Ford lies music, including the evocative "Red River Valley" and "Shall We Gather at the River" themes woven into Ford's soundtracks. In Ford's cavalry westerns, particularly *Rio Grande* (1950), the music is key to atmosphere, meaning (through lyrics), and the establishment of camaraderie. When the Sons of the Pioneers, allegedly a group of cavalrymen sitting around a campfire, sing the haunting "My Gal Is Purple," John Wayne walks alone beside the Rio Grande, lost in his memories of the past, his

Not every film with a memorable song and dance is a musical, as proved by Rita Hayworth's famous "Put the Blame on Mame" in *Gilda* . . .

failed marriage, his loneliness, and the sudden physical presence of his wife, who has arrived to reclaim their son from cavalry service. The music, the setting, the lyrics, all bring specificity to an audience about subtext, feelings, and characterization. But what if the music in a western moves away from the campfire? How far can music be taken before the genre is changed? I'm not talking about the overtly musical westerns, such as *Calamity Jane* (a 1953 Doris Day vehicle), *Red Garters* (a 1954 musical satire of westerns, starring Rosemary Clooney), or *Annie Get Your Gun* (a 1950 adaptation of a Broadway musical that was never a real western in the first place). I'm asking, What about Howard Hawks's *Rio Bravo* (1959)? Trapped inside

his jailhouse, awaiting the arrival of deadly foes, sheriff John Wayne and his deputies, Walter Brennan, Dean Martin, and Ricky Nelson, pass the time, trying to keep calm. Nelson plays his guitar and sings, and the entire group launches into a rolling version of "My Rifle, My Pony, and Me," accompanied by Brennan on the harmonica. (Only Wayne does not sing, as is appropriate: he is John Wayne.* He looks on, pleasure and apprecia-

. . . and by Marlene Dietrich's gold-painted legs in a spectacular harem production number in the nonmusical version of *Kismet*.

* Ironically, John Wayne once played a singing (dubbed) cowboy in B films. By the time of *Rio Bravo*, however, he was the legendary western hero John Wayne, separated from everyone else by his royal status. He would not sing.

tion written on his face.) It cannot be denied that Martin and Nelson, two pop singers of the era, are in fact doing an anachronistic musical number, as audiences of the day would expect from them. It's a wonderful moment in the movie, and as bizarre as it is, it works. It's the coming together of a group that must face death and danger, and it shows their resilience, their self-control, and their newly defined camaraderie. But does this musical interlude, which is not like singing "Happy Birthday" or a bunch of sea chanties, make *Rio Bravo* a musical? No, it doesn't. Again, musicals are not defined simply by the performance of a musical number. They must be defined by the purpose of that number, the frequency of other numbers, and the inciting of audience expectation of that number.

Sometimes there's a reason a musical number is in a movie that doesn't seem to call for one, but the reason is external to the plot. For instance, in 1939's *Love Affair*, Irene Dunne sings three times: first, a classical song while Charles Boyer's grandmother (the unacceptable Maria Ouspenskaya) plays the piano; second, when she tries out for a job in a nightclub ("Dance, My Heart"); and third, when some schoolchildren join her for a rendition of "Wishing," a song that became popular as a result of the film, with Dunne adorning the sheet music. Why does *Love Affair*, a melancholy romance, have three musical moments?

It has been established from the beginning that Dunne used to be a nightclub singer, but she's now being kept by a wealthy man (Lee Bowman). Thus, she can sing while Ouspenskaya plays, and that makes sense; it's improvisational and lovely. And when she breaks free of Bowman in order to become worthy of Boyer, it's logical she would return to her former profession in a nightclub. But—after she's run over by a car in the New York streets and becomes crippled—why does she sing with schoolchildren? In particular, why does her hospital nurse wheel her over to a schoolyard, so three little girls can join her while she sits in her wheelchair, strums a ukulele, and helps them do an all-out rendition of "Wishing"? There's a plot "reason." The school principal (called "Pickle Puss" by the students) needs an excuse to come out and offer Dunne a job as the music teacher for the school—even though she's crippled, he doesn't know who she is, and she's never taught school before. Later, when Dunne's not getting better, the children (and "Pickle Puss") come to visit her in her apartment and sing "Wishing" for her. Does any of this make sense? Or make the movie a musical? Not really. But the music defines Irene Dunne: When she's moved by Boyer's grandmother, she sings. When her heart is full of optimism and joy, she sings. And when she's desperate and trying to keep her spirits up, she sings, even though musical performance is not the operating mode of the movie. The decision for the songs is about stardom, character, audience expectation, and sheet music sales . . . not about genre.* If the songs were removed from *Love Affair*, it would tell the same story in the same emotional tone. The music doesn't define it.

Purpose is everything in any sudden musical rupture in a movie. *Margie* (1946), starring Jeanne Crain, capitalized on postwar craving for a sense of "the old days" by presenting a sweet story set in the 1920s. It's about a high-school girl who falls in love with her French teacher. The movie is not a musical, but it found purpose in the good use of period songs of the flapper era, as when Margie watched from her upstairs window while her popular next-door neighbor (Barbara Lawrence) and a boyfriend play a record and do an impromptu dance to "A Cup of Coffee, a Sandwich, and You." In *Congo Maisie* (1940), Ann Sothern (again) stops an angry mob of murderous African tribesmen by emerging from a colonial station wearing a low-cut sequined gown and a feathered headdress à la Ziegfeld. She advances toward them, dancing and singing "St. Louis Woman," and performing some grade-school magic tricks. The magic scares them, but it's the song that stops 'em cold. A worthy purpose.

Sex was often a musical purpose. An improvisational use of music helped Hollywood solve one of its biggest censorship problems: establishing sexual attraction and the fulfillment of it. If a nonmusical couple suddenly "sang" together—well, an audience could understand what that meant. When Clark Gable and Claudette Colbert launched themselves into the group mix bawling out "The Man on the Flying Trapeze" in *It Happened One Night* (1934), their whole relationship changed. When Robert Williams and Jean Harlow "sang" an argument about whether or not he'd wear the spats she'd bought for him in *Platinum Blonde* (1931), their playful back-and-forth, their pushing into each other's rhythms, acted out a specific kind of love scene; and when Myrna Loy and Walter Pidgeon sang and danced around the streets of New York City on a late-night get-together (*Man-*

---

* Irene Dunne could sing, and her earlier movie career had put her in many musicals, among them the prestigious 1936 *Show Boat*. Her singing in *Love Affair* was not a surprise to audiences: some might have expected it, and most would have welcomed it. The singing, however, isn't necessary to the plot, only useful to her character definition and her stardom, as is her warbling of "I'll Get By" to Spencer Tracy in *A Guy Named Joe* (1943). She's a wartime ferry command pilot just singin' to her fella.

Proof, 1938), an audience knew it was only a matter of time until Pidgeon's fiancée, Rosalind Russell, would be out of his life. Loy and Pidgeon, playing nonmusical characters, skip down the block, arm in arm, their voices joined in perfect sync, easily slipping into the pretense that they *are* characters in a movie musical. Audiences understood the comic reference and what it said about them. It wasn't just their song and dance that said "sex" or "love"; it was their union—physical, improvisational and thus spontaneous, and coming out of them in spite of themselves.

A perfect example of how specific purpose tips the balance lies in *Ace Drummond*, a nonmusical Universal serial made in 1936, created by the celebrated World War I flying ace Eddie Rickenbacker. Under no circumstances could *Ace Drummond* be thought of as a musical. It's been built for adventure and excitement, and for a young audience; and yet the daring air ace, who roves the world of danger, *sings*. In the first episode ("Where East Meets West"), Ace (played by John King) is a passenger on an airplane in Asia. As the plane takes off, it hits severe air turbulence, and a woman on board becomes frightened. To calm her, Ace sings. (King is a good singer, as it turns out.) The song is "Give Me a Ship and a Song." The lyrics roll out: "Give me an open sky and a plane to fly . . . Give me a motor's roar and a plane to soar." Ace is cheerful and happy; and hearing his jolly ditty, everyone perks up, including the frightened lady.

The next thing that happens is that the copilot is shot and the pilot is wounded. Ace races forward to take the controls and straighten everything out until the pilot gets a grip on himself and nobly says he can carry on. Ace then informs everyone he's going to bail out (over Mongolia) and take a look down below to find out what happened. Within a few minutes of episode one's brief running time, Ace Drummond has calmed a passenger, evaded bullets, rescued a floundering airplane, reassured the pilot, bailed out, and . . . sung a number. He does not sing again, but if you decided to come back next week for episode two (and, really, why wouldn't you?), you would find he does. *The Invisible Enemy* finds Ace hitting the ground (presumably in Mongolia, which looks mysteriously leafy). He folds his parachute, fights off some enemies, rescues the captured heroine (Jean Rogers), and drives her away in a conveniently waiting horse cart. And then he sings again. It's the same number: he still wants a ship and a song. None of this makes any sense, but the same song has economically performed two different functions in two weeks: reassurance and romance. Perhaps the idea is that the all-American hero really does have to do it all, which includes singing. (Certainly Ace's song charms the heroine, who giggles the whole time.) The point is that Ace's singing doesn't make the film a musical—it's just an unusual and strange form of characterization. Ace Drummond is a hero. He can do anything—so he does. (Perhaps later, he will tap-dance his way out of a dungeon.)

The Ace Drummond "characterization"-by-song is silly and unjustifiable, but sometimes a single song in a nonmusical is an important key to character definition and thus essential. *Torrid Zone* (1940) stars James Cagney, Pat O'Brien, and Ann Sheridan in a hard-hitting, fast-talking movie about two tough guys who work South American plantations. They fight, trick each other, and nearly destroy each other: male enemies locked in employment competition. However, the film opens up on the sound of Ann Sheridan's voice. While about thirty seconds of plot pass (Pat O'Brien rips a wanted poster off a wall, yells at a local policeman, walks across a street and into her saloon), Sheridan's voice is heard singing "Caballero" underneath on the soundtrack the entire time. She's singing in a run-down cabaret. Her performance shows she knows how to take care of herself and she knows how to control a crowd of leering men. Although she never sings again, neither the movie nor her character would be the same without the song. Her musical performance establishes her. She is defined by it as feminine, desirable, glamorous, but also tough and humorous.

When Cagney and O'Brien take over the film, everything shifts to their banter and maleness, their goals and competition. If the movie didn't start with a major focus on Sheridan, she'd get lost in their fisticuffs and angry exchanges. The song allows her to mark her place before the noisy men start banging around. Even though she'll later deliver sassy dialogue and some sexy moments, it's the song that puts her on a level with Cagney and O'Brien. Her costars have to compete to rule their world as the story unfolds; she owns hers from the beginning.

Sheridan's song *is* musical performance, but not the sort that defines a film as a musical—it's characterization, no more. This occurs in many murder mysteries and film noir movies in which a beautiful femme fatale is given a song to sing as an explanation of the danger she represents. Ava Gardner sings just once in *The Killers* (1946). She's not playing a professional singer, she's just noodling around with the piano player at a party. Yet when he hears her, Burt Lancaster's goose is cooked. He has heard her siren song.

Could *Gilda* be *Gilda* if Rita Hayworth didn't sing "Put the Blame on

Mame"? (The irony is that except for a brief moment reprising "Mame" with her guitar, Hayworth *doesn't* sing "Put the Blame on Mame." She's dubbed.) The iconic "Put the Blame on Mame" defines *Gilda* the movie, Gilda the character, and also Rita Hayworth's persona and legendary status. As Gilda, she performs "Mame" in defiance, an act of anger and rebellion against Glenn Ford, their marriage, and her whole life. In some movies, Hayworth might shoot Ford instead. Or have an affair with his best friend. Or kill herself. In *Gilda*, she makes her point and reveals her desperation by humiliating herself in a pseudo-striptease in front of a night-club audience by singing and dancing. A serious movie like *Gilda* can't be effective (or be taken seriously) if, all of a sudden, a character turns up on a casino/nightclub floor and does a polished song and dance. *Gilda* has previously explained that Gilda is a dancer, but more importantly, it *shows* us that she's one. Hayworth runs away from Brazil and is hired to enter-tain in an Argentine nightclub, where the audience is treated to a number ("Amado Mio") that could be in any musical film. Hayworth, caught in a spotlight and dressed in a sexy gown with a bare midriff, sings and dances before a nightclub audience, so there's no later plot mystery as to why and how Gilda can get out there and pull off that Mame thing. She's a pro. And, of course, the audience of the day knew Rita Hayworth could dance, which made them expect her to do so and helped them accept her doing so even if Gilda is more femme fatale than song-and-dance gal.

Gilda is not a musical, even though Hayworth was a musical star for the audiences of 1946. Although she had appeared in nonmusicals as she climbed to stardom (*Only Angels Have Wings, Susan and God, The Lady in Question*), she had reached the top through her wonderful dancing (and extraordinary glamour) in two musicals with Fred Astaire (*You'll Never Get Rich, You Were Never Lovelier*), one with Gene Kelly (*Cover Girl*), one 20th Century–Fox color success, *My Gal Sal*, and Columbia's *Tonight and Every Night*. To express Gilda's frustrations, it was suitable for Hayworth to sing (dubbed) and dance. Yet *Gilda*, the movie, is a film noir with danger, suicide, murder, corruption, Nazis, and barely submerged sexuality. *Gilda*, a nonmusical, is nevertheless defined by the musical performance of "Put the Blame on Mame." In fact, Rita Hayworth's career has also been defined by it: it's her "Play it, Sam," her "Tomorrow is another day."

Musical performance in a nonmusical isn't always used to define charac-ter; it can supply plot meaning. (Everybody gets why Dooley Wilson has to sing "As Time Goes By" in *Casablanca*.) *The Prizefighter and the Lady*

(1933), starring Myrna Loy, Otto Kruger, and Max Baer, is the story of a young prizefighter (Baer) who falls in love with a gangster's girl (Loy) and faces various problems as a result. It's fundamentally a woman's picture, as the story focuses mostly on Loy, just reaching her stardom at MGM. However, the movie begins by focusing on the character played by Walter Huston, a drunken ex-boxing manager who sees a hunk of a guy (Baer) lifting large beer barrels in a speakeasy. Huston gets sober fast and turns Baer into a fighter, so it's also a boxing movie. Or a women's boxing picture. What is of interest is that it needs musical performances to make both genres work . . . but it's not a musical.

Loy plays a singer in a nightclub owned by Kruger, her jealous lover. Twice in the film she takes the stage to stand by a piano in front of an orchestra to sing "'Cause I'm Just a Downstream Drifter." Both times she displays bare shoulders, wears jewels and satin, and is bathed in an isolating spotlight. The first time she sings, she realizes to her surprise that she's falling in love with Baer. The second time she sings is after she's married to him. This time, she realizes Baer is being unfaithful to her with the blonde who's sitting at their table. The two performances of the song aren't just defining her character; they're telling the audience about her character's inner self and providing plot information. The first time she's dreaming of a love she thought she'd never find or have, and the second time she's realizing that the love wasn't what she thought it was. No acting from Loy is necessary, only her lip-syncing to the music. (She's dubbed.) The audience understands. This is explicit (and common) usage of music in a nonmusical.

There's a matching musical number for Baer. On the night before he fights for the heavyweight championship against Primo Carnera (the real-life heavyweight champion, playing himself), Baer (who in real life was also a successful boxer) is advertised as appearing onstage with a chorus of beautiful girls. After an audience is alerted to this via posters, the proscenium arch appears, curtains open, and out comes Max Baer (in tight pants and T-shirt), who proceeds to sing and dance with a chorus of extra-small female dancer/singers who make him look even bigger than he is. And, yes, Baer actually dances and (unlike Loy) sings, and he's fully adequate for the task. He not only does steps, he performs a routine on the rings, showing off his perfectly formed body. It's a fully developed, choreographed, and costumed musical number. After that, there's a ten-round fight in which he and Carnera beat each other bloody.

Why does *The Prizefighter and the Lady* have Baer perform a complete and traditional musical number? Maybe because he's an adequate singer/dancer and MGM is trying to develop him as a movie star and wants him to strut all his stuff. Maybe because he's a real hunk in his T-shirt, or maybe someone felt the movie needed to distract everyone from its plot. Whatever the motive, whatever the madness, the musical number speaks the language of film. It tells the audience that Baer's character, Steve Morgan, is an irresponsible egomaniac, not worthy of Loy and unappreciative of her, and furthermore too stupid to know he ought to be home in bed the night before he takes on Primo Carnera, who is twice his size. The music is character, plot, and full explanation. And an audience used to seeing musical numbers in many places in motion pictures takes it as it was intended: Baer is wrong about everything, and Loy is a real lady for sticking by him. He doesn't deserve her, so he's going to have to be beaten bloody, and then apologize. *Music* develops both Loy and Baer at crucial moments and defines why and how they will fall in love, have trouble, and resolve things happily. And yet *Prizefighter and the Lady* is not really a musical, and neither Loy nor Baer is a musical performer.

All these examples of movies that are not musicals, but contain musical moments or even rely on musical performances to develop aspects of plot and character, are important to the understanding that the genre evolved in a complex manner. It was never a case of "singing and dancing is singing and dancing, and that's a musical, folks." The performance of music—the acts of singing and dancing—were singular modes of telling audiences things, ways to make them feel and understand in specific ways. Movies always used music for many different things: Character. Suspense. Forward movement. Mood. Attitude. Warning. Shock. And for music itself. It was never "just" music, and that is particularly true if the music involves the performance of a musical selection. The *genre* of the musical—in which songs and dances are the *purpose*—is different from having one or two numbers thrown in somewhere in the frame.

As a result, the definition of a musical is not simple; nor are musicals themselves "simple," although being thought of as "simple" is part of the history of the genre. *Stormy Weather*, of 1943, is a prime example of how complicated a seemingly "simple" musical could be. *Stormy Weather* is an entertaining movie containing a minimum of plot, a maximum of musical talent, and an unpretentious presentation. (Along with *Cabin in the Sky*, also from 1943, it's one of two African American musicals made inside the studio system during World War II.) The parade of talent includes

Lena Horne, Bill "Bojangles" Robinson, Fats Waller, Cab Calloway, the Nicholas Brothers, the Katherine Dunham dance troupe, and more. When Lena Horne sings the title song, which became a signature hit for her, the visual presentation is cinematically sophisticated, a full characterization for Horne, a plot development, a showcase for spectacular talent, and yet easy to follow and enjoy.

The plot setup is simple. Bandleader Cab Calloway is "puttin' on a show for soldiers" and rounding up musical stars to appear in it. It's patriotic, but it's also a ruse to bring former lovers Robinson and Horne together again. After Calloway's band performs a number (with him splendidly attired in a fabulous white zoot suit with matching hat), Lena Horne sings "Stormy Weather."

The setting for Calloway's "show for soldiers" is a strangely contrived space. It's a large hall with a traditional curtained proscenium-arch stage, so it looks almost like a high-school auditorium. There's no real orchestra pit, and a set of stairs leads down off the stage to the floor, where the band sits. Out in front of the band is a "nightclub" dance floor, and beyond and around that area are tables and chairs for patrons to sit, order drinks, etc. Thus the set contains a performance stage, steps to get down off it, a place to dance, and a place to sit and enjoy a show, but it is not a traditional theater nor is it a nightclub. It's just kind of a space to film in.

Lena Horne begins her performance of "Stormy Weather" on the proscenium stage. As the Calloway band starts the introduction to the familiar strains of her hit song, thunder is heard, lightning strikes, and the curtains part. Horne, onstage, is positioned on a small set that suggests a room. It has a door (she's leaning against it) and a window. She moves toward the window and begins to sing. The window is open, and outside in the streets it's raining heavily, the wind is blowing, and people are scurrying for cover.

Horne continues her song by leaving the window area, walking down the steps on the front of the stage and out onto the dance floor. The patrons at the tables (including Robinson) are seen to be watching her in medium close-up. Horne goes on with her song, moving about the tables, but at the sound of the wind and thunder and the sight of more lightning (now inside the nonstage area) she runs back up the stairs and takes the stage again. She returns to the window, still singing, and closes it, although viewers can see through it, to heavy rain outside.

The camera then moves forward, taking the viewer past Horne, through the closed window, and out into the street itself, leaving the "puttin' on a show" area. The people in the rain-drenched street are soaked but dressed in zoot suits (for the men) and tight jackets and slit skirts (for the women). They dance, executing a full routine in this new space, which has its own set (sidewalk, lampposts, store windows, stairway to an el train). As the music (nonvocal) continues, heavy clouds can be seen and more lightning strikes over the image of the lead dancer. This dancer is the famous Katherine Dunham, and the people in the streets are her dance troupe. Suddenly, the camera takes the viewer toward Dunham as more lightning strikes over her image. Her street clothes disappear, the street disappears, and she is seen wearing a leotard with a dance skirt over it. The wind blows the costumes off her troupe so they are also in leotards. Dunham and her dancers then perform a modern dance (their specialty) against billowing curtains that have appeared behind them. (Lightning continues to flash back there.) When the camera first moved toward Dunham, she appeared to be "thinking," and the combination of camera movement and cutting relocates the viewer into an abstract universe, allegedly inside Dunham's head. After a full dance number, one of the longest in the movie, the lyric of the song ("keeps rainin' all the time . . .") is heard, and the image shifts back to the busy street with Dunham and her group once again in street clothes. The rain has stopped and they scurry away. The camera backs up through the window and onto the stage set to find Lena Horne singing as she leans against the closed window. A viewer can still see the empty street outside. As the camera pulls back farther, Horne is bathed in a spotlight onstage. Then the curtains that opened up to reveal her are closed.

This performance of "Stormy Weather" has one arena for the song in the nightclub, another arena outside in the street, and a third arena, a "thought" or emotion inside a dancer's head. The song travels easily to these spaces, each one establishing a new area of musical performance (and a new type of cinematic presentation). When Horne is onstage, she sings directly to the camera. When she goes out into the nightclub audience, she is observed singing *to them* as she moves around the room. When she goes to the window, she sings to herself, isolated from any audience. When the camera goes outside to find the dance troupe's space, Horne disappears— everything, including the nightclub and the rainstorm, disappears for the fantasy number. This is how musicals work: establish a real place, go into musical performance that is easy to understand (performer in nightclub), and progress into the abstract, taking the viewer along. There is nothing simple about it. It's a complex movement through time and space, although presented matter-of-factly. And while it happens, Calloway's plot keeps unfolding, with Horne's loss and loneliness, Robinson's confusion, and the question about the resolution of their relationship. The number is a number, but also the setup for plot resolution with a happy ending.

For many years, the attitude toward the musical film was that it existed only for entertainment or escape, and therefore the form was not—maybe even could not be—thoughtful or meaningful. (If so, why is it so hard to make a good one?) The simplest idea about the genre was that it would never be serious, that there would be no darkness, no despair, no "bad stuff" in it. How, then, do we explain *Gold Diggers of 1933*, in which there is a musical number that contains a breadline and a shooting as well as a miniature World War I (with bleeding soldiers) and the tragic aftermath in which a war hero, with his medal pinned under his ragged jacket lapel, has become a bum begging for help? The Andrews Sisters are torpedoed right in the middle of an onboard ship rendering of "Shoo-Shoo Baby" in *Follow the Boys* (1944) and are never seen again. Janet Blair and Marc Platt, the singing/dancing secondary leads in the 1945 Rita Hayworth vehicle, *Tonight and Every Night*, are obliterated by a Nazi bomb dropped on their jolly London pub. (To help warn potential patrons, the August issue of *Screenland* labeled the movie "A great dramatic musical.") *The Gang's All Here*, surely one of the most "escapist" of all musicals, released in 1943 during World War II and featuring comedy, color, kaleidoscopic images, and Carmen Miranda and some penile bananas, still contains a little scene in which the hero is shown slogging through the jungle in combat.

Musicals are not always about escape and certainly are not always happy; nor do they eschew bad things such as murder. Musical "escapism" might be true for some musicals, but not others. *Show Boat*, one of history's most famous and groundbreaking musicals (filmed in 1929, 1936, and 1951) contains alcoholism, miscegenation, and attempted murder. *Down to Earth* (1947), a peppy Technicolored Columbia musical that presented Rita Hayworth as Terpsichore, the goddess of dance, and which bestowed on her the famous tag "Love Goddess," contains a murder. And there's Cecil B. DeMille's astonishing 1930 *Madam Satan*, a musical version of his 1920s silent films about marriage, infidelity, and fashion, which *The New York Times* called "a strange conglomeration of unreal incidents." *Madam Satan*'s finale takes place on a zeppelin during a masquerade party. When the zeppelin is hit by lightning and torn loose from its moorings, disaster occurs. ("The controls are smashed! Get all these people into para-

Charles B. Middleton takes aim at the orchestra leader while the chorus line endorses his music criticism in *Murder at the Vanities.*

chutes!") Through an extended sequence of chaos, thunder and lightning, screams and panic (throughout which the band plays "Where Do We Go from Here, Boys?"), men dressed as pirates, bandits, and toreadors—and women dressed in almost nothing (but adorned with pheasant feathers and spectacular jewelry)—struggle into parachutes and jump for their lives.

The little-known but totally amazing 1934 *Murder at the Vanities* has just about everything. Directed by Mitchell Leisen, the film is a murder-mystery musical, set in a theater during an opening-night performance. While the police arrive and begin investigating murder backstage, the musical show runs onstage. Music can be heard throughout the movie, and from time to time the audience is shown the numbers that are occurring while the investigation progresses. (It's a sort of musical *Noises Off.*)

Murder at the Vanities has comedy that is tough-minded and risqué, but two brutal murders occur. One of the victims is a female private detective (Gail Patrick), who's killed by a hatpin stuck directly into her heart. Her body's stashed up in the fly gallery, and her blood drips downward. As the show progresses, a chorus line of nearly nude women take their places inside large flower "buds" as singer Gertrude Michael walks in front of these growing plants, singing to the audience to love "Sweet Marijuana"—yes—and enjoy its positives.* One of the bare-shouldered chorines feels something splash on her naked flesh during the song. She looks. Blood! She screams. In an epic number entitled "The Rape of the Rhapsody," an all-white orchestra wearing period costumes is shoved offscreen by Duke Ellington's band and a romping chorus of African American maids led in song by Michael, who sings, "Oh lawdy if they have bandannas/they'll go to market singing dirty hosannas." Then the white orchestra leader returns, wielding a machine gun to "shoot" Michael and the whole lineup—mass murder always being a good idea for a musical number—but Michael is shot for real.

Musicals, really good musicals, are difficult to make. The wonderful thing about the form for those who make them is that audiences often don't expect them to be good, they just expect them to be musical. Many musicals are excuses to show talented people (or even not-so-talented people) singing and dancing and solving a small plot problem. But to make a really good musical—one that succeeds in taking the audience into a musical universe, and finding a way to move its characters from nonperformance mode to performance mode and back again—is a challenge. If the job of the audience is to accept music as meaning, then the job of the filmmakers is to find the way to make them accept it without question. This was the business task of Hollywood filmmakers, and it becomes the history of the genre and its evolution. Hollywood had to learn how to make *movie* musicals.

A movie musical is built around the idea that songs and dances can be used to tell a story, or used in part to tell a story, or used to tell part of

---

* The studio defended the lyrics by writing the Hays Office the following: "There is, of course, no indication of the use of any narcotics nor are there any girls smoking cigarettes or anything to indicate that this is a song about narcotics . . . nor do we believe that it is evident to many thousands of people who do not know what marihuana [sic] is that this song has anything to do with narcotics." (They got away with it.) In fact, *Murder at the Vanities* is a prime example of what could be gotten away with, which is why the Production Code for censorship was about to be enforced. It was based on a play by Earl Carroll and Rufus King. Carroll was a showman famous for his "Vanities" presentations, which featured sexy showgirls wearing as little as possible. Carroll made no pretense at "art"; he just paraded his girls. *Murder at the Vanities*, a 1933 book musical on which the movie is based, was his biggest hit. The movie introduced the hit song "Cocktails for Two" (by Arthur Johnston and Sam Coslow), performed by Carl Brisson, a sort of Danish Maurice Chevalier.

a story. Musicals are defined not just by singing songs or doing a little dancing, but by the concept of music. A working definition of a musical is that it's a stylized presentation of life, where "reality" is presented not through the actions normally associated with everyday life, but through musical performance. Characterizations, depth, plot points, subtexts, are not absent; they're just on the screen in a form not usually associated with them: the musical number. "Reality" is established inside a song and dance, which is why people sometimes think they're trivial. Musicals dispense with other kinds of action, with serious dialogue and lengthy discussions—e.g., "Never Gonna Dance." (In some films, individuals don't perform the music: it's layered over them on the soundtrack. Some performers in musicals perform performance: They can't sing and are dubbed. They can't dance and are used only for faked close-ups.) Unlike genres that are driven more by dialogue, character, or story, such as westerns and gangster films, musicals can be set anywhere, anytime, with unfamiliar sets of characters and conflicts. Musicals are unrestricted except for the need to be musical in some way—mostly by defining themselves as musical, by having music be feeling and explanation. Although some musicals are *all* music (*The Umbrellas of Cherbourg*), most musicals are a finely balanced, carefully juggled mixture of musical and nonmusical sequences. When a team sets out to make a musical, the key task is to reconcile those two opposites into a happy coexistence. Of the two conflicting elements—music and nonmusic—it's the music that has to determine the style, structure, and movement of the film. If the music is wrong or bad, the movie will fail. If the plot is wrong, it can work if it's buoyed up by the music. (It's better if neither is wrong, but if both are wrong, the movie is a flop.)

Musicals have to find the answers to a series of questions. How soon should an audience learn that people in the movie are going to start singing and dancing, and not always doing those things because they're vaudevillians? What should be the relationship between the music and the plot? How many musical numbers can be sustained in a plot, and how often—and at what intervals—should they appear? What works best when the movie has to shift from everyday life over into musical performance? How can a movie move from the nonmusical universe to the musical and back again?

When people in Hollywood began making musicals after sound made it possible, they inherited a tradition that had already been established regarding "types." There were the musical revue, the operetta, the opera, the backstage musical, the Cinderella story set to music, the biography, the love story, etc. Filmmakers could and did embrace all these approaches, but they also went beyond what had come before. They learned how to develop original film musicals to showcase uniquely talented musical performances, and they developed cinematic solutions and created specific business strategies to make musicals. They turned a theatrical form into a cinematic one.

This development took place over decades; it was a set of trials, successes, and failures. The history of Hollywood is not a "Eureka!" story, like the discovery of radium, or like Hollywood's *Madame Curie* chose to tell the story of the discovery of radium. The history of the musical is a question of the business finding a way to keep the format fresh and to please viewers with its assets. A brief summary is simply that at first, Hollywood mostly made movies in which the film told a story, and there were songs and dances added in; if you took the songs and dances out, you'd have a story that made sense. This practice shifted more to one where the audience was given movies with songs and dances that were key to everything, and there was a fairly irrelevant little story to contain them; take out the plot and you had an entertaining set of musical numbers left. But eventually, Hollywood turned the musical into an integrated art form, in which it made movies with songs and dances and stories interrelated, and you could remove neither. Movies in which people sang and danced for a living (which provided an excuse to do a number) morphed into movies in which people sang and danced as they lived. And yet both forms can be observed from the beginning, and after the more integrated type became the norm, the old "backstage" ones continued on. Progress wasn't always smart business.

To accomplish this creative and historical development, Hollywood had to make a lot of musicals and learn a lot of lessons. They had to face the music.

II

Origins:
The Arrival of Sound

UNLIKE MOST GENRES, the film musical has a clearly delineated starting point. The arrival of sound made it possible. This does not mean, however, that there isn't fog surrounding that very same chronological marker. Although film historians are well aware of the facts regarding the introduction of sound into the movies, the average person's sense of that event goes something like this:

BOOM! Sound fell out of the sky on an unsuspecting Hollywood. No one saw it coming. No one had even thought of it. ("Actors are supposed to *talk*? Is everyone crazy?") The film business was shocked, *shocked*, when, unexpected by anyone, a movie was released—*The Jazz Singer* in 1927—and Al Jolson, the popular singing star, yelled, "You ain't heard nothin' yet!" just before he got down on one knee and sang "Mammy." The movie business was plunged into chaos, and famous silent stars had to slink away into the night, gone forever, and why? Because sound revealed that they couldn't talk. Or that they talked like Lina Lamont. Or, in the latest version of this myth, the Oscar-winning 2011 movie *The Artist*, they could speak only French. (The *Artist* "stars" rescue their careers by tap-dancing, a very appropriate plot choice.)

This "story" of the arrival of sound is not accurate, but like all good legends, it has just enough truth to keep it alive. It's been embraced by the public largely because the film business itself embraced and heavily promoted it. The business found *The Jazz Singer* to be an easy explanation for a complex issue. A classic example of how movies defined the arrival of sound by using *The Jazz Singer* is demonstrated, appropriately enough, in such movies as *Singin' in the Rain*. Invited to a producer's home for an after-premiere party, the reigning silent stars of the day are treated to a little demonstration of sound film. Some laugh. Some are repulsed

("It's *vulgar*"). All are shocked, but go on partying after being warned that "over at Warners" they're making an "all talking, all singing movie called *The Jazz Singer*" (which actually was not "all talking" and "all singing").

The truth is that *The Jazz Singer* did not bring on the arrival of sound, nor was that film even the beginning of musical presentation on film. Sound

The Jazz Singer and Al Jolson take the world by storm as New Yorkers line up to see—and hear—what all the excitement is about.

had been available in some form or another from the beginning of movies. Thomas A. Edison, after all, had invented the phonograph before he started trying to make "motion" pictures. He didn't approach movies thinking about how to add sound. He invented a sound-reproducing machine and then tried to figure out how to put a picture with it. Edison introduced his first sound movie in 1896 in a crude process he called the Kinetophone. His labs were always tinkering with sound, trying to link it to an image, and he had workable systems in place by 1906, but none really succeeded. Sound—the lack of it—was acknowledged as a problem from the beginning of motion pictures, but when the business ingeniously made an art form out of "silent" pictures, everyone bought in and moved on . . . except the inventors, who kept on looking for technological solutions. For them, it was about science. The problem was twofold: synchronization and amplification. They could get one working but not the other—they had loud or they had intelligible—but they kept trying, because they felt the audience wanted sound.

For exhibitors, it was a matter of getting customers in the door. In the beginning, they didn't assume the public wouldn't miss sound; they tried to solve the problem. Some of their ideas were clumsy; some were a little silly. Actors stood behind the screen and spoke the dialogue (loudly). A phonograph played the dialogue as the picture ran (a sort of crude sound-on-disc idea). Actors stood to the right of the screen, wearing costumes and making entrances and exits, speaking their lines—two shows for the price of one. There was also an idea that worked beautifully: musical accompaniment by orchestra or piano. When silent film rapidly developed into a sophisticated art form beloved by the public, moviegoers didn't actually miss sound, really, so why bother to add it? Films began to always have some form of musical accompaniment, and when a highly successful road show such as *Birth of a Nation* (1915) went across the country, it was accompanied by a "traveling sound man" to provide sound effects: ringing, banging, gunfire, etc.

Meanwhile, science soldiered on. All over the world, inventors were always trying, but they weren't entertainers, and their little sound movies were often just pictures of themselves talking. Over time, various processes were introduced and played with. Alice Guy Blaché, the pioneering female French producer/director, actually made many experimental films with sound and image for Gaumont during 1906 and 1907. By 1913, over one hundred American-made singing and talking films had been released, and ads in movie magazines claimed "The Talking Motion Picture Is Here." But it wasn't—not yet. D. W. Griffith rented a synchronizing system called the Kellum Process for sound inserts for his 1921 *Dream Street*, and the film was released with a prologue spoken by Griffith himself, praising sound.

By the middle of 1924 there were about thirty theaters already wired for sound in America, with fifty or more in the process of being wired. By 1925, Western Electric had a working sound movie system, and in 1926 Warner Bros. bought it and created the Vitaphone partnership to produce and distribute sound films.* On August 6, 1926, Warner Bros. presented its first all-sound movie program at their theater in New York. The program was billed as "AN ALL SOUND EVENING," and it consisted of two Warners Vitaphone shorts and a feature, *Don Juan*, starring John Barrymore, that had a full musical accompaniment with sound effects from start to finish. (There was, however, no spoken dialogue.)

Throughout 1926, audiences were treated to short films and features that had some form of sound attached through the Vitaphone system. This process made it possible for any form of sound—orchestral, vocal, dialogue-related, sound effects—to be recorded and then reproduced on discs which would be played in sync with projected images with the necessary amplification to be heard throughout a large theater. Two kinds of sound motion pictures were released throughout 1926 and 1927 with the Vitaphone system: full-length movies with synchronized scores and sound effects (*Don Juan*, *The Better 'Ole*, *When a Man Loves*, *Old San Francisco*, *The First Auto*) and short films that presented audiences with successful vaudeville routines, operatic arias, and skits. These sound movies were in theaters for a full year before *The Jazz Singer* premiered in October of 1927.

Among the 1926 Vitaphone sound-on-disc short-film releases are such things as the tenor Giovanni Martinelli singing "Vesti la giubba"; the New York Philharmonic playing Wagner's *Tannhäuser* overture; and Elsie Janis, "the great stage and vaudeville favorite and outstanding entertainer of the war days, assisted by a chorus from the 107th Regiment," singing, among other favorites, "When Yankee Doodle Learns to Parlez-Vous Français." Most significantly, there's a 1926 Vitaphone short featuring Al Jolson singing "When the Red, Red Robin (Comes Bob, Bob, Bobbin' Along)," "April Showers," and "Rock-a-bye Your Baby with a Dixie Melody." On a June 17, 1926, sound disc, Will H. Hays, the president of the Motion Pictures Producers and Distributors of America, gives a speech in which he welcomes Vitaphone to the motion-picture industry. In addition to paying tribute to the four Warner brothers for their forward thinking, Hays points out that "service is the supreme commitment of life." It's worth noting that Hays also commented on the wonderful thing the new invention was going to bring to movies: music. "In the presentation of these pictures, music plays an invaluable part . . . Vitaphone shall carry symphony orchestras to

* Around the same time, Fox Film developed a sound-on-film system, the one that would ultimately prevail and replace sound on disc.

the town halls of the hamlets . . . It has been said that the art of the vocalist and instrumentalist is ephemeral, that he creates but for the moment. Now, neither the artist nor his art will ever wholly die."

During the time frame of 1926–1931, the Vitaphone shorts (which continued beyond the establishment of the sound feature film) presented some of the most famous acts from vaudeville and also showcased popular entertainers of the era from Broadway, radio, on-the-road tours, and opera: Jack Benny, Fred Allen, George Burns and Gracie Allen, Edgar Bergen and Charlie McCarthy, Lou Holtz, Bert Lahr, Joe E. Brown, Jack Haley, Helen Morgan, Beniamino Gigli, and many lesser-known personalities.*

These Vitaphone shorts are fabulous time capsules. They allow a modern audience full access to what vaudeville actually was, and some of it is delightful (George Burns and Gracie Allen doing their famous "Lamb Chops" musical skit). Some of it is appalling ("A Hebrew salesman walked in . . ." from Eddie White, who was himself Jewish). Some of it is simply astonishing: Chaz Chase, a comedian whose act consisted of eating his own clothes. Chase, who billed himself as "The Unique Comedian," also ate lighted matches, cigars, and his ukulele. When someone asked his daughter if he actually ate all that stuff, she explained that he stored it in his cheeks, spitting it out later. (However, she pointed out, he wouldn't eat just any old thing. "He didn't eat glass.") Chase also danced. What a man!

The Revelers is five guys, four of whom sing harmony and one who plays the piano (they're the 1927 inspiration for the German group, the Comedian Harmonists). *Horace Heidt and His Orchestra* is pretty much just that: Horace Heidt and his orchestra, enhanced by megaphones, banjos, guitars, guys in sweaters with an H on them, a bunch of tap dancers, twin pianos, and a dog. However, due to the Vitaphone shorts (and the soundtrack films), audiences in America had been exposed to sound and to musical sound in the movies before *The Jazz Singer* came around. In fact, it's my impression, from interviewing people who worked during this era, that the coming of

---

* The presence of movie shorts—comic, musical, dramatic, newsworthy—continued throughout the studio-system era. They were shown ahead of the night's feature film. During these early years, there's often slightly off-color or politically incorrect material in them, much of which is musical. For instance, Harry Ross, an emcee and performer, in a short entitled "Frankfurters," sings a risqué song complaining about his insatiable girlfriend: "Even when it was Yom Kippur, I had to slip her . . . frankfurters." (A modern blogger commented that he hoped they were Hebrew National.) There were also dramatic "playlets," with men who later became movie stars: Spencer Tracy in *The Hard Guy* in 1930 and Pat O'Brien in *Crime Squares* in 1931.

sound never surprised Hollywood at all. They had always assumed it would happen some way, sometime, in some form. What surprised them was that sound brought on the death of silent film, which was so successful, so loved by the public, and had reached such an artistic pinnacle by 1927. They had assumed silent and sound films would coexist.

The calendar year of 1927 is considered to be the official year in which sound took hold. Warner Bros., with its Vitaphone process, put into production five full-length movies that had sound incorporated into key scenes: *State Street Sadie*, *Glorious Betsy*, *Midnight Taxi*, *When a Man Loves*, and, of course, *The Jazz Singer*. Except for the last, these films are almost totally unknown today; and although people discuss it a lot, *The Jazz Singer* is rarely seen. Almost all the sound it presents has Jolson singing. His first onscreen song is "Dirty Hands, Dirty Face," after which he speaks his famous words ("Wait a minute, wait a minute, you ain't heard nothin' yet . . .") and then he introduces his next song, the better-known "Toot, Toot, Tootsie."* There is very little spoken dialogue in the film, and the only recorded back-and-forth conversation is between Jolson and his mother, but there *is* plenty of music. Not only does Jolson sing the two songs mentioned above, he also does "Blue Skies," "Mother of Mine, I Still Have You," and "My Mammy" and the traditional Jewish "Kol Nidre." Films that were shot silent with sound added, such as *The Jazz Singer*, were called "part-talkies." Part-talkies were not always musicals.†

The success of these films (the part-talkies), particularly *The Jazz Singer*, inspired the business to try out a full sound feature, the "all-talking" concept, and a transition to sound took place. During this transition period, there were four types of exhibitions going on simultaneously, depending on where one lived or attended movies: (1) silent features, a business-as-usual format; (2) a program that was a roster of all-sound shorts like the Vitaphone releases; (3) a group of movies in which sound was incorporated into key scenes; and (4) the first "all-talking" pictures.

Warner Bros., pleased with its success with shorts and features in 1927,

---

* Songs for the young Jake Robin were prerecorded on the track, as in "My Gal Sal" and "Waitin' for the Robert E. Lee," in which there's no synchronization between Jake's wavering mouth and the piano player's beats.

† The idea that movies could be "part-talkie"—that is, have some sound in them, but only where it seemed appropriate or necessary or interesting—might make it possible to think of all musicals as part-talkie . . . the other part being people not talking, but singing and dancing.

put six all-talking films into production, all of which would be released in 1928, the year sound moved into place and the transition from silence to sound really began. These movies were: *Lights of New York, The Lion and the Mouse, On Trial, The Terror, The Home Towners,* and *The Singing Fool* (which was a musical starring Al Jolson). The first of these "talkies" to go into general release was the gangster movie *Lights of New York,* which is

thus officially the first "all-talking, all-sound" full-length motion picture and should take its place in film history accordingly. *Variety* reviewed *Lights of New York* by saying, "Here is the first 100% all talking picture . . . a real pioneer in the sense of being the first all-talker." *Lights of New York* (not a musical) ran fifty-seven minutes and was directed by Bryan Foy; its star was Cullen Landis, an unknown today, and it was a very, very bad gangster picture. (Huddled together around a telephone sitting in the middle of a table, which is obviously where the microphone is hidden, one of the group

In *The Jazz Singer,* Al Jolson sings "Blue Skies" and chats with his mammy (Eugenie Besserer) while his cantor father (Warner Oland) looks on and . . . *listens.*

of gangsters carefully intones: "We . . . will . . . take . . . him . . . for . . . a . . . ride.")

Since *Lights of New York* was clearly recognized at the time as the first all-talking movie, why does the myth persist that it was *The Jazz Singer*? The business always knew the truth, and would even admit it when it fit its purposes. In a 1947 short film, *The Sound Man* (shown on Turner Classic Movies on October 2, 2017), the narration clearly identifies *Lights of New York* as "the first all-talking full-length feature" and further identifies *In Old Arizona* as the first *on-location* all-talking feature (the mike is cleverly concealed in a cactus).* First of all, *The Jazz Singer is* a film in which there is sound: lines of dialogue *are* spoken, and someone *does* sing. But *The Jazz Singer* also had what Hollywood has always been able to make valuable use of: the kind of offscreen pizzazz that could make cash registers sing. Offstage, outside the theater, there was drama surrounding *The Jazz Singer*. The Warner brothers were in financial trouble, mostly due to the innovative and far-seeing efforts of Sam Warner, who believed in the future of sound. Sam more or less forced sound on his brothers, and *The Jazz Singer*'s big success—along with their investment in the Vitaphone process—saved their studio. Just the day before the premiere of the Jolson film, Sam (who was married to a famous and glamorous movie star of the era, Lina Basquette) dropped dead. His death brought real-life melodrama to the opening of *The Jazz Singer*, and so there was a great deal of emotion the night of the event. Al Jolson himself appeared, cried openly for Sam, and then went out into the audience and personally shook the hand of each customer. These events play out like one of those old movie montages of expository headlines: STUDIO ON THE VERGE OF BANKRUPTCY! YOUTHFUL BROTHER DROPS DEAD! GLAMOROUS STAR DEVASTATED BY LOSS OF HUSBAND! ON EVE OF HIS DREAM PREMIERE, ENTREPRENEUR LOSES LIFE! JOLSON CRIES FOR FRIEND! And if all these offscreen theatrics weren't enough, there's the movie itself. It has Al Jolson, an icon of his times, singing some of his most popular songs, getting down on one knee to emote, and uttering a line that is perfect for the announcement that sound has arrived: "You ain't heard nothin' yet." You didn't, of course, hear all that much in *The Jazz Singer* either, but the movie had Jolson and his theatrics and his music. He *does*

---

* The short was part of a series made by the Motion Picture Academy to promote the film business. With cooperation from all the studios, it contains clips from what were then current movies, *The Bishop's Wife* and *The Jolson Story*.

speak the famous tag line, and he *does* get down on one knee, and he *does* sing. Who needs a bad gangster film like the dull *Lights of New York,* starring Cullen Landis, who has no charisma? History be damned! Hollywood went with a better cast, a better story, and a better dramatic context, officially proclaiming *The Jazz Singer* as the first sound film. (As John Ford's films tell us, when the legend becomes fact, print the legend.)

The Jazz Singer is mostly silent, but when Jolson sings, it's atomic. He had a blockbuster ability to put a song across, and he was performing material (except for "Mother of Mine, I Still Have You," written for the film) that he had been selling to audiences for a long time. He had the handle on how to deal with live audiences: he talked to them, ad-libbed to them, and promised them things before, during, and after his songs. Thus his "dialogue" in *The Jazz Singer* is casual, easy, conversational, *and musical.* When he says, "Wait a minute, wait a minute, you ain't heard nothin' yet," the line was an old familiar friend he'd often used onstage. And it's all about music. Jolson introduced sound to the American moviegoer by introducing it as music.

The success of *The Jazz Singer*—and its legend—are grounded in one important thing: music. It was the beginning of something new: the musical film tradition. As Hollywood began to tell its own story about the arrival of sound, *The Jazz Singer* emerged as a perfect way to put the event onscreen. Big star, perfect tag line, offscreen drama, unexpected financial rescue, and simple one-line, one-song musical format. It worked. It was short, punchy, easily understood, and, of course, it was musical, music being the one new thing that audiences were really going to get from sound. Thus we have the myth of *The Jazz Singer* as the first sound movie. Even cleaned up, it's the myth of an audience's first glimpse of a great singing star, even though they'd already been able to see him (and hear him) in a Vitaphone short in 1926. Watching *The Jazz Singer* today, after all of that, is a bit of an anticlimax. It's not a great film, or even a very interesting one. (Frank Capra's 1929 movie *The Younger Generation* is also about Jewish assimilation, and it's a much better, deeper, and more cinematic version of that tale.)

Historians agree that from 1926 to 1931, a transition to sound took place in American cinema; but there has always been debate about how long the transition took, as well as about how difficult it actually was. Considering what a technical, artistic, economic, and business upheaval the arrival of sound meant, it was on the whole accomplished without any great disruptions. Very few stars lost their careers, and some who did were fine with it, or really lost out because of other reasons.* The business was at the same time coping with something that was in the long run much bigger: the Depression, and its effect on audiences and the economy. There are two schools of thought on the transition: (1) that it was slow, difficult, and took at least three years, and (2) that it was quick, and took about forty-five minutes on a Friday. The first group of historians are those who study exhibition, technology, and distribution, and the second are those who study films as art. Both sides are neither wrong nor completely right. The business system, with its financing, equipment changes, and theatrical venues that had to retool, rebuild, and re-equip, are correct that it was a slow process. The artists themselves, working inside, quickly found ways to compensate and accommodate: boom mikes, soundproof camera booths, adding sound over photographed images, using cutting to provide action, etc. I interviewed two film directors who were key to the transition to the sound era: Frank Capra and Rouben Mamoulian. Both felt that artists (such as themselves) were able to return to good filmmaking with sound added within a very brief time frame. (My conversations with Capra were particularly extensive. As a man who studied science and technology before he entered the movies, he was undaunted by technological changes.)

It's logical to assume that different aspects of the transition moved at different paces. What everyone can agree on is that Hollywood coped, moved forward, and never looked back. The arrival of sound changed things in all areas, and one of the most important of those areas was in relation to the creation of the musical film. The arrival of sound inspired more musical films than most people realize, as the newness of musicals drove the popularity of sound films forward. Starting in 1929 and continuing until early 1931, the market was flooded with musicals. In 1929, Hollywood began hiring sound-related performers and technicians of all types, including, of course, musicians, arrangers, songwriters, ex-vaudevillians, singers and dancers, choreographers, and composers—all were in demand to create the suddenly possible, and thus excitingly new, musical genre.

Publicists, agents, movie magazines, and newspapers fed the public's interest in the new technology. There were articles on how sound worked,

* Vilma Banky's ethereal image did not match her guttural Hungarian accent, but she had just married and was happy to retire. The Talmadge sisters were glad to stop working and live like the rich women they were. John Gilbert, contrary to popular opinion, had a fairly lengthy and reasonably successful sound career. His problems were more personal, such as his drinking and his bad relationship with Louis B. Mayer.

with the prediction that sound on film would soon outperform sound on disc (it did) and on "voice doubling." In the beginning, fans were not lied to, or kept in the dark, about a star's inability to sing. In an article entitled "The Truth About Voice Doubling," the July 1929 *Photoplay* clearly explained that Richard Barthelmess "did not sing in *Weary River*, and, of course, he didn't play the piano. Johnny Murray sang . . . while Frank Churchill played . . . it was done very neatly." Johnny Murray was under contract to provide Barthelmess's voice for the entire year of 1929, just as Debbie Reynolds's character was supposed to do for Lina Lamont (Jean Hagen) in *Singin' in the Rain*. Fan magazines touted new movie personalities, especially those who had been successful in musical venues, such as Broadway, vaudeville, and nightclubs: Norma Terris, Maurice Chevalier, Marilyn Miller, Helen Morgan, Gertrude Lawrence, Helen Kane, Irene Bordoni, Frank Fay (who brought his wife, Barbara Stanwyck, to Hollywood with him), and Vivienne Segal, among others.

Many musicals of all types were offered to the public in 1929; these films are almost totally unknown today, partly because of availability issues, but also because audiences don't have the patience for the often clumsy cinematic presentation they offer. Many of them feature famous names (Fanny Brice in *My Man*, singing the title song plus "Second Hand Rose," "I'd Rather Be Blue," "I'm an Indian," and "If You Want the Rainbow (You Must Have the Rain)"). The 1929 list includes the all-black *Hearts in Dixie* (with "forty negro spirituals, folk songs, cakewalks, folk dancers, strummin' banjos," and billed as having "More than Sound—Life Itself!"); *The Pagan*; *Fox Movietone Follies*; *Close Harmony*; *Queen of the Night Clubs* (starring Texas Guinan); *The Desert Song* (the Sigmund Romberg operetta); *Syncopation*; *Honky Tonk* (with Sophie Tucker); *Broadway*; *On with the Show* (with a Technicolor insert); *Not Quite Decent*; *The Time, the Place, and the Girl*; *Innocents of Paris* (with Maurice Chevalier, and the ads tell audiences to pronounce it "She-val-yay"); *Rio Rita*; *Hit the Deck*; *Hallelujah* (another all-black musical, this one directed by King Vidor); *Dance of Life*; *Marianne* (with Marion Davies); *Sweetie*; *Red Hot Rhythm*; *The Hollywood Revue of 1929* (with Joan Crawford doing a thumping tap dance); and many others. The history of the musical begins in this transition period, and the movies that were made illustrate a mini-lesson in what would happen over the coming decades: innovation and experimentation coupled with a grounding in what was already known and familiar from vaudeville and Broadway. There would be the tradition of the revue—a lot of unrelated musical presentations and a few funny skits (which would remain alive into the war years with patriotic variations such as *Thank Your Lucky Stars*, *Star Spangled Rhythm*, and *Hollywood Canteen*, and carry on to *New Faces* (released in 1954); the backstage musical, which would never really go away, with its boy-meets-girl plots; and musicals such as those by Lubitsch and Mamoulian, in which music is integrated into the story and is used to express character, to advance the plot, and to make comments on events. The idea of the integrated musical, which is often attributed to the Arthur Freed unit at MGM, was part of the earliest years of sound. Here is where a history emerges which can be tracked forward from movies in which people sing and dance for a living toward movies in which people sing and dance as they live; and yet both forms were thought about and produced from the very beginning. Among these 1929 releases are films of differing value that illustrate where the talking musical started out and where it was going to go: the Marx Brothers in *The Cocoanuts; Show of Shows;* Janet Gaynor in *Sunny Side Up;* and *The Broadway Melody*.

The Cocoanuts, the Marx Brothers' first movie, is a prime example of early musical adaptation. It is a functional filming of their Broadway hit of the same name. *The Cocoanuts* stars the four brothers with the inevitable Margaret Dumont; a beautiful young Kay Francis as a villainess; singing star Oscar Shaw as the leading man; and singer/dancer Mary Eaton as the female ingenue. The original play was by George S. Kaufman and Morrie Ryskind and the music by Irving Berlin. *The Cocoanuts* was filmed at the Astoria Studios in Long Island in the spring of 1929, and the resulting movie proved a hit. The brothers were appearing on Broadway nightly in *Animal Crackers* during the shooting, working all day on the movie and pumping it out onstage at night. The movie shoot was inevitably slowed by the need to use new sound equipment and, according to Harpo's autobiography, *Harpo Speaks*, by unexpected on-set laughter from people who would forget that all sounds were being picked up by the microphones. Director Robert Florey, according to Harpo, was especially vulnerable: "Florey couldn't help breaking up. When he laughed, he laughed so hard he drowned out everything else on the sound track."

The Cocoanuts is a direct adaptation of stage to screen, literally a photograph of the show. At first, the business was more or less content with this simple method of creating musicals. The general idea was that a musical was something you saw only in a theater; previously, you couldn't see one on the movie screen, because there had been no sound. Therefore, the

task was to transfer the stage show onto the movie screen as accurately as possible—lift it up and relocate it. The purpose of the camera would be to put the movie viewer in the best seat in the Broadway house. Many of the 1929–30 musicals are shot as if to make it possible to look straight ahead and see the full theatrical presentation, and if you look left or right, to have an unobstructed view of the entire panoply. (This is what movies could do for you!) *The Cocoanuts* illustrates this method. Although it probably shouldn't be viewed as anything other than a Marx Brothers vehicle—stories of how they turned the script into their own creation are legendary—the filmed *Cocoanuts is* a Broadway musical put on film.

In its review of *The Cocoanuts*, *The New York Times* indicated that the camerawork was harmless. That was considered a compliment at the time: the idea was that a movie camera should never get in the way of what

Four (count 'em!) Marx Brothers (Zeppo, Groucho, Chico, and Harpo) knock audiences out with their fast-paced jokes in *The Cocoanuts* . . . and there's singin' and dancin', too!

was good, which was the proscenium-arch original show. The camera's role was to photograph. That it might have some specific, interesting, or (God forbid!) artistic thing it could do in musical presentation seemed unthinkable. "Don't interfere" was the mantra of most early Broadway adaptations.

The "young" leads, Shaw and Eaton, sing both together and alone, but pretty much always sing the same song. Even Harpo's obligatory harp solo is the same song. (During tryouts, when numbers were being cut, Berlin is reported to have said, "My God! Any more cuts and this will be a musical without any music!") Shaw and Eaton sing in the crooned-over, stretched-out style of the day: "I'll dreeeeeeeeaammm of youoooooo." The musical numbers are shot in two basic styles: Here we are in the theatre seats looking at the proscenium arch and aren't we lucky?!" and "Here we are in our movie seats looking at the new medium of sound film and aren't we lucky?!" There's not much of the latter, but there is some. The camera occasionally relocates itself onstage. During the love duets, it moves in for medium close-ups, so the two good-looking youngsters can be fully appreciated. Bits of business are revealed very specifically as inserts so the audience can clearly see how a handkerchief is dropped to be picked up. (This was a common silent-film device.) Once in a while, a viewer sees the legs of the dancers as they trot by, and there's a glorious moment in which a kaleidoscopic overhead crane shot shows chorus girls forming patterns with their bodies. It's a pre–Busby Berkeley moment, but relatively brief, and it is abandoned quickly and presented more as a stunt than as an interesting development for showing dance on film.

The chorus girls of *The Cocoanuts* aren't really dancers; they're more like a marching drill team. Their steps are simple, and anyone could do them. The girls are all short and somewhat plump, pretty rather than glamorous, and certainly not providing viewers with a line of dance that is athletic and visual. They poke around the stage, prancing like little ponies and smiling their heads off. (Such dancers were actually called "ponies.") The brothers are, of course, hilarious, and know what they're doing.* The screen medium does not inhibit them or slow them down at all. (When Dumont, in her first turn as Groucho's stoogess, tells him he wouldn't love her if she weren't rich, he replies, "I might, but I'd probably keep my mouth

---

* *The Cocoanuts* has four Marx brothers (Groucho, Harpo, Chico, and Zeppo), with Zeppo assigned a very small role as Groucho's hotel assistant. (Nobody cared.)

shut." This is the movie in which he famously tells her that when they meet secretly in the moonlight, she should "wear a necktie so I'll know you.")

The Cocoanuts clearly reveals what a 1929 Broadway show was like. It's obvious that the Broadway musical of the day didn't care much about the art of the motion picture or even about the art of the Broadway show. There's no reason for the music, and no story or character that really matters. Above all, there's no real emotional connection between the music and the characters performing it. Whether show or movie, *The Cocoanuts* is about plot, or event, never about character or emotion. It is an excuse for some great comedy routines, some nice songs, and a few cheeky dances that reveal panties and plump legs.*

Show of Shows, running a long 128 minutes, is another example of what in the beginning everyone thought the musical could (and even should) be. It's an elongated Vitaphone short, one act after another glued together in trainlike effect by the presence of Frank Fay. It's highlighted by a spectacular two-strip color sequence featuring the young and ravishingly beautiful Myrna Loy and singer Nick Lucas, who was well-known at the time. What the movie accomplishes is the fundamental idea of bringing vaudeville to the masses. It's an expensive, varied presentation in which the "best seat in the house" concept is maintained, except when the camera does its magic, through a cut to bring the performer closer (via a medium shot) in a way that even the best seat could never provide. That was the magic of the original musical film: good sound, access to stars, faithful reproduction of a proscenium spectacle, and a closer look at the talent. The movie contained vaudeville skits, a touch of highbrow Shakespearean class (John Barrymore as Richard III from *Henry VI, Part 3*), color (the Loy episode), names such as Winnie Lightner and Beatrice Lillie, and a look at "formations" of the sort that preceded Busby Berkeley. Girls dance out and across the stage on differing platform tiers, wearing dresses that are white in front and black in back (with wigs to match: blond in front, brunet in back). Naturally, they turn back and forth. Girls also come out in shorts and proceed upstage to climb ladders that are concealed so they appear to be walking up walls marked by large argyle patterns of Xs. And if all that weren't enough, sixteen pairs of real-life sisters who work in the movie business come out two at a time to sing their names in a number called "Meet My Sister": Dolo-

---

* What was fresh in *The Cocoanuts* was the antic Marx Brothers blasting onto the screen with their verbal assaults, just as they were doing it in the theater itself at the time.

res and Helene Costello, Alice and Marceline Day, Ada Mae and Alberta Vaughn, Molly O'Day and Sally O'Neil, Shirley Mason and Viola Dana, and Sally Blane and Loretta Young among them.*

In its day, *Show of Shows* must have seemed beautiful, exciting, and sophisticated. Men in tuxedos . . . women in elegant gowns . . . ironic humor . . . beauty . . . and famous names talking! The Myrna Loy Asian number is introduced by Rin Tin Tin! He barks it up big-time. It would seem that a revue like this would be enough for any audience: after all, wasn't this the sort of thing that Broadway had to offer? The musical film could be the Broadway revue for everyone who couldn't get to New York. What else did it need to be? *Show of Shows* assumed that the movie musical should record and replicate vaudeville and/or Broadway and leave it at that.

This idea continued past *Show of Shows*. Sound brought on an excitement over musical films, particularly when audiences realized there would be more treats like *Show of Shows*—an example was *King of Jazz*, released in 1930. The "King of Jazz" was Paul Whiteman, a man as popular in his own time as rock stars are today. Whiteman mainstreamed jazz music by putting together a large band that officially brought African American music into the white world. Carl Laemmle Jr., head of Universal Pictures, signed Whiteman up to appear in a sound movie in 1929 and brought him to Hollywood with great fanfare. Whiteman and his group boarded the "Gold Train," a gold-painted train that was sponsored by Old Gold cigarettes, and arrived to be covered by the Universal payroll for months before they actually did anything. Signing Paul Whiteman for the movies was one thing; creating a story that could star him was another. Whiteman was corpulent, slightly balding, and not a young man.

Universal chose John Murray Anderson, a New York producer who was a sort of low-budget alternative to Florenz Ziegfeld and his extravaganzas, to direct *King of Jazz*. While Ziegfeld owned Broadway, Anderson owned Greenwich Village, where he produced his own singing-and-dancing revues. Anderson had no experience in movies, but he had produced what were called "prologues" for the Paramount theater chain. ("Prologues" are those things James Cagney is producing in *Footlight Parade*—that is, extravagant live musical numbers that appear onstage before the movie

---

* *Photoplay* magazine mused, "If they could guarantee us Lillian and Dorothy Gish doing a black bottom, the world would be a better place."

starts. No doubt Anderson's prologues could not rival those Cagney, in the guise of Busby Berkeley, was putting on. Trying to do "By a Waterfall" on stage might have been a bigger challenge than Anderson could handle.) *King of Jazz* brought audiences something they could never have imagined: not only Whiteman's music, beautifully recorded, but also amazing Technicolor (two-strip) sequences. The movie presents the first film appearance of Bing Crosby as part of the Rhythm Boys trio; an extravagant "It Happened in Monterey" Mexican number with Jeanette Loff; a beautifully recorded presentation of Gershwin's *Rhapsody in Blue*, which had originally been commissioned by the Whiteman Orchestra; and John Boles singing "Song of the Dawn." The soundtrack is historic: the first feature-length film to use a prerecorded soundtrack made independently of the filming. *King of Jazz* brought spectacle to the masses and introduced the sort of imaginative and awe-inspiring entertainment that musicals might bring, but it cost nearly two million dollars to make and did not turn a profit after its initial release.*

Sunny Side Up is, as the credits announce, "an original musical comedy," and as such, it is an important film in the transition-to-sound era. It wasn't developed from a Broadway show, so there was no impulse to photograph it as if the moviegoer had been transported to a theater. It simply begins as if there's sound in the universe, and we're in a movie house watching and listening to a musical world. In that world are the adorable Janet Gaynor and the stalwart Charles Farrell, a very popular love team from the silent era who prove they can make it across the sound barrier with ease.

Sunny Side Up opens with a cacophony of sound that is loud and emphatic, no doubt dazzling the audiences of the day. As a single camera tracks around and up and down an East Side New York City tenement area, sound is laid over the image to show a world of ethnicity, noise, laughter, music, screams and yells, moving vehicles—the works. The glory of sound. A world of sound. There's a constantly switching point of view on what can be heard as an audience is "walked" around a tenement street. This camera movement with the accompanying shifting tones, tongues, and modulations is a kind of musical number in itself. The movie that follows is a very

---

* It was rereleased after musicals made a comeback in 1933, but in a version that was cut from 105 minutes to 65 minutes. Today it can be seen in magnificent restoration, and there is a book, *King of Jazz*, chronicling its history, written by David Pierce and James Layton. There is also a relevant biography of John Murray Anderson, hilariously titled *Out Without My Rubbers: The Memoirs of John Murray Anderson as told to Hugh Abercrombie Anderson.*

American story, one of a rich boy and a poor girl, of dreams and democracy, of tenement rooms and Long Island mansions. What will make it significant is that the leading characters in it don't play professional musical performers, so they have to find a believable reason to sing and dance. The film also has to find a way to present a big, superscale musical number without anyone wondering where it came from. This marks *Sunny Side Up* as truly an "original" movie musical, even if it's a bit old-fashioned in plot and, for the most part, does not violate the basic "backstage" musical concept.

The first musical presentation after the opening establishment of sound/image is done by Gaynor. Having set eyes on the wealthy and handsome Farrell, she picks up a zither, sits down in a chair in her modest little apartment, starts strumming, and, after looking at Farrell's photograph in a newspaper, sings—almost as if she's talking to herself in music—"I'm a Dreamer, Aren't We All?" Gaynor is held in the frame in medium close-up as she sings, and her little song, put forth sweetly, shyly, in her reedy little voice, is an acting tour de force. She's charming, funny, sad, winsome, a little discouraged, a little encouraged. She's magic. Show me the person who can resist Janet Gaynor in this intimate moment of talking/singing

Janet Gaynor gives out with the title tune at a block party in *Sunny Side Up,* an original Hollywood musical.

about her inner life to an audience! Gaynor is adorable, and it's no wonder she won the first Academy Award for Best Actress based on *Sunrise*, *7th Heaven*, and *Street Angel*. She's not a great singer, but her ability to make a song meaningful in the context of a movie is peerless. An audience is going to be asked to understand why a rich boy like Farrell falls in love with her, why she's worthy of that love, and why she even deserves it, too. In this song, all that—and more—is put across with a motionless camera, a zither, and a little woman who understands that sound affords her the opportunity to act through song lyrics. Gaynor goes on to perform this song two more times: when, exposed as only a poor little shopgirl, and not a socialite, she has to sing it in front of an audience who know who she really is; and finally, when she has had to accept the loss of the love of her life (which is temporary, of course—this *is* a musical). She thus sings the song first to establish her character, then to provide drama, and finally to reflect the hopeful philosophy of the film. Gaynor is by turns upbeat, downbeat, and überbeat. *Sunny Side Up* knows how to present a musical number as more than a musical number, and thus it is an important moment in the early development of the genre—it marks a beginning of sorts for musical performance that's more than just singing a song. Gaynor's role in *Sunny Side Up* is an example of how a silent-film star could successfully add music to her earlier persona and move forward to become an even bigger star. She portrays an ordinary working girl, and the genius of her performance is that the majority of her musical offerings are designed to confirm her as a nonprofessional. Without sound, Gaynor is ethereal, radiantly childlike without being unreal emotionally. With an ability to sing to her audience and with an opportunity to speak saucy dialogue and muse wistfully aloud, Gaynor added to her former image a more modern self: a perkier, more optimistic and capable presence. Her glow became a sparkle.

Gaynor's second number takes place at a block party with an amateur performance lineup. There's a little boy who has to go to the bathroom trying to recite a poem before it's too late, some other cornball offerings, and Gaynor coming out to sing "Sunny Side Up." She comes on like an amateur with a good-sport willingness to join in. When she goes up on the makeshift neighborhood stage to perform her contribution to the fun, she's wearing an off-the-rack print dress and holding her props: a top hat and a cane that seem too big for her. She stands for a minute, as if she's afraid to start, then smiles at her audience and uncorks a truly insignificant little singing voice: "Be like two fried eggs/Keep your sunny side up!" When she starts a soft-shoe routine to follow her vocal, her tiny feet in her little shoes make her look like someone's daughter dancing in the kindergarten recital. She's no Ethel Merman, but she doesn't need to be. She owns the concept of someone who's just getting up onstage to perform, counting on the goodwill of her audience to accept her as a working girl who will sing and dance because it's the tenement block party.

With Gaynor in *Sunny Side Up*, the "naturalistic" musical begins to take form. The movie shows itself to be a wonderful grab bag of what may lie ahead, not only by being an original creation for film, but also by having simple songs sung for established reasons, or sung for no established reason. Gaynor sings to explain herself. Charles Farrell's numbers are explained by his preparations for a "charity show" to be done at his mom's Long Island estate. He's *rehearsing*. All his numbers are rehearsals, with one exception: a break is made when he simply stands looking at a photo of Gaynor and sings "If I Had a Talking Picture of You."

Sunny Side Up understands the possibility of using a song for character intimacy, but it also provides the audience with a gobsmacker of a big musical number. It could be called Busby Berkeley–ish except he wasn't on the scene (he was over at Goldwyn making *Whoopee!*). Presented logically as part of the big charity-show finale, "Turn on the Heat" appears from behind a water-fountain curtain that is lowered for it to begin (a gimmick Berkeley himself would use later, in 1943's *The Gang's All Here*). The chorus girls trot out to gyrate behind a lyric being sung by the third lead (Sharon Lynn), who is Gaynor's rival for Farrell. First the girls are dressed as Eskimos standing outside tiny igloos. As the lyrics roll out ("Turn on the heat, turn on the heat/Get hot for Papa or Papa will freeze"), the girls bump and grind. Slowly the igloos begin to melt, and the girls shed their fur parkas and hoods. Ultimately they strip down to their skivvies; all the snow and ice are gone; and out of the ground begin to sprout . . . trees! The trees grow upward, getting bigger and bigger, finally producing bananas that grow and elongate. Presumably Papa will not freeze, and also presumably, Busby Berkeley saw this number and finally was able to create his own bananas in a latter-day Carmen Miranda number. (The dance numbers in *Sunny Side Up* were created by Seymour Felix.)*

* The film was directed by David Butler, with songs by DeSylva, Henderson, and Brown. Gaynor was supported by comic El Brendel and song-and-dance specialists Marjorie White and Joe Brown in this highly successful movie. Farrell and Gaynor made a total of four musicals together, even though neither of them was truly a musical performer.

Seen today, *The Broadway Melody* puts on a proud display of sound. It embraces music, although it doesn't quite embrace the camera. It's still an important step forward, and not just because it was the first musical to win the Best Picture Oscar. Planned by Irving Thalberg, the famous MGM producer, *The Broadway Melody* featured an original screenplay that would lay out the template for the backstage movie musical, and it also boasted a score written especially for the film. Most historians credit *The Broadway Melody* as "the first" in the categories of original musical screenplay, backstage tradition, original score, use of prerecorded music, and, of course, the Oscar. Its love song, "You Were Meant for Me," became a standard, and its success motivated the studio to create a series of *Broadway Melody* movies for 1936, 1938, and 1940. It was also remade by Metro in 1940 as a vehicle for the young Lana Turner, *Two Girls on Broadway*.

The song-and-dance man who played the lead, Charles King, was the sort of performer that sound brought to Hollywood. Born in 1889, he'd been a professional since 1908 and had introduced some important songs on Broadway: "Play a Simple Melody" in 1914's *Watch Your Step*, "Nellie Kelly, I Love You" in *Little Nellie Kelly* (1922), and "Sometimes I'm Happy" from *Hit the Deck* (1927). He was a consummate pro, and easily fit into the role of a confident songwriter/singer/dancer that *The Broadway Melody* needed. His movie career was brief but significant. In addition to introducing both "Broadway Melody" and "You Were Meant for Me," he later appeared in 1930's *Chasing Rainbows*, in which he introduced Franklin Delano Roosevelt's campaign tune, "Happy Days Are Here Again." He died in 1944, his other two movies being *The Hollywood Revue of 1929* and 1930's *Oh, Sailor Behave!* (one of my favorite film titles).

The Broadway Melody opens up with a proud and confident usage of musical sound, not unlike *Sunny Side Up* does. The difference is that *Sunny Side Up*'s world is a tenement street, and *The Broadway Melody*'s is a Tin Pan Alley music company. There's a cacophony of voices, accents, musical instruments, songs, and conversations, all of which are about musical professionals rather than normal street folks. A guy is pitching his new song, instrumentalists are knocking out a hot jazz tune, singers are harmonizing, a piano player is banging away, a quartet is giving out, arguments are underway—it's an atmosphere of excitement, possibility, competition, all with a real New York vibe, delineated and created through sound, primarily musical sound. It's a bold statement that this movie is going to embrace sound, use it as an asset, and treat it like an old friend even though it's new and challenging. The dialogue feels improvised, and thus natural and real.

The first musical to win the Academy Award for Best Picture: *The Broadway Melody*, made by MGM, the studio that would become famous for the genre. Left to right: Anita Page, Charles King, Bessie Love

Much of it overlaps (so much for the idea that overlapping dialogue was invented decades later). "Hot dog!" someone remarks with enthusiasm, and it's a reflection of how any viewer (even today) feels in the middle of the energetic, exciting, and wonderful world of New York City.

The Broadway Melody's opening credits have an upbeat rendition of "Give My Regards to Broadway" laid over a typical aerial shot of the tip of Manhattan. When the story moves into the Tin Pan Alley scene already described, the hero is singing the title song, "Broadway Melody." When the two leading ladies arrive fresh from "the West," they are sassy, argumentative, and slangy. "Ain't it swell?" is their overall evaluation, and "And how!" is their form of approval. "Ska . . . rew!" is their order to leave. They toss off lines that describe their world—"ironing our clothes on mirrors." It's all energy and color until a shock hits the audience when an intertitle suddenly jerks the action back to the silent era. Throughout the movie, intertitles cut in: "The girl's apartment" . . . "The Final Dress Rehearsal" . . . "Three months later," etc. Almost all of them are unnecessary, and so rapidly has the movie established the sound universe that they seem to come from another planet. Only in preparation for showing a musical production number does the film feel free to let these titles go. Instead, an alleged audience member holds a program on which the oncoming musical presentation is announced: "The Wedding of the Painted Doll" and "The Boy Friend." (This "program" tradition would continue in musicals for decades.)

The Broadway Melody is a backstage musical, which means that, unlike in *Sunny Side Up*, there will be no need to explain musical performance. The characters are in show business and thus they sing and dance. They perform their music onstage for audiences, in rehearsals for their bosses, for each other to receive feedback, and at parties to provide entertainment. There is no challenge as to how to transform space from a nonmusical world into a musical world. The film just has a world, and people in it make music to earn a living. There's one possible disconnect in this regard. The plot concerns a songwriter who has made his place in New York. Having succeeded, he sends for the girl he plans to marry, who is also a performer. She brings along her kid sister, now grown up and a great beauty, and when the songwriter sees the sister, etc., etc., etc. The sister returns his feelings, but both of them love the third wheel too much to do anything about it. And yet, the songwriter composes a song for the kid sister, and sings it to her outside the performance arena and outside any plot excuse for him to do so. The song is "You Were Meant for Me" and he sings it in "the girl's apartment." He sings. She reacts. This is an apparent violation of the backstage concept, and perhaps the beginning of integrating song into characterization and story. But is it really? He *is* a songwriter. He *does* sing all the time. He has earlier written "Broadway Melody" for her sister. And the leading lady and leading man of a Broadway musical would often sing to each other (with no explanation) at a Long Island weekend party or some similar setting. There appears to be no intention, no real understanding of this possible disconnect by any of its performers or by its director. Nevertheless, it is a kind of prescient moment.

The Broadway Melody contains one other very important element in the development of the musical genre: an ability to contain inside its comedy, romance, and music a highly dramatic and sincerely tragic moment. When Bessie Love (playing the rejected sister) realizes that King and her more beautiful younger sibling, Anita Page, are actually in love with each other—something that hadn't previously occurred to her—there is a moment in her backstage dressing room that is deeply dramatic. Love stands with her back to the audience, and a deep silence falls between her and King, Page having run out in tears. The silence is held, proving that moviemakers still understood its value, even though the new technology was allegedly shattering it forever. The movie has made the very best use of sound that it possibly could, but the dramatic high point uses the silence that had made cinema an art form to that date. (It boded well for the future of the movies: sound might be king, but silence would be the queen mother.)

After the plot moves on and Love releases King, who leaves her, she sits down at her dressing table and begins to use tissues to remove her makeup. While working on her face, she begins to sob, crying uncontrollably, and finally breaking out into hysterical laughing while she sobs. Love is great in this scene, which undoubtedly helped move *The Broadway Melody* to Oscar-status, but she's also defining the future of the genre. There will always be room for tears and tragedy inside the seemingly lighthearted musical. Love's scene is echoed in Judy Garland's hysterical breakdown in her dressing room while talking to Charles Bickford about her husband's alcoholism in the 1954 *A Star Is Born*. Garland, too, has just done a happy number (for the movie camera in this case), and she has to repair her makeup in front of a mirror.

The Broadway Melody points to the future. Its musical numbers are impressive, and the songs are excellent. What it lacks is innovative dance and innovative camerawork to present the dance. The dancing has an acrobatic quality, something that often appears in early musicals, especially the Vitaphone shorts that reproduced vaudeville acts. (Physical movement was physical movement. Dance could and did belong to tumblers and acrobats as well as tappers and ballet practitioners.) The main thing about the way the dances are shown is that the camera refuses to get into them. The musical numbers are horizontal. They move across the screen as they would across the stage, from left to right, or from right to left, or back and forth. When and if the filmmakers decide to take a viewer closer, the camera goes up to the footlights, or perhaps just onto the apron or over into the wings to allow a closer look. The depth of the dance, the incorporation of the camera in some way into the movement of the dancers, is not really present in any coherent or sophisticated manner.

In 1929, there was one other important musical that promised a bright future for the genre: *The Love Parade*. It was not a Broadway adaptation, and it went beyond the two successful "original" musicals, *Sunny Side Up* and *The Broadway Melody*. It starred Maurice Chevalier, Jeanette MacDonald, Lillian Roth, and Lupino Lane. This was the first time Chevalier and MacDonald would be paired, but not the last. It was MacDonald's film debut, and she began in a very different sort of musical from those she would later be associated with, her famous operettas opposite Nelson Eddy. *The Love Parade* is one of the sophisticated and cinematic efforts of Ernst Lubitsch, the imaginative German director who became celebrated for his famous "touch," which was his sly visual style that presented unexpected behavior and comment and clever innuendo. He's one of the true pioneers of the sophisticated development of the musical film, and *The Love Parade* was his first. He followed it with *Monte Carlo* (in 1930), with MacDonald, this time co-starred with Jack Buchanan and Zasu Pitts.*

The Love Parade and *Monte Carlo* are part of the transition to sound, but the sophistication and cinematic mastery they represent, while appreciated, is somewhat jumped over in historical discussions. A simple trajectory is laid out: here's *Jazz Singer*, then *The Broadway Melody*, and then musicals die until they are resurrected by Busby Berkeley. Lubitsch, however, cannot be overlooked. Everything in his world was about performance. His silent films were visual musicals, lyrical images for the eyeball. His ability to glide, to hide, to move his plots forward unexpectedly and always at a graceful pace, allowed him to easily embrace musical numbers. Lubitsch became a key figure in the creation of fabulous musicals, his pioneering work sometimes not seen as the innovation it was because it was so deftly entertaining and because it was so divorced from reality. *The Love Parade* is practically the embodiment of the transition to sound, a textbook lesson in what the issues were, the problems that were being faced. On the one hand, as characters sing and/or dance, sometimes the camera doesn't move, and the songs are performed in front of a backdrop; on the other hand, the camera moves fluidly, some songs are shot creatively, and sound is used as a whole new set of meanings. Depending on what part of *The Love*

---

* *Paramount on Parade*, to which Lubitsch contributed three musical sequences, came out in 1930 between these two films.

Parade you're looking at, you're either seeing a work of cinematic genius that's solving the problems of sound and embracing the new possibilities, or you're watching a clumsy example of how no one knew what to do other than stand in front of a camera and sing, keeping in everyone's sightlines. MacDonald (as Queen Louisa) sings her first song (the film's hit, "Dream Lover") in the tradition of an operetta. Beautifully dressed, she sings, and that's pretty much it. But when she comes out to review her troops for "March of the Grenadiers," Lubitsch lays the song over the images, so that a viewer is experiencing a separation of sound and picture, and yet a clever juxtaposition of both. Queen Louisa is seen riding her horse, but then everything she is reviewing is shown—soldiers, drums, trumpets—while the recorded track is heard.

Another clever separation of soundtrack and image occurs during Chevalier's delightful song "Paris, Stay the Same." While he sings about the wonderful women of Paris, those charming ladies he will miss since he's been recalled to Sylvania, an audience is shown what he's singing about. Sexy, gloriously dressed, sipping champagne and smoking cigarettes, these beautiful and sophisticated creatures are intercut with his singing. The women are elegant creatures—and expensive looking. The wonderful Lubitsch touch is that after Chevalier finishes singing, his valet begins to sing the same song, and an audience is shown *his* beautiful ladies: maids, waitresses, and girls of his own social stratum. This is adorable, but it's not the punch line. From master to servant, yes, from high-class ladies and would-be ladies to servants, yes; but then Lubitsch cuts to Chevalier's dog. The audience is treated to the sight of the well-groomed poodles he'll be missing.

In *Monte Carlo*, MacDonald sings "Beyond the Blue Horizon" as the world races by outside her train window; she throws open the window and embraces that world. Here, the possibility of a musical number moving through time and space without dancing or the specific physical movement of a character is demonstrated. Music liberates. Music releases. Music travels. It can be *heard* to move, and the image can be *seen* to move. A character can sing/talk to viewers about what's being seen and what's being felt at the same time. MacDonald is embracing the world through song and "talking" to the people outside her windows . . . or so it seems, thanks to cutting, sound recording, and the wedding of sound and image.

Lubitsch's musical skills are also on display in another 1930 feature, *Paramount on Parade*, a compendium of numbers and sketches directed by dif-

"I have a system that never fails...."

ferent people: Dorothy Arzner, Rowland V. Lee, Frank Tuttle, and Edward ("Eddie") Sutherland, and eight others, including Lubitsch. As a musical, the film falls into the typical transition-era variety show format. Lubitsch directed three segments, all musical: *Park in Paris*, *Origin of the Apache*, and *Rainbow Revels*. The *Apache* number is a great satire working off the traditional dance of the pimp and his woman in which they beat each other up. Maurice Chevalier and Evelyn Brent, beautifully dressed in evening clothes, begin arguing, then indulge in a wild "Apache" fling, ripping each other's clothes off. The joke is that they're really a happily married couple, and they end the dance by getting beautifully redressed and going out on the town. In *Rainbow Revels*, which was shot in two-strip Technicolor, Chevalier is a chimney sweep surrounded by a chorus line of beauties wearing very little, while he sings "Sweepin' the Clouds Away."

Other creators besides Lubitsch began thinking more about the medium itself. In *Whoopee!*, a lively filming of Eddie Cantor's stage hit, Busby Berkeley was the choreographer. He and the film's producer, Samuel Goldwyn tried to be more inventive and not just photograph a play. Berkeley did not use multiple cameras to "capture" the stage play from different seats in the house and thus different vantage points. He used only one camera

In Ernst Lubitsch's delicious *Monte Carlo,* Jeanette MacDonald and England's famous music-hall star Jack Buchanan take a gamble on a little flirtation.

to provide close-ups of the faces of dancing girls, and in a bold move he put it overhead to create what would become one of his signature moves: the creation of a kaleidoscopic effect as the audience looked down on the girls doing formations. The use of only one camera meant that the audience felt more a part of the musical presentation, and as if they had a more intimate relationship with Cantor. This imaginative use of cinema is not consistent in *Whoopee!*, which is often stagebound, even static, but it's a beginning. *Variety* picked up on Busby Berkeley's first work in *Whoopee!*: "Nifty numbers staging by Busby Berkeley, inclusive of one fine overhead shot of the girls, besides some Lady Godiva stuff of the girls riding down the trail astride horses." *Variety* knew that "Lady Godiva stuff" was going to go over well with audiences.

The creation of musicals, both good and bad, was prevalent throughout 1929 and into 1930. *Sally* showcased the popular Marilyn Miller ("Now the screen has robbed the stage of its most prized possession"). Other successful musicals of the two-year period included *The Vagabond Lover* (with Rudy Vallee); *Glorifying the American Girl*; *Love Comes Along*; *Pointed Heels*; *Nix on Dames*; *High Society Blues*; *The Girl from Woolworths*; and *Paramount on Parade*. Lawrence Tibbett was brought from the Metropolitan Opera to sing in MGM's *The Rogue Song*, co-starring Laurel and Hardy and directed by Lionel Barrymore. Dennis King, a Broadway leading man, came to do *The Vagabond King* ("with Jeanette MacDonald," who would be there long after King was gone). Silent stars with voices, such as Ramon Novarro, were turned into musical stars with movies like *Devil-May-Care*, and Joe E. Brown was hired to re-create his Broadway success *Hold Everything*. New stars emerged, such as Nancy Carroll, a cute little redhead whose name is almost unknown today. She was a chorus girl on Broadway as a teenager, and while dancing in a show in California was spotted by a Paramount talent agent. Something of a cross between Clara Bow and Janet Gaynor— tiny, big-eyed, both sweet and saucy—Carroll became a big-name star in this era, heavily publicized in the November 1929 *Photoplay* as "a pretty little New York girl, all peaches and cream, an Irish lassie." Of her first "all-talkie," *Close Harmony* in 1929, the May *Photoplay* review said, "Her voice is clear and resonant." In 1929 she also appeared in *The Shopworn Angel*, *Sweetie*, and *The Dance of Life*. Of the latter, *Photoplay*'s September review said that Carroll "comes in for a big share of the laurel wreath. She is natural and charming and uses her head for something besides her permanent wave . . . This little girl has climbed to the top of the sound film successes."

The Dance of Life, an excellent early film that's an honest portrait of backstage life, was based on a highly successful play from the 1927–28 Broadway season (called *Burlesque* and written by Arthur Hopkins and George Manker Watters). It was an important step forward not only for Carroll, who played the role originated by Barbara Stanwyck, but also for the musical genre. Released in August 1929, it was enhanced by starring the original leading man, dancer Hal Skelly, with Ralph Theador, Charles D. Brown, Dorothy Revier, and Oscar Levant in his film debut. It kept the theme song, "True Blue Lou," Skelly's big moment as a singing clown with tragic undertones, and wowed audiences with the addition of a two-strip Technicolor sequence. Evaluated by *Variety* as "sturdy box office stuff . . . an intelligent and fairly faithful adaptation," *The Dance of Life* was a hit, and its story became the basic template for vaudeville musicals: the hero is a suc-

The adorable Nancy Carroll, big-name star of transition-to-sound musicals, but forgotten as time went by

cessful comic who becomes an alcoholic; he deserts his wife, but she goes on loving him anyway.* It was a flexible plot: tragedy and comedy could both be grounded in the hero, and the backstage setting allowed all sorts of musical numbers to be easily included. (*Variety*'s review labeled Carroll "a looker" and explained the significance of the title change: "The switch in the title from *Burlesque* to the more alluring *Dance of Life* was smart. The play's original title is only known in New York, Chicago, and a few key cities; for exhibition purposes *Burlesque* might be a detracting screen moniker." *Variety* was subtly suggesting that patrons might think the movie was a grind-house effort; the new title gave the material more class, but the movie's real importance became the emergence of the brief stardom of Nancy Carroll.

---

* The "Burlesque" story was remade as *Swing High, Swing Low* in 1937 with Carole Lombard and Fred MacMurray and as *When My Baby Smiles At Me* in 1948 with Betty Grable and Dan Dailey.

Some of the new stars, unlike Carroll, endured (Jeanette MacDonald), and some were even more meteoric and rapidly disappeared, such as Alexander Gray. The handsome Gray was an industrial engineer who had a voice and studied singing as a sideline and was thus perfect musical star material. He began singing professionally and had a minor success until he was cast in the Chicago touring company of *Desert Song* as the Red Shadow and Jack Warner gave him a screen test. He was given the movie lead in *Sally*, co-starred with the famous Marilyn Miller. He lived a story of unexpected stardom, a plot right out of one of Hollywood's musicals. As the last months of 1930 approached, however, and studio bosses reviewed their bottom lines, they began to rethink musical films. Profits were beginning to shrink, and the public appeared to be getting tired of them. They had become used to sound, and just having songs and dances no longer ensured success at the box office.

There is almost universal historical acceptance of the idea that musicals disappeared from the screen from late 1931 up until the release of *42nd Street* in 1933. Pity the poor musical: born in 1927 and laid in an early grave in late 1931—or so most movie history tells us. (When it comes to Hollywood history, the simpler the better: "*The Jazz Singer* is the first sound film.")* Reading *Variety* reviews of movies from January 1, 1929, forward toward *42nd Street* (March 14, 1933) reveals a somewhat different picture. *Variety* was a trade paper, and the comments in its reviews were directed at the business itself. *Variety* reviewers were sharp-eyed, intelligent about innovations in cinema, and always tough about what might or might not become a hit. A casual history, unintended but grounded in what was really happening with musicals, emerges from reading these reviews. Since *Variety* reviewed movies as they were released into theaters, it's possible to see what movies were going to be "out there" for audiences to attend or not attend. Did musicals actually disappear? It's important to remember that a release date was exactly that—a *release* date. After a picture was let loose, as it were, it flowed out into America and often wouldn't reach a small town for as much as a year. After the first big premiere and large-city openings, the rest of the country waited for the film to arrive. A 1930 release could become a 1931 viewing choice for rural and small-city audiences.

* There's also "No real violence appeared on American screens until *Bonnie and Clyde*," "*Fatal Attraction* was a landmark film" (apparently, no one had ever seen *Play Misty for Me* or even *Attack of the 50 Foot Woman*), and other oversimplifications.

This explains why a genre might seem "dead" to the business but hadn't disappeared for moviegoers, who were still consuming it.

Starting in 1928 and continuing to 1933, *Variety* (as well as other trade papers and movie magazines) followed a common practice of identifying films as musicals or at least as having musical numbers. This identification had been inspired by the arrival of sound: Music! Songs! Exhibitors and audiences would want to know. "All Dialogue with Songs" was a common subhead for any film being reviewed, and the purpose was simply to say the movie was not just a talkie with dialogue only, but a musical one. (For example, *So Long Letty* from 1929 and *Puttin' on the Ritz* from 1930 were so identified.) This was good business practice. As talkies became the norm, the tag line was shortened to "with songs." (*The Hot Heiress* of 1931 was so defined.) Clarity was of great importance in these reviews. *Fifty Million Frenchmen* (reviewed April 1, 1931) was explained as "a musical with songs removed." Because *Frenchmen* had been a big Broadway musical hit, it was important to *Variety* to make sure potential buyers were aware that this was the *plot* of the show, not the show itself. Similarly, *Variety* knew what would not play in Peoria. For *Pagliacci* (1931), a film of the opera, the reviewer warned that the film ("the first time a grand opera has been seen in its entirety") wouldn't make money, because they "didn't turn it into a moving picture . . . but merely screened the opera." *Variety* always praised musicals for spectacle. *Happy Days* (February 19, 1930), shot on wide-angle film in the Fox Grandeur process, was described as having much to draw patrons: "Dixie Lee singing and 32 girls doing tap and jazz routines . . . Ann Pennington in 'Snake Hips,' wriggling . . . a whole minstrel first part . . . four tiers of 86 people . . . a leader and 32 girls in intricate maneuvers . . . Janet Gaynor and Charles Farrell . . . singing . . . 'A Little World All Our Own' as they build a miniature cottage while they sing."

Throughout 1928, 1929, 1930, and early 1931, *Variety* reminds us of the delights of musicals, but abruptly, in the March 18, 1931 review of *The Hot Heiress*, a warning note is sounded. "Now that the musical era in talkies is over, song spots in films must be hand-picked. When the songs don't fit, they are worse than useless. When all the songs fit, there will again be an important place for theme music on the screen." The comment on songs is as right today as it ever was, and no modern analyst could put it any better; however, the pronouncement in a review about the musical era being over seems to come out of nowhere. It's clear that although musicals were still around for those who wanted them, the genre's huge popularity—and the audience excitement over sound—had begun to decline.

From the date of the *Hot Heiress* pronouncement onward, there *are* fewer musicals released, but there *are* musicals, and sometimes during this "dead" period the reviews reveal a yearning for them. The July 14, 1931, review of *Children of Dreams* says that "there is talk of a musical talker revival." Even with *Fifty Million Frenchmen* (the "musical with songs removed"), the reviewer muses that "maybe a couple of good songs and good voices could have helped." Regarding Lubitsch's *Smiling Lieutenant*, *Variety* (May 27, 1931) says the film "is a blow to those who had hopes that this release might speed resumption of musical films," because it has "a poor quality of tunes." ("Otherwise," says the review, "it's a smart comedy.")

On September 29, of the same year, *Palmy Days* with Eddie Cantor gets a good review, and the work of Berkeley is cited: "[A] point to be noted is the dances staging by Busby Berkeley . . . with an overhead camera view." There are positive reviews for *Her Majesty Love*, *Delicious*, and others; and on March 29, 1932, both *Girl Crazy* and *One Hour with You* ("100% credit to all concerned . . . a money picture") are greeted with enthusiasm. On August 23, 1932, *Love Me Tonight* receives a total rave, praising the film for how well its musical numbers are "blended in." Throughout 1932, musicals such as *Way Back Home*, *Dancers in the Dark*, *Harlem Is Heaven*, *The Phantom President*, *The Big Broadcast*, *The Kid from Spain*, and *The Girl from Calgary* are reviewed. Musicals did *not* entirely disappear, and the ones that played were not all failures. Furthermore, reviewers began to understand the use of musical numbers in a movie. The designations "with songs" or "with songs removed" or, most interestingly, "with songs, but not a musical" (for *This Is the Night*, April 19, 1932) showed how the business began to understand that just having a musical number performed inside a plot didn't necessarily turn the film into a musical.

The difference between the business's attitude toward musicals and the audience's is an important issue. Costs were a factor, because the business had begun to feel the effects of the Depression, and the risk of making a movie that was expensive (with musicians and spectacles to pay for) but might not be popular was a negative.* As 1931 unfolded, Hollywood began

---

* In 1930, MGM stopped production in September on *The March of Time*, an expensive and ambitious musical being directed by Charles Reisner. It was to have three sections with musical performers of the past, present, and future, among them Weber and Fields, Fay Templeton, Buster Keaton, and Ramon Novarro.

to lose confidence in musicals as an easy way to make money, but it never entirely gave up on them. It *is* a fact, however, that fewer musicals were made during 1931 than previously, and some ads for movies with light-hearted names carried the tag line "This Is Not a Musical" in case audiences didn't want to see one. In 1932, there were still fewer musicals in release, and that year might be considered the bottom of the barrel for the format. This is ironic, considering that this year was also the depth of the Depression. For those who want to label the appeal of the musical as simply "escapism," it's important to realize that in the worst year of the Depression, musicals were at their nadir of popularity.

To be historically accurate, it's also worth noting that although 1932 hit a low point for numbers of musicals *produced*, there were highly successful (and influential) ones out there, some of them releases from late 1931: there was a whole lot of shakin' goin' on. Eddie Cantor appeared in *The Kid from Spain*, Janet Gaynor and Charles Farrell in *Delicious*, Marilyn Miller and W. C. Fields in *Her Majesty, Love*, the comedy duo Wheeler and Woolsey in *Peach-O-Reno* and *Girl Crazy*, and George M. Cohan and Jimmy Durante in *The Phantom President*, among others. Two of the greatest and most influential musicals were made: Lubitsch's *One Hour with You* and *Love Me Tonight*, both with Jeanette MacDonald and Maurice Chevalier. In 1932, Hollywood also offered Marlene Dietrich singing "Hot Voodoo" in *Blonde Venus*, Bing Crosby as himself in *The Big Broadcast*, and Dick Powell as a singer in *Blessed Event*. Nelson Eddy was put under contract, and Mae West and Fred Astaire were packing for the trip to California. Musicals may have lost popularity, but the development of future musical stars continued. The celebration of the return of the musical in 1933 should be tempered by the understanding that musicals never fully disappeared.

As the calendar turned over to 1933, the Irene Dunne vehicle *The Secret of Madame Blanche* ("with songs") was reviewed, reflecting what was apparently on everyone's mind in the business.* Although the review indicates that musicals had not been much missed, it says, "Some music and singing . . . is pleasant to hear for a change . . . more than welcome . . . more of this could be stood." More of it was about to be stood.

On February 14, 1933, the man who had become associated with the genre and with the beginning of sound, Al Jolson himself, appeared in movie houses in *Hallelujah, I'm a Bum!* ("with songs"). An odd duck of a

---

* The film was not a musical. It was a *Madame X*–type tearjerker, but because Dunne played a music hall singer, "with songs" was accurate.

film, it nevertheless was welcomed with open arms, and a month later, on March 14, 1933, a *Variety* reviewer responded to a movie called *42nd Street*: "It's a musical . . . and it'll be socko." Suddenly, the musical format became a Hollywood innovation. Its originality was going to separate the movie musical from its stage mother, and open up a whole new creative world.

III

1933:
A Musical Year

O F ALL THE FILM-HISTORY-MADE-EASY CONCEPTS, the one that has the strongest claim to truth is "In 1933, *42nd Street* brought on the rebirth of the musical film." When *42nd Street* was released in March of 1933, audiences *did* fall in love with it. It was a musical wow, with its gobsmacking musical numbers, its romantic duo of Ruby Keeler and Dick Powell, and its "go out there and become a star" backstage story. *42nd Street* was fresh and funny, visually staggering, an easy marking place for the "rebirth" of the musical, which actually had not been dead, but was only playing possum, as it were. Looking back on 1933 today gives perspective. It was a year of musical innovation led off strongly by *42nd Street*, but actually featuring *four* major influences: two directors (Ernst Lubitsch and Rouben Mamoulian) and two dance creators (Fred Astaire and Busby Berkeley).

Lubitsch and Mamoulian

Ernst Lubitsch and Rouben Mamoulian were highly influential men in the transition-to-sound era. They also were important in musical film history because they incorporated cinema into their numbers and thus contributed to the advancement of the art form. Both saw in movie musicals an opportunity to do something new with what formerly had been a stage-bound tradition. Although Lubitsch made only four really important musicals during the transition period, and Mamoulian's movie work was largely nonmusical, they are key to what makes 1933 a seminal year.*

---

* Mamoulian's musical films include *Applause; Love Me Tonight; The Gay Desperado; High, Wide and Handsome; Summer Holiday;* and *Silk Stockings*. He was fired from the 1959 *Porgy and Bess* before shooting began and was replaced by Otto Preminger.

During 1929 and 1930, as has been discussed, Lubitsch's *The Love Parade* and *Monte Carlo* were hits, and his three musical sequences in *Paramount on Parade* were successful. As musicals began to lose their initial impact, however, he made two other major films: *The Smiling Lieutenant* (1931), with Miriam Hopkins, Claudette Colbert, and Maurice Chevalier, and *One Hour with You*, a March 1932 release with Jeanette MacDonald and Chevalier.* Although he did not have a big 1933 musical release comparable to *42nd Street*, some of his musical work would have been in circulation during that time frame so that his influence was being felt. Lubitsch was greatly respected in Hollywood, and his commitment to sophisticated musical films during 1931 and 1932 did much to keep the genre on the mind of the industry.

He was, in fact, a natural for the musical film. His instincts were rhythmic, and his silent movies are often great examples of movement, cutting, and physical exuberance. In the delicious *The Oyster Princess*, a German silent in 1919, a wedding celebration scene depicts the wedding party, the guests, and the servants—everybody!—indulging in a dance that traverses all through a huge mansion with great physicality and joy. An onscreen orchestra blows their instruments while their leader boogies around, setting the pace, keeping constant movement onscreen and inspiring the viewer to "hear" music. Add a song lyric and it's a latter-day big-time musical number worthy of any MGM effort. (An original score was composed for *The Oyster Princess* in its own day.) The spontaneous quality of Lubitsch's silent comedies is musical in essence, so it's logical that he could—and did—step up to direct some of the most influential of the early examples of the genre.

Ernst Lubitsch, it is always said, is a master. What is he a master of? He is a master of what is *not* shown on the screen. For every filmmaker, there is always, lurking around the edges of the frame, a dangerous element: the rest of the story, the part that distracts the audience, the part that makes no sense, the part that questions, the part that kills the fun. Lubitsch was the master not only at keeping those parts at bay, but also at dictating to an audience what they should be thinking instead. He has an imaginative elliptical technique through which a viewer becomes a kind of participant in the storytelling process. He moves his stories quickly forward through

---

* Lubitsch's musical magnum opus, his version of *The Merry Widow*, would be his final musical until 1948, when he undertook the Betty Grable film *That Lady in Ermine*. He died of a heart attack shortly after filming began and the movie was completed by Otto Preminger.

time, showing an audience how to fill in the gaps. He puts the audience in the position of writing their own jokes in their heads. His ability to make the audience his partners in storytelling was unparalleled, and has been much celebrated.

From 1929 to 1932, Lubitsch's four musicals all replaced the explanatory title cards used in the silent era with song lyrics (and musical innovations). Silent-film audiences had been trained to supply thoughts and feelings for actors whose faces were shown to them in beautiful close-ups. Lubitsch replaced those "thinking" and "feeling" moments with songs and dances and musical elements. His films were fundamentally operettas, but operettas restyled with his famous "Lubitsch touch"—which has been defined as many things, but really means his wit and the ability to translate it into cinematic terms. Lubitsch worked in two onscreen story arenas: Paris (or the Riviera or some other sophisticated place) and Ruritania. For the former, he had fashion, wit, sex, and a cutting-edge sophistication; for the latter, he had sentimental plots, cutout characters, class restrictions, and romantic conventions that were always well established. What he did with both settings was amazing: he made them into charming jokes without cruelty, sexy relationships without smut, and deliciously entertaining worlds that Americans could enjoy. Lubitsch made Americans love both Paris and Ruritania, and accept them as settings for their own escapist dreams. In an era in which sound was new, and moviegoers heard the "deze-dem-doze" sound of real American accents, the rat-a-tat of machine guns, and the hot jazz that was taking over popular music, Lubitsch carved out a place in their hearts for the Old World. He is always given credit for his European sophistication, which he deserves, and for his bringing that quality to Hollywood. But he didn't leave things there. His movies celebrate unexpectedness, the breaking of class barriers, the embracing of secret sexuality, and an exuberant romantic zing that is, in fact, very American. In a sense, he gave audiences an Americanized European flavor . . . or perhaps a Europeanized American flavor.

One Hour with You did not originate as a Lubitsch film. The directorial responsibility had been assigned to a newcomer, the gifted George Cukor, with Lubitsch as supervisor. His "supervision" quickly turned into taking control. Unhappy with the script, Lubitsch (aided by Samson Raphaelson) began rewriting his own silent masterpiece *The Marriage Circle* to replace the original plot. The end result was strife, and a court case (*Cukor v. Paramount*, New York Supreme Court) in which Cukor filed suit to block the premiere. Scott Eyman, in his book *Ernst Lubitsch: Laughter in Paradise*, quotes Lubitsch from the deposition he gave in court: "Cukor's work lacked the Continental flavor which was essential to this type of picture. We also felt that the dialogue was not pointed in the right ways and was not spoken as effectively as it should be. We particularly noticed that all of the actors overplayed their parts and in the silent parts were even grimacing." In the end, Cukor was (by agreement) allowed out of his contract with Paramount so he could work with David O. Selznick at RKO. The final title card for the movie read, "Directed by Ernst Lubitsch, assisted by George Cukor."

As a result, *One Hour with You* turned out to be a Lubitsch film. It makes bold use of the unnaturalness of the musical form* by breaking the fourth wall aggressively and using direct camera address, a choice that was uncommon in the studio-system years. Without the need to account for transitioning into musical-performance mode, the movie becomes a fluid, seamless effort, a delight to watch and hear. Characters speak from the film directly to viewers, and discussions occur about singing. MacDonald tells Chevalier at one point to stop singing because "the orchestra is gone." When husband Chevalier is torn between his wife (a delightful and youthful MacDonald) and Mitzi, his would-be seducer (Genevieve Tobin), he sings about his dilemma right to the camera, in medium close-up: "I love my wife, but ooooohhh, that Mitzi!" Earlier, he has asked us, as audience, very directly what we would have done if Mitzi had tried to seduce us. What a bad thing! And he loves his wife! A terrible moment! ("But oooooh, that Mitzi!") What, after all, would you do? "Well, that's what I did, too," he sings.

One Hour with You demonstrates early in musical history that it isn't necessary to have artificial barriers (or concrete explanations for performance) between the audience, the characters, and the music. The problem for this format—as opposed to the easier-to-do backstage story—was that there were very few Ernst Lubitsches available to make it work (as George Cukor had found out).

In the early years of musical experimentation, Lubitsch's films, particularly *One Hour with You*, stand out—if everyone had followed its lead, the

---

* *The Smiling Lieutenant* and *One Hour with You* are both charming, but the former has very little music. What it does have is a great deal of fun. When Chevalier's mistress (Claudette Colbert) and his wife (Miriam Hopkins) discuss things musically, Colbert advises Hopkins that no man like Chevalier will ever be interested in her unless she piques that interest. "Jazz Up Your Lingerie" is Colbert's musical advice, and the two women find sympathy and sisterhood.

history of the musical would be very different. It's a movie closer to the operetta tradition than to the backstage musical, since its characters sing rhymed dialogue to one another. They do not go onto a stage and do "numbers." They sing as they talk and talk as they sing. The artifice of the musical is proudly on display, and without any apologies. Since the movie is also about exposing the artificial restrictions of society, it's a perfect wedding of music and plot. As will be happening in musicals in later decades, the movie announces itself as a movie and asks the audience to accept the fact. This postmodernist approach (in 1932) was completely acceptable to both audiences and filmmakers. It was easier, cheaper, and safer for the movie business not to emulate *One Hour with You* . . . but it could have done so. Experimentation is part of Hollywood's history; it's just that no one thinks of Hollywood that way. The musical genre offered a perfect opportunity for filmmakers to play with cinema, and some did so. Most, however, wanted to find great stars and let them sing and dance with no need to explain anything and no need to complicate matters with self-reflexivity.

Rouben Mamoulian is often described as "the poor man's Lubitsch." No one, really, is anyone's Lubitsch, and the statement is unfair to Mamoulian, who was highly respected for his work in the transition-to-sound era. (He is not as well-known today.) He was inventive in solving various aesthetic problems encountered from the new technology. (Andrew Sarris called him "an innovator who ran out of innovations.") Mamoulian didn't fear sound (as was also true of Lubitsch and men like Frank Capra and William Wellman). He has been credited by writer Tom Milne with transition innovations that include the use of subjective sound (in 1931's *City Streets*), the use of a subjective camera, a 360-degree pan, and colored filters (*Becky Sharp*, 1935, the first full-length movie shot in three-strip Technicolor), the use of nonrealistic sound (*Love Me Tonight*, 1932), and the liberation of the camera and the soundtrack in *Applause* (1929), for which he insisted the camera be allowed to move and for which he recorded by using two microphones and two channels, combining the tracks during printing. Only *Applause* and *Love Me Tonight*, among these films, are musicals, but Mamoulian's other films develop cinematic issues important to musicals: color, dream sequences, sound recording, and camera movement. Rouben Mamoulian is a significant part of musical-film history.*

---

* Mamoulian later, in the 1940s, directed the original Broadway productions of the stage hits *Oklahoma!* and *Carousel*. Before he came to Hollywood, he had also directed operas and Broadway shows. He was not a novice or a newcomer to the concept of musical presentation.

Maurice Chevalier and
Jeanette MacDonald,
husband and wife in
One Hour with You, a
musical version of the
silent *Marriage Circle*.
They still have issues,
but now they can sing
about them.

Applause, Mamoulian's first movie, starring singer Helen Morgan, was
a melodrama with music, and a harbinger of things to come: the serious
musical. The story is full of old-fashioned mother love and sacrifice, but
it clearly demonstrates potential for what musicals will be able to achieve,
largely because of the openly emotional performance by Morgan, a great
singer. In a show-business story, she plays an aging burlesque queen who
sings "Give Your Little Baby Lots of Lovin'," "I've Got a Feeling I'm Falling," and "What Wouldn't I Do for That Man?," one of her greatest hits.

Mamoulian establishes immediately in the opening sequence of *Applause*
that his camera won't be intimidated and locked down by sound. From a
close-up of a closed storefront, the camera tracks backwards and enters a
burlesque house, moving past the musicians in the orchestra pit. It pans up
and tracks along a row of plump dancing legs leisurely pumping up and
down—a bit too plump to give the kick a snap. Continuing to move, the
camera pans up finally to show the dancers with their sad, tired faces, bored
to death as they bump and grind their way around the stage.

Love Me Tonight, released late in August 1932, has everything any musical could possibly need except for two things: color and dance. It's one of
Mamoulian's best films, and certainly his best musical, but it also reflects the
influence of Lubitsch's earlier musicals as well as the work of the French-

man René Clair, which perhaps accounts for Mamoulian's reputation as an innovator having faded. In fact, there is no choreography per se in the movie—that is, no dancing. The film from start to finish may be seen, however, as one long piece of total choreography. It essentially makes up for its lack of color by being witty and imaginative and for its lack of dance by presenting a rhythm of editing and artificial "movements," including slow motion and speeded-up action. The opening is an extended fifteen-minute sequence in which all the major characters are introduced and their relationships established while the film travels from Chevalier's tailor shop in Paris to MacDonald's castle in the country. It has often been said that this movie is just one long musical number.

Love Me Tonight plays with the romantic operetta, slyly poking fun at it, yet delivering its glamour and romance. The celebrated musical team of Lorenz Hart and Richard Rodgers wrote nine original songs, and all of them were beautifully integrated into the charming script by Samuel Hoffenstein, collaborating with Waldemar Young and George Marion Jr.

The film's opening uses one song—"Isn't It Romantic?"—to travel across time and space, linking Chevalier to MacDonald. Thus it is music that first brings them together and music that tells the audience they belong together and promises that they will be together. The entire movie becomes

Jeanette MacDonald fears she might not measure up, but Maurice Chevalier knows his job in *Love Me Tonight* because "the son of a gun is nothing but a tailor."

musical space, and there is no "break" from the so-called "realistic" world in which there is no singing and the "unrealistic" in which there is. Mamoulian skillfully sets up a total musical universe with an almost fairy-tale quality to it, mostly through a highly skilled interweaving of songs and action. He recorded the entire musical score before he started shooting the film, allowing him to create a great harmony between sound and image.

The charm of *Love Me Tonight* lies partly in its sophisticated use of fantasy, a "Sleeping Beauty" fairy tale in which a very Paris-hip Prince Charming of the lower classes drives out to a rural world of wealth to collect a bill he's owed and ends up awakening a luscious young woman whose dead husband was over seventy when he wed her. The opening of the film (the main debt to Clair—a debt that is repaid in kind when Vincente Minnelli uses something similar for *An American in Paris*) is a joy to watch. Paris wakes up in the early morning, and it wakes up to "music," a concert of sounds: a street being swept, a carpenter and shoemaker going about their jobs, etc. It's a world in which ordinary things are musically rhythmic, and in it lives Maurice Chevalier. The sequence ends by moving to the signature sight of his straw hat hanging on the wall of his shop, linking him as a character to his own musical persona and presenting him in the film as part of this wonderfully musical Paris. The movie then assures viewers that all this music extends beyond the boundaries of the city by using "Isn't It Romantic?" to move from Chevalier to MacDonald. Chevalier hums and sings, and into his shop comes a contentedly plump prospective bridegroom who picks up the tune and takes it outside, where it's heard by a taxi driver, whose customer (a composer working on a score as he rides) then carries it onto a train where the military troops riding with him pick it up. They sing it out as they march the countryside and are overheard by a band of Gypsies, who transform it into something more romantic as one of them runs to serenade Princess Jeanette, who is sighing on her balcony. She then sings the song herself. "Isn't it romantic?" Every detail is perfect in this transition of song across time and space, including the adjustment of the lyrics to accommodate the narrative. ("Isn't it romantic?" sings the cab driver, and then "At last I've got a fare" as the composer gets in. The composer sings, as he listens, "Isn't that romantic? . . . I think I'll take that down," and he jots the music on his paper.) The song begins in the early morning in Paris and by the time it arrives at MacDonald's balcony, it's night. "Isn't it romantic?" Yes, it is. From Chevalier to MacDonald, it surely is. It's also cinematic, funny, charming, and inventive.

Love Me Tonight has only one musical number that uses a conventional presentation: Chevalier performs "The Poor Apache," a typical cabaret number, for guests at the chateau's masquerade party. All the other musical moments are cinematic. Chevalier's "Mimi" is performed as direct address to the camera. "Love Me Tonight" is sung by two people who are seen to be asleep—their voices come from offscreen, laid over their sleeping close-ups as "thought" performance. Chevalier's arrival at the castle is a musical joke in which, as he runs upstairs, the tempo of the music speeds up, and as he slows down, the beat slows down, too. When he is revealed to be a tailor and not a baron, as was thought, the characters of the film (including all the servants in the kitchen) sing their shock ("The Son of a Gun Is Nothing but a Tailor"). None of them are professional singers, so the musical presentation becomes an example of the nonsinger performing a number. (And when the news is first heard, a maiden aunt, shocked to the core, knocks a vase off a table—the sound is as loud as a bomb exploding—a delightful aural joke.) When the weekend guests go on a hunt, the horses, the stag, and the people all move in both slow motion and normal movie speed, according to the needs of the music and its rhythm. When MacDonald's doctor examines her to find why a beautiful and apparently healthy young woman is constantly languishing abed, the two have a conversation in music.

Love Me Tonight has never really been surpassed for its organic integration of music, plot, and character. Music drives the plot in every way. At its foundation it is a very funny and original script, and in contrast to so many musicals that have great songs and dances but pedestrian scripts, *Love Me Tonight* is a felicitous wedding of the script, all the musical components, and the possibilities of sound cinema. Everything is accomplished with wit and sophistication, but also—most importantly—with music. *Love Me Tonight* showed everyone in the film business what the musical could be.*

At the film's end, Mamoulian presents a hilarious parody of Russian montage, and perhaps even a bit of a dig at Lubitsch's "Beyond the Blue Horizon" from *Monte Carlo*. As MacDonald rides masterfully out astride her horse to catch her lover and remove him from a speeding train, there's

* Indicative of Mamoulian's total mastery of cinema, *Love Me Tonight* includes three zoom shots. Zooms are thought of as an invention of the 1960s but were available in the 1930s and appear in other movies: *Private Worlds* (1935) and *Prestige* (1931), for example. Zoom lenses had to be hand-cranked and were not easy to use, so no one embraced them. Frank Capra, when asked why, said, "We had taste."

a mélange of pounding horses' hooves, train wheels, and country peasants all singing in the fields until MacDonald, bold and dynamic, hands firmly planted on her hips, stops the train and reunites with Chevalier. It's a great feminist reversal of a finale, all set to the tune of the title song.

In 1937, Mamoulian would direct another unusual musical, which would be better known if it were more easily available: *High, Wide and Handsome*, starring the lovely Irene Dunne, the handsome young Randolph Scott, and the sensuous Dorothy Lamour three years before her first *Road* picture. The songs, music by Jerome Kern with lyrics by Oscar Hammerstein II, includes the charming "The Folks Who Live on the Hill" and the rollicking "Allegheny Al," among others. The film is innovative because it weds an utterly realistic story based on historical fact to musical performance. The plot concerns the discovery of oil fields in Pennsylvania in about 1859, which created a conflict between the farmers who find the oil on their land and the railroad tycoons who try to block their efforts to lay pipelines to carry it to market cheaply. Against this conflict—shot on location and presented as truth, and tough truth at that—is played a story involving Dunne and Scott and romantic songs, all shot on artificial sets. Dunne plays a circus performer who's stranded on Scott's farm, where there's moonlight, soft hills, and apple blossoms that he can shake down off the trees onto her—it's a place where she can sing to the chickens and the pigs. The realistic world of competitive business is mixed with the world of romantic operetta, but it works. *High, Wide and Handsome* is a movie that illustrates the "reality" and "unreality" modes of musical movies that would be overtly and self-consciously articulated later in film history. Its world of farmers, music, rural locations, sets, and dangers carries the hint of the future *Oklahoma!* all over it. Mamoulian is a major force in mixing the sense of realism available to movies into a musical format.

Astaire and Berkeley

Just as Mamoulian and Lubitsch made musical stories cinematic, Fred Astaire and Busby Berkeley made *dance* cinematic. Each in his own way made choreography that fully accepted—and furthered—the idea that, for the audience, movie dances were not taking place under a proscenium arch. Both men thought about the differences between presenting choreography onstage and inside a film frame. There would be no restrictive idea that a viewer was sitting in a seat in a Broadway house. Each man uniquely embraced what the use of a camera—a single eye—could do to bring excitement and fresh appeal to a dance: coming in close on a dancer . . . changing perspectives . . . giving an unusual angle . . . enhancing the rhythm through cutting . . . using special effects.

Astaire made a direct statement: "Either the camera will dance, or I will dance." His goal would always be the integrity of the performance. He was aware that in the early years of cinematic musicals, the ability to use multiple cameras to photograph a dance from different angles had brought excitement and newness to choreography. Furthermore, being able to cut a dance apart and shift viewing perspectives—something that could never happen for a viewer inside a Broadway theater—made dance-on-film even newer and more inviting. Cutting to reactions, both from other performers, either onstage or in the wings, and from the "audience" sitting in the alleged theater, or cutting to close-ups of tapping feet or feet flying across a stage—these options inspired a new look for dance. It was a basic idea, and a worthy one: let the audience in the movie house see what the audience in a theater could never see, because that's what movies could do. Astaire rejected these ideas because they broke up the dance, destroyed its line and thus its poetry, and distracted viewers from his movements. He demanded control of the camera, and essentially asked it to follow the dance, respect the dancers, and bring greater emotion to the viewers by making the dancing mean something in the story or by showing dancing in a way that made them feel like a part of it. Astaire was not anti-cinema. He embraced such things as slow motion, traveling mattes, and special effects. But he wanted to dance in the center of the camera's eye.

Berkeley also had a philosophy of camera usage: the camera itself will dance, and under my control. When Berkeley began his movie career, he, too, was in a working environment that often used four cameras and four crews to film a musical number, with the dancing/singing being filmed from four different directions so that an editor could assemble the shots to provide what was thought to be an exciting innovation—varied perspective for the viewer. Berkeley used one camera in a one-eyed position. He, like Astaire, understood that cinema was about wedding the camera's eye to the audience's eye for maximum control. Berkeley's approach was a sort of "Nobody move!" type of dancing, because it depended on formations, multiple images, repeated visuals, all of which were given to the viewer by the

From Astaire's earliest days as a movie dancer in *Top Hat* . . .

movement of a camera through time and space. His dances were detached from the narrative of the movie, but they often told stories inside themselves. Although sometimes his dances had no dancing, just movement and formation, when he presented actual dancing it could be like a deployment of troops: an advancing army of tappers, as in "Lullaby of Broadway" in *Gold Diggers of 1935.*

When Berkeley directed large troops of dancers, his primary concern was still the movement of the camera. Astaire and Berkeley are the yin and yang of the 1930s birth of really cinematic musicals. They both understood the three fundamentals of excellent movie choreography: the camera, the dancers, and the viewing audience. Berkeley can be defined as totally cinematic; he just wants an audience to watch. Astaire is a master of cinema who asks a viewer to react as well as view—he adds participatory joy. Astaire wanted as few cuts in one of his dance numbers as possible, and those that are there were hidden or masked, so as not to spoil the rhythm and line. Berkeley incorporated cuts *into* the rhythm of his dance routines.

Fred Astaire, that most continental and debonair of men, was a quintessential American. He was born as Freddie Austerlitz in Omaha, Nebraska, and everything that defined him can be seen as midwestern: hard work, integrity, ambition, loyalty, lack of pretension, and the ability to be sophisticated in the most natural way. His modesty and unbloviated conversations about himself can also be defined by his origins. When he began dancing in movies, there were few precedents for photographing dances imaginatively, except, of course, for Busby Berkeley's methods, which wouldn't work for a soloist like Astaire; yet he seemed to have an instinct for the camera, and he learned by doing. He was a perfectionist, and a quiet thinker, astute in his observations: "In the old days," he said later in his life, "they used to cut up all the dances on the screen. In the middle of a sequence, they would show you a close-up of the actor's face or his feet, insert trick angles taken from the floor, the ceiling, through lattice work or a maze of fancy shadows. The result was that the dance had no continuity. The audience was far more conscious of the camera than of the dance." Astaire would not dance in movies if he could not control his own numbers—how they looked, how they

. . . to his musical finale in *Finian's Rainbow*, he was the epitome of professionalism and perfection.

sounded, and how they could be experienced. That's why Gene Kelly, himself an innovator of presenting dance on film, made the clear statement: "The history of dance on film begins with Astaire."

Singing—the sound of a song—is a satisfying part of musicals. The lyrics are an intimate dialogue with the viewer, but the singer is usually up close and personal. Singing creates direct intimacy, whereas dance brings the freedom of vicarious physicality: the ability to jump, twist, turn, leap, and soar; to join with others in a line of synchronized movement; to embrace a partner and perform together to music, perfectly in step, perfectly joined, something to feel in our hearts, in our souls, in our brains, and in our bodies. And the dance was never more perfectly presented on film than by Fred Astaire.

He began in films in 1933 with two movies, *Dancing Lady* and *Flying Down to Rio*, neither of which fully established him as the definitive artist he would become. *Dancing Lady*, his movie debut, had him appearing as himself, dancing with Joan Crawford (who became a lifelong friend). It was his felicitous pairing as a second lead, opposite Ginger Rogers, in *Flying Down to Rio* that was the beginning of his opportunity to become not only a legendary performer but also an unparalleled influence on American dance. Astaire would remain in Hollywood and in the movies for the rest of his life, never returning to the stage, thus asserting his influence over the movie musical. Although he was also successful in his television specials in the 1960s and 1970s, it was his movie work that inspired George Balanchine to say, "He is the most interesting, the most inventive, the most elegant dancer of our times. . . . He is like Bach, who in his time had a great concentration of ability, essence, knowledge, and a mastery of music. Astaire has that concentration of genius. You see a little bit of Astaire in everybody's dancing."

Astaire has little to do in *Dancing Lady* except in the film's grand finale, for which he's partnered by Crawford in her early years as one of MGM's greatest lookers and most popular stars. As a dancer, Crawford was untrained but capable. Her dancing style was unpolished, and her tapping is from the Ruby Keeler school, which means hitting the floor hard and giving it all you've got. (Later, dubbing taps allowed most women tappers to be lighter on their feet. Dancers like Eleanor Powell and Ann Miller could knock it out either way, of course. Powell's powerful tapping inspired Astaire to remark, "Ellie can lay 'em down like a man.") Astaire has an early scene in which he's called on at rehearsals by Clark Gable to show Craw-

ford a routine. ("Good evening, Mr. Astaire," she says.) Later, he appears in the final number, his place to shine, and shine he does. The number is significant because it's Astaire's first real appearance as a movie dancer, and because the number itself is cinematic. Crawford and Astaire are first seen dancing in evening dress. She's wearing big puffed sleeves, a layered, ruffled formal gown set off by a gold band around her small waist, and he's in white tie and tails. The song is "Heigh-Ho, the Gang's All Here." What catches attention is that after the first part of the number, the two dancers are lifted skyward on a platform and carried magically across time and space to another world: a Bavarian set where they present a second song,

Astaire's dancing debut in movies was with an unexpected partner, Joan Crawford, in *Dancing Lady* (1933).

"Let's Go Bavarian." And Bavarian they go, with Astaire in lederhosen and Crawford in a dirndl and long blond braids. (It's pretty unforgettable.)

It's 1933. Before the full influence of Berkeley had taken hold. The dance ("musical ensembles by director Sammy Lee and Eddie Prinz") breaks down the proscenium arch. Astaire and Crawford are supposed to be appearing in the opening night of a stage show, but they are rising above and away from the other dancers, being carried (allegedly) within the theater to a second place—a transposition that could really have been accomplished only by closing the curtains and changing sets and costumes. The musical has gone Hollywood! Astaire observed the importance of the camera and its movement and the possibilities of using editing and dissolves in dances while rehearsing and shooting this, his first real dance on film. *Dancing Lady* is often dismissed as an "unimportant" Astaire, but it's not only where he began, it was his eye opener; and it must not be forgotten that any MGM movie starring Joan Crawford and Clark Gable—not to mention Ted Healy and his Stooges, Franchot Tone, Robert Benchley, Winnie Lightner, May Robson, and Nelson Eddy (as "singer")—is not a minor movie. Astaire began at the top in star power, but he also began at the top in terms of production capabilities.

Astaire's next nine films are legendary due to his RKO pairing with Ginger Rogers. (There would be a total of ten, with the final entry being made at MGM.) This major musical relationship is discussed later in "Pairs," (pp. 249–261). By 1935, after his first three movies with Rogers, Astaire was fully defined as a dominant male dancer, and in his famous signature number "Top Hat, White Tie and Tails," from *Top Hat*, the complete movie-dancing Fred Astaire is on display.

To compare what Astaire brought to musicals with what Berkeley did, it's useful to first compare *Top Hat* to *42nd Street*. Astaire is essentially the auteur of *Top Hat*, as Berkeley is of *42nd Street*, even though neither of them directed his movie. *42nd Street* is rooted in America during the Depression, and *Top Hat* is rooted in an elegant world with a European setting. *42nd Street* has songs and dances that almost all come at the very end of the movie, in back-to-back presentations; they're not related to the story or integrated into it. There's a frank and open divorce of music and plot, and the songs exist only for their entertainment value. In *Top Hat*, the songs and dances are mostly integrated into the plot. They demonstrate emotions, as in "Cheek to Cheek," or further the plot, as in "No Strings." They introduce the dramatic or narrative possibilities of dance to the musical.

At the time it was released, *Top Hat* was greatly praised for its "spontaneity," as Arlene Croce has pointed out. It's a lively movie with a smooth integration of plot and music; but seen today, it's a bit of a hothouse flower, and "spontaneous" is not the word that leaps to mind. However, there's no question that the dances are fabulous, and they appear to be happening because feeling and circumstances have inspired them.

Astaire's signature can be seen in everything he did, but his iconic title number from *Top Hat* reveals his genius. It is a solo unrelated to the plot, but the song supplies the title of the movie, and the top hat will always be associated with Astaire. (He never understood that, saying, "At the risk of disillusionment, I must admit that I don't like top hats, white ties, and tails. . . . I don't look like a movie star, and I don't act like a movie star.") Astaire plays a professional dancer in *Top Hat*, so the audience is not surprised to find him in the wings of a theater, in the middle of the opening night of a new show. A smooth and familiar transition leads the viewer into the "Top Hat" routine. Astaire is backstage preparing to go on. In a conversation with his friend (character actor Edward Everett Horton), Astaire learns where Rogers is (Venice) through a telegram that Horton hands him. Grabbing it joyfully, Astaire tells Horton to prepare to go to Venice "with wings on" as he does a lean-back, high-kick step that efficiently, through a cut, lands him onstage, still clutching the telegram in his hand. As the music plays, the audience sees a full lineup of men dressed identically to Astaire in top hats, white ties, and tails. The men part into two opposite groups, and Astaire is seen at the back of the stage. He then walks down to the front and they regroup behind him. Seen in medium close-up, he's holding the telegram and starts to sing the lyric: "I just got an invitation through the mail . . ."

Astaire is impeccably dressed, adorned with white handkerchief in the pocket, a white boutonniere above. He carries a cane, which he swings loosely, casually. While he sings the lyrics, he's seen in a medium close-up until he begins to dance a little bit in front of the chorus of men. Astaire's singing style is as perfect as his dancing: rhythmic, easy, conversational. Irving Berlin said, "It's nothing new to say that Fred Astaire is a great dancer. But what was even more important to those of us who ever wrote songs for him was that he was also a great singer. Fred was responsible for more hit songs than many of the top singers. He knew the value of a song and his heart was in it before his feet took over. I'd rather have Fred Astaire sing my songs than anyone else." As he sings, Astaire "dance/walks" in front of the line of men. No one could walk like Astaire, just as no one could dance like Astaire. He rocks a bit from side to side and swings one of his arms loosely, his whole body without a tense nerve in it, walking the way great drummers often walk: as if they're responsible for the rhythm of life. Astaire sings: "Oooh . . . I'm . . . puttin' on my top hat!" and the lyrics become a dance of words. The identical "gents" behind him look a bit bored as he sings, appropriate for their class and manners; but when the dance begins in earnest, they stop moving. *He* dances, they imitate, and then he surpasses them. If the dance were a narrative—and in its way it is—they would seem to be intimidated. They leave the stage.

Astaire is left alone. There's a floor, a horizon line at the back of the stage, a drawing of puffy clouds in the sky, a series of white globular street lamps in descending order of size, and a drawn outline of the Eiffel Tower. And Astaire. To the sound of "Top Hat, White Tie and Tails," dressed in the clear black-and-white that only the old film stock could provide, Astaire dances against a gray-and-white world that sets him off in a sharp contrast inside a perfect frame. He is the center of what the audience inside the story would see as their proscenium stage, and the movie audience would see as the center of the movie frame. He is exactly the right distance from the bottom of the frame, and from the top, and from both sides: not too obviously in the middle, but realistically and aesthetically in the perfect place. He can be observed head to toe as he dances, twirls his cane, and turns in circles at a faster and faster speed. Suddenly, the lights dim down onstage and the music grows softer. Astaire seems to have gone somewhere else, leaving the viewer behind—off to a *misterioso* world. A little secret place inside the dance! As he dances, he's like a teenager trying things in front of a mirror, doing little poses, complicated steps, checking to see if anyone else is behind him. He's having a musical conversation with himself—it's a private dance, expressing his inner life. Up comes the music again, and the chorus of men returns. In an amazing tapping tour de force, using his cane as a mock gun, Astaire begins to shoot them down one by one: *Pop! Pop!* As the music plays, Astaire dances across their line, using his "gun," making his feet do a machine-gun rat-a-tat until they are all gone. Victory! Astaire has mowed down all his imitators or would-be top-hat wearers. He shows them, us, and himself: Astaire is the man in the top hat who simply "reeks of class." And no one can dance like he does.

This could be the end of the musical presentation, but it's 1935, and *Top Hat* is a musical that has learned to understand the genre. The curtain closes, and the film cuts to a group of elegantly dressed older men in a theater box, Horton standing behind them, and they are clapping wildly. It then cuts back to the stage, an open curtain, and the chorus line of men. Astaire comes out for his bow in front of the line of dancers, and the curtain is then pulled. As Astaire comes out again to take a solo bow in front of the curtain, he takes a mock shot with his cane at the applauding audience! They laugh and clap even more. The film then cuts to a view of the pit orchestra and its maestro, continuing to play "Top Hat" until their image disappears and transfers viewers to "Venice," where a small group of musicians dressed in movie-Italian clothes is sedately playing "Top Hat."

This dance is perfection in itself, but it is also perfectly presented: an excuse is made for why we're seeing it; a smooth lead-in takes us there; the photography respects the integrity of the dance and the dancer; and when the routine is finished, we are reminded where we are, and why. The final intelligent presentation is made by taking us away from the theatrical performance space to an allegedly "real" one through the same music, played differently, and on to the next set and the next scene, which will be a dialogue scene, not a musical number. Astaire did not direct *Top Hat* (Mark Sandrich did), but his understanding of how to go into a musical presentation, photograph it, and come out of it is one of the most important elements in the "Top Hat" number.

After *Top Hat*, Astaire thrilled audiences with a great many fabulous routines that showed his understanding of how to present dance on film. His first days in the movies, in the year 1933, offered him the opportunity to reconfigure his choreography for the medium of film. From there onward, he was a dancer who would become a movie star who would become a legend who would become immortal. Over his decades, he set a standard for movie dances. His solos included cracking-hot tapping, as in his "Let's Say It with Firecrackers" Fourth of July dance in *Holiday Inn*; the special-effects driven "Shoes with Wings On" from *The Barkleys of Broadway* and his dancing on the ceiling in *Royal Wedding*; his bullfighter routine in a Paris courtyard in *Funny Face*; his tribute to tap dancer Bill Robinson, "Bojangles of Harlem," in *Swing Time*; and many, many others. Astaire's basic understanding was that it was all about keeping the dancer the key visual element inside the frame, seen head to toe unless the choreography was designed for something else. He knew all film dances must be planned for cuts and camera movements, that dance on film was dance on film and not dance on the stage or in a nightclub. This understanding was part of the growth and development of the American musical film.

(top) In his thirty-five-year movie career, Astaire partnered with many besides Ginger Rogers. Some were famous dancing stars: Rita Hayworth, *You'll Never Get Rich* . . .

(bottom) Ann Miller, *Easter Parade* . . .

(top) Vera-Ellen, *Three Little Words* . . .

(bottom) Eleanor Powell, *Broadway Melody of 1940* . . .

(top) Cyd Charisse, *The Band Wagon* . . .

(bottom) and Leslie Caron, *Daddy Long Legs*.

(top) Some were unexpected: Joan Fontaine, *A Damsel in Distress* . . .

(bottom) Joan Leslie, *The Sky's the Limit* . . .

(top) Betty Hutton, *Let's Dance* . . .

(bottom) Jane Powell, *Royal Wedding* . . .

(top) Paulette Goddard, *Second Chorus* . . .

and (bottom) Lucille Bremer, *Ziegfeld Follies.*

Some were forgotten: (top) Marjorie Reynolds in *Holiday Inn*.

And some appeared only on television: (bottom) Barrie Chase.

Some, like him, became movie legends: (top) Audrey Hepburn in *Funny Face* . . .

. . . and (bottom) the inimitable Judy Garland, *Easter Parade*. Astaire called her "the greatest entertainer who ever lived . . . or probably ever will live . . . an amazing girl . . . it was one of the greatest thrills to work with her."

One partner worked only behind the scenes. Astaire considered him a friend and equal, Hermes Pan, dance assistant, chalking it out for *Roberta*.

Astaire's physical grace was not limited to his dancing. Is there anything more lyrical than Fred Astaire, clad in a tuxedo, casually walking an English country road, swinging along through a misty, tree-lined world, hand in pocket, singing to himself. "A foggy day . . . in London town . . . had me low . . . had me down." He twirls a bit, sings a bit, looks as if he's on his way to play golf or do nothing, yet he's duded up to the gills in a perfectly tailored tuxedo. He stops, sits on a fence in a softly swirling fog, and creates an intimate moment with the audience. He sings what's in his heart, but ever so lightly, ever so casually, laying it on with ease and contained joy. He dances, too, but it's his walk—that little sway from side to side, that tiny swing to his body, that one arm moving gracefully, rhythmically—that makes it all work, that makes it unique. A touch of class, a touch of Nebraska, and more than a touch of genius. For over five decades, that was Fred Astaire onscreen. Rarely is Fred Astaire described as a "movie star." He's called a dancer, or perhaps a legend, but not really a movie star. And yet he *was* a movie star, and a big one for a long time. There's a quality to his presence on film—always, very simply, that he's Fred Astaire, the one and only. In his first film he played himself, and in his second, his character was named "Fred Ayres." *Easter Parade* and *The Barkleys of Broadway* were about the situation a famous dancer finds himself in when his female partner leaves him. *Royal Wedding* is about a famous dancing couple who are brother and sister, and the sister leaves him to marry an English nobleman (as his own sister Adele did). *The Band Wagon* is about an aging dancer, whose movies included one in which he wore a top hat, etc., etc. Astaire's movies became self-reflexive, but never to his diminution. "I'll go my way by myself," he sings in *The Band Wagon*. Astaire was unique, and as brilliantly partnered as he was, from Rogers to Garland to Charisse to Hayworth, Miller, and Caron, he was always in a class "by himself."

Francis Ford Coppola, an underrated director of innovative musicals, gave Fred Astaire the perfect cinematic send-off. In 1968, when Astaire was nearly the age of seventy, Coppola cast him in what would be his final musical performance in a plotted musical. The show was a screen adaptation of the Broadway hit *Finian's Rainbow*, with book and lyrics by E. Y. Harburg and music by Burton Lane. (Fred Saidy also worked on the original book.) The musical was a hit in 1947, but because its plot involves racial issues coupled with fantasy and whimsy, Hollywood had never thought of it as a surefire hit. It had been twenty-one years since the show was created when Coppola put together the movie, which starred the British singer Petula Clark, character actor Keenan Wynn, Tommy Steele, Don Francks, and Astaire. The filmed *Finian's Rainbow* was not a success. What had seemed daring in 1947 seemed awkward in 1968. The score, however, provided beautiful and witty songs: "Look to the Rainbow," "Old Devil Moon," "The Begat," "That Great Come-and-Get-It Day," "When I'm Not Near the Girl I Love," and "How Are Things in Glocca Morra?"

Astaire plays the key character of Finian, and his old friend and collaborator Hermes Pan created his choreography. Every move Astaire makes is perfection, including his performance of a lovely Irish jig and a slow-moving piece using a cane and different levels. But it is the movie's ending that gives Astaire his envoi, his cinematic send-off. Astaire, youthful, trim, and energetic, dons a tweed hat and a long blue scarf, picks up his cane and bag to make an exit after his daughter's wedding, and then twirls. Around his neck is a bright orange neckerchief, tied with that little touch of fashionista perfection that marked out Astaire's personal style. He's off . . . "to find me a rainbow." He kisses his daughter and moves away from the crowd, ascending a little hill as he exits. He pauses, turns, and suddenly taps his cane on the ground: *Tap! Tap!* "Hey, hey," he then calls out. "Goodbye, me friends, I'll see you all in Glocca Morra!" Petula Clark begins singing the lovely song about a perfect utopian place, fondly remembered from the past, stressing the words "May we meet in Glocca Morra someday." Astaire is then seen in long shot, twirling and twisting and dancing, moving out and away from the camera into the far distance. As the full cast sings out about a future meeting date in a magical fantasy setting, Astaire moves farther and farther away. A rainbow appears, and then he's gone. Nothing like him will ever be seen again.

Busby Berkeley was about as different from Fred Astaire as could be imagined. Born in Los Angeles in 1895, he became a lieutenant in the US Army during World War I, where his work was creating and staging military parades. (It figures.) After the war, he began staging army camp shows for soldiers, and this led to work in the theater as both an actor and a choreographer. His first major success was in the latter area; and the show that defined him permanently as a dance director was the successful 1927 Rodgers and Hart musical *A Connecticut Yankee*. Berkeley's sense of dance as abstraction was already evident in his Broadway career. From his beginning as a creator of dances, he worked from what he had learned in the military, thinking in terms of formations and maneuvers and not about the individual dancer as a human form. In 1930, he arrived in Hollywood, brought there by Samuel Goldwyn, who hired him to stage the dances for the filming of the Eddie Cantor stage hit *Whoopee!*

Whoopee! was billed as "a musical comedy of the Great Wide West" with "dances and ensembles staged by Busby Berkeley." (The film's director was Thornton Freeland, himself a man who had choreographed large groups of dancers for the stage.) Shot in the early two-strip Technicolor process, *Whoopee!* reveals the ethnicity of early Broadway shows with its attitudes toward the leading lady marrying a Native American (a no-no, until it turns out he was adopted) and its Jewish jokes. (When the Native American protests his unsuitability by reminding Cantor "I went to your school!," Cantor says, "You went to a Hebrew Indian school?") *Whoopee!* acknowledges the arrival of sound with its opening number—"The Wildest of Cowboys is He"—by cleverly starting with the sight of a real landscape with real cacti and real riders on horseback racing across it, and then smoothly transitioning into the riders arriving at what is clearly the original stage set. The boys and girls of the chorus burst through the back gate of the set onto the stage and enthusiastically open the movie with the rousing number. Berkeley immediately establishes his credentials as a man who will not be bound to the stage. The dance is seen from the front, but also from above and in a kaleidoscopic pattern. The dancers bend over each other to create a snakelike wave, which is seen from overhead as they weave up and down. It's a boisterous opening number made new and fresh by Berkeley's touches of unusual camera views that transform the original routines.

He also shows his stuff in an ensemble dance number ("Stetson") later in the film, in which the chorus taps and the camera moves past them to observe each individual. The camera sits still while each pretty chorine comes toward it to smile and put her hat on. The girls ultimately switch hats from head to head, and the camera makes its first "Berkeley journey" through the spread legs of the chorus girls, an image that will occur over and over in Berkeley's work. There's also a Ziegfeld Follies parade of girls wearing "Indian maiden" getup. In the end, the movie is a perfect example of various styles on parade in an early musical: the standard Broadway show with a star like Cantor; the Ziegfeld Follies parade of women in flamboyant costume (Ziegfeld was a coproducer of the film); and the future of the 1930s musical scene in Berkeley's unusual camerawork.

After *Whoopee!* Berkeley went to MGM to create dances for the movie that introduced successful comic Bert Lahr to American audiences, *Flying High* (a 1931 release). Lahr was hired to play the role he originated in the Broadway show of the same name, that of an aviation mechanic named Rusty.* His costar was the rubber-bodied comic Charlotte Greenwood, in a role originally played onstage by Kate Smith. The show's music was written by the famous songwriting trio of Henderson, DeSylva, and Brown, but the Broadway score was dropped except for the title tune and a new one provided by Dorothy Fields (lyrics) and Jimmy McHugh (music).

Seen today, Berkeley's work is not only the most interesting aspect of *Flying High*, it's practically the only thing that can be fully enjoyed. Except for his role as the Cowardly Lion in *The Wizard of Oz*, Lahr's reputation in the movies has not endured. He should be the king of the genre (not just

---

* Lahr also appeared on television in 1951 in a shortened version done as part of the NBC television series *Musical Comedy Time*.

the forest!), because his shtick is musical: everything he says is a song and every move he makes is a weird modern dance. His comedy is all about rhythm, timing, repetition ("Hiya, sporty, sporty boy, hiya sporty boy" and "I finally said it, I finally said it"). Every statement is a musical recitation as he echoes himself. His comic persona comes from another universe, with a strong absurdist quality, which is what made him perfect for the original American production of *Waiting for Godot*. He makes strange noises in his throat, particularly the "mmmnong, mmmnong, mmmnong" he's famous for. When he makes something amusing out of nothing, such as repeating an unfunny line of dialogue—"It's out of order, it's out of order"—he makes the first sentence information and the second one an emphasis that becomes comic. ("Is that thinkin'?" he asks, and then, "Or is that thinkin'?," making an audience realize that not only is it *not* thinking, but it's hilarious that he even suggests it is.) Lahr was a comic who made unnatural behavior funny because it was inside a matter-of-fact and naturalistic frame. (My students today say he seems crazy to them, unfunny, possibly even dangerous. Such is what happens as times change.)

Busby Berkeley's madness is a different story. Although his work is usually associated with Warner Bros., or possibly with his 1943 Fox success, *The Gang's All Here*, connoisseurs also know him for his Goldwyn movies, which began with Cantor and *Whoopee!* But few remember that *Flying High* was really his first chance to choreograph and stage dances the way he wanted (he was more restricted when creating for Cantor's stardom). Availability often defines history, and access to *Flying High* is limited. Nevertheless, it is the first full-out Busby Berkeley movie.

Berkeley's work hits a viewer right in the face. There's no hesitation, no compromise, and no doubt about who's in charge. After the leading lady (Kathryn Crawford) sings "I'll Make a Happy Landing" for no apparent reason, a chorus of young women enter. The Berkeley tradition appears: the girls are stationary while the camera tracks swiftly past them. They are seen in medium close-up, posing and smiling, as each one is revealed to be pretty, young, and sexy. Then the presentation takes off into cuckoo land: a fleet of tiny airplanes on a string morph into girls and then into a group of tap-dancing aviators, and then into an airplane formation seen from overhead. The formation then turns into an undulating chain. The dancers, seen from the front, form a line with men in back, women in front; the men wave their hands in one direction, standing up, while the girls bend forward and wave theirs (in white gloves) in the opposite. The dancers then spell out the names BYRD, HAWKS, and LINDY. There's a kaleidoscopic overhead of more formations; and to end the piece, the camera once again passes by the lovely girls in close-up, and finally irises out on the original singer. It's all right here in *Flying High*: everything that Berkeley will use to create his unique dance world is in place; it will only be escalated, intensified, made more abstract and sexual in future films.

The movie progresses through various skitlike scenes, with the main emphasis being on the relationship of Lahr and Greenwood, who chase around and fall down and grapple with each other. A parade of character actors involve themselves in the action: Guy Kibbee, Charles Winninger, Hedda Hopper, Pat O'Brien. The underlying sexuality of Berkeley's style emerges. Female aviators need to take a physical so they can enter a flying contest. These girls are all "young and healthy," as Berkeley would later have it at Warners. They wear satin blouses and skirts (and the nurse, too, wears a satin cap and uniform), and the doctor (Winninger) tells them to strip. Seen from their knees down, they drop their clothes and walk forward, later to be seen in black bras and panties, with the bras nicely decorated with little black bows. One girl lies down on a bed and leans back, raising one of her legs up a little to be examined by the doctor, who appreciates her black outfit and matching black high heels. (It's almost a shot from a porno film.) Music plays during all this, and the girls do a few formations and then exit, to be followed by a routine between Winninger and Lahr that contains wedding-night jokes, gay jokes, urine-specimen jokes, narcotics jokes, and enema jokes. Flying high indeed!*

Berkeley has one other piece of major choreography in *Flying High*, set to the tune of "We'll Dance Until the Dawn." It, too, is readily identifiable as a Berkeley routine, with girls, formations, overhead shots, different levels and platforms. *Flying High*—and MGM, a studio that would become famous for musicals but never for Berkeley's, although he would be rehired there in the 1940s—played a significant role in his career.

After *Flying High*, Berkeley returned to Goldwyn to choreograph three Eddie Cantor films: *Palmy Days* (1931), *The Kid from Spain* (1932), *Roman Scandals* (1933). *Palmy Days* ("dances and ensembles by Busby Berkeley") opens with a Berkeley fantasy: beautiful young girls, seemingly hundreds of them, as they prepare for their workday inside a bakery. (Signs say "Glorifying the American do-nut," "Our bread is well bred," and "Eat our cake and have it too.") Since the girls are surrounded by sweets all day, they're required to do calisthenics and gymnastic routines led by Charlotte Greenwood, who advises them to "reach for a pickle instead of a pie." As she sings "Bend Down, Sister" (what a song!), the girls are presented in what is clearly Berkeley's style. Reminded in song that they shouldn't "be hasty with French pastry . . . you wanna be thin," the girls walk toward the camera, one at a time, to be seen in medium close-up, smiling, then turning

---

* Lahr's work, with its verbal incongruities and strange patterns and rhythms, really needed a live audience for him to play his rhythms off.

away as their movements become a sort of dance. They are also seen in typical overhead Berkeley kaleidoscopic shots; they tap out routines; and they work with a visual variation of the gold-coins from *Gold Diggers of 1933* (using pie plates). The opening is pure Berkeley—an audience-grabbing mixture of sex, music, humor, and dance.

Throughout the movie, Berkeley is not allowed to interfere with Cantor, however. With a script partially written by Morrie Ryskind, a Marx Brothers favorite, the jokes (however corny) fly fast, and Cantor is able to make them fresh through his strong, but faux-innocent, eyeball-rolling presentation. (Asked how many girls work in the factory, he replies, "About half." When a list of employees is torn in two "to cut staff," it seems very much like a Harpo Marx idea.) Cantor entertains in blackface ("There's Nothing Too Good for My Baby") without any female accompaniment, but when Cantor is forced to go in drag to hide himself from crooks, Berkeley is given the opportunity to do a big swimming-pool scene (a great preparation for his later work with Esther Williams at MGM), which presents the troupe of girls later to be known as the Goldwyn Girls, a bunch of beauties who appear in Goldwyn musical comedies as late as Danny Kaye films in the 1950s.

The Kid from Spain, well directed by Leo McCarey (with "numbers created and directed by Busby Berkeley"), again opens on a sexy Berkeley vision, of girls waking up in bed and having to get dressed while the audience ogles them. A young blonde (some say it's the teenage Betty Grable)* says directly to the camera, "We're opening this story/By giving you a peek/Into our dormitory/Where all the pretty girls sleep." Another asks, "Will you turn your head/While we get out of bed?" The girls are sexy, the lyrics are sexy, and the routine is sexy. The girls parade up and down stairs in black see-through lace, advancing to a swimming pool (again), where they dive in and perform water-ballet routines seen by an overhead camera. The sophisticated and detailed formations show off their rear ends while they dive; they spread their legs wide and they dress behind illuminated screens that allow viewers to see their shapes in shadow. These visions of sex and beauty and naked bodies are not really integrated into the plot in any particular way. The ideas that Berkeley had for *Whoopee!*—the nascent beginnings of Berkeley as a distinctive visual artist—are being allowed to develop and grow and even dominate running time.

* Grable was in the chorus of *Whoopee!* and at an early age became a "Goldwyn Girl."

In *Roman Scandals* ("production numbers directed by Busby Berkeley"—his shifting credits on his Goldwyn films suggest backstage arguments over billing), the numbers show that Berkeley knows how to present a traditional tap routine, well coordinated, in a "narrative" song and dance for a song if he's required to do so. "Build a Little Home" has dancers tapping out a traditional routine even though Berkeley never thought about steps in his dances. He thought about bodies, space, and camera movement—all united as movement to represent the physical release of dance, but through the camera itself, not in front of it. For Berkeley, a woman and her body are an abstracted image designed to be viewed by a moving camera from whatever unusual or interesting angle he can devise. *Roman Scandals* is most famously known for its "slave market," in which women are seen chained up, wearing long, long blond wigs designed to cover their supposed nakedness. There's all kinds of weirdness: men with whips, a dancing brunette who does a fine hootchy-kootchy gyration and then jumps to her death (the incorporation of death into a musical number also being something Berkeley will develop further at Warners). It's clear that his sense of movie dance is already in place.

The main difference between the early Berkeley choreography at Goldwyn and the more celebrated Warner years is that the Goldwyn films are about the Goldwyn Girls and not getting in the way of the great (and very popular) Eddie Cantor. There's no indication that anyone believes in Berkeley's own vision as anything important—it's just useful to show off the sexy females and set up Cantor. As significant as Berkeley's earliest movie work is, it's really after he moved to employment at Warner Bros. that he became the visual force we think him to be today.

Warner Bros. was a studio that cared very little about stars, although they made and championed some of the best. Warners also had no real commitment to music or dance, so they were very willing to focus only on abstract sex, which is why Berkeley's real fame came after he was put under contract by Warner Bros. and moved there to do the choreography for *42nd Street*. For this film, Berkeley would establish a pattern in which he conceived and directed his dances entirely separately from the rest of the film. (Astaire, who insisted on a very close collaboration with his director, also conceived his dances separately, working with his longtime associate Hermes Pan.) For *42nd Street*, Berkeley knew his goal: "What I wanted to do was create for the camera. The way-out musical had never been tried. A lot of people used to believe I was crazy, but I can truthfully say one thing: I gave 'em a show."

42nd Street was actually based on a book, and not a very good one, by Bradford Ropes. The novel is a backstage plot in which, like in the movie, an impresario is puttin' on a musical show called *Pretty Lady*. The plot may be similar, but the ambience is not. The novel features a leading lady whose morals are in the gutter, a leading man who's a gigolo, and all sorts of topics that wouldn't go over easily with a mass audience: homosexuality, the seduction of a minor, gangsters, a horrible stage mother, and more. It was 1933, and censorship existed but was not yet enforced (1934 would be the key year for that), but the novel's story was both morbid and sordid, and not what Warner Bros. would want to use for a mass-market musical. What the novel had that was useful was a solid backstage plot and multiple story lines that allowed the movie to accommodate both a dramatic story and a musical story.

42nd Street contains the moment that if it weren't there, everyone would have to pretend it was: Warner Baxter takes hold of Ruby Keeler's arms and passionately tells her, "Sawyer, you're going out a youngster, but you've got to come back a star." It's one of those wonderfully cornball lines (like "You've gotta have heart") that works because it doesn't work. It made

The movie that revived the musical genre in 1933: *42nd Street*, with Ginger Rogers, Ruby Keeler, and Una Merkel rehearsing for stardom

42nd Street into a seminal film, the one that has to be referred to when you're satirizing the genre. It's the "This town ain't big enough for both of us" or "Is this the end of Rico?" or "We'll always have Paris" of the musical film. When the line actually occurs, it's an absorbing moment. Warner Baxter, who delivers it, had won the Oscar as Best Actor (for *In Old Arizona*) in the 1928–29 race. He was an established silent-film star who had made the transition to sound; he had played in stock, worked on Broadway, and was a very popular leading man. He treats the scene seriously, and brings to it his understanding of movie acting, backstage Broadway, and the

Berkeley's choreography tools on display: legs (*Dames*) . . .

importance of being believable in the moment. The young actress he speaks his line to, Ruby Keeler, is playing an inexperienced dancer and is in fact an inexperienced movie actress. In their backstage pep talk, Baxter looks as if he really means it. She looks as if she's waiting for him to stop speaking so it will be her turn. There's an offscreen truth to what is happening: *42nd Street* partly depends on this pretty but blank young woman's ability to appeal to viewers. Baxter has the good sense to look really worried about that. After all, what is it that's going to make this girl a star? Her ability to put over a pop tune ridiculously titled "Shuffle Off to Buffalo"? Baxter and the movie audience bond in dubious prayer. Keeler, a pretty young girl with a sweet demeanor and no visible acting talent, tap-dances in the hit-it-hard style of her era. She stomps the floor, slightly bent over, and leans into it, her elbows out, making plenty of noise.

The number begins spectacularly with a train stretching across the stage that will break in half and swing back to reveal the characters on board. As would be true for many of Berkeley's numbers, the singing and dancing will tell a story. Clarence Nordstrom and Keeler are newlyweds on their way to Niagara Falls, so there's plenty of innuendo. In one upper berth, Una Merkel and Ginger Rogers are perched in sexy pajamas. Merkel is eating an apple (Eve) and Rogers has a peeled banana (no explanation needed). They sing, "When she knows as much as we know/She'll be off to Reno."

The movie has two other fully produced audience spectacles: "Young and Healthy" and "42nd Street," the grand finale. The first has Dick Powell singing amid girls, girls, girls, all blond, and after he kisses the one he's singing to (Toby Wing), the image leaves the ground, taking viewers into a kaleidoscopic world where girls wear short costumes. The camera not only presents them in interesting overhead formations, it again travels lasciviously through their spread legs. In the "42nd Street" number, Keeler sings and dances, and then the camera pulls back to reveal that she's on the top of a taxicab. She climbs down and moves out into the streets of New York. There are governesses spanking babies, newsboys, cops on horseback, street peddlers, even a drunk coming home late and starting to beat up on his girl. She jumps out a window onto the roof, finally being helped down in time to start dancing off with another man just before the drunk comes out the door and stabs her. An army of dancing guys and gals advances toward the footlights and then turns into skyscrapers to present an urban skyline, with Keeler and Powell on top, waving happily at The End. And yes, it does sound crazy, but it was new and fresh and spectacular. In their day, Kee-

ler and Powell were charming, and the movie was grounded with performances by experienced people like Baxter and Bebe Daniels. At this stage of Berkeley's work, the studio apparently felt some need to act as if everything happening on stage was plausible: there are often cuts at the end of numbers to the sight of an audience in their seats, clapping enthusiastically.

42nd Street took audiences by storm. In what amounted to a total rave, *Variety* was clear in assessing the film's financial potential: "a money picture for any type of house." Busby Berkeley was singled out—"Using his earlier style from Cantor pictures . . . breakaway scenes, dissolves, overhead camera angles, iris-ins-and-outs," etc.—revealing how the business understood the use of cinema to take musicals to a new level of originality. (The review is a reminder to those who think old movie audiences bought the Berkeley numbers as legitimate stage pieces. The review points out that these dances are for the movies because they obviously "exceed what could really be done.")

The success of *42nd Street* (it was nominated for Best Picture) took Berkeley immediately on to his next movie, also a 1933 release: *Gold Diggers of 1933*. In *Gold Diggers* there are four big production numbers: "We're in the Money," "Pettin' in the Park," "The Shadow Waltz," and "Remember My Forgotten Man." They are perfect representations of the different modes in Berkeley's work. Each allegedly begins on an actual theater stage . . . and then flies off somewhere else. Each begins with a key performer singing the lyrics to the song: Ginger Rogers for "Money," Dick Powell for "Pettin'" and "Shadow," and Joan Blondell for "Forgotten Man."* These numbers are not spaced carefully throughout the narrative.

* "The forgotten man" was a term used by President Franklin D. Roosevelt in a campaign speech in which he spoke about how two in ten men in America were unemployed—former soldiers. Roosevelt said they were "the forgotten man at the bottom of the economic pyramid." According to Leonard Maltin's invaluable historical research on the movie, printed in his *Movie Crazy* ("A Newsletter for People Who Love Movies," no. 21 [summer 2007], pp. 1–15), the song was intended to be sung by Blondell, but in the final film that is not what happened. "Joan Blondell recites the lyrics one time through, then the great African American singer Etta Moten, perched on a tenement windowsill, performs the tune to a bluesy orchestral accompaniment. At the end of the sequence Blondell reprises the song one last time, pouring her heart out, and revealing a lusty contralto voice . . . In

Berkeley's multiples, elevations, and repetitions: *Gold Diggers of 1933*, with girls, girls, girls—and violins . . .

. . . and (next page) *Gold Diggers of 1935* with girls, girls, girls—and pianos

The film opens on "We're in the Money" but it's more than half an hour before the second number, "Pettin' in the Park." (During this period of running time, Dick Powell sings to Ruby Keeler across the gap between their apartments, and he sings a tune for Ned Sparks at a tryout, but these are not real production numbers.)

Gold Diggers of 1933 was not actually directed by Berkeley. That task went to Mervyn LeRoy, and it shouldn't be forgotten that a lot of what makes *Gold Diggers* work was the skill LeRoy brought to keeping up the pace and showcasing the wit of female stars like the young Ginger Rogers and the veteran Aline MacMahon. The movie, however, is a musical, and it's Berkeley who directed the musical numbers, and it's significant that many movies that Berkeley did not direct are nevertheless called "Busby Berkeley movies." When one of his visual extravaganzas appeared in a film, it was what the audience talked about and remembered. (There were other choreographers doing large-scale musical numbers with unique camera angles—for instance, Thornton Freeland and Seymour Felix—but their formations had a predictable quality that Berkeley's could blow out the door.)

Nineteen thirty-three was Berkeley's year. With his dances for *42nd Street* and *Gold Diggers of 1933*, he made his mark. Boldly, he took the attitude that the movie's story didn't matter—it was just the excuse for the true reason any-

Dick Powell and Ruby Keeler, who became musical stars in Berkeley movies, getting ready for "Pettin' in the Park" in *Gold Diggers of 1933*.

---

fact, Blondell's final chorus was recorded by a Los Angeles–based vocalist named Jean Cowan, known for her bluesy style." Berkeley explained that he chose Blondell for the number even though "Joan Blondell can't sing, but I knew she could act it. I knew she could 'talk it' and put over the drama for me." "Remember My Forgotten Man" was the last segment of *Gold Diggers* to be filmed, in April of 1933. According to the Daily Production and Progress Reports from Warner Bros. (available in the USC archives), forty singers, nineteen orchestra members, one piano player, two bit singers, eighty-one men, and one hundred girls were called for the filming. This was the sort of army Berkeley liked to assemble. Dressed as soldiers, male extras were going to march on treadmills, with women cheering them along down below.

one would want to watch the movie: his choreography. And he further took the attitude that anyone who wanted to complain that his musicals couldn't actually be performed in a theater was someone who just didn't get it. He, after all, had been staging dances for the theater successfully for years, and did they imagine he didn't know that? Berkeley just plowed ahead, acting as if the movies were not the theater, nor should they be. They could do something unique and fascinating that only they could do . . . so why not embrace that idea? Berkeley more than embraced it: he hugged it almost to death.

In his years of Warners success, Berkeley came up with one spectacular development after another, including girls behind transparent shades undressing and redressing, and girls in tin-can dresses that would need a can opener to remove. "The Shadow Waltz" dressed women in flower-petal skirts. *Footlight Parade* (1933) had girls in cat suits, a full narrative with marching soldiers in "Shanghai Lil," spectacular underwater photography in "By a Waterfall" (a true forerunner of his Esther Williams movies), and the story of the "Honeymoon Hotel," in which all the guests are named Smith. *Gold Diggers of 1937* tells us "All's Fair in Love and War," with giant rocking chairs, and females singing that the perfect husband is "a nice old man with lots of wealth / But not in the best of health." There's a warning that "love is just like war," followed by an actual mini-musical ("War"), set in a World War I no-man's-land trench. It's a real battle of the sexes set to music, in which females stop to spray perfume on themselves and the men surrender when they kiss them. There's bugles and guns and a marching female army . . . Berkeley constantly topped himself.

Two of the most detailed and spectacular of Berkeley's black-and-white numbers from his Warners years are "I Only Have Eyes for You" from *Dames* (1934) and "Lullaby of Broadway" from *Gold Diggers of 1935*. Both represent a high point of Berkeley's visual imagination, but they are grounded differently: the first in a "realistic" narrative setting and the second in pure abstraction. Both contain internal developments that can be logically viewed as character and/or plots.

"I Only Have Eyes for You" presents Keeler and Powell allegedly doing a number on a proscenium stage. Keeler is waiting outside a production of *The Merchant of Venice* while the ticket seller (Powell) finishes work for the evening. After the last ticket is sold, the two "walk" through the city, board the subway, and ride to the end of the line. While they're walking, he sings the song to her—they are in a crowd but alone in their love. As

Powell sings the words "they all disappear from view," the crowd around them disappears through the use of an optical, an effect that can only be done in film. When present, the crowd, including a cop, all sing the song, too. On the subway, the other riders disappear, and Powell replaces (in his head) every female face on the advertising signs with Keeler's. One of these Keeler "heads" detaches from its sign and appears alone, set against a black background. It then multiplies. The "heads" move around inside the frame in a formation, turning from side to side, connecting and reconnecting, forming into one large head, banding together into a human shape made out of Keeler heads. These images finally fall forward, revealing a second universe *inside*, one with pretty girls dressed like Keeler, all in white, with dark wigs, moving up and down on staircases, across revolving bridges, swaying and swinging their skirts. It is a world of Ruby Keelers, so it's a world in which it isn't possible to have eyes for anyone else. The audience is then taken inside a third, even deeper universe, in which each girl carries a huge cutout of Keeler's head. These again unite to form one single head, and the camera advances toward the eyeball on its face. Keeler herself then rises up from inside the image to emerge from the eyeball. When the number returns to the original space of the subway car, Keeler and Powell awaken, and he carries her across the railroad tracks, singing their song again. And it's raining! All on stage! After this, the sign of a typical New York City audience clapping enthusiastically for the number appears, returning the movie audience to "reality." The presentation of this song in *Dames* is something of a statement about the moviegoing experience itself. A viewer leaves the grounded "reality" that the film has presented and enters first the dream world created by the filmmakers, which goes beyond plot and characters, and then his or her own personal world of dream and romance. If the New York audience had actually seen "I Only Have Eyes for You" in front of them on a stage in 1935, they probably would have run shrieking from the theater.

"Lullaby of Broadway" is perhaps the most written-about and analyzed of Berkeley's numbers, at least from a cinematic standpoint. ("Remember My Forgotten Man" would be the one for the cultural historians.) It's an important example for many reasons, not the least of which is that it forces people to remember that despite the oft-repeated adage that no one danced in Berkeley's numbers, they sometimes *did* dance, and dance quite spectacularly. Ruby Keeler, after all, was a tap dancer, and James Cagney was a real hoofer who did some of his best dancing in *Footlight Parade*. "Lullaby of

Broadway" is Berkeley's tap-dancing magnum opus. It tells a "story" about Manhattan socialites arriving home "early in the morning" after a night of partying, coinciding with the proletariat getting up to go to work. It begins with a black screen and the voice of Wini Shaw singing as the camera moves slowly toward a small image of her, continuing in a single take until she's full-frame. She turns her head around, so a viewer is looking down from above her. She leans back, puts a cigarette in her mouth, and suddenly her face turns into a map of Manhattan. Berkeley's daring and visual imagination were never more abstracted or surprising, and the cigarette gesture has an insolence—even a decadence—that is accomplished with great simplicity and bravado. As the audience is taken down into "Manhattan," the map of Shaw's face becomes her map of existence.

In early-morning New York City, contrasts appear: the workers get up and do their jobs in a "workers' ballet," followed by a "Broadway baby" (Shaw) getting out of a taxi, just arriving home. "Sleep tight, baby," say the lyrics, "the milkman's on his way." She takes the milk from the driver, pours some into a dish for the kitten outside her door, and enters her apartment, where she undresses and goes to bed.

This is enough for any one musical presentation, but the song and the dance continue. The clock outside her window advances to 6:45 p.m. as she sleeps all day. When she rises, it's dark outside, and she begins her round of activities not previously witnessed, going from nightclub to nightclub, carousing until she and her escort (Dick Powell) arrive in a place that can only be thought of as the Nightclub in the Sky: a vast, layered space with a blackened floor, jazzed-up orchestra, and vaulting stairways. They watch a tap-dancing army of men and women—the Advance of the Proles, but in tap shoes! The army rat-a-tat-tats down some stairs and across the dance floor, moving back and forth, up and down, in a display of real dancing power. It's a cacophony of irresponsibility, punishment, and wild abandon. Powell and Shaw dance, she runs away out onto a balcony, playfully closing the glass doors behind her. Powell rushes to her, kisses her through the glass door, as the crowd pushes against him. The pressure opens the door and pushes Shaw over the balcony. She falls to her death! A clock on a tower shows it's 4:30 a.m. The camera takes the viewer back to the map of Manhattan and to Shaw's face. She removes the cigarette, turns her head around to fully face the audience again, and sings, "Listen to the lullaby of old Broadway." Then her face recedes back to where it came from, wherever that was . . . which, really, was the very strange mind of Busby Berkeley.

The distinctive Berkeley style involves visual patterns, formations, mathematical precision, repetition, and a kind of internal logic designed to transport the viewer into Berkeley's inner world. A Berkeley number begins with a specific indication that it is taking place on a stage, or in a nightclub, or in a specific, detailed, and physically delineated musical space. He locates where the viewer is in the narrative and in relation to the frame. At some point, he crosses a boundary of perception and releases a viewer from *that* place, letting go of all pretense to realism. His work is the audience's liberation from time and place. In his most elaborate spectacles, the image moves toward a place onscreen—such as Ruby Keeler's eyeball—and enters it, and behind it, on the other side of reality, is a new and different world. It's as if he stops the clock of the movie, dilates time, and moves into another dimension. Berkeley is the sci-fi expert of the movie musical. Did audiences accept it? They had no trouble, because Berkeley made it so clear that they had been released into spectacle. By doing what he did, he made everyone realize once and for all that musicals could break down the proscenium arch and move into the fantasy life of the spectator. His camera goes into your head and plays with the logic of looking, the sense of seeing, and the multiplication and mathematics of objects that are moving in front of our eyes. Berkeley didn't really change dancing; he changed musicals. He added to the development of the genre artistically because he showed visibly onscreen that an audience could go to another space within the frame, and in that space could be an unrealistic level of musical performance, something surreal and new and different.

Berkeley's career at Warners began to slip as the late 1930s arrived. His personal life was a shambles. (He married six times and found nothing but misery until his final marriage, to Etta Judd, in 1958.) In 1935, Berkeley, a heavy drinker, was driving legally drunk in Los Angeles and became involved in a three-car automobile crash, and three people were killed. (Berkeley himself was badly cut and bruised.) An eyewitness testified that he had been speeding and had changed lanes and swerved into another car, hitting it head-on. Berkeley underwent three trials for second-degree murder but was finally cleared of charges. He survived the scandal, but his erratic lifestyle undoubtedly contributed to the various professional setbacks he would soon encounter. Songwriters Al Dubin and Harry Warren, who worked closely with Berkeley at Warners, called him "the madman," and it wasn't a joke. His personal problems led inevitably to career issues, and Berkeley's unusual and spectacular musical presentations also became less new, less appealing to audiences. He left Warner Bros. for MGM, a studio that wanted spectacle but wanted glamour and lavishness more than innovation, so he clashed with his bosses over ideas and left in 1943 to go to 20th Century–Fox, where he made one of his best movies: the truly astonishing *The Gang's All Here*. Ultimately Busby Berkeley faded from the limelight until an interest in nostalgia brought him back to Broadway for a revival of *No, No, Nanette* with Ruby Keeler in 1971.

Berkeley's musicals can never have the dramatic force of those by someone like Vincente Minnelli because of their lack of integration with the narrative. They can never have the grace and elation of Astaire's astonishing art of dance. They can never contain the specific intellectualism of the art of the dance that Gene Kelly's developed. What they do have is something no other musical numbers have: an unexpected amazement that makes a viewer gasp. Berkeley is the man who tells a viewer that the proscenium arch is a lie and who boldly proves that cinema is not theater. In the end, his problem was that there was no place to go with his style. It was spectacle, and audiences like narrative. But Berkeley was an experimentalist who proved audiences could and would accept abstraction at their local movie house. They were willing to read images set to music and absorb them into their own private feelings and thoughts.

The four talents—Lubitsch, Mamoulian, Astaire, and Berkeley—are absolutely key to the emergence of the musical as a true American movie genre after the transition-to-sound era. Their movies are historical touchstones and stand alone in their innovative and imaginative approaches, and yet it's important to remember that there are always amazing, undiscovered musicals that defy these historical pronouncements. In *Hooked on Hollywood*, Leonard Maltin describes an obscure musical from 1933 that is about as innovative as it gets and might be celebrated as "historically significant" except for one important thing: almost no one has ever heard of it and fewer have ever seen it. It's an RKO movie called *Melody Cruise*, starring Charlie Ruggles, Phil Harris, Helen Mack, Greta Nissen, and Chick Chandler, and directed by Mark Sandrich, who would go on to do Astaire-Rogers musicals.

Melody Cruise is pre-Code sexy, and moves along at a peppy pace, running only 76 minutes. Its "historical significance" lies in what Maltin identifies as "an endless procession of flashy camera tricks and musical ideas." These include, among others, showing girls in disconnected spaces around the ship, all singing "He's Not the Marrying Kind," with one line assigned to each separate group before cutting to another. In other words, *Melody*

Cruise of 1933 was a modern musical, predating Streisand's "Don't Rain on My Parade" journey of song in *Funny Girl* in 1968. Why wasn't its originality noticed at the time? Why isn't it on the list of innovative musicals? Well, for one thing, its goal was very clearly fun, not art. It didn't capture the attention of any critic or analytical voice, and it had no key musical star for audiences to hold on to in memories. This is the significance of artists such as Lubitsch, Mamoulian, Astaire, and Berkeley. They *were* noticed— and remembered—for making interesting things happen and they did it more than once. *Melody Cruise* was a bit of a one-off, with no Irving Berlin, Jerome Kern, or Cole Porter helping it out to provide hit songs. But it's important to remember *Melody Cruise*. Throughout musical history, oddities like it happened. Movies would break the fourth wall, connect singing and dancing performances across time and space, and allow actors to "talk" through songs and demonstrate their feelings through dance. But those things were taken for granted, merely observed. It would be almost a decade or more after 1933 before movies would begin to consciously *point* at such things, announcing: *This is art*. But the casual creativity of *Melody Cruise* exists and should not be forgotten; it, too, was a part of the progress (and it provides an opportunity to see a very young Betty Grable in a bit part!).

With the impact of the four talents of Lubitsch and Mamoulian, Astaire and Berkeley, 1933 brought the musical genre forward toward its future: cinematic usage, the beauty of dance, text and subtext, abstraction and experimentation. The possibility of an art form that could play on Main Street, USA, was secured.

IV

Stars and Strategies

HOLLYWOOD WAS ALWAYS ABOUT TWO THINGS: stars and stories. The studios developed stars and created specialized stories adapted to fit them ("vehicles") or else featured them in already established popular genres that worked for their talents (westerns, melodramas, gangster films, or, of course, musicals). Starting right at the beginning of musicals in 1926–27, and really taking hold in 1933, when the musical established itself as a permanent, reliable form of movie that any studio could manufacture, the musical star vehicle became a staple of the business.

Studios were making product to sell, so they wanted to find a way to repeat success. To be able to shape a musical around a single star in a specific kind of story would be smart business. Build the story around the talent. Choose songs to suit that story and that talent. Then make lots and lots of movies like that. Discussions of Hollywood musicals seldom address the issue of how an individual performance style affects the overall presentation of the movie. Hollywood understood this, and actively searched out interesting and varied musical performers, developing a strong tradition of musicals created for and defined by a specific performer: the star musical. Musical performers were the auteurs of their films; they appeared in vehicles designed especially for who they were and what they could do musically. Judy Garland sings, but she also dances, and she presents a trembling and touching presence. Astaire dances, but Astaire also sings, and he's a peculiar combination of impeccable sophistication and Nebraska brashness. Film stories could be made to fit.

Consider the difference between Judy Garland and her daughter Liza Minnelli. Both had serious acting chops, and both represented a curious mixture of vulnerability and enduring strength. Both could sing and dance at a top level, as well as do comedy and tragedy. Yet they project an opposite emphasis. Garland creates a relationship with an audience that says, "I'm vulnerable. I really need you. I might break down here. I probably won't make it through this unless you help me, love me. If you do, I'll make it." Minnelli goes in the opposite direction. "Get back, I'm gonna blast you," she says. "I can do this by myself, and I will. I'm not my mother, don't worry, I'm not gonna break down. I'll get us all through this." Minnelli works both with her mother's persona and against it, but she is also fundamentally working off it. As her famous mother's daughter, she had no other choice, but the point is, movies could be made to work for both these women—or for any other musical star. Once musicals were a securely established film genre, finding the stars to carry them became the first real business motivation.

Stars

Jolson, Crosby, and Presley

A comparison of the films of Al Jolson, Bing Crosby, and Elvis Presley illustrates how the specific talents and personalities of three singers were used to create star musicals. Jolson, Crosby, and Presley are legendary singers of the twentieth century. Each of these men had his own personal style. Each had a legendary stardom in more than one medium. Jolson was tops in vaudeville, radio, theater, and movies; Crosby owned the fields of radio, movies, TV, and recording; and Presley had movies, TV, and records and was also the master of the concert-performance tour. Fame for these men lasted until death and has continued beyond, especially in the case of Presley. Although Jolson had a period of approximately three years in which his career began to fade, and Crosby eased into retirement mode after 1970 (but still occasionally performed), all three were working professionals to the end. Each represented his own era. What they shared is what spurred Hollywood to build movies around them. Each had a voice unlike any other singer's. Each had physical moves that marked him out: Jolson's energetic use of arms and legs, Crosby's laid-back stance, and Presley's hip-gyrating sexuality. Jolson was the unschooled boy who grew up in vaudeville and forged his way to the top with his ability to excite a live audience through the electricity of his personality. He was the guy who had to do it without amplification, right in front of his audience. Crosby embraced the jazz rhythms that began to entertain the mainstream at the end of the 1920s, and defined himself through his voice by singing in front of bands and on radio. He owned the microphone, defining the transition between the live performance and the recorded one. He was comfortable with the new medium of the motion picture and became one of its greatest stars during what is now known as the Golden Age of Hollywood. Presley represented the teenage spirit of his own era: the hot young guy who woofed and wailed, swinging his hips and snapping his fingers, taking the old Jolson moves forward into rock and roll and open sexuality. Each of the three singers had his own sex appeal; each had his own distinctive talent; each had various nicknames. Jolson was Joely, Mammy Boy, and the Jazz Singer (even though he seldom sang jazz). Crosby was Bing, Der Bingle, the Groaner, the Crooner; and Presley was the King, Swivel Hips, the Hound Dog Man. But none of that mattered. Each one was just who he was, a unique musical presence: Al Jolson, Bing Crosby, Elvis Presley. All three were legends in their own time and beyond. Hollywood bought that quality and used it, understanding that who they seemed to be was who they could be on film. It was a surefire formula for success. From the beginning of the sound era to the final collapse of the studio system, 1927 to 1969, the films of these men represent the *star* musical.

Jolson

Al Jolson was born Asa Yoelson in what is now Lithuania in 1886. His father was a cantor, and hardship drove him to America to look for a better life. Forced by poverty to leave his family behind, the elder Yoelson spent four years alone in the new country, working in Washington DC, until he could afford to send for them. Al Jolson arrived with his mother, his two older sisters, Rose and Etta, and his older brother, Hersch, in 1894. The mother died in childbirth within a year. Having by all accounts been his mother's favorite, Jolson, only eight years old, became restless and unhappy. He found solace in his discovery of the world of entertainment, and he and his brother became street singers. When Hersch left home at age fifteen, Jolson soon followed. The brothers made their way forward; by 1904 they were in vaudeville. Jolson was exposed to all the show business traditions of the era, including blacking up. It was inevitable that he would try it, and it seemed to liberate him, provide him with a mask behind which he could be free to let himself go into all-out musical performance. Since a white man blacking up with burnt cork was common in those days, Jolson didn't think about whether it was racially offensive or not; it was an available vaudeville shtick to him, and one that worked for his voice, his moves, and his action. He just did it, as did many others. By 1906, Jolson had become an enormous hit as a blackface singer. In 1908, he was invited to join the famous Dockstader Minstrels. When the Shubert brothers, Broadway impresarios, bought out Dockstader, they inherited Al Jolson as part of the package. By 1911, Jolson was onstage at the Winter Garden in *La Belle Paree*. He became an enormous personal hit, and moved up to fame and fortune. By the time Jolson was twenty-six, he was a well-known Broadway star, and soon after he became a household name.

After *The Jazz Singer* put Jolson in the movie spotlight, the canny Warner brothers knew that it was good business to capitalize on the press and hype generated by the film's success. It is a testament to Jolson's fame, his success in *The Jazz Singer*, and his powerful personality that Warners would even consider him as a viable movie star. He was forty-one years old, short (about five-eight), with a big head and a big grin, but not conventionally handsome. One of his biographers, Michael Freedland, described Jolson's look as that of a "Roman emperor." He wasn't a matinee-idol type (although he thought he was), but he carried himself the way he nicknamed himself, as "the World's Greatest Entertainer," and in that lay his potential. He thought he was great—and he *was* great—and he could sell himself to audiences whether they were actually live in front of him or just out there in a dark movie house. His confidence was astronomical. He strutted around dressed in cashmere jackets, tailored suits, handmade shoes, and fur coats. He smoked a big cigar and knew how to wield it like a high-stepping majorette with a baton. He exuded power and confidence. But could this come across onscreen? It was one thing to headline a new technological innovation and another to have only a personality to sell: would the interest in Jolson carry forward? *The Jazz Singer*, after all, was a fluke: it had been a novelty to hear the great Jolson talk and sing in the movie house.

The three Warner brothers knew business and knew customers. Although they were famous for treating stars like dirt (as opposed to MGM, where they were revered), Warners understood that Jolson was a star, and he could enter movies as a star in order to play his star self and perform his own famous star hits—and that if he did, they'd make money. In the end, Jolson would make eight feature musicals at Warner Bros. from 1928 to 1936, and five of them would have him playing a character named Al. It was how the public saw him, and the way they best believed in him. Even if he was called Bumper, Gus, or Joe, as in the other three, audiences were thinking of him as Al. He "retired" from show business after *The Singing Kid* in 1936, but returned in 1939 under contract at 20th Century–Fox and made three movies there that year, in one of which (*Hollywood Cavalcade*) he played himself. His final movie, back at Warners, was 1945's *Rhapsody in Blue*, about the life of George Gershwin, in which he also played himself. Thus it perhaps can be said that Al Jolson, more than any other movie star, literally played himself onscreen.*

Jolson's second film—*The Singing Fool*—was his real movie test. "Produced with Warner Electric Apparatus," *The Singing Fool* is a perfect example of how a movie musical was built to fit an already established musical personality, to bring Jolson the Great to the masses who couldn't see him any other way. His costars were Betty Bronson and Josephine Dunn, and he was given the big entrance reserved only for those that moviemakers knew the audience was atwitter to set eyes on. After a quote from no less than Henry Wadsworth Longfellow about how important singers are (on a title card), the audience is told (on another card) that they will now see "the beginning of the workday for some and the end of the playday for others." The story begins outside a speakeasy called Blackie Joe's. A limo pulls up, and another title card tells everyone that a young woman is saying "You would bring us to a joint like this" to her escort. *The Singing Fool* is part talkie, part nondialogue sequences, but when title cards are used, there is music on the soundtrack. The shot-silent opening scene uses that crutch—music to cover—as a hand-held camera moves through a crowded scene of drunken revelers. The viewer is located behind a round table carried by a waiter who is going to set it up for the new arrivals. As he moves,

---

* Jolson was advertised as "a legend in his lifetime" for 1928's *The Singing Fool*, which would become one of his greatest hits. Jolson was indeed "a legend in his lifetime," one of the most legendary of America's singing stars, but although many know his name today (mostly in association with *The Jazz Singer*), few realize just how great a star he really was—not just on Broadway but also in the movies. A survey of American movie musicals done in 1980, with all rental income from a musical's initial release period adjusted for inflation, ranked *The Singing Fool* number 18 on the list of successes, topping more famous entries such as *Oklahoma!*, *Guys and Dolls*, the 1951 *Show Boat*, *Singin' in the Rain*, *An American in Paris*, *The Wizard of Oz*, *Cabaret*, *Gigi*, the 1954 *A Star Is Born*, and many others. Furthermore, the 1946 *The Jolson Story*, a musical biography made during the star's lifetime, was itself ranked number 9, and *The Jazz Singer* was number 26. Jolson put rear ends in the seats.

Al Jolson . . . showing off his pizzazz

he twists and turns, the table turning right, then left, always in a forward motion among a boozed-up, hot-time-in-the-old-town atmosphere. The waiter carrying the table is Al Jolson. When he sets it down and is shown in close-up, a title says he's "a waiter by ambition, a song writer by nature, and a singing fool." It's a star entrance all right, because only after he's seen does recorded sound enter—it had to wait for Jolson. *The Singing Fool* is barely underway, but it has set up what will become the Al Jolson musical format: fun, high energy, a 1920s atmosphere, with him as an ambitious show-biz guy. Jolson says he's going to sing a ballad for the first time, dedicated to Molly, the girl he loves, and then he does what he does best: he sings—"It All Depends on You." He's shot in medium close-up, and he acts out the drama of the song as he sings it. Jolson has the power of a lifetime of performance experience. His musical "self" had been forged in front of audiences. There's no way he's going to let a single eye wander away from him even if, on a soundstage, he has to imagine them. He's a perfect example of a singer whose stage personality is so strong it carries over onto film without a hitch. He never pretended to be anyone but Al Jolson, either onstage or on film. In this film, he'll stop an audience's applause by saying, "One moment . . . one moment . . . you ain't heard nothin' yet," a reprise of his famous line from *The Jazz Singer*. Later he'll tell them, "I'll sing a thousand songs," a comment he was famous for making to a theater audience. Later, in case anyone missed it, he repeats the "You ain't heard nothin' yet" line. He sings loud. He jukes and he jives. He sways and he shakes. He winks and he smirks. He never lets up, even when he's singing a sentimental ballad. Viewers are confronted with an electric presence. Jolson's material is corny, often racist and misogynist, and he's consummately old-fashioned in almost everything he has to give. And yet. When he begins to perform, it's like Frankenstein's monster starting to move. The doctor looks up into the heavens in disbelief and cries out incredulously, "It's alive! It's alive." And Jolson *is* alive. Eternally alive, and that's what made him a star. He considered himself one, and he wasn't going to let anyone forget it.*

Even though not romantically handsome, Jolson's face is a good movie face. He has big eyes, sharp cheekbones, and a highly defined profile. He has a rich, distinctive speaking voice, and he exudes a tangible sexuality. It's an unpolished Clark Gable–ish sexuality. He's smooth, but not suave. In *The Singing Fool*, Jolson sings his second song almost immediately after his first. It's one of his most famous: "I'm Sittin' on Top of the World." His performance is shot in alternating medium close-ups and full-frame long shots so that he can do one of his highly physical improvisatory dances. His moves are spontaneous, unchoreographed, and natural to his performance style. He moves both his arms and his legs, sways his hips, and taps his feet. His waiter character skyrockets to fame immediately after singing these two songs. Why wait? This "skyrocketing" reflects how musicals were styled for their lead performer without any pretext that things were

---

* Even as late as 2015, a modern personality like Rod Stewart told interviewer Scott Hudson that he "spent most of his teen years in his bedroom playing with his model train and listening to Al Jolson records." Stewart said it was those records that initially helped him develop his trademark gruff vocal impressions that led to his inclusion in the Jeff Beck Group.

otherwise. A montage of sheet music appears, and it's basically sheet music from Jolson's own parade of hits. Hollywood was confident in its knowledge of audiences, counting on them knowing that Al Jolson was Al Jolson, so that in any of his movies, he'd naturally *be* Al Jolson. The audience is suddenly, without any further plot development, deposited at the Club Cliquot, where "Al" is now both the owner and the star. Welcomed by the riotously happy audience, he belts out the big Jolson hit "Rainbow 'Round My Shoulder."

The Singing Fool has an unoriginal plot. Jolson marries the wrong woman, and she uses him to further her own career. She's unfaithful, but Jolson is blindly devoted to her. (When he tells her of his love, she replies, "Let's not get into a gab fest at this hour of the night.") But it is the little boy they have that matters in this marriage, because he gives Jolson the opportunity to sing "Sonny Boy" to the lad when he wakes up in the middle of the night. When Jolson sang a song like "Sonny Boy," he *acted* the number, sometimes reciting part of the lyrics. His verbal delivery has a conversational quality—it never sounds like dialogue. He's always casual and confident, with impeccable timing and the sense that he's in total control. He uses slang, often throwing in Jewish words (referring to things as "kosher," etc.). This improvisational element to Jolson's song delivery is one of his unique qualities.* Jolson was born in the nineteenth century, but he was a twentieth-century artist in his approach to rhythm and improvisation in his singing.

"Sonny Boy" is given plenty of screen time, establishing what will be the main musical focus for the remainder of the movie. When his two-timing wife leaves him, taking the boy with her to Paris (her departure note is signed "Hastily, Molly"), Al hits the skids, recovers, climbs to the top again, and then hears that Sonny Boy is very ill in the hospital. (And just about that fast.) This gives him the opportunity to sing "Sonny Boy" a second time, after he picks the little tot up out of his hospital bed and carries him to a chair. After the number is over, Al carries the child back to bed, lovingly putting him down and covering him. (Behind Al, we can see the doctor looking at the kid and shaking his head.) When Al goes into the

---

* Elvis Presley, who cited Jolson as a favorite and an influence, often "recited" or "talked" part of his lyrics to his audiences. Crosby, too, played with lyrics, but his approach was more of the true scatting jazz singer. Jolson was not really a "jazz singer," but the improvisational, or dramatic, portions of his delivery of songs are linked to the jazz tradition of playing with musical format.

How most people
picture Al Jolson: in
blackface, down on one
knee, hard-selling "My
Mammy"

hallway, the mother's scream is heard, but Al doesn't understand his child is dead. (It's a bit of a shock to the audience, too, who have naturally expected that the sound of Al Jolson singing "Sonny Boy" will get him up on his little legs to dance the polka.) Al tells the doctor to take good care of his son, do everything for him, etc. Then he walks brokenly out, down a long corridor. Al Jolson is no actor, but he *is* a performer. He gives this scene the old silent-film razzmatazz, and his exit is a perfect setup for the grand finale. Back at the theater, no one expects Al to go on, but he says no, he'll feel better if he works. "I'll be there," says Al Jolson. The stage manager intones, "He's a real trouper, and he'll go on." This is Al Jolson's climactic presentation of Al Jolson, and the completion of the film as a star vehicle.

Throughout the movie, it can be seen that Jolson's background is that of a stage performer, not because he's a ham, or old-fashioned, although both of these things are relatively true. It's because he never looks a coactor in the eye. He keeps his own face turned to the camera, always looking out toward where he remembers is the place his audience would be located. In his last big scene, he finally lets the camera take charge. He begins to blacken his face. (Ironically, there has always been an African American valet present in his dressing room, but there has been no blackface number so far.) Since blackface was Jolson's signature, the audience knows this will be his final number, and they know it will be "Sonny Boy." The movie strings the audience along, pumping up the anticipation. Jolson blacks up slowly, intercut with shots of a minstrel show coming out onto the stage. He puts on his woolly wig, fighting tears. He comes out of his dressing room and slowly, sadly enters the stage, the spotlight hitting him. His "Sonny Boy" music comes up, but he says he can't, and everyone starts to panic, but the philosopher stage manager says it's gonna work. Jolson says he's gonna try, adding for the orchestra leader: "Play that again, will you?" Up comes the music again, and this time he sings. Yes, he sings, seeing his son's face in front of him. Jolson starts low and pumps it up, giving it everything he's got, and the crowd jumps to its feet when it's over. He collapses after the curtain falls. "I'll never quit again, and as long as there are people who'll listen to me, I'll never quit again," he promises. And that's Al Jolson, folks. He didn't know how to quit, and he didn't know how not to sing a thousand songs, and he didn't know anything but show business and singing his brains out. (And he made sure that no one got in his way.) Warner Bros. understood that, and built its Jolson films around that character. In *The Singing Fool*, they had located his screen self. After that, they found plots to incorporate his famous songs and to allow him to breeze on confidently, suffer a little, do his thing, and always consistently be the Al Jolson he had spent a lifetime projecting to audiences.

After the enormous success of *The Singing Fool*, Jolson did *Say It with Songs* (1929), *Mammy* (1930), *Big Boy* (1930), *Hallelujah, I'm a Bum* (1933), *Wonder Bar* (1934), *Go into Your Dance* (1935), and *The Singing Kid* (1936), all of them maintaining the same pattern Warners had established for his songs and his personality.

In Jolson's career, there were only three challenges to his established musical presence and storyline: the unusual film *Hallelujah, I'm A Bum*; his work with Busby Berkeley (*Wonder Bar*); and his costarring with his young wife, Ruby Keeler (*Go into Your Dance*). Not one of these challenges threw him off track or in any significant way changed the basic pattern Warners had developed to sell him in movies. *Hallelujah, I'm a Bum* (1933) is of interest because it's one of the few Jolson films that isn't about show business and in which he doesn't play a character who was clearly based directly on who he was as an entertainer. Costarring Madge Evans and Frank Morgan, *Hallelujah* is an unusual musical, and, in fact, an unusual film. Called a "Depression curio" by Leonard Maltin, the film is well directed by Lewis Milestone, cowritten by Ben Hecht and S. N. Behrman, and features songs by Rodgers and Hart that have rhyming dialogue. (Rodgers and Hart even make cameo appearances as a photographer and a bank clerk.) *Hallelujah* is an example of the offbeat political movie of the Depression years (others include *Gabriel over the White House*, *The Phantom President*, *Wild Boys of the Road*, and *Heroes for Sale*). Jolson is excellent in the film, and his best friend and companion is African American. They are two hoboes who spend their winters in Florida and the rest of the year in New York as denizens of Central Park.*

Jolson's character is dubbed "the Mayor of Central Park." (Frank Morgan plays a lesser being, the actual mayor of New York City.) Jolson's Bumper is "a gentleman of leisure," meaning that he does not work. The plot has him saving a young woman who tries to commit suicide, only to find she's an amnesia victim. (Amnesia: the movie disease.) When he falls in love with her, Bumper gets a job (with the mayor's help) to pay her rent. This character is unusual for Jolson's films because not only is he not defined initially as an entertainer, he is a man unconcerned with fame, success, wealth, or even purpose. Jolson demonstrates that he *can* put his power to service in a story; he *can* pull himself down and into a character. Whenever any kind of movie star—musical or dramatic or comic—was cast in a role that was the opposite of what the audience expected of him/her, the business called it a "departure." Bumper is a "departure" for Jolson, although he's still charismatic, the center of attention, the solver of problems, and—naturally—a guy who can sing. There is no fundamental change to the entertainment Goliath that was Al Jolson. This time, however, he sings as he lives; he doesn't sing for a living. There's a lot of music: the title song (well done by Jolson), "My Pal Bumper," and "What Do You

---

* When Bumper (Jolson) goes back to work, having once been a performer, he puts on blackface while his friend solemnly watches him do it. No comments are made, as was true in *The Singing Fool*. These scenes are uncomfortable for modern audiences. A jaw-dropping scene takes place in *The Singing Kid* in 1936. Jolson—in full blackface—performs with Cab Calloway and his orchestra in a nightclub in which *all* the patrons are African Americans.

Want with Money?" But most of the music is also the film's dialogue, a modern approach to musical films.

Hallelujah hits a high point in a musical trial sequence in which people who have to live in the park, the Depression victims who are Bumper's friends, conduct a hearing regarding their disapproval of his decision to go to work. Jolson sings his defense: he's fallen in love. During this sequence, Jolson is singing about his inner life, acting directly through his singing, and not just putting over a song. In so doing, he reveals why he was such an effective entertainer and why he could be a successful movie star. He had always understood how to channel emotion out of himself and into a set of words that are musical. (This was why "My Mammy" and "Sonny Boy" worked so well.) He doesn't make a big deal out of *acting* his numbers, the way latter day singers like Barbra Streisand would do; and although there's a great deal of talk about left-wing politics ("Pardon me, Egghead, you talk like a Red" and "She dresses like a capitalist"), Jolson doesn't forget to deliver his trademark line: "You ain't heard nothin' yet."

Busby Berkeley entered into the Jolson movie mix in *Wonder Bar* (1934), for which he created the dances (the film was directed by Lloyd Bacon). Jolson's star persona had to be mixed into a large all-star cast and contend with Berkeley's over-the-top, fantastical production numbers. *Wonder Bar* was a variation on MGM's 1932 *Grand Hotel*, set in a "grand hotel" or "wonder bar" of nightclubs. There are several interlocking dramatic stories, each one of which has to be resolved in eighty-four minutes of plot—plus production numbers. Besides Jolson, the movie features Dick Powell, Dolores del Rio, Kay Francis, Ricardo Cortez, Guy Kibbee, Ruth Donnelly, Hugh Herbert, and Fifi D'Orsay. Jolson is given the usual star entrance early in the film when he blows in to the Wonder Bar (which is decorated with a gigantic poster of his face). He's full of good cheer, energy, and "Oh, baby!" greetings for everyone. He sings "Vive la France" in his classic style, dancing around, snapping his fingers, getting down on one knee while the camera remains locked on him.*

Wonder Bar defies the conventional idea that musicals are always escapist, with no real drama or hardship. Jolson's Paris nightclub is a major crime zone. A diamond necklace is stolen, adulteries abound, gigolos lurk, and a customer tries to cut his wrists with a razor. Dolores del Rio and Ricardo

---

* He's afraid of nothing. "Boys will be boys!" he calls out to an obviously gay couple, adding a lascivious "Woo!" (The film's trailer promised "the Gayest Rendezvous on Earth.")

Cortez take to the nightclub floor to perform their tango ("The Gaucho Dance"), and their personal conflicts enter into their routine. He throws her hard to the floor, pulls her hair, and brutally cracks his whip into her face—twice—and across her body. Although no marks are shown, she registers her pain. When they exit the floor, an abandoned knife is shown, and a telltale drop of blood. She has stabbed him. (He dies, and the problem of his corpse is solved by sticking it in the car of a patron who every day threatens to run his car off a ledge, and finally conveniently delivers on his threat, solving the dead-body problem.) All this in eighty-four minutes. Jolson pays no attention to any of it, acting as if it's all a day at the office for him, which it apparently is, and just waiting his turn for the spotlight. He ignores Berkeley's amazing routine with a black marble floor, hundreds of girls in matching gowns moving in and out among moving marble columns until the grand moment when the camera rises up to show the typical overhead kaleidoscope effect. He just follows it with a long comedy routine with a stooge, full of language jokes and vaudeville double entendres, after which he sings a hearty "Ochi Chornye" and gets the audience to join in. Nothing stops him.

The musical shoot-out—and the challenge to the Jolson definition—arrives when he has to appear in the middle of a number created by Berkeley. Jolson vs. Berkeley! It's a Godzilla vs. Mothra moment, and Jolson shows no concern. He comes out the way he always does, and socks it to the audience. (Overwhelming Busby Berkeley's visuals is Jolson's ultimate proof that he really *is* the World's Greatest Entertainer.) Seen today, the number is a horror, but it's also one of those moments from the past that remind us how things once were. A blackface Jolson, dressed in rags in a backwoods setting, talks to a little girl and sings "I'm Goin' to Heaven on a Mule." Allegedly set on a nightclub stage, the number then opens up into a massive visual fantasy in the typical Berkeley manner. Jolson is seen riding to heaven on a mule, knocking on the door, and being admitted by St. Peter, Gabriel, and a chorus of children ("Hi-De-Ho!"). Everyone is in blackface. Neatly avoiding the "Chute to Hell," Jolson travels forward through the Pork Chop Orchard, the Possum Pie Grove, the Fried Chicken stand, cheerfully singing, "Watermelons are blowin' in the breeze." (St. Peter says, "You ain't seen nothin' yet!") Everybody's singing and dancing, while Jolson reads a Yiddish/Hebrew newspaper and a huge melon opens up so the tap-dancing star Hal LeRoy can do his thing. The level of racism and insensitivity in this number is astonishing, but no one seems the least concerned or even aware, especially Jolson, who, no matter what visual shock or inventive camera movement occurs, keeps his place in the center of things and never lets go of his own musical persona. Even in the midst of "15 Big Stars," as the trailer claimed, Jolson took pride of place, advertised as "that greatest of entertainers, Al Jolson."

Go into Your Dance (1935) costarred Jolson with his wife, the *42nd Street* tap dancer Ruby Keeler. (Keeler and Jolson had wed in 1928, although he was forty-three and she was only nineteen. Jolson had already been twice divorced.) In *Go into Your Dance*, the dances are staged by Bobby Connolly, not Berkeley, so neither Keeler nor Jolson is overwhelmed by visual imagination, although the numbers have a glamorous style. Jolson is introduced in a big sombrero and a Mexican serape, wearing a wide grin and a radiant shine. Even at the age of forty-nine, he still has a lean look and the intense energy that drives his musical engine. His delivery of dialogue by this time in his movie career is slangy and almost gangsterish. "I'll be there, baby," he promises a woman, "but not a word to Winchell." When he wants a cocktail, he says, "Spray me with it." He's a natty dresser, neat and precise, and his musical presentation hasn't lost its verve. He sings "Mammy, I'll Sing About You" and still uses expressive gestures, still performs within the song, and still gives a drama to his lyrics without losing the beat of the music.

Keeler and Jolson perform two big hit songs together: "About a Quarter to Nine" and "She's a Latin from Manhattan." Even when paired with the youthful Keeler, Jolson prevails, by doing one of his blackface numbers toward the end and, before his finish, telling Keeler (who's been shot, again defying the law that musicals contain no trauma), "Baby, you ain't heard nothin' yet." After the shooting, which apparently inspires *him* to perform, the blackfaced Jolson does his solo version of "Go into Your Dance," doing his hip-swaying, back-and-forth wiggle. Warners billed Jolson and Keeler as "the World's Greatest Musical Combination" and "What a team!" Adding that the film also had "100 fast-stepping cocktail cuties," the trailer dropped Keeler and went straight to promoting Jolson. A character actor says, "I'd know him through his black face, blue face, or what face . . . I've seen him on stage lots of times." The movie, the ad assures, "was made to thrill the entire world." When it came to Jolson, no superlative was too great.

By 1936, and the final picture of Jolson's star run at Warners, the concept of the musical vehicle for a specifically defined movie star was firmly in place. It's clear in watching *The Singing Kid* that Hollywood had figured out that if you have an established star to sing what he sings and do what he does, you can get away with a lot. The public would buy tickets just for the star and the songs. Near the end of the movie, Jolson ditches a rehearsal, and with his cronies alongside him walks out into the city streets. He begins to sing and, during the ensuing stroll through the town, an audience sees and hears a mixture of weather, traffic, city noises, and events, both real and unreal, as the musical group—the Jolson posse—sing and dance while the city characters go about their business of selling, jostling, riveting, etc. It's an amalgam of unreal elements (the musical performance) and real elements (a normal day on a city street). The scene culminates with everyone, whatever performance universe they're in, dropping down dead on the sidewalk while Jolson climbs atop their bodies to belt out "Mammy." The strange mess ends with a cut that shifts Jolson and the dead into blackface as they all come alive! This extended musical and narrative sequence is an obvious presentation of the two choices that moviemakers now understand are available for musicals: performance as a profession or performance as an emotional expression. So what was going on with *The Singing Kid*? Was it creation or desperation? Experimentation or bungling? One thing is certain: Jolson could run out of plots, tricks, and devices, but as long as he didn't run out of songs, the audience didn't care. Moviemakers knew it. Just have him sing and carry the show . . . clear proof that the musical star vehicle existed.

After *The Singing Kid* (with Jolson again playing a Broadway star, but with special appearances by artists such as Cab Calloway, Wini Shaw, and the Yacht Club Boys), he was off the screen for a period of about four years. He was fifty years old, and Keeler had become a Warner Bros. star. Jolson roamed restlessly about, playing the horses, keeping himself busy, and finally agreeing to appear in 20th Century–Fox musicals. In 1939 he was given good billing in *Rose of Washington Square*. His name was still news, but the real stars of the film were Alice Faye and Tyrone Power, in a thinly disguised version of Fanny Brice's personal story of the arrest of her husband, Nicky Arnstein. (Brice sued.) Jolson was really playing a supporting role: a guy who was really just himself. He sings some of his own standards, "My Mammy" and "California, Here I Come," and his old electricity is still there.

After *Rose of Washington Square*, Jolson made only three movies, *Hollywood Cavalcade* (1939), in which he played himself, *Swanee River* (1939),

and *Rhapsody in Blue* (1945). In *Swanee River*, a biopic about the famous songwriter Stephen Foster, he plays E. P. Christy, the originator of the American minstrel show. In *Rhapsody in Blue*—another biopic, this one about George Gershwin—Jolson again played himself. His star self finally overpowered his movies, and he could only be seen either as part of his own history (Christy) or as Al Jolson; and he finally returned to the height of fame because of two movies that were in fact his own biopics. Jolson could never really be anyone but himself, which is why he is so clearly the template for the movie-musical singing star who has vehicles built around him and his personality.

Jolson was a musical Rasputin—no matter what, he just didn't give up. After *Swanee*, he was restless and bored in retirement, so he was among the first to volunteer to entertain the troops during World War II. Pushing himself as he always did, flying into war zones, doing long shows in

Larry Parks portraying Jolson (with a sign to help) in the movie that brought Jolson back to the top of the heap, *The Jolson Story*

less-than-supportive weather and accommodations, he ultimately collapsed, only to recover and begin touring army hospitals. After the war ended, Jolson was approached by Columbia Pictures about a possible biographical movie. With an ego like his, it was inevitable that he did not, *could* not, believe that anyone could possibly play Al Jolson but Al Jolson, so his response was "Am I too old for this?" (He was sixty-three.) When told that the plan would be to have a younger actor portray him, he was incredulous. Who could duplicate his voice, his moves, his energy and passion? Given the power of his performing, it wasn't an unreasonable position for him to take. Many actors were tested, among them Richard Conte (later famous for playing gangsters as late into his life as the *Godfather* movies), Jose Ferrer (who would become the Oscar-winning husband of singer Rosemary Clooney), and Danny Thomas (who would star in a remake of *The Jazz Singer* in 1953). The genius of the resulting movie, the 1946 *The Jolson Story*, was to use Jolson himself on the soundtrack, but to have a young actor (Larry Parks, who earned an Oscar nomination for his portrayal) learn to imitate his moves and lip-sync to his recordings.*

The Jolson Story secured the Jolson legend and kept his name alive for another generation. It was a gigantic hit: the biggest box-office-grossing film of the year. The movie acts as if Jolson had been practically dead at the end of the 1930s and no one had ever heard of him, or if they had, they'd forgotten him. Since he worked throughout the war, and since his last movie had been made in 1945, and since *The Jolson Story* went into general release in 1946, there's only a very short time in which Jolson was not an active performer. But the movie makes drama out of his retirement, and sold the idea that although he'd been out of the limelight, his "old" style of singing was still viable.

The miracle of *The Jolson Story*, and it *is* a miracle, is that although it starred no big names (Parks was new, and his leading lady, Evelyn Keyes, had never become a real star), and with no musical performances in it other than the Jolson imitations, it managed to do what might seem almost impossible: capture a sense of the Jolson vibrance and energy without Jolson's physical presence. The creators of the movie found the answer of how to

---

* In only one performance, "Swanee," Jolson himself is seen in long shot, actually performing the dance and the very special hand moves required, replacing Parks. Jolson was very particular about everything connected with him, and in this case, he insisted Parks needed to be replaced: only *he* could do "Swanee."

put Al Jolson on the screen without having Al Jolson on the screen: keep him singing the music and have almost nothing but music, song after song in a headlong rush, a continuation of the "build the movie around the star" concept.

The plot is slight: young Jewish boy does not want to sing in the synagogue like his cantor father—he wants showbiz. Instead of turning this into a tragedy, à la *The Jazz Singer* itself, the movie just shoves it aside, with his parents agreeing within minutes to let their young son go on tour with a vaudeville show. In fact, all through *The Jolson Story* any problem that surfaces is shoved aside in a similar manner. The boy Jolson is a hit in his vaudeville act with the man who becomes his lifelong friend and mentor (Steve Martin, a fictional character played by William Demarest). When a potential crisis arises—the boy's voice changes and he can't sing—this is sloughed off with his game whistling. When his voice is restored, and he's now Larry Parks, the crisis of Martin not wanting him to sing (since the whistling is working) is shoved aside by an opportunity to put on blackface and go on as a soloist in another star's place. Success! And then on the road with the Dockstader Minstrels, he climbs over hostile competition, from the chorus line to a quartet to a duet. Nothing gets in the way of Al Jolson. After his parents give up their objections to his career, they become a sort of running Yiddish joke. Cantor and wife they may be, but they pick up showbiz lingo and start spouting box-office returns and talking like *Variety* headlines. Comedy relief is supplied by these "parents" and by one other device: the horseradish joke. Everyone eats his mom's horseradish, including him, claiming it won't be too hot, and guess what—it is too hot! When Ruby Keeler refused to allow her name to be used, Jolson's wife was renamed Julie Benson (a shoving aside of its own kind).* She becomes the star of such films as *42nd Street*, *Flirtation Walk*, and *Go into Your Dance*, all Ruby Keeler movies, as the audience would know. When she becomes unhappy because Jolson works all the time, he quits rather than lose her, but when Dad, Mom, "Steve Martin" (who's always around), and the Jolsons go out to a nightclub and he's asked to sing, the final crisis musically appears. He sings his head off, happy as a lark, and "Julie" realizes she's just plain all wrong about what Al Jolson should be doing. Instead of being

---

* Also conveniently shoved aside were the death of Jolson's mother when he was a boy, Jolson's two earlier wives, and the son (Al Jolson Jr.) that he and Keeler adopted. *The Jolson Story* cares little for fact—and not much for plot, either.

home with her, he should be in nightclubs singing encore after encore. She politely points this out to his papa and calmly walks out. No use creating a fuss. Everybody, including the audience, knows she's right. Behind her, Al sings on: "April Showers," the first song he sang to her earlier in the picture. The End.

The decision not to complicate anything and just let Larry Parks *be* Al Jolson was genius, and it paid off. The movie speeds along like an express train, barely stopping to set up and resolve its issues. It's song after song, with close-ups of Parks, who does an amazing job. There are more than eighteen songs: "On the Banks of the Wabash," a bit of "Ave Maria," "When You Were Sweet Sixteen," "By the Light of the Silvery Moon," "Blue Bell," "Ma Blushin' Rosie," "I Want a Girl (Just Like the Girl That Married Dear Old Dad)," "My Mammy," "I'm Sittin' on Top of the World," "You Made Me Love You," "California, Here I Come," "The Anniversary Song," "Waiting for the Robert E. Lee," "Rock-a-Bye Your Baby," "There's a Rainbow 'Round My Shoulder," "About a Quarter to Nine," "Liza," "She's a Latin from Manhattan." All were Al Jolson hits, and he gives them all he's got, which was still, even in 1946, more than almost any other performer could muster.

The Jolson Story realizes, although it claims otherwise, that the audience still knew who Al Jolson was and cleverly shapes the story to be: do you still want him, remember him, want his style of singing? The movie tells the audience what its answer is: yes, you do, you know you do. And they did. By cleverly stringing song after song together, many superimposed across montages of postcards, sheet music, record labels, or *Variety* headlines, with Parks's face lip-syncing close-up, the movie became like one of Jolson's evenings in which he gave the audience all he had and as much as it wanted, singing and singing and singing, never letting down or growing tired. The movie itself became the embodiment of an Al Jolson performance. Jolson is depicted in the film interrupting the script of an overly long Broadway show by saying, "Let's get to the finale—everybody's tired, and we all want to go home." He then tells them the rest of the story, and the show is finished, the plot cast aside. "Turn up the lights," he says, so he can see their faces. Then he sings "You Made Me Love You," a perfect musical explanation of the Jolson career.

Jolson's career was reborn, if it was ever really dead, and he returned to radio, recording success, and newspaper headlines. The success of the movie spawned a 1949 sequel, *Jolson Sings Again*, also a success, but not a smash hit like the original. *Jolson Sings Again* carried on the same approach to what mattered about Jolson: music. It started out with a printed settling of "Julie" once and for all: "This is the rest of the story of Jolson . . . Julie saw the old spell come over him and [she] walked out of his life." The first image puts Jolson right back in that nightclub of the final "The End" of *The Jolson Story*, and continues with him (supported by family and the ever faithful "Steve Martin") going back home to find "Julie" packed up and gone. The rest of the movie tells how Jolson first tries to find her and then goes back to work, but finds it hard. ("I used to live for this . . . It's hard work now.") The story of his entertaining the troops leads to collapse, then to remarriage to an Arkansas-born nurse (Barbara Hale), a true-to-life character: Jolson wed his final wife, Erle Galbraith, in 1945. There's a bit about his wasting time owning racehorses and prize fighters and visiting Europe. His mother dies (he's not there for the big finish, so mercifully the audience is spared). Lip service is paid to a new kind of singing star: Bing Crosby. He's always on the radio. ("There was a time they played Al's records.") The horseradish joke is revived, this time for "Steve Martin." Mostly, *Jolson Sings Again* is about two things: another long list of songs—all the ones not used in the earlier movie, such as "Baby Face," "Red, Red Robin," and "For Me and My Gal"—and the making of the movie *The Jolson Story*. It's interesting that in both movies about Al Jolson, *The Jazz Singer* is more or less passed over. This is because the two movies were made by Columbia Pictures and *The Jazz Singer* was a Warner Bros. movie. ("Never give the competition any credit," is a Hollywood motto.)

Jolson Sings Again is about what mattered to Jolson and the studio in 1949: the 1946 success of *The Jolson Story*. Mom may die, but nobody sings "My Mammy." Erle and Al Jolson adopted two children, Asa Jr. and Alicia, but there's no time for that here. Jolson's biggest crisis is when he doesn't get name billing (he's lumped with "and many others" and billed under Gene Kelly) at a benefit he agrees to do. The important news is that making *The Jolson Story* made Jolson sing again. Audiences for the sequel loved what was, for the time, a wonderfully self-reflexive movie that seemed to give them a glimpse behind the scenes. While "Jolson" sits in a darkened screening room, someone slips in and takes a seat. On the screen, "Jolson" watches Larry Parks lip-sync in close-up to one of his recordings ("Toot, Toot, Tootsie"). When the lights go up, "Jolson" jumps up to demand "Who is that?" He's told, "Meet a young fella named Larry Parks." So Al Jolson meets Larry Parks—or, as the audience loved, Larry Parks meets

Larry Parks. Later, "they" stand side by side, looking into a mirror, while "Jolson" teaches Parks his moves; and while Larry Parks is being filmed playing Al Jolson, "Al Jolson" stands on the set by the camera, silently mouthing the words and doing his own moves alongside. They meet again at the preview in Santa Barbara, which is, of course, a smash success. Parks was so believable that Jolson cracked, "When I die, they'll bury Larry Parks." The film ends, letting us know that the next time Jolson appears at a benefit, he is billed *over* Gene Kelly.

Jolson was on top until his death in 1950.* On radio, in movies, or television, Al Jolson—wherever he might be—was always alive, perhaps the liveliest, most vibrant performer in the history of the business. (If Al Jolson and Ethel Merman had had a baby, the world would have been looking at a musical machine.) Jolson's accomplishment in becoming a movie star is surprising and a tribute to his charisma. His entire life was devoted to live performance, to pleasing his audiences, talking directly to them, and catering to them. He was famous for shenanigans that ignored prepared material, stage books, and directions. He would arrive late, tell the audience to excuse him while he blacked up right in front of them, talking nonstop or singing while he did it. He rang curtains up and he rang them down. He'd invite audiences to come "next door to a little café" after the show and he'd go on singing for them. He ordered boxes of chocolates and had them distributed throughout the house. Nothing mattered to Al Jolson but Al Jolson—and his audience. *He* was the show, not the play or the story, and certainly not any costars.

A personality like this, with his confident ego, inevitably didn't endear itself to everyone. George Burns described Jolson's marital failures by saying, "It was easy enough to make Jolson happy at home. You just had to cheer him for breakfast, applaud wildly for lunch, and give him a standing ovation for dinner." Sigmund Romberg, who wrote some of the music for Jolson's hit show *Bombo*, called him "Simon Legree in blackface." Jolson feuded with his older brother, who had helped him in the early years, and their relationship was never really resolved. Jolson spoke very freely about his competitors as lesser talents. He once said, "I'll tell you when I'm

---

* Jolson had risen to the call to entertain troops in Korea, going there against doctors' orders. He collapsed and was sent home and died shortly afterward of a massive heart attack. He more or less died with his boots on, which was just the way he would have wanted it. For him, audience applause was everything. He was sixty-four.

going to play the Palace. That's when Eddie Cantor and George Burns and Groucho Marx and Jack Benny are on the bill. I'm going to buy out the whole house, and sit in the middle of the orchestra and say, 'Slaves! Entertain the king.'"

Jolson's greatest rival: Eddie Cantor

But no matter how hard Jolson might have been to deal with, no one denied his talent. The great Eddie Cantor admitted, "I couldn't compete with him." Robert Benchley wrote, after seeing him onstage in *Big Boy*: "When Jolson enters, it's as if an electric current has been run along the wires under the seats where the hats are stuck. . . . He speaks, rolls his eyes, compresses his lips, and it's all over. You are a member of the Al Jolson Association." This quality is what made Warners build movies around him, tailored to who he was and what he could do. One has only to think about how such great performers as Lunt and Fontanne, electric onstage, came across as two dull and relatively unattractive actors in their movie

Ethel Shutta and Eddie
Cantor in the movie
version of their famous
stage hit, *Whoopee!*

The Guardsman to realize just how special Jolson was. He could juice it up
for an audience when he had no audience—on a movie soundstage. If he
knew someone was watching, or even if he knew someone *might* be watching, he went gonzo into his song and dance. That was the quality that came
across even onscreen, and made him one of the early definers of the movie
star musical.

There were other successful male singers in Jolson's era, of course.
Perhaps his greatest rival was Eddie Cantor, a great audience favorite
and durable star, yet not well-known today. Cantor appeared in twelve
full-length movies in the 1930s and, like Jolson, was a "personality" singer
who sometimes did blackface and who had a highly successful stage and
recording career, as well as a top-rated radio show. Also like Jolson, Cantor
was already highly established when he began making movies after sound

came in. He was born in 1892 on Manhattan's Lower East Side, and by 1907 he was in vaudeville. He was such a hit he went on to star in six versions of the *Ziegfeld Follies*, as well as book musicals such as *Make It Snappy* (1922) and *Kid Boots* (1923). Cantor's movie career paralleled Jolson's biggest years. He began appearing in musical shorts in 1929, when sound got rolling across the nation. In these shorts he performed numbers he had made famous on Broadway, such as "Now That the Girls Are Wearing Long Dresses."

Cantor's feature debut was in *Whoopee!* (1930). He sang the title song, plus "A Girl Friend of a Boy Friend of Mine" and "My Baby Just Cares for Me," in his signature style, which included prancing around the stage, jumping up and down as if he'd just sat on a cactus, clapping his hands, waving a big handkerchief, and rolling his big eyes. (Cantor's nickname was "Banjo Eyes," also the name of one of his Broadway shows.) He was a distinctive performer, with great popularity and success in theater, radio, and films, and he was also a songwriter ("Merrily We Roll Along"). Heard on radio as early as 1921, Cantor went on NBC's *Chase and Sanborn Hour* in 1931 and continued to be a major radio star on various shows through 1953. He also made successful appearances on television in the 1950s and even had his own TV show. Like Jolson, he had a biopic made on his life, *The Eddie Cantor Story* (1953), which starred Keefe Brasselle, a modestly talented actor whom Hollywood tried futilely to turn into a star and who certainly was no Cantor look-alike. (Also like Jolson, Cantor performed his own songs.) But the movie was a flop. J. Hoberman, writing in *The New York Times* while reviewing a set of DVDs that presented four of Cantor's Samuel Goldwyn musicals, said that his "impact on Hollywood history today seems negligible," and quotes film historian Henry Jenkins as positing that moviegoers outside large cities did not like Cantor: "Subsequent Goldwyn productions strove to make Cantor more acceptable to a national audience. He became less 'New York'—less risqué, smart-mouthed, and Jewish." This is typical "the hicks didn't get it" punditry. Vaudeville was full of eyeball-rolling, innuendo, prancing about, and Jewish humor (which read as ethnic to people who were not Jewish, and thus they could grasp its meaning from their own immigrant backgrounds). An entire national audience liked Eddie Cantor. The real problem for Cantor is the modern audience, who find him misogynist, racist, and homophobic. (Hoberman understands that because of this, Cantor's work "may find its ultimate place in the more rarefied realms of racial, gender, and cultural studies.")

Despite insensitive material (indigenous to the times), Eddie Cantor had pizzazz and wattage of his own. No performer stays on top as long as Cantor did in vaudeville, Broadway shows, movies, radio, and television without having a broad audience appeal. When Cantor bursts onstage to perform the hit song "Makin' Whoopee" in *Whoopee!*, he's funny, he's original, and he's amazing. Today they'd put him on Ritalin, but he's beyond modern; he's in a time frame of his own, which is where a great performer ultimately lives. He works hard to entertain, rolling his eyes and clapping his hands and giving it all he's got. (A serious movie rival to "the World's Greatest Entertainer," Cantor was a top-ten-ranked star in 1939.) He and Jolson were contemporaries, and the same manic energy that it takes to keep a live audience in their seats is as present in Cantor as it was in Jolson. The differ-

ence is that Jolson is higher octane: he's all about himself, but himself singing the song. He does what used to be called "putting it over." Cantor was more generous to an audience, more about giving than taking. He brought joy onstage and gave it all away.

Cantor understood the difference between himself and Jolson. When Jolson died in 1950, Cantor had lived with the inevitable competition most of his life. (Cantor died in 1964, at age seventy-two.) He called Jolson "a man of the people . . . a childlike spirit . . . overflowing with love of humanity." He said competing with Jolson was like "a midget trying to touch a giant's head." The strain of dealing with someone like Jolson surfaced ever so slightly as Cantor added, "Jolie had human frailties, just like any other man. I say that in all sincerity and with my heart full of love. . . ." However little bitterness or annoyance crept in, Cantor demonstrated clearly that he fully understood Jolson's power by saying that the man was "six acts of top billing rolled into one," because Jolson was "his own lighting and his own scenery," concluding with this summing up: "He was more than an actor or a singer or an entertainer . . . he was an experience." It took someone who had performed in his own era and had observed him up close both on and

Eddie Cantor and Al Jolson, two old friends and show-business legends, circa 1948

off the stage for years to fully grasp how electric Jolson really was. Eddie Cantor got it.

Crosby

Jolson's stardom was created by using his already developed performing personality: Warners put him in movies that fit him. The same was true for Bing Crosby, a band singer, recording artist, and radio star who entered motion pictures in 1930 in *King of Jazz*, but his movie persona was not pre-

A young and attractive Bing Crosby hits the big time in movies, cast opposite Marion Davies in *Going Hollywood*

defined; it grew on film. He was born Harry Lillis Crosby Jr. in Tacoma, Washington, in 1903 and studied at Gonzaga University for a time, but music drew him away. He started playing drums and singing with a local band, and then joined the band's piano player, Al Rinker, in leaving Washington for Los Angeles in 1925. Rinker and Crosby were put under contract by Paul Whiteman in 1926, and with a third musician, Harry Barris, they formed a group called the Rhythm Boys and began appearing regularly with Whiteman's popular dance band. In the 1930s Crosby was hired as a solo artist to sing on the radio for CBS; in August 1931 he signed a contract to do a fifteen-minute weekly show on the network, creating a large following. Because he was relaxed, good-looking, and charming, the movie business inevitably sought him out. His motion picture career was, like Jolson's, shaped to accommodate his looks, his physicality, his style of singing, and the surface personality he projected. The difference was in their levels of fame at movie entry point.

Most people today don't realize what a great star Bing Crosby became. He was a success in short films and features, but also in radio, television, and records. (He did not appear in stage musicals; he performed in front of live audiences in personal appearances, radio/TV tapings, and on bandstands, but he had no Broadway or vaudeville career.) As a singer, he had thirty-eight number-one-hit singles, more than either Elvis Presley or the Beatles, and his recording of "White Christmas" was the best-selling record for over fifty years. He was a top-rated radio star, the first recipient of the

Grammy Lifetime Achievement Award (in 1962), and an inductee into the Radio Hall of Fame (in 1996). (He sang on the radio at least once a week from 1931 to 1962.) In 1948, he was voted the most admired man in America, outranking President Truman, General Eisenhower, and Jackie Robinson. Most of the records he set outside of movies will never be equaled. He was even inducted into the World Golf Hall of Fame (in 1978) and

Crosby's 1930s stardom required him to carry movies that didn't have much besides him: *She Loves Me Not*, with Kitty Carlisle . . .

. . . and *Waikiki Wedding*, with Shirley Ross.

had his face on a 1994 commemorative US postage stamp in the "Legends of American Music" series. And these are only a few of his awards and statistics.

As impressive as all these facts are, it is in the field of the motion picture that his record surprises most people today. Bing Crosby was a bona fide movie star. Not including shorts, cameos, joke appearances, and voice-overs, Crosby made more than sixty-three movies (and all but a few were musicals). He won one Oscar for Best Actor and was nominated for a second, and his box-office record was phenomenal. Only John Wayne and Clint Eastwood, over time, have been as consistently ranked at the top as Bing Crosby was. He was named to the top ten box-office list first in 1934, and then again in 1937, and from 1940 to 1954 he was on the list every year. He ranked number one from 1944 to 1948. In 1949, he was second only to his frequent movie partner Bob Hope. Crosby's record means that, starting in 1934, and hitting the peak in 1940 and holding on to it well into 1955, for a solid twenty-two years the American moviegoing public loved Bing Crosby on the silver screen as much as they loved anyone. And yet he appeared in very few really good movies—but that's the definition of a star: their "vehicle" is all about their individual talent and can be "carried." (Crosby, Jolson, and Presley all appeared in movies that would not be much without them.) The business capitalized on star quality.

If you stood Al Jolson and Bing Crosby side by side, they would not seem particularly different in physical assets. Neither is conventionally handsome, but both project strong personalities, and both of them are attractive as a result. They have big heads on smallish bodies, but that doesn't matter in the movies; the camera could disguise height in both men and women. Short people who were well proportioned did not look small inside the frame, and that was true for both Jolson and Crosby (Crosby was about five foot seven, although he claimed five-nine). But the medium could not hide certain types of defects: Crosby's ears stuck out. Until about 1934, in the film *She Loves Me Not*, Crosby's ears were taped down and stuck to his head in the same way Clark Gable's were. (For both men, this ceased to be a problem once they were established. It seemed not to matter anymore, at least not to their fans.) Both Jolson and Crosby have large, expressive eyes, but Crosby's were soft and cowlike, and Jolson's glittered.

The difference between Jolson and Crosby is their style of singing, suggested character, and energy level. Crosby is a nonchalant performer. Nothing seems to matter much. Whenever he appeared in front of a live audience, Crosby didn't run out and leap onto the stage the way Jolson did. He ambled out, and he was no flashy dresser. He wore sports slacks and jackets, short-sleeved shirts, and some kind of old hat to cover his advancing baldness. He did not wield an aggressive cigar—he puffed on a slow-burning pipe. Both men have charm, but Crosby's is relaxed and Jolson's is ferocious. Bing Crosby often said that one of his earliest musical influences was Louis Armstrong, but that his all-time favorite performer was Al Jolson. His own performance style, however, was the opposite of Jolson's. On film, Crosby is laid back, easygoing, a jokey kind of guy whose every comment seems to be ad-libbed. He was someone audiences could imagine knowing, running into down at the barbershop or over at the ball game. Both Jolson and Crosby make their dialogue seem as if they just thought of it, that they made it up, but Jolson hit every line hard: every syllable counts; he wants you to pay attention. Crosby lays the words out in an offhand manner that suggests it doesn't matter if you grasp what he said or not. He plays with lyrics, riffing, and shifting meanings; Jolson gets everything that can be had out of the specific words. Crosby even whistles casually, in a lyrical, tuneful way, where Jolson whistles sharp and clear, like a racing train. Each man plays with the song being sung, making it his own, but Jolson exaggerates glissandos, while Crosby scats a kind of "Oooo-oooooh, let's go cuddle in a corner" quality. Neither man just leaves a song alone, but neither kills it with the "I am brilliant" quality some modern singers use. There's a fundamental respect for what the lyrics mean. Both can find the drama, the heart, the meaning. Both absolutely sing *to* the audience, each performing in his individual way.

The difference between Crosby and Jolson as singers leads to the difference in the movies that were created for them, and shows again that studios adapted musicals to fit the talents they hired. Although Crosby spent his first years in show business doing live performances from a bandstand, in a nightclub, or in front of audiences, he is a creature of the radio microphone era, whereas Jolson was the man who grew into full maturity always doing his thing in front of a live audience. Jolson learned to work an audience directly, and carried that electric, pump-it-up style into the modern media. Crosby learned how to move an audience by working through a recorded form to reach them. Since his audience was not physically present, his style developed accordingly. He reached them by being less bombastic, more romantic, more conversational. He worked *closer*, with intimacy in his voice and manner. Jolson sang to (and *at*) an audience; Crosby sang to an individual. Significantly, this meant Crosby's movie-musical characters did not *have* to be showbiz people. The way Crosby sang—his croony, jaunty, warm and mellow style—meant that his movie character could be an ordinary kind of guy. His stories could be fairly simple, often stressing comedy, and certainly making him a romantic lead. He was put forward as just like one of the folks in the audience, who had a value system like theirs and who knew what really mattered in life.

Gary Giddins, the leading interpreter of Crosby and his influence, has said that Crosby's "key attribute as a troubadour of American song was his capacious appreciation for its diversity, his disposition to follow music wherever it led." Giddins's summation was that Crosby "knew instinctively that as long as he kept in mind who he was, he could make any style his own." Giddins described Crosby's voice as having "an echoey and pleasing throatiness" which "served as Bing's signature sound." For the average person listening to Crosby on the radio, it was a new sound. Crosby was different. He was a shift from tenor to baritone, a movement away from the Billy Murray/Chauncey Olcott Irish lyrical voice; and he was not ethnic or New Yorkish like Jolson and Cantor. He "oohed" into the microphone, giving rise to his definition as a crooner. His voice had personality—he joked a song, he whispered a song, he wooed a song. Other singers mostly just sang; Crosby made a number a private interaction with the listener. And he could "speak" all forms of American: country and western, Hawaiian, patriotic, comedy, love, Irish—there was no musical conversation he couldn't have.

In the beginning, Crosby appeared as himself or a member of the Rhythm Boys in *King of Jazz*, *Reaching for the Moon*, and in 1931's *Confessions of a Coed*. In 1931, his radio success led him into two-reelers made by Mack Sennett that stretched into 1933. He usually played himself, or at least a character named "Bing Bangs" or "Bing Fawcett." In each of these seven shorts, Crosby would wander in, amble around until a minimal plot set him up to sing one of his most popular tunes of the day: *I Surrender Dear* (1931), *One More Chance* (1931), *Dream House* (1932), *Billboard Girl* (1932), *Blue of the Night* (1933), and *Please* (1933). In 1933's *Sing, Bing, Sing* he reprised several of his hits. During this successful run of short films, which introduced Crosby as himself to movie audiences, he also appeared as "Bing" in the Paramount feature *The Big Broadcast*, in which all he does is sing "Please" and "Here Lies Love." In 1933, however, he made a Paramount feature called *College Humor*, in which he played "Professor Frederick Danvers," and that film might be considered his official feature-movie debut as a musical actor, although he has little to do but sing some of his own already established radio hits. (Bits of "Memories of You," "Learn to Croon," "Please," "Just One More Chance," and "I Surrender Dear" are all incorporated into one of his "lectures" as advice to his class. "Down the Old Ox Road" is reprised as an overview of campus life.) He introduces "Play Ball" and "Is This Really Love" and, in general, hangs around among the other stars, Jack Oakie, Burns and Allen, and Richard Arlen.

The first significant film starring Bing Crosby—the one that proves he is a musical star with a persona of his own, who cannot be upstaged or wiped off the screen—is 1933's *Going Hollywood*, a vehicle built not for him but for Marion Davies. Contrary to her misunderstood reputation as the model for the untalented Susan Alexander in *Citizen Kane*, Davies was a charming and talented performer. Her lover, the powerful (and powerfully wealthy) William Randolph Hearst, made sure she had her own production unit, Cosmopolitan Pictures, to create vehicles to showcase her soft blond beauty, her comedy timing, and her musical skills. One of the movies styled especially for her was *Going Hollywood*, and her costar was the new young talent Bing Crosby. He stole the picture.

Crosby is strongly presented in the movie, and even though it's Davies's own company, a generous amount of time and focus goes to him, not her. Davies looks beautiful, and she has her own musical numbers, but Crosby is the standout news, officially moving from radio star to movie star. Previously, he was in the movies because of his radio success, defined as a radio success, and singing the songs he had popularized on the radio. Here he *begins* as a radio star, but that's the base of his character—an already established platform from which he moves (literally, in the plot) to become a Hollywood movie star.

The credits of *Going Hollywood* say clearly: Marion Davies in *Going Hollywood with* Bing Crosby. The plot, however, recognizes Crosby's already established status in his own medium: radio. His first song is right up front, but he sings it unseen, over the radio, while Davies listens. Her character has been quickly established in the opening minutes as a French teacher in a rigid girls' school. She longs for "music . . . life . . . love," and she hears those things in Crosby's voice, which inspires her to pack and, nearly penniless, leave the school behind. While Crosby sings "Don't waste the night in wishing" in "Our Big Love Scene," Davies is photographed in close-up, radiantly lit, her blond hair shining and her huge eyes sparkling. It may be a Marion Davies picture, but it's Crosby's voice that dominates the image and is the only thing being heard. And what's more, it's Crosby's voice that is enveloping her character, motivating her character, providing emotion for her character, and claiming both the visual moment and the plot. Davies shows up at Crosby's apartment just as he's preparing to leave New York for Hollywood to try making movies. He's hungover, cranky, egotistical, and involved with a French star (Fifi D'Orsay) who's accompanying him to California. While Crosby packs, a group of technicians are recording his new number, "Beautiful Girl." Thus, the first two musical presentations of the movie feature Crosby, not Davies.*

The departure from Grand Central on the *20th Century Limited* is a singular musical presentation. *Going Hollywood* is a movie in which characters will sometimes "sing as they live"—the excuse for performance is not always rehearsal or direct professional presentation. As Crosby packs to leave, he's being recorded in his apartment, so that the action onscreen depicts a man who can sing anywhere, anytime, for any reason. His next number (the title song) is a borderline extravaganza: maybe it's people singing and dancing because they're professionals and that's what they do . . . or maybe it's a musical world and everyone in it sings and dances just because they do. An audience is clearly told (in dialogue) more than once that Crosby's departure for Hollywood has been set up as a "big publicity sendoff," so there could be a reason why everyone at Grand Central is singing and dancing, but since all the people coming and going at the station, including the train's porter, are involved in the number, and since young women ride baggage carts around, and even reporters are singing, "Going Hollywood" has to be seen as an integrated musical presentation.

* "Beautiful Girl" is later used in *Singin' in the Rain* as a "crooner" number.

After he jumps onto the train and stands at the back on the little platform, Crosby launches directly into "Out where they say / Let us be gay / I'm going Hollywood." In medium close-up, he moves a little bit from side to side, adding a slight rhythmic shake to his shoulders, and jazzing up the lyrics, scatting a bit. (If this presentation were taken up a few notches, Bing Crosby would be Elvis Presley.)

There's a lot happening in *Going Hollywood*. Davies sings and dances, imitates D'Orsay, and does good comedy work. D'Orsay herself does a number, and there are painful minutes given over to a trio of comics known as the Radio Rogues. None of this detracts from the timeless quality of Crosby. He's allowed to play his character drunk (he does it well) and is given room for a dramatic scene. After quarreling with Davies (they've fallen in love, of course), his character embarks on an all-night binge that ends up in a dive in Mexico. In the dark, shadowy atmosphere, which shows women dancing together and an optical presentation of cocktails and blurred vision, Crosby sings "Temptation." He's photographed in close-up and given subjective point-of-view shots. He's also beautifully lit, every bit as much as his leading lady. (The movie is well-directed by Raoul Walsh.) Between his jaunty and lively "Goin' Hollywood" song and dance and this moody, broody love song with a subtext, Crosby shows everything he can do. He's loosely comic and improvisational, yet he presents some passionate acting. He's absolutely at the cutting edge of male singing performance for the year 1933. He's got It in the male category. The film ends with a spectacle: a wow number that looks like a dream setting for Cinderella's ball. There are masses of people, Davies is singing and dancing in a spectacular costume, but in the middle of it, dramatically featured (as he returns from his booze fest to resume responsibility and revive Davies's love), is Bing Crosby. He's come back from Mexico and he's *there*. And, P.S., he's never going away again.

After *Going Hollywood*, Bing onscreen was Bing onscreen. He was more than a voice on the radio for fans: he was now a physical presence they recognized and adored. Starting in 1934, Crosby began an astonishing run of successful films, churning them out. In 1934, there were three (*We're Not Dressing*, *She Loves Me Not*, and *Here Is My Heart*); in 1935, another four (*Mississippi*, *Two for Tonight*, *The Big Broadcast of 1936*—a cameo only— and *Millions in the Air* (as the singing voice for another actor). From 1936 until 1962, he made two or three hit movies per year. Some were mere comedy cameo appearances in a Bob Hope movie (such as *The Princess and the*

Pirate) or just as a big joke, as a singing voice on loan to a homely actor like Eddie Bracken in *Out of This World*). But he was working consistently, and also making records and appearing on radio and, later, television.

All the Crosby films were successful, all were personally adapted to his musical self, and most were relatively cheap to make. All that was needed was a simple plot, a costar or two, and Bing leaning against the fireplace with a pipe in his hand, singing. Or standing by a tree, singing. Or strolling down the street, singing. Things could be juiced up by having him dance, or perform with other big-name stars; but really, the public came to watch Bing and listen to his voice. Aging was not a problem for him, since youthful energy wasn't his thing. He had nothing to worry about as the decades rolled by.

After his musical movie self was defined, Crosby's career settled into a groove that accommodated different aspects of his musical ability, but always presented him in one of five types of Crosby star musicals:

1. Dramatic story films in which he sang, such as *Going My Way* (his Oscar winner) and *The Country Girl* (his other Oscar nomination)
2. A series of seven comedies (with music) costarring him with Bob Hope; the famous *Road* pictures
3. Movies that had something special to them as *musicals*, such as his pairings with Fred Astaire (*Holiday Inn*, *Blue Skies*) or Danny Kaye and Rosemary Clooney (*White Christmas*)
4. Movies that were directed by well-known auteurs: Billy Wilder's *The Emperor Waltz*, Frank Capra's *Riding High* and *Here Comes the Groom*, or Leo McCarey's *Bells of St. Mary's**
5. And, finally, movies that can only be labeled as films with no special distinction other than Crosby's presence (*Welcome Stranger*), the tailored star musical of the type that exists only to present the star cheaply and quickly.

No matter what level of director or costar he had, or whether the emphasis was comedy, drama, or music, all these films were clearly geared to Bing Crosby. They are all star vehicles.

---

* McCarey also directed Crosby in *Going My Way* and won Oscars for both writing and directing the film.

Going My Way is a prime example of the musical nonmusical—the dramatic film in which Bing sang. Because of its sentimentality, its clichéd characters, and its oversimplified presentation of religion, modern viewers are often shocked to realize it was voted Best Picture of the Year by the Motion Picture Academy (beating out *Gaslight*, *Double Indemnity*, *Since You Went Away*, and *Wilson*). *Going My Way* was given ten Oscar nominations, with seven wins, including not only Best Actor for Crosby but also Best Supporting Actor for Barry Fitzgerald. It was one of the biggest box-office hits of the year. *Going My Way* didn't need to explain why Crosby, the priest, was a musical performer. The fact that Crosby was playing a priest was no problem for moviegoers, because the character was so clearly musically defined. They knew in advance that if they were going to a Bing Crosby movie, even if he wore a Roman collar, it would have to be in some way a musical.* The music is woven into the plot, and Crosby's musicality is defined as coming from his prior life, his former interest in music and desire to be a songwriter. Father O'Malley (Crosby) thus is nothing more than a Bing Crosby who became a priest—which he considered doing in his

Crosby in his iconic role in *Going My Way*: Father O'Malley, the singing, piano-playing, baseball-loving, problem-solving priest, surrounded by (left to right) Fortunio Bonanova, Risë Stevens, Frank McHugh, and a bunch of "swingin' on a star" kids

* Such expectations became a problem for a movie of 1944 entitled *Christmas Holiday*, which starred both Gene Kelly and Deanna Durbin but was *not* a musical or even a musical nonmusical, despite Durbin's singing two songs. It was a dark noir about a murderer played by Kelly. People wanted their money back.

own life. The film has five musical numbers: "Too-Ra-Loo-Ra-Loo-Ra!" (done twice), "Going My Way" (also done twice), Schubert's "Ave Maria," "Swinging on a Star," and the Habañera from *Carmen*. In addition to crooner Crosby, the film features the Metropolitan Opera star Risë Stevens in an important role.

Going My Way ambles along with a low-key tale of a progressive, hip young priest who's assigned the problem of getting a failing parish back on track by taking over from the aging traditionalist played by Fitzgerald. As Crosby tools around in a St. Louis Browns baseball cap and jacket, he shapes up juvenile delinquents, solves a mortgage problem, takes Fitzgerald golfing, withstands the downer of a church fire, and writes a hit song to bail out the church financially. It's a pile of junk, but sitting on top of it, like a diamond in the mud, is Crosby: calm, confident, casual—but above all, musical. The film was a move toward an actual acting performance for Crosby, and he proved himself to be more than capable. As is almost always true for great pop singers, he knows how to deliver a line, because his sense of timing and rhythm has been honed by music.

Crosby makes *Going My Way* work. He's a modern element in the frame, always seeming to ad-lib a bit, always seeming to raise an eyebrow a bit, always seeming to have the outsider's point of view. He's cool, and he's wise. Crosby establishes without effort a place in the movie that is not the place the movie is living in. He doesn't undercut the religion or the sentiment, but he suggests slightly that accepting it is a choice done only by accepting, not committing. Above all, he hints that there might be a *new* way of dealing with these old ideas of religion, morality, and behavior. That new way is demonstrated by the cool stuff Father O'Malley embraces: the pop culture of baseball, songwriting, appropriate conniving, and a little bit of golf. It's *your* way, he tells the audience, and it's okay: I'm Bing Crosby, and *I'm* doing it. Crosby is able to do this and still keep his character honest, and the way he does it is through the use of music—*his* style of music. Crosby's singing builds in the needed element of relief from religion for the viewer.

If the musical numbers were removed from *Going My Way*, the story of the film would still have all its elements in place. (Crosby's character could save the parish by writing a best-selling novel instead of a hit song.) However, it seems unlikely the movie would be as charming, or as popular as it was. It is Crosby's matter-of-fact singing that cements the idea that his priest is modern yet also believes in the Church and its ideals. The trappings of pleasure—sports and music—are outer coverings, and it's okay for Crosby to wear them because underneath he has his Cassock—and his "Ave Maria"—and the Church. By casting a well-established musical star, adapting a religious story and character to *his* star musical persona, and by working multiple musical numbers into the seemingly real and naturalistic world of a city parish, the film makes a fairy tale believable. (It also knows its limits—there are no dance numbers in *Going My Way*.)

More than almost any other male musical star (the notable exception being Sinatra), Crosby tackled real dramatic roles.* Although his voice is heard on the soundtrack under the credits for *Man on Fire* (1957), he does not sing at all in the movie. It's his "departure" movie and as a result, his least-known and least-popular film. He gives a strong performance of a tormented father, angry at his core at his wife's leaving him for another man. The edge that often surfaced in Crosby's ad-libs and humor is magnified into a real anger, and it's a bit ugly. But his most successful dramatic role, not counting *Going My Way*, is in his second nomination for Best Actor, *The Country Girl*.

The Country Girl is Grace Kelly's Oscar-winning movie, and although she gives an acceptable performance, it's hard to believe she's the downtrodden wife of a drunken ex-star who pushes her around and keeps her almost as a servant. She's too beautiful, too patrician. Crosby is superb as the drunk, and William Holden is outstanding as the theater director who decides to take a chance on him for the lead in his new Broadway show. ("The guy has to act while he's singing and sing while he's acting," he says.) The statement is an excellent description of Crosby as a star. Holden and Crosby are two great actors in the American movie-star tradition. When they reach the turning point, a big dramatic scene, Crosby understands they are essentially "singing" a duet, and he must adapt to the rhythm of his costar and take the lead for himself according to the "lyrics" they are delivering. He has the ability to play the melody (pretending to be confident, happy-go-lucky, and genial) and still keep the undertones (the frightened and devious drunk). In his "audition" for Holden's character, he re-enacts what had been his character's biggest success, which could easily be a charming soliloquy from an earlier Crosby movie. But later in the film, he swings from one mood to another mood to still another in a three-step

---

* Female singers such as Garland, Streisand, Julie Andrews, and Doris Day also succeeded in non-singing parts.

acting tour de force. First he's drunk in a bar and joins in with the lounge singer's little number, called "Love and Learn Blues." Crosby, of course, can really sing it and really swing it. For the first time in the movie, his character seems to enjoy singing, to revel in the gift of his talent. He's loose, funny, riffing along and enjoying every minute of it. He knows everyone in the bar loves him, and it's safe, anonymous, and he's drunk anyway. Next and almost immediately, he shifts to another mood, expressing deep rage and an ugly anger. In a third shift that escalates his rage, he breaks down and becomes a broken, crying man, admitting he's been lying about his wife to save himself. Crosby was an actor who could sometimes be romantic, sometimes comedic; but in *The Country Girl* he proved he could also be dramatic at a surprising depth. His approach to his dramatic scene in the bar is not unlike his approach to singing a musical number. In fact, since it begins as a Crosby song, it's almost operatic as it moves to conclusion. Audiences accepted Crosby's dramatics as part of his musical self: they lived with him as a man who appeared at the movie house in various star vehicles with music. *The Country Girl*, for them, was just a tough-minded one. (Crosby lost the Oscar to Marlon Brando in *On the Waterfront*.)

Crosby had a quality that never gets articulated: a huge star, he could nevertheless easily fold himself into a singing duo. That was a characteristic that neither Jolson nor Presley had. They could, of course, sing duets, and Presley was terrific when dancing with Ann-Margret, his best movie love interest; but to be part of a pair meant a kind of bonding, the creating of a harmonious fusion of equals, and Jolson and Presley were singles. Crosby didn't *compete*. He slid in alongside a partner and was comfortable there. If the script had him insult a rival, be mean or indifferent to a partner, he'd play it that way; but he was also willing to be someone's on-film musical equal. Jolson wasn't about to accept the idea he could ever even have an equal, and if he had encountered one in his era—he didn't—he would have ramped up and blown him/her off the stage. Presley didn't seem to care one way or the other. His self-confidence made him a generous partner to the point of seeming indifference. He was loose and unfazed by the idea of an equal. He was, after all, the King. Crosby, however, could pair up: with Danny Kaye, with Fred Astaire, with Rosemary Clooney, with Barry Fitzgerald, but most spectacularly with the great comedian Bob Hope.

In 1940, Paramount Pictures—with no credit for inspiration or foresight—paired Bing Crosby with Bob Hope (a relative newcomer, having made his feature-film debut in *The Big Broadcast of 1938*) in a movie called *Road to Singapore*. The low-budget comedy had originally been planned for Fred MacMurray and Jack Oakie, but when that couldn't be scheduled, the studio did what studios did: threw in two other guys they had under contract. In so doing, they ensured Hope's stardom (which was already in place), used Crosby's musical definition effectively, and defined a legendary pairing the public embraced and never abandoned. Bing Crosby and Bob Hope went on to make six more *Road* films, for a total of seven: *Road to Zanzibar* (1941), as well as to *Morocco* (1942), *Utopia* (1946), *Rio* (1947), *Bali* (1952), and *Hong Kong* (1962).

Hope and Crosby were one of the great musical-comedy teams of the Hollywood era. With Hope, Crosby was masterful, which was not easy: Hope himself was also a powerful, unstoppable force on radio, the stage, in person, and in the movies. Hope might seem to be one of those actors who could never be a pair—he had a Jolsonesque dominant energy—but he was deceptive. Think of him singing "Thanks for the Memory" in *The Big Broadcast of 1938*. It became his theme song, but it wasn't introduced as a solo—it was a duet with Shirley Ross. The two of them sing the lyrics with an easy banter between them, a wry humor, and a heartfelt melancholy. History has defined Ross as a minor star, and she's not a great singer or actress or beauty; but paired with Hope in this number, she's sensational, partly because Hope connects to her, gets in her vibe, and creates a shared moment. On radio, he was a perfect foil for Jerry Colonna, who was a big radio star but never a movie personality, and he was an excellent costar for both Lucille Ball and Paulette Goddard. He could pair up, but he never found a better mate than Crosby; and except for Dorothy Lamour (who could handle one or the other of them individually or both of them at the same time, and has been underrated for it), neither ever had a better partner.

Hope and Crosby, Crosby and Hope. Hope has one of those "Look out, I'm on, and I'm comin' at ya!" movie personalities. Crosby makes the audience come to him on his own terms. They're a perfect marriage. Crosby is a great singer, but Hope can sing, too. Hope started as a dancer, but Crosby can hoof it when he has to. Both can be funny and both can be serious. Obviously, Crosby can go deeper on the serious side and Hope can ramp the comedy up higher, but they mesh. And it's Crosby's ability to pair up that drives the connection.

Crosby and Hope are not a simple wedding of two opposites, the way movie comedy teams often are. They both have larceny in their souls. Crosby plays the smarter of the two, the one who can usually victimize

A comedy trio who knew how to hit the road: Bing Crosby, Dorothy Lamour, and Bob Hope in *Road to Utopia* . . .

the other. They share an amazing ability to ad-lib, and their timing makes overlapping ad-libs possible. Hope is always just a shade dumber, more often the victim, and Crosby is the guy who gets the girl, and the girl is always Dorothy Lamour, the glamorous version of Margaret Dumont. (Even when Hope seems to get the girl, in *Road to Utopia*, after an accident separates the threesome, leaving Hope and Lamour to marry, when Crosby visits them years later, their son is played by—Bing Crosby—one of those jokes the censors decided to overlook.)

The *Road* pictures break the fourth wall constantly, and Hope and Crosby are two guys made for that particular stance.* They easily reject illusion, and by doing so, enhance it. They have the ability to make an audience feel that their pointing out the fakery makes everything more realistic—which, of course, it does. In *Road to Morocco* their first song completely shatters reality in a wonderfully comic way. As they ride across the desert on a

---

* Another movie comedy that broke the fourth wall with modern skill was the 1941 film version of the 1938 Broadway hit *Hellzapoppin'*. Both starred the comic team of Ole Olsen and Chic Johnson in an "anything goes" farce that refused to recognize any conventions. The movie also had Martha Raye, Jane Frazee, Mischa Auer, Shemp Howard (of the Three Stooges), Hugh Herbert, and Robert Paige. Olson and Johnson were famous for being willing to do anything for a laugh, and the movie, unavailable until recently, has had a legendary status as a comic masterpiece among people who have never seen it. Perspective is being restored, but the fourth wall is, without a doubt, not only broken, but shattered.

camel ("It's only a kangaroo!" Hope has exclaimed when they first discover it), their song refers to the fact they'll be sure to meet Dorothy Lamour, that they have solid studio contracts so nothing is going to happen to them, etc. They are talking to us, singing to *us*, doing a comedy routine, breaking the illusion, giving us the plot, reminding us of their *Road*-picture formula, and moving forward in the frame and in the story—and interacting with each other. Crosby was at the peak of his popularity, so *Road to Morocco* is highly musical. Three song numbers are presented almost back to back within minutes after the title song: "Ain't Got a Dime to My Name" by Crosby, "Constantly" by Lamour, and the big hit, "Moonlight Becomes You," by Crosby.

Crosby didn't falter when lifted out of his star-designed vehicles and put into auteurist material. He could adjust, although some directors were more on his wavelength than others. Musical stars who defined their own films were seldom paired with directors who had singular cinematic styles (exceptions being Kelly, Astaire, and Garland). Studios felt that one stylist was sufficient for any movie. Crosby's long career meant that he would, of course, be paired with directors who were tops, and he smoothly adjusted to their personal universes: his method was Bing Crosby Comes to Cap-raland, or Wilderville, or wherever was relevant. In his career, he made movies with Billy Wilder, Frank Capra, Leo McCarey, Charles Walters, and received his second Oscar nomination in one by a respected but lesser

. . . and the makeup department's idea of how all that traveling would age them

light, George Seaton. His movies with each director illustrate his defined musical star self, and how working *with* it made a successful movie and working against it created problems.

Billy Wilder's *The Emperor Waltz* (1948) was one of Crosby's least successful films, and Wilder's, too. Crosby didn't belong in a musical Austria, wearing lederhosen; he was more at home in King Arthur's court (his 1949 remake of Will Rogers's *A Connecticut Yankee*) than in Ruritania. But the main reason for the failure of the film, which is really quite charming, is that Crosby isn't given enough music. Crosby plays, not an American, but *the* American: the one we all imagine ourselves to be (happy and easygoing) and the one Europeans would like us to be (rather naive, a bit lazy, and unthreatening). Crosby is a consummate American type, but never the hard-driven, rags-to-riches immigrant guy who builds, works, grasps, and controls. Sometimes he's a character who has that in his past (*High Times*) or a guy whose family has money and he needs to escape it (*Road to Singapore*). Even when he's counted among the wealthy, as in *High Society*, the musical remake of *The Philadelphia Story* with Crosby in Cary Grant's role of C. K. Dexter Haven, he's not really a rich guy. He's got the mansion, the manners, and the clothes, but not the actual dough-re-mi. He makes his living as a songwriter, hanging out with Louis Armstrong and other musicians who've come to Newport for the jazz festival and blending in easily with two reporters (Frank Sinatra and Celeste Holm).

In Wilder's film, Crosby sings only three songs, plus some words (which are brief) to Strauss's "Emperor Waltz" at the film's finale, but the film is an attempt to make what would have been a sophisticated Lubitsch comedy about the classes, a world Crosby would never live in, and therefore a mistake. It's not a star vehicle. The plot is potentially clever: high-born European countess (Joan Fontaine) meets an American traveling phonograph salesman in Franz Joseph I's Austria. They hate each other, but their dogs (her poodle and his mutt) fall metaphorically in love. Crosby is loose and slangy, and sings beautifully; Fontaine is lovely, lavishly overdressed, and properly haughty; and the dogs do their stuff—but the film has one foot in replicated 1930s froth and the other in postwar Americanism. It is an example of a fine director with a strong personal style being asked to adjust his ideas and his sophistication to the Crosby musical star universe and not really doing it.

Crosby fared much better with auteurs Leo McCarey and Frank Capra. In addition to *Going My Way*, Crosby was directed by McCarey in the highly successful sequel to the story of Father O'Malley, *The Bells of St. Mary's*. *Bells* is a better movie than *Going My Way*, although Crosby makes both work equally for his character. For once, he has a top-level actress as a costar, the radiantly beautiful and talented Ingrid Bergman. Her performance as a nun brings believability to Father O'Malley's world, which the fake hoke of Barry Fitzgerald could not do. Both the comedy and the drama are elevated by her presence; Crosby and Bergman are an excellent onscreen pair. Crosby gives Bergman a lightness and joy she doesn't always have, and she gives him a credible gravitas suitable to his "priesthood."

Crosby fit perfectly into Frank Capra's postwar world, appearing in two films, *Riding High* (1950) and *Here Comes the Groom* (1951). The first is a remake of Capra's 1934 hit *Broadway Bill*, about a racehorse owner (a perfect role for Crosby, a track fan), and the second is about a foreign correspondent looking for a home for two children he wants to adopt from war-torn Europe. Capra and Crosby were perfect for each other, and Capra had no trouble absorbing the Crosby style and character into his universe, or directing a musical number. In *Groom*, Crosby and his costar Jane Wyman (the first Mrs. Ronald Reagan) swing out in a charming improvisational song and dance to Hoagy Carmichael and Johnny Mercer's Oscar-winning "In the Cool, Cool, Cool of the Evening." Back in 1932, Capra had made a film called *Platinum Blonde*, in which his hero, played by Robert Williams, is essentially Bing Crosby without the music. Williams died tragically just before the movie's release; otherwise he would surely have become a big star. Crosby is very much like him, with the same easy manner that Capra made good use of.

The only other "auteur" film Crosby made was 1956's *High Society*, directed by the underrated Charles Walters. It's a proper musical, with great stars (in addition to Crosby, Sinatra, and Holm, there are Grace Kelly, John Lund, and Louis Armstrong). Crosby adapted easily in his role as a kind of singing Cary Grant.

To understand the Crosby magic on film is to understand the star-musical vehicle. Although he was in some very good movies (*Bells of St. Mary's*, *High Society*), he was never in any great ones. He carried his movies, and most of them were very thin in what they had to offer other than him. Paramount, his chief studio, put him where the public wanted him: singing, lazing along, romancing a bit, philosophizing a bit, and, if paired with Hope, yukking it up quite a lot. By 1947, Crosby was a national institution. Americans didn't have to wait for his latest movie to arrive at the local theater: they could hear him every day on the radio in some form, or play his records. He was a part of everyone's daily life, with his voice as familiar as a neighbor's or even a family member's. Few stars with that level of fame would have found themselves hitched to a vehicle like *Welcome Stranger* (1947). It's a formula film, crafted seventeen years after Bing Crosby first entered movies, only two years after his Oscar win, and at the peak of his box-office power. He's forty-four years old and at the very top, but he's not given much to work with: his character has a pipe, some songs, a profession (in this case, he's a doctor, not a priest).

Welcome Stranger has no quality that defines it. It's a classic example of how Paramount created lackluster vehicles for Crosby without having to worry about much more than having him sing a few good tunes. Directed by Elliott Nugent, with songs by Johnny Burke and Jimmy Van Heusen, *Welcome Stranger* costars the lovely Joan Caulfield, a soft blond with a minimum of talent, and the ever-mugging, ever-scene-stealing Barry Fitzgerald. Crosby and Fitzgerald were being teamed again after their terrific success in *Going My Way*, and the pairing demonstrates Crosby's ability to claim the screen as his own. No matter how much Fitzgerald does, and he does plenty, his cutie-pie old codger has to live in Crosby's world. Crosby owns the screen. He rents out a section, very generously, to Fitzgerald, and without any obvious fear of being upstaged. The film was advertised as being a reunion of the two stars from *Going My Way*, back together again as if they were Greer Garson and Walter Pidgeon or Fred and Ginger. As to Caulfield (rumored to be one of Crosby's most important off-screen romances), she didn't matter much. Crosby didn't need a costar; he only needed a leading lady. If he was paired with another star—a Hope, a Grace Kelly, an Ingrid Bergman—that was okay, because he couldn't be upstaged. If no name was available, no name was needed. He'd carry things along, and Caulfield (very pretty and very unobjectionable) was someone he could carry with ease. And there was always Fitzgerald lurking in the wings to fill out the spaces.

In *Welcome Stranger*, Crosby is part of an organization called the Physicians and Surgeons Placement Bureau, which assigns doctors to temporary jobs, acting as replacements until a permanent doctor can be found. He arrives in a small town in Maine, already enemies with the doctor who has come to fetch him. They meet cute. (After all, their relationship is the real romance of the movie.) Neither knows who the other is, and they clash over a newspaper, over Crosby's singing on the train ("This is a washroom, not a cabaret," says Fitzgerald), and over Crosby's getting the last order of brook trout in the dining car, the one that Fitzgerald has been salivating for. Crosby is the opposite of what Fitzgerald feels is an appropriate small-town doctor. He wears loud sport jackets ("California getup"), and has been a hotel physician, a ship's doctor, a personal doctor for a rich man, etc. As soon as he's filled in the two-month gap until the new doctor can arrive, he'll be off to Guatemala. He's a good doctor, but what he really does is sing. ("The doctor's as good as Frank Sinatra," says a townswoman.) Because he's Bing, nobody wonders why Crosby is singing. Nobody wonders why he and Fitzgerald are acting like some old married couple—they saw *Going My Way*.

Like Jolson, Crosby had his rivals. Dozens of "crooners" appeared during his lifetime, and whereas most of them were content to be radio or TV stars, a number of them attempted film careers unsuccessfully: Dick Haymes, Perry Como, Vic Damone, Eddie Fisher, and Tony Martin, for example. Bing Crosby is often discussed in relationship to Frank Sinatra, and a sort of pseudo rivalry between them was created for the media. They were never really rivals, however. Crosby's movie career began in 1930 and he was a star by the mid-1930s. His movie career was spent largely under contract to a single studio, Paramount, where vehicles were built for him. Sinatra had only a brief period of such handling, in his "skinny guy who's shy with girls" years at MGM. Sinatra hit it big in the early 1940s, so the two men were actually a decade apart. Sinatra's career took a nosedive at the end of the 1940s, but then took an unexpected turn upward when he won Best Supporting Actor of 1953 for his role as Maggio in the film adaptation of James Jones's best seller *From Here to Eternity*. Before then, Sinatra was a singing star who sometimes made musicals; afterward, he was a dramatic actor who sometimes made musicals. To the world, of course, he was always FRANK SINATRA, SINGER, but in the movies, he stepped away from the genre he was born to inhabit. His musicals can be divided into two distinctly different periods: his young years as a crooner, and his later years as an actor/singer.

Sinatra's first Hollywood movies (well chronicled in Tom Santopietro's *Sinatra in Hollywood*) presented him only as an unnamed singer standing in front of Tommy Dorsey's band. In *Las Vegas Nights* (1941), he sang "I'll Never Smile Again," and in *Ship Ahoy* he sang "The Last Call for Love" and "Poor You." In *Reveille with Beverly* (1943), he was identified as Frank Sinatra, singing one of his hits, "Night and Day." In 1943, he made his film debut as an "actor" in an RKO movie, *Higher and Higher*, with Michèle Morgan, Jack Haley, and Marcy McGuire. However, he did not play a character: he played himself as if he *were* a character. Nearly a half hour goes by on screen before he appears, and then the doorbell of a mansion rings, McGuire (the maid) answers the door, and a skinny young guy holding a bouquet of flowers says, "Good morning. My name is Frank Sinatra." The maid, a bobby-soxer, faints into his arms. It's clear that no one feels confident Frank Sinatra is movie material unless he appears as

The young and dreamy Frank Sinatra in his starring debut, *Higher and Higher*, with Marcy McGuire and Barbara Hale

the phenomenon he's become: himself, the singing heartthrob of teenage girls. Sinatra performs "I Couldn't Sleep a Wink Last Night," "The Music Stopped," "You're on Your Own," "Lovely Way to Spend an Evening," and "I Saw You First." Singing was what he was there to do, and he did it well. Next time out in a feature, *Step Lively* (1944), he was paired with Gloria DeHaven, George Murphy, and Adolphe Menjou and given an actual role as "Glenn Russell." The movie was a remake of the Marx Brothers comedy *Room Service* (originally a hit play), and Sinatra sang four songs by Jule Styne and Sammy Cahn.

After *Higher and Higher* and before *Step Lively*, Sinatra appeared in the Warner Bros. 1944 short, *The Road To Victory*, a patriotic booster with an all-star cast including Bing Crosby, Cary Grant, Dennis Morgan, and Jack Carson. Sinatra sang "There'll Be a Hot Time in the Town of Berlin." He then appeared in a second, more fully developed patriotic short in 1944, this time filmed by 20th Century–Fox and released in 1945: *All-Star Bond Rally*, which ran a full nineteen minutes and trotted out star royalty: Bob Hope as emcee, with Betty Grable, Fibber McGee and Molly, Bing Crosby, Harry James and his band, and . . . Frank Sinatra, who sang "Saturday Night Is the Loneliest Night of the Week." Sinatra, no longer standing anonymously in front of a band or playing a version of himself, is a different presence on film. He takes the stage with supreme confidence, elegantly dressed in suit and tie, singing beautifully, and delivering little joke lines as if he's as big a name as anyone else in the frame. He looks like a movie star, and offstage the wheels were in motion for him to become one.

According to Santopietro, when Louis B. Mayer saw (and heard) Sinatra sing "Ol' Man River" at a wartime benefit, he turned to one of his minions and said, "I want that boy." Louis B. Mayer got that boy. In 1945, Sinatra signed a contract with MGM and began the first phase of his movie-musicals career. His contract allowed him to continue making records, sing on the radio, take twelve weeks of vacation per year, and own publishing rights to some of the music in his movies. Sinatra was not a standard seventy-five-dollar-per-week, seven-year-contract hire.

From 1945 to 1949, Sinatra made six A-list musicals for MGM: *Anchors Aweigh* (1945), *Till the Clouds Roll By* (1946), *It Happened in Brooklyn* (1947), *The Kissing Bandit* (1948), and *Take Me Out to the Ball Game* and *On the Town* (both 1949). He also made an award-winning short film that was a plea for tolerance, *The House I Live In* (1945), two sales trailers, and one dramatic film, *The Miracle of the Bells* (1948), in which he played a priest. In *Till the Clouds Roll By*, he sang only one number. In the grand finale, he stood on a pedestal wearing an immaculate white suit in front of an all-white orchestra—against a hot-pink background—and sang "Ol' Man River," the song that had inspired Mayer to hire him. *Life* magazine called it "the cinematic low point of the year." The ludicrous plan of featuring a white singer doing music written about African American life keyed to an African American voice brought on decades of scorn for Sinatra and MGM.

Sinatra's MGM musicals presented him as a character designed to match his youthful appearance. He had a lean and hungry look often tactfully described as "underfed," but he was downright skinny, all sharp elbows, high cheekbones, and big eyes. He was like a gawky wallflower at the prom. His famous musicals costarring Gene Kelly cast him accordingly, with the two men paired as opposites: Kelly as a worldly-wise wolf with a way with dames, and Sinatra as a naive kid too shy to ask a woman on a date, much less tell her he loves her. In *Anchors* and *On the Town*, Kelly and Sinatra are sailors on leave; and in *Ball Game*, they're members of a turn-of-the-century baseball team who, with comic Jules Munshin, form a trio of "Tinker to Evers to Chance" double-play artists (who also sing and dance). Much is made in these films of Sinatra being scared of women. In *Ball Game*, singer/dancer Betty Garrett, his romantic lead, actually picks him up and carries him off the ball field, singing "It's Fate, Baby, It's Fate." In *On the Town*, she's a super-aggressor, trapping him in her taxicab, pressing him to "Come Up to My Place." Sinatra acts terrified. These onscreen shenanigans, designed to fit with Sinatra's looks in the mid-to-late-forties and to appeal to his teenage fans, appear almost shocking today, since audiences have long been aware that in real life Sinatra was already a confident ladies' man.

MGM didn't know what to do with the young Sinatra, casting him in *The Kissing Bandit* with Kathryn Grayson and stalling his career . . .

Sinatra and Kelly were a simpatico pair onscreen, and became lifelong friends. Their costarring might have become a nasty competition, but they possessed different skills and were comfortable together.* Kelly was happy to discover that Sinatra, when taught, was surprisingly light on his feet and could be put directly into the musical action through dance. (On a TV talk show, after watching a clip from *Anchors Aweigh* of the two of them dancing the "I Begged Her" number, Fred Astaire commented, "Frank surprised me there. He was really dancing.")

Sinatra's singing was never tampered with at MGM; this meant that, though he could be a comic foil or the butt of Garrett's lust, or hang around

---

* Sinatra was billed above Kelly in *Anchors Aweigh* and *Take Me Out to the Ball Game*. For *On The Town* they are co-billed above the film's title, Kelly to the left and Sinatra to the right.

shyly while the women went for Kelly, when he sang everything changed. The sound of his voice suggested a different Sinatra: he had a haunting passion, depth of feeling, sensuousness, and the hint of an edge that bore no relationship to a naive young sailor. When he sang a ballad like "I Fall in Love Too Easily" (in *Anchors Aweigh*), or when he rolled out a fast-paced happy tune like "Yes, Indeedy" (in *Ball Game*), he gave off a genuine joy in life. In his music, Frank Sinatra revealed what lay ahead in his career: the ability to project emotion.

Sinatra's only musical flop at MGM was the movie he ridiculed (and hated) for the rest of his life: an operetta-style musical set in old California, placing him opposite Kathryn Grayson. *The Kissing Bandit* was a fiasco. He said watching it was "a sadistic form of torture." Sinatra wore ruffled shirts and tight pants, and was cast as the shy son of a notorious bandit who had always kissed the women he robbed—making them grateful to lose their money and jewels. In a sailor suit or a baseball uniform, Sinatra seemed to be what females called "cute" in those days; in ruffles he looked silly and out of place. Sinatra's vibe was always modern, cutting-edge. Later in life, when he appeared in period films such as *Can-Can* and *Dirty Dingus Magee*, he defined the era on his own terms: musically hip for *Can-Can* and comically raunchy for *Dingus*.

. . . but he later found his ring-a-ding self and put it to good use in the title role of *Pal Joey* at Columbia.

Everything changed for Sinatra in 1953. Prior to *From Here to Eternity*, his career as a singer had waned, and his movie-star status had gone with it. (His personal life was also in turmoil, with a messy divorce from his first wife and a headline-grabbing romance with, and subsequent marriage to, superstar Ava Gardner.) In 1950 and 1951, he was seen in two dubious films, *Double Dynamite* and *Meet Danny Wilson*. Both were unsuccessful. *Meet Danny Wilson* was a musical of sorts, with Sinatra as a nightclub singer who gets mixed up with racketeers; it had been shot in 1948 and held back from release until 1951, a comment on its quality. *Double Dynamite* was a disaster. *The Kissing Bandit* may be foolish, but at least Sinatra sings. In *Dynamite* he plays a meek bank clerk erroneously accused of robbery. Sinatra's famous "comeback" in *Eternity* is not exaggerated. His Maggio was truly a rebirth for an artist who had risen to the very top and fallen to the very bottom.

After *Eternity*, Frank Sinatra made forty-three feature films (including cameos), but only seven were musicals. His recording career, his TV life, his movies, and his fame soared to newer and newer heights, but he neglected his natural genre. This is particularly significant considering that his level of success meant he could do whatever he wanted in those years. None of his seven musicals—with the possible exception of *High Society*—was outstanding. The great loss to the history of movie musicals was his departure in 1956 from *Carousel*, in which he had been cast to play Billy Bigelow but was replaced by Gordon MacRae. (See pp. 346–8 on Rodgers and Hammerstein musicals.) His first film released after *Eternity* was *Suddenly* (1954), in which he played a political assassin, and the next was more a dramatic picture than a musical, though he did sing and was paired with Doris Day: *Young at Heart* (also in 1954). The movie was a remake of a 1938 Warner Bros. hit, *Four Daughters*, based on a novel by Fannie Hurst. Sinatra took over the role originated by John Garfield: a cynical musician drifting through life. He sings five songs, and for the first time brings to the screen the aura of a man who's been to the bottom and back. He's a different Sinatra from his happy sailor days: he's thirty-nine and looks older, seeming hardened and disillusioned. The movie gives him a dynamic entrance, with his back to the audience when a door is opened. He turns in close-up, a cigarette dangling from his lips, his blue eyes burning, and seems to be saying, "I'm back and this is the way I look . . . I'm not a kid . . . I've failed and recovered." Particularly when he sings "Just One of Those Things" or "One for My Baby," Sinatra shows he's an artist, not just a crooner or a cute guy or even a skilled actor. He reveals the potential for legend.

After *Young at Heart*, Sinatra made a string of dramas and comedies in which he didn't sing or simply sang the title tune on the soundtrack, as in *The Tender Trap* (1955) and *Come Blow Your Horn* (1963).* Mostly, he

---

* In 1955, Sinatra appeared on TV in a musical version of *Our Town* in which he played the Stage Manager and Paul Newman was George Gibbs.

made dramatic pictures in which he undertook challenging roles: *Not As a Stranger* (1955), as a young doctor; *The Man with the Golden Arm* (1956), as a heroin addict; *Johnny Concho* (1956), as a neurotic western hero; and *The Pride and the Passion* (1957), as—perhaps the most ridiculous role he ever played—a nineteenth-century Spanish revolutionary who, alongside Cary Grant and Sophia Loren, drags a huge cannon across the landscape. Sinatra wears a black wig and speaks in a Spanish accent. Why was he making junk like *Pride* and not a musical? As if he were asking himself the same question, after shooting a cameo for Mike Todd's *Around the World in 80 Days* (which would be released in 1956), Sinatra did appear in four "mature" musicals during this time span: *Guys and Dolls*, released at the end of 1955, *High Society* in 1956, and *Pal Joey* and *The Joker Is Wild* in 1957. His final two musical films followed: *Can-Can* in 1960 and his last, *Robin and the 7 Hoods*, in 1964.

Sinatra's "mature" musicals present him as the opposite of his younger self. Once the shy fella who didn't know how to get a girl, the older Sinatra is characterized as a cynical guy who knows how to con a "chick." He became the "been there, done that," jaded but attractive grifter. He was a natural to inherit the Gene Kelly role in *Pal Joey*, and the movie version was adapted for the character to be a singer rather than a dancer. He was just right for gambler Nathan Detroit in *Guys and Dolls* (and could also have been a better Sky Masterson than Marlon Brando, who couldn't sing well enough to handle songs like "Luck Be a Lady," a Sinatra concert staple). He played the Jimmy Stewart role in *High Society*, the musical version of *The Philadelphia Story*, and was singer/comedian Joe E. Brown in the musical biopic *The Joker Is Wild*, which introduced one of his signature songs, "All the Way," by Jimmy Van Heusen and Sammy Cahn. These four musicals were well tailored to Sinatra's older screen persona, and gave him terrific songs to sing. He did "You're Sensational" and "Well, Did Ya Evah!" in *High Society*, and "It's All Right with Me" in *Can-Can*, "The Lady Is a Tramp" and "I Didn't Know What Time It Was" in *Pal Joey*, and the title tune in *Guys and Dolls*, among others.

To the end of his movie career, Sinatra continued making dramatic and comedic films, playing gamblers, detectives, cowboys, and war heroes until his final movie, *The First Deadly Sin*, in 1980.* He developed a wiseguy brio, and around him seemed to hang an aura of something dangerous or

---

* He did a brief cameo playing himself in 1984's *Cannonball Run II*.

unpredictable. He embraced those qualities, appearing in movies that might be thought of as his "thug" years, nonmusicals such as *Tony Rome* (1967) and *Lady in Cement* (1968). After he retired from movies, in his television musical shows he seemed to mellow somewhat; as *Newsweek* put it in 1982, "Age has softened his sinister aura." Sinatra died on May 14, 1998, at the age of eighty-two.

When Sinatra sang on film, he gave the audience what they expected of him: the warmth of his voice, his amazing timing, his personal way with lyrics. Every song he sang was his. He had a great career in musicals, but he's much more than the sum of his movie musicals and is not limited to being defined by them in the same way someone such as Gene Kelly is. Sinatra was an excellent dramatic actor, easy and natural and skilled, but when he appeared in musical performances, the only man present on screen was—and is—Frank Sinatra.

Most of Crosby's "rivals" appeared after he had already reached a legendary status. During his rise to fame, in the 1930s, there were two who didn't last: Rudy Vallee, who preceded him but soon faded, only to come back as a nonsinging comedy figure in the 1940s, and Russ Columbo, who died tragically, leaving historians to speculate about what might have happened had he been there to rival Crosby.

Russ Columbo was not only a first-rate singer but also a composer, someone who might have reshaped the history of American male popular singers had he lived. He wrote two songs that were significant in advancing Crosby's career, "Prisoner of Love" and "You Call It Madness (but I Call It Love)." Columbo started his career as a band singer with Gus Arnheim, but also formed his own band. He was in several early musicals, among them *Dynamite* (1929), *Broadway Thru a Keyhole* (1934), and *Wake Up and Dream* (1934), but he died in 1934 at the age of twenty-six, the victim of an apparently accidental gunshot wound that is the subject of much speculation in Hollywood scandal histories. (In handling a friend's antique gun, Columbo was unaware it was loaded. Various stories account for how it was triggered, with the bullet allegedly ricocheting off a table and striking Columbo in the face, killing him instantly.) He was romantically involved at the time with Carole Lombard, and his death made big headlines. Columbo has been compared in retrospect to both Crosby and Sinatra; his singing style was the popular crooning of the day, à la Bing, but his intonation is often said to be similar to Sinatra's.

The young man who was a successful rival to Crosby, Dick Powell

(1904–63), is someone people rarely think of in this connection because he left his singing career behind. Dick Powell was a handsome young tenor from Mountain View, Arkansas. He was slim and boyish and was put in movies mostly to sing key numbers and to romance an equally young, slim girl. He was a top-ten-box-office star in both 1935 and 1936, two years, significantly, in which Crosby did *not* appear on the lists. His career began in 1932, around the same time as Crosby's, and continued through the 1930s during Crosby's rise to glory. Like Crosby, he came out of radio with a strong following. Unlike Crosby, however, he had a slightly jumpy—or peppy—quality, and he had a somewhat malicious twinkle in his eyes that, coupled with a crooked little grin, made him just a tad devilish. He was at ease, but not laid back—there was a hint of naughtiness, the innocent-looking kid who puts the tack on the teacher's chair.

Like Crosby—and Jolson and Cantor and everyone else used to make star musicals—Powell became "typed." He was the jaunty juvenile, a young up-and-comer who could be cast in a backstage musical, paired with a good-looking costar and given an opportunity to sing some hit songs. After a string of successes in Warner Bros. musicals (the Busby Berkeley–dominated *42nd Street*, *Gold Diggers of 1933*, and *Dames*; two well-directed Frank Borzage military musicals, *Flirtation Walk* and *Shipmates Forever*, plus others), Powell became tired of juvenile roles. Unlike Crosby, he wanted out of the vehicles that were being built for him. Aware that his youthful days were waning, he made a sudden career shift into the crime and dark detective dramas of the 1940s and early 1950s that are now labeled film noir. (As early as 1936, he was quoted as saying, "I'm not a kid anymore, but I'm still playing boy scouts.") Beginning in 1944, he changed his image, a difficult thing to do in Hollywood and proof of his ambition and intelligence. He appeared as Raymond Chandler's Philip Marlowe in *Murder, My Sweet* (1944, based on *Farewell, My Lovely*), and Powell was unpredictably successful as a tough guy. Speaking Chandler's hard, dry "I'm bored and I'm tough" dialogue on the soundtrack of *Murder, My Sweet*, Powell was excellent. He turned himself into a cynical grown-up and opened up new possibilities for himself.

From 1944 onward, he appeared in some very good films: André de Toth's downbeat noir about an unhappy insurance salesman, *Pitfall* (1948); Anthony Mann's *The Tall Target* (1951), in which he was a detective trying to prevent the assassination of President Lincoln; and Vincente Minnelli's *The Bad and the Beautiful* (1952), an excellent film about the movie business. He sometimes did comedies (*Reformer and the Redhead*, 1950; *Susan Slept Here*, 1954), in which his ability to deliver lines was impeccable; and he became a director, stepping behind the camera for movies such as *Split Second* (1953), *The Conqueror* (1956), and *The Enemy Below* (1957). ("The best thing about switching from being an actor to being a director is that I don't have to hold my stomach in anymore.") Powell, like Loretta Young and a few others (including Crosby), saw the potential in the television business, entering it full force in 1952 as producer, director, and occasional actor for his Dick Powell Productions. He died of cancer in 1963, allegedly one of the richest of the Hollywood stars. Powell is an underrated movie presence—he was not only a brilliant businessman, but a shrewd judge of his own abilities.

Since his career unfolded alongside Crosby's, why is Powell never thought of as a serious rival to Der Bingle? Powell had a voice, a distinctive presence, the ability to do both comedy and drama, and the same sharp sense of how to get rich that Crosby had. The Powell/Crosby comparison illustrates one of the issues of musical-film development. Powell's voice was beautiful but light, and his physical presence suggested juvenile roles. His career is split into halves: the 1930s juvenilia and the 1940s–early 1950s grown-up roles. Crosby glided across the decades, seemingly ageless, seemingly the same guy from start to finish. Crosby had the better voice, of course, and the deeper talent, but his uniqueness is illustrated by the career of Powell, who had to find a way to break his musical-star mold to keep his stardom alive.

The main issue for the Crosby rival Dick Haymes was that he just didn't have the sharply defined personality that suggested a type of movie character to inspire a studio to build movies around him. Haymes was not a specific type—he was neither a juvenile nor a mature lead, neither a comic nor a dancer, and not particularly bad or good. He just was handsome and sang beautifully, in movies like *State Fair* (1945), in which he helped popularize Rodgers and Hammerstein's "That's for Me." But the movies of the era understood that Bing Crosby, the original crooner, was the one you could turn into a movie star, because you could, in fact, build a musical universe around him.

Crosby had another potential rival, his younger brother Bob. (Bing stayed close to his family, and brothers Everett and Larry remained in his show business life, Everett as his business manager and Larry as his publicist.) Brother Bob found his own musical fame. When band leader Ben

Pollack began neglecting his organization in 1935, his musicians decamped and reformed under the leadership of their musical director, Gil Rodin. Needing a frontman, they offered the job to Bob Crosby, which is how he got started. (He once remarked, "I'm the only guy in show business who made it without talent." Gary Giddins said, "The musicians in his band would not have disagreed with him.") Bob had a decent baritone, a friendly manner, and a good bandstand personality. When a smaller version of the band, an octet, was formed and labeled the Bob Cats, the name stuck for all of his later groups. The Bob Cats were described by Duke Ellington as "a truly gut-bucket band with a strong blues influence." The musicians included drummer Ray Bauduc, Matty Matlock, Billy Butterfield, Joe Sullivan, and others. Bob Crosby, however, doesn't seem really relaxed the way his brother did, nor does he register strongly inside a frame. Coming across him in a minor role in a movie, he also doesn't particularly resemble Bing. When he begins to sing, however, the likeness emerges; and as you listen, he disappears and Bing Crosby rules. As a result, Bob Crosby was never a serious threat to his older brother in terms of movie stardom—or any other kind, either. Bing Crosby once said, trying to prove he was ordinary, "There are a lot of guys like me." But even his own brother couldn't be him—nor could his oldest son, Gary, who of the male singers among Bing's children came closest to having his own success.

Crosby's final musical was *Robin and the 7 Hoods* in 1964, and it costarred Frank Sinatra, Dean Martin, and Sammy Davis Jr. The cool kids of the 1960s invited the old man who had been cool before they knew cool was cool to join them in a musical romp that nobody took particularly seriously. Crosby enjoys himself. He has nothing at stake, since he's not the star who has to carry the film. He's very casual, and appears to be ad-libbing all his lines in the old *Road* tradition with a touch of W. C. Fields's colorful vocabulary thrown in: "You gentlemen find my raiment repulsive?" he asks Sinatra and Martin when they object to his character's lack of chic flash in clothing. Crosby plays a clever con man who disguises himself as square, and his outfits reflect a conservative vibe in the eyes of the cats who are looking him over. The inquiry leads into a number, "Style," in which Sinatra and Martin put Crosby behind closet doors for a series of humorous outfit changes, to try to spruce him up. Crosby comes out in a plaid suit with knickers and then in yellow pants and an orange-striped shirt. Martin and Sinatra keep on singing—and hoping—while Crosby models a fez. He finally emerges with a straw hat, a cane, and a boutonniere in his

Three great talents, singing and dancing about style, which they've all clearly got plenty of: Frank Sinatra, Bing Crosby, and Dean Martin in *Robin and the 7 Hoods*

tuxedo lapel, looking like a dude. In his own low-key way, taking his spot in the center, right between the other two, Crosby joins in the song and begins to take musical charge. Sinatra is clearly digging Crosby, the older man he always wanted to emulate.* Both Sinatra and Martin are perfectly willing to let Crosby be the focus. He's earned it. He's the original that the other two wanted to become. He was there when Sinatra and Martin were still kids. He's Bing Crosby! The three men begin to do a kind of old man's strut, singing and dancing perfectly together ("... his hat got a little more shiny ... "). The audience is looking at the three dominant male singers of

* It wasn't the first time the two of them had presented movie gold. In *High Society*, they did a show-stopping version of "Well, Did You Evah!" The addition of Dean Martin puts the cherry on top of the icing on top of the cake.

the era from 1940 to 1977. They're having fun, showing everyone exactly not only what makes a pro, not only what makes a star, but what makes a legend.

Crosby, Sinatra, and Martin were three major male singing stars whose careers overlapped, with the emergence of their stardom in that order. They had distinctly different approaches to the cinematic frame. Sinatra's entrance, even if he seemed cool, indifferent, and casual, was tantamount to kicking the door down. Crosby slipped in from the side, all low-key and "Don't mind me." Martin, perhaps as a result of having to stand around for years while Jerry Lewis swung on the chandelier, always established himself as outside the frame: "I'm just hangin' loose out here and watchin' the action." These three men were all really good actors—great actors, even—but their singing defined them, and in that race Bing was the pacesetter. Although both Sinatra and Martin are probably better known today, and Sinatra is the gold standard of male singers, his role model was always Crosby. Nobody could upstage Crosby, partly because he was so good at appearing not to care. When he was present, everyone else seemed to be sweating it out.* Crosby never lost it. He presented himself to any audience as if the very idea weren't in his brain pan.

Crosby was a shrewd businessman; in his private life, he owned 15 percent of the Pittsburgh Pirates, built the lucrative Del Mar racetrack, and started his own television business, Bing Crosby Productions, which was hugely successful with such hits as *Ben Casey* and *Hogan's Heroes.* One of his smartest moves was providing the funding for an early electronics lab, so that he became a pioneer in the development of both audio and video tape recording in the late 1940s and early 1950s. He left behind an alleged estate worth about $130 million, making him one of the richest men in Hollywood at the time (Bob Hope and Fred MacMurray were his contemporary equals).

At the end of his life, Crosby was wealthy and respected and did only what he wanted to do. The surface looked smooth, but just as *The Country Girl* showed the public a dark side to the characters he could play, offscreen,

* *Robin and the 7 Hoods* was Crosby's valedictory movie, his final appearance in a Bing Crosby type of role. He made only one more film, a remake of *Stagecoach* (1966) in which he portrayed the drunken doctor originally embodied by Thomas Mitchell, a nonsinger who got an Oscar for Best Supporting Actor for the role). In 1972, he made an uncredited cameo appearance in Bob Hope's *Cancel My Reservation*, an old tradition between them, and he also appeared as himself as one of the star presenters in 1974's tribute to old musicals from MGM, *That's Entertainment.*

there was a parallel dark side to his personality. It was not a secret that the young Crosby was a heavy drinker; he never hid the fact. His first wife, a former star named Dixie Lee, herself suffered from alcoholism. As their four sons grew up, Crosby was revealed by them to be a difficult—perhaps abusive—father, although his family with his second wife, actress Kathryn Grant Crosby, testified to a happier home life. Watching him being interviewed on TV by Barbara Walters in 1977 is revealing. He's BING CROSBY, beloved American icon, successful businessman, movie star, TV producer, singer, actor, etc. He's as laid-back and blue-eyed as ever. His relaxed and charming air is combined with a seemingly open honesty. There's a "Whatever you want to ask me, Barbara" quality about him. He's cool with anything. And then Walters asks him what he would say to his daughter if she decided to live with a man before she was married to him. Crosby's eyes go steely, and without skipping a beat he tells Walters he would say, "Aloha. Aloha on the steel guitar." Crosby could be cold and tough.

That same year, a TV special, *Bing Crosby's Merrie Olde Christmas*, was taped in London. It would be his last TV appearance, aired just five weeks before his death. He did a duet with David Bowie in which Crosby sang "The Little Drummer Boy" and Bowie counterpointed with "Peace on Earth." It was a very odd pairing indeed, but Crosby looked utterly calm and comfortable alongside a much younger man whose musical style—never mind his clothes—was decades outside the limit Crosby had set for himself. (If anyone looks nervous, it's Bowie.) It didn't matter. In an obituary tribute to Bowie, AP's David Bauder wrote, "The culture clash made it an immediate classic—the World War II era crooner with one of rock's wildest personalities. It was hard to imagine them in the same room, let alone standing around the piano. Yet neither man looked down upon the other." Able to partner someone, anyone, right to the end, Crosby remained who he was, straightforwardly "rum-pum-pum-pumming" his song, easy, relaxed, and musically defining the moment. David Bowie was counterpointing him, not vice versa.

In his later years, Crosby became a man who liked to keep out of the limelight as much as possible. He died in Spain, shortly after playing eighteen holes of golf, having shot a very respectable 85, winning his match. His last words were purported to be "That was a great game of golf, fellas." (As is always true with legendary performers, these facts are disputed. Gary Giddins says Crosby actually said, "Let's go get a Coke.") This casual, unprofessional, easy trot offstage suited Crosby's image as "just an ordinary guy."

In interviews throughout his career, Crosby was modest, laid-back, and matter-of-fact. About his phenomenal success with the Irving Berlin song "White Christmas," he said: "A jackdaw with a cleft palate could have sung it successfully." He summed himself up by claiming he had just been lucky. (*Call Me Lucky* was the title of his autobiography.) "Honestly," he said, "I think I've stretched a talent which is so thin it's almost transparent over a quite unbelievable term of years." One of his most self-deprecating quotes was "Everyone knows I'm just a big, good-natured slob." Everyone actually didn't know that offscreen, but onscreen was where it mattered. When he was awarded the Oscar for his performance as the warmhearted, super-wise priest of *Going My Way*, Crosby said in his acceptance speech: "This is the only country in the world where an old, broken-down crooner can win an Oscar for acting. It shows that everybody in this country has a chance to succeed. I was just lucky enough to have Leo McCarey take me by the hand and lead me."

Crosby maintained his modesty to the end of his life. In 1954 he admitted, "I don't sing anywhere near as good as I used to, and I feel sincerely that it's getting worse." He wrote his own epitaph as "He was an average guy who could carry a tune." Carry it right to the bank, as it turned out, riding the musical vehicles the business built for him.

Presley

Elvis Presley is just as big a name today as he ever was, and his career has a unique feature not shared by Jolson or Crosby: he's supposed to still be alive even after he's dead. People claim to have seen him. (I once had a Duke alum tell me that Elvis had been his graduation speaker in 1997, twenty years after Elvis's death. Well, that's Duke for you.) Presley is the only one of the three who died an early and tragic death, the circumstances of which serve to feed his legend. In the tabloid-fame sweepstakes, Elvis Presley wins. However, in motion-picture history, he paid the highest price. Jolson and Crosby appeared in vehicles especially designed for them, but Presley had to carry the can for twelve years in mostly lackluster films designed not so much to showcase him as to exploit him.

Elvis Presley was the King (but not to Crosby, who said, "Let's face it.

Sinatra is the King"). Crosby did, however, pay tribute to Presley, frankly stating, "He helped kill off the influence of me and my contemporaries, but I respect him for that. Because music always has to progress, and no one could have opened the door to the future like he did." Presley was well aware of both Jolson and Crosby, his predecessors. He named Jolson as his idol, and sang one of Jolson's hits ("Are You Lonesome Tonight?") as a tribute. (Presley's own version became a huge hit, and in it he not only sang but used Jolson's own method of reciting the lyrics, turning them into a dialogue.) Presley was aware of his own place in the singing tradition: he could belt it out, he could croon, he could mesmerize live audiences, and yet he took pop singing to a new place, the world of rock and roll. Furthermore, he understood what rock and roll represented: the rejection of earlier, tamer forms and the embracing of the world of the teenager. He gloried in rock and roll's outlaw quality, and had no fear of it being thought of as seriously dumb. He embraced the dumb and made the world take it seriously.

Presley's movie stardom came as a result of his other stardom: that of the singing idol, the teenage heartthrob who turned out to be able to attract any age, any sex, and to keep fan ardor alive. This earlier success was also true for both Jolson and Crosby. Jolson was indisputably a huge star when he appeared in *The Jazz Singer* and moved on to his movie career, and Crosby was a highly established radio and recording success when he, too, began his movie stardom. But Elvis Presley was a sensation, an overnight whirlwind who roared to the top in 1956 with a single hit song, "Heartbreak Hotel." He's closer to Sinatra in the sort of adulation he had inspired *before* he appeared in movies.

Jolson was in the right place for the transition to sound, and Crosby was there for the peak of the musical genre and the microphone era. Presley was not that lucky in the timing of his movie career. He came in just as the great days of Hollywood studio filmmaking were winding down, and he hit his speed during the 1960s. Films were large-scale and international; and musicals made money only if they were expensive blockbusters or cheapo teen flicks set on a beach with a blanket and a gaggle of surfboards. Presley, however, made his films work. He starred in thirty-one movies as an actor, all moneymakers. He himself lost patience with these assignments, gained weight, and finally became disillusioned about movie stardom. The public didn't quit him, and neither did the cinema. He quit the cinema, but never quit his public, and they, to this day, have never quit him, either.

Although he was a top-ten box-office draw for seven years, Presley appeared in only a few really good movies. His first, *Love Me Tender* (1956), was one of them. It was a highly credible debut for a performer who most people felt would never be able to act. *Love Me Tender* presented Presley to movie audiences in an unexpected way: as a hot teenager, but not a modern one. The movie was set in the Civil War era. While his older brother (Richard Egan) is away at war, Presley falls in love with his girl (Debra Paget). He sings several songs, among them "Love Me Tender," which is the old song "Aura Lee" with new lyrics. Presley is young and handsome in the 1950s sideburned style, and he looks as if he has the potential to become a real movie personality—sort of a singing Valentino. His second film is also a respectable effort: *Loving You* (1957), the story of a publicist (Lizabeth Scott) and a country-western singer (Wendell Corey) who discover a

Elvis Presley and his guitar in one of his vehicles, *Clambake*

gas-station attendant (Presley) who can sing. Presley was more confident and comfortable than in his first movie, and the critics who had ridiculed the idea of Presley as an actor began to be a bit kinder. His third and fourth movies, *Jailhouse Rock* (1957) and *King Creole* (1958), were emblematic of who he was and what he could do, and the reviewing establishment began to admit that maybe he was going to be good, after all. In *The New York Times*, Howard Thompson threw in the towel after seeing *King Creole*: "As the lad himself might say, cut my legs off and call me Shorty! Elvis Presley can act. . . . Acting is his assignment in this shrewdly upholstered show-case, and he does it." Years later, in 1987, one of his *King Creole* costars, Walter Matthau, said of Presley, "He was an instinctive actor. He was very intelligent. He was not a punk. He was very elegant, sedate, and refined and sophisticated."

In 1958, Presley began serving two years in the army (to fulfill his era's required universal-military-training law) and was unable to make films. He returned in 1960 with two releases, *G.I. Blues* (which was designed to capitalize on his army service) and *Flaming Star*, which is the film that proves Presley could have done more with his movie career had he been allowed. Directed by the masterful Don Siegel, *Flaming Star* presents Presley as a half-breed caught in a war between his parents' peoples. After the first ten minutes, he doesn't sing again. Many critics think *Flaming Star* is Presley's best film, largely because he plays a character other than himself, and the action is not restricted to musical numbers. And this Presley "departure" film was a success.

After *Flaming Star*, however, things quickly go downhill, sliding into a formulaic pattern of songs, girls, locations, and speed, all with titles like *Girls! Girls! Girls!* (1962), *Fun in Acapulco* (1963), and *Kissin' Cousins* (1964), in which Presley plays an army officer and his look-alike bumpkin Tennessee cousin—two Presleys for the price of one! In 1964, he appeared in *Roustabout* (as a guy who joins up with a carnival headed by no less than Barbara Stanwyck) and *Viva Las Vegas* (with Ann-Margret). These are the last two films of his career with any real credibility. Some of the titles of those that followed say it all: *Tickle Me* (1965), *Harum Scarum* (1965), *Girl Happy* (1965, featuring Gary Crosby, Bing's oldest son, as one of Elvis's singing costars), *Clambake* (1967), *Easy Come, Easy Go* (1967), and *Live a Little, Love a Little* (1968). It was one long slide of predictable plots and settings intercut with songs that became hit records until Presley finally walked away. In his final year of feature films, 1969, there were three releases: *Charro, The Trouble with Girls*, and *Change of Habit*. (In 1970 and 1972 he was covered in two documentaries about his touring career, *Elvis: That's the Way It Is* and *Elvis on Tour*.)

Elvis Presley onscreen played a list of similar characters, all of whom combined sex appeal with a fundamental decency and wedded competence with machinery and a desire for speed. Outlaws, gas-station attendants, playboys, criminals, entertainers . . . a half-breed, a GI, a boxing champion, a pilot, a trapeze artist, a race-car driver, a singing cowboy, a helicopter pilot, a riverboat gambler, a frogman, a doctor . . . none of it mattered. It was always Elvis the public wanted, and it was always Elvis they got. Sometimes he played a musical performer; sometimes he did not. Either way, he sang and danced. The concept of explaining why he would break into song and/or dance was totally unnecessary: he came to movies as who he was, needing no establishment, no explanation, and no time wasted. Just bring him on—and that's what these films did. He was the star, and everyone else was shoved to the side.* Three musicals illuminate the Presley film career, and all are star vehicles in the tradition that was conceived and honed in the 1930s Hollywood studio system: *Jailhouse Rock*, his signature film; *Viva Las Vegas*, the most entertaining of his formula films; and *Clambake*, an example of the film formula pit he fell into.

Jailhouse Rock is loved by Presley fans and embraced by people who know nothing about him because it is, in effect, his *Jolson Story*. It is his presumed biography. Jolson's act was cleaned up for his public, eliminating wives and children and a dead mother, but Presley's was dirtied up—times had changed—throwing in a jail sentence and wiping out his loving parents and a world of friends. *Jailhouse Rock*, of course, was never meant to be *The Elvis Presley Story*, but it's the story everyone feels really *is* the story of how an Elvis Presley could emerge. It incorporates his bad-boy image, his rock-and-roll-outlaw self. (Jolson's movie only incorporates his hit parade of songs, which was enough; but Presley's tale is more interpretive, more mythic, partly because it makes no actual claim to being his biography—which it isn't.)

The credits for *Jailhouse Rock* appear atop a charcoal sketch of Presley,

---

* Presley sometimes was paired with a well-established singer, such as Nancy Sinatra at the peak of her white boots fame in *Spinout*; or he might appear with a name-actor near the end of their career, such as Lizabeth Scott or in their older years, such as Barbara Stanwyck, or Angela Lansbury, who played his mother in *Blue Hawaii*, but mostly, an Elvis movie was an Elvis movie.

arty yet earthy. He presents his backside and wears tight pants, his iconic version of the Betty Grable over-the-shoulder pinup of the World War II years. The story is about Vince Everett, a boy who gets into a bar fight and is sent to jail, sentenced to one to ten years on a manslaughter charge. To the public of 1957, this seemed right for Presley. Surely someone who

Presley's most iconic movie image: *Jailhouse Rock*

sang that way, dressed that way, snarled that way—and swung his hips that way—was a jailbird. Where else could such behavior come from? The movie confirmed Presley as an outsider, a rule breaker, and that's certainly what he was in his music and in his unusual looks and clothes. He was like an alien force. That touch of "the other" that he put in the spotlight inspired teenagers everywhere. It was what they wanted to be. It also contains the 1950s inner cry of teenagers, the "Get me out of here" frustration of youth's increasing quarrel with the establishment that would erupt fully in the 1960s.

In *Jailhouse Rock*, Presley is already the classic young version of himself: lots of hair, sideburns, an insolent yet often polite presence. The secret to his success was this naughty-but-nice mixture. He's a jailbird, in on a manslaughter charge, *but* it wasn't his fault. The guy picked a fight with him, and because Presley is so tough, he struck him hard and he just fell backwards and died. (The unfortunate victim had taunted Presley by saying, "Run along, sonny, before I mess up your hair.") Presley handles women both politely (he was defending a barfly when the fight broke out) and roughly (he grabs his leading lady for a romantic clinch and treats her however he wishes.) Presley's costar, Judy Tyler, plays an "exploitation manager" (one of my favorite movie jobs). She helps Presley cut a record, and her sage advice puts him on top ("Put a little fire in it"). Their first love scene takes place on the sidewalk in front of her sedate parents' home, in the dark of night. He's been rude to her family, and she says, "I think I'm gonna just hate you," to which he wisely replies, "No . . . you ain't gonna hate me . . . I ain't gonna *let* you hate me," and sweeps her up into a hot kiss. When she sputters about his "cheap tactics," he gives it to her straight: "That ain't tactics, honey. It's just the beast in me." Audiences loved the beast.

When Presley's character becomes a big success in *Jailhouse Rock*, he turns into what we now know is the full Elvis. He's a surly young man, the musical James Dean. When he sings "Treat Me Nice," he's loose, moving around, snapping his fingers, shifting his legs from side to side, rising up on his toes, shaking his head. "You know I'd be your slave / If you ask me to," he sings, "But if you don't treat me nice / I'll walk right out on you." Loving but dangerous. Willing to do what you want but only on his own terms. All the confusion and contradiction of youth is contained in his image, his movements, and his song lyrics.

The high point of *Jailhouse Rock* is the number always used in clips to define Elvis: the "jailhouse" number. It makes the outlaw element specific, as does the reminder that his character served fourteen months in prison. This number is choreographed, and Presley dances with a team of chorus boys, little mini-Elvises. He showcases his patented style, long hair swept up and back, a bit hanging over his face, his sideburns fully on display. He's the turned-up-collar Elvis who was easily caricatured as six inches of thick black hair on top of a delicate face with a full, sensuous mouth. In many ways, a smaller, simpler number that Presley does in *Jailhouse Rock* is truer to his most common movie presentation. It's just him and a backup group beside a swimming pool. Elvis wears a sweater and sings one of his biggest hits: "Baby I Don't Care." The "Jailhouse Rock" number has become iconic and definitive because in retrospect Presley is seen more as a bad-boy, outlaw type and because the number has the traditional "musical" presentation of "puttin' on a show." Presley is allegedly "dancin' the Jailhouse Rock" in front of TV cameras, and thus he performs within his performance, the layering that musicals thrived on. But Presley movies always depended on something simple and effective: Presley just singing in front of friends, or with little kids, or to himself all alone as he wandered around. Just Presley. Just singing. After all, these movies were designed partly to sell his records, and fans didn't need anything but Elvis in his sweater, with a turned-up collar, going up on his toes, swinging his hips from side to side and snapping his fingers, camera focusing on him in the center of the frame, cutting going from medium long shot (to take in the hips) to close-up (to stress his almost feminine beauty). "He became a heel overnight," his former cellmate says of him, but he's swiftly on his way to becoming a good guy again, because that's Elvis. He gave his audiences everything they wanted of him. *Jailhouse Rock* illustrates how Elvis could and would become a star in carefully designed vehicles. It begins the process of turning his simple songs into fully rehearsed choreography. He becomes more than a singer of hit records: he does numbers, and the basis of his on-screen musical self is defined. *Jailhouse Rock* is truly his signature piece.

Viva Las Vegas is the best template of the Presley formula of songs, speed, sex, and settings. It's the best partly because it paired Presley for really the only time with his female counterpart, the hip-swinging, sexy, hot young singer/dancer Ann-Margret. She had previously made only three films, *Pocketful of Miracles* (1961), a remake of *State Fair* (1962), and the prestigious musical *Bye Bye Birdie* (1963), in which she set the frame on fire as the teenage girl selected to give one last kiss to a rock-and-roll teen idol who is leaving for the armed forces. Ironically, that particular character, Conrad Birdie, is a thinly disguised parody of Elvis himself, inspired by the frenzy set off when he left for his mandatory military training. Ann-Margret stepped up out of a Broadway-derived Elvis satire (*Birdie* was a huge stage hit) to play opposite the real man who had inspired the movie that gave her stardom. *Viva Las Vegas* is an entertaining musical that knows what it's doing with Elvis Presley but, significantly, also knows what it's doing with Ann-Margret. She was the only leading lady he ever had who could match his overt sex appeal.

Ann-Margret throws down the challenge to Presley, and he definitely takes it. She comes right at him with her own brand of sass, and he enjoys it.

(They became real-life lovers and later good friends, and it shows onscreen. They're a trashy, flashy version of Bogart and Bacall.) *Viva Las Vegas* is at a point in Presley's movie career where he can still come alive, and he and Ann-Margret romp all over town. Faster and faster. Hotter and hotter. Wiggle-waggling and swaying and shaking and finally, in one scene, collapsing in laughter together for the sheer silliness of it all. Presley's first film, *Love Me Tender*, shows what he could have been. *Jailhouse Rock* shows exactly who he was; and junk like *Harum Scarum*, *Tickle Me*, and *Clambake* shows what he sadly became. But without *Viva Las Vegas*, the charm of Presley on film cannot be fully understood.

Viva Las Vegas is fun. It shows off the real on-location Las Vegas, the Hoover Dam, and the original casino strip that made the city famous. It's the real/unreal gambling city, the Vegas that defined the concept. Viewers can ogle the Flamingo, the Tropicana, the Sahara, the Desert Inn, the Golden Horseshoe, and the Sands. It's noisy, wild, open, a little low-class, and far more exciting than the upper-middle-class haven it's become. There's no Bellagio with a ritzy spa and an art gallery, no couture shopping, and no pricey restaurants featuring French cuisine. No, sir. It's Las Vegas, baby, and there's tight pants, boat-long cars, hamburgers, and, of course,

Elvis Presley with his female counterpart in on-screen sex, Ann-Margret, out on the town and ready to live it up in *Viva Las Vegas*

Elvis Presley as a race-car driver and Ann-Margret as a pool manager in a flashy hotel decorated in aqua and orange. It's the original Sin City, a chic destination for those with money who are in the know. Elvis's Vegas is a place to boogie.

Clambake was Elvis's twenty-fifth movie in eleven years, one of three released in 1967. Not since the earliest years of cinema had anyone been cranking movies out at that rate. By 1967, when *Clambake* was released, the studio system was really finished, but Elvis would go on after *Clambake* to release another six films. *Clambake*, at number twenty-five in release, very clearly represents the rut that Elvis had been shoved into. Its trailer announces "ELVIS!" and tells audiences that "it's a bikini bake!" "Elvis go-goes on water . . . go-goes wild with bikes," but other cast members are ignored. It's just ELVIS! That was the whole point of his oeuvre.

Presley's movies were, of course, designed to showcase him (and not much else), but they were also viewed by his handler, Colonel Tom Parker, as useful for spurring his record sales. In the trailers for Presley movies, there's always an unusual feature: onscreen, big, colorful letters tell viewers that the songs Presley will sing in the movie are available on RCA Victor Records. In other words, in selling the movie, they are selling the records, and what's surprising is that there's a hint that if the audience doesn't feel like seeing this latest stinker about race drivers or helicopter pilots or whatever, they can skip going and use the money to buy the records of the songs Presley will be singing, since they probably will be the only really good things in the movie. It was a red-flag shout-out that could never have happened in the old days of Hollywood. (Most musical stars were not allowed to have separate recording contracts if they were under contract to the studio itself. Stars like Betty Grable and others never made records. Exceptions were people like Sinatra, Crosby, and Jolson, who had established themselves with lucrative record contracts prior to signing with studios.) The Presley movies were a means to an end: Presley as a recording artist and a live concert performer who packed 'em in. His movies were the icing on the cake. They were also solid business investments. Producer Hal Wallis said, "A Presley picture is the only sure thing in Hollywood."

Clambake has a simple, barely developed plot because it has a simple (and single) purpose: to showcase Elvis Presley. His leading lady is Shelley Fabares, and his arch-rival is Bill Bixby. Both are television faces to attract a young crowd; and for the older audience there's Gary Merrill, standing around with a pipe in his mouth, and James Gregory, standing around with a cigar in his. Pipe and cigar define their characters: kindly and philosophical boat owner who will support Elvis's desire to do something on his own (pipe), and Elvis's father, a loudmouthed, hard-driving oil tycoon (cigar, extra long). Elvis is given a romance and a rival and a comic pal (Will Hutchins). And, of course, there are a bunch of others: young women in bikinis and a playground full of kids (who are there so he can do a number called "Confidence").

Clambake demonstrates that no one cared very much about quality in these movies. Within its opening few minutes, Elvis is established as rich, dissatisfied with his idle life, and in conflict with his father. At a gas station, he changes places with a cyclist who is on his way to a water-ski instructor's job at a Miami hotel. He sings "Who Needs Money?" as he cycles (and his "other" drives his red convertible) to Miami, passing plenty of Florida scenery on the way. Minutes! In only a few, the movie has clearly, almost carelessly, presented plot, conflict, music, and scenery. The Presley formula is in place. The plot is very similar to part of *Viva Las Vegas!*, but there's no Ann-Margret (Fabares doesn't sing or dance). Instead of Las Vegas, there's Miami Beach, but there's less commitment to selling it. The Presley formula presents Elvis as a good guy who is smart and likes to win, who will be misunderstood by the girl, supported by an older male, and who will successfully remodel a racing machine (in this case a boat) and win a big race. Along the way, he'll sing and dance a little in two numbers, wander around alone at night singing romantic songs, and deliver the title tune (over the credits as well as in the film itself).

Like all of Presley's lighter musicals, *Clambake* is cheerful, fast-paced, rhythmic, but its comedy is weak, its plot is nil, and its conclusion foregone. The songs are not good songs, but Elvis gives them all he's got. He's already beginning to thicken up slightly, but even if his waistline has expanded, he still looks good. He knows what is required of him. Nobody in this movie is unprofessional, but the whole thing feels slightly uncommitted. There's no moment that gives an audience Elvis's old spark. "C'mere," he commands Fabares, who is holding a rose and preparing to leave his presence. She obediently comes to him. He takes the rose and tosses it, gives her a Kleenex, and commands, "Blot!" She removes her lipstick accordingly, and he pulls all the pins out of her upswept hair. The audience awaits the hot kiss, but nothing happens. She just leaves, and then Elvis sings a plaintive "You Don't Know Me." What happened to the beast in him? The fire he had for doing these movies has clearly gone out, and the studio feels no need to rekindle it. Movies like *Clambake* have decided it doesn't matter. Nothing matters. Whatever Elvis's character needs magically appears: money, a job, a boat to drive in the race, a scientific lab for him to prepare his "goop" (that's what it's actually called), which is an invention to strengthen the boat hull. Everyone drinks from the Fountain of Presley. Presley himself, however, was becoming increasingly bored making these foolish movies, which were much more fun in the beginning, mostly because he found it fun to do them.

Presley never made much effort to explain why he was always the star, had to be the star. Sounding a bit like Bing Crosby, he once explained his appeal by simply saying, "Some people tap their feet. Some people snap their fingers, and some people sway back and forth. I just sorta do 'em all together, I guess." However, what other performers had to say about Presley is an amazing list of accolades from all kinds of people. Leonard Bernstein said, "Elvis is the greatest cultural force in the twentieth century. He introduced the beat in everything: music, language, clothes, it's a whole new social revolution . . . the sixties comes from it." John Lennon said, "Before Elvis, there was nothing," and Carl Perkins, a contemporary who worked with Elvis, said, "This boy had everything. He had the looks, the moves, the manager, and the talent. And he didn't look like Mr. Ed like a lot of us did. In the way he looked, way he talked, way he acted—he really was different." Eddie Murphy said, "He had such presence. When Elvis walked into a room, Elvis Presley was in the fucking room. I don't give a fuck who was in the room with him, Bogart, Marilyn Monroe." Dick Clark put it in more sedate terms: "It's rare when an artist can touch an entire generation of people. It's even rarer when that same influence affects several generations. Elvis made an imprint on the world of pop music unequaled by any other single performer." Phil Spector put the final spin on what everyone else was saying with eloquent simplicity: "You have no idea how great he is, really you don't. You have no comprehension. It's absolutely impossible. I can't tell you why he's so great, but he is. He's sensational."

As someone who was there as a teenager when Presley first hit the airwaves with "Heartbreak Hotel," I can attest to his impact. Elvis Presley was the guy we were all looking for: a bad, bad boy . . . only not really. And he gets rich. Perfect! Presley was young and Valentino-like handsome. He didn't follow style; he *set* style. His sideburns, tight pants, longish hair, and brightly colored outfits—not to mention his later glitter and sparkle—set a trend that changed fashion and inspired imitators. Presley didn't need to smoke a cigar or a pipe as a trademark. He was smokin' hot.

Jolson, Crosby, and Presley shared something indefinable, and not just the magic of their unique talents and personalities. On film, each managed to inject just a touch of irony into his performances. Each had a way of suggesting to audiences that movie watching was a partnership in a conspiracy of believable/unbelievable nonsense. "I'll sing for you," each of them seemed to say, "and I'll act this stuff out, but you and I know it's all just a wee bit silly." Jolson, Crosby, and Presley were great offscreen, on records, and on TV, and their movie performances demonstrate the conspiracy approach that many great film stars projected. It's the "You know what I'm thinking" relationship that makes viewers feel connected, feel elevated and respected, and feel deeply entertained and, yes, even loved, that makes the great movie star. Jolson, Crosby, and Presley all managed this, each in his own way. Jolson ad-libbed, looked directly into the camera, and was often self-referential in his repeated tag lines, such as "You ain't heard nothin' yet." Crosby also ad-libbed. He kept just outside the boundaries any film set up, and often undercut seriousness with a casual shrug or eyebrow lift. He riffed lyrics under the main thread. Presley let himself be his own critic of whatever he was in the midst of: if it was fun, he had fun and showed it; if it stunk, he walked through it and made no effort. About his own image, he was always amused; his tongue-in-cheek presentation of himself, which had conviction even as it had humor, was one of his greatest assets. Presley was both accessible and mysterious. He was the modern version of Jolson and Crosby, but he was used to define a star musical in exactly the same way as they had been.

The creation of the musical star vehicle was not an exclusive movie phenomenon—Gertrude Lawrence, Ethel Merman, and Maurice Chevalier had whole shows written for or shaped to their unique gifts (as had nonmusical theatrical performers). But the movie version was an important step in the history of musicals, as it linked the genre to the business's plan of creating stars for profit. The knowledge that the star system would work with musical performers helped ensure the future—and the longevity—and the profitability—of the format: musicals could be locked down as a formula with a set of guidelines to follow. It also helped the business understand what it had in the musical film: how it was the same as all other movies, but how it was also different. Jolson, Crosby, and Presley—and the stories of their musical careers—illustrate the emergence of the star vehicle, the securing of the star vehicle, and the reproduction of the star vehicle. Each man's career in movies is part of that three-part understanding.

Al Jolson's impact on the movie musical is primary. Not only is he the man most people think defined the format with *The Jazz Singer*, but he is actually the man who defined the musical star vehicle with his powerful personality. With Jolson, the motion-picture business learned that it could buy a solidly established musical performer, famous for a style of singing and for a set of familiar songs, and use his established personality in the movies. The name would draw; the definition was already in place. All that had to happen was finding a story that fit what was already known. The Al Jolson movie only had to have Al Jolson, and all he had to do was sing his stuff. His movies would need no additional musical performers (competition) and no characterization for him since he brought his own. He could ad-lib all he wanted, and if he needed room for sentimentality (dead child, broken marriage) so he could sing one of his sad songs, that would be okay, too. Because Jolson was a very *now* kind of performer—immediacy was his thing—his films could have modern settings and stay close to the theater or nightclub world (which saved money). An Al Jolson star vehicle would be all about him as the public understood him, and yet, unique as he was, the Al Jolson movie could be used as a template for any similar dominant personality.

The Bing Crosby model grew organically out of his singing style. No prior personality for him was known to the audience when Crosby was first developed. All anyone knew was the sound of his voice, so a valuable lesson was learned: a musical star could be shaped out of music that people had only heard (Crosby's radio success). Because he was a voice first and an image later, Crosby's on-film world could be a world of other people. His star vehicles could contain comedy and romance, because he represented an actual person, not a powerful Broadway star who was iconic before he started in movies. Crosby could be real, and the star vehicle presented him that way. The story could be found in his voice. Bing Crosby, the only one of the three men who became an old-fashioned style of Hollywood movie star and was thought of as such, offered the truest, most reliable template for the star vehicle: a singer/actor with a persona that audiences would believe in and return over and over again to see in any story.

Elvis Presley's movie career is the one that confirms the concept of star vehicle and uses it. In his era, the idea of a "movie star" was no longer the thing it had once been. Moviegoers were no longer naive, buying fan magazines for fantasy stories about their idols. They bought the tabloids and read about clay feet. All Presley had to do was step up into the vehicle—now a hollow shell—and ride it. It no longer mattered what the business wanted to do with him. He came to movies a ready-made package to be put on the sales shelf. All movies had to do was let Presley be Presley; he was an amalgam of the Jolson idea and the Crosby phenomenon. The star vehicle was still usable, but it no longer mattered in the same way. With Presley, it was all just "Let's rock-and-roll."

Merman and Martin, Day and Durbin

There's always a mystery surrounding any kind of stardom. The public could be unpredictable in whom they would embrace, and talent and beauty—presumably the two prerequisites for the motion picture—were not always validated by the public. Great stage actors such as Katherine Cornell, Tallulah Bankhead, and Lunt and Fontanne could not become movie stars. Great beauties such as Gwili Andre and Elissa Landi and Anna Sten and handsome men such as Alan Marshal and John Carroll and Hurd Hatfield didn't make it to the top. When it came to musical ability, stardom was more predictable, because it was difficult to make a musical star out of someone who couldn't sing or dance. (The phenomenon of the nonsinger, nondancer in a musical would have to wait for the modern era.)

But there's a subtle quality to the issue, which is the problem of defining stardom: what is it anyway? We assume stars of musicals are successful because of their ability to sing and dance well, but do we value a western star because of the way he sits on a horse or ropes a steer? Hollywood was especially shrewd at developing female musical stars out of women with some glamour, a good work ethic, and no particular musical talent. Dubbing singing and doubling dancing (in long shots) was doable. But when there was real talent, then real effort was made by the studios. They taught women how to be both stunning *and* musical at a very high level. Two big-name female stars (primarily in television), but who also appeared successfully in musical movies, can be compared in order to see what Hollywood taught: Lucille Ball and Carol Burnett. They are more than a generation apart in age. Ball began her career in the studio system of 1930s Hollywood, and Burnett began her career on the stage in 1950s New York. But Ball, well taught by the old system, was still a star when Burnett had her own musical variety show on television. The two women admired each other and became friends. In a 1969 episode of Ball's *Here's Lucy*, an excuse to do a musical show and have Burnett as a guest star was invented. Lucy's own children (who appeared in her show) go to a school that needs a new gym, and they will "put on a show" à la Mickey and Judy and con Burnett into appearing in order to raise money.

This lame premise, old even in the 1940s, allows the two pros, Lucy and Carol, to perform an extended musical number together. It contains the songs "Lullaby of Broadway," "You've Come a Long Way from St. Louis," "Mention My Name in Sheboygan," etc. Burnett is superconfident and multitalented, but she's a performer, whereas Lucille Ball is a *star*. Ball works *with* Burnett but nevertheless gives a little flip of her hair, adds a little moxie to her prance, and manages to grab the eye away from her partner. And she holds on to it. Burnett pumps it up and out, delightfully so, but Ball takes it easy and goes small—the very definition of movie stardom. (Don't compete. Just control the eye.) Ball had the benefit of years of movie training to prepare her how to stay alive in the frame and seem natural, never belting her vocals or pushing her dance kicks too hard. She had been shown how to be a musical star on film. This is no knock on the immensely talented Burnett, a major talent. It's an explanation of Hollywood musical vehicular stardom. Talent could be enhanced, guided, even invented.

It's a curious issue, however, that when it came to females in musicals, beauty was more of an issue than good looks were for a male. Men who were not "lookers" became musical stars (Donald O'Connor, Red Skelton, Danny Kaye, including even, as some claim, Fred Astaire) because they *could* sing and dance, but that was not as true for women.* On the contrary, if a woman was beautiful, alluring, and sexy, but possessed only modest musical skills, she was likely to be developed for musicals or at least tried out in the genre. Exceptionally beautiful women who became popular with audiences could be cast in musicals: Lana Turner and Janet Leigh, for example. Neither was an originally trained performer, but both were taught basic dancing at MGM and, after they were established, appeared in a few musicals. There were also female musical stars who rose up in movies largely because of their looks, even if they had talent. Rita Hayworth, unquestionably a capable dancer, could not sing and had to be dubbed. Vera-Ellen and Cyd Charisse did not sing and were limited in performance range. These women became successful musical stars anyway. Women like Hayworth had musical vehicles created for them, but Vera-Ellen and

---

* In fact, many handsome men were starred in musicals (George Montgomery, Tyrone Power), and no attempt was made to pretend they were musical. Their roles did not require them to sing or dance.

Charisse were partnered with bigger-name stars and did not define their films.

Great Broadway singing stars seldom became famous movie stars (with Julie Andrews a notable exception). Men like Alfred Drake, John Raitt, Harve Presnell, and Ezio Pinza didn't translate well from stage to screen. Women who had supporting roles onstage (Betty Hutton, June Allyson) moved upward into the movies; understudies (Shirley MacLaine) were discovered and hired by studios; women who replaced original stars for the road shows could succeed (Irene Dunne in *Show Boat*); and women who went to Hollywood to reprise their own famous roles (Barbra Streisand in *Funny Girl*) could remain; but in general, Broadway singing stardom and movie singing stardom were different. Broadway was always about the music, the song itself, and Hollywood was always about the star personality. A Broadway performer *had* to be able to sing—night after night, show after show, getting through the number on pitch in front of a packed house. When the movies made a musical, the creating of the number involved multiple takes, dubbing, and a final edit to select the best moments of the performance and cut them together. Not only was the creative process totally different—live vs. filmed—but the audience relationship was different. On Broadway, the audience listened to the singer—who was sometimes very far away—and the music and the song were what mattered (which, of course, included the quality of the voice). In the movies, empathy between the star and the viewer was everything. The singer was brought up close, and the song became personal. The song matters in both cases, as does the musical talent, but it's the balance between the importance of the voice and the importance of the personality that defines the relationship between the listener/viewer in theater audiences and film audiences. This inevitably meant that the looks of the musical performer—the way he or she photographs—was very important in movies.

There were five great singers of the 1920s–1940s era who were women with real personalities and highly original style, but who were not beautiful: Sophie Tucker, Fannie Brice, Martha Raye, Ethel Merman, and Mae West.*

---

* England produced a popular singer who wasn't beautiful, either, but who had a terrific soprano voice: Gracie Fields, known affectionately as "our Grace." She was a good actress and a highly successful comedienne, a top box-office draw in England in the 1930s, and also the decade's highest-paid female star. She appeared in musicals like *Sing As We Go* (1934), *Sally in Our Alley* (1931), and *Look Up and Laugh* (1935). Her working-class persona endeared her to the British. When she agreed to star in some Hollywood films, they weren't musicals, and she insisted they be shot in England: *Molly and Me* (1945), and *Holy Matrimony* (1943).

All five made movies, but only Mae West became a real leading-lady-type movie star. All five of them did comedy as part of their personae, since the tradition in America for the nonbeautiful female lead or supporting actress was the need to be funny as compensation. Each of these women compensated in her own way. Tucker apparently didn't give a darn. She brought an amalgamation of American singing styles—jazz, blues, Yiddish—and perfect comedy timing to her performances. She crossed ethnic borders and put it all together with the zing of the melting pot. She was the Last of the Red Hot Mamas. Who needed beauty? Brice presented herself as if she were beautiful, except when she felt like presenting herself as childlike or a comic version of a woman who wanted to be beautiful. Brice had talent to burn, so she took control of her own image and worked the way she wanted to in whatever medium she felt like taking on. Mae West was a better-looking version of Sophie Tucker: slimmer, younger, sexier; she made jokes about men's attitudes toward women. She usurped male power for herself. There would be plenty of sex, but she'd decide who and when and why, and the why might be diamonds or it might be pleasure. Either way was a good time for Mae. Her singing ability was the least of the five, but it was distinctive, and her ear for a song's subtext was impeccable. When she droned out "Easy Rider" or "Frankie and Johnny" or "I'm an Occidental Woman in an Oriental Mood for Love," she made it a come-on—but always a come-on of the sort that allowed her to mutter under her breath her famous putdown as she paraded down a runway in *I'm No Angel* to the catcalls of panting males: "Suckers!" West was fabulous, but she made only eleven movies, even though she beat the odds.

Martha Raye is the closest competition to West for being thought of as an actual movie star; she was also a success in almost any performing arena she tried, including vaudeville, stage, film and TV, nightclubs, recordings, and, later in life, as a "female Bob Hope" who entertained overseas troops. (If she had tried, no doubt she'd have been a major force in rodeo clowns.) Raye was a Butte, Montana, girl, born to vaudevillians who put her on the stage as soon as she could do anything to enhance the show. By her teenage years, she was a real trouper and knew almost no other life. (It was said she had so little schooling that her scripts had to be read to her.) While appearing on Broadway in *Calling All Stars* (1934), she was spotted by Hollywood talent scouts and brought to California, where she made her film debut in a musical short entitled *A Nite in the Nite Club*. Her feature film debut came two years later, in 1936, but at the top of the heap, cast in the Bing Crosby vehicle *Rhythm on the Range*. She wasn't Bing's leading lady—that was the beautiful Frances Farmer. Raye was the comic relief, and *Variety* reviewed her by saying she was "a female Joe. E. Brown" (a big-mouthed comic of the day) but that "with material and handling she should go far." Her big moment came when she sang what would become a defining number for her all her life, the comic "Mr. Paganini."

Raye had two major assets: a powerful, beautiful singing voice, and a set of broad comedy skills that matched her looks. She was a tiny woman, but she had a big mouth, long, skinny legs, and big boobs. (Her private life was pretty outsized, too. She married seven times, won the Jean Hersholt Humanitarian Award, and was awarded the Presidential Medal of Freedom for her service to the military.) Raye's looks caused her to be labeled by Hollywood as a clown as much as a singer. She accepted that definition and adopted a comic stance. She'd bug her eyes, stick her elbows up, and teeter back and forth on very high heels, turning her knees outward

in order to look gawky and ridiculous. She was willing to purposely over-act and do any sort of comic pratfall, but when she sang, she really sang. She had a full, rich voice and a distinctive way with a lyric. From 1936 to 1944, she made twenty-two feature films with such costars as Betty Grable, Bing Crosby, and Bob Hope. In 1947, Charlie Chaplin personally chose her to star with him in *Monsieur Verdoux*, his black comedy about a man who kills his wives for their money. (He knew what he was doing. The Raye episode is the highlight of his film.) Raye worked all her life, returning to the screen in 1962 to costar with Doris Day and Jimmy Durante in *Billy Rose's Jumbo*. Although at that time she'd been off the screen for fifteen years, she was still funny, dynamic, a distinctive comic . . . and a great singer.

Three female singers who never found top movie stardom were Martha Raye, kickin' her heels up in *Keep 'Em Flying* . . .

Merman

Ethel Merman was the true star of the pack. She was always a great singer, and when she was onstage in *Gypsy*, in 1959, she showed audiences that she could act a complex role, too. She didn't try to mess about with a song: she stood up straight and hurled it out there as if she were throwing a 100-mph fastball. Every word of the lyrics was crisp and clear and audible to the very back row. No words were slurred; nothing got lost across the rows. The common description of Merman's singing is "belting." She "belted" it out of the park, and for this reason, the most common opinion about Merman as a movie star is the simple idea that she was too big for the screen, too loud, too brassy. Watching Merman in a movie, however, presents a slightly different impression. She's big and brassy and loud, all right, but she has an inherent glamour that is seldom remarked on.

Ethel Merman, a secretary by trade (and by all accounts a darned good one), started performing at private parties in the mid-twenties and then began appearing in nightclubs. When a Warner Bros. agent heard her sing, he helped obtain an exclusive six-month contract at the studio for her, but her first full-length movie was for Paramount: *Follow the Leader* (1930). Since her movie contract allowed her to continue appearing in clubs between assignments, she accepted a gig at the Palace in New York and was invited to audition for a role in the new Gershwin musical, *Girl Crazy*. She was hired immediately when the Gershwins heard her sing "I Got Rhythm," and she began rehearsing during the day for the Broadway show while still performing at night at the Palace. When *Girl Crazy* opened in October of 1930, she was an instant hit because of her peppy personality and her amazing lung power. It was that ability to hit the people in the back row that kept her on Broadway, and after *Girl Crazy* closed, she appeared in such hits as *George White's Scandals* and *Take a Chance*, to great success.

Hollywood had kept her on its radar, and in 1934 she returned to Paramount to appear in a Bing Crosby musical, *We're Not Dressing*. Based on J. M. Barrie's famous play *The Admirable Crichton*, the movie was a screwball comedy that enjoys a cult reputation today. Its cast is an amazing lineup of now-legendary performers: in addition to Crosby and Merman, it features the youthful and beautiful Carole Lombard and the comedy team of Burns and Allen. The young Merman is cute, bouncy, and a dominant personality. She's fresh and confident and a good comedienne. Nevertheless, it's clear that because she wasn't conventionally beautiful, Hollywood wasn't quite sure who she should be onscreen.

Merman was next cast with another great musical star, Eddie Cantor, in 1934's *Kid Millions*. In one of those Hollywood decisions that make everyone think the place was run by madmen, Merman plays Eddie Cantor's mother (he was seventeen years older), but she does get a great song, Irving Berlin's "An Earful of Music," and she appears in the grand finale, a visual Technicolor fantasy inside an ice cream factory. (The rest of the film was in black-and-white.) She was cast with Cantor again in 1936 in *Strike Me Pink*. Her appearance in the movie is surprising today, as she is presented

as a torch singer, wearing glamorous clothes and photographed in intense close-ups. (Merman had always done torch songs in her nightclub acts. It was *Girl Crazy* that brought her fame as a belter.) Modern audiences are often astonished to come across Merman playing a nightclub singer named Joyce Lennox. It's not the nightclub singing that amazes, but the kind of singer she represents. It's her first real appearance in the movie, and she sings a torch song, "First you have me high, then you have me low." The voice is strong, the diction is clear, and the full mezzo-soprano tone that booms out is pure Merman, but the look is something else. Merman is wearing a black dress with a deep, square neck, a black tam adorned by a diamond clip, and a big diamond bracelet. She's shot in noirish lighting against

. . . the young and attractive Ethel Merman, singing with *Alexander's Ragtime Band,* led by Tyrone Power . . .

a black background, and she's seen mostly in an intense close-up that, as her brassy voice is heard, presents her, eyebrows plucked in a thin 1930s line, as a figure of great glamour and chic. She is lit for beauty, dressed for fashion, and positioned under a lone streetlight. Even though it's not how modern audiences think of Merman, she was good-looking enough—and with a good figure as a young woman—that the idea of her as a glamorous chanteuse was not a crazy one. What was going to define Merman in the long run, however, would not be what an audience was looking at, but what they were hearing. What a voice! She blasts off the screen, and in that sense, she definitely is too big for the frame.

There's something inexplicable about Ethel Merman. I saw her onstage in *Gypsy* and she was beyond terrific; she was epic. She filled the theater, and by that I don't mean her big voice reached out to the back rows. That's a given. It was that she *filled* the theater: from the back of the house to the back of the offstage area, ceiling to floor, row by row, seat by seat, customer by customer, she occupied every inch of space. That's an experience that movies cannot duplicate. On film, Merman didn't fill the entire frame. Instead, she nailed down her spot, feet firmly planted in what would become a familiar stance in which she bent her elbows, held her arms straight out in front of her, and rocked them backwards, elbows going up, then back down, and then arms forward again. Merman rocked. The movies captured how she was filled with song when she sang. When she started singing in movies, that was all she was going to do, sing it out, full of rhythm and making the song the most important thing for her and, by extension, for the audience. She was better at presenting a character in movies than she's given credit for, but mostly she seemed unconcerned about "acting." She wanted to sing. That, she knew, was her ace in the hole.

Merman was always determined, yet matter-of-fact about her success. She figured, why wouldn't she be a success? Who could hit it out of the theater the way she could? She wasn't particularly thrilled with her film career at the end of 1934, so when she was offered the starring role in Cole Porter's *Anything Goes* on Broadway, she agreed to play the signature role of Reno Sweeney, which became the final definition of her persona. It was the first of five Porter shows she would star in, and its score gave her great songs: "I Get a Kick out of You," "You're The Top," "Blow, Gabriel, Blow," and the title song. When the movie version was cast, Merman was signed for the role she had originated, but the movie focused mostly on Bing Crosby. It was a Paramount film, and Crosby had become a major star for the studio. One reviewer sounded a warning note, saying that Merman didn't come across "on screen as magnificently as she does on stage." This became the easy explanation of why Merman never became a real movie star, but it's perhaps more true that her sensational stage career intercut her movie appearances, drawing her away and locking her into the other medium. Following the movie of *Anything Goes*, Merman returned to the stage for another Porter hit, *Red, Hot and Blue*, after which she bounded back to California to make two more movies. One was a Sonja Henie starring vehicle, *Happy Landing* (1938), and the other was the legendary *Alexander's Ragtime Band* (also 1938).

Merman can be seen at her best as a young woman in *Alexander*, one of the top box-office draws of the year. It is an example of a foolproof movie in the most simpleminded way possible: twenty-nine Irving Berlin songs, a minimum of plot, and song after song performed by a high level of talent. *Alexander* is movie-musical formula, but not easy to do, because it relies on something elusive: solid talent and star power. It's got Irving Berlin's songs . . . and 20th Century–Fox's Murderer's Row of box-office star names. The female singers are Merman and the lovely Alice Faye, plus two of the handsomest leading men of the era, Tyrone Power and the musical Don Ameche, supported by a cast of character actors and specialty performers including Jean Hersholt, Jack Haley, Helen Westley, Paul Hurst, Dixie Dunbar, Ruth Terry, John Carradine, and Chick Chandler.

Merman is at ease amidst the starry lineup. She doesn't appear in the film until it's half underway, but she enters looking bright and sassy. Power is told he ought to hire her for his band because "when she sings, it'll probably knock you out." Merman does a few bars of two standards, "Say It with Music" and "A Pretty Girl Is Like a Melody." She performs four big numbers with singer/dancers behind her: "My Walking Stick," "Everybody Step," "Pack Up Your Sins and Go to the Devil," and "Heat Wave." She also stands up and sings "Blue Skies" at a party; and one number that was shot and recorded for her was deleted before release, "Marching Along Through Time."*

Merman is pretty, and she has a great figure. She photographs well from the front, but not as well in profile. She's at ease, delivers her lines with punch but doesn't overact. She's got spark and life inside her, and when

---

* Two other numbers were also cut: Don Ameche singing "Some Sunny Day" and Jack Haley doing "In My House" with Wally Vernon and Chick Chandler.

she sings she's dynamite, as she always was. But she doesn't really seem to care, and what she has, despite her great voice, was available in lots of other energetic, pretty young girls. In contrast to Alice Faye, Merman didn't look like star material to Fox. Faye is a movie personality, giving off a haunting quality, an unusually melancholy air for a central figure in a musical plot. As many have said about her, Faye seems vulnerable, and that, combined with her own unique singing voice, made her the movie star Merman never became. (Faye is discussed in "Studio Styles.") Nevertheless, Merman's a well-cast contrast to Faye, brunette to blonde, hard to soft, and she performs (and acts) with an engaging style. She looks cute and has a charismatic energy. Had she been an ordinary musical performer, she could perhaps have become a successful sidekick or a second-lead movie star, but before the release of the hit *Alexander's Ragtime Band*, Merman had left Hollywood for another foray into Broadway-show hits.

Merman's movie career was not a failure. It can be divided into two sections: the years of her youthful success, in which she made nine feature films, lasting from 1930 to 1940, and the latter years, in which she had become the famous stage queen and award winner Ethel Merman of Broadway and was invited to return to California. During that time frame she appeared in two 1950s successes: the role she originated in *Call Me Madam* (1953) and a show-business family story, *There's No Business Like Show Business*, in 1954.* In between these two periods, the thirties and the fifties, she became the Amazon Queen of the Broadway musical.

Merman was never really happy with the way her films turned out, but she appeared in some very big hits and always nailed her part. No one could upstage her, not even Bing Crosby, the very handsome Tyrone Power, the lovely Alice Faye, the ice-skating sensation Sonja Henie, or the eyeball-rolling Eddie Cantor. When Merman was on, Merman was on. Her impact, however, was not like Jolson's: on film, she held herself in a kind of reserve and let her voice do all the work for her. Celluloid diminished her power to reach out and grab a live audience by the throat, but it didn't diminish her personality or her ability to sing like nobody else. Merman on film—what she was and what she could have been—is not on the same

---

* After that, she did comedy roles in five movies across three decades: *It's a Mad, Mad, Mad, Mad World* (1963), *The Art of Love* (1965), *Journey Back to Oz* (1974), *Won Ton Ton, the Dog Who Saved Hollywood* (1976), and *Airplane!* (1980). (She also appeared as herself in the patriotic *Stage Door Canteen* in 1943.)

level of disappointment as the attempted movie career of her contemporary Mary Martin. It's a curious thing that two women who became legends on Broadway could never become stars in musical films. The movie business really worked hard to turn Martin into a star in a concentrated effort during the late 1930s and early 1940s, and then just gave up. Since stardom was apparently the only goal either she or her studio bosses wanted, Martin bolted.

Martin

The strange case of Mary Martin proves that musical stardom is linked to elements of personality that *must* be seen onscreen or no real movie career can emerge. Those who saw Martin onstage speak of her effervescence and her audience appeal. Martin made stage history with her breakthrough performance in *Leave It to Me!* in 1938. She did a sizzling pseudo striptease at an allegedly Siberian railroad station, singing to a chorus of male dancers (one of whom was Gene Kelly) the provocative lyrics to "My Heart Belongs to Daddy." She went on to such triumphs as the lead in *One Touch of Venus* (1943), *Lute Song* (1946), *South Pacific* (1949), *The Sound of Music* (1959), and *I Do! I Do!* (1966). Either *South Pacific* or

. . . and Mary Martin, whose heart belongs to daddy in the Cole Porter biopic *Night and Day*, where she recreates the number that made her a Broadway star

The Sound of Music alone would have ensured her legend. She was also a resounding success in the medium of television, with her repeated performances as *Peter Pan* (the first on stage in 1954, and then for TV in 1955, '56, and '60) and on June 15, 1953, Ford's fiftieth anniversary show, performing a thirteen-minute duet medley with Ethel Merman. And yet, Mary Martin, a legend in her own time, was a flop in the movies.

Sometimes an explanation for why someone doesn't become a star can be found in a single photograph. Mary Martin appears on the cover of *Hollywood* magazine in June of 1942. Right away, it's obvious she's not really cover-girl material; she's no Hedy Lamarr or Lana Turner or Ingrid Bergman. Every attempt, however, has been made to glamorize her for the photo. Her mouth is garishly red, red, red. She has bare shoulders, long, dark-pink gloves, diamond earrings, and masses of coiffed and rolled hair stuck under a large black hat adorned with a massive light-pink cabbage rose festooned with green leaves and stems. Her gloved hands are resting on her chin, and she's really reaching for a sultry look. Her eyelids are drooping in what is meant to be a bedroomy manner. Inside the magazine however, an article tells readers that Martin "considers her most important job being a mother." Who *is* this person? The cover photo reveals the problem: Hollywood didn't know what to do with her.

But the film business believed in Mary Martin's talent, and did everything it could to make her a star, which proves that shaping a movie to fit the personality can only work if there is a specific and clear personality to shape, one that audiences can see and believe in. Martin, who looked a good deal like the sublime comedienne and actress Jean Arthur, could not make a distinctive mark for herself in movie musicals. Her natural Texas effervescence didn't come across on the screen. She began with a quick bit in *The Rage of Paris*, provided the vocals for Margaret Sullavan in *The Shopworn Angel*, and dubbed for Gypsy Rose Lee in *The Battle of Broadway*, all in 1938. This debut year went well enough that the business began to work with her, featuring her in a series of films onward to 1946.*

Martin's film career is an example of never finding the way to present a musical performer in a specific kind of story that works. First she was cast in *The Great Victor Herbert* (1938) as half of a bland young couple who sing Herbert's songs. She then appeared opposite Bing Crosby (a high-profile showcase for her, a maximal opportunity to become a success) in *Rhythm on the River* (1940), then opposite Jack Benny in *Love Thy Neighbor* (also in 1940), then again with Crosby in *Birth of the Blues* (1941). Also in 1941, she was given a plum role as the lead in *Kiss the Boys Goodbye*. Every effort was made to showcase, including a nice comedy role in *New York Town* (1941) and her own spot in the patriotic all-star *Star Spangled Rhythm* in 1942. She

---

* She made one additional film appearance, in 1953's *Main Street to Broadway*, in a cameo as herself, one of several big-name Broadway stars, such as Ethel and Lionel Barrymore, Shirley Booth, Rex Harrison, Lilli Palmer, Helen Hayes, Henry Fonda, and Tallulah Bankhead.

was then off the screen until 1943, when she appeared in *Happy Go Lucky* and *True to Life*, a comedy with songs. She finished out her movie career playing herself in *Night and Day* (1946).*

Studying Martin's film debacle is revealing. Opposite Crosby in *Rhythm on the River*, she can't find her groove, and Crosby, relaxed and easy, wipes her off the screen. *Birth of the Blues* has the kind of songs Crosby loved to sing ("My Melancholy Baby" and "St. James Infirmary" and the title tune), and the film is another of his personal star vehicles. Martin has little room to claim her own territory, and she's lost in the mix. *Love Thy Neighbor* moved her away from the Crosby threat, but paired her with Jack Benny *and* Fred Allen, two guys who, in their quest to outdo each other, also left little room for anyone else. The story caters to the idea that they are having a famous radio feud, which means they are front and center. Martin is better in this film, but she cannot steal the frame away from Benny and Allen (as well as Eddie "Rochester" Anderson, Verree Teasdale, and Virginia Dale). By the time she arrives at *Happy Go Lucky*, her name did not mean anything to moviegoers because she hadn't established herself. The film is her first in color, and she's perky and charming; but again, she's playing opposite established personalities: Dick Powell, Eddie Bracken, and Rudy Vallee. What's even more horrible for her, the female-sidekick role is eaten up by Betty Hutton, who performs the slangy comedy song "Murder, He Says." Hutton has the distinctive personality that movie musicals crave. Stories can be built around her crazy behavior and her wild, over-the-top-musical performances that are unlike those created by any other female musical stars. In *Happy Go Lucky*, it is easy to see why Mary Martin did not become a star in films. She has no in-the-frame definition. She can't compete with someone like Hutton, who owns the movie space. There was a word used to define the emergence of a star—the player was said to "register." It meant hit the cash register, but it also meant to imprint the self on the minds of the viewers. Mary Martin, on film, did not register. Was this because she looked like another already famous star (Arthur)? Was this because she wasn't given good enough material? The mystery of stardom in the movies is the

---

* In *Night and Day*, in her one number, Martin comes into her own, because what she comes into *is* her own: she performs her showstopping "My Heart Belongs to Daddy," and finally moviegoers can see why she became a star. But she's not carrying the picture, and the number is an out-of-context "and then he wrote" number from the autobiography of Cole Porter. And Cary Grant plays Porter. Again, it's not Martin's show. Grant eclipses her without doing anything—something he could not do with a singer he'd play opposite two decades later, a blonde from Ohio.

mystery of stardom in the movies. Film was not Mary Martin's medium. As it turned out, she didn't need it.

Day

While Mary Martin was trying hard but not succeeding in the movies, and Ethel Merman had returned to Broadway, Doris Day, née Doris Kappelhoff from Cincinnati, Ohio, was becoming a successful band singer, with one really big hit under her belt: her 1945 recording of "Sentimental Journey" with Les Brown's band. (It's a classic, still great.) Day's life story and her climb to fame have been well documented in two excellent books, Tom Santopietro's *Considering Doris Day* and David Kaufman's *Doris Day: The Untold Story of the Girl Next Door*. As Santopietro points out, the stories about how a star of Day's magnitude are found vary according to the teller. What matters regarding the history of musicals is that in 1947, Warner Bros. was looking for someone, preferably a bouncy blonde, to play the lead in a new musical they were planning. Opinions vary, but most historians think Warners wanted Betty Hutton for the role. Hutton was the bounciest of the bouncy, and she, too, had a successful recording in 1944 ("It Had to Be You," number 5 on the charts); but she was under contract to Paramount and negotiations didn't work. However it happened, Day was ultimately signed for the part in the movie that was titled *Romance on the High Seas* and released in 1948. It would be her first movie, her introduction to the public as a singing personality on film. Billed fourth in the credits and on posters, after Jack Carson, Janis Paige, and Don DeFore, Day had no previous acting experience in films, so Warners took no chances on her. They surrounded her not only with the names above her in the credits but also with solid troopers such as S. Z. "Cuddles" Sakall, Oscar Levant, Eric Blore, Franklin Pangborn, Fortunio Bonanova, the Page Cavanaugh Trio, and the popular calypso singer of the day, Sir Lancelot. They assigned veteran Busby Berkeley to stage the musical numbers, and put the movie under the direction of the skilled Michael Curtiz (whose other credits included *Casablanca* and *Mildred Pierce*).*

Looking at *Romance* today, it's obvious that Warner Bros. doesn't yet

OPPOSITE Doris Day in *The Pajama Game*: the band singer who became an all-time female box-office champion

* Day was first signed by Michael Curtiz Productions, as he was the first to recognize her potential. Since he was under contract to Warner Bros., he sold her to his own studio.

know exactly how to define Day's personality: they're winging it, trying her out. Some studio bosses had felt she was slightly Betty Huttonish, so there is a tinge of Hutton in her role; others had been reminded of Ginger Rogers, so the writers have thrown in a touch of the Rogers wisecracking character. Warners finally decided to showcase Day in *Romance* as Hutton (Day is a little zingy, a little crazy, and she does specialty numbers) mixed with Rogers (wised-up and funny, but fundamentally American and down-to-earth). To this mix was added what Day herself had: an easy, likable personality, a bit of the tomboy, but kind and sweet—and, of course, with great musical chops. Day wasn't beautiful; she was pretty, however, very pretty, and she was appealing and had warmth. She starts out the movie as a gum-chewing showgirl, and by the end, when it had become clear to the studio that she was going to succeed, her character has more class, more tenderness, and Day's natural grace is allowed to emerge.

What audiences saw in Doris Day was that, unlike most other movie stars, she seemed to really be a normal person like them. She was blond, blue-eyed, lightly freckled, and had a big grin with slightly protruding teeth. (American moviegoers love female stars with teeth: Gene Tierney and Loretta Young as well as Doris Day.) She had a sense of humor that came across, and she had a three-dimensional presence. She seemed rounded and real, with actual hips and long legs. No one who ever interviewed Day or wrote about her failed to mention that they found her unexpectedly sexy. More men (and women) wrote about Day and defined her body and personality as "sexy" than ever did Marilyn Monroe. Monroe was defined as a sex object, or a sex goddess, a fantasy of sex that was glorious but unreal. Day was defined in reality as well as on film as sexy. (No one has suggested that maybe the reason Day was always defending her virtue in her later movies was because so many wanted to rob her of it.)

Romance set the pattern for Day. In the rest of her musicals at Warners, she always played a "real," down-to-earth kind of American girl, usually one working somewhere, probably in a nightclub, but always dreaming of something else: travel, wealth, success, love. The cheap, slightly low-class quality glimpsed in the early scenes of *Romance* was altered to make her more of a "good joe" kind of gal, with a solid work ethic. The cheapness (no doubt coming from the Hutton idea but going toward Jean Harlow) was replaced by a perkier, more likable version of what Warners had been trying to assign to her with the slang and the lack of manners and polish. Her movie bosses smoothed her out, shined her up. What no one would ever alter in any Day musical was her singing style, and the way she could put the song over to the audience, as if she were talking directly to them.

Warner Bros. could not have set Doris Day up for stardom any better than it did in *Romance*. She was given wonderful songs: "I'm in Love," "Put 'Em in a Box, Tie 'Em with a Ribbon," "The Tourist Trade," and, in particular, the song that would become a big hit, the lyrical "It's Magic," written by Jule Styne and Sammy Cahn, perfect for her voice and her style. Day had been standing on a bandstand since she was a very young girl, singing directly to an audience as if she were talking to them. She knew how to put over a song. Never mind that on the studio set she had no real audience: she did what she had learned to do, and she was easy, relaxed, and humorous. She *did* have a touch of both Hutton and Rogers, but also a touch of Bing Crosby, Frank Sinatra, and Lana Turner. She had a lot going on, and the public saw it—saw it and loved her. By the time the movie ended, and the audience had taken in all of *Romance on the High Seas*—a thoroughly charming and very underrated musical—Doris Day had established herself as Doris Day, her own unique self. Warners need not have worried. She was immediately put under scrutiny for long-range stardom, to become one of those "star vehicle" musical players. In Day, the movies found a woman

"A star is born" when Doris Day appears in her first movie, *Romance on the High Seas*, playing an unknown singer on a budget, dreaming of a fancy shipboard vacation.

other women could like, whom men could want, and that everybody could believe was out and about in the world in some way. She had *working* credibility. The studio immediately began to promote her, and crafted a second vehicle for her to begin shooting as fast as possible. Day's second film (*My Dream Is Yours*, 1949) began a successful run of movies created especially for her. *Dream* was followed quickly, to capitalize on her rising popularity, by *It's a Great Feeling* (also in 1949). Over the next few years, from 1950 to 1954, she made journeyman musicals for Warners that were all successes because of her: *Tea for Two* and *The West Point Story* in 1950; *Lullaby of Broadway*, *On Moonlight Bay*, and *I'll See You in My Dreams* (all in 1951); *April in Paris* (1952); *By the Light of the Silvery Moon* and *Calamity Jane* (both 1953); and *Lucky Me* (1954).*

These musicals were, at best, flimsy. They are all star vehicles. *Romance* was the best of them, although two charming period pieces (*On Moonlight Bay* and *By the Light of the Silvery Moon*) are excellent, and *Calamity Jane* is very popular with her fans. Her other musicals had plots created out of the Warners grab bag, songs recycled from other Warners films (often from Busby Berkeley movies) and choreography that was sometimes good, sometimes clichéd. Her costars, with the exception of James Cagney in the weak *West Point Story* and maybe Howard Keel in *Calamity Jane*, were never top-of-the-line film names. Gordon MacRae, Gene Nelson, Ray Bolger, Robert Cummings, et al. were talented but were not big *movie* names. These men were billed second to Day, because after *Romance* Warner Bros. understood that in Doris Day they had the real thing.

They also understood that if Day was going to become the dominant musical star that they were certain she could be, having her dance would strengthen her appeal and widen her range. In her first three movies (*Romance*, *My Dream Is Yours*, and *It's a Great Feeling*), Day was cast as a singer because at the time she was not a dancer; however, Warners learned she had originally planned to become one. In 1937, when she was thirteen, her right leg had been shattered in a near-fatal car accident, and she became

---

* Day was a working contract player at Warner Bros., which meant she was assigned films according to their needs and desires. In 1951, during this time period, she also made *I'll See You in My Dreams*, a dramatic musical biopic about lyricist Gus Kahn (Danny Thomas), and although Day sang many of the songs, her basic role was a dramatic one as Kahn's often domineering wife. She appeared as herself (with James Cagney, Virginia Mayo, Ruth Roman, and Gordon MacRae) in 1951's *Starlift*, and in 1950's dramatic *Young Man with a Horn*, starring Kirk Douglas as a musician, she played a band singer. These movies were not musical vehicles built for and around her.

a singer because she couldn't become a dancer. "I thought I was through forever with a dancing career," she said in a 1950 interview with James Padgitt of the *Dallas Times Herald*. Warners had doctors examine her, and when they gave her clearance, she cautiously began rehearsing tap routines for her fifth movie,* *Tea for Two*, with Gene Nelson. When she first realized that, having given up her dreams of a dancing career and settling for becoming a top-ranked singer, she was really still able to dance, Doris Day came on like gangbusters. She taps out into a happy glory in all her numbers in *Tea for Two*.

Tea for Two is harmless enough. There's no use getting mad at it, but it's a feeble remake of the Broadway success *No, No, Nanette*, which featured the tune that became the title, the charming "Tea for Two." The musical numbers were directed by LeRoy Prinz, but Gene Nelson and his wife, Miriam, a choreographer, contributed much to helping Day regain her confidence and also helped create Day's dances. The Nelsons were friendly, kind, and supportive to Day, and he was a lucky choice for her first onscreen dancing partner. Nelson was a good-looking young man with an easy, athletic style of dance, a sort of relaxed Gene Kelly. He represents a male example of how musical stardom could elude a truly attractive and talented player. Nelson was an excellent dancer, a real rat-a-tat-tat tapper, and he was at ease in front of the camera. After being introduced in *I Wonder Who's Kissing Her Now* (1947) and playing alongside Gordon MacRae and June Haver in *The Daughter of Rosie O'Grady* (1950), he fell to mostly supporting roles. Why is debatable, but Hollywood already had one dancing Gene, and Nelson was perhaps a bit bland in his screen presence. He may not have become a top movie star, but he did not disappear off the history pages. He played Will Parker in the 1955 filmed version of *Oklahoma!*, directed Elvis Presley (in *Kissin' Cousins* and *Harum Scarum*), starred in and directed television shows, and had a final triumph as Buddy in the Broadway musical success *Follies* in 1971.

By the time of *Lullaby of Broadway* in 1951, Doris Day was in full confident flower as a singer/dancer in movie musicals, and Warner Bros. had learned how to shape a movie to her image. Day was always presented as friendly, open, humorous, sexy, warm, down-to-earth, honest—and peppy.

---

* It was actually her sixth movie, but the fifth to be released. It's the first time in her career that she received top billing, and she was supported by both a singer (Gordon MacRae) and a dancer (Gene Nelson) for the new dancing Day.

Warners showcased her energy. Day had a strong work ethic, and she conveyed a no-nonsense aura to her audiences: no Ruritanian princesses for her. The Warner Bros. Doris Day star-vehicle definition was clear: put her at the center; give her multiple songs and dances; support her with a comedy lead such as Phil Silvers or Billy De Wolfe; throw in "Cuddles" Sakall; get her a romantic leading man whether he can sing or dance or not; recycle some plot that's been seen before; adapt it to popular songs that the public knows; and have Doris Day play a warm-hearted, all-American, tomboyish girl. With a little sex. For over a decade, that was the Doris Day musical career.

By *Lullaby*, Doris is a confident musical movie star. She's capable of singing comedy numbers, Latin numbers, heartbreaking numbers, any kind of vocal that's in the book. She can put a song over as well as any singer who was ever in the movies. The fact that she can also dance—and not just tap, but really *dance*, as a romantic partner, a comic cutup, a balletic swan, or whatever was needed—meant that Doris Day

Doris Day rose to even greater success when she became the dancer she'd always wanted to be, rolling out like Fred Astaire in *Lullaby of Broadway*.

could, and did, carry her specially designed musical star vehicles.

The trailers that Warner Bros. developed in Day's early years to sell her films reflect how quickly she was brought along, and how the way she was showcased changed. For *Romance on the High Seas*, the studio knew they had something in Day, but what? Not being sure, they opened the trailer with blond Doris and brunet Janis Paige singing a little duet about the film's charms, both shot in medium close-up. Doris Day looks pretty and perky and she claims the screen away from the very talented Paige. As the trailer moves into selling the movie, it identifies the strong cast in the following order, with the traditional medium shots with their names underneath: Jack

Carson, Janis Paige, Oscar Levant, S. Z. Sakall, Don DeFore . . . and last, sixth in line, the "GAL-amorous Doris Day." It's up to her to earn more the next time, and she does. By the time of *It's a Great Feeling*, the trailer says, "You are invited to attend the Coming Out Party of a glamorous New Star . . . yes, it's that great day Doris Day." In *April in Paris*, she's top-billed over Ray Bolger, and the trailer says, "Here's Doris as Dynamite Jackson" and "Doris is really tickin'." Now she's just "Doris," no other identification needed. Only two or three years have passed, and Doris Day has established a musical persona and become identifiable by her first name.

Doris Day was a great musical-comedy star, but also a very good emotional actress. As she developed and her career moved forward, she began to appear in more dramatic roles. She made two dramatic films in which she didn't sing: *Storm Warning* (1950) and *The Winning Team* (1952) and two in which she did, *Young Man with a Horn* and *Young at Heart* (1955). *Young Man with a Horn* was a dramatic story loosely based on the tragic life of the great jazz musician Bix Beiderbecke, starring Kirk Douglas as the horn player. Day played a band singer, and she did four fabulous numbers, among them a great version of "Too Marvelous for Words." (Harry James doubled for Douglas on the soundtrack, and the film's album was a success.) It wasn't a stretch for Doris Day to play a band singer, since she had spent a fair amount of her young life being exactly that, but her role gave her moments of dramatic intensity that she more than met. *Storm Warning* also gave her an intense dramatic role as a woman married to a cruel Ku Klux Klan leader (Steve Cochran). Day was costarred with Ginger Rogers (playing the main role, as Day's sister) and Ronald Reagan as a district attorney bent on ridding the community of the Klan. In 1952, she appeared again with Reagan (they became lifelong friends) in *The Winning Team*. Reagan played the baseball pitcher Grover Cleveland Alexander, whose supportive wife (Day) helped him overcome

Doris Day would have been a star if all she did was sing and dance, but she proved herself over time in a flexible and varied career. She had her "tomboy" roles, as in *Calamity Jane* . . .

... and her pretty-as-a-picture leading-lady musical vehicles at Warner Bros.: *April in Paris* (with Claude Dauphin) . . .

various health and alcohol issues. Warners always knew Day could act and that she was able to create a believable character. What is unusual about her career is that around 1955, only a few years into one of the most successful musical careers of any female star, Day's dramatic work bled into her musicals. In 1955 she appeared in two serious musical movies: *Young at Heart*, with Frank Sinatra, and *Love Me or Leave Me*, with James Cagney. In both films, she was linked to music, which gave her the opportunity to sing. As stated earlier, *Young at Heart* wasn't exactly a musical; it was a drama about a musical family. Four daughters play instruments or sing, so it *might* be called a musical, but it would have to be labeled a dramatic one. Day takes the role of the most tragic daughter and plays it well. In the biopic *Love Me or Leave Me*, which she made for MGM, she plays a real-life musical star, Ruth Etting. However, it is not a lighthearted movie, as Day marries James Cagney, who ultimately shoots (but does not kill) the man she really loves.

These two films are followed by a role that is one of Day's greatest performances, as Jimmy Stewart's wife in Alfred Hitchcock's remake of his own film with the same name, *The Man Who Knew Too Much*. (The original was released in 1934, the remake in 1956.) Day's character is a former popular singer, which gives her the excuse to be able to perform the ubiquitous hit song "Que Sera, Sera" to her son when she puts him to bed. Stewart sedates her before he will tell her that their son has been kidnapped. In the moments she has before losing consciousness, Day's hysteria over her son, anger at her husband's lack of respect in his decision, and her increasing drowsiness is a dramatic highlight.

The Man Who Knew Too Much is an example of the ambiguity of defining musical films. How can the movie *not* be a musical when it stars Day and she sings "Que Sera, Sera," one of her greatest hits, and not only sings it once, but sings it as the key element to finding her kidnapped son and releasing him from his captors? Singing a song, even if it's sung by Doris Day, and using it as a key plot element, does not make the film a musical; but what is illustrated is that if you develop star vehicles around a singer for a long enough time, the public accepts a performer as "musical," which means they can sing anywhere, anytime. Few performers could be defined that way and have it be credible, but Doris Day is the prime example of some-

. . . her dramatic biopics, as a gangster's musical wife, singer Ruth Etting, opposite Jimmy Cagney in *Love Me or Leave Me* . . .

. . . and her strong
dramatic career,
as Jimmy Stewart's
frightened wife in
Alfred Hitchcock's story
of a kidnapping, *The
Man Who Knew Too
Much* . . .

one who could sing and was always welcome to do so. In fact, her audiences were unhappy if she *didn't* sing somewhere in a picture, and were willing for her to do it any old way. This is the phenomenon of the musical star vehicle. It allowed Day's singing to become a useful plot device for Alfred Hitchcock. (In the earlier version of the film, the mother was a crack shot, and used her rifle to help her daughter escape.)

Her next film was a thriller, *Julie*, released in 1956; she was featured in a role that seemed designed to enlarge her moment of hysteria from *The Man Who Knew Too Much* into a full-length experience. Playing an airline stewardess chased by a husband who's announced he's going to kill her, she spent the entire film being afraid and hysterical.

A great singer, Doris Day had always made her songs about communication. She found the story behind her first big hit, "Sentimental Journey," and she told that story underneath the lyrics. She was an actress who sang, and a singer who acted her lyrics out. When her famous lyric "Once I had a secret love / That lived within the heart of me" (in *Calamity Jane*) is heard, cornball song that it is, Day lifts it up to a revelation. The fact that emotional communication through music was her forte—both lightheartedly and seriously—made her the perfect choice for dramatic leads. Day was an ironclad box-office movie star because Doris Day could act and Doris Day could sing. (Later, the world would also learn that Doris Day was a terrific light comedienne.) After 1955, Day made only two more purely musical films of the old-fashioned generic definition: *The Pajama Game* (1957) and *Billy Rose's Jumbo* (1962). Her other movies were either dramatic (*Midnight Lace*, 1960) or comedic (*Pillow Talk*, 1959; *Lover Come Back*, 1961). Almost all of her films, however, found a way for her to sing. Her public wanted to hear her, and filmmakers understood that. So she just sang. Sometimes it made a lot of sense, as when she's rehearsing for a school musical in *Please Don't Eat the Daisies* (1960), and sometimes it didn't need to. In *The Tunnel of Love* (1959), Day and her husband (Richard Widmark) go to a neighbor's party, and as they dance on the patio, she sings a song. The rest of the dancers don't even look at her; no attempt is made to explain or justify.

The career of Day illustrates how the business used a star with her flexibility to the max. Once she was well established as Doris Day, beloved movie-star singer, it was assumed the audience would never question why she was singing or when she was singing. Filmmakers knew how far to push it. (She does not, for instance, sing in *Midnight Lace*, where she again played a wife who is being terrorized into a state of hysteria. Pausing to rip off a number just didn't fit in.) In a light comedy, it was easy to work a number into the plot, such as having Day and costar Rock Hudson sing "Roly Poly" in a bar scene in *Pillow Talk*. There's a piano player who encourages everyone to do a drinking song, and guess who takes over the number? Day and Hudson are in the bar so they join in when it's their turn. They enter the bar not as musical performers, and they depart not as musical performers; but in between, Doris Day is Doris Day.

Day's last two real musicals were both superior, but only *The Pajama Game* was a real hit. Both it and *Jumbo* presented a Day who had learned how to fuse her dramatic capabilities into her musical performances without becoming heavy-handed. After *Love Me or Leave Me*, she was always an actress who sang, and that ability to mold a dramatic force into her songs elevated her to the position she occupies today in retrospect: she's a legend. Her musicals are not throwaways. In *The Pajama Game*, she's Babe Williams, a hard-nosed working woman, and some of the grit and independence that had fueled Day's life was allowed to be seen onscreen.

The Pajama Game was one of Broadway's biggest hits of the 1950s. Based on Richard Bissell's 1953 novel, *7½ Cents,* the story concerns labor negotiations in a pajama factory, not necessarily a toe-tapping idea, but an eclectic score with clever lyrics (by the new team of Richard Adler and Jerry Ross) lifted the material into a bouncy entertainment. In the movie, Day brings high energy and real zip to her character, and she handles her

. . . but many people remember her mostly for her romantic comedies: *Send Me No Flowers*, shown where she's never supposed to have been, in bed with Rock Hudson . . .

. . . sizing up a distinguished Clark Gable in *Teacher's Pet* . . .

melancholy reprise of the hit song "Hey There" perfectly. With direction by Stanley Donen, the participation of George Abbott, dances by Bob Fosse, and costars such as John Raitt, Eddie Foy Jr., and Carol Haney (all from the original Broadway cast), Day was surrounded with as much care and talent as she had been in her first Warner Bros. musical, *Romance on the High Seas*. This time, however, she was unquestionably the star, and no longer a chattel on the Warner Bros. roster. (She had become a freelancer, and Warners had to lure her back with a high salary to obtain her services.)

Is it possible that a big Broadway success with a distinctive pedigree of its own can be made into a star vehicle? The original starred Janis Paige as Babe, and it was one of her biggest successes. Removing Paige and inserting a strong and well-established movie star automatically changed a show with personality of its own into a Doris Day star vehicle. The moviegoing public couldn't—and didn't—want it any other way. They were trained for the Doris Day musical, and her zippy performance and superb rendition of the hit songs overrode anything and anyone else. Once established as the definition of a musical universe, Doris Day, like all the great ones before her, could maintain her dominance of the frame.

. . . and thinking it over when Cary Grant makes his move in *That Touch of Mink*. Musicals, dramas, comedies, holding her own with the leading male stars of her era: Doris Day did it all for over three decades.

In *Billy Rose's Jumbo*, Day was again surrounded with big-name personalities: Jimmy Durante and Martha Raye and a long list of famous circus headliners. The movie adaptation of the show, which originally hit the boards in 1935, was designed by MGM (*the* maker of musicals) to be big, big, big. The book was officially twenty-seven years old, but MGM bosses figured that with the truly beautiful score by Rodgers and Hart, with Busby Berkeley's final film choreography, and with Doris Day, top box-office draw, front and center, things would automatically just become new and fresh. Most people didn't agree, largely because the film is long and takes on an almost epic structure. The director, Charles Walters, was a veteran of musicals, and himself an excellent dancer, and he understood how to do musicals. At the center, Day is appearing in what was thought of as her "musical comeback," since she had not appeared in a pure musical since *The Pajama Game*. When she sings "Little Girl Blue" (and also "My Romance"), she is plaintive and touching, at the peak of her ability to tell an audience through music what she was feeling, really feeling, deeply inside. *Jumbo* is a favorite among many musical fans, but it was a failure in its day, a flop at the box office, and the butt of many bad reviews from New York critics who felt too sophisticated for an elephant, a circus, and a blonde from Ohio. Seen today, *Jumbo* reveals that as a singing actress, Doris Day could make any musical into her own star vehicle. She had never needed any help with that process, not even at Warners in 1948 with *Romance on the High Seas*. By the time of *Jumbo*, she is an artist, pure and simple. What a shame she wasn't cast in the movie versions of *South Pacific* and *The Unsinkable Molly Brown*, both of which were fine without her, but she was the perfect choice for both and would have delivered the music to perfection. Her album of *Annie Get Your Gun* with Robert Goulet—another project she'd have been excellent for—is proof of what a great show tune singer she really was. Doris Day, aged ninety-seven, died a legend in 2019.

Durbin

Female singers *could* be developed as musical auteurs, as Doris Day was, and another great career of a female musical star confirms this: Deanna Durbin, a child star of the 1930s who grew up onscreen and finally became impatient with not being allowed to do more mature roles. Durbin and Judy Garland were contemporaries, and both at one time were under contract to MGM. Garland remained there, but Durbin was signed by Universal Pictures, where she not only became a star, but was reputed to have saved the studio from financial ruin.

Durbin's story is a show-business fairy tale. Born in Canada, she was brought to Los Angeles as a baby when her family made the move to California. Early on it was discovered that she had a beautiful singing voice, and since she was in Los Angeles, right under the noses of the studio-system moguls, it was inevitable that as she performed around town, she would be heard and seen. By the time she was thirteen, in 1935, she began a profes-

sional career. A very pretty, vivacious girl with great self-confidence and a glorious voice, she was swept up into the movie business, and in 1936 she made her feature-film debut: *Three Smart Girls*. She was an immediate hit, clearly presenting a very specific personality to the viewing audience: peppy, sweet, charming, a girl who could and did fix any problems, a very American form of Cinderella. Understanding what they had, Universal Pictures, not noted for outstanding musical films, went into high gear to promote Durbin and to build musicals around her. It wasn't hard: write a screenplay about a little girl who is associated with adults who have problems (divorce, no money, loneliness, whatever) and have her solve those

The radiant Deanna Durbin, singing with joy in *His Butler's Sister*

Deanna Durbin became a star "overnight" in her feature film debut, *Three Smart Girls* (Durbin on left, with Barbara Read, Nan Grey).

problems, singing about six songs while she did it. Some of her songs were operatic (Durbin had a classic soprano voice) and some of them were pop tunes. She could do both. At the beginning of her career, the formula was about a preadolescent girl; then it changed to be about a teenage girl; and then about a young woman out in the world. Durbin got tired of it, and she quit pictures, flat-out quit at the top—a showbiz rarity.

Durbin and Day shared the quality of being believable as normal human beings. The durability of their careers is linked to this quality. Day shifted with the times and with her own aging process, and she was successful at remaining in the public eye as Doris Day for decades, becoming the female star with the longest reign among the top ten box-office draws. Durbin could have lasted longer, but didn't want to. She left show business for happiness as a wife and mother, living in France.

Durbin's quality as a radiant presence onscreen was linked to her ability to sing for people as if it were a natural act. She was established from the beginning as "a little girl who sings," and any old pretext could be used. Durbin sang in her movies because she was a young girl who knew a song, or because someone was ill and wanted to feel better, or because someone at a party asked her to do so, or because she was playing the piano and looking at some sheet music, or because she was happy riding her bicycle, or because an old man needed to be crooned to sleep, or whatever. But really, Deanna Durbin onscreen in a musical sang because she could and she was good at it, and she shared her gift with any listener . . . or so it seemed. The genius of the Durbin career was that the movies she was in were designed to let her sing for joy, a joy that came across to the audience.

One of the best things about building star vehicles for a young woman like Deanna Durbin was that her youth offered a basic plot concept that could be stretched for years: she was a young girl who would grow up, and that meant school plots, parental plots, growing-up plots, first-date and first-kiss plots. Durbin didn't need the subgenres of the musical, such as the backstage musical or the adaptation of a famous operetta or Broadway musical (they were expensive to acquire). She began in the Depression, so a story about starving musicians could be developed (*One Hundred Men and a Girl*, 1937); she made films in World War II, so a job in an airplane factory would work (*Hers to Hold*, 1943); she could be topical as well as the emerging teenager. This gives Durbin's films a variety as well as a familiar sameness, and offered her the opportunity to play in quite original movies. *It Started with Eve* (1941) is a likable little screwball comedy that puts her into one of those crazy situations: she's pulled in off the rainy streets to pretend to be Robert Cummings's fiancée, to satisfy the dying wish of his

Deanna Durbin and Leopold Stokowski, two household names of the 1930s, costarring in *One Hundred Men and a Girl*

super-wealthy father (a scene-hogging Charles Laughton)—and then, of course, the old man doesn't die and she has to stay on.

Durbin was a vehicular star who tested the boundaries of musical definition. She played in plots, and she sang in them. Sometimes the fact she was a great singer was a motivation for her (wanting to become a successful singer) and sometimes it was just that she had a nice voice and could sing to people. This allowed her to be defined as a lovely and very real young girl. Durbin could make a very sentimental lyric seem not only less corny, but meaningful. She could sing something old-fashioned, and her youth gave it credibility as something that had once been important to older people or as a way of life that was believable. In *Nice Girl?* (1941) she sits at a piano playing a simple song while her father and her two sisters listen and add their own music. The lyrics are sung slowly, sweetly, as she looks at her family members eye-to-eye, from one to another, and sings: "Turn the hands of time for me, / Let me live my memory, / Once again I long to be / Beneath the lights of home . . . / In that little old sleepy town . . . / Not a thing but moonbeams run around." Durbin is playing a small-town girl, and since she is singing "beneath the lights of home," (the song's title), even if the lights are Hollywood kliegs, there's a simple honesty to her. Like all the really popular movie stars of her day, Deanna Durbin had truth in her performance, and hers came from her own family background but also from her talent as a singer of lyrics. Like Day, she treated music as communication, not just performance. Unlike Day, her career has no trajectory toward mature dramatic roles.

In 1936, when she begins in *Three Smart Girls*, Durbin's a Little Miss Fix-It. She sings three songs, provides comedy relief, and plays a strong-willed, smart girl who not only can get what she wants, but can get other people to hand it over to her with a smile. She becomes the center of every other character's world. In 1948, near the end of her career in *For the Love of Mary*, she sings three times, plays light comedy, and is a strong-willed young woman who can get what she wants, and who has the President of the United States, all nine Supreme Court justices, the United States Navy, and everyone else she meets trying to make her happy and see that she gets what she wants. She is the center not only of every character's world but also, apparently, of the entire United States government. It's progress of a sort, from preadolescent to White House telephone operator, but everything else is pretty much the same. The audience went to a Durbin movie to see a star they loved in a familiar type of story, and to wait for her to sing. (In *Mary*, there's no explanation of why a young woman with a fabulous soprano voice is working as a telephone operator.) The pattern has been set for the star musical vehicle: Deanna Durbin will sing because Deanna Durbin sings, period. *For the Love of Mary* was her last film to be released (although it had been shot before her penultimate release, *Up in Central Park*. She had made twenty-one films in eleven years, and some were box-office smashes. All were successful. Sizing up her progress, Durbin announced, "I was the highest-paid star in the poorest material." She married her Frenchman, leaving Hollywood and leaving America, and keeping out of the limelight for the rest of her life. She died on April 17, 2013, at age ninety-one.

Durbin—and Doris Day—represent the phenomenon defined by Jolson, Crosby, and Presley, with the obvious difference: they are females. Female stars usually have shorter careers than male stars. Perhaps this will change, but history shows us that a woman who is aging has a harder time finding roles to play than a man. Day and Durbin are unique in that Day switched from her musical vehicles to dramatic roles to comic roles and over to television, always maintaining her recording career and thus defying the odds. Durbin just quit. "I'm tired of playing little girls," she said, "I'm a woman now."

There were other lovely young women stars who could and did sing, with vehicles built around them. Judy Garland is in a legendary class by herself; but Jane Powell, the latter-decade Deanna Durbin, became one of the most successful, and she was able to add a high level of dancing skill to her movies, which allowed her to be cast with someone like Fred Astaire, as in *Royal Wedding* (in which she played a version of his dancing sister, Adele). There was Kathryn Grayson, designed for operetta material and a solid second-tier movie star, but there were others who could not be turned into singing stars around whom vehicles could be successfully built. Dinah Shore, a lovely young woman and huge recording star with a really good popular-music singing style, and Rosemary Clooney, one of the finest female pop singers of all time, and Ginny Simms, a particularly pert and pretty girl who had the personal backing (to say the least) of Louis B. Mayer—none of these could become the vehicle stars that Day and Durbin could. It wasn't as easy as all that to be able to carry cookie-cutter movies to success year after year just because you could sing. But the business knew it *might* work; and when they could make it work, they made it work. It was a cheap form of musical to make, and a lucrative one at the box office.

Durbin and Day prove that the musical vehicle could fit either men or women, but they also show that women found it harder to keep going, and were often unwilling to be famous. Durbin ran away from it, and Day retired with her reputation intact, but unwilling to work or accept prizes and lifetime-achievement awards. During her long period of reclusiveness she could presumably have stepped forward to make a Doris Day vehicle movie any time she wanted to. We should have been so lucky.

Eleanor Powell, Dancer

Male stars who were dancers (Astaire, Kelly, Dan Dailey, Gene Nelson, Donald O'Connor, Ray Bolger, Bobby Van, and others) were all men who could sing, and singers (like Crosby and Sinatra) could dance when they had to. The big-name women stars who were singers could not always dance well, although some could learn to get by; but singers such as Kathryn Grayson and Jeanette MacDonald were not dancers. Women dancers who could not sing were difficult to create vehicles for: they had to be dubbed, and voice matching could often be a problem. Rita Hayworth had more than one dubber and thus more than one singing voice, but her beauty and extraordinary dancing ability carried her. Even so, she was most often cast in musicals opposite someone like Kelly or Astaire or Sinatra. To build star vehicles around women who were limited in the singing range seemed to pose problems for Hollywood musicals. There are very few, if any, female nonsinging dancers who carry their musicals alone.* The

* There is no female dancing star who is not either dubbed in as a singer or bolstered by her male dancing partner. Sadly, female dancers tend to have shorter careers than men. The exception regarding longevity of stardom is Ginger Rogers, but her goal in leaving Astaire was to free herself to become a dramatic actress and thus extend her career, a goal she achieved in spades (although at the end of her life, she was appearing onstage in musicals and touring with a musical act). Judy Garland was a singer who became a wonderful dancer, and she unquestionably carried musicals without a big-name male performer opposite her (e.g., *Meet Me in St. Louis*, *The Harvey Girls*), but she is not defined as a dancing star.

One woman who danced, and who could also sing, might have become a dancing star had she not sunk into alcoholism: Lillian Roth. She's charming in Lubitsch's *The Love Parade* and is seen to the best of her 1930s potential in DeMille's *Madam Satan*. Backed by two jazzy musicians, Roth, wearing a low-cut blouse and a very short skirt, grabs a top hat and cane and delivers a sizzling number called "Low Down." It's a wow. Somewhat of a musical Clara Bow type, she high-kicks her hat out of the frame in her loose-limbed dance with an African American vibe. She was a real star, but only for a short time in films. Roth wrote a frank autobiography about her career descent, *I'll Cry Tomorrow* (1954), which became a best seller and was made into a successful 1955 biopic, starring Susan Hayward.

phenomenal and highly unusual exception was Eleanor Powell, who for a brief period of movie history (1935–45) was a star of highly successful musicals.* She made a total of only thirteen films after MGM signed her, a relatively small output in the days when movies were being ground out on a regular basis. In ten of these she was the leading lady or was co-billed with another name star, such as Nelson Eddy or Robert Taylor. In two, her only contribution was the performance of a specialty number.

Powell was a personality difficult to build stories around. Nevertheless, she was a musical performer of such unique qualities that MGM, her home studio, decided to create star vehicles for her. It was something of a challenge, as a female dancer seemed to the studios to be more difficult to move about in a plot. (A man could dance anywhere, apparently, more easily than a woman could. No one seems to know why, but perhaps dancing seemed somehow aggressive when a woman did it alone in the streets.) For whatever reasons, Eleanor Powell was restricted to a form of backstage musical, but the format worked for her. The studio managed to find ways to put her onstage for spectacular production numbers and grand finales, and also to allow her to just be tappin' around outside in the world, or in her apartment, or in her dorm room with friends. Wherever she danced, and whatever the excuse, and despite the brief length of her stardom, Eleanor Powell, as long as she lasted, was a spectacular dancer. She wasn't always very lucky

------

Another popular singer/dancer was Jessie Matthews, a British star who was rumored to be first choice to star with Fred Astaire in *Damsel in Distress*. Matthews was an apple-cheeked, dark-haired talent nicknamed "the Dancing Divinity" and "the English Ginger Rogers." She appeared in a string of successful British musicals, among them some directed by her husband at the time, Sonnie Hale: *Head Over Heels* (1937), *Gangway* (1937), and *Sailing Along* (1938). But her most famous musical was the film version of *Evergreen* (1934), in which she had also starred onstage (where it was called *Ever Green*). Long after her career fizzled out in the war years, Matthews became so popular in England on radio as Mrs. Dale in *Mrs. Dale's Diary* that she was awarded an OBE by Queen Elizabeth in 1970. Another exceptionally popular British dancing star was Anna Neagle, a top box-office draw for over two decades. Her lightweight musicals were produced and directed by her husband, Herbert Wilcox, and Neagle's success led her to Hollywood to make three of them: *Irene* and *No, No, Nanette* in 1940 and *Sunny* in 1941, with Ray Bolger. Neagle was also paired beautifully in her British films with Michael Wilding (best known as Elizabeth Taylor's second husband) in a series of musicals, the best of which is *Spring in Park Lane* (1948). Wilding (who can unexpectedly dance with personal zing) dreams of physical union with Neagle as expressed through a charming dance. His unpolished but capable physicality makes him seem to be an ordinary and very real young man who has just fallen in love. He's professionally amateurish . . . or perhaps amateurishly professional. Either way, it works.

* Powell *was* dubbed, and sometimes sang. The studio worked hard to match her voice. In *Broadway Melody of 1936*, the dub doesn't sound much like her. In *Broadway Melody of 1938*, her dub has a lighter, more feminine tone, slightly higher and better linked to how she really sounded.

in the quality of her star vehicles, however. She was not only the victim of weak plots, she was the victim of downright goofy ones. In *Ship Ahoy* (1942), with Red Skelton, she plays a professional dancer who is persuaded by foreign agents (disguised as government officials) to carry a "magnetic mine" to Puerto Rico when she sails. The plot crisis finds her forced to tap out a desperate Morse code to warn everyone the ship's in danger—right in the middle of her onboard performance. (Powell rises to the occasion, and everyone in the film acts as if it all makes sense.)

Powell is a strong, hard-hitting tapper. She could dance with speed and power, turning in rapid circles, revolution after revolution around the floor, and bending backwards with spectacular ease. Yet she has a softness to her that Ann Miller, also a great tapper and a glamorous star, never had. Powell's tap rhythms are intricate and truly syncopated. When she dances, it's a show-stopping spectacle. She spins, she leaps, she kicks and slides. She does the splits. She is acrobatic, and represents the transition between the thumping style of Ruby Keeler and the much lighter form of tapping female dancers did later. Powell, like Miller and Keeler, learned to tap-dance when it was still necessary to pound out the sound of the tap for an audience that was sitting right there in front of you. When movies made it possible to record taps and even overdub them beyond any human level, they didn't need the help. Powell's big numbers, like those that take place on battleships, are spectacle, but not sensation. They work off the mechanics of Busby Berkeley, but they aren't an imitation. They go through similar motions, almost a physical homage, but they're not credible as Berkeley-ish. They show the influence of Berkeley, but they are designed to focus an audience on a single dancer: Eleanor Powell.

Powell's phenomenal dancing is well illustrated by the finale of her hit film *Born to Dance* (1936), which costarred her with the young Jimmy Stewart.* The grand number was designed to showcase her and let her be the final image of the movie, the thing the audience could best take home so they'd eagerly await her next film. It begins with Frances Langford singing "Swingin' the Jinx Away," followed by Buddy Ebsen singing and dancing. When the camera locates Powell, attired in a short military costume com-

---

* MGM was not yet quite sure what to do with Stewart. He could sing a little, dance a little, and had a relaxed charm that worked well in light comedy. On the other hand, he could be a villain, as in *After the Thin Man*, and they even considered him for one of the Asians in *The Good Earth*. Here, they talked themselves into his being groomed as a leading man in musical comedies. Luckily for Stewart, Frank Capra came along to save him.

plete with epaulets, belt, big gloves, and a drum-major hat, a patriotic theme is introduced. The outfit is covered in sparkles, and she wears dark hose and shoes with low heels. She's atop a turret on a ship and slowly taps down the stairs until she hits bottom and swoops out into a spectacular routine at top speed, flashing her big smile. Her taps are crystal clear, crisp, and delineated. She uses spins, kicks, bends. She stands on one foot, her leg vertically extended alongside her face, and then easily bends backwards (twice) as if she's made of rubber. She then bends backwards again to touch the floor behind her with her palms, moving onward into a snappy tap-strut that merges into a long shot of her tapping, shown head to toe, stopping only to kick the back of her own head. After a series of spectacular Rockette-style kicks (she turns and spins after each one), she finishes off with a forward flip into a standing salute to the audience. This high-speed smorgasbord of

The unparalleled Eleanor Powell in one of her spectacular military routines, bending back with ease in *Born to Dance*

amazing physical feats, any one of which would have made her a star, is cut to appear as one extended number executed by Powell without stopping. Such cuts in movies could enhance a dancer's routine, as the routines were sometimes performed in stop/go sections that allowed dancers to rest, but Powell was a physical phenomenon with her rapid spins, bends, and kicks that never lost track of her rat-a-tat-tat taps, and she did some of these challenging dances in one take. She was the master of the continuous one-take spin punctuated with splits and back flips. The fact that she was also pretty and charming and harmlessly likable elevated her to the very top of screen dancers, but only for a decade.

The high point of Powell's career in terms of partnering a male dancer came in *Broadway Melody of 1940*, when she and Fred Astaire combined for a series of timeless routines.* Astaire always paid tribute to Powell's abilities; and her tapping that needed no embellishment in after-dubbing was a challenge he embraced. Their magnum opus together is their extended, incomparable final routine to Cole Porter's "Begin the Beguine." Against a black sky studded with stars, dancing on a liquid-black mirrored floor, Astaire and Powell flow sensuously across the screen dressed in pure white, a last gasp of 1930s glamour as 1940 dawns in Hollywood. When the music changes to a more upbeat tapping session, they wear more casual clothes and, reflected in the mirrored background of the set, they let it rip in a boogie-woogie version of the music that allows them both to tap it all up and out. A viewer has the sense that, for once, both are experiencing relief that the person on the other side of the dance is not going to mess it up or not be perfect. Their eyes meet, and neither ever looked happier in a dance number. At one point, the music drops out as if the orchestra just can't handle their pace, and they escalate the intricacy and power of their steps with a tribute to what good dancers can really do when the opportunity arises.

Powell's extravagant production numbers would inevitably go out of style. How many battleships can anyone twirl around on, and how many crazy set pieces with giant drums and Hawaiian fire pits can be worked into a plot? She didn't seem to mind, however, and left films for marriage to actor Glenn Ford, motherhood, and a long life of religious work. While she was onscreen, however, Powell was the proud definer of a kind of star vehicle that no one but her could possibly have executed.

* Powell never danced with Gene Kelly on film.

Swim and Skate: Williams and Henie

One would not necessarily imagine that musicals could be made out of water, but the business found two serendipitous uses for H_2O: chlorination and refrigeration. Heat it in a swimming pool or freeze it into an ice rink. Find two lovely young women who could dive in it or glide over it. Then add some songs and dances. Only Hollywood would imagine this could work. Two of the oddest types of musical star vehicles that became successful in the years of the studio system were the swimming musicals of Esther Williams and the ice-skating films of Sonja Henie. Let's face it, even making one successful film with a nonprofessional who is cast because of her athletic prowess was a long shot, but to imagine that many films could be made over years, and that the individual swimmer and skater could reach the top of the box office, was simply unbelievable. And yet it happened. Twice. Champion swimmer Esther Williams and three-time Olympic gold medalist Sonja Henie defied the odds. Henie was on the top-ten-box-office list in 1936, 1937, 1938, and 1939, while Williams appeared in both 1949 and 1950.

The great breakthrough lay in the business realizing that an athletic performance was akin to a musical performance. Since musicals presented singing and dancing as physical acts in a real world, why not present the physical acts of championship swimming and skating as if they were singing and dancing? And to be secure, why not set the athletic acts inside a movie in which other actors—real musical performers—were also doing what they did best? A movie like that could become more than just a musical universe—it could become an *athletic* musical universe. This was the approach that two different studios (MGM for Williams and 20th Century–Fox for Henie) discovered, developed, and maintained for a remarkably long run.

Williams

Esther Williams was an L.A. girl who had won three national swimming championships by the age of sixteen. When Louis B. Mayer put her under personal contract, he saw her as a potential rival to the success of 20th Century–Fox's Henie. If skating could work in the movies, why not swimming? Mayer knew that it might be difficult to create a female-driven

swimming story. However, MGM had already had success in finding a story format for a male swimmer: they had made the concept work for the Olympic gold medalist Johnny Weissmuller in the *Tarzan* films, devising plot devices such as struggles with crocodiles, fast swims to rescue various people and animals, high dives off vined trees, etc. Studio technicians had worked effectively with underwater photography, and Weissmuller had starred both in the water and under it for a decade. Could this work for Williams? Mayer didn't picture her as a female Tarzan. She looked like a wholesome California girl, not a jungle exotic. Mayer hoped to develop her into a major A-list MGM movie star—with a little swimming thrown in. He didn't envision her solely as a musical swimming star. After all, she was attractive enough to play any type of role. A typical development plan

Sonja Henie, three-time gold-medal Olympic skating champion, up on her toes and ready to count the house (*Wintertime*)

OPPOSITE: Esther Williams, champion swimmer, a multimillion-dollar mermaid (*Bathing Beauty*)

("bring her along") in bit parts and shorts began for Williams: a small role in *A Guy Named Joe* and a featured part in one of the Andy Hardy films (which often showcased young women with potential; Lana Turner, Donna Reed, and others had undergone the Andy Hardy treatment).

Unlike many contract players, both male and female, Williams was not easily intimidated. "I was a champion," she said, "and I knew that being able to get to the end of the pool first just might mean there were other things I could do, too." She grew impatient with her development process and pushed Mayer for more. When MGM decided that she was too beautiful to be ignored, and that they should just take a chance on her, they featured her in a movie carefully designed *around* her: *Bathing Beauty* in 1944, originally planned to be a Red Skelton vehicle, its story and title adapted to showcase Williams. The final film, as released, shows clearly how MGM hedged its bets about her in case the public didn't take to her or she got lost in the mix of Skelton, music, comedy, and sparkling Technicolor.

There was no losing Esther Williams. She was tall, exceptionally good looking, with a slim figure, perfect posture, an easy smile, and a charming, relaxed manner that was utterly natural. There were other girls like that around, but Williams had something most of them didn't have: an incredible self-confidence that made her comfortable in the frame and always, as it were, the first to the end of the pool.

MGM went all out in her "star" launch vehicle. Williams was not given something beyond herself to do: she would play a swimming instructor. She would be surrounded with established musical stars: Harry James and His Orchestra, with his singer Helen Forrest; Xavier Cugat and His Orchestra, with his singer/dancer Lina Romay; the Latin favorite Carlos Ramírez, a famous baritone from South America; the comic antics of the already established Red Skelton; and for a perfect villain, Basil Rathbone. Carefully planned and constructed, *Bathing Beauty* did its job and made Williams a star.

Williams enters the film in a short cape. It's bone white with colorful red, green, and yellow flowers stitched onto it in the Mexican style. She has pink ribbons in her braided hair, bare legs, and hot-pink high heels. With a big smile, she walks to a high diving board, sheds the cape to reveal a hot-pink (fluorescent, really) bathing suit. As she climbs the board's ladder, she looks over her shoulder with a flirty smile à la Betty Grable and then executes a swan dive. (The dive is in long shot. Rumors say Williams never did her own diving unless it was off a low board or the side of the pool.)

When Williams surfaces, she begins her first challenge for real MGM stardom. She swims to music. Her backstroke is strong and physically provocative. She has a way of turning her chin toward her shoulder that looks very come-hither, whether it's approved Olympic technique or merely MGM razzmatazz. She smiles and she splashes. She glides and she grins. As Williams had said, she knew how to get to the end of the pool first, and she didn't let the studio down.

Throughout *Bathing Beauty*, the lineup of experienced MGM musical stars protects Williams like a phalanx of football tackles hovering around a quarterback running with the ball. In a series of specially designed clothes, Williams acts as if there's no possible problem. Besides her introductory swimming number, she owned the grand finale: a spectacular water ballet with girls, girls, girls, sparklers and tiaras, music and dance, and plenty of swimming. Water ballets—or aquacades, as they were often called—had become popular at outdoor parks around the country, at Sarasota Springs in Florida, and at the World's Fair of 1939–40, and audiences were happy to see one on film.

After *Bathing Beauty*, MGM began to trust Williams. Ultimately, she was allowed to carry her movies, even dance and sing a little bit. (She was part of a duet with Ricardo Montalban that introduced the hit song "Baby, It's Cold Outside" in *Neptune's Daughter* in 1949.)[*] Whatever the studio handed her, she could do. She swam underwater with Roman statues, with the cartoon figures Tom and Jerry, and with seaweed, roses, ribbons, and colored yarn in her hair. And there was a bonus to Esther Williams. Because of her intelligence and her onscreen and offscreen self-confidence, she could believably be cast as something other than a swimmer. In her movies, which were always in Technicolor, she sometimes played a professional swimmer or entertainer, but she also portrayed the owner of a baseball team, a Wave, a health-and-fitness advocate, and a bathing-suit designer and entrepreneur. Williams was the all-American girl who would move away from next door because she had other things she wanted to do. She became a unique kind of movie star; but without the musical format and the carefully crafted star vehicles MGM built for her, she might have struggled.

MGM shaped her films as "swimming musicals." *On an Island with You*

---

[*] Costars Red Skelton and Betty Garrett reprise it, and Garrett becomes the aggressor, trying to keep Skelton in her apartment as he tries to resist. The song was about the battle of the sexes in two directions.

(1948) illustrates the clever plan her home studio invented to both showcase her and cover for her. Williams had nothing to apologize for—she was a champion swimmer and a hard worker—but she was not a singer or a dancer or an actress. As was true for so many Hollywood stars of the studio system, she could, however, sing enough, dance enough, and act enough to be not only acceptable, but likable. Nobody thought she needed to do a Lady Macbeth turn to give her gravitas. She had beauty and poise, and she could hold the frame in the light entertainments she headlined without being eclipsed. *On an Island with You* is an Esther Williams picture. She's the center point. However, she is supported by two leading men, Peter Lawford and Ricardo Montalban; by a comic relief, Jimmy Durante; by a gorgeous dancing female second lead, Cyd Charisse; and by the music of Xavier Cugat and His Orchestra.

The structure of *On an Island with You* makes sure to let the audience know they are in a "musical universe." The movie opens up on Williams swimming to music in a tropical lagoon with a troupe of female swimmers, and when she separates herself from them, stepping ashore to reveal long hair and a fetching two-piece sarong, Montalban (in a navy uniform) is strumming a guitar and singing to her; thus, the musical universe is fully set up and endorsed. But she breaks the illusion when she suddenly says, "Oh, I'm sorry, I forgot my line." The camera then moves to reveal that what the audience hasn't been shown is a film crew photographing a "Rosalind Reynolds movie."

The action soon shifts to a neon sign advertising "Xavier Cugat and His Orchestra" at the Royal Aloha Hotel. Over the next twenty minutes or so, a series of musical numbers is performed, only one of which involves Esther Williams, all of which take place at the nightclub. First, Cugat and the orchestra do a "nightclub act" presentation of their typical Latin song and dance. After a brief plot establishment of the stars and their movie coworkers sitting alongside the nightclub floor, Montalban makes a polite "Would you like to dance, Yvonne?" request to tablemate Charisse. They take the floor and do a well-choreographed-and-rehearsed tango as if by accident. Then Durante is brought onstage by Cugat, introduced as an ex-vaudevillian, and he does a full-out routine to a song called "I Know Darn Well I Can Do Without Broadway (But Can Broadway Do Without Me?)." During these musical offerings, the nightclub music is always playing, so that the audience experiences not only a continuous, nonstop musical presence, but three extended "numbers," none of which involves any performance by the film's star. She sits at the table, turned to the side so viewers can see her full-length white lace bare-midriff formal gown and can participate in her pleasure at all the musical action that she herself is observing. This nightclub sequence is a major portion of the movie, and it is followed by a scene in which Montalban and Williams, who are to be married, join each other in the swimming pool. They "swim/dance" to a musical accompaniment that is not explained, nor does it need to be. They are watched by Lawford and Charisse, from different vantage points, in a sad and lonely way, since each of them is in love with one of the swimming duo.

The "choreography" of the swim/dance is clever. Williams and Montalban, who was not much of a swimmer, fake it beautifully, moving arms, turning around in the water, smiling happily at each other. This is not one of Williams's spectacular water extravaganzas; it's just a wee bit of water to put her in the pool and to make her a part of the performance lineup. Cugat, Montalban, Charisse, and Durante were all legitimate musical stars. (Montalban was also a serious actor, and he developed that part of his career more fully as he advanced. However, he appeared in many musicals, including Broadway shows.) Williams does not sing during the romantic swim, nor is she really dancing, but the effect is skillfully created that she, too, is musical. (What she was was aquatic.) And since Williams will end up with Lawford and Montalban with Charisse, those two stars are included (through cutting) in this simple but effective romantic-swimming choreography. Plot, character, music, and water.

MGM did more with Williams than just put her in a pool. Most of her movies had a modern setting (exceptions included her turn-of-the-century *Take Me Out to the Ball Game* and the crypto-Roman *Jupiter's Darling*). Esther Williams appeared in a world that was designed totally for her, a permanently Technicolored world that only MGM would envision. It was a world of casual, comfortable luxury that always featured Olympic-sized swimming pools and Williams in stunning wardrobes. It was a modern world with large, open rooms, eight-foot-long couches, bold color blocks of turquoise, orange, and hot pink, and hotel rooms the size of football fields. She wore clothes with wide shoulders and straight skirts (all designed to flatter her flat swimmer's tummy), strapless bathing suits, formal gowns, and sundresses (to showcase her swimmer's shoulders), bare-midriff halters and shorts. It was a movie design that created a transition between the art deco of the 1930s and the mid-century modern of the late 1950s and 1960s.

The Esther Williams musical universe endorsed the concept of resort vacations. It was a sort of travel poster for destinations that featured nightclubs, floor shows, swimming exhibitions, and a comfortable, easy way of life that had no poverty, no racial tensions, and the kind of glamour that was attainable. Her movies have not been recognized for their ability to sell the American dream life of the late 1940s and early 1950s, the postwar prosperity and "You can have it all" mindset. Williams walked in this world with her supreme self-confidence and an utter sense of her ability and right to belong anywhere. She was more of a female role model than has ever been properly acknowledged.

Henie

Esther Williams as a musical star is a phenomenon, but Sonja Henie as one really pushes the envelope. Williams, after all, was a gorgeous, statuesque American girl who could sing, dance, and act a bit. Henie, with her Norwegian accent, did not sing or dance, and her acting consisted of flashing a lovely smile and showing off a pert personality. To take a chance on her becoming a star was a real long shot. A specialty-number featured performer, perhaps, like Hazel Scott, or even a sidekick player like Carmen Miranda. To become a star was unexpected.

What helped Sonja Henie become an American movie star was not insubstantial. She was an international celebrity, an established personality. Americans had seen her in newsreels, clad in white fur, skimming over the ice at the Olympics, even being presented to Hitler at the 1936 Berlin games. Darryl Zanuck signed her for 20th Century–Fox in 1936 without even finding out how she photographed or whether or not she could sing or dance. She could skate, and that was all he wanted to know. The studio launched her career with *One in a Million* (1936) and took the same precautions that MGM would take nearly a decade later with Esther Williams. *One in a Million* told a story about a young Swiss girl who was preparing to compete in the Olympics as an ice skater (why push an audience too far?). The owner of an all-girl orchestra (Adolphe Menjou) spots her and tries to lure her away to skate to his music, and that's pretty much the story. Henie's love interest was played by Fox stalwart Don Ameche, there to pick Henie up if she fell over. The grand finale was a lavish ice show with Henie skating at Madison Square Garden. And like Williams and her swim-

ming, Sonja Henie could really skate, flashing around the ice, toe-dancing on blades, waving her rear, and putting on a real exhibition. Along the way, the movie featured plenty of other talent to carry her: the comedy of the Ritz Brothers, singer Dixie Dunbar, Borrah Minevitch and his Harmonica Rascals, Nick Castle's choreography, and songs that included the title tune. Henie was protected, but she *was* cute and perky, and she knew how to be adorable. And like Williams, Henie had the self-confidence that comes with a high level of athletic achievement.

Water: hot, with Esther Williams in *Million Dollar Mermaid*, and . . .

Henie's films at first presented her simply as a girl who could skate (and ski) because she was from Scandinavia, where everybody did those things. Later, she played a professional skater. Because of her extreme fame as a skating queen, the Henie musicals felt no real need to overexplain why she was skating to music in the middle of a plot. She was like Rin Tin Tin: he was a dog, so he barked. She was a skater, so she skated. Audiences had no questions about either action.

The musical film is now recognized as an American art form, but at the time the studios were making them, they were thinking only of the business—the bottom line. The Sonja Henie ice-skating musical is an example of how careful studios could be when venturing into unfamiliar territory. The decision to start making specially designed musical vehicles for one star was not made lightly. After her initial success in *One in a Million*, 20th Century–Fox was very eager to go on making Sonja Henie movies, but wary that she might have been a fluke, a one-hit wonder with her bowling-alley ballet on ice. Her fan mail indicated otherwise, and her own record of hard work and success boded well for her ability to adjust to the rigors of Hollywood. The businessmen of Fox studios knew, however, that it would be the test of her second movie that would let them know whether she was really bankable. Should her films even continue to be musicals? How much could she be developed as an actress or a comedienne? Could she really be one of their star-vehicle people? She had looks and a certain kind of fresh glamour, and moviegoers found her accent to be charming and not a liability. Her English was clear and understandable. But she didn't really sing, and her dancing, while okay, was best showcased on the ice,

. . . frozen, with Sonja Henie in *Sun Valley Serenade*. Either way, it takes a lot of people to create a wet musical number.

where she herself had defined the concept of ice dancing.* What should her next film be was the question, and given that it was always best to get a potential star back out on movie screens as soon as possible, the answer needed to be found quickly.

Henie's second film was a 1937 movie called *Thin Ice*. (The title was more descriptive than might have been desirable.) The first decision made was to pair Henie with a good-looking young man who was definitely on his way to a major stardom: Tyrone Power. Power had made two successful screen tests in 1935, appeared in two small roles in 1936, and stepped up later that year in a major "debut" film as a leading man, *Lloyds of London*. His star appeal was immediate, and his success so astonishing that Fox showcased him in no fewer than five movies during 1937, one of which was *Thin Ice*. (Three of these films paired him with the beautiful and already established Loretta Young: *Love Is News*, *Café Metropole*, and *Second Honeymoon*.) That Power was chosen to be Henie's costar in 1937 indicates that Fox believed that Henie's ice-skating musicals would continue to be successful if planned carefully.

Henie and Power were a solid team, and would be reunited in 1938 for *Second Fiddle*. The difference between *Thin Ice* and *Second Fiddle* is the difference between building a musical around a potential star and building one around an established star. *Thin Ice* is low-budget, with unknown songs. *Second Fiddle* was more expensive and has an Irving Berlin score. *Thin Ice* has clumsy ice numbers, and *Second Fiddle* has fancy, expensively costumed ice "ballets." In *Second Fiddle*, Henie is photographed in close-up and medium close-up during her ice numbers, and the rink has been reduced to a size that will enable her to be the visual focus of every audience eye. During the time between *Thin Ice* and *Second Fiddle*, Power and Henie had conducted a highly publicized love affair, and they had become beloved to fans who followed their romance avidly. Both had become bona fide movie stars.

In *Thin Ice*, 20th Century–Fox has not yet learned how to photograph Sonja Henie's skating routines, nor have they fully understood that she could be front and center in the storyline. Her role is that of—what else?—a skating instructor at a hotel in the Alps. Power is—what else?—a

---

* Henie did occasionally do a credible dance routine. "If I can do it on ice skates, I can do it on a dance floor," she tells Cesar Romero in *Wintertime*. And it was true. It was just more interesting on ice.

prince. The plot shenanigans that lead these two to true love are tedious and predictable, with Power posing as a newspaperman, Henie having a venal uncle (Raymond Walburn, born for the role), all sorts of back-and-forths that are of little interest but designed to fill the running time, even though it's only seventy-eight minutes. There is musical support from the singing comedienne Joan Davis, who leads an all-girl orchestra and performs two numbers: "I'm Olga from the Volga" and a yodeling song, "My Swiss Hilly Billy." She plays no role in the movie other than "leader of the orchestra who performs two songs." It's clear she's a time filler and a Henie support system, should it be needed. The Fox studio team does not forget its basic musicals lessons, however. The credits of the film roll out underneath a song entitled "Overnight!," an obvious reference to Henie's sensational first film debut. Within minutes after the story opens, inside the hotel, before Henie appears, the all-girl orchestra performs a number in which a singer who'll never appear again sings "My Secret Love Affair." There is no character development, plot originality, or coherence to *Thin Ice*.

What there is works. Power is handsome and relaxed, and Henie knows what she's supposed to do. She plays a naive girl, so her matter-of-fact line delivery (without "acting" nuance) fits her character. She looks pretty, wears nice clothes, and smiles. When the time comes, she skates out in front of the cameras at full speed, spinning, jumping, twirling, doing her famous trademark move of running on tiptoe on her skates. She's clad in white furs, sparkling costumes, crowns of cellophane and diamonds . . . all very ritzy. There's only one problem: the rink she skates on is gigantic, and she is mostly seen in long shot. She's accompanied by a large number of other skaters, male and female, all in lavish costumes. Her number is treated as a moving tableau and the viewer is placed in a stationary position—not a good seat in the Broadway theater, but a good seat in a hockey arena for an Ice Capades show. Sonja Henie needed camerawork that was cinematic, that would take a viewer in close to her, that could focus in on her spinning feet, that could follow her around the rink and isolate her from a skating troupe, putting her in a movie spotlight, letting her be the star she was born to be. Her routines are also interrupted by cuts away to Power (in various disguises as he pretends not to be who he is) watching her. The primary technical mistake of not understanding that the audience wants to be close to musical performers, because they are giving us a vicarious musical-performance experience, mars *Thin Ice*. The studio at first thought Henie's success was due to spectacle: masses of skaters forming snakelike conga lines, crisscrossing on the ice, speeding around the perimeters, and presenting Rockette-style formations. They did not yet understand that it was her personality the audience loved. She needed to be seen as Fred Astaire would be seen, head-to-toe in the frame, in the center of the action, carefully matching her skating to both lyrics and musical rhythms. After the success of *Thin Ice*, this issue was corrected. The size of her skating rink was adapted to locate her in the center of a smaller space, and her camerawork was completely revamped to change her routines from an Ice Capades show to a Sonja Henie appearance. Her star-vehicle format finally emerged.

Henie's routines were photographed with enormous fluidity and skill, beautiful lighting, and superb production designs. Twentieth Century–Fox was not stingy in presenting their ice star, whose sparkle and dimpled smiles were easy to capture, but whose ice numbers were expensive and difficult to shoot. The hot lights needed for movies in her day melted her ice. Looking closely at any one of her fancy routines, you can see that at times she's skating through a layer of water. She's in a puddle, which was not only difficult for her, but dangerous. The studio had to constantly stop and start her productions, taking time to refreeze her ice, needing to be careful about her falling and injuring herself. The photography of an ice show required judicious planning and strategic cutting, with elaborate camera booms and long arms that stretched out over the ice to provide close-ups of Henie. As her success grew, the need to create ever more elaborate spectacles on ice drove the studio to a frenzy of strategic planning. The Sonja Henie ice routine would often present a sequential event, in which she would leave the ice to return with a new and different costume, to be accompanied by an entirely new scenic design as well as her recostumed ice troupe. This resetting the scene allowed for a change in musical pace, a different song, an exciting reboot for viewers, but it also allowed the production team to have time for ice maintenance. It was a learning process for the studio, and the goal was always not only to present Henie properly, but to present her musically to her best advantage.

Fox worked hard to find variety for Henie's skating routines, and it became a real challenge to come up with something new. (Once, but only once, she was towed out in a bird's nest, dressed like a bird, beak and all.) Henie was lifted up and down by cranes, by other skaters, and by ropes. She hung from a tree branch, was towed over the ice in various conveyances, was rolled in posed on lavish sets she'd step off to skate. She turned, she twisted; she jumped up onto things and she jumped down from things. She skated alone, she skated with a chorus of men, she skated with a chorus of women, she skated with a chorus of men and women. She skated with a partner, she skated with two partners. She did military numbers and she did conga lines, Latin rumbas, and Irish clog dances. She did ballet. She did comedy skating and romantic skating. She did fashion parades. She skated on black ice and she skated on white ice. She was watched while she skated by bandleaders (Woody Herman), costars (countless dark-haired males), and envious rivals (countless second leads). She wore feathers, sequins, dirndls, tutus, ribbons and bows, diamonds and emeralds. There was no end to the embellishments and variations that 20th Century–Fox created for Sonja Henie; but in the end, it added up to the same thing: Sonja Henie, Olympic champion, took the ice and skated. That was what you paid to see, and that was what you got. The Sonja Henie movie was a musical star vehicle.

By the time Henie became a top moneymaker for Fox, there's a clear change in her movies. In *Sun Valley Serenade* (1941), one of her biggest hits, Fox is still building *around* Henie, but now not to prop her up but to showcase her more effectively. No longer concerned about her accent or her inability to sing or her acting skills, the studio gave her a real character to play—not Hedda Gabler, but a character, and an aggressive one at that. She's a Norwegian war orphan adopted by Glenn Miller's band as a publicity stunt. They think she's a baby, but when she arrives, she's a voluptuous and rather man-hungry young lady. This allows Henie to be inside the action, appear in more scenes, and dominate other people in the plot. It keeps her on the screen even when she's not skating, and it makes her skating more interesting, more personal and natural. For instance, Sonja Henie skates on the Sun Valley ice rink without it having to be a show-business presentation. She just goes out and skates, and everyone on the rink pulls off to watch her. And the reason the adopted war orphan skates and skis like a champion is . . . she's Norwegian! She's not a professional ice skater. A Sonja Henie film is now a Sonja Henie film and nothing else; yet there's also a handsome leading man (John Payne), comic support (Milton Berle and Joan Davis), a rival leading lady (the beautiful Lynn Bari), and, as happened in *Thin Ice*, a musical group that is just there, with no real explanation: here it's the Nicholas Brothers and Dorothy Dandridge, dancing to Harry Warren and Mack Gordon's "Chattanooga Choo Choo," a song that was nominated for an Academy Award and, as recorded by Glenn Miller, became the first-ever certified gold record, selling 1.2 million copies.

Sun Valley Serenade presents musical performance as if it were natural and casual in all ways. The Nicholas Brothers' number sneaks in with that kind of casualness, but it bears no relationship to anything else, nor is anyone evidently worried about that. The Brothers have never been seen or mentioned previously in the film, nor will they be seen again. Why they are in Sun Valley doesn't matter; they are just there. They are introduced as part of a simple afternoon rehearsal of the band, and yet there's a fully designed set for the number—a cutout train in a station just sitting inside the ski lodge.

What happens in the Nicholas Brothers' number is a riff on the Busby Berkeley tradition of transitioning inside a number to a different musical universe from a natural space, which had itself been first turned into a musical performance space. There is nothing else like this in the movie. As the Miller band waits for the hero to show up (he's late, off skiing with Henie), they decide to rehearse "Chattanooga Choo Choo" while they're doing other things: sitting around, playing cards, waiting. The music starts up, and the band's famous Tex Beneke suddenly stands, puts down his saxo-

A "rehearsal" out of nowhere in *Sun Valley Serenade*, with the fantastic Nicholas Brothers, Dorothy Dandridge, and the "Chattanooga Choo Choo"

phone, and strolls casually over to members of the Modernaires, who are in the middle of a card game at the table. They *sing* "Hi, there, Tex" and then go forward with the song. The little group then moves over to a nearby table where the final singer of the group, Paula Kelly, is knitting. She joins in the song. Beneke and the Modernaires are actually singing one of the greatest hit songs of Miller's career (one that anyone attending the movie would be hearing on the radio and jukeboxes), but they are singing it as a backstage rehearsal, a casual act, because they know it so well that this is all they have to do. This familiarity, this nonchalance, is violated suddenly when the movie cuts to a nearby set where there's a fake railroad train with smoke billowing out the back. Dorothy Dandridge (at that time the wife of Harold Nicholas) is seen in full costume, prepared for performance, with a parasol, a shiny black dress, and tap shoes. She's moving between the Brothers, who are themselves wearing straw hats and tweed suits. None of these three is dressed as if at a ski resort, but rather as if they're all at a southern train station. They sing and dance to "Choo Choo" and, as always with the Nicholas Brothers, the dance is spectacular. (Dandridge exits onto the train while they do their most elaborate routine, and rejoins them afterwards.) Before the number concludes, the camera again reveals the band, sitting at tables, clearly in the same performance space as the Brothers and Dandridge, who are apparently, like Tex Beneke and everyone else, just rehearsing. There is no explanation for why a full set exists for a dance number at a ski resort; the audience has been trained to accept any kind of musical number in a Sonja Henie ice-show movie. But the movie will later go to elaborate lengths to justify a number in which people sing and dance to "The Kiss Polka," setting it up as an activity, naturally done, by people who are staying at the Sun Valley lodge.

Sun Valley Serenade is Henie's best film. It allows her room to perform, create a character, and fill up the space with dialogue scenes, which means she skates less. In her big finale, however, she skates on black ice, dressed all in white, and surrounded by white: white trees, a chorus in white, her partner in white. The routine is very long, extended to accommodate her stardom and also to reflect the style of Busby Berkeley. This beautiful finale recycles the film's music; and although she's surrounded at first with a chorus, and then goes on to a duet with a skating partner, Henie finally skates alone. This is how her movies were shaped to end, and to remind everyone that Sonja Henie, *Musical* Ice-Skating Star, was what they paid to see.

By the time of *Sun Valley Serenade*, Sonja Henie had become a capable movie star. She was a very pretty girl, and enhanced by Fox's makeup artists, she looks lovely. Her movies reflect the formula of the "athlete as musical star" concept by always surrounding her with other talent. Both Henie and Williams played females who could get what they wanted, and who often dominated the men in the frame, never allowing themselves to be used or kicked around. Henie was by nature a bubbling, effervescent personality. Her huge popularity extended to moviegoers of all ages, but young girls adored her. A line of Sonja Henie dolls (always wearing tiny ice skates), coloring books, and paper dolls sold well, as did her line of skating costumes and winter hats.

The Henie career was relatively brief. She was no pushover for a studio to handle, and could be temperamental, although always disciplined. After her success in *One in a Million* she had been signed by Fox for a total of nine more movies, and she quickly starred in one after another. The titles say it all: *Thin Ice* (1937), *Happy Landing* (1938), *My Lucky Star* (1938), *Second Fiddle* (1939), *Everything Happens at Night* (1939), *Sun Valley Serenade* (1941), *Iceland* (1942), *Wintertime* (1943), and *It's a Pleasure* (1945). All in all, Henie made only ten films for Fox.* When she was done with movies, she was still a famous professional skater, and she went on the road to headline her own ice show, raking in millions over time. She retired in 1960, at the age of forty-four, and returned to her native Norway, living lavishly and becoming a patron of the arts. She died from leukemia in October 1969.

In 1985, Henie's brother Leif brought out a tell-all book entitled *Queen of Ice, Queen of Shadows: The Unsuspected Life of Sonja Henie*, cowritten with Raymond Strait. Leif described his sister as the possessor of a Scandinavian sense of humor, "which is akin to zero," and a woman who "wasn't the least bit interested in anything if it didn't involve her personally." He quoted coworkers who had nothing good to say, among them producer Milton Sperling ("She didn't need a stage mother. She was her own stage mother") and one of her skating partners, Marshall Beard ("She was a hard-nosed bitch and maybe you think I'm putting her down. Not at all. She had the balls of a brass monkey"). The book was an unflattering portrait, culminating in the description of the siblings sitting on opposite sides of their mother's deathbed, arguing back and forth. Sonja, annoyed that the nurse hadn't addressed her formally by her married name, lunged at the woman, wrestled her to the floor, dragged her into the hallway, and tried to throw her off the balcony. (Henie was reported to be strong as an ox.)

---

* Her final film, *The Countess of Monte Cristo* (1948) was not made for 20th Century–Fox. It was a Universal release, and gave her an eleventh movie credit.

After hearing the news her mother had passed away, her first words were "Go get her jewels." Upon receiving them, she went through them, holding up a pearl necklace and remarking, "I think I'll have another strand added to these and make a new necklace." In her will, Henie disinherited all the members of her family. Queen of Ice indeed. However, her funeral was a Norwegian national event, attended by King Olav V and the royal family. In the end, to her countrymen, she was a three-time Olympic gold-medal winner and a ten-time world figure-skating champion who had spent a few years on the Hollywood movie screen before returning to her homeland.

Pairs

Star vehicles in Hollywood were not always built for a single artist. The business always understood that "boy meets girl" was a good story idea, so that casting two people who looked good together, seemed to complement each other, and could, of course, stand each other long enough to get through a scene, would be good box office. The business set up an efficient (and economical) system to pair a top female star with an up-and-coming male star, or a top male with a young female. This became standard practice, as when Clark Gable was cast with relative newcomer Lana Turner in *Honky Tonk* (1941) and *Somewhere I'll Find You* (1942) or when Greta Garbo was paired with Robert Taylor in *Camille* (1937). The casting of two people whom the public embraced as a genuinely believable couple was more or less accidental. The business tried out combinations, always looking for the magic that would ring at the cash register. What worked or didn't work is part of the mystery of stardom, the unanswerable questions of why this one and not that one, why those two and not these two. Movie audiences loved to see William Powell and Myrna Loy play Nick and Nora Charles so much that they were delighted to have them paired in anything (they made a total of fourteen films together, six of which were *Thin Man* movies). Audiences embraced Greer Garson and Walter Pidgeon as a married couple, and loved them as a unit in nine movies, including *Blossoms in the Dust* (1941), *Mrs. Miniver* (1942), and *Mrs. Parkington* (1944).* Why

---

* The final appearance of Powell and Loy in a film has Loy doing a cameo in Powell's starring vehicle *The Senator Was Indiscreet* (1947). As a surprise for the audience, she emerges as the senator's

wasn't Garson in sync with Gregory Peck? When he was her handsome costar in *The Valley of Decision* (1945), fans wrote in demanding Pidgeon. Why wasn't Loy's partner Clark Gable? They were successful together in *Wife vs. Secretary* (1936), *Too Hot to Handle*, and *Test Pilot* (both 1938). Nobody knows the answers to these questions, really, although everybody can generate the punditry to supply speculations. There's no recipe for picking two people to star together who can generate a chemistry the audience will buy. It's always a puzzlement. And luck more or less fueled the pairings that succeeded.

Musicals embraced the idea of costars because the majority of films in the genre were love stories, and that usually meant songs and dances designed for a man and a woman to execute. However, there were challenges involved for musicals that precluded the simple idea of "Here's a new female, let's put her with Fred Astaire." It wasn't possible to throw two people together only because one was being developed to appeal to the mass audience. The musical designed for *two* people presented problems beyond looks, personality and voice compatibility, and chemistry. In a musical film, musical ability had to be considered first: there had to be musical talent. A singing voice could be dubbed, but there were other considerations: Did the voices blend together? Was the actor's musical style operatic or Broadway-trained? Would the heights match up? Musical pairs were harder to cast than nonmusical, and yet the business worked hard to create them, because once found, they were a goldmine. In the 1930s and late 1940s, Hollywood created three musical pairs that became legendary: Nelson Eddy and Jeanette MacDonald, Fred Astaire and Ginger Rogers, and Mickey Rooney and Judy Garland.

MacDonald and Eddy

The most popular singing duo ever to appear in movies was Jeanette MacDonald and Nelson Eddy, who at MGM made eight successful operettas together. They are unequaled in film history; yet they are often derided, and at best are seldom taken seriously—except by their large numbers of

---

wife at the very end. Garson and Pidgeon were assigned a similar cameo usage, acknowledging their popular pairing. In *The Youngest Profession* (1943), a story about young fans who seek autographs, Garson and Pidgeon play themselves, out on a publicity tour to New York City. They invite the fans to tea: Garson pours; Pidgeon smokes his pipe.

devoted and loyal fans. It's probably true to say that no one likes MacDonald and Eddy except the public; but given their endurance, it might be better said that nobody likes them except everybody who's seen them. Most of the people who make fun of them have never actually *seen* a MacDonald/Eddy movie, and their knowledge of who or what they were is linked to comic skits by Carol Burnett or Benny White, or possibly to Madeline Kahn's fabulously funny rendition of "Ah! Sweet Mystery of Life" when Frankenstein's monster makes personal contact.* The real MacDonald and Eddy are more talented, more charming, and more versatile than rumor would have it. The eight films they made are, in chronological order, *Naughty Marietta* (1935), *Rose Marie* (1936), *Maytime* (1937), *Sweethearts* (1938), *The Girl of the Golden West* (1938), *New Moon* (1940), *Bitter Sweet* (1940), and *I Married an Angel* (1942).

When Eddy and MacDonald were first costarred, there was a significant imbalance in their careers. MacDonald was already a star. She entered movies in 1929 and had formed a successful musical pairing with Maurice Chevalier, although the two of them didn't get along well, and they weren't really musically simpatico. Chevalier was a music-hall singer, a boulevardier who floated on French charm, winking and rolling his eyes and generating sexual innuendo. MacDonald could handle that, but she was a soprano with a trained voice, and she had serious aspirations for her singing career. She had also begun in movies under the direction of one of the great masters, Ernst Lubitsch, and her early years at Paramount had taught her to have high standards and expect only the best.

When MacDonald moved from Paramount to MGM in late 1933, her new studio set about preparing her first showcase, *The Cat and the Fiddle* (1934), and then undertook a longer-range plan for her to star in the role she coveted, the title role in *The Merry Widow* (also 1934). Lubitsch was set to direct the latter, which would be her final pairing with Chevalier. The two films did well, but the delicious *Merry Widow* revealed the truth to MGM: MacDonald and Chevalier really were out of tune. His saucy music-hall style, in which he often "talked" his lyrics in a raspy French accent, was in sharp contrast to her lilting soprano. MacDonald was a hit with fans, how-

* A notable exception was their famous contemporary Noël Coward, whose operetta *Bitter Sweet* was made into one of their movies. Coward wrote in a letter to his secretary that "no human tongue could ever describe what [they] have done to it. It is, on all counts, far and away the worst picture I have ever seen. MacDonald and Eddy sing relentlessly from beginning to end looking like a rawhide suitcase and a rocking horse respectively."

The most popular singing duo in movie history in their screen debut as a pair: Jeanette MacDonald and Nelson Eddy (fetching in his coonskin hat) in *Naughty Marietta*

ever, and the studio began to look around to find a better musical fit for her. On their roster they had a big blond guy from Providence, Rhode Island, named Nelson Eddy. They took a look at him.

Eddy had been put under contract by MGM in 1933, but in nearly two years had only done bit parts in three films:* *Broadway to Hollywood*, *Dancing Lady*, and *Student Tour*, hardly an auspicious lineup. He was insecure about acting in the movies and hoped to become a major name on the recital circuit instead. He wasn't pushing himself forward as a movie star, but MGM saw that he was tall, blond, blue-eyed, and handsome in a solid and substantial way not always found in baritones. Louis B. Mayer considered Eddy as a costar for MacDonald, but also considered teaming her with Allan Jones, a classically trained tenor who was himself a handsome man with an easy and relaxed charm. In the end, however, Mayer chose Eddy to be MacDonald's next costar, and MacDonald approved the choice.

Naughty Marietta was a 1910 Victor Herbert operetta that featured a rhapsodic score designed to be sung by highly trained singers. The show produced a remarkable list of hits: "Ah! Sweet Mystery of Life," "Tramp, Tramp, Tramp," " 'Neath the Southern Moon," "I'm Falling in Love With Someone," and "Italian Street Song." The original production ran for 136

---

* MacDonald had *starred* in thirteen.

performances in New York, and was already something of an old-fashioned vehicle twenty-five years later when MGM adapted it to introduce its new singing team, following the tradition of putting an established name (Mac-Donald) with a newcomer (Eddy).

The movie version of *Naughty Marietta* was given great care by MGM. In every way it's a lavish production, with superb sets, costumes, and musical arrangements. It was nominated for 1935's Best Picture Oscar (losing to *Mutiny on the Bounty*), and it won the Oscar for Best Sound Recording.* It's a peppy 104 minutes of music, action, and comedy—not things usually associated with the MacDonald/Eddy team or for that matter with operetta in general. It has a great deal of music, and events never die on screen while viewers wait for another song. A trailer designed for a latter-day re-release defined *Naughty Marietta* as "the film acclaimed as the Greatest Musical Romance of all time," brought back for its "adventure, magnificent production, golden voices, and true love story." The ad copy was echoing audience responses.

The movie opens up in Paris on MacDonald's singing along with a bird in a cage, trilling away, and it will be nearly half an hour until newcomer Eddy is seen onscreen. MacDonald portrays a playful French princess, full of fun and a friend of the common people who knows what she wants in a man: to see him "standing tall and strong." She's trying to write the lyrics to a song her music teacher has composed; she has only a few bars of it so far, but she knows it's important. (It's the first notes for "Ah! Sweet Mystery.") The film's opening is designed to quickly establish MacDonald as democratic (and thus open to a new life in Louisiana), musical, and full of feisty charm, with the ability to write music. This takes very little screen time, and the movie moves quickly to her dilemma: she's going to be wed against her will to a tired old nobleman, and we all know how useless *they* are. Quickly she becomes a runaway princess by assuming the identity of her servant, Marietta, who had signed up to become a "casquette girl" (a group of females being taken to Louisiana to become brides for the men who were taming the land there).

Naughty Marietta moves quickly toward its important goal: finding Nelson Eddy in a Davy Crockett hat. On her way to him, MacDonald sings,

* The script for the modernized *Marietta* (as opposed to the original 1910 production) was written by John Lee Mahin and the married team of Albert Hackett and Frances Goodrich, writers known for their wit and impeccable pace and story construction.

chats democratically with the other women, and is captured by a group of surly pirates. (And these are not operatic pirates wearing feathers on their hats and parrots on their shoulders. One of them calmly shoots dead an old lady traveling with the group. It's a bit of an audience gasper, since people think they're watching a harmless operetta.) The women are rescued by . . . Nelson Eddy (in his hat) and his singing male chorus of woodsmen. The first time any audience really *saw* Nelson Eddy in a movie was in this image: hat, leather pants, fringed jacket, marching along in front of a male troop of backwoods types, lustily singing the hearty "Tramp, Tramp, Tramp." Eddy is always described as "wooden" and criticized for being a stiff actor, but here he is, a big man, uncommonly good-looking, moving along with energy and pace, singing with self-confidence in his beautiful baritone voice. He sounded good; he didn't look wooden; and as far as not being a great actor, they were used to that in movie heroes. To date, for light operetta, they'd had to make do with stars like Dennis King (not very good-looking), Ramon Novarro (good-looking but short), Tullio Carminati (ditto), and Lawrence Tibbett (tall but not very good-looking). Nelson Eddy was a welcome find.

When MacDonald and Eddy meet and interact, their chemistry onscreen is obvious as they play out a sort of musical *Taming of the Shrew* relationship. MacDonald has been set up as a decent person, so the movie is safe in having her be challenging, difficult, and temperamental with him. She's also saucy, flirtatious, and bold. (To get free of having to marry one of the backwoodsmen, she tells the governor she's not a "nice girl" and is taken to the bad part of town and given a "house" for her work. The censors were not pleased.) Eddy is calm, having decided she was what he wanted the minute he saw her. He holds his ground, and he can do it. His bulk—or woodenness—is put to use as a reliable masculinity to, as it were, offset or take care of her flightiness and aristocratic inexperience in the real world. He's clearly not a great actor, but that never seemed to worry Eddy—he hadn't asked to be a movie star. He had self-confidence in the frame, and his substantial presence makes him seem to be a real man (for a baritone) and a suitable "standing tall" kind of guy for MacDonald. And so they banter and flirt and then sing about it. They sing *for* each other, and they sing *to* each other. They sing joyously and they sing romantically. They sing music people like or people hate, but Nelson Eddy and Jeanette MacDonald sing to each other the way Fred Astaire and Ginger Rogers dance with each other. What they feel and think comes to an audience through their song. The high point of their musical collaboration comes when MacDonald suddenly finds the words for the song she has been trying to write. She sings it to him across a crowded room at a moment of plot complication when she's being forcibly taken back to Paris, and he's in danger of arrest if he tries to rescue her. She sings "Ah! Sweet Mystery of Life" to him as her pledge of love

and also her farewell, and he receives it as such. Ignoring all danger (and everyone else in the room), he sings it back to her, and as she draws near him, they sing together, alone in their love, their sacrifice, and their music. It may sound corny, but it works, and that's why Eddy and MacDonald are still the most famous singing duo in motion-picture history.

Why do Eddy and MacDonald work as a musical team? First and foremost, their singing styles and voices blend together beautifully. Physically, they're attractive; she is utterly feminine and, for operetta, he is solidly masculine. More importantly, they have a real chemistry together in their dialogue scenes. MacDonald's persona is that of a coquette who will flirt but who gets huffy if someone tries to take liberties with her. On the surface, her films

MacDonald and Eddy in their most lavishly produced and ultra-romantic film, *Maytime*

hint, she's perhaps spoiled, but underneath she's a strong woman of quality. Eddy plays against her flighty character with calm humor. He's not bothered by her bad behavior—the implication is that no matter what she does, he can handle her. He's amused by her and will take no nonsense. MacDonald and Eddy understood these roles, and how to fit them together. Working side by side, both musically and in dialogue, they easily present a couple who meet, are attracted, clash over small matters, setting off sparks, and fall utterly in love in a way that brings music out of them. Their secret was this: they are believable *musically*. The MacDonald/Eddy coupling contains a submerged echoing of real love, suggesting the possibility that these two people cannot live without each other because their music unites them, makes them sexier and saucier and more alive than they otherwise would be. Many of their fans actually believed them to be in love; others thought they hated each other. Either way, it's chemistry. When MacDonald leaned toward Eddy and he leaned back, something happened that was palpable.

No matter how lavish the films became, as in the beautifully costumed and mounted *Maytime* (1937) or the Technicolored *Sweethearts* (1938) and *Bitter Sweet* (1940), MGM never lost its understanding of what made the MacDonald/Eddy films successful: music and romance. A certain simplic-

MacDonald and Eddy in the last of their musicals, still in love and still on key, *I Married an Angel*

ity was maintained for the MacDonald/Eddy duets, but always enhanced by the understanding of how to cut between two stars, building not only the song but their relationship through music. In the 1936 *Rose Marie*, Eddy paddles a canoe across a moonlit lake with MacDonald riding along in front of him. There's just the two of them, the canoe, the paddle, the lake, the trees, the sky, and the moon. They engage in bantering dialogue, with a discreet sexual undertone. Eddy begins to sing "Rose Marie" (her character's name) and MacDonald ignores him. As he continues, she begins to listen—he's good! She gives a little nod of her head to acknowledge it, and then begins listening with pleasure. The song plays out in a cutting rhythm from Eddy singing alone in the frame to the two of them in the beautiful setting, wedded through song, over to her alone in the frame, listening and being moved. There's characterization, plot development, physical beauty, and subtext through music. "Rose Marie" rings out, and the audience is isolated in the emotion of the song, encouraged to own it for themselves.

Nelson Eddy comes to life when Jeanette MacDonald plays opposite him. He is much less interesting in his movies without her (*Balalaika*, with Ilona Massey, 1939, or *The Chocolate Soldier*, with Risë Stevens, 1941). In these he becomes the wooden object he's thought to be.* MacDonald came to her films with Eddy from the deliciously funny and tantalizing Paramount musicals of Lubitsch and Mamoulian; she cut her movie teeth on sexual innuendo and a flirtatious presence. She brought those qualities into her MGM movies with Eddy, and he responded to the best of his ability. For his part, he gave her stability, grounding her in a more human and likable character. He never appeared to be in direct competition with her, as Chevalier had. In short, they were perfect opposites who fell in love onscreen.

MGM always did right by the "singing sweethearts." The production values of all their films were outstanding. However, as Eddy and MacDonald moved forward through their eight movies in seven years, there was not always consistency. *The Girl of the Golden West* and *I Married an Angel* are weak entries, but *Rose Marie* and especially the beautiful and sentimental *Maytime* were excellent. The Technicolor of both *Bitter Sweet* and *Sweethearts* played up MacDonald's beautiful red hair and blue eyes. To fans and general audiences, it all worked. Until times changed and their type of operetta went the way of the dodo bird, Eddy and MacDonald were the king and queen of the singing-star musical vehicle.

Jeanette MacDonald and Nelson Eddy were never equaled by another singing-star couple, but MGM tried. There were single movies that had critical and popular success, such as *Seven Brides for Seven Brothers*, starring the diminutive Jane Powell with the burly Howard Keel, but the movie was made a success by its director, Stanley Donen, with his understanding

---

* MacDonald, on the other hand, could reproduce her attractiveness and play effectively with others. She generates a virginal sexuality to contrast with Clark Gable's very nonvirginal heat in the nonmusical *San Francisco* (1936), in which she sings, but it's an earthquake spectacular, not really a musical.

of presenting dance on film, and by its exuberant choreographer, Michael Kidd. Powell and Keel were excellent together, and appeared in summer stock in later years as the leads in *South Pacific*, but they did not become a movie pair. The greatest effort made at MGM to re-create the magic of Eddy and MacDonald was directed at finding the perfect match for their beautiful and busty young soprano Kathryn Grayson. Grayson, too, was cast opposite Keel, and they were not unsuccessful, appearing in lavish Technicolor versions of Broadway hits. They were the logical choices for Magnolia and Gaylord Ravenal in the 1951 version of *Show Boat* and seemed the best studio choice for the 1953 *Kiss Me, Kate*. Despite being rumored to hate each other offscreen, they were successful, but the excitement and magic of Eddy and MacDonald eluded them.

Grayson was better matched with newcomer Mario Lanza. Grayson and Lanza appeared in two movies, one of which was Lanza's introduction to audiences, *That Midnight Kiss* in 1949. He was an energetic movie presence—good-looking and bursting with health. In the beginning of his fame, he took the country by storm. His most important asset was his truly glorious tenor voice. Lanza had begun singing as a child, but had been somewhat derailed by time spent serving in the army during World War II. A high-school dropout, he resumed singing after the war and soon was doing concerts and singing opera. Movie talent scouts spotted him, and MGM smelled money every time they looked at him or heard him boom out a popular tune: unlike many opera singers, Lanza could sing pop songs without seeming to be slumming. He also exuded a sense of being just a regular guy and could be cast as a truck driver, a shrimp fisherman, or an ordinary soldier. He was perfect for the postwar era, when democracy infused the musical. Gone was the world of top hats and silk dresses, nightclub ritz and country estates. In had come Gene Kelly in loafers, and veterans banding together to create musical shows helped by gals who were secretaries. Lanza, son of a disabled vet, a kid who had worked in his grandfather's grocery store, was an operatic tenor who could be made into a musical companion for Grayson. *That Midnight Kiss* ("introducing Mario Lanza") was a showcase designed around him, bolstered by Grayson, already a star, and a supporting cast that included Ethel Barrymore, José Iturbi, and Keenan Wynn. Lanza plays a delivery man who has "studied music a bit" and who now, postwar, has opened his own trucking company on a GI loan. Grayson was given a wardrobe of Technicolor clothes featuring lime green, lemon-drop yellow, and sharp blue, with the occasional

The pair that MGM hoped to turn into another MacDonald and Eddy, with no luck: Kathryn Grayson and Mario Lanza in *That Midnight Kiss*

soft, warm pink for eyeball relief.* Lanza could handle his deluxe launch; onscreen, he's not a stiff stick, he's expressive and has internal life, and he conveys the sense that he loves to sing, that he has fire inside.

MGM presented Lanza carefully. He had not been trained as an actor and had a minimum of education, but this somewhat rough-edged quality heightened his appeal as a singer for movie audiences. All he really had to do was sing, and that he could do. His stardom soared; he made eight hit movies in ten years, but his personal demons emerged. He was temperamental, gained weight easily, and rejected the discipline that Hollywood stardom required. The studio scheduled him for the lead in *The Student Prince* (1954), but his weight was so much a problem he was replaced by Edmund Purdom onscreen, and only his voice was used. Audiences began to tire of him. Lanza's career—a quick rise to the top, a high level of stardom, including the cover of *Time* magazine, and the coveted title role in a Caruso biopic—was inevitably going to have an equally spectacular crash into the pit. Lanza was dead by the age of thirty-eight, his final days in Europe spent seeking how to regain his MGM status.

Lanza and Grayson as a movie duo were patterned after Eddy and MacDonald: banter, conflict, opposition, then a clinch. They're good enough

---

* Grayson, a coloratura soprano, had the ability to costar with almost anyone without any noticeable change in her persona. She was foolproof.

together, but times had changed, and they couldn't become the new Nelson and Jeanette. There would never be a "new MacDonald and Eddy."

Astaire and Rogers

Why was Ginger Rogers the one for Fred Astaire? Everybody knows the alleged quote from Katharine Hepburn: "He gives her class and she gives him sex." A remark like that inevitably suggests that she was classless and he had no sex appeal, which if it were true would mean that neither of them could have become the stars they were, whether together or apart. Is there no passion in Astaire's lifting his hands to draw Rogers to him, to their breathless connection as he openly seduces her in their "Night and Day" from *The Gay Divorcee*? Is there no class in Rogers's delivery as she resigns herself to dance with him one last time in *Swing Time*? Clever quotes are fun, but Astaire and Rogers both had a talent, a work ethic, and a determination to be the very best they could be. The basis of their success lies in that professionalism and not in easy labels that don't account for their versatility or their willingness to do whatever was necessary. It also lies in the upbringing of two kids who were taught by their mothers to play to their strengths and make it happen where they could and create the illusion that it was happening where they couldn't. Thus, Astaire put love and sex into his dancing and Rogers put class into the way she carried herself and into whatever silly line she had to utter, decade after decade.

Astaire has already been discussed as a solo dancing star and as a major influence on movie choreography. He'd been a star for seventeen years in vaudeville and on Broadway (paired with his sister, Adele) before he made his movie debut in 1933. What about Rogers? She'd won a Charleston contest at the age of fourteen and, driven by her stage mother, Lela, had gone into vaudeville with two other girls as Ginger and Her Redheads. She'd already made nineteen movies when she was first cast with Astaire. For her, the Astaire musicals were an interlude on the way toward what she really wanted: to be thought of as an actress (and she finally made it, with an Oscar win for *Kitty Foyle* in 1941). Her early film persona was a bit brassy, but attractively sassy, and she played an American female who couldn't be messed with. Offscreen, she was independent, strong (even tough), and determined to be who and what she wanted to be. She was never a woman without resource, and she could do comedy, drama, and any kind of musical

Astaire and Rogers, Rogers and Astaire, sublime together in ten musicals from 1933 to 1949: from first to last (opposite) *Flying Down to Rio* . . .*The Gay Divorcee* . . . *Roberta* . . . *Top Hat* . . . *Follow the Fleet* . . . (this page) *Shall We Dance* . . . *Swing Time* . . . *Carefree* . . . *The Story of Vernon and Irene Castle* . . . *The Barkleys of Broadway*

with great skill. She was a natural athlete, with the strength, intelligence, and suppleness to learn Astaire's routines and to stand up under the challenge of his professionalism.

Always meeting the highest standard was bred into both Astaire and Rogers, and their onscreen musical performances find them both at the top of their game. There is much less written about Rogers than about Astaire, for obvious reasons: he was their choreographer, and the man who dictated how their dances would be photographed and edited. But there was balance and equality between them regarding song, dance, and performance. Astaire is a singer with a singular style, and is underrated as an actor. He's no Hamlet, but he doesn't have to be, and his ease, his charm, and his rhythmic, casual delivery of lines makes them believable. He's never tense as a character, or out of sync with anyone else who's talking in the frame. Rogers was essentially an actress who danced, and she had her own set of strengths. When she meets Astaire's character again after a long absence in *Follow the Fleet*, her ability to bring tears to her eyes at seeing him makes their dances more credible, more specific. The faraway, transported look on her face at the end of the "Night and Day" dance in *The Gay Divorcee* is that of an actress who knows what she wants to put across.

They began together in *Flying Down to Rio*, in essence the very opposite of most Rogers/Astaire movies. It's spectacle, not elegant simplicity. Dances such as "Carioca" and the iconic girls-on-airplane-wing title number present an overstuffed frame as a challenge to the eye and are nothing like the dancer-focused presentations that become characteristic of their later films. "Carioca" goes on and on, featuring different singers (among them the great Etta Moten in close-up); whirling dances in contrasting costumes; shifting settings; and different dance floors. There's always too much to look at. Rogers has a small role in the film and is not an equal plot partner. (The movie appears to be setting up Astaire to become a comic second lead.) If nothing else, the movie reveals how strong a personality Astaire really was. Not handsome, small and wiry, and nothing like a 1930s musical romantic lead, his easy banter, relaxed presence, and, above all, his spectacular dancing dominate the show and establish him forever as a star, not to be denied. And when Rogers joins him, she brings her own strong 1930s presence into play in a "whatever you give me, large part, small part, comedy, dance, or drama, I'll do it and nail down my corner." Her own confidence is equal to his, and she immediately establishes herself, matching his charm, and adding her own zing. Together they create a world that is owned by the two of them in a way that everyone in the audience can appreciate. Although there's some clutter in the dance numbers in their next film, *The Gay Divorcee* ("The Continental") and other films, there's never again the visual mess of *Flying Down to Rio* in their work. *Flying* is a happy and entertaining film, but the lack of dance-focused choreography and the emphasis on spectacle was never again the format of the Astaire-and-Rogers movie.

Once paired, Astaire and Rogers just fit. They are both slender and the right height for each other. Astaire likes to move a woman rapidly around the floor in an intricate pattern of steps, and on a dance floor Rogers could fly. She was light and could be twirled up and around. She was flexible, especially in her remarkable back, which suited Astaire's desire to have his female partner sway backwards and forwards from the waist up. She was very pretty, but not so beautiful that she wiped him off the screen, and both could laugh with ease on camera. And, crucially, Rogers fit perfectly with Astaire in their dialogue scenes—they're not great only when dancing with each other, they're great when *talking* to each other. Their banter is like a musical number, with the same kind of pauses and checks and balances that their choreography has. *Carefree*, one of their minor movies (it has a loony plot, but great songs by Irving Berlin), demonstrates their skill at verbal choreography. Rogers, at the suggestion of her fiancé (the eternally, delightfully inadequate Ralph Bellamy), comes to see Astaire, who is for once not playing a dancer. He's a psychiatrist (the kind we're all looking for: a dancing psychiatrist). Rogers is willing to meet Astaire, but when she accidentally hears him refer to her as "dizzy, silly," and "in need of a good spanking," her mood changes. She will make it hard for him. (This is the traditional "meet cute" clash that marks the beginning of the onscreen Astaire/Rogers relationship.)

In a dialogue scene played in Astaire's office, he directs her to a chair. She chooses another. He tries to redirect her. She refuses. He moves around the room in puzzlement. She holds her place.

He speaks: "Let's get to know one another."

She replies: "Why?"

He: "I have to know my patients' minds as well as I do my own."

She: "Why?"

He: "You do understand the purpose of psychoanalysis?"

She: "No."

Their dialogue is a dance number: *rat-a-tat, bump, rat-a-tat, bump, rat-a-tat, bump*. The two actors play the dialogue in a rhythm they're both familiar with: back and forth, back and forth, back and forth. He leads, she responds. He talks in a fluid line, leading her, and she challenges in return. To watch them work as actors is to see a musical pair who are completely inside each other's timing, perfectly matched. They know each other's moves, but not just because they've already worked together: they understood each other's moves both in dance and in dialogue from the first moment they took the floor in *Flying Down to Rio*, which is why they became a pair who found success in musicals.

There are no dance teams that rival Astaire and Rogers—or Astaire and anyone else—on film. Dancing duos tend to be specialty acts, such as the famous ballroom team Veloz and Yolanda, who often appear in nonmusical movies to swirl around a ballroom in tuxedo and gown, as they do in 1940's *Pride of the Yankees* when Gary Cooper (portraying Lou Gehrig) and Teresa Wright (as the woman he'll marry) go on a date to a nightclub. Gene Kelly and Judy Garland made three films together (*For Me and My Gal*, *The Pirate*, and *Summer Stock*), all of which contain excellent dance duets for them. Kelly seems happier than usual to have a partner. (He's emotionally a soloist.) The musical success of Kelly and Garland is not linked to their dancing together as much as it is to the meshing of their personalities. They were friends offscreen, and it's possible to believe in their friendship—they seem like real pals. Offscreen, Garland was always supported by Kelly, no matter what was going on in her personal life. Kelly also danced well with Cyd Charisse, but they were never a "pair," and Garland and Mickey Rooney were song-and-dance costars, not a dancing team. The only other true movie dancing team was Marge and Gower Champion, and they were supporting actors, not real stars, even though they did headline one musical, *Everything I Have Is Yours*.

The Champions make a good comparison to Astaire and Rogers in terms of what a "dancing pair" really means. Astaire and Rogers were *individuals* who were successfully costarred and paired. The Champions were a team, and although they had personality—particularly Marge, who could be comedic—they did not dance with others. They were a dance team, period. Each could do a solo number, and did, but they were defined as a dancing pair and nothing else. Gower Champion later became a successful Broadway director and choreographer, and he was the driving force behind their success. Without Marge, however, he was bland: she gave the team what personality it had. Their married status and long years of collaboration made them smooth. They could dance at high speed across a large open space, use props effectively, dance around obstacles and up and down stairs without losing their highly coordinated steps. They were in perfect sync . . . but there was a visual problem. Gower was a small, thin man, perfectly proportioned, but on a different scale from Marge, who had solid legs, a full face and body, and a chunkier look. She was, luckily, shorter than he was, and that helped, but the Champions were not well matched in the frame. The skilled cameramen of the studios shot their routines carefully to disguise this factor, and their costumers did what they could; but carefully watching them reveals the problem. They are drawn to different-size scales. The Champions were ambitious, and their routines were often highly stylized, removing them to a dream world set against a black background and incorporating tap, ballet, and athletics. Their routines were a synchronized swim of dance, with matching gestures and movements, perfectly in tune with each other. The Champions are good, but they cannot generate the subtext of Astaire and Rogers. Narrative subtlety and meaning—acting performance in dance—is not a part of who they are. They have no poetry, no mystery.

Astaire and Rogers, as everyone in the universe has already written, are sublime together, and Rogers tends to cancel all competitors even though Astaire did have other fabulous partners, starting with his sister, Adele, who by all accounts was a lively sprite, super simpatico with him on the dance floor. But he also had Cyd Charisse, as in the elegant "Dancing in the Dark" from *The Band Wagon*, which literally demonstrates two people falling in love through dance. There was the remarkable Eleanor Powell, who could match his tap-dancing grace effortlessly and still be as powerful a tapper as any man; the long, lithe Barrie Chase, who joined him on his TV specials; and Lucille Bremer, who although not the greatest dancer was well matched to him physically and could bring drama to their duets. Astaire also partnered women who were primarily singers but who, when necessary, could work well with him (Judy Garland, Jane Powell). He danced with top stars who weren't really dancers at all but who managed it in his arms (Paulette Goddard, Joan Fontaine). He had partners who've been overlooked and underappreciated (Joan Leslie in *The Sky's the Limit*) or disliked and overly criticized (Betty Hutton in *Let's Dance*). He danced with partners who were too short for him (Leslie Caron), too tall for him (Ann Miller), or had less personality (Vera-Ellen). He danced with men (Bing Crosby, Jack Buchanan, Gene Kelly); he danced with couples (George Burns and Gracie Allen, Jack Buchanan and Nanette Fabray); he gave dancing glamour to obscure females (Sarah Churchill, Marjorie Reynolds, Virginia Dale, Joan Caulfield); and once he was paired with a woman as physically unique and stylishly legendary as he himself was (Audrey Hepburn). Astaire danced with a coatrack, across the clouds, and up the walls and over the ceiling, with a store full of empty shoes, with firecrackers, in slow motion and in both black-and-white and color. Whenever he danced, and whoever he danced with, he was perfection; but for audiences, the partner for Fred Astaire was Ginger Rogers, first, last, and always. After his sister, Adele, retired, Astaire was never anything but a solo dancer, *Fred Astaire*, except when he danced with Rogers. With her, he was classified officially as half of a dancing pair of movie stars: Fred and Ginger, Ginger and Fred.

It has, however, often been said that Astaire's favorite dancing partner was Rita Hayworth, who, like him, had been dancing professionally since her early years. In the two films they made, *You'll Never Get Rich* (1941) and *You Were Never Lovelier* (1942), Hayworth is stunningly beautiful and alive, and when she and Astaire dance she effortlessly matches him with a shared joy in their movements. In addition to "I'm Old-Fashioned" from *You Were Never Lovelier*, they are particularly beautiful together in "So Near and Yet So Far" in *You'll Never Get Rich*. The dance, credited to Robert Alton, the "dance director" of the film but no doubt worked on by Astaire, caters to Hayworth's Latin background. The music flows over a rumba beat, and Hayworth uses her arms, her shoulders, and her hips in rhythm with Astaire's own graceful moves. Having danced all her young life with her father, Eduardo Cansino, Hayworth has footwork in the flamenco tradition: plenty of it. She moves her feet with ease, stepping lightly, swaying and bending to Astaire, lifting her magnificent shoulders, maintaining the flamenco posture of a straight back. In *Lovelier*, the choreography for "I'm Old-Fashioned" (credited to Val Raset, but clearly Astaire's style) is, by contrast, light and airy, almost delicate. Their feet seem almost never to touch down, moving so quickly they generate no sound until the dramatic point when Astaire hits hard with one step, changing to a more Latin beat, and finally a jazzed-up excitement. Astaire and Hayworth are a wonderful dance duo. When they swing out in the fast-paced, hot-tapping "Shorty George" number, she's hep and fresh and up-to-speed. When they dance in the moonlight, her radiance dominates and something primal rises up in a way it never did between Astaire and Rogers. As they play their characters in dialogue, however, they don't have the same chemistry that Rogers and Astaire had. Hayworth seems happy to be dancing but still a bit remote, and her unbelievable looks distract a viewer from anything else onscreen. When Hayworth and Astaire danced, the partnership was fabulous, but only when they danced. The two films they appear in, however, are Columbia features, and Columbia was not yet a studio noted for remarkable musicals. (Soon enough, with 1944's *Cover Girl*, a star vehicle created for Hayworth that would pair her with the up-and-coming Gene Kelly, the studio would understand better what it could do with musicals at the box office.)* Hayworth was spectacular, but whether she was Astaire's favorite or not, one has to think about Ginger Rogers. Ginger Rogers! In the end, Rogers is the best because she had the best of him in their ten musicals together, and she never disappoints. Their legendary pairing in all types of numbers—romantic or dramatic, comic or serious—is always perfection.

The studio that made all but one of the Astaire/Rogers films, RKO Radio Pictures, did everything it could to support their talents, as the movies they made were popular and profitable. Astaire and Rogers paired is the high point of American movie musicals. Any one of their movies, or any number in it, has something worth discussing. Their fifth film together, *Follow the Fleet*, reveals the essence of what made them great together. It isn't really the best of the Astaire/Rogers films (that would probably be *Swing Time*) or the most iconic (*Top Hat*) or the first (*Flying Down to Rio*) or the last of the RKOs (*The Story of Vernon and Irene Castle*) or the one in color (the MGM-made *The Barkleys of Broadway*) or the one that brought them together as leads (*The Gay Divorcee*), etc. It's just "the fifth one," but it has a little zing to it and it has some differences from the others that make it worth focusing on.

In *Follow the Fleet*, Astaire plays a sailor, and a gum-chewing,

---

* *You'll Never Get Rich* was Hayworth's first major dancing role. She had done only a one-scene dancing appearance (billed as "dancer" under her real name, Rita Cansino) as a soloist in a nightclub in the 1935 *Dante's Inferno*, starring Spencer Tracy, and two minor musical roles in *Paddy O'Day* with Jane Withers and in 1940's *Music in My Heart*. Her brief dance in the Tracy film is a textbook example in how to spot a potential star. In a low-cut satin gown, wearing orchids on her shoulder, she and her partner do a series of intoxicating spins featuring her spectacular footwork. It's a wow—audiences forgot that the ship she's dancing on is just about to catch fire and sink. In 1942 she also made *My Gal Sal*, on loanout to Fox, costarring Victor Mature, as well as *You Were Never Lovelier*. Hayworth, despite her later success in *Cover Girl*, *Tonight and Every Night*, *Down to Earth*, and other musicals, never looked more at ease than in her movies with Astaire. She was different with him, confident and obviously having fun. Along with *My Gal Sal*, the Astaire movies show an audience a Hayworth who's playful, teasing, amused. The "love goddess" tag—the "Gilda" curse—was not yet weighing her down.

cigarette-smoking kind of sailor at that.* Rogers is a dance-hall girl, and that dance hall isn't the Silver Sandal of *Swing Time* or the Broadway stage. In other words, Astaire and Rogers in *Follow the Fleet* are a little bit *common*, or at least as common as they could ever pretend to be. There's a lot of music for them; both of them sing, do solo dances, and duets with the other. (It's a movie in which Ginger herself has a solo dance, which was unusual.) In addition, there's handsome Randolph Scott (still in his musical-comedy phase, before he became a western star) and Harriet Hilliard (who sings two offerings) as the central romantic couple, and even two future stars in bit parts: Betty Grable and Lucille Ball. The movie is an entertaining romp, with music composed by Irving Berlin. Two contrasting dances show the range of the Astaire/Rogers pairing and reveal how much they could accomplish together: "Let Yourself Go" and "Let's Face the Music and Dance."

The song "Let Yourself Go," a strongly rhythmic piece with a solid dance beat, is first sung by Rogers on the bandstand as "part of her job." She's dressed in a feminized satin sailor suit, with an anchor decoration and a jaunty captain's cap. In the plot, Astaire has just shown up, not knowing she's there, because his ship's in port. They rediscover each other, and the audience quickly learns through dialogue that he once asked her to marry him and she said no because she thought marriage would ruin her career. She's ended up here, and he's ended up in the navy and they're both rueful, a little mad but not mad, and obviously still in love. Their relationship will not be the focus of a "Will they?" story—that will be Scott and Hilliard's plotline.

After a few minutes of exposition and some other music, the audience is shown the darkened dance floor and treated to the sound of a slightly bluesy, lazy kind of version of "Let Yourself Go." An announcer says it's time for the weekly Saturday-night dance contest, and dancers take the floor, ready to go. Astaire and Rogers walk into frame, and although they don't hear the announcement, they hear the music and see other dancers. So what do they do? As casually, as easily, as if it could ever be possible for the two of them to walk past a dance floor and hear music without dancing!— they turn to each other, still talking, and roll out onto the floor, all rubber legs and banging taps. The audience sees that they were not only born to

---

* Astaire even chews gum with style, holding his mouth slightly off-angle, and creating a distinct arrhythmic movement that calls attention to itself. With Astaire, gum chewing is almost a number.

dance but born to dance together, and what's more, it's so natural to them that they do it without even realizing it's happening. In fact, they continue their conversation about their relationship as they do it. Suddenly, Rogers realizes they're in the dance contest, and as an employee she's not supposed to enter. Fred doesn't care; he wants to dance. She tries to escape, so he challenges her: does she fear she can't do it anymore, can't be as good as he is? That's it. They go for it.

Challenge was the basis of many of the Astaire/Rogers routines. They both danced at and with each other, and a cranky relationship or a meet-cute competition was often where they started in their plots. In "Let Yourself Go," they are past that point in their friendship/love affair, so they start out to prove something through dance. (This is the opposite of what happens in the charming "Pick Yourself Up" dance in *Swing Time*, in which Fred pretends he can't dance and she has to teach him.) As they hit the floor, they suddenly spot some serious competition. After studying a couple of hot tappers, they unite at once. From then on, they up the ante of their dance, going into a swirl of tapping, letting loose with a dynamic routine that features their bodies rocking back and forth and really knocking it out. This dance is not sacred. It's not about falling in love. It's not about losing each other. It's hoofing at the highest level, and it's about putting away, once and for all, any other couple who could imagine they could beat out Fred Astaire and Ginger Rogers on a dance floor. In this dance, they aren't Astaire and Rogers, they're Fred and Ginger, and they get down. In doing so, they stay true in their dance to the characters they're playing: a sailor and a dance-hall girl.

Later in the movie, however, an entirely different dance is presented to the beautiful "Let's Face the Music and Dance," a song that could be the theme song for Depression victims. It's one of the most iconic of all the Astaire/Rogers pairings. The number has a timeless detachment from any place or plot. It's a dance the two characters perform on a proscenium-arch stage in front of an audience, and they are not expressing themselves directly. It's not about them or their situation or their love or their characters. Thus, sailor and dance-hall girl that they are, they become other "characters" in the number, and these "characters" have a story to act out that is not part of *Follow the Fleet*. The dance is unconnected, and thus can and does exist entirely on its own as the definition of the Astaire/Rogers pairing.

"Let's Face the Music and Dance" is restricted to the stage. An orchestra begins to play, and curtains open up to show a gambling casino in which the tuxedoed Astaire, surrounded by friends and well-wishers, gambles until he loses all his money. His friends move away from him as the curtains close, only to reopen quickly to show Astaire out on a promenade beside the ocean. Lights twinkle, the water sparkles, and the broad walkway is backed by what is probably the backside of the casino, although the design, which is really too busy for the scene, is somewhat ambiguous. It provides patterns of light and darkness, and square blocks and shapes, to distract a viewer's eye. Astaire smokes, and former friends pass him by, cutting him dead, until he realizes he's now completely alone, friendless, and penniless. Out of his pocket he takes a small silver gun, while behind him Ginger Rogers walks out to the ledge overlooking the water. She's clad in one of her over-the-top 1930s ball gowns, this one dominated by a big fur collar and made out of glittering metallic beads.* She goes to the ledge to jump, but Astaire pulls her down. She's unwilling, so he shows her his own despair—no money and the gun. When she tries to grab the latter, he throws it toward the water.

To this point, the little story has played out on a legitimate stage-bound area, and it will continue to maintain that restriction, as well as the idea that the two characters in the movie are pretending to be two other characters, unlike themselves, as they dance. Astaire sings the song to Rogers, lures her to forget suicide and accept things as they are. He does this by singing the lyrics of the song: "There may be trouble ahead . . ." He persuades through song. At first she resists, holding her chiffon handkerchief carefully, her beads shimmering in the light, but he lures her. Finally, she gives slightly and enters his mood, his music, and his dance. They begin a dazzling flow of turns, jumps, spins, and dips, ending in an unexpected throw-back of their bodies, followed by a high step, a dip and a kneel, and an exit offstage. The "number" has ended for both its audiences, the one inside the film and the one inside the movie house. This dance is a performance-within-a-performance. Astaire and Rogers are not dancing

---

* Ginger Rogers's dresses often drove Fred Astaire crazy. This one is reputed to have weighed over thirty pounds, and during filming, when one of the sleeves smacked him in the face, he literally saw stars and didn't know where he was. (There is also the famous feathered dress that molted onstage while they danced to "Cheek to Cheek.") The beaded dress may have been a dangerous weapon—possibly lethal—but it's an important part of the visual beauty of this dance. Because it's heavy, it swings hard, seeming to embody a desperate anger or frustration. It brings intensity and drama to the dance story. And Rogers wears it beautifully.

to show us how their characters fall in love but to show us how their characters (who are already in love) perform a dance onstage. This changes things. To some, this dance seems a bit cold, with its distracting background of the looming edifice with sharply delineated lines and geometric shapes. Rogers's metal gown, the "suicide" story, and the strange two-part setting, switching from the gambling club to the outside of the casino—all these things may seem off-putting to some. But the unrelated setting and story free the dancers from narrative restrictions, and the dance is beautiful, dramatic, and unusual, full of strange movements that are uncommon in the usual Astaire/Rogers routines. The dance is free to be baroque, even rococo, rather than reflect the usual deco clarity and simplicity of line. There's nothing else like this dance in their films. Isolated as it is, it seems pure and really perfect.

Astaire and Rogers are an elegantly attractive couple. As a young woman, Ginger Rogers was pretty but not gorgeous, and Astaire was not a conventionally handsome leading man. This worked well for their pairing. If Astaire had been handsome in the matinee-idol tradition, everything between them would have shifted in the wrong direction: he wouldn't have had to woo her. If she were more beautiful, he might have seemed unworthy of her glory. As it is, when he sets out to woo her, the delicious surprise that not only was he worthy of her, but she would have to earn him on the dance floor, gave depth and resonance to what was happening between them. As a man who is more than just another pretty face, Fred Astaire brings to a movie not only his dancing—and his great singing style, and his fashionable ease in wearing clothes—but also his *character*. One had to be handsome to play a leading man in the movies in those days, but Astaire wasn't. He had something more—genius. And he's *interesting* to look at, different, fascinating. She has something more, too—a believable quality that American audiences responded to and that kept her a star for decades. These qualities open the door to something: the wonderful secret that always unfolds for the audience in a Fred Astaire/Ginger Rogers movie. He's just a guy, but suddenly, for some reason, he will begin to dance, and then it happens. An audience can see he is beautiful, timelessly beautiful. She sees it, too. She begins to soften and glow and flow toward and into him, uplifted into her own realm of excellence by his attention. Astaire and Rogers were the promise that movies made to ordinary viewers: inside you, behind your looks, there is something else, something desirable and special and eternal. Like Fred and Ginger.

Rooney and Garland

Mickey Rooney and Judy Garland never found better emotional musical partners than each other. They were both showbiz kids, born in trunks, and put to work by families that didn't exactly give them the best of childhoods. Rooney was performing publicly at the age of seventeen months, and Garland by the time she was two and a half. When they first appeared in movies together, in *Thoroughbreds Don't Cry* (1937), he was seventeen and she was fifteen, but both were already experienced pros who knew what they were up against: the practical need to keep their careers going. They would appear in ten movies together, although not all were musicals. Two were all-star shows that featured them performing numbers: *Words and Music* (1948), in which Rooney played Lorenz Hart and Garland played herself, so they paired for "I Wish I Were in Love Again," and *Thousands Cheer* (1943), in which they didn't perform together at all. They were together for three of Rooney's Andy Hardy movies: *Love Finds Andy Hardy* (1938), *Andy Hardy Meets Debutante* (1940), and *Life Begins for Andy Hardy* (1941).* Excluding *Thoroughbreds*, which was not a musical (Garland sings one song out of nowhere), there were only four musicals that actually presented them as a team: *Babes in Arms* (1939), *Strike Up the Band* (1940), *Babes on Broadway* (1941), and *Girl Crazy* (1943). It's a tribute to the power of their musical talents—and also to their dynamic pairing—that the idea of the Rooney/Garland collaboration is based on only four films.

Rooney and Garland are not like MacDonald and Eddy or Astaire and Rogers: They weren't two people who had worked their way up in show business and unexpectedly clicked when put together, generating an unexpected natural chemistry. Garland and Rooney were show-business born and bred, and they knew it was their job to pair up perfectly with *anyone* they were stuck with. That had been beaten into them as kids. So when they finally paired up with each other, their mutual professionalism was

---

* The three Andy Hardy films are not musicals, although Garland, cast as Betsy Booth, the daughter of a famous Broadway star, is given an opportunity to sing, because her future at MGM was guaranteed as a songstress. In *Love Finds Andy Hardy* she sings "In Between," "It Never Rains but What It Pours," and "Meet the Beat of My Heart"; in *Andy Hardy Meets Debutante*, she does "Alone" and "I'm Nobody's Baby." But in *Life Begins* she doesn't sing: four songs had been recorded ("Abide with Me," "America," "Easy to Love," and "The Rosary") but none was used. The key point is that Garland sang, but didn't perform musically with Rooney in these movies. *Thoroughbreds* was a horse-racing film in which Rooney plays a jockey.

atomic, and for them personally it was therapeutic. Each found a partner who was going through what the other one was going through. They bonded offscreen, and onscreen they did their jobs at the highest possible level in honor of that bonding. Garland and Rooney leap onto the screen with a "Wow! Pow!" energy. People took it as the excitement and promise of youth rather than as the sometimes pill-fueled neurosis of showbiz kids. Rooney said later in life: "Judy and I were so close we could have come from the same womb." Astaire and Rogers are possibly the most physically compatible couple ever seen onscreen, whether or not they are dancing. Every move they make suggests they were born to be united in dance, which isn't true for Rooney and Garland. Despite their obvious friendship, they are not physically and vocally unified, nor do they project a secretly held subtext of emotion. They are too young, too inexperienced in real-life feelings, and working too hard. Rooney and Garland are a pair who project consummate professionalism. Theirs is not an emotional link; it is the connection of exploited children who understand each other the way no one else possibly can. They can do anything musical the movie needs, but there's the sense they know they *must* do it coupled with their shared joy in the knowledge that, hideous though it might be for them at times, they *can* deliver. They project the relief of the no-risk situation for a couple of child stars who realize they've been paired with someone else who can do the job. They *survive* together as much as they perform together.

Their movie chemistry was manufactured by mixing pure talent with pure talent. They sang, they danced, they played musical instruments, they rode bicycles. They did comedy and they did drama. They generated a high-octane wattage that ultimately exploded and nearly killed them.

Garland and Rooney, like Astaire and Rogers, had very big separate careers. Garland is one of the musical film's most iconic figures. More books have been written on her than on any other Hollywood performer except for Marilyn Monroe, who isn't thought of primarily as a singer or dancer. It's often been Garland's stormy personal life that has attracted biographers as much as her ability to sing and dance, but there's no question she's a legendary figure in Hollywood's history. If she had made only *The Wizard of Oz* (1939), she would have earned her place; but she appeared in movies with both Fred Astaire and Gene Kelly, headlined her own star vehicles, was Oscar-nominated for both musical and dramatic performances, starred in a memorable TV show, and brought audiences to standing ovations in the theater. Although she died in 1969 at the age of only forty-seven, she

racked up a substantial list of outstanding musical moments in movies, and as a result she is revered to the point of idolatry.

Garland is sometimes thought of as unreliable and a trainwreck, but it's possible to make an argument for her as the consummate pro. She soldiered on despite everything. She partnered with the most dynamic musical performers of her era and she held the frame opposite stunning female competition, some who could sing and/or dance (Ann Miller, Cyd Charisse) and some who only had to stand there to grab the audience's attention (Lana Turner, Hedy Lamarr). Garland could fold herself into a duet comfortably, becoming a perfect costar and friendly companion, or she could carry even the weakest vehicle all by herself. Garland sliding smoothly into "For Me and My Gal" with Gene Kelly or clowning extravagantly with Astaire in "A Couple of Swells" are examples of how easily she adapted, how competently she could do whatever was asked of her musically, and how strong she was as an actress, never losing her character as she entered a musical number. In movies that she had to carry—*The Harvey Girls*, for instance—she's amazing, funny and touching and musical, turning what could have been a forgettable programmer into something really good.

(Her uncertain but eager-to-live character travels alone to the Wild West to marry, only to find herself in a Cyrano de Bergerac dilemma.) Garland lifts every scene. She makes "On the Atchison, Topeka, and the Santa Fe" unforgettable; wrings true poignance out of a minor song, "It's A Great Big World" as part of a trio that includes lesser talents Virginia O'Brien and a dubbed Charisse; and dances with gusto and skill to "Swing Your Partner Round and Round." There's no need to even mention her total ownership of "Somewhere Over the Rainbow" in *The Wizard of Oz*, and, of course, her rendition of "Have Yourself a Merry Little Christmas" in *Meet Me in St. Louis* is one of cinema's greatest musical moments, nailing the inevitable disappointment of the bummer holiday for all eternity. Yes, little Margaret O'Brien breaks down hysterically and takes over the scene, but it's Garland who drives her to become our surrogate weeper. Judy Garland was reliably entertaining in movie musicals from childhood to death.

Garland was a tiny woman (four foot eleven) with a big voice. She had about her the aura of a lost lamb, albeit one with a huge and saleable tal-

. . . and on Garland's TV show, older and legendary, with a lifetime of performance behind them

ent. She grew up on film, and the American public had the opportunity to watch it happen. At first she looked eager to please, a little uncertain about whether or not she would be liked, but not at all uncertain about belting out a song. Garland was a bit chunky and rather awkward and insecure looking in her earliest film appearances, but when she sang, all that fell away—she was transformed into something else. Her singing is effortless, even when it's designed to be emotional or a painful confession about inner feelings. She always knew how to sell a song, and she grew into a confident performer, but she never lost all of that youthful, tremulous quality. When she became a woman who seemed to carry genuine sadness inside her, audiences bonded to her for life. Most of her musicals contain a moment when she, alone in the frame, sings a sad or melancholy or moody song, seemingly to herself in a contemplative moment, but really directly to the viewer. This "Garland moment" was her signature. Wistfully, sadly, yearningly, but powerfully, she put an audience into an emotional musical conversation that made each person feel as if she were singing directly to him or to her. This ability to create privacy and intimacy is the mark of a star. Garland could do it when she was just a kid: in *Broadway Melody of 1938*, with "Dear Mr. Gable," and in *The Wizard of Oz*, singing "Over the Rainbow." Not many people want to sing the song today: there's no way to overcome the image of Judy, Toto, and a sepia-toned haystack. Over and over again, Garland would sing a plaintive tune in her "Garland moment": "I Cried for You" (*Babes in Arms*), "But Not for Me" (*Girl Crazy*), "Better Luck Next Time" (*Easter Parade*), "The Man That Got Away" (*A Star Is Born*). People either liked this emotional relationship or they didn't, but Garland had a glorious voice, and no matter how anyone felt about her presentation, the sound of her singing was always a gift. And the singing was not all Garland had: she could act, she could do comedy, she delivered lines with her own quirky, natural rhythm, and she could dance. Her dancing was not a smooth and polished performance, but she brought energy and commitment to every routine. She's a bit ragged sometimes, and fakes it a little in the whirls, but she's a pleasing dancer to watch because she knows it's supposed to be fun and she gives it everything. Garland has moments of dancing on film that endure.

When Judy Garland partners Fred Astaire or Gene Kelly, she keeps up, and her personality is strong enough to match her partner's. When she takes on a solo, it's possible to see what she could really do, as she brought the same individual personality to the dance that she did to the song. In

The Pirate she plays a repressed young woman from an unsophisticated environment who becomes accidentally hypnotized and releases herself through a wild dance ("Mack the Black"). "Don't call me poor soul," she warns just before she takes off, swishing the red-and-black skirt she wears underneath a virginal white blouse. She puts all her manic, even neurotic, energy into her dance. When she does "Get Happy" in *Summer Stock* or "Lose That Long Face" in *A Star Is Born*, she becomes the showbiz brat, born and raised, who knows it's up to her to make it go, and make it go she does. She was never better than when she took on as a dance partner the seven-year-old Margaret O'Brien in *Meet Me in St. Louis*, a musical moment that required her to act as well as sing and dance. Playing older sister and younger sister, Garland and O'Brien stage an allegedly impromptu performance at a teenage party in the family home. Garland warbles "Under the Bamboo Tree" while O'Brien (a terrific actress and also a child who'd had ballet lessons) follows her lead. Garland has to sing, dance, steer O'Brien, keep on her marks and under the key light, and also render a sensitive performance of an older sister making sure her little sister doesn't screw up, ruin the act, or misbehave. Garland juggles it all like the pro she always was.

As I've written elsewhere, Mickey Rooney had talent to burn—and he burned it. He was what in movies was called "a little guy," standing not much over five foot two. He had a boyish face, a wide grin, a shock of unruly hair, and a kind of gee-whiz demeanor that translated to moviegoers as an all-American optimism of the boy-next-door type. But Rooney was never a boy next door, unless you were renting next to a casino or a racetrack. He burned the candle at both ends in the most spectacular way, chasing women, drinking, carousing, gambling, all the while he was embodying the epitome of an American high-school boy, Andy Hardy. That's how good an actor Rooney was.

Over nine decades, until his death at age ninety-three in April of 2014, Rooney appeared onscreen in dramatic and comedic roles, earning Oscar nominations for Best Actor for *Babes in Arms* (1939) and *The Human Comedy* (1943) and two more for Best Supporting Actor, for *The Bold and the Brave* (1956) and *The Black Stallion* (1979), and winning two honorary Oscars, one in 1939 and one in 1983. The fact that he was considered important enough to movies to be given two honorary Academy Awards with forty-four years in between meant that he had gigantic staying power. Rooney's musical talent was prodigious. He sang; he danced; he played the drums, the piano, and the banjo; and he composed music. Yet he isn't limited to being a musical star; if anything, he's considered a dramatic actor or a comedian and seldom mentioned for his musicals—except those with Garland. It was the pairing with her that showed moviegoers what he could do with song and dance. Significantly, he had made no real musicals before her, and made almost none after.*

Judy Garland and Mickey Rooney were cast musically as typical American teenagers with typical American teenage problems. (They were anything but. And by the way, even if they were, what typical American teenager has the problem of having to put on a show to save his or her family financially? Or to save a college from financial ruin? Or any of the problems they faced, even in the allegedly more realistic Andy Hardy movies?) Two numbers show what Garland and Rooney could do together, and what their audience appeal really was: one from their first "grown-up" movie, *Babes in Arms*, and one from their last, *Girl Crazy*. When *Babes in Arms* was released (in 1939), it marked three firsts: the first all-out musical they did together; the first starring the two of them to be produced by the Freed Unit; and the first movie directed by Busby Berkeley at MGM. It was also Rooney's first chance to star in a true big-budget musical and show off his singing and dancing skills. In 1939 Rooney was at his peak. He had made fifty movies and had been a star for five years. He was *seasoned*. He had been listed among the top ten box-office draws during 1938, and had been named number one on that list in 1939, the year he was awarded a special Oscar for his contributions to the motion picture. Garland's stardom was newer, but she had established herself in *The Wizard of Oz*, and MGM believed in her future.

Babes in Arms was a huge hit. It abandons most of the Rodgers and Hart score written for the stage version, retaining only the beautiful "Where or When" and the title song. The story establishes the pattern that would be maintained throughout the four Rooney/Garland musicals: young people face a problem of some kind, and their solution will be to put on a musical show; Rooney will hurt Garland in some way, which will inspire her to sing

---

* His one other really significant musical is *Summer Holiday* (1948), with Gloria DeHaven, although *The Strip* (1951) cast him as a drummer who gets mixed up with gangsters and who is living in a nightclub world populated with musical performances by Louis Armstrong and others. He appeared on Broadway later in life in the hit show *Sugar Babies* (1979–82) and thus became redefined as a musical performer. His appearance as the tragic Lorenz Hart in *Words and Music* was a dramatic role that gave him limited musical-performance moments—one of which was, as mentioned, with Garland.

a sad love song; they will duet together; others will provide some music; and the movie will end with a big-bang all-out musical finale. All four films were made at MGM with Arthur Freed as producer and Busby Berkeley as director.

The "puttin' on a show" formula served Rooney and Garland well. It's in the great active American tradition of "Let's solve our problems by doing something." Also important: no one had to take it seriously. Some modern writers feel that audiences believed it in some naive way, but what audiences did believe was that kids would (and could) put on a show, as in high-school plays, Girl Scout Christmas programs, and community theater. That didn't mean anyone thought the show was going to be good, or move to Broadway, or make everyone rich and famous. It meant fun in real life, and usually it was done by young kids around a neighborhood during dull summer days. (I appeared in one with a group of my friends when I was seven years old. We called it "The Great K.D. NATCH Circus," and my job was to twirl a baton for the audience, even though I didn't know how to twirl a baton. It hardly mattered, since the magician didn't know how to do magic tricks, the clown was crying and wanted his mother, the acrobat couldn't turn a cartwheel, and the tap dancer was barefoot. What the heck, we were "puttin' on a show" in the tradition of Mickey and Judy! It wasn't real, but neither were *they* as far as we were concerned. We just liked them.)

Babes in Arms starts out by showing Rooney being born backstage at the Palace Theater in New York City during his father's vaudeville performance. As Rooney says on the DVD of *Babes in Arms*, the movie about kids "puttin' on a show" is "almost autobiographical." When an announcement of the birth is made, the audience all sing "Rock-a-Bye Baby" along with Rooney's father (played by Charles Winninger). Everyone believes they're secure in vaudeville, but then the sound motion picture arrives: the sound of "Broadway Melody" from the film of that name; a clip from the "Singin' in the Rain" number from *The Hollywood Revue of 1929*; and the *Variety* headline GARBO TALKS (Garbo, of course, was an MGM star).

What we see today in *Babes in Arms* is that although Rooney and Garland found relief in each other, there's a kind of manic horror in some of their work. They are two young people playing teenage uncertainty, but their mutual neuroses were real even if their circumstances in the movie weren't. Crazy pokes through. As they sing "Good Mornin'" (more famously known from *Singin' in the Rain*), Rooney plays the piano and

Garland sings, but the number escalates as it progresses. "Sell it, Ma, sell it!" he commands her. They are beyond professional; they are desperate. When they perform for their parents in their second number, Rooney frantically plays piano, slaps a bass, jumps around from instrument to instrument. Garland sings "against" Betty Jaynes, the soprano second lead who plays Rooney's sister. (She's a sort of Deanna Durbin phantom; Louis B. Mayer always regretted losing Durbin.) Rooney pounds the keys, slaps the bass; Garland sings, twirls around the room, and they jump on the piano stool—there's a push, a drive, a madness that fuels the number.

The finale of the movie is cut in half: a bifurcated version of the show they put on, half of which takes place in their small town and half of which appears on Broadway at a later time. This musical ending, like the endings of all their four "puttin' on a show" movies, has a frenzied quality. The first half is an unfortunate minstrel show, with Mickey and Judy (and everyone else onstage) in blackface. It's a terrible stereotype, and the music (old songs like "Banjo on My Knee," "I'm Just Wild About Harry," "Ida," and "Moonlight Bay") can't make up for what the audience is seeing. The racial insensitivity is overwhelming. The second half of the show is patriotic bang-bang with such lines as "We've got no Duce, we've got no Führer / But we've got Garbo and Norma Shearer . . . / We've got Nelson Eddy, lots of others, / We've got three of the four Marx Brothers." (The lyrics were the smug boast of MGM, since all these stars were under contract to the studio at the time.) The final extravaganza contains a great deal of marching, marching, with Rooney impersonating Franklin Delano Roosevelt and Garland his wife, Eleanor. (Rooney's impressions of famous people were a part of these movies. Earlier he had given viewers both Clark Gable and Lionel Barrymore.)* What our country needs right now, say Rooney and Garland, is DANCE! And dance they do, with the entire cast swinging out into a wild jitterbugging, tapping, marching chaos of movement, which is finished off—inspiring some relief—by the words "The End" on the screen. (Whew!) During World War II, this frantic quality would fuel many musicals and bring other performers to stardom (Betty Hutton, most conspicuously); but the pairing of Rooney and Garland, with their youthful exuberance (and possibly pill-ingested energy), all under the direction of the manic Berkeley, kicked it off.

* His best is his manic Carmen Miranda, executed in full drag in *Babes on Broadway*. He was dressed in this outfit when he was introduced to Ava Gardner on set. He became her first husband.

The last of the "puttin' on a show" musicals* was *Girl Crazy*, and Rooney and Garland are at their best. He shines in the first (and almost immediate) number, in which, as a carousing college boy who drinks too much, he shows up at a nightclub where Tommy Dorsey is playing. He's pulled onstage, pushed around by a lineup of chorus girls, and then June Allyson (not yet a star) comes out to do a specialty number, singing "Treat Me Rough" à la Betty Hutton. Rooney has to give a "drunk" performance while also responding to the choreography, Allyson, the club "audience" watching, and the subversive lyrics. For her part, Garland is more beautiful than she had ever been in her early years. It's less than five years since *Babes in Arms*, but both stars have grown in presence, confidence, and ability. They don't seem to be kids anymore, and yet they're still youthful and credible as college-age. They are seamlessly both musical and dramatic, and Garland is now as great a star as Rooney. At the start of their pairing, he was the star and she was a super-talented beginner. This film recognizes who she has become and who she will be forever, and if anything, she's given more to do than he is. (Rooney has a great deal of comedy shtick, and most of it doesn't hold up well, whereas Garland has more music, and everything she does seems as modern as the day it was shot. At the time the film was released, the balance between them might have seemed more equal.) The amazing Gershwin songs are perfect for them, and the plot is stuffed with music, a lot of it. The Tommy Dorsey orchestra, an audience favorite of the era, was also featured. Except for the finale ("I Got Rhythm"), the choreography is done by Charles Walters.†

Girl Crazy is high octane like the Gershwin music that drives it, full of American zest and energy and thus perfect for the hard-driving, high-stepping sass and strut of the more mature Rooney and Garland. Even the lovely and romantic tune "Embraceable You" is staged with nonstop movement around a ballroom. Garland sings the lovely lyrics ("you irreplaceable you") as she moves behind a long tableful of young men who are help-

---

* These musicals are also called backstage musicals, although technically Rooney and Garland are not playing professionals who are "backstage." They are also known as "barnyard musicals," although no particular barnyards show up in them. Because I am from the farmland, where there are real barnyards, I always call them "puttin' on a show" musicals.

† Walters ultimately became a director of musicals, among them some of the most entertaining and unpretentious of Hollywood's output: *Easter Parade*, *Summer Stock*, *Good News* (1947), and *High Society*. Walters's musicals are favorites of most musical fans for their excellent dance numbers, handling of star performers, and sheer entertainment value.

ing her celebrate her birthday. The camera moves with her as she glides smoothly along, and it never abandons her, letting her rest only when she sits down at her new piano (a birthday gift from the chorus) to play—and she really could. When she climbs onto the piano, they pull her back and forth across the floor, and finally she dances with all of them, then taking on one partner (who is Walters). Except for the poignant "But Not for Me," the numbers all reflect movement, energy, and a kinetic spirit that fits with the setting, the story, and the star team. Their duet, "Could You Use Me?," shows clearly how Rooney and Garland have meshed. They are perfectly in sync in a comedy song and dance, and both of them display acting skills that are smoothly woven into the music.

Garland has three special numbers all her own: "Bidin' My Time" which she performs with a cowboy quartet rather than Rooney; the lovely "Embraceable You," with its mobile camera tracking around the ballroom; and one of her greatest solos, "But Not for Me," exquisitely shot with shadows falling on her dress and her face (by cinematographer William Daniels, who was Garbo's favorite). The finale, the last of the Rooney/ Garland musical blockbusters, is a frantic mélange of tap dancing, singing, fringed whips being cracked, and guns being fired by cowboys. It's Busby Berkeley's choreography and his last time to yell at Garland off camera; she looks almost hysterical at moments. As platoons of cowboys and cow-girls march up and down, back and forth, and the Dorsey band blasts the music, the number comes to a wow finish as a large cannon is drawn up and fired. Rooney and Garland are lifted up and down inside a circle of dancers, and then brought into close-up as they sing: "Who could ask for anything more?" It was a great ending for a cycle of star vehicles that paired two unbelievably talented performers.

The last sight anyone had of Judy Garland and Mickey Rooney together was when he guested on her 1963–64 TV show, *The Judy Garland Show*, on CBS. They have beached up there, the flotsam and jetsam of early fame, both reflecting the pain of celebrity, lost stardom, exhausting lifestyles, too much booze and pills, too many marriages, and maybe too much talent discovered too young. Both look old and tired before their time, and in the photos taken during rehearsals, they seem wary and skeptical. And yet as they sit together, leaning against each other, his arm across her lap, her head tilted toward his, you have the impression that when the bell rings, they'll leap up and win the prize, if only because they know that they can count on the other to do his/her half. At the end of their pairing, Rooney and Garland don't have much left in the tank, but together they can make it add up to more. Theirs was the love affair of professionals, and the only one that lasted for either of them. She gave him credit for teaching her what she needed to know in movies and when asked who was her favorite costar, never hesitated to say "Mickey Rooney." When the TV show was finished, Rooney took Garland's hand and led her down to the audience. He said, "Here is the love of my life."

Strategies

GENRE MOVIES DON'T ALL HAVE THE SAME THINGS. There's not always a schoolmarm or a saloon singer in a western, and some shootouts are unconventional. How about one with a harpoon, as in *Terror in a Texas Town* (1958)? (A Norwegian sailor walks the walk in the lonely street, gunless, and heaves his harpoon at his opponent, taking him down.) There are genre hybrids, cross-pollinations, varied tones such as a comic western (*Blazing Saddles*, 1974) or a musical western (*Red Garters*, 1954). There are subplots that appear so frequently they themselves begin to be thought of as genres: the "slasher movie," which is a horror film with knives. Genre can't always be quickly identified. What if the first image is rain pounding on the windowpanes of an old dark house as lightning flashes and shrieks and moans are heard? Sounds like horror. On the other hand, maybe it's a comedy. Or maybe inside the house the zombies are doing the Watusi and it's a musical. Once the movie business found a generic definition, it began to develop it, vary it, and create subgenres for it. These manipulations became business strategies, designed to keep an established story format fresh for customers. With musicals, there was always one happy issue: the songs were what counted, and you could keep writing new ones. The plots didn't matter as much. And yet the business needed reliable stories. As Hollywood moved through the transition to sound, the 1933 establishment of the musical as original genre movie entertainment (as well as a tone to be laid over other genres), and the understanding that musical movies could be developed around specific star personalities, it also realized that plot variations could be reliable moneymaking strategies. Various ideas, creations, experiments, and inspirations appeared, disappeared, reappeared, and finally solidified into studio policy. (Historical developments in Hollywood are seldom straightforwardly linear.) The studios settled into using story types and established forms such as opera, operetta, and the "showbiz" story. They borrowed and musicalized genres like the biopic. They expanded the practice of adapting and remaking successful Broadway material into films by using dramatic films as a foundation for a musical translation: stir in music and a new film with a reliable story was created. They also practiced their usual form of financial acumen: they created a B musical, a cheap reference to the more expensive original. These strategies not only paid off; they became basic subgenres in the definition of the musical . . . and they could all easily be used as star vehicles.

Biopics

An easy way to make a musical would surely be to tell a story about a musician, right? It seems simple enough. Just take a composer, a singer, a dancer, an impresario, an opera star—anyone connected with music—and tell what happened to him or her . . . with music. It didn't take long for the filmmaking business to start making musical "biopics" (as biographical films are jauntily known). Very few stand up on modern viewing, however. Biopics about musical performers were often movies thrown together around a star, or around a famous song (which was usually the title of the film), or just around a series of musical numbers, and that was that. They are seldom distinguished films.

And yet there are so many of them! There are movies about bandleaders: (*The Glenn Miller Story*, 1954, *The Benny Goodman Story*, 1955, *The Fabulous Dorseys*, 1947, *The Five Pennies*, 1959, about Red Nichols); about classical composers: Robert and Clara Schumann and Johannes Brahms (*Song of Love*, 1947), Mozart (*Amadeus*, 1984), Rimsky-Korsakov (*Song of Scheherazade*, 1947), Chopin (*A Song to Remember*, 1945), Liszt (*Song Without End*, 1960), Grieg (*Song of Norway*, 1970); about opera stars: Enrico Caruso (*The Great Caruso*, 1951), Marjorie Lawrence (*Interrupted Melody*, 1955),

Grace Moore (*So This Is Love*, 1953), Jenny Lind (*A Lady's Morals*, 1930); about popular song composers: DeSylva, Henderson, and Brown (*The Best Things in Life Are Free*, 1956), Rodgers and Hart (*Words and Music*, 1948), Paul Dresser (*My Gal Sal*, 1942), George Gershwin (*Rhapsody in Blue*, 1945), Jerome Kern (*Till the Clouds Roll By*, 1946), Victor Herbert (*The Great Victor Herbert*, 1939), Stephen Foster (*Swanee River*, 1939), Dan Emmett (*Dixie*, 1943), W. C. Handy (*St. Louis Blues*, 1958), John Philip Sousa (*Stars and Stripes Forever*, 1952), Scott Joplin (*Scott Joplin*, 1977), Gilbert and Sullivan (*Topsy-Turvy*, 1999); about choreographers: Bob Fosse (*All That Jazz*, 1979), and dancers (*The Story of Vernon and Irene Castle*, 1939); about performers: the Dolly Sisters (*The Dolly Sisters*, 1945), Eva Tanguay (*The I Don't Care Girl*, 1953), Marilyn Miller (*Look for the Silver Lining*, 1949), Gertrude Lawrence (*Star!*, 1968), Jane Froman (*With a Song in My Heart*, 1952), Ruth Etting (*Love Me or Leave Me*, 1955), Billie Holiday (*Lady Sings the Blues*, 1972), Al Jolson (*The Jolson Story*, 1946), Blossom Seeley (*Somebody Loves Me*, 1952), Helen Morgan (*The Helen Morgan Story*, 1957), Fanny Brice (*Funny Girl*, 1968), Nora Bayes (*Shine on Harvest Moon*, 1944), George M. Cohan (*Yankee Doodle Dandy*, 1942), Lillian Russell (*Lillian Russell*, 1940), Lillian Roth (*I'll Cry Tomorrow*, 1955), and Ray Charles (*Ray*, 2004); about piano players: *The Eddie Duchin Story* (1956); about drummers: *The Gene Krupa Story* (1959); about strippers: Gypsy Rose Lee (*Gypsy*, 1962); about impresarios and night club owners: Sol Hurok (*Tonight We Sing*), Florenz Ziegfeld (*The Great Ziegfeld*, 1936), Texas Guinan (*Incendiary Blonde*, 1945); about country music singer/composers: Loretta Lynn (*Coal Miner's Daughter*, 1980), Woody Guthrie (*Bound For Glory*, 1976), Hank Williams (*Your Cheatin' Heart*, 1964), Patsy Cline (*Sweet Dreams*, 1985), and Johnny Cash (*Walk the Line*, 2005); about singing groups (*Jersey Boys*, 2015) and many more. A complete list would be overwhelming, if this one isn't.

Most of these movies are scorned, even though they were "only musicals" and no one expected much anyway. Debates about historical accuracy for movies about important people (Lincoln, for example) are endless, but the musical category seemed to be less significant. The purpose of the musical biopic is music: musical performance and/or the story of musical composition or the challenge of the musical life. It's not teaching fact; it's presenting music. Nevertheless, musical biopics have come in for their own scorn, as in the case of *The Dolly Sisters* (1945). Rosie and Jenny Dolly were identical twins, not just sisters. They were brunettes, not blondes (although

Betty Grable and June Haver portrayed them). And their lives were any-thing but uniformly successful, both personally and professionally: multiple marriages, gambling addictions, and suicide plagued them, none of which turns up in their biopic. In the musicals category, perhaps the most scorned example is *Night and Day*, the alleged story of the life of composer Cole Porter. Gone is the fact he was neither tall nor handsome (he's embodied by Cary Grant); gone is the story of his homosexuality; gone is the truth about his classmate Monty Woolley, who plays his "former Yale professor"; gone is any understanding of the complex relationship Porter had with his wife, Linda. And yet watching the movie—and listening to it—conveys a sense of Cary Grant as Cole Porter that has a curious appropriateness. Grant is the epitome of a certain casual sophistication grounded in a hard-working, hardscrabble background. He was a Cockney who pulled himself out of poverty into the role of "Cary Grant," a Cole Porter–ish creation if ever there was one. Grant *is* the lyrical world of Porter: the guy who always knows what to say, says it simply and charmingly, with a little twist of bit-terness or jabbing humor, the guy who never fools himself about love, who is both funny and dangerous, who knows how to dress, how to act, and how to woo. The songs of Cole Porter—who was not born poor like Grant but was a midwesterner who created his own sophistication—are the concept of a "Cary Grant." Furthermore, just to listen to the lyric "do do / That voodoo / That you do so well" is to hear the staccato, broken-rhythmic delivery, the punching out of the words, that is the vocal style of Grant. The "Judy, Judy, Judy" line that imitators invented to sound like Grant has the same "voodoo that you do" structure. If Porter's music and lyrics were magically turned into a human being, they would, in fact, turn into Cary Grant. So why not Grant as Porter? And Porter's gay yearning is all over his lyrics (which *are* in the film). His marriage is presented with meaningful subtext: first he tries to escape Linda—he turns down her offer of support and love—and after he finally does marry her, he avoids her by working nonstop and never spending time alone with her. There is an undercurrent of aural and visual truth to *Night and Day* that is cinematic and runs under-neath the surface like some suppressed melody waiting its turn to surface.

A few biopics stand out for being truly musical biographies as opposed to being just musicals—or just biographies. What mattered, of course, was music, but there were other challenges to the biopic, primarily in whatever was the true story of the musician's life. Was there drama? Was there even any kind of a story, and if not, could one be invented? (Invention of "facts" was never a no-no for Hollywood.) Concurrently, was there too much drama, or drama of a sort that didn't seem salable to a current audience? (*Night and Day* ignored Cole Porter's homosexuality, while his latter-day biopic, the 2004 *De-Lovely*, told the audience about almost nothing else.) Many musical stars had no real story: born in showbiz, worked in showbiz, died in showbiz. Others were too forgotten to be of interest decades later. It was hard to create plots that weren't just "And then he/she wrote . . ." for composers, or "And then I sang . . ." for performers.

Four biopics illustrate the problems of the form and what the business accomplished with them: *Till the Clouds Roll By* (1946), *Yankee Doodle Dandy* (1942), *Love Me or Leave Me* (1955), and *The Great Waltz* (1938). All four of these films were successful. Two are personal stories about American songwriters: Jerome Kern (*Till the Clouds Roll By*) and George M. Cohan (*Yankee Doodle Dandy*); one tells the story of a performer who popularized the songs of her era, Ruth Etting (*Love Me or Leave Me*); and one is the story of a European composer whose music is known to everyone, Johann Strauss Jr. (*The Great Waltz*). These musicals identify some things that can make a biopic successful: a dramatic human story with a murder (*Love Me or Leave Me*), music that adapts easily to the rhythms of film editing (*The Great Waltz*), a wealth of popular songs to be used (*Till the Clouds Roll By*), or music with a patriotic theme (*Yankee Doodle Dandy*).

George M. Cohan (1878–1942) and Jerome Kern (1885–1945) were contemporaries, and both had a big influence on the popular music of their era. Both wrote songs that are now standards. Kern had thirty-eight shows on Broadway, and eight of them were made into successful movies. Cohan himself appeared in a dual role in a successful movie musical, *The Phantom President* (1932), which had songs by Rodgers and Hart.* Two of his successful stage musicals were made into movies (*Little Nellie Kelly*, 1940, with Judy Garland, and *Little Johnny Jones*, 1929). Both biopics were being planned within the lifetimes of their subjects. *Yankee Doodle Dandy* in 1942 and *Till the Clouds Roll By* in 1945 represent the pros and cons of musical biopics and make a good comparison. The films were reviewed and received in opposite ways. *Yankee Doodle Dandy*, starring James Cagney

---

* Cohan also made three silent films, *Broadway Jones* (1917), *Seven Keys to Baldpate* (1917), and *Hit-the-Trail Holliday* (1918), none of which, obviously, were musicals. His only other film (*Gambling*, 1934) is considered "lost" and is unavailable for viewing. Based on a play by Cohan, it's a murder mystery about gamblers and has two songs, "My Little Girl" and "Dr. Watson and Mr. Holmes." The first is by Cohan and the second by Bernie Hanighen and Johnny Mercer.

(who won the Best Actor Oscar), was hailed as excellent entertainment, and audiences turned it into a financial success. On the other hand, *Till the Clouds Roll By*, starring Robert Walker, was denounced by critics. The movie *did* make money, mostly due to its parade of MGM stars performing great Jerome Kern numbers. Seen today, the evaluation of Cagney's performance remains solid, although many find the movie too patriotic (it was designed to lift morale in World War II), and most people still find *Till the Clouds Roll By* tedious in its plot but delightful in its musical numbers.

If no factor other than the leading performers was considered, *Yankee* and *Clouds* vary enormously. James Cagney, who deserved his Oscar win, is one of Hollywood's most charismatic and legendary movie stars. Cagney's dancing *contains* his energy, keeping it coiled inside as if, although he's giving out all anyone could want, there's plenty more if he needs it. His unique presence—brash, wily, simultaneously both reassuring and dangerous—and his astonishing ability to tap, sing, and control his body make him an obvious choice to play a dynamic stage performer. He's a dynamic *film* performer, so it all translates perfectly, and in George M. Cohan, Cagney found an iconic role.* Robert Walker was a fine actor, but he had no musical ability (or at least none ever shown onscreen). His movie persona was that of a shy young all-American guy, somewhat hesitant and sweet. Even when he played a villain, as in Hitchcock's *Strangers on a Train* or McCarey's *My Son John*, he was effective because he seemed so likable, so charming. While Cagney is banging out taps and challenging rivals and dominating the frame (beautifully) in *Yankee*, Walker has nothing much to do in *Clouds* except stand around representing decency and a cerebral talent. Audiences could grab on to Cagney, but found no way to connect to Walker, who nevertheless did his best with a colorless role.

The two biopics have much in common: they are traditional stories about real-life composers, recounting an American success story with falsifications of facts to present a more interesting and "shaped" narrative. They both contain death scenes, family conflicts, and happy marriages. They are not only about real people, they present portraits of other real people who

---

* For audiences, he *became* Cohan, and stood as the audience's mental picture of him so much that in 1955, when Bob Hope played Eddie Foy in *The Seven Little Foys*, Cagney was asked to reprise his role in a bit in which he and Hope, playing the two legendary showmen, dance on a table together in what is one of the really great musical moments buried in a so-so movie. Hope and Cagney are real dancers, but they also know how to dance in character, ad-libbing through the routine, teasing, challenging, tapping—two old pros, legends portraying legends.

Two World War II biopics: James Cagney dancing up a storm as George M. Cohan in *Yankee Doodle Dandy* . . .

were musical stars (Eddie Foy, Marilyn Miller, etc.). Both have montages of famous Broadway show marquees, to illustrate the passage of time and touch base with audience awareness of just how famous the biographical subjects were. Each film has an extended musical number that re-creates one of the subject's biggest hits: *Little Johnny Jones* in *Yankee Doodle Dandy* and *Show Boat* in *Till the Clouds Roll By*. Both stories span many years and are told in flashback, using narration.

Where they differ is what makes one musical work while another doesn't.* The most significant difference that affects audience enjoyment is simple: although both men are successful composers of popular music, one of them (Cohan/Cagney) is also a performer and the other one (Kern/

* *Till the Clouds Roll By* is in color, and *Yankee Doodle Dandy* in black-and-white; the former was made at MGM and the latter at Warner Bros.

Walker) is not. Cagney can thus perform Cohan's music himself, so audience involvement is greater with Cagney than with Walker. Cohan can also be seamlessly integrated into the musical episodes of his story in a way that Kern can't. For instance, Cagney tries to sell his song "Harrigan" by performing it with his love interest (Joan Leslie). An audience can identify with Cagney's *character*, while they can only identify with Kern's *music*. Although there is a hoked-up "family" mini-problem in the Kern movie, involving the daughter (played by Lucille Bremer) of his friend and mentor (Van Heflin), there is no real development of an emotional connection between Kern and her character. The script of *Yankee Doodle Dandy* provides a flesh-and-blood character for Cagney: a selfish, egotistical man who nevertheless wins respect, whereas the Kern character is too good to be true. He never loses his temper, never faces a crisis, never does much of anything, ending up a bore. (The biggest excitement in Kern's onscreen life comes when he does *not* go to Europe on the *Lusitania*, which was sunk by the Germans. Kern misses the boat—and so does the movie.) This comparison is furthered by the fact that George M. Cohan was born into a show-business family—his parents and sisters are all musical characters. He had to struggle against poverty and the ups and downs of a precarious profession. He had to fight for success, and the plot shows him scraping

. . . and Robert Walker as Jerome Kern in *Till the Clouds Roll By*, with little Joan Wells and Van Heflin (standing)

Biopics: the real persons and how Hollywood presented them. George M. Cohan, natty in his hat . . .

. . . and James Cagney, sartorially similar (*Yankee Doodle Dandy*)

his way upward. Kern was born relatively well-off. The audience meets him only after he's grown up and starting his career. His entry into show business apparently wasn't overly difficult, and once launched, he never suffered a down period. (Kern was preparing to write the score for the 1946 hit *Annie Get Your Gun* when he collapsed and died of a heart attack.) The difference in the basic biographies of Cohan and Kern robs the latter's story of one of filmdom's basic biopic staples: the rags-to-riches story of a guy who, in a very American way, fights for success and rises up not only because of talent but also because of hard work and a feisty nature. Cohan is a typical American hero, with his energy and comic ways, while Kern seems passive and dull. MGM counted on Kern's beautiful music being enough for audiences.

MGM—and other studios, too—made biopics like the Kern film (e.g., *Words and Music*, about Rodgers and Hart, or *Deep in My Heart*, about Sigmund Romberg) to showcase a roster of musical stars performing famous songs. The composer was an excuse, and whatever his life might be could be suppressed, repressed, tarted up and dramatized, or basically ignored. The point was to showcase the stars in a sort of updated version of something like 1929's *Show of Shows*. Today, the stories seem tedious, and a viewer waits from number to number, trapped in a star performance musical nightmare. Sometimes the performances are worth the wait: June Allyson and the charming Blackburn Twins in "Thou Swell" in *Words and Music*; Lena Horne singing back-to-back "Where or When" and "The Lady Is a Tramp" in the same film, gorgeously gowned in white with purple and lavender accents; Jose Ferrer and his singer wife, Rosemary Clooney, doing a duet of "Mr. and Mrs." in *Deep in My Heart*; Judy Garland as Marilyn Miller in *Till the Clouds Roll By* washing dishes and singing her heart out with "Look for the Silver Lining" (the number was directed by Vincente Minnelli). But one waits for these gems and, while waiting, has to sit through some pretty swampy plot progress. In those days, audiences loved musical numbers and were willing to wait if they had to for each emergence of a major star to do a few minutes of music. Even in the days of first release, these biopics did not draw audiences because of the composers themselves but because of the stars and the promised performance of the music. "Thou Swell" alone shows how deep the talent roster went in those days. June Allyson was a top box-office star serving her studio, available for a single number, and the Blackburn Twins were popular dancers who appeared in several first-rate musicals. They were good-looking, able to do tap, a little ballet, and modern dance with great exuberance and real skill. They were minor supporting talent, but major talents inside the frame. For every set of Blackburn Twins, considered specialty players, there were literally hundreds of others who never made it onscreen at all except as extras or members of the chorus.

Yankee Doodle Dandy is not designed to show off a musical talent roster like MGM's, but rather to present Warners impressive cast of famous character actors, all playing real historical people in nonmusical support-

The young and beautiful singer Ruth Etting . . .

. . . portrayed by a glamorous Doris Day (*Love Me or Leave Me*)

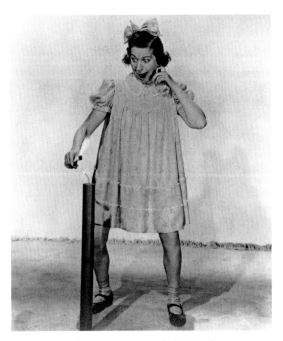

Fanny Brice in her comic guise as Baby Snooks . . .

. . . and Barbra Streisand's re-creation, with hair bow, ankle socks, and flat shoes (*Funny Girl*)

ing roles that provide plot development and colorful, believable characterizations. The large supporting cast of *Till the Clouds Roll By* is different: a remarkable roster of famous musical performers under contract to MGM, but their "support" comes only through performing a musical number and then disappearing. This means that the people who perform Kern's music are just the people who perform Kern's music. The person who performs Cohan's music is Cohan himself in the guise of the unique and utterly alive and energetic James Cagney. *Yankee Doodle Dandy* thus is making a story with music. *Till the Clouds Roll By* is making music with a story. The main actor in *Yankee Doodle Dandy* provides the music, with supporters providing comedy and drama. The main actors in the Kern film provide drama and comedy (not much), with the supporting cast there only to perform disconnected numbers. Ironically, this means that *Till the Clouds Roll By* is more musical than *Yankee Doodle Dandy*, but with less satisfying results.

A comparison of the scripts for the two movies locates the basic discrepancy of quality. Each film has its raison d'être: *Yankee Doodle Dandy*'s is patriotism, because it was released in the early days of World War II, and *Till the Clouds Roll By*'s is a celebration of the life of one of America's most successful and popular songwriters. *Yankee Doodle Dandy* is written as a brash portrait of a typical American. *Till the Clouds Roll By* means to be reverent. (MGM decided to take a deified, slightly pompous attitude toward Kern due to his recent death, and no studio could be more pompous than MGM when it made up its mind.)* The script of *Yankee Doodle Dandy* tries to unite onstage musical numbers with offstage events by moving back and forth inside a musical performance. When Joan Leslie sings the Cohan number "The Warmest Baby in the Bunch" (an immortal lyric), she doesn't realize Cohan hasn't obtained permission from the theater owner for her to do so. Offstage, he's involved in a fistfight to keep her from being removed from the spotlight. She performs; the backstage fight is revealed; she goes on performing; the backstage fight gets worse; etc. The movie cuts back and forth between plot and music. *Till the Clouds Roll By* tries to present its superstar numbers as minimusicals in and of themselves, uninterrupted, so that an audience can enjoy Judy Garland or June Allyson or Dinah Shore on her own terms.

The two scripts also contain many parallels, some of which are ludicrous. Cohan goes to the White House, Kern goes to MGM. Cohan goes "over there" to the European war, and Kern goes "out there" to Hollywood. Where script and performance really make a difference is in the two death scenes. When Cohan's father (Walter Huston) dies, two great movie actors, Huston and Cagney, play out an honest emotional situation in which neither one misses a beat. The scene

* Kern died just before production began, in the film's planning stages. Cohan died on November 5, 1942, at age sixty-four. The film had premiered in New York on Memorial Day to great success and went into general release on June 6th. When first approached in 1941 about the biopic, Cohan asked, "Would anybody go to see it?," adding that he didn't "want to be connected with a box-office flop." He needn't have worried.

Billie Holiday with her trademark gardenias . . .

. . . and the showstopping Diana Ross, who portrayed her in *Lady Sings the Blues*

includes a motif that has been emphasized throughout the movie: when the Cohan family finished a number, the son always said, "My mother thanks you, my sister thanks you, my father thanks you, and I thank you." When Cohan speaks these words to his dying father, it is a true family moment, a son saying goodbye to his father. When Kern says goodbye to his mentor as he dies, there is no such connection and no echoed motif. Robert Walker and Van Heflin are both excellent actors, but there's no real emotional build. They have nothing to work with.*

Both movies, as musicals, are very aware of the proscenium arch. Since they're about Broadway composers, they remain wedded to the sense of an accurate presentation of the musical performance onstage. As a result, both films share a strength (consistency of theme and biographical truth) and a weakness (flatly presented numbers that are less lively and modern). A biopic that is a musical must finally be judged on its music and its musical performances. Each of these movies does, in fact, at some point break

Cole Porter, elegantly turned out as always . . .

* There's always a "test of time" bottom line to movies. Although *Till the Clouds Roll By* ends up the loser on the biopic scale, it has an ace up its sleeve: the wonderful music of Jerome Kern and some great performances by MGM's best. It uses nearly fifteen minutes of screen time right at the start to re-create the opening night of Kern's *Show Boat*. Kathryn Grayson is Magnolia, Lena Horne is Julie, and Tony Martin is Gaylord. There's no arguing with Kern as a composer or musical innovator.

the proscenium-arch tradition. *Till the Clouds Roll By* shows two unrelated back-to-back numbers using different costumes (with June Allyson) in a re-creation of *Leave It to Jane* that would not happen onstage, but its main break with tradition comes in the numbers done by Judy Garland, portraying Marilyn Miller. Although the movie was directed by Richard Whorf, a journeyman former actor under contract to MGM, Garland's numbers were directed by Vincente Minnelli. Garland has two major sequences: an alleged re-creation of Miller's rendition of "Look for the Silver Lining" as she originally did it onstage and a presentation of two other hits, "Who?" and "Sunny." The Minnelli-directed musical presentations create their own reality and their own miniplots. "Look for the Silver Lining" begins offstage in Miller's star dressing room, with a fashionably dressed Garland removing her own clothes, putting on a waitress costume, and dirtying her face to play a little scullery maid who will be washing dishes as she sings. Garland is called for her entrance, and she walks along backstage, greeting

. . . and Cary Grant (with Alexis Smith), dressed as the suave soldier Porter never was in *Night and Day*

stagehands, as she prepares to "go on." The camera tracks with her, setting up a postmodern peep at "backstage" before her "onstage" entrance. First an audience sees Garland as a glamorous, self-confident woman who dismisses her dressing-room guest and begins turning herself into her opposite: a poor little waif. She then walks onto a "stage"—pretty cavernous for Broadway—and washes dishes, singing about her dreams and reminding herself to "look for the silver lining." The musical performance has been set up to give a viewer a little plot, a shift in characterization through music, and a full musical onstage performance. Not only does this work within the context of the film itself, but it comments on Garland and how Minnelli, her husband at the time, saw her as the person she really was (chic, sharp) but also understood the film persona she had created for her fans (a sad/ funny little figure). As Garland sings, the camera never leaves her, creating the "Fred Astaire" tight frame around her so audiences can become deeply involved in her song.

Garland's other two songs, "Who?" and "Sunny," are highly cinematic. They involve a vivid use of color, swirling images (the entrance of a circus troupe), and a rapidly moving camera (lifting, dropping, involving heavy usage of booms and cranes). An audience sees Garland alone, Garland with a group, Garland leading and Garland following, but always Garland as the central figure of the musical performance. The space inside the frame takes on a depth the proscenium stage doesn't have, and the experience of watching becomes almost three-dimensional. The camera leads the viewing eye deep into the frame, creating the feeling of becoming a part of the performance itself. Inside this fairly unsatisfactory musical, *Till the Clouds Roll By*, lies an important historical revelation. Vincente Minnelli was to become one of the most important factors in developing the American film musical into an original art form. The almost shocking difference between the way the numbers he directed look today and the more pedestrian and conventional remainder of the film is a harbinger of what is to come. It's also important to realize that much of what will be attributed to the influence of Gene Kelly is already visible here: the attempt to make dance kinetic and to shape the two-dimensional experience of dance on film into a deeper, more three-dimensional format.

Yankee Doodle Dandy breaks the arch in a patriotic presentation of the Cohans doing "You're a Grand Old Flag," one of Cohan's hit songs. The number contains marching bands, armies of class-conscious workers, and superimpositions of the American flag. It has the Lincoln Memorial in it! The camera moves wildly, almost taking off as if it's searching for Busby Berkeley, whose influence is clearly felt. (It's a Warner Bros. film, after all, although well-directed by Michael Curtiz.)* The visual presentation has a

---

* Dances were credited to Seymour Felix, LeRoy Prinz, and John Boyle.

sense of depth, space, movement, and narrative internal logic that marks it out as cinema, not theater.

Both *Clouds* and *Yankee Doodle* are biopics that tell stories with plots, but the bottom line for both is music as much as—if not more than—drama. *Love Me or Leave Me* is an exemplary biopic of the dramatic variety. It succeeds because it treats the story of Ruth Etting, a famous vaudeville and radio star in the 1920s, as a dramatic event in which the leading character just happens to sing. Etting performs on the radio, in nightclubs, and on Broadway, and during rehearsals or while being filmed. She sings because, in the tradition of the backstage musical, it's her job. The film's focus is on the intense story of Ruth Etting (played by Doris Day) and the mentor who became her husband, gangster Moe "the Gimp" Snyder (James Cagney). Cagney, although a musical-biopic veteran, does not perform music in the film, but he has a musical-performance rhythm and clearly depicts an appreciation for Day's musical ability. The story uses songs to comment on the advancement and ultimate deterioration of the relationship between Etting and Snyder through music. When things are upbeat, Day sings "Stay on the Right Side, Sister"; when she feels forced into a relationship with Snyder, "You Made Me Love You"; after he exploits her, "Mean to Me"; "Shaking the Blues Away" when she tries to lose herself in work; when she feels degraded, "Ten Cents a Dance." When she falls in love with another man and has to leave him, two newly composed songs reflect her situation: "I'll Never Stop Loving You" for the man she falls in love with, and "Never Look Back" as she is forced to leave him behind.

Love Me or Leave Me is successful because it has at its core what most biopics lack: a true dramatic story, involving Etting's difficult relationship with a gangster who furthered her career, and her ultimate dilemma when she falls in love with another man. Snyder shoots his rival, which happened in real life; he served a prison sentence for it. (Etting and Snyder wed in 1922 but divorced in 1937. Unhappy later about her relationship with pianist Myrl Alderman, Snyder shot him on October 15, 1938, but Alderman recovered from his wounds. Three days later, his wife sued Etting for alienation of affection, but he and Etting wed on December 14, 1938, during Snyder's trial.) The story department didn't have to invent this perfect tale of 1920s gangsterism, nor did they have to hide the love affair, since Etting gave her legal permission to tell her story. There was no drama to be invented, and none to suppress. The story of Ruth Etting was a good movie tale, and that made her a perfect subject for a biopic. Having Doris Day to play her, and having Cagney to portray the gangster—his cinematic DNA—lifted what might have been an ordinary movie to the top. It also didn't hurt *Love Me or Leave Me* that the 1950s brought a great revival of the 1920s gangster story to Hollywood and the songs had become popular once again. The script did not sugarcoat the story—it paints a hard-hearted picture of Etting's desire for success and where it took her—but its strength, as must always be true for a musical biopic, lies in the music. When Day sings, emotional truth rolls out. No fancy camerawork is needed. It's an old-fashioned biopic because it can be. The story was there, the music was there, and the integration between the two was a straightforward thing. A woman was a singer, and she had big trouble in her life. Day and Cagney are excellent, and Cagney received an Oscar nomination for his performance. Day, in her challenging dramatic role, proved herself to be a true actress. The film ends with the two characters finally separated, and Day singing what had to be the perfect torch song for their failed relationship, "Love Me or Leave Me." The movie is one case of a biopic actually telling an honest story of two people, with the natural music woven into it.

Movie imagination at work: Cornel Wilde as Frédéric Chopin, with furniture and ruffled sleeves, in *A Song to Remember* . . .

In the movies, the act of creation—writing, composing, even inventing—is generally represented by the furrowed brow, facial anguish, and masses of crumpled pieces of paper lying around on the floor. To write a novel, apparently, one rips sheets of paper out of a typewriter for about a minute, and *voilà!*—out comes *War and Peace*. The difficulty of musical composition varies according to whether the music is a popular song (in the film of that name, Ann Sothern and Robert Young toss together "Lady Be Good," a complicated lyric, just by noodling together around a piano for a few minutes) or what was called "highbrow" (in *A Song to Remember*, Cornel Wilde suffers over the fall of Poland and women and children starve while his Chopin brings forth a polonaise). An example of a movie that actually found a way to wed cinema to the act of composition is the 1938 success *The Great Waltz*, the story of Johann Strauss Jr., directed by Julien Duvivier—and it became a success without the benefit of any big name box-office stars.*

The Great Waltz, full of the Viennese schmaltz of Strauss's waltzes, is a superior biopic—it's an all-out lavish production by MGM. A modern audience may or may not appreciate it, but its linkage of the act of composing to film cutting, camera movement, and specifically inspirational images is impeccable. It's a highly sophisticated film, concentrating mainly on

. . . and Fernand Gravet as Johann Strauss Jr., with violin and ruffled shirt, plus a wife (Luise Rainer), a mistress (Miliza Korjus), and the blossoms of the Vienna Woods

* In 1934, Max Gordon produced *The Great Waltz*, a lavish Broadway show about Johann Strauss Jr. that originally ran for 298 performances. The 1938 MGM film is not a filmed version of the Broadway show; it's almost totally different, with lyrics composed by Oscar Hammerstein II. There are actually two other biopics of Strauss entitled *The Great Waltz*. In addition to this one, the best, there's a wooden 1972 version (also from MGM) with beautiful singing by Mary Costa, lyrics by Robert Wright and George Forrest, and choreography by Onna White. Max Liebman produced a television version in 1955.

music rather than plot, presenting extended musical passages that immerse a viewer in a whirl of sound and movement. (The script, well written by Samuel Hoffenstein and Walter Reisch, has its occasional sly barbs. When Strauss debuts his orchestra to a totally empty restaurant, his future mother-in-law tactfully says, ignoring his failure, "You have a wonderful son, Mrs. Strauss." His own mother replies, "I warned him.")

The Great Waltz is a smart biopic. It gets the issue of accuracy out of the way immediately with a prefilm title card: "We have dramatized the spirit rather than the facts of his life, because it is his spirit that has lived—in his music." (So don't bother to write us.) The movie then concentrates on showing Strauss (Fernand Gravet) conducting his own music or playing his violin with his orchestra, counterpointed by the joyous response of ordinary people. An opening title of the film instructs the audience that it is "Vienna in 1844," a time when "nice people" didn't dance the waltz. The film then opens with two very brief negatives to establish Strauss's "struggle." A banker fires him and refers to his music as being "fiddle-dee-dee on paper." Then there's a disastrous debut of his first orchestra. As he plays *Artist's Life*, the famous opera singer Carla Donner (Miliza Korjus in her movie debut)* and a troupe of friends just happen to pass by, hear the music, and come in to listen more closely. Across the empty space, in a series of extreme close-ups, Strauss plays his violin and Donner reacts, their eyes telling of their attraction through the music (his are dark and intense, hers wise and sparkling). Theirs will be a passionate love affair, expressed always through music: her singing his compositions. (Never mind that Strauss has a noble little wife, played by Luise Rainer in one of her "Let me suffer, I'm after an Oscar" roles. Rainer, famous for her ability to cry in front of a camera lens, was known as "the Viennese teardrop.") *The Great Waltz* delivers a fairly mature plotline. Donner is Strauss's muse, but they will separate for noble reasons even though they are musically born to be together.

After Donner and her entourage leave, the disappointed café owner fires Strauss and says, "Open the windows and start your cleaning" to his staff. Once the windows are open, and the people outside hear the music, Strauss's career is made! There's never a moment when the people of Vienna don't respond to a Strauss waltz with wholehearted enthusiasm. The people in

---

* Korjus ("Pronounced gorgeous," said the ads and trailers for the film) was brought to MGM in the hopes she could be another Jeanette MacDonald. Although she is attractive, and not dead or stiff onscreen, Korjus was a somewhat shrieky soprano who did not catch on with the public.

the streets, hearing the music through the open windows, respond. Whatever they're doing—strolling, casually talking, playing cards, rocking in chairs, knitting—is abandoned. They rush forward and stream into the café, where they listen, applaud, and when a polka begins, they twirl, swirl around the dance floor in a dance that has energy, passion, and kinetic joy, all enhanced by the sound of the music and the rapid movement of a tracking camera. The dances were staged by Albertina Rasch, and they stress speed in movement, attached to a circular turning that billows the female dresses outward. The camera shows the whole troupe dancing, and the film cuts to insets that show feet rapidly moving, the tempo enhanced by the billowing skirts, with the visual movement adding even faster pacing.

All the musical moments of *The Great Waltz* are presented with this combination of cinema and music, and all are fully developed and extended. On the other hand, plot scenes go directly to whatever the trouble is, having characters state their issues so the film can move on. *The Great Waltz* is an example of a reversal of the relationship between musical numbers and plot in the musical film: lengthy numbers intercut by plot rather than vice versa.

The significant scene for the biopic is one in which the act of creation is defined musically onscreen. As Korjus and Gravet drive in a carriage through the Vienna Woods at dawn, they collaborate on the writing of *Tales from the Vienna Woods*, one of Strauss's most famous waltzes. It's neither more honest nor more true than any such scene, and it contains the usual felicitous accidents that trigger composition. But it plays out with credibility, and is followed by a scene in which it is made clear that Strauss has spent the day working with an orchestra to write the necessary pages to make the song into a true musical composition. The main thing it has is viewer participation. Once the music begins to roll out, the joy of Korjus and Gravet, accompanied by the carriage driver (the superb character actor Christian Rub), is infectious. The creation of the music is presented as accidental, then inspirational, then problematic, and then triumphant—a miniature example of what actually happens as an artist struggles to make something work. It is an exemplary scene because it defines creation with cinematic tools.

The "writing" of *Tales from the Vienna Woods* plays out in plot, setting up the "composing" scene. After an accidental meeting during a revolutionary uprising, Strauss rescues Donner, who's ungrateful, as she and Strauss have had a previous falling out. They cannot be separated, however, because of the danger, so they struggle through the night of uprisings.

As morning nears, Strauss is able to hail a carriage, and the only place to go that's not barricaded is the Vienna Woods. As the beautiful light of dawn breaks through the trees, Strauss and Donner are seen asleep in the open carriage. It's very silent in the woods except for the sound of twittering birds. It's six a.m. when Strauss wakes up, and the coachman has stopped the carriage. After a brief conversation between them, which wakes Donner up, the composition begins.

The coachman takes his seat and begins to drive. To the sound of the horses' hooves, rhythmic and steady, Donner and Strauss are yawning in the carriage. A goatherd's horn is heard in the silent woods. The horses pound along, setting a rhythmic base. Strauss and Donner are seen in medium close-up, the sunlight of the woods around them, the movement of the carriage steadily providing movement inside the frame. A new sound enters: sheepherders' instruments. The carriage speeds up; the two occupants look around them. Back and forth the film cuts, from one to the other, then to the sight of the sun-dappled woods and to the sheep- and goatherders with their flocks, enhanced by the intermingled sounds of hooves, horns, and birds. Suddenly, a melodic line is heard when the coachman has brought out his harmonica and begun to play. The two musicians, Strauss and Donner, laugh out loud as they listen and begin to relax. The carriage speeds up a bit more, and the sound of many birds is heard. The accidental collaboration of harmonica, birds, horses, and herder instruments inspires Strauss to sing out "*da da—da da—da yum-bum-bum*" over and over as he hears the possibility of a composition in his head. Donner picks it up. When he finally becomes stumped, unable to continue, she triumphantly sings a bridge for him—"da *da!*"—that carries the tune forward. At the perfect moment, a French horn trumpets into the tune, blown by a uniformed coachman on an expensive closed carriage that rides past them at just the right moment. Their own coachman begins to sing to his horse, "Come on, my Rosie, come on, my Rosie!" Strauss and Donner stand up in the carriage, singing, repeating the lead tune of *Tales* over and over, Donner swinging her hat in time to the music, Strauss in an ecstasy of delight, both of them bathed in the light of dawn coming through the trees.

The movie then cuts to a nighttime scene, after the carriage has taken the actors to a closed open-air restaurant "the Grinzing Garten," where the finished composition is being played. It's suggested that Donner has waited while Strauss orchestrated the music, and the restaurant band is now playing his finished song. (The restaurant is not open to customers because of the revolution the night before.) Donner then sings the lyrics (like all the film's lyrics set to Strauss's music, they were written by Oscar Hammerstein II). Again, Strauss and Donner are united in music. As she sings, she moves through the frame, leaning first to one side, then the other, twirling around in circles, advancing forward in the space, giving in to the music, in ecstasy because of it. Strauss joins her, twirling her around in a rapid waltz. As he bends her backwards, her hat falls off, and they move and move and move and the camera never lets them go. They dance to his music; she sings; and just as in every Strauss waltz there comes a moment of intensified rhythm and sound, that moment of release comes to their characters simultaneously. Around and around and around, until they finally kiss. Composing *Tales*, has taken nearly thirteen minutes of screen time in a 102-minute movie,* and it has also taken two musicians from dislike to passion, allowing them to share in composition as an act of love and sex, in "the night, the moon, and the music," as the lyrics say. (No paper was wadded up.) *The Great Waltz* is more than a biopic; it's a true film musical. Every visualization of the act of composition links sound and image. An audience not only hears what Strauss hears in his head but also what he sees in his mind.

A musical biopic was a restricted kind of musical. It could never be better than its subject (and the star chosen to play him or her) and the music that filled that person's life. That was the bottom line of the biopic. However, great performers often ended up with lousy biopics (*The Eddie Cantor Story*), and witty, talented composers had their stories told as lumpkin tales with no personality (Rodgers and Hart in *Words and Music*). Undertaking a biopic could give a Hollywood studio many problems, not the least of which could be a lawsuit from living ex-wives, friends, and family. (Even when a movie wasn't acknowledged as a biopic, telling a show-business musical story might inspire trouble. Fanny Brice sued 20th Century–Fox over *Rose of Washington Square* for just telling a story that echoed hers, without using her name.)

Despite the problems and the many lame examples, biopics have never been abandoned by moviemakers. Even today, they are constantly made for both film and television, and some of them are still musicals: *Ray* (2004), *Walk the Line* (2005), *Jersey Boys* (2014), *Straight Outta Compton* (2016), *Bohemian Rhapsody* (2018), et al. The modern musical biopic tends to be

---

* The carriage ride uses about five, and the scene with the orchestra six, with an approximately two-minute transition in which Donner dries her clothes and listens as the finished piece begins.

a superior product, as the creators have learned to try to tell the true story (and thus find a real drama), cast top-of-the-line actors, and validate the musical talent. They also no longer have the censorship restrictions that once limited the screenwriting process. Jamie Foxx won an Oscar for his portrait of Ray Charles, Reese Witherspoon for portraying June Carter; and the form has become a more biographically reliable presentation. The musical biopic was a studio strategy that has stood the test of time.

B Musicals

Musicals attracted moviegoers partly because they had physical beauty in everything inside the frame. They were often lavish, even careless, expenditures of money. Big star names. Excess and spectacle. Girls, hundreds of girls, all tapping their brains out. Acres of drapery hanging suspended from nowhere. Dancing and singing, huge orchestras, gorgeous costumes, amusing sets, beautiful sets, or complex sets that revolve, rise up, and even turn upside down. Musicals were not cheap to make. However, whenever any type of movie became a success in Hollywood, the system created the Walmart version. Because of the success of the musical film as a genre, Hollywood was inevitably going to try to make cheap ones. It wasn't a genre that would lend itself easily to stinginess, but Hollywood would do anything to make a buck.

There *was* a Hollywood B musical, but "B" in Hollywood did not mean second-rate. It meant low cost. It meant untried stars and writers and directors, people being groomed for a higher level of work, people who had found success somewhere else, like radio and records, or people who had slipped down from a higher level for whatever reason. It meant recycled furniture, small sets, dresses off the department-store rack (or reused from A productions). "B" was not an evaluative term; it meant a movie usually designed to run under seventy minutes, cost as little money as possible, and not feature big-name movie stars. It meant efficiency. It meant something designed for the bottom half of the bill or for playing in the small-town market. It meant economy and smart business practices. It meant strategy.

The B musical was created out of scraps lying around: songs that were in the public domain or already established hits, or perhaps work that composers under contract had done that everyone knew would never make the hit parade. Basically, it meant reusing as much as possible, but making it look new and fresh.* These movies demonstrate clearly how the musical format was defined, both on the screen and behind the screen. Because they are shadows of their richer, more mature cousins, they show what the musical was designed to do for the audience, and how the people who made musicals saw the task. They are like blueprints for their better selves, or practice pads for a future product. Their purpose is more forthrightly monetary than it is in the artier examples of the genre.

B musicals came in a variety of types. Some were built around musical personalities that a studio hoped would become stars—Dennis Morgan in *Tear Gas Squad* (more about that later)—or around a star or pair of stars that a studio hoped to turn into big names: Debbie Reynolds in *I Love Melvin* or Marge and Gower Champion in *Give a Girl a Break*, both from 1953. Sometimes they emerged from low-budget studios like Monogram or Republic that featured their own contracted musical stars (Belita in *Lady, Let's Dance* for Monogram). Sometimes they tried to cash in on an imitation of a successful pair: Universal developed knockoff movies for Donald O'Connor and Peggy Ryan, a low-budget version of Mickey Rooney and Judy Garland. The O'Connor/Ryan musicals were bouncy, youthful, and successful—but cheap. Sometimes Bs were thinly plotted movies that featured radio stars or popular bandleaders of the day. The B musical was a grab bag, a bargain basement of leftovers or available-to-sell material. Even "highbrow" musicals involving classical music or opera were created during the time frame of B musicals: *Carnegie Hall*. B movies cross a spectrum: seriously musical films, with stories incorporating musical numbers, over to fragile structures that just go from number to number, often just an opportunity for a popular singing star to walk in and do a hit song. One thing was certain, however: unlike other kinds of B movies—gangster, horror, social problem, comedy—the B musical *had* to have musical talent. There was no faking it on a low budget when there were no distractions of lavish clothes and sets. As a result, the history of the B musical is often a revelation of popular musical performers who couldn't act or weren't attractive enough for stardom—and of talented musical performers who never became popu-

* B movies are not the same as "programmers," which were an "in-between" use of a star, designed to capitalize on time available on a star's contract. Programmers had good production values and protected the star name, but were more expensive than the movies on the studio's B roster. A programmer could be shot fairly quickly and sold on the star's name, and they were useful as vehicles in which to try out newcomers who might become stars.

lar. Bs were star vehicles from the used car lot. It's possible to slum one's way through these films stumbling over talent after talent and observing the way singer/dancers looked in an era that had no television to record their performance.*

One of the most curious B musicals is inexplicably called *Tear Gas Squad*. It's inexplicable for many reasons. First of all, it has no tear gas squad. It does have some tear gas, right at the end, but really it's a movie with more songs than gunfire. It's a 1940 movie made by Warner Bros., which explains the title: Warners was a studio that had more confidence in gangster movies than in musicals. But it had a young man from Milwaukee under contract whose name was Stanley Morner. He could really sing, possessing a beautiful tenor voice. He was also good-looking, with a charming smile and a matter-of-fact and thus natural acting style. He'd been around a bit, singing "A Pretty Girl Is Like a Melody" in the 1936 *The Great Ziegfeld*, only to have his voice dubbed later by Allan Jones. When he was signed by Warner Bros., his name was changed to Dennis Morgan and the studio cast him in a lineup of B movies to see whether the public took to him or not, and if they did, whether they liked him best in westerns, women's pictures, gangster movies, or perhaps, since he could sing, musicals. *Tear Gas Squad* is about a nightclub singer who sings dressed as a cop (Morgan) who decides to become a police cadet to woo a girl. (Warners had the uniforms in wardrobe.)

This "tryout," or looking for type, was standard studio procedure. (Gene Kelly, surely a definitive musical star, also appeared in the war film *Pilot #5* in 1942, the drama *The Cross of Lorraine* in 1943, the Mafia story *Black Hand* in 1950, etc., during his first movie decade.) Morgan appeared in *Illegal Traffic* and *Men with Wings* in 1938. By 1940, he was the star of *Tear Gas Squad*, a B musical designed to give him a shot as a singer without spending too much money. The way Morgan is wedded to song in a comfortably criminal environment is very clever and reveals how sneakily a musical star could be tried out and developed without risk in a B movie. The film opens up on Morgan dressed as a cop, but the camera pulls back to reveal that he's only *dressed* as a cop. He's actually performing in a nightclub. Morgan soon stepped up to A-level stardom at Warners, largely as a musical star.

---

* There *were* "soundies" during the 1940s: jukeboxes that had visual accompaniments for the records played. It was possible to see the performers at the same time as listening to their music. Soundies were the forerunners of MTV.

And then there's a 1941 Columbia film called *Time Out for Rhythm*. Directed by the workhorse B director Sidney Salkow, this film demonstrates how easily a low-budget musical could be made once the rules of the genre were familiar to an audience. *Time Out for Rhythm* has no real characters, no real story or nuance, just a referential plot on which to hang musical numbers. It begins in the "Zodiac Club," a nightclub in which Rosemary Lane is singing a weak number: "Did Anyone Ever Tell You?" Bingo—we have a musical film with a typical nightclub setting. Rosemary Lane, one of the singing Lane Sisters (the others were Priscilla and Lola), was a star who had never made it big, but who had appeared in many Warner Bros. films: *Hollywood Hotel* (1937), *Gold Diggers in Paris* (1938), and *The Boys from Syracuse* (1940), etc. Priscilla Lane became a star of sorts at Warners, but Rosemary's career slowly fizzled out. Although she was a singer, and although *Time Out for Rhythm* constantly refers to her as a singer, and although she opens the film with a song, she never sings again. She's served her purpose: establish the genre. When her number ends, her costars Richard Lane (no relation) and Rudy Vallee are arguing about her. Before this discussion can be resolved, a group of Harvard college boys come in, a fight breaks out, and the nightclub is destroyed. Lane and Vallee then continue their discussion in the wreckage, deciding to form a producing partnership. Vallee is a great developer of musical-show ideas, and their collaboration will be a bond of unbreakable friendship. When all this is over, only about two minutes of film time have elapsed. We've had music, argument, wreckage, fistfights, undying friendship established, and the future of major characters defined. But not really. It's all just been referred to, and audiences accept it because they understand the B film tradition. Other movies, better movies, more expensive and better-developed movies, would have filled in the gaps, but no one expected that to happen at the bottom of the bill.

Time Out for Rhythm, without challenge or conflict, also moves forward in time and musical success. Glen Gray and his Casa Loma Orchestra do a low-budget number, "The Boogie Man," using a play on the words "bogey" for scary and "boogie" for jivy. Lighting and cutting and camerawork create a shadowy, film noir atmosphere that is visually arresting, with clever uses of instruments lit against a black background, and piano keys moving without human hands touching them. The fact that this number has nothing to do with anything doesn't matter: this is what the film has—Glen Gray—and this is what we're gonna get. When the orchestra finishes, on come the Three Stooges, out of nowhere, to do a routine involving falling off chairs, bumping into walls, and knocking over furniture. They finish with a comedy knife-throwing act in which the knife thrower wears glasses and can't see. There is no music for any of this, and no plot advancement; action stops for the Three Stooges' routine, rather as if the audience were in a vaudeville house and the Stooges followed Glen Gray. *Time Out for Rhythm* provides musical numbers and comedy routines, but no real plot; thus, the numbers do not have to be integrated into the story, since there really isn't much of one, anyway. That is the essence of the B musical.

The movie lurches rapidly forward, giving reference to standard musical story ideas: disappointment in love, singer leaving show to marry, singer returning from marriage to recover fame, new girl found and promised lead, quarrels among friends, etc., etc. There is mention of auditions for a television show, which provides the excuse for numbers to be presented visually, as if they were on a Broadway stage. Six Hits and a Miss, a popular singing group of the 1940s, sing "Time Out for Rhythm" along with singer Joan Merrill, a popular radio star of the day who was quite pretty and who Columbia thought might be made into a star. (Merrill plays a singer named Joan Merrill—it's that kind of a movie.) But the key element of the movie, and the one that makes it watchable today, is the "new girl" who will be discovered. Playing a maid and tap dancing around the apartment while she dusts is the young and talented Ann Miller. Presenting a song called "A-Twiddlin' My Thumbs," she sings, dances, smiles, and steals the show. From then on nothing else matters. Others will sing again, and the Stooges will bang around, but Ann Miller is the central event with her amazing tapping and her strong personality.

Time Out for Rhythm is not much of a movie, but it's proof of genre. It is also proof of star showcasing and development, and proof of financial acumen. It demonstrates clearly how the business of filmmaking worked, and how weak movies could be turned into moneymaking strategies. Let's face it, it's a mess. The Stooges team up with a popular radio comedy act of the day, Brenda and Cobina (Blanche Stewart and Elvia Allman); Rudy Vallee sings with Joan Merrill; Rosemary Lane ditches Richard Lane three times and then marries him; plot points are announced rather than performed; Glen Gray and the Casa Loma Orchestra perform; and everyone works hard in a Carmen Miranda–ish number with music by Eddie Durant's Rhumba Orchestra. It finally ends when Ann Miller comes on to finish off the title song, "Time Out for Rhythm." When it's all over, we know three things: Ann Miller will become a star, Allen Jenkins can tap dance,* and low-budget musicals can be made to work, because the audience has been taught that music, not plot, matters. That was the triumph of the B musical.

B musicals are often sad little events as they work to achieve their goals. *Lady, Let's Dance* (1944) is an example of a Monogram Picture starring Belita ("the Ice Maiden"), a British ice skater who was brought to Hollywood as potential competition for Sonja Henie. Belita was born in Hampshire, England, in 1923 as Maria Belita Jepson-Turner. Her background was not one of poverty: her father was a military officer and her mother the daughter of a royal physician. Furthermore, Belita was not a one-trick pony. She could not only skate but also do ballet (she studied with Anton Dolin), ballroom dancing, Latin numbers, a bit of tap, play the violin—and in case none of that worked, she spoke four languages. ("She skates, she romances, she dances," promised the film's posters.) She was raised by a

The unstoppable Belita, ice-skating "rival" to Sonja Henie, but for less money, in *Lady, Let's Dance*

* Jenkins was a popular comedy star, often used as a tough-talking gangsterish type. He did not sing and dance in movies, but like many performers of the era, he had learned to do musical work for vaudeville. When Miller does one of her centerpiece numbers, "Obviously the Gentleman Prefers to Dance," Jenkins is her partner. And he *can* dance!

classic example of the driving stage mother; Belita was trained for stardom as soon as she could walk. An excellent athlete, she took to ice skating more than anything else and qualified for the 1936 Winter Olympics at the age of twelve. By fourteen, she had turned professional, and soon she migrated to Hollywood (thanks to the Henie phenomenon) and first skated in a Hollywood movie as one of the ice dancers at Republic Pictures in *Ice-Capades*, in which another European skater trying to cash in on the Henie craze, the Czech Vera Hruba Ralston was billed low as "ice dancer." Belita moved up to "Belita, Star on the Ice" in her next movie, Monogram's *Silver Skates* (1943),* but her biggest musical movie as a Sonja Henie would-be is *Lady, Let's Dance*. It was Monogram's stab at turning her into a star, and she was optimistically billed over the title. The credits include not only "Dances staged by Dave Gould" but also the announcement that all "ballet under the personal direction of Michael Panaieff."

Lady, Let's Dance is nevertheless the cheap version of a Sonja Henie film. Belita plays a war refugee working as a waitress. Her character name is Belita—why waste anyone's time and money trying to think up a name when she already had one, and it was the one you were trying to promote? That mind-set defines the look of the film. Why have two chairs when only one person is going to sit down? Why have two outfits for daytime for the leading lady when she can wear the same one twice the way real people do? Why spend any money if you can possibly avoid it?—and that includes the attitude toward the music. Belita can dance to Beethoven's Fifth or to a bagful of popular tunes, so there's no need to hire songwriters. What we can do, reasoned the studio and the producers, is spend money on what we are trying to promote: Belita as an ice-skating star to rival Sonja Henie. We can drum up a couple of new numbers, throw in some Ice Capades comedy skaters (Frick and Frack), and get a leading man (James Ellison) who has a recognizable name but can spend most of the screen time off somewhere trying to find a job and fighting in World War II.

As a result, *Lady, Let's Dance* has a bit of a plot, a few cheap sets, and a tiny conflict, but otherwise has only what a musical is supposed to have: costumed numbers featuring the star. Four popular orchestras of the day were thrown in, the biggest name being Henry Busse with "the sensational Hopkins Twins from the San Francisco Watercade in their famous

---

* She was billed third after costars Kenny Baker and Patricia Morison, and featured in an impressive four-and-a-half-minute routine called "Love Is a Beautiful Song."

water waltz" as an added attraction.* However, it's Belita who has to carry the film. (Her character says she was educated in England, to explain her accent, but the plot says she's the skating champion of Holland.) Belita dances with a partner to a ballroom rendition of "Green Eyes," rehearses a "Ballet Modern," and then stars in a nightclub doing the "Snow Queen Ballet." In this she does ballet, then a semitap, then a sexy routine to "St. Louis Blues" . . . all in her tutu. Quickly—time matters in the B musical—Belita becomes the star of an ice show. (She had found success as a dancer, but good advice is handed to her: "You can get a million toe dancers" but an ice skating star "ain't so easy to find.") It's a very grand ice show, *Glamour On Ice*. There are two back-to-back huge production numbers. The first is "A Bit of Gay Nineties," which features some old tunes and a number written especially for the movie by Dave Oppenheimer and Ted Grouya, "In the Days of the Beau Brummel" (or, as they sing it, "Beau Brumm-ELL"). It's a sort of Currier and Ives skating scene. The second presents Belita skating to "Silver Shadows and Golden Dreams" (by Lew Pollack and Charles Newman, played by Mitch Ayres and His Orchestra). A brief plot episode follows these triumphs, in which Belita proposes the show add the comedy team of Frick and Frack, who fall down later for laughs in two numbers of their own: "The Gay Nineties" (which economically allows for the recycling of costumes from Beau BrumELL) and a "Swiss Frolics" number. Belita then does what is really a very lovely routine, ice skating with a male chorus dressed in top hats and tails. She becomes "the darling of the ice world," which is illustrated by a montage of posters announcing her shows: *Golden Skates*, *Dancing Skates*, *Skating in the Sky*, *The New Frozen Follies* (as opposed to the Old one), etc. While these posters roll by, they are alternated with a wartime combat montage of Ellison fighting, a large image of his helmeted face superimposed over war footage. (This mixture of combat and music, a strange generic combination, also turns up in *The Gang's All Here, Up in Arms,* and other wartime musicals.)

The movie has no real plan, no real story, only Belita. The final fifteen or so minutes of the film are just ice-show material: an audience can take a good look at Belita, who is a bigger woman than Henie, fuller-figured, not a tiny little creature. As a result, she doesn't skate with the speed and delicacy of Henie, but she's an excellent athlete, can jump as many as seven times as she skates in a circle, can do a mean splits in the air and on the ice,

---

* Also featured were the bands of Eddie LeBaron and Lou Brenz.

and can use her ballet training excellently to present a lovely ice routine. Like Henie, Belita didn't sing, and her B studio didn't pay for dubbing. Her film ends with a big finale. Her war hero has returned home and is now in a wheelchair, with no explanation . . . he's just in a wheelchair. Belita says, "I don't care if I ever skate again. I just want to be with you." He shapes her up fast, saying her career was what he was fighting for, and she shouldn't let him down. Belita, who is very pretty, blond, and at ease with line delivery without being a real actress, knows what to say. She'll skate, but "just for you." The final big number, "The Spirit of Victory," is a mind boggler. Belita skates in front of a gigantic replica of the Statue of Liberty to Beethoven's Fifth. The End. Belita lacked Henie's twinkle and sparkle, which is what kept her from stardom, but she could skate. And a B musical model worked perfectly for someone like her. She became—briefly—a B movie star.

Attempts were made to stretch Belita past the skating genre to prolong her stardom. Her 1946 movie, *Suspense*, was—true to its title—such an attempt.* It was an ice-skating musical film noir. *Suspense* had shadowy lighting, implied menace, two murders, and an avalanche. In case none of that worked, Belita did skate. She does a Cuban number in which, while Miguelito Valdés sings, she whips around the ice with real attitude, not just skating, but doing an interpretive dance on ice. She bends her back, waves her arms sinuously, and presents her body in a sexy way. It's a little like watching the young Rita Hayworth dance: it's less about choreography than about showing off a spectacular physical presence. To prove to audiences that Belita could be in movies that were full of "suspense," her finale combines that title with the glamour of skating. In a "Jaws of Death" ice number, Belita skates out wearing black to do a jump through a hoop adorned with dangerously positioned daggers; she's so good a skater, an audience is told, that she can jump through (at high speed) precisely at the right point—enough to endanger her life, but not harm her. Unbeknownst to her, but made very explicit to the audience, is the bad news that the villain has cleverly repositioned one of the knives so that there's no way she won't be impaled when she jumps. (No one backstage apparently has noticed this redesign.) The result was not much suspense, but plenty of Belita, who for the most part, never really got off the ice in her career.

---

* In fact, Belita is probably best known today for her starring roles in three excellent film noir movies—besides *Suspense*, two nonskating stories, *The Gangster* (1947) and *The Hunted* (1948). She also is known for dancing a key part in Gene Kelly's *Invitation to the Dance*.

One of her other contemporaries, however, did manage the leap, as it were: the Queen of Republic Studios, Vera Hruba Ralston, a Czech ice skater who arrived in America in 1941, and signed a long-term contract with Republic Pictures in 1943, supported by its head man, Herbert Yates, who left his wife and children for her in 1947, although they did not marry until 1952. (He was forty years her senior.) Her first movie was *Ice-Capades*, followed by *Ice-Capades Review* in 1942.* Ultimately, Yates liberated her from the ice rink. She began playing dramatic roles (*The Lady and the Monster*, in 1944) and, thanks to the influence of Yates, never skated again.

B movie skaters like Belita and Ralston became movie personages because of the success of Sonja Henie, of course. Henie's stardom even inspired MGM to try an ice-skating movie, inexplicably pairing Joan Crawford and Jimmy Stewart in a mess called *The Ice Follies of 1939*. Both look wobbly but skate gamely, like the pros they are. The movie ends with an extended ice show in color (the rest of the film was in black-and-white). *Ice Follies* presents a number on skates ("A Song for Cinderella") as a scene from a movie being watched by a fancy premiere audience that includes Crawford and Stewart side by side. (It was an early moment for Crawford's fans to see her true coloring: she was a redhead with piercing blue eyes. They also got to hear her sing. Because she had a fairly good voice, MGM was always considering making her do musicals, but her onscreen persona was not well suited to song and dance, as they learned in 1953 with *Torch Song*.)

B musical stars either moved up (Ann Miller) or disappeared (Belita). A rare exception was the lovely Jane Frazee, who became an authentic star in twenty-seven B musicals from 1940 (her feature debut in *Melody and Moonlight*) to her retirement from feature films in 1951 with *Rhythm Inn*. She went on to costar in the popular Joe McDoakes shorts as Joe's wife Alice from 1954 to 1956, when the series ended. Although she moved into television, and appeared as a regular in a series called *Beulah*, Frazee ultimately quit show business and went into real estate. That was a B star's trajectory: leading lady to selling houses. Frazee in her day, however, was much loved and very successful. She'd been a child star, touring in an act with her sister, Ruth. When they grew up, they kept on singing together on radio and in nightclubs until Frazee broke into movies for studios like Republic.

---

* The Ice-Capades were traveling ice shows that began touring America in 1940, lasting until 1997. Both Belita and Vera Hruba worked as skaters in these tours. The two movies have Ralston billed in the cast as "Ice Skater" and "Ice Capades Skater" respectively. The first stars James Ellison and Jenny Coleman and the second Ellen Drew and Richard Denning.

Frazee had different types of musical successes, from hits such as the Abbott and Costello vehicle *Buck Privates* (1941) to westerns like *Swing in the Saddle* (1944) and topical entertainments like *Rosie the Riveter* (1944). She starred in the film version of *Hellzapoppin'* (1941), Roy Rogers movies (*Springtime in the Sierras*, 1947), and movies that featured great jitterbugging by Donald O'Connor and Peggy Ryan (*Get Hep to Love*, 1942). In *San Antonio Rose* (1941), she and the Merry Macs introduced two of the year's biggest hit songs, the title tune and "The Hut-Sut Song." Whatever she appeared in, she was always pretty, fresh, and capable in both dance and song, although not outstanding in either. A typical Frazee musical, and one of her most successful, was the 1947 *Calendar Girl*, made at Republic, a B studio that made bottom-of-the-bill features. The movie ran a lavish (for a B film) eighty-eight minutes and was a period piece, which meant Republic believed in Frazee's ability to make a film pay off. Playing with singers Kenny Baker and William Marshall, leading man James Ellison, "other woman" Gail Patrick, and character actors Victor McLaglen and Irene Rich, Frazee sailed along through a highly adequate musical presentation, well directed by Allan Dwan. (Dwan had begun his career in silent films, and had the skill and experience to put anything up on the screen with pace and style.) *Calendar Girl* is surprising because, B movie that it is, from a B movie studio, it nevertheless knows how to imitate its betters. (Republic was a B studio that moved up to producing A films such as *The Quiet Man*. *Calendar Girl* reflects the studio's transition, aspiring to and almost looking A level.) The movie opens up onto Frazee, seen in a window, singing (for no reason) about how "A Bluebird Is Singing to Me." The movie rolls forward very fluidly, with songs laid in very simply, and so often that up to a point, the world is a musical universe, with all its characters happily singing and dancing around. It presents a world in which music flows naturally, and the proceedings are full of high spirits and a great sense of joy. *Calendar Girl* shows very clearly why B musicals succeeded. They imitated expensive A musicals and, anxious to present music as cheaply as possible, eliminated a great deal of plot—and thus, by accident, often created quite a sophisticated and well-integrated musical entertainment. The B musical had no pretense except for occasionally pretending to be an A. Let Frazee sing in the window like Judy Garland in *Meet Me in St. Louis*, for instance. And find a star like Frazee, who was a bit of Alice Faye, a bit of Betty Grable, and a bit of Janet Blair . . . and enough of herself to make fans like her work and want to see it often for over a decade.

World War II brought many talent-packed B musicals into production to fulfill the big need for movies as cheap entertainment. *Private Buckaroo* (1942) is typical. It has no real plot to speak of, other than "Hey, folks, it's wartime and people are gonna get drafted, and we all like to listen to music." It opens into a nightclub where the very popular Harry James band is performing "You Made Me Love You," one of their greatest hits. James's band singer, Helen Forrest, comes out and does the vocal, singing it pure and straight in the style of the day while James blows his typical sweet, sharp horn. This event has set up the film, and the rest is pretty much more of the same: Dick Foran, cast as a singer with the James band, comes out and sings the title tune. The James band does another number, and then Joe E. Lewis does a comedy song, "I Love the South," and the Andrews Sisters do one of their hits, "Three Little Sisters." Then everyone enlists in the army: this movie is going to last only sixty-eight minutes, so there's no use wasting time.

After the mass enlistment, there will be a series of "shows" and a minimum of plot. Foran will sing "I'm in the Army Now"; the Sisters will ride in a jeep singing "Six Jerks in a Jeep" (three soldiers are driving them); Harry James will play for a USO party and the Sisters will do "Steppin' Out Tonight"; Foran will play the piano and sing a lugubrious "Nobody Knows the Trouble I've Seen" in a sort of Nelson Eddy–ish manner. Next there'll be a matinee show, with James doing an instrumental, the Andrews Sisters singing "Don't Sit Under the Apple Tree," and Peggy Ryan and Donald O'Connor dancing with a troupe of other young couples. (O'Connor and Ryan were stars at Universal, but O'Connor has no spotlight in the dance, and only a few moments of plot dialogue.)* Ryan gets a solo spotlight in the dance, and the youthful troupe are hot jitterbuggers, dancing with acrobatic skill and great athleticism. Foran sings "We've Got a Job to Do," and the Sisters swing out with "Johnny Get Your Gun Again." The men then march off to war. The lyrics ring out: "This war is yours and it's mine / We've got to back up that line / We've got a job to do." And that's a wartime B movie for you, a great business strategy.

The trick of the B movie was to throw a few softballs of plot the audience's way. There's a blond romantic lead for Foran (Jennifer Holt) and a cartoonish little girl who has all the answers (Susan Levine) and a touch of plot about Foran being an egotist who has to learn to be part of the troops,

---

* He didn't even get billing.

etc., etc. But really? The plot's a lame attempt that no one needed anyway. *Private Buckaroo* is just a few jokes (mostly from Mary Wickes and Shemp Howard, without the other Stooges) and a lot of music right out of the jukebox and alive "onscreen" in front of audiences.

The war years also brought B musicals that specifically reflected the era. Besides teenage jitterbugging and military camp and enlistment movies, there were movies that presented women working in war plants (and singing) as well as pseudo-liberated women's stories and Good Neighbor policy musicals with Latin music and settings, such as the ritzy 1944 (at ninety minutes) *Brazil*, with Tito Guizar and Virginia Bruce, set in Rio—that is, the Rio of California

Frances Langford's starring movies were all B films. Langford was a very popular radio singer who had toured military zones with Bob Hope. She had a substantial career making B films about strong women, such as the well-made and directed *Bamboo Blonde* (1946), *Swing It, Soldier* (1941), and the very interesting *Career Girl* of 1944. The credits say the film stars "Miss Frances Langford," and the releasing company is PRC Pictures, a B House if there ever was one. Langford plays a girl from Kansas City who wants to try for her own career, although her hometown boyfriend says she should come home and start her real career as his wife. She tells him off, saying she has talent, she will stay, and if she decides to come home she'll buy her own ticket. When she runs out of money and can't find work, in a depressed and defeated mood, she decides she will have to marry to survive. When she calls him, the scene shows her sitting dejectedly at the telephone, and all she's allowed to say is "Yes, James" over and over again. It's satisfying—and surprising—to note that this musical, in which Langford sings several songs, ends with her becoming famous and *not* marrying him.

The B musical fulfilled a need that would ultimately become the definition of modern movies: niche programming. With low costs in production, stars, and composers, the B musical could easily satisfy a rural, small-town, or specific musical desire. Audiences of the 1930s and 1940s liked to see the people they were listening to on the radio, and so many musicals of the era featured radio personalities who just came on to do their thing while the movie stops dead to accommodate them. The Radio Rogues, Kate Smith, Morton Downey Sr. all appeared, as radio, especially in the 1930s, was somewhat of a rival to the motion picture. (It's what brought Bing Crosby to movie stardom.) A low-cost movie that could star (or at least show) a popular radio entertainer was a good B movie idea: 1945's *Radio Stars on Parade* had a flimsy plot about two agents getting mixed up with gangsters, but it was only an excuse to present Skinnay Ennis and his band, singer Tony Romano, the Town Criers, and the Cappy Barra Boys. Inexpensive musicals were built around swing music and popular bands (*Swing, Sister, Swing*, 1938), singing cowboys (*Boots and Saddles*, 1937, and *Melody Ranch*, 1940, both with Gene Autry, and *Cowboy and the Senorita*, 1944, with Roy Rogers), radio stars, and singing comediennes (Judy Canova in *Hit the Hay*, 1945, and *Singin' in the Corn*, 1946.)

The singing cowboys were niche performers, but they weren't obscure or minor cultural figures. Gene Autry, the single most successful example of the type, was ranked among the top ten box-office draws in 1940, 1941, and 1942, the year he enlisted in the Army Air Force for World War II. Autry is the man who really popularized the singing-cowboy concept for a wide audience, and his "westerns" took place in modern settings and always mixed action with song. His decision to leave his huge career in movies, radio, personal appearances, and recordings to serve his country in the war opened the door for a member of the Sons of the Pioneers, Roy Rogers, to advance to leading-man status. Rogers was himself ranked in the top ten in 1946. Both men endured as stars, with Autry becoming one of the wealthiest men ever to appear in motion pictures. The singing-cowboy concept grew out of his fame as a singing radio star and successful recording artist.

A typical Autry film such as *Boots and Saddles* was shot in eleven days in Lone Pine, California, costing about $43,000. Autry's studio was Republic, the B organization that would later move into A level production, but in the 1930s was highly successful financially by making films like the typical Autry musical western: low-cost, popular star, few expensive sets and costumes. Autry was paid $5,000 per film, and given a stipend for using his own clothes and his own horse and for doing publicity. Since the Autry movies had modern settings, it was never necessary to generate specialized sets, carriages, stagecoaches, costumes, etc. Autry's songs often had already been popularized by him on his radio show. He was a musical phenomenon, equally celebrated as a singer and as a cowboy. He reached A level status in B level material. According to TCM's Jeremy Arnold, *Boots and Saddles* "became the first Autry film to play a Broadway movie house and the first to garner a review in *The New York Times*."

The singing-cowboy movie is an example of how unpredictable the history of musicals could be: a western figure, grappling with cattle rustlers, thieves, arsonists, land grabbers, and all sorts of problems, could perform a song in the middle of the action without jarring an audience. The issue regarding the musical—why is this person singing in this movie?—seemed not to touch these modern cowboys, who rode along with their guitars and warbled about sagebrush, roses, and San Antonio. In a B musical, lack of

The handsome man who put the singing cowboy into the cash register, becoming a top-ten-ranked box-office star: Gene Autry with his horse, Champion, also a looker

expensive development created a filmed universe that didn't seem to need rules or to be believable in the same way as other movies. An audience accepted disconnected and illogical events in Bs; they seemed to know that poverty accounted for making do and getting along with things as well as possible. It was, no doubt, something they understood and accepted from their own lives.

The niche musical had room for horse-faced comediennes like Judy Canova and gawky dames like Joan Davis. Davis—who always looked put-upon, as if she hadn't been invited to the party—was the comic relief in many movies, among them some starring Sonja Henie (*Thin Ice*, *My Lucky*

Star), Shirley Temple (*Just Around the Corner*), and Alice Faye (*Wake Up and Live*; *Sally, Irene and Mary*). She became a headliner later in life with *If You Knew Susie* (with Eddie Cantor, 1948) and found top-rank fame as star of her own television series, *I Married Joan*. Her musical numbers usually featured a loose-limbed, awkward dance and a self-deprecating lyric. Canova was what was then called a "hillbilly comic." She yodeled, did pratfalls, and defined a female slapstick type of comedy in films. She was, however, a capable singer and could also play the guitar. Called "the Jenny Lind of the Ozarks" and "the Queen of Corn," she was a feature player in nearly twenty movies, such as *Sis Hopkins* (1941), *Puddin' Head* (1941), and *Joan of Ozark* (1942)—a pioneer of the female comic who cares nothing about how she looks but only about how the audience laughs. (Canova also appeared in early TV.)

There were B movies that also revealed how white musicians were quietly usurping black music, movies like *I Love a Bandleader* in 1945, which costarred bandleader/comedian Phil Harris with the popular African American comic actor Eddie "Rochester" Anderson, a key figure on Jack Benny's radio and TV shows. In *I Love a Bandleader* a thin story provides an excuse for unrelated musical numbers set in a nightclub. Whether they're being rehearsed or being performed for club patrons, the numbers need no explanation and no coherence. In fact, a very postmodern tone of breaking the fourth wall occurs three times in the movie, to confirm that the story really isn't the point. Harris plays a wall painter who gets bumped on the head, which renders him that most cinematic of casualties: the amnesiac. He suddenly finds himself able to lead a band—logic is not the point of this musical—and he muses that if he's a bandleader, maybe he's Harry James . . . "or even *Phil Harris*!" He also refers to Rochester as being connected to a "Mr. Benny."

I Love a Bandleader exists for music and only for music. There's a quartet of singing African American female musicians, a guitar player, a piano player, a bassist, and a drummer all doing a jazzy number, and, of course, Rochester's own musical performances. (Rochester was the first moon walker I ever saw, in 1939's *Man About Town*, with Benny, Dorothy Lamour, and Betty Grable. Forget your Michael Jackson!) When Phil Harris sings his famous "That's What I Like About the South," it's definitely black patter he's performing. He's channeling black culture and making himself famous—and seemingly unique—while doing it. He is actually usurping black culture, an early cinematic example of white performers doing crossover. (Bing Crosby and the Rhythm Boys were an even earlier example, and of course Elvis Presley would be a famous later one.)

While white performers were usurping black music and style, the "black circuit" was making low-budget musicals with African American performers. These films were designed to play in theaters in the South that were

The cheapo musical plan: lots of people to fill the frame: the Jivin' Jacks and Jills surrounding Dan Dailey and Grace McDonald (front and center), with Peggy Ryan to the left of Dailey and Donald O'Connor to the right of McDonald, in *Give Out, Sisters*

specifically for ethnic audiences. *The Duke Is Tops* (1938), reissued as *The Bronze Nightingale*, is an example of one of these musicals, and is particularly noteworthy for being the movie debut of Lena Horne. She's not the star billed over the title: that's Ralph Cooper. It's a true B movie in that its production values are very cheap, but it runs a full eighty minutes. Horne looks very young, is radiantly beautiful, and has stardom written all over her. She sings several numbers, among them "Let's Be True to One Another" and the big finale, "Harlem Is Harmony." It's a show-biz story that presents one specialty number after another, all of which are excellent.

The B movie came in all genres, with westerns claiming the highest number made and horror a close second. Crime and gangster movies, which would become examples of early film noir, were popular, too, as were cheap comedies. Although many musicals were made, they were more labor-intensive, and as the 1950s unfolded and studios were under financial and legal pressures, the practice of creating low-cost B films slowly began to diminish. The double feature became a rare event, so there was no need for "the bottom of the bill." The B musicals that had covered niche areas began to be the rock-and-roll presentations of the 1960s that were often labeled "exploitation films." "Niche" was a genteel word that "exploitation" laid bare. Either way, the ability of the business to extend the musical genre, and adapt it into low-budget presentations that used musical talent that was not necessarily mainstream, is a development of generic marginality that came easier to musicals than to any other type of movie.

By 1960, the studios still existed, but the former factory system of the "golden age" was no longer in place. The B movie more or less morphed into the "exploitation" film—that is, a movie that could be sensationalized by linking it to current events, newspaper headlines, or parental topics of concern. "Exploitation" became a word in the film trade that indicated an opportunity to advertise, sell, and heavily promote a movie that had no particular merit other than it *was* capable of being sensationalized. Musical exploitation films were made to sell teenage recording artists, African American performers, or anything that seemed to be popular enough for audiences to want to see, but not popular enough—or reliable enough—for mass-market appeal, so that the money spent to make the movie had to be minimal. The so-called "beach-blanket movies" of the 1960s were a sort of B musical exploitation phenomenon: *Beach Party* (1963), *Pajama Party* (1964), *Bikini Beach* (1964), *Muscle Beach Party* (1964), *Beach Blanket Bingo* (1965), et al. These movies often starred musical performers Frankie Avalon and Annette Funicello, but they were designed to feature anybody who had a hit record: the Supremes, the Four Seasons, the Righteous Brothers, "Little" Stevie Wonder, etc.

In its own era, the B movie was a welcome option. It cared little for lavish accoutrements and even less for logic, but its very cheapness made its performances seem attainable. It was a knockoff piece of furniture. All it cared about was singin' and dancin', which today makes it a valuable example of the form, an honest record of popular music, and a showcase for straightforward and unadorned musical performance. Today a B musical is a wonder to behold. Consider only five World War II B musicals with

Donald O'Connor. There's *Give Out, Sisters* (1942) in which the sisters are named Andrews and they give out with, among others, their celebrated "Pennsylvania Polka" while O'Connor and Peggy Ryan do an authentic jitterbug with the Jivin' Jacks and Jills, who include Tommy Rall, and there's also singer Grace McDonald and dancer Dan Dailey Jr. for good measure. There's also *When Johnny Comes Marching Home* (1942) and *Top Man* (1943). In addition to O'Connor the former boasts singers Allan Jones, Gloria Jean, and Jane Frazee, while the latter has O'Connor and Ryan in a patriotic story about high-school kids volunteering at a defense plant, riveting their brains out, stopping only to do some great numbers along with singer Susanna Foster, Borrah Minevitch and his Harmonica Rascals, Count Basie and His Orchestra, and—wait for it—Lillian Gish as a concerned wartime mom. (You never know who you'll find in a B.) There's 1942's *Get Hep to Love* and 1943's *Mister Big*, both with O'Connor, young and fresh and multitalented. Sit down and let these movies hit you with their jitterbugging, swing dancing, silly (but briefly present) plots, overwhelming optimism, and astonishing musical names—all seen in under seventy minutes—and you'll be ready to declare *Trocadero* (1944) a masterpiece. It's the story (allegedly) of how the Club Troc (a real Los Angeles nightclub) went from restaurant to dance club, surviving Prohibition, the Depression, and family ownership squabbles. Columnist Erskine Johnson tells the story—a really irrelevant event—but who cares when it's intercut with musical numbers to die for: the Stardusters with Gus Arnheim and his band; Wingy Manone and His Orchestra; Ida James singing "Shoo Shoo Baby" with Bob Chester's band; songs by Rosemary Lane and Johnny Downs; Matty Malneck and his Orchestra doing "Louisiana Lulu"; and even Dave Fleischer presenting an original little animation with a character called Snippy, which makes up for the horror of the very dated and unfunny Radio Rogues, who were a hit at the time. Yes, the B musical is a marvel; it got to the essence of the genre and can never be dismissed as history, cinema, culture, or entertainment. It was an important business strategy.

Opera and Operetta

Hollywood was always a scavenger, and as sound arrived, two tried-and-true musical sources were obviously available: opera and operetta. It's an insight into Hollywood's ideas about its audiences that from the beginning, operas were not thought of as potentially making a lot of money down at the local movie house. That is, not if they were presented as *operas*, which were clearly thought to be too highbrow. Moviemakers, however, were interested in two things that opera had: stars and stories, both reliable box-office elements.

The movie studios had never been above stealing plots from operas: *La Bohème* made a beautiful silent vehicle in 1926, directed by King Vidor and starring Lillian Gish and John Gilbert, but based on Henri Murger's 1851 novel, not Puccini's opera. Variations of *Carmen* would include everything from Rita Hayworth seducing Glenn Ford (again) in 1948's *The Loves of Carmen* and the all-black, modernized *Carmen Jones* (in 1954) with Harry Belafonte, Dorothy Dandridge, and Pearl Bailey. Gershwin's *Porgy and Bess* was filmed in 1959, and despite the wonderful music and excellent performers (Dandridge, Sidney Poitier, and Sammy Davis Jr.), it has mostly been forgotten due to unavailability of prints. Operas, except for their plots and cultural variations, were not very attractive to Hollywood filmmakers.

Opera *stars* were a different matter. Geraldine Farrar appeared onscreen in silent films, simply because she was famous and loved by fans who wanted to see her, as in *Carmen* in 1915, for example. Mary Garden also appeared in silent films. Grace Moore, Lily Pons, and Gladys Swarthout made musical movies in the 1930s, and Risë Stevens in the 1940s. Mario Lanza, never really an opera star, became a hit in the 1950s, and Lauritz Melchior briefly became a lovable character actor in Technicolor MGM musicals in the late forties and early fifties. Helen Traubel, Robert Weede, and Ezio Pinza made musicals, although Pinza was stuck in a turkey with Lana Turner (*Mr. Imperium*, 1951). (His famous role in *South Pacific* went to the younger, handsomer Rossano Brazzi, who was dubbed by Giorgio Tozzi. Pinza died a year before the film's release.) In 1982, Luciano Pavarotti would take a flier in a movie called *Yes, Giorgio*, but a flier it was. Hollywood was always willing to have someone like Jeanette MacDonald *play* an opera singer, so she could belt out an aria from *La Traviata* or *Faust* just before she let 'em have it with a rousing "San Francisco . . . open your golden gate," but that was not the same thing as presenting opera stars on film. (As much as she wanted to be a real opera star, MacDonald became a movie star instead.) Hollywood, however, was always looking to find a real opera star who could "cross over." Using attractive opera singers in lighthearted musicals was not the same risk as making operas into movies.

The question was, could an opera star sing a pop tune as well as serious music? The studios wanted to play it safe. In case too much of the audience didn't want opera, they hedged their bets by having the singer "go popular" with tunes that didn't work for their highly trained voices. Alas, in general, very few could swing out, and thus very few could muster even a brief stardom by fitting into the democracy of the Hollywood musical. This was particularly true of the men: Tullio Carminati, Lawrence Tibbett, James Melton—none of these became real movie stars. During the 1930s, opera stars who were good looking enough (and had enough personality) were brought to California by almost every studio. None of them ever really became long-lasting stars.

Lily Pons and Risë Stevens were two beautiful opera singers who almost had movie careers. Hollywood recruited Pons in the 1930s for her beautiful coloratura voice, her petite look, and her exceptional popularity with Metropolitan Opera audiences. Pons appeared in three musicals in the mid-thirties: *I Dream Too Much* in 1935, *That Girl from Paris* in 1936, and *Hitting a New High* in 1937. Stevens, a mezzo-soprano, was cast opposite Nelson Eddy in 1941's *The Chocolate Soldier*. She also had a plum role as the singer who had been in Bing Crosby's life before he became a priest in *Going My Way*. Yet neither woman became a movie star. Pons was dark-haired and lovely, but lacked screen presence, and Stevens just didn't catch on. She was, however, able to extend her career into radio and television, appearing in original TV musicals like *Little Women* in 1958. She also played the leading role of Anna in Lincoln Center's 1964 production of *The King and I*. (Both Pons and Stevens appeared as themselves in the 1949 movie *Carnegie Hall*, as did Pinza and others.)

Of all of the classical singers who tried for movie stardom, perhaps the prettiest was the now nearly forgotten Grace Moore. Wisely, the business put her in modern movies, not operettas, and her star rose accordingly. Moore, "the Tennessee Nightingale," was portrayed onscreen by Kathryn Grayson in the 1953 biopic, *So This Is Love*. Moore might be better known today had she not been tragically killed in an airplane crash in Denmark in 1947. She made only nine films, but her glorious soprano voice was one of the finest to be heard in the movies.

Pop music was not a problem for Moore. Although she made her opera debut in 1928 at the Met and toured extensively, singing in Paris, Monte Carlo, and London, she actually began her career on Broadway in such shows as *Hitchy-Koo* in 1920, and she introduced Irving Berlin's "What'll

I Do" and "All Alone" in the *Music Box Revue*s of 1923 and 1924. Her first movie was *A Lady's Morals* (1930), followed by *New Moon* (also 1930). Other films included *Love Me Forever* (1935), *The King Steps Out* (1936), and *I'll Take Romance* (1937). *One Night of Love* (1934) was her greatest hit—the film that made her a true movie star and earned her an Oscar nomination. The movie, one of the top box-office draws of 1934–35, told a banal story about a young American soprano who goes to Italy to study but becomes torn between a career (represented by her impresario, opera singer Tullio Carminati) and romance (represented by Lyle Talbot). In *One Night of Love* Moore sang pieces from *Carmen*, *Lucia di Lammermoor*, *Madama Butterfly*, and *La Traviata*, and a popular title song created for her by Victor Schertzinger, with lyrics by Gus Kahn. Moore's *One Night of Love* inspired Hollywood's further interest in having opera singers as leading ladies, but she was the standout of the lot. (Moore was a kind of highbrow Doris Day.) The best example of her appeal is the 1937 *When You're in Love*, costarring her with Cary Grant, who had been in Hollywood since 1932 but who was in his seminal year of moving up into real stardom. (He also appeared in *The Awful Truth*, *The Toast of New York*, and *Topper* that year.)

Grace Moore is a beautiful blonde, and she sparkles onscreen. *When You're in Love* reminds any viewer who wants to dismiss her as a minor figure that she was very definitely a star. The film begins, after the Columbia Pictures logo, with a medium close-up of Moore singing, her hair perfectly coiffed, her gown an extravaganza of its own, and her visual power on display. After a few minutes, the title comes up: "Miss Grace Moore in . . . " It's *Miss* Grace Moore, and she's not only billed *over* the title, she's singing before the movie even starts. Everything she wears in the film is custom-designed to hide her slightly thick waist, but she looks elegant, often in stark black with diamond brooches and clips, or stark white with dramatic trims. Even when she's supposed to be relaxed and human, she's elegantly gotten up in a plaid shirt and carefully fitted loose pants. Write-ups of Grace Moore often refer to her as "icy" or "glacial." In this film, perhaps because of the amazing warmth generated by Cary Grant, she's regal, but relaxed. She has a casual and confident acting style, and she and Grant play in an improvisational mode as they enact the typical "We hate each other, which means we're meant to be together for eternity" scenario. The movie was both written and directed by Robert Riskin, and it has snappy dialogue and believable comedy.

Moore and Grant play characters stranded in Mexico, she without visa and he without money. She hires him to marry her so she can obtain her papers, and of course they fall in love. The film uses a lot of intense close-ups, particularly of the handsome Grant staring adoringly at Moore, his eyes warm and his dimple on display. His loose and naturalistic style liberated Moore, and together they are quite good in a pleasant film. Moore sings Verdi, Puccini, and Schubert, plus "Siboney" and, to a modern audience's shock, Cab Calloway's "Minnie the Moocher." (This song was cut before release and reinserted later, so that some prints today do not contain it.) To see a very blond, very delicate white female suddenly swing out into "Minnie" is what is called a showstopper. It stops you, all right. Moore shakes her hips, waves her arms, and is generally unafraid of tackling material that is alien to her singing world. As she works it to death, one has only to picture Cab Calloway, steppin' around, gettin' down with it, loose and jazzy, to realize what a nutty mistake this really was. Moore, however, can command the frame, and when she sings such songs as "Siboney," she's beautiful and lyrical.

Miss Grace Moore and Mr. Cary Grant know what you're supposed to do *When You're in Love.*

"Siboney" is an example of how a musical number in a film can transform something ordinary into something fabulous, and it illustrates the evolution of the musical. It's 1937, and all focus of story, performance, and technology is on the music. The number becomes a visual and musical dialogue between Moore and Grant. She sings; he watches her sing. The watching takes place in a darkened nightclub in Mexico. There's a huge crowd, packed together at small tables. It's a world of joy, noisy and glamorous, a place where the audience never went and couldn't really go, that special movie place of promises, beauty, release, and sex. The lighting makes use of deep, dark shadows, and the swaying musicians (dressed in big sombreros and serapes) stand at the foot of a stairway. Moore is dressed in a dark dress with a long V-neck, covered in little faux diamonds. At the point of the V is a flower the size of Rhode Island, and she casually holds a chiffon handkerchief that could be a table-cloth. When she sings, she's in softly lit darkness, but her face shines. She glows, and Grant, watching her, is shot in intense close-up. His appreciation for her music, her beauty, and her sex appeal are openly delineated on his face. (This was why Cary Grant was a star for decades: he was comic, witty, acerbic, but he was also romantic and desirable, and he knew how to make audiences believe they knew what he was thinking and feeling.) This musical interlude between Grant and Moore could be a throwaway, but it's an interlude to get lost in, to dream about, and to feel anything you want to feel. It represents the reason Hollywood was so successful for so many years, and it's a definition of stardom without words, only images. It is also a definition of the power of performed music in movies. If an opera star, like Moore, could wield that power, then Hollywood was willing to build a movie around her.

Opera stars might be a business challenge, but operettas were different. They were a logical choice for Hollywood to turn into mass-market movies. Hollywood didn't have to invent the form or write or create it. Operettas were ready-made, highly popular; and the often beautiful and sentimental songs and stories appealed to the era. As soon as sound arrived, Hollywood embraced them, putting them onscreen, where they stayed for a remarkably long time. Today operettas are largely thought of as nothing more than old-fashioned musicals, flawed by a lack of dance numbers for the leads and overly sentimental by modern standards. However, operettas ("little operas" or "singing musicals") were originally promoted enthusiastically. Ads screeched out: OPERETTA! on a movie poster, confident the term was a positive box-office draw. *The Rogue Song* was advertised in 1930 as "the Greatest Operetta Ever Produced," featuring a large photograph of the star, Lawrence Tibbett, and a drawing of the Metropolitan Opera House, where he had "thrilled thousands" with his singing. *Married in Hollywood* (1929) was proudly sold as "the first Viennese operetta to hit the screen, with music by Oscar Straus."

Photographing sound movies was, of course, a problem at first, which affected the quality of these early operettas. The cameras were set within glass-windowed soundproof booths in 1929 when what is labeled "the first operetta with sound" was filmed: Sigmund Romberg's *The Desert Song*,

starring John Boles. Ads proclaimed it "the first Music-Play to be produced as a complete talking and singing picture."* By the end of 1929, the problem of camera noise had been mostly resolved. Where at first sound cameras had to be set inside soundproof structures (called "ice boxes"), which were hot and uncomfortable for the cameraman and which restricted camera movement, by 1930 small containers that covered the camera (called "blimps") were being used to repress noise and allow freer movement. With the new freedom, Hollywood turned immediately to adapting more and more successful (and established) operettas to the screen. The calendar year 1930 brought *The Rogue Song, The Vagabond King, Bride of the Regiment, Sweet Kitty Bellairs, Captain of the Guard, Song of the Flame, Dixiana, The Lottery Bride, Golden Dawn, Viennese Nights*, et al.

Hollywood shrewdly looked for operettas that had the potential to provide more than just songs and dances, which was why *The Desert Song*, with its desert setting, Riff warriors, intrigue, and excitement in addition to its melodies, was its first choice. Based on Sigmund Romberg's 1926 operetta, which was itself hugely popular, *The Desert Song* was made into a musical movie three times: in 1929, 1943, and 1953.† In other words,

* The same ad also announced "exotic dancing girls . . . a chorus of 132 voices, 109 musicians, and Romantic wild Riff horsemen."

† The highly popular (and very versatile) Sigmund Romberg (*The Student Prince, Maytime*, etc.) had a long

while the studio system was functioning, a version of this reliable property came out nearly once a decade. Audiences didn't mind a repeated plot in an operetta. It was the songs, the music that delighted them; the music could

be listened to over and over. The three versions of *The Desert Song* are a miniature history of musicals. The first version, with John Boles as the Red Shadow, is stilted, bound in by camera restriction, but with some two-strip color sequences. The 1943 version had three-strip Technicolor added, and was freshened with an updated, modernized plot: it's the Nazis the hero is fighting! Dennis Morgan is the Red Shadow, and there's swift, capable direction by Robert Florey which emphasizes action. Topical updating was present in the 1953 version also: in the days of the Cold War, calling a hero "Red" anything seemed unpatriotic, so the Red Shadow name was dropped. He's just a regular old rebel, played by Gordon MacRae opposite Kathryn Grayson. The third version, also in color, stressed beautiful costumes, romance, and more plot than song, and also added more choreography (by LeRoy Prinz).

and successful Broadway career, and twelve of his operettas were made into movies in addition to *The Desert Song*. Romberg wrote the music, Otto Harbach and Oscar Hammerstein II the book and lyrics, with support from Frank Mandel on the book.

OPPOSITE, TOP *The Desert Song* was so popular it was made into three movies over three decades, with three different singing Red Shadows. First was John Boles, obviously under the influence of Rudolph Valentino . . .

. . . then came Dennis Morgan (opposite, bottom), tousled and energetic . . .

. . . followed by Gordon MacRae (this page), sharing the frame with the inevitable Kathryn Grayson.

The three Red Shadows (Boles, Morgan, and MacRae) are distinctly different actors.* Boles was a handsome Texan who had seriously studied voice and had appeared on Broadway in *Little Jesse James* (1923). Because of his exceptional good looks, he was brought out to Hollywood to become a fairly successful silent-film star in the later period of silents. When sound came in, he was perfectly positioned, having had vocal training and looking as he did like an Arrow collar ad. His was the privilege in starring in the 1929 *Desert Song*, officially the "first" Broadway show to be filmed. And it looks it. If any movie could be said to be ill at ease, it's this one, and ditto its star. But Boles was pleasant-looking, with a nice voice, and he made a credible Red Shadow. (His leading lady was Carlotta King.)

Dennis Morgan was a more relaxed performer, and he was skilled at banter, a talent that was put to good use when he was paired with Jack Carson to become a second-string Bing Crosby/Bob Hope combo in a series for Warner Bros. (*Two Guys from Milwaukee*; *Two Guys from Texas*; *It's a Great Feeling*; *The Time, The Place and The Girl*). Morgan was a very good Red Shadow. Gordon MacRae had no acting skill, but his full baritone handled the Romberg music perfectly. He came across as good-natured and easygoing. His was a rather casual Red Shadow—kind of a guy waiting his turn to sing rather than a guy all worried about Riff wars.

Shifting cultural attitudes are reflected in the three heroes: Boles plays the original character, a man who pretends to be shy and inept who is secretly the Red Shadow (a variation of the Zorro/Scarlet Pimpernel concept). Morgan is an American hero, appropriate for World War II; and MacRae in the 1953 version is a Frenchman. In 1929, the old-fashioned original plot is maintained along with its hero; in 1943, the action is updated to World War II; and in 1953, the plot is safely relocated out of the Shadow's "Redness" and into a neutral Allied zone. The women shift from being a society girl to a professional singer to the general's daughter. The Riffs go from being the evil enemy to being helpers to being the good guys.†

Three Red Shadows, three leading ladies, and three very similar and yet different versions of *The Desert Song* within the time frame of less than

---

* A logical choice to be a Red Shadow, Nelson Eddy, was not a Warner Bros. contract player. He got his chance on TV in 1955 when *Max Liebman Presents* starred Eddy with Gale Sherwood in an acclaimed adaptation that featured him in live performance.

† The 1943 version takes its location seriously since the war brought news from the area. There is even a reference to the *real* Riff leader, the Berber chief Abd el-Krim.

twenty-five years. Why so many *Desert Song*s? There are solid reasons: a beautiful, melodious score that contains some of Romberg's best and most romantic compositions ("One Alone," "The Riff Song," the title song); a contemporary setting (in its day); an exciting story with implied action onstage which could be transformed into real action onscreen. And, of course, a title that everyone knew, with songs that everyone knew, and over it all, originally, the influence of Rudolph Valentino as a dashing sheik who carries women off whether they wanted to be carried off or not (with the understanding that they *did* want to be carried off, at least safely so, at the movies).

The 1929 *Desert Song* gives a viewer an idea of what the original stage show was like, and the 1953 version reveals how dated a concept that had become. The 1943 version, however, shows what Hollywood could do with an operetta with a little bit of rewriting, some clever casting, and a sharp director who knows how to get an operetta up on its feet and dashing across the desert.

The original Broadway *Desert Song* had an exotic quality that tapped into the times. The Riff uprisings of the 1920s had inspired interest in sheiks, desert nights, and glamorous dashes on fast horses across the sands. The most dominant cultural touchpoint was, obviously, the Valentino movies *The Sheik* and *Son of the Sheik*. The setting, the music and lyrics, and the erotic connection to Valentino made *The Desert Song* seem fresher, sexier, and more entertaining than other operettas that were still being set in Vienna and a European prince-and-princess environment.*

The Dennis Morgan/Irene Manning *Desert Song* was released into movie theaters in 1943, in the depths of World War II. The story was cleverly updated to link the Red Shadow's bravery to current events. Morgan plays an American who has fought in the Spanish Civil War (the movie is set in 1939) and has come to French Morocco to help the Riffs block a German railroad. (North Africa was a popular locale for movies during the war, from *Casablanca* to *Sahara* to *Five Graves to Cairo*, etc.) To freshen the Romberg score, three new songs were written: "Fifi's Song," "Long Live the Night," and "Gay Parisienne." LeRoy Prinz created a sensuous choreography with harem girls in the popular Hollywood hootchy-kootch style.

---

* The original show had a song called "It," a topical number that played on the popularity of Clara Bow, the 1920s "It" girl.

The 1943 *Desert Song* is an example of Hollywood's tinkering with old material to make it timely, while still maintaining respect for the music and following the guidelines that were in place regarding musicals. Purists are offended, but it was smart business. Robert Florey, the director, was French, a former art director with a strong sense of visual style and the ability to keep a film moving. His *Desert Song* is as much an action picture as it is a musical, featuring an extended battle scene between French troops and the Riffs, exciting chases across the desert sands, and colorful intrigue in the Casbah. Although there's stirring music on the soundtrack, the first use of music in the plot is when Morgan gives the Riff signal on a piano that he appears to be merely noodling at; the film has been underway for several minutes, taking time to establish its very modern political plot before introducing itself as a musical. It makes clear it's not an operetta from the 1920s.

Florey's *Desert Song* shows that it's possible to update a plot without losing its base elements. Morgan covers his face with a red burnoose, but he's called El Khobar rather than the Red Shadow. The enemies are the Germans, but they are not specifically named as such until the final confrontation, when "Berlin" is heard to be the master manipulator. The French forces who have opposed the Riffs join Morgan and help defeat the enemy. The biggest battle of the film is well shot, well cut, and orchestrated to add movement and involvement. What this *Desert Song* achieves is the ability to bring to life the implied story of the operetta, all the action, danger, fighting, and riding across the frame at high speed that can't be achieved onstage. The music is seamlessly incorporated, and the frame doesn't go dead so the romantic leads can sing a ballad. The old plot seems fresh, timely, and upbeat as the story flows along. The running time is ninety minutes, and a full story is told, "with songs." The leading lady, Irene Manning, whom Warners hoped to make into a star, is bland but has a lovely voice, and she's updated for a modern point of view by appearing as "the new singer from Nice." Dance is folded into the action in a natural way: an exotic native dancer plus the onstage performances by Manning and her troupe. As a result, this *Desert Song* does not play like an operetta but instead like a low-budget action/adventure film with a significant cast of character actors (Bruce Cabot, Victor Francen, Gene Lockhart, Curt Bois). And yet once the film is underway, the gloriously romantic Romberg music swells up and is strongly present.

Operettas, however, were not all so adaptable. They harked backward, not forward, and except for the singular (and unexpected) success of the MacDonald/Eddy collaborations, soon enough they were relegated to only an occasional variation of the musical genre. The operetta was a rather dead thing onscreen. The exception is a fine piece of filmmaking that is also a great operetta, the 1934 *Merry Widow* directed by Ernst Lubitsch. The movie musical had just turned its important 1933 corner when *The Merry Widow* was made into a hit film by MGM.* In 1934, the enforcement of the Production Code went into effect, and MGM was a studio that cared about conforming. Thus Lubitsch needed to downplay his usual sexual innuendo and up-play a sort of civilized sexuality, which he managed to do. Lubitsch's *Merry Widow* shows where the musical could go, how it could become cinematic and separate itself from theater. All the tools of cinema—camera movement, cutting, set design, lighting, use of space—are woven into the movie to integrate song and dance into the plot and define the characters and their romance. The goal of musical history would ultimately be to achieve what *The Merry Widow* already achieved; but in the commercial world of Hollywood, progress was not always embraced.

The original operetta premiered in Vienna in 1905. The first American production starred Ethel Jackson and Donald Brian and opened at the New Amsterdam Theatre in New York in 1907. With its varied and beautiful score, its charming tale of romance with a dash of comedy, and its Parisian settings, it was a howling success everywhere. Hollywood made two versions, the Lubitsch in 1934 and a lavish but overstuffed remake with Lana Turner and Fernando Lamas in 1952. (Turner was dubbed by Trudy Erwin.)†

The 1934 *Merry Widow* shows why operettas stayed alive: they could be transformed into something modern and cinematic, and, of course, they had the wonderful music that had been alive in the culture since they were originally launched. Unfortunately, most operettas didn't get the kind of treatment that Lubitsch gave *The Merry Widow*, so the form began to wither and die despite MacDonald and Eddy. By 1952, when *The Merry Widow* was remade with Turner and Lamas, the fizz was gone. The stars,

* By all logic, *The Merry Widow* should have been a Paramount musical rather than an MGM: it has Lubitsch to guide it, and Jeanette MacDonald and Maurice Chevalier as its stars.

† The celebrated silent version, released in 1925, starring Mae Murray and John Gilbert and directed by Erich von Stroheim, was obviously not a musical.

TOP, LEFT Three *Merry Widows* graced the screen: the Erich von Stroheim silent classic with Mae Murray, bent backwards by John Gilbert—no music but plenty of heat . . .

TOP, RIGHT . . . The Lubitsch bonbon, with Jeanette MacDonald and Maurice Chevalier at Maxim's, with the fizz of a great French champagne . . .

despite an offscreen romance, generate no heat, no frisson of cranky attraction that has to be resolved the way the MacDonald-and-Chevalier relationship did. The Turner/Lamas version is sumptuously produced in color (the first color version of the operetta), filled with velvet and silk, posh accoutrements, detailed sets, and carefully designed costumes for both men and women. Everything about it says money, but not much says class. It does have the music, and it does have a little comedy, but it stresses the frustration of romance more than the joy of it. It can be labeled as a full-bodied red wine as opposed to the highest-quality champagne of the 1934 version.

Lubitsch's *Merry Widow* is a delightful operetta onscreen. It's witty, sexy, beautifully produced, and very musical. As a movie, it has always suffered in comparison to Lubitsch's earlier MacDonald/Chevalier vehicles (*The Love Parade*, *One Hour with You*) because it's an MGM production, not a Paramount, and the general feeling is that MGM was not as sophisticated or willing to be risqué as the more European Paramount. The difference is not

just studio policy: the censorship crackdown and the agreed-upon enforcement of the Code may have led MGM to conform more willingly than some other studios. But *The Merry Widow* is nevertheless still a Lubitsch production, with his trademark elimination of specific continuity explanations. What MGM always gives is top-rate production values, and *The Merry Widow* has clothes, furniture, and visuals of a very high caliber. It also has MacDonald and Chevalier, who, whatever their offscreen relationship might have been, are always deliciously pitted against each other in sug-

. . . and the MGM Technicolor extravaganza with Lana Turner and Fernando Lamas—maybe a good red but not much sparkle.

gestive sexual combat. Lubitsch's ability to make visual jokes is on display. When the heavyset king goes out for the evening, and the slender Chevalier sneaks in to "visit" the queen as soon as he departs, the king discovers he's forgotten his uniform belt and sword. He returns to retrieve it, leaving the audience outside the door, expecting trouble. Nothing happens. The king emerges, absentmindedly talking to himself, walking his long corridors, fastening his belt around his large middle. Suddenly, he stops. Wait—the belt is half his size! This clever deferral of the king's discovery that Chevalier has unrobed (or at least, since it's post-Code, unbelted) avoids a clichéd scene, involves the audience in figuring out the joke, and delivers a punch line in a visual and highly unexpected way. Lubitsch is still very much functioning as Lubitsch.

The Merry Widow as a film is one of those one-step-forwards that the musical movie often took. It's not a backstage story; it's not an original movie script or score; it's not fresh and new with its music . . . it is an old operetta first produced in 1905. Ah, but it's a *movie* operetta, well aware of what cinema can do and right on top of the issue of singing and dancing within a filmed context. Even seen today, it's modern, and its comedy holds up.

The Merry Widow accomplishes what musical films need to accomplish: It establishes the parameters of its filmed world immediately in its opening. The audience is told it's in Marshovia (through a title) and shown a map of Europe. There's no Marshovia visible . . . so a magnifying glass appears onscreen, cleverly positioned to enlarge: MARSHOVIA. This not only says everything about the little kingdom that anyone needs to know, but also establishes immediately that this particular operetta will be a funny musical, not a sadly romantic one. Comedy established first, then on to the music. Uniformed men, marching in order, are seen moving through the narrow streets of the capital city, marching, marching, in an impressive display of military power—although they are singing "Girls, Girls, Girls" and have to break their lines and separate to march around the cows that are wandering the streets. Everything is perfectly set up: Marshovia isn't really there on the map, and thus it isn't real, so it'll be okay if people sing or, for that matter, do anything else unreal. The country is a joke, with its cows, but the opening also cleverly undercuts the typical operetta tradition. There'll be no sacrifices or heartbreaks here. (And in case any audience member didn't get this, the king will soon be seen reading his newspaper, *The Morning Moo—for Table and Stable*.)

The Merry Widow doesn't need any logical reason for singing to occur, and yet it takes audiences into its universe on a careful three-step progression for acceptance: first, with the soldiers marching and singing (which is logical); then with Jeanette MacDonald hearing gypsies performing underneath her balcony, so she goes out and sings with them, the beautiful "Vilia" (which is also logical); and finally, after MacDonald looks into her diary to see if it's filled, and it isn't, she writes in it, saying, "I thought that this day would be the day my heart would find romance," and then she begins to sing her emotions: "I thought that this day would be the day / And my heart would learn to dance." The opening minutes of *The Merry Widow*, a graceful movie, are cinematic perfection, particularly *musical* cinematic perfection. Since the secondary characters in this movie will never sing—only MacDonald and Chevalier have this privilege—music gives them a private place in which to relate to each other and to play out their romance. Music will be the playing field on which their love will be defined. It also proves that they are made for each other. Music will eliminate their difference in wealth and rank; it will eliminate their problems; it will both bring them together and separate them from everyone else. They are linked by music, defined by music, and united by music yet they always sing separately. Finally, they will dance together in the acceptance of their love, twirling and swooping to "The Merry Widow Waltz." In the end, they have to dance—get physical with each other, as it were. Accept each other, and unite their bodies in music. (Albertina Rasch created the waltzes.)

Criticism has been made of *The Merry Widow* regarding the lack of big, staged choreographed dance numbers. It's primarily a singing musical—it is, after all, an operetta—and its only true dance number is the grand finale that features the "Merry Widow Waltz," and that is also intercut by plot scenes. Some feel this lack of dance is a flaw. Watching *The Merry Widow*, however, quickly erases this idea. The film is full of energy, and has a "dancing" forward motion to its narrative. Movement is everywhere. It's in the film's editing, the pace of its dialogue, and it's in the sparkle of a sequin, the swirl of a floor-length gown, and the tip of a top hat. It is integrated "dance" designed for the movie frame, the dance of the eye across space.

Chevalier's arrival at Maxim's illustrates *The Merry Widow*'s type of dance. He enters in a whirl of movement that carries him forward into a riotous atmosphere, with waiters, patrons, and "girls, girls, girls," all moving, twisting, turning. The camera rushes an audience out onto a dance floor, following a troupe of can-can dancers who run out to begin their entertainment. The audience doesn't sit down at the tables and watch this dance to its completion, but that doesn't diminish the sense of choreography. This

Mario Lanza, the last operatic box-office star developed in Hollywood, was honored to be chosen to play *The Great Caruso*.

entrance into Maxim's, the action that follows it, the song that's sung by Chevalier ("Girls, Girls, Girls"), the women who rush to him and attend him, moving forward, backward, and around him, his own happy greetings to everyone he meets—it all adds up to a musical number that is danced. It's just not conventional. During this extended sequence at Maxim's the music of the "Merry Widow Waltz" is tantalizingly woven into the score (as it is throughout the film), and a portion of it is presented so that Chevalier and MacDonald can dance together for a spell in a private dining room. She almost—almost!—succumbs to his seductive charms, as she begins to sing the lyrics to him while he twirls her about the floor. They even kiss . . . ah, but she goes home when the "girls, girls, girls" appear. Her departure is a Lubitsch tease.

The famous waltz appears in full form at the Embassy Ball when the guests take to the floor to waltz around. The whole world seems to be dancing as the beautifully dressed men and women glide across a decorative floor, all reflected in the mirrors that line the walls. While the dance takes place, the drama of the Chevalier/MacDonald romance (will they or won't they?) intercuts. The lovers go outside to resolve their issues. ("I've just come out of the shrubbery. Big doings in the garden," Edward Everett Horton cables the king of Marshovia, reporting on their progress.) *The Merry Widow* reminds again the importance of Ernst Lubitsch to the history of musicals. Kudos to him for masterminding Hollywood's greatest operetta film and ensuring the operetta as a viable business strategy.

Transformations and Adaptations

As has been discussed, from the beginning of musical history Hollywood relied on Broadway for material. It was such an easy business strategy: just buy the rights to a successful show and turn it into a musical movie: *The Cocoanuts* (1929), for example. Even when, within the first full year of sound, the original Hollywood musical appeared, studios went on buying and filming Broadway shows. Such "adapting" continues today in a curiously reversed format: now Broadway buys original Hollywood musicals and makes them into stage shows, such as the Broadway versions of *Singin' in the Rain*, *An American in Paris*, and *Seven Brides for Seven Brothers*.

Hollywood "adapted" from anywhere and everywhere. Theater, of course, was a great source for many movies, whether musical or not. *The Philadelphia Story* was first a hit on Broadway, starring (and written for) Katharine Hepburn. MGM bought the rights to make it into a hit movie, starring Hepburn with Cary Grant and Jimmy Stewart, and later made it into an original musical called *High Society*, starring Grace Kelly in the Hepburn role, costarred with Bing Crosby and Frank Sinatra. Adaptations were fluid. The 1942 film version of the hit play *My Sister Eileen* became a 1955 movie musical also called *My Sister Eileen*, starring Janet Leigh, Jack Lemmon, Betty Garrett, and a young Bob Fosse (also doing his first credited choreography for a film).* Lubitsch's movie *Ninotchka* became the Broadway musical *Silk Stockings*, which in turn was made into a movie with Fred Astaire and Cyd Charisse. The 1933 nonmusical, *State Fair*, starring Janet Gaynor and Lew Ayres, became a movie musical—the 1945 *State Fair*, starring Jeanne Crain, Dana Andrews, Dick Haymes, and Vivian Blaine—which in 1962 in turn became a remake starring Pat Boone, Bobby Darin, Ann-Margret, and Alice Faye.† The nonmusical movies called *Daddy Long Legs* (1919 and 1931) became the musical *Daddy Long*

---

* This movie, with songs by Jule Styne and Leo Robin, should not be confused with the Broadway musical adaptation, *Wonderful Town* (1953), starring Rosalind Russell (in the role she'd played in the nonmusical 1942 film) and Edie Adams, with music by Leonard Bernstein and lyrics by Betty Comden and Adolph Green. Russell also starred in a 1958 TV version of the show on CBS.

† In 1969 the St. Louis Municipal Opera, a large outdoor theater, presented yet another adaptation, complete with prize hogs and a midway. In 1996 this version was reduced in size and presented on Broadway by David Merrick as a final "new" Rodgers and Hammerstein show. Songs from both movies and from other Rodgers and Hammerstein musicals (including one cut from *Oklahoma!*) were rounded up. *State Fair* was durable.

Legs (1955) with Astaire and Leslie Caron. *Bachelor Mother* (1939), with Ginger Rogers and David Niven, became *Bundle of Joy* (1956), with Debbie Reynolds and Eddie Fisher. There are countless examples of this practice, with the prizewinner perhaps being *Kismet*. The stage play, a Broadway hit for actor Otis Skinner, was made into a movie three times (1920 and 1930, both starring Skinner, and in 1944, with Ronald Colman), and then into a Broadway musical in 1953, which became a 1955 MGM musical. Technically, that's *Kismet* to *Kismet* to *Kismet* to *Kismet* to *Kismet* to *Kismet*.

In 1927, Broadway changed a nonmusical source into a musical: the successful Edna Ferber novel *Show Boat*, which was turned into a legendary show that would itself be adapted into a film three times: in 1929, 1936, and 1951. Tracing the adaptations of the novel *Show Boat* into the Broadway hit and on to three film versions was accomplished by music historian Miles Kreuger in *Show Boat: The Story of a Classic American Musical*. Kreuger identifies the original show as "the birth of the modern musical," and almost everyone agrees with that assessment. Ferber's novel was published in 1926;* the Broadway adaptation, with music by Jerome Kern and book and lyrics by Oscar Hammerstein II, opened in New York on December 27, 1927.† *Show Boat* took everyone, both critics and audiences, by storm, and its enormous popularity, still alive today, made it inevitable that Hollywood would want to make it into a movie. The hit show had opened, however, just as sound was becoming easily available, so the studio that purchased the rights (Universal Pictures) began its adaptation as a silent film: the novel and its story without the Kern/Hammerstein music. *Show Boat*, the film, thus became a miniature lesson in the history of technology: in 1929, shot silent but released later with some sound added; in 1936, presented after movies had solved the problem of sound and had arrived at a peak of black-and-white artistry; and again in 1951, when color and location shooting were available and the studio that presented the film, MGM, was at its own peak of creativity. Each of the three *Show Boat*s reveals something

---

* The book had been serialized in a magazine, *Woman's Home Companion*, from April to September of 1926, and its official publishing date was August 1926. It became an immediate success.

† The Broadway show was produced by Florenz Ziegfeld and starred Norma Terris as Magnolia, Howard Marsh as Gaylord, Charles Winninger as Cap'n Andy, Edna Mae Oliver as Parthy, Helen Morgan as Julie, and Jules Bledsoe (not, as many people believe, Paul Robeson) as Joe. Robeson had been the original choice for the role, but delays in production had prevented him from accepting due to other commitments. (He was Joe in the first London production, which opened in May 1928, and in the 1936 film.)

about movie musicals and musical history. The first version cannot repro-duce the show's music because it's technically not possible; the second has solved that problem and can concentrate on story and character as well as both music and cinema; and the third counts on color and the success of what had become a legendary property to sell the material.

The book presented adaptation challenges right from the beginning. It is a saga, covering a show-business family over five decades, and involving many characters and many subplots, some revealed through elaborate flash-backs. It includes miscegenation, alcoholism, desertion, gambling, murder in self-defense, a drowning, a giant storm on the river—all potential prob-lems in one way or another, and a lot to deal with. One of Hammerstein's best contributions was the taming of the novel. At the time, he was a young man who had successfully collaborated on musical books with Otto Har-bach. (The Harbach/Hammerstein collaborations were highly successful: *Wildflower* in 1923, *Rose-Marie* in 1924, and *Sunny*, with music by Kern, in 1925, and the latest, the blockbuster Romberg musical *The Desert Song* in 1926.) Hammerstein's challenge was similar to the one that always faces a

An enduring and beloved property became an enduring and popular movie-musical source, starting with the first *Show Boat* in 1929: Joseph Schildkraut and Laura La Plante, with banjo but no sound . . .

screenwriter adapting a novel to the motion picture: the need to compress events into a two-hour format, eliminate characters accordingly, simplify the plot to create a clean line with a more direct purpose, and organize the story's chronology for clarity. Hammerstein was able to do this, choosing to focus the musical stage play on the character of Magnolia. When completed, the Kern/Hammerstein *Show Boat* gave audiences something groundbreaking: a musical that was delightfully entertaining but also seri-

. . . Irene Dunne and Allan Jones in 1936, with sound, plus heart and soul . . .

ous, with tragedy and comedy intertwined. It was coherent and tightly constructed, but took the time to fully develop its characters. The music and the story were well integrated, and no song or dance was external or inappropriate to its tone and purpose. There was no moment in which a character said "I was thinking about ancient Persia . . ." and on came a harem of dancing girls. Everything was about what it was supposed to be about, with no meanderings and no unrelated moments. In other words, the musical stage play that was the book of *Show Boat* was written as if it were a screenplay. The material was perfect for adaptation.

What *Show Boat* brought to the Broadway stage was a change from the era's popular lighthearted musical comedies that featured specialty numbers, unrelated songs, and a frequent lack of dancing from the principal characters. *Show Boat* was a musical play rather than a musical comedy, but not an operetta set in faraway Ruritania. It was a story about American issues and the American past, a complex tale about a woman, Magnolia, who grew from innocent youth into a sadder but wiser maturity. It incorporated the American musical vernacular of spirituals, patriotic music, and known rhythms, but it presented a trunkful of new and glorious music, all of which furthered characterization and expressed inner feelings of the singers. In short, it was indeed, as Kreuger has noted, "the birth of the modern musical."

. . . and Kathryn Grayson and Howard Keel in 1951, with beautiful Technicolor but not much else.

The 1929 movie version of *Show Boat* was not available for screening for many years. It was a silent film that starred Laura La Plante as Magnolia and Joseph Schildkraut as Gaylord, but as the film was completed and prepared for release, the need for sound—particularly for the glorious Kern and Hammerstein music—became apparent. A second version of the movie was created with an eighteen-minute sound "prologue" in which the original Broadway cast was photographed and recorded singing the songs. Some sound effects and bits of dialogue were also added to the main feature. The 1929 *Show Boat* movie was thus first a nonmusical and then a musical of sorts.*

* During the transition-to-sound period, films undergoing preparation as silent movies were often recalled to have one or two sections of sound added. These movies were nicknamed "goat's glands movies" in reference to a medical procedure devised by a quack doctor named John R. Brinkley in which the glands of goats were transplanted into humans as cures for a long list of illnesses, among them impotency. I first heard this rare term at a conference on sound that took place in the early

The first *Show Boat* reveals how strong the original story really was, and how different from the usual musical comedy libretto. It remained a Broadway musical comedy, but it was not limited to that definition. It rose above, showing that musicals could be both serious and comic; in short, that they could be an art form in their own right. The fact that the story of the novel, as adapted, could stand alone as a movie was significant.

It is the 1936 *Show Boat* that transfers the historical significance of the original musical to the screen, and that shows what a movie musical could be—and should be. It adapts a cinematic point-of-view, lifting *Show Boat* off the stage and into the new art form under the direction of the very talented and sensitive James Whale. The movie's success begins with its impeccable casting of the roles, particularly with having Paul Robeson, the original choice for Joe, appear to sing "Ol' Man River" and "Ah Still Suits Me." For Magnolia, the movie cast Irene Dunne, the beautiful singing star who had replaced Norma Terris in Boston just after the post-Broadway tour got underway. (Kreuger points out that many erroneously believe Dunne had understudied Terris, but this was not true; Dunne was brought in specifically as Terris's replacement.) Gaylord Ravenal was played by Allan Jones, a handsome tenor who was the star of many movie musicals from 1933 to 1945. (Jones, the father of singer Jack Jones, became famous for his signature song, "The Donkey Serenade," which he first sang in 1937's *The Firefly*, which costarred him with Jeanette MacDonald.) Helen Morgan played Julie and Charles Winninger was Cap'n Andy, Helen Westley was Parthy, and Hattie McDaniel was Queenie.

James Whale was an odd choice to direct the landmark musical. A British stage director, he had arrived in Hollywood in 1930 to direct one of his biggest stage successes, the play *Journey's End*. He stayed on in California and became famous for four of Hollywood's most iconic horror films: *Frankenstein* (1931), *The Old Dark House* (1932), *The Invisible Man* (1933), and *Bride of Frankenstein* (1935). His movies were marked by a sensitivity that presented flawed characters sympathetically; they had a macabre comedy within them, and were beautifully shot and lit for an atmospheric, brooding quality. Whale knew how to suggest a subtext to audiences; his ability to present a complex musical with depth of character and feeling was clearly present. The 1936 *Show Boat* is not just the best of all the filmed *Show Boat*s; it's also one of the very best examples of the musical format on

_____

1970s at Eastman House in Rochester, New York. I thought I had perhaps imagined it, but Kreuger also refers to the term in his impeccably researched book.

The greatest *Show Boat* of them all: Paul Robeson, Irene Dunne, Hattie McDaniel, and Helen Morgan, four brilliant performers, hangin' around the galley in a musical mood

film, one that has stood the test of time and will no doubt continue to do so. Everything about it is cinematic, but without overwhelming or destroying the original story and characters. Above all, it respects the music and the intentions of the book.

"Respect" for the music of any original Broadway show being adapted into film was always debatable. The 1936 *Show Boat* is an example of Hollywood's common practice of purchasing a musical and then changing it. Whale's version cuts a few songs from the stage play and adds three new ones, all written by Kern and Hammerstein, so the mood and style of the music matches: "I Have the Room Above Her," "Ah Still Suits Me," and "Gallivantin' Around."* In fact, it was a common practice for Hollywood to

---

* Kern's musical style was one in which he often incorporated songs already known to his audiences into his books. The 1936 *Show Boat* reflects this by using "After the Ball" and "Goodbye, My Lady

purchase a musical and make changes in the plot and characterization—no one apparently cared—but it's surprising to note how often successful scores were altered. Songs were dropped, used only as background music, assigned to different characters, or replaced with new songs. People always wonder why Hollywood would do this. It seems crazy to buy a musical with great songs and not use them, but the business had serious (and legitimate) reasons for this practice. A movie musical was more of a plot structure than a Broadway show, and thus there were often too many songs to be easily incorporated into a ninety-minute movie. Sometimes the musical-movie star couldn't sing well enough to handle a particular number, or dance well enough, or seem credible as a person who could or would do either with a particular song. New material that accommodated movie stardom would be written to better showcase a star—lyrics and style that matched the star's persona. And besides, the studios owned music publishing houses. A new song meant a new hit, which meant more money from sheet-music sales. Why pay royalties to another firm? Creating hit songs for recording and sheet-music sales was a cottage industry for Hollywood, and every piece of sheet music that featured a movie on the front (with a movie-star photo to catch a customer's eye) was also a successful promo for the movie.* Dropping good songs for newer, lesser ones seems like an idiotic practice, but the bossmen of the studios were shrewd businessmen who knew how to make a buck.

Whale showcased his singers and their music through cutting and camera movement and angles. When the great Paul Robeson sits by the river-

---

Love" as well as by inserting "Bill," a song Kern had written in 1917 with P. G. Wodehouse, not Hammerstein.

* An example of extreme cutting is the truly awful movie version of *The Boys from Syracuse*, which originally had a dazzling score by Rodgers and Hart, including "Falling in Love with Love," "This Can't Be Love," and "He and She." The movie version, starring Allan Jones, Joe Penner, Irene Hervey, Rosemary Lane, and Martha Raye, was reduced to a seventy-three-minute running time by cutting three major songs—and then replacing them with two new ones. The Cole Porter stage hit *Panama Hattie* starred Ethel Merman, but the movie replaced her with the pretty and softer Ann Sothern. Sothern could sing, and had a charming personality, but she wasn't a big-voiced belter like Merman. Some of the *Panama Hattie* songs weren't right for her, so the movie kept a few, but built around her with two singers with strong personal singing styles: the comic deadpan Virginia O'Brien, who sang "Fresh As a Daisy," and the stunning, show-stopping Lena Horne, who was given Porter's "Just One of Those Things" as a specialty number. Horne was not as lucky in her own starring film *Cabin in the Sky*, in which one of her best songs, "Ain't It the Truth?," shot in close-up while she's taking a bubble bath, was cut from the final release. She's fabulous-looking and sings with amazing personality—a loss to film history, although it later was used in an MGM short.

side, whittling and watching the world go by, he begins to sing "Ol' Man River." Traditionally, he would be shot in medium close-up, so that an audience could experience his singing by viewing him up close, isolated in the pleasure of his voice. Whale gives the viewer the song and the voice and the personality, but he does more. He approaches Robeson via camera movement, executing an amazing 360-degree pan around him, increasing a viewer's participation and excitement and extending the view, showing Robeson in context. Around him are his fellow African American men at work, "body all achin' an' racked with pain." What Robeson sings—"ya gets a little drunk an' ya lands in jail"—is then shown in a series of images. The song fully expresses Robeson's character, but it also provides a significant social context.

When Jones and Dunne sing "You Are Love" on the top deck of the show boat at night, the soft lighting and romantic glow enhance their relationship. When McDaniel, Robeson, Morgan, and Dunne fool around in the boat's kitchen, singing, they are improvisational, realistic, and musical all at the same time. When Julie (Morgan) agrees to sing a song known "down on the levee," she presents a lilting "Can't Help Lovin' Dat Man." McDaniel and Robeson join in, and Dunne jumps down off the table and moves around the space, everybody swaying and singing, and Dunne executing a remarkable shuffle. ("Look at that gal shuffle!" exclaims Robeson.) In its day, the scene had no agenda other than to say that Julie and Magnolia are friends and Magnolia has learned Julie's songs and dances and feels comfortable with Joe and Queenie. (Today, Dunne's dance is startling, and her eyeball rolling is often seen as offensive.) When Dunne gets one chance to survive by performing well at a big-city New Year's Eve nightclub party (after she's been deserted by Gaylord), she's terrified, out of her element, and stiffly unsuccessful. Unbeknownst to her, her father, Cap'n Andy, is in the audience, and when he stands amidst a crowd of revelers to call out to her, "Smile, Nolie, smile!," the emotional realism of her response and subsequent loosening up to win the crowd as she warbles "After the Ball" is a perfect wedding of song, performance, dramatic crisis, camera movement, lighting, and crowd control.

Since Dunne is not singing a new song but is presenting a standard that the audience already knew, the directorial concentration could give full attention to her and her performance. No one needed to concentrate on a "new song" for its lyrics and meanings. Once the song begins, familiarity puts everyone at ease, and the scene becomes about what it is supposed to be about: Dunne's fear, her father's love and support, and her response, which takes her to triumph and a life of fame. As Dunne, a very good actress, slowly relaxes, and begins to sway back and forth as she dances, ultimately sweeping out into a full waltz, singing her heart out, waving her beautiful fan, and charming everyone, the camera locates her properly, the cutting works to her advantage, and the costume and lighting give the audience a beautiful (and emotional) experience.

The cast of the 1936 *Show Boat* is perfect. Having the chance to see and hear Paul Robeson alone is worth watching the entire movie, but there's also the legendary Helen Morgan repeating her success from the original production. When she sings "Bill," Whale gives her the greatest respect. He honors the intensity of the moment and the purity of her performance by eschewing any camera tricks. He holds on her, finally going into intense close-up with a portrait lens. (Morgan was not the modern world's idea of a torch singer. Her voice is light and high, but it has a crystal purity to it.)

A miniature re-creation of *Show Boat* from the opening scene of the Jerome Kern biopic, *Till the Clouds Roll By*, with (from left) Lena Horne as Julie, Virginia O'Brien as Ellie May, William Halligan as Cap'n Andy, and Bruce Cowling as Steve

Morgan is only thirty-six years old, but she seems older, bowed down by tragedy, not just in her characterization of Julie, but in her very soul. Morgan was an alcoholic, and she *was* bowed down, but she could sing.* Her ability to present "Bill" with credible but understated emotionalism is one of the 1936 *Show Boat*'s finest moments. She makes the song an anthem for female passion and disappointment in men, but with delicacy and dignity. She doesn't wail and she doesn't beat her chest and she certainly doesn't kill the lyrics with "performance." She just sings, and as the camera presses down on her, coming in so close that she can hide nothing, she turns her face slightly away, almost in shame, but unwilling to deny her truth. Whale's presentation of Morgan singing "Bill," and his understanding of how to show her pain honestly without detracting from a lyrically beautiful song, is perfection. It's an important moment for musicals—this is how Judy Garland will be shot and edited; this is how a singer in a musical can "speak" to an audience with a song and its lyrics, but also with a subtext of personal feeling that only a camera can reveal. It's about how the musical film can establish intimacy . . . about why audiences will love musicals for decades to come.

The 1951 *Show Boat* has everything anyone might want from a musical: great songs, an all-star cast, colorful dances, lavish production values, a fabulous-looking show boat especially constructed for the shoot—absolutely everything—except what counts: a heart and a soul. Despite the best efforts of everyone involved, it's slickly commercial, having the confidence of its reliable material with nothing else required. The cast consists of top MGM headliners: Kathryn Grayson as Magnolia, Howard Keel as Gaylord, William Warfield as Joe, Joe E. Brown as Cap'n Andy, Agnes Moorehead as Parthy, and Frances Williams as Queenie. Superstar Ava Gardner was given the role of Julie, with the studio overlooking the fact that Lena Horne was available and would have been perfect. Gardner was beautiful, talented, and growing as an actress—but not yet there. Her singing voice wasn't strong enough for the role, but she wanted to do her own singing. Test recordings were made; she just couldn't do it. She was dubbed by Annette Warren.† Although by 1951 the script was tried and true, changes were made. The 1936 film has a long separation between Magno-

---

* Morgan would be dead within five years (in 1941) of cirrhosis of the liver.

† Gardner's voice was used on the MGM soundtrack recording.

lia and Gaylord: they don't reconnect until they are old. The 1951 movie shortens their separation to a mere three years, diminishing the sadness of their story, losing the sense of a lifetime of loss and melancholy. A second alteration also diminished tragedy: Julie is made the instrument of their reconciliation. Instead of her disappearing into the night, clutching a bottle, Gardner is allowed to be the savior of the leads and to enjoy her good deed, with the hint that her life may take a turn for the better now.

Making their movie debut in the 1951 version are dancer/singers Marge and Gower Champion in the roles played by Queenie Smith and Sammy White in the 1936 version. White and Smith play the couple for what they were meant to be: two ordinary song-and-dance people, just making a living on a show boat and hoping to please an audience enough to stay employed as they move on in life. The Champions play them as if they're a couple of Copacabana headliners. Their numbers come across as a slick, modern nightclub act, supremely sophisticated, so that the nostalgic world of the show boat and its era are destroyed when they perform "Life Upon the Wicked Stage" and "I Might Fall Back on You." Robert Alton did their choreography, which is out of place with its ritzy costumes, props, settings (a revolving couch, quick costume changes, etc.), but mostly for its attitude. In the "Wicked Stage" number, Gower Champion mocks the era the action is set in with a series of quick costume changes that satirize early melodrama. White and Smith were presented simply as two old-timers who knew how to do a mean cakewalk; the Champions do a mixture of dance styles, showing off their dancing lessons, as it were. They were an instant hit, however, and moved on to a solid career with MGM.

The 1951 *Show Boat* did not advance the artistry of the musical film. It was a candy box, but the kind you buy at the drugstore. Yet making multiple versions of a property remained a lucrative Hollywood strategy, as has been seen not only with *Show Boat*, but also with *The Desert Song*. Additionally, there were two *Rose Marie*s: the Eddy/MacDonald and a bad 1954 version with Ann Blyth and Howard Keel; *Roberta* was made with Astaire and Rogers in 1935 and again as *Lovely to Look At* with Keel and Grayson, Red Skelton and Ann Miller, and the Champions in 1952; and both *Girl Crazy* and *Rio Rita* were remade. Comparisons inevitably reveal a basic movement forward from a stage-bound presentation with an immobile camera to a colorful and skilled technological event, but seldom an advancement in terms of understanding what a movie musical can be.

The greatest opportunity to consider the difference between Broadway shows and the musicals made from them lies in four classic Rodgers and Hammerstein successes: *Oklahoma!*, *Carousel*, *South Pacific*, and *The King and I*. The shows opened on Broadway in, respectively, 1943, 1945, 1949, and 1951; the film versions were released in 1955, 1956, 1958, and 1956.* The four Rodgers and Hammerstein hits have become legendary Broadway shows, with glorious, melodious scores which featured impeccably matched lyrics and literate and intelligent books. But the movie versions of these fabulous shows do not represent the best of the American Hollywood musical. Their assets don't disappear on film: the music, the dance, the characterization, and the integration between book and music haven't blown out the door in translation. However, these adaptations remain stage pieces and never

The definition of a classic adaptation: terrific music, great performances, star power, historical significance, in Gershwin's *Porgy and Bess* (1959), with Sidney Poitier, Dorothy Dandridge, and Pearl Bailey

---

* *Flower Drum Song* (1958) and *The Sound of Music* (1959), two other Rodgers and Hammerstein shows, were also made into movies successfully. Both received mixed reviews when they opened, but the movie *The Sound of Music* was a gigantic hit. Hammerstein died of cancer in 1960, and the fruitful collaboration ended. Rodgers and Hammerstein also collaborated on *Allegro* (1947), *Me and Juliet* (1953), and *Pipe Dream* (1955), all unsuccessful and none made into movies. They also did one movie, *State Fair* (1945; see pp. 400–1), and an original television musical, *Cinderella* (1957).

truly lift off the ground to become cinema. They're like the dancing hippos in Disney's *Fantasia* (1940). To the beautiful sound of the "Dance of the Hours" from *La Gioconda*, the hippos roll out, sweetly clad in pink tutus, spinning and turning, up on their little hippo toes, keeping perfect time with the beat. All is in place: music, image, costumes, setting, color, concept. There's only one thing wrong: they are hippopotami—and we can *see* they are hippopotami.

One of the main goals of a musical film is to provide an audience with a vicarious sense of release through singing and dancing. We want to feel that we're musical, that we can do it ourselves if they'd only let us. At the very least, we need to feel that those people up on the screen are doing it *for* us. A good musical provides the vicarious joy of performance, of physical freedom through dance, of losing inhibitions through singing. By the time the Rodgers and Hammerstein musicals were put on film and released, this lesson had been learned, not only by Hollywood filmmakers but also by audiences. Viewers went to the movie adaptations of *Oklahoma!*, *Carousel*, *South Pacific*, and *The King and I* expecting to have that experience—and were sadly let down. What they saw was what everyone assumed would be enough—a moving record of four great Broadway musicals—but a stage play is a stage play and a movie is a movie. By the mid-1950s, when these movies were released, audiences had experienced the kinetic energy of original movie musicals, had danced in the wet streets with Gene Kelly and across the ceiling with Fred Astaire. The adaptations were hits (except for *Carousel*), but the experience of watching them was something of a let-down even at the time, and certainly has become even more disappointing over time.

There are four different directors for the movies—Fred Zinnemann for *Oklahoma!*, Henry King for *Carousel*, Joshua Logan for *South Pacific*, and Walter Lang for *The King and I*—but except for the latter, which is the best movie of the four, they are all made less by one characteristic: reverence. The material has been approached as if it's sacred, and in so doing, the shows have been lifted up and relocated to the movie screen just like in the old days of the lame adaptations of the transition-to-sound era. This time, of course, there's magnificent color, wide-screen CinemaScope vistas, perfect sound recording, and the Todd-AO process . . . *but* . . . there is present in all four movies a dominant horizontal line: the look of the stage set as it would be seen by a theater's viewing audience. The eye is asked to travel *across* more than *into*. Cutting excludes rather than draws in. It's fair to say that the opportunity to hear beautiful music and experience legendary stage musicals has been faithfully adapted to the motion picture screen. But nothing else. What progress for movie musicals is made by these films? None.

Oklahoma! was the first of the Rodgers and Hammerstein musicals to be filmed. It opens on a beautiful sight: row upon row of wide-screen corn through which the camera moves, revealing a majestic landscape and ultimately locating Gordon MacRae riding a horse and singing "Oh, What a

Beautiful Mornin'." He's riding along against the landscape, singing great music, an apparent immediate establishment of the perfect musical universe. (Never mind that he's a bit of an upscale singing cowboy, or that Charlotte Greenwood, when she appears, is "churning" butter by working the churn the way someone who's never seen a real churn would work it.) Soon enough the real problems emerge. The beats between song and dialogue are not cinematic; events are played out in theater style, and there's a deliberate artificiality. (This was the first and last musical Zinnemann ever directed.) It's a filmed stage play—with some real locations—but primarily a movie that is proud to be theatrical because theatricality is considered proof of

Big-budget productions of successful Rodgers and Hammerstein Broadway shows included *Oklahoma!*, with Shirley Jones and Gordon MacRae in a surrey with some fringe on top . . .

superiority, a display of pedigree. Forward movement stops dead while someone sings a song. Everyone speaks in unnatural performance style: "When she acts thataway" and "Don't be agin' Jud." This pseudo-dialect is part of the original piece, but hearing it on film, with each dropped *g* hit with a sledgehammer, makes the characters seem false and diminishes audience involvement. When it's time for "Kansas City" and Gene Nelson (as Will) begins his dance, the frame is largely held to a horizontal line. When Gloria Grahame as Ado Annie sings "I Cain't Say No," the camera holds still in medium close-up while she delivers the number. Her song ends. Boom. Pause. Wait. Character may now talk. This style does not reach out and involve a moviegoer in the performance: The viewer is set up as a watcher from a seat, not a participant in the music. No kinetic experience is provided. This style is not an accident of incompetence—it's a predetermined policy. Maintaining staged artificiality takes the life out of the material, which is DOA onscreen.

When the highly celebrated dances by Agnes de Mille appear, it's clear that her choreography was designed for the proscenium arch and not for the moving camera. The dancing moves sideways across the frame and is presented as if it were on a stage. The dancers' feet are often cut off, and the "modern" dance today looks dated. When the lovely young Shirley Jones (as Laurey) sings, standing on a set against a fake background, she's not presented as confiding in the individual viewer. She's providing a photograph of what it would be like to sit in a theater and hear someone sing a beautiful song like "People Will Say We're in Love." The abandonment of real location for the stylized sets of the Broadway show shatters the tonal integrity. The proud claims of the trailer that sold the movie—"Now All the World Is a Stage"—have come to be all too true. *Oklahoma!* was an important Broadway show—one of the most successful of all time—with beautiful and varied music and historically important dances. The movie adaptation does not do it justice because it is not a true adaptation but a too-faithful re-creation of the theater experience.

Carousel was even less successful than *Oklahoma!*, and is the weakest of the Rodgers and Hammerstein adaptations. *Carousel* presents the horizontal line again, along with troupes of faceless characters moving around in busy backgrounds that do not direct the eye. The dancing has lots of acrobatics—exhilarating onstage as a troupe runs out full of energy to execute them—but without that same spirit on film. I've seen *Carousel* three times onstage and have never failed to cry. The movie can't generate that same emotion, because the performance—both of the story and of the music—doesn't engage with the viewer.

Gordon MacRae has a very good voice, but the character of Billy Bigelow needs an actor, and he has no skill. He was never supposed to have played Billy. The role was assigned to the movie star best suited for it—Frank Sinatra. Sinatra was just shy of forty years old at the time, a seasoned performer in movies, and the man with the voice *and* the person-

ality to play an on-the-grift carnival barker who, having fallen in love for real, tries to reform and can't. *Carousel* has a mixture of glorious music, romance, tragedy, comedy, and fable—Sinatra could deliver all of it. The story of his abrupt departure has many different versions. Sinatra showed up for costume fittings, publicity photographs, and even prerecorded some of the songs, among them a duet with costar Shirley Jones of "If I Loved You." He seemed excited, challenged, and happy to be undertaking the role, but when the cast and crew assembled in Maine to begin work, Sinatra

. . . MacRae and Jones ride on the *Carousel* of love . . .

got out of his car, took one look around, and got back in his car. What he saw was elaborate camera equipment. Twentieth Century–Fox was planning to shoot some sequences in both CinemaScope and CinemaScope 55, a new process, which would require Sinatra to do those scenes twice. He was heard to say, "I signed to do one movie, not two." He left without explanation, never to return. Two biographers, Tom Santopietro and James Kaplan, have speculated. Kaplan: "What accounted for Sinatra's abrupt departure? The mystery has echoed down through the decades, taking on a kind of haunted quality because of the magnitude of the missed opportunity: all the world seems to agree that Frank, with his real-life raffishness and existential doubts, not to mention his astounding voice, would have made an amazing Billy Bigelow. Could he have been scared?" Santopietro wrote: "Through the years, some have muttered that Sinatra was actually more concerned about whether he had the tools to successfully pull off the role, utilizing the two cameras dustup as an excuse." Most musical fans feel Sinatra's departure from *Carousel* is one of the great losses to movie history (along with Merman in *Annie Get Your Gun* and *Gypsy* and Doris Day in *South Pacific*). No one is ever going to know for sure why Sinatra left *Carousel*, but he gave a great gift of the role to Gordon MacRae, who did the best he could with it.

South Pacific at least had an idea about how to reconcile the difference between the stage and movies. After the pompous presentation of an overture (without the usual explanatory word, "Overture," that would traditionally appear onscreen for the duration), the breathtaking images of the Hawaiian island of Kauai, where location shots were selected for their beauty, appear onscreen. The definition of "cinematic" was to be a picture-postcard look at the beauty of the South Pacific, a travelogue approach. At least it was something, but unfortunately director Josh Logan also opted for a use of color that infused the entire screen to indicate mood (yellow for happy, blue for sad, reddish for erotic). It's the equivalent of a gel being laid over a frame, and, when combined with smoke and mist, it becomes lifeless onscreen, draining the realism out of a story that has serious issues. One of the joys of the stage version of *South Pacific* is the fun of seeing a woman actually wash her hair onstage ("I'm Gonna Wash That Man Right Outa My Hair"), and the whole idea is destroyed by a movie adaptation. An audience is left with a cute little song, but no real punch.

South Pacific has two major leads who do not do their own singing: Rossano Brazzi in the Ezio Pinza role and John Kerr as Lieutenant Cable

(dubbed by Bill Lee).* The Mary Martin role, Nellie, is played by Mitzi Gaynor, a durable singer/dancer whose career longevity is surprising. (A child ballerina who retired from movies in 1963, she continued working in nightclubs and on television for decades.) Gaynor does a credible job, but even if Martin had been young enough to have played the role she originated, or if Doris Day had been cast, would the filmed *South Pacific* be more worthy of the show? Not with its flat look, dubbed singers, and corny use of smoke, mist, and color overlays.

The King and I is a worthy adaptation. The sets and costumes are lavish, and its two leads, Yul Brynner and Deborah Kerr, are both real actors. The

. . . *South Pacific* with Mitzi Gaynor, hair washing on her mind . . .

---

* The original Bloody Mary, Juanita Hall, was cast, but since she couldn't hit her high notes—she was fifty-seven years old—she was dubbed by Muriel Smith. Hall did do her own singing in the 1961 movie version of *Flower Drum Song*.

role of the King was owned by Brynner, who had originated it onstage and who defined it utterly. His confident performance (which won him the Best Actor Oscar that year) enlivens the frame and adds drama, humor, and the intended depth to the story. Kerr, one of the loveliest (and most talented) actresses of the era, couldn't sing, and was dubbed by Marni Nixon; but her skill as an actress, particularly in having to play against show-stealer Brynner, balances the relationship. Although the imaginative dances by Jerome Robbins are often flattened out, there's life and energy in the film, and it doesn't have empty backgrounds and dead air onscreen. The presentation of the show-stopping choreography for "The Small House of Uncle Thomas" is undiminished.*

The most effective of the filmed Rodgers and Hammerstein musicals is, of course, *The Sound of Music*, which finally turned their work into a real movie, and which finally found a leading lady who could sing, act, dance, and put them all together. (*The Sound of Music* is discussed fully in chapter VI, related to Julie Andrews's career.) An adaptation of a hit Broadway musical, Hollywood learned, could only be as good as its talent both in front of and behind the camera. It would never be enough to just photograph a stage play, a lesson that had been learned in the transition to sound but that had to be relearned in the 1950s, even when the films made money.

. . . The King and I, with Yul Brynner in his star-making title role . . .

Movie musicals made from nonmusical movies are a special category of adaptation. They're not as much adaptations as translations: a film that doesn't have music has to change its language of communication with the viewer. It has to undergo a musical rewrite. Instead of having a boy and girl play a love scene in which they try to say how they feel in dialogue, the boy and girl have to sing to

* Jerome Robbins, a major Broadway choreographer, did not have a huge movie career. Besides *The King and I*, he did the dances for *West Side Story* (and was codirector with Robert Wise). His choreography for both *Gypsy* and *Fiddler on the Roof* was used as the basis for the film versions, and his ballet *Fancy Free* was the inspiration for the one in *On the Town*.

each other, "speaking" in lyrics, and then express their feelings physically by dancing together. The film is dilated at certain plot points to accommodate a musical number that shows the audience musically the essence of the scene's emotion. For instance, in *High Society*, as Grace Kelly prepares to remarry, she reminisces about her first honeymoon in a flashback. Her ex, who still loves her (Crosby), is seen singing "True Love" to her.

Nonmusical-to-musical "translation" was very popular, and the way it was done, how it worked or didn't work, is another demonstration of how the business learned to make musicals. There were a great many "translations" from movie drama/comedy to movie musical, and most were successful—so successful, in fact, that it might seem that the act of "translating" was an easy task: just insert music into key scenes and star two people who can sing and dance. This was anything but true. Consider how director Clarence Brown's beautiful film version of Eugene O'Neill's

. . . and Deborah Kerr as the schoolteacher he hires to teach his children, but who also gives him a lesson or two

original stage play *Ah, Wilderness!* (1935) was transformed into the musical *Summer Holiday* (1948),* created by the Arthur Freed unit at MGM and directed by Rouben Mamoulian.

Ah, Wilderness! is a lovely and tender film, sensitively directed by Brown, who had a strong feeling for small towns and rural attitudes. The original play on Broadway starred George M. Cohan as the father, but the Brown film starred Lionel Barrymore before his scenery-chewing, lovable-old-curmudgeon years. It's deliberately nostalgic, warmly human, set in a specific era, with a clear plot situation, a strong set of characters, and an attitude that can easily have music added. At the base of *Ah, Wilderness!* is a family story, but there's also a love story, a comedy, and a positive portrait of America—all elements that can motivate (and have motivated) successful songs and dances for musicals in the past. Hollywood often mined these elements—family, small towns, and/or patriotic events—for musicals such as *Meet Me in St. Louis*, *Two Weeks with Love* (1950), *In the Good Old Summertime* (1949), *Excuse My Dust* (1951), *Centennial Summer* (1946), and others. O'Neill's *Ah, Wilderness!* was a success and became not only *Summer Holiday* but also, in 1959, a successful Broadway musical called *Take Me Along*. Ironically, later in his life, Eugene O'Neill wrote a play about his family that was an honest portrait of their tragic relationships: *Long Day's Journey into Night*. (I hope I don't ever have to see a musical based on that particular version of his world.)

The movie *Summer Holiday* was designed to be faithful to *Ah, Wilderness!* but also to turn it into a Technicolor movie set with an ice-cream parlor, a charming old-fashioned town, a roomy private home, and a sentimental and über-nostalgic use of period machines and ideas. It was imagined as a re-creation of what O'Neill had called his "comedy of recollection," but it lacks the sincerity and innocence of *Ah, Wilderness!* It's phony—a hyped-up never-never world of invented cultural references. The director chosen by the Freed unit, Rouben Mamoulian, was a sophisticated European. He had earlier been associated with the stage success of *Oklahoma!*, a show that was definitely a New Yorker's idea of the Midwest, even though an enjoyable and highly successful one. Mamoulian's usage of and attitude toward the sets, costumes, and characters of *Summer Holiday* is

---

* Made in 1946 but not released until 1948, *Summer Holiday* was a commercial failure. It cost $2,258,235 and grossed only a little over $1,609,000. Part of the problem was that the production ran into trouble with postwar labor strikes, which delayed its completion. It took 113 days to shoot.

closer to mockery than to respect, although the finished film is not a satire. The problems of *Summer Holiday* illustrate the issues musicals would ultimately master regarding the integration of music and plot, the use of song for characterization, and the need for careful mastery of narrative structure regarding insertion of music at proper plot points.

The task of *Summer Holiday* is to develop all the main relationships through song, which is what a good musical should do. Sadly, it doesn't enrich any of the play's relationships through music. No set of characters—or even a single character—becomes the audience's identification point musically. The film has four sets of characters with underdeveloped musical potential as duets or solos: Richard and Muriel, the young lovers; the father and the mother; Uncle Sid and Cousin Lily; and Richard's brother and sister, Tommy and Mildred.* Casting is an issue. In the dramatic film, Richard is played by Eric Linden, a young actor who was known for playing sensitive teenage characters. In *Summer Holiday*, Richard is played by Mickey Rooney, who in 1948 was twenty-eight years old and twice divorced. He's loaded with talent, but innocence is no longer in his repertoire, if it ever was. (Even as Puck in 1935, Rooney was a wiseass, and his great strength was playing a kid who always knew the score.) The lovely but clearly mature Gloria DeHaven plays his girlfriend, Muriel, and insecure teenaged lovers they are obviously not. As the father and mother, Walter Huston and Selena Royle are capable performers but generate no warmth together, nor do they provide the grounding in honest family life that Barrymore and Spring Byington do for the original.† Sid and Lily (Frank Morgan and Agnes Moorehead) are the key characters linked to the truth in *Ah, Wilderness!* Underneath their relationship is real sorrow and loss. Sid drinks too much, and Lily is unable to forgive him for something that happened eighteen years before. The seeds of disappointment, lack of forgiveness, and frustration that become the full story in *Long Day's Journey into Night* are present in *Ah, Wilderness!* in the relationship of Sid and Lily. When it is removed in *Summer Holiday*, the story collapses around it

---

* In the movie *Ah, Wilderness!*, Richard's younger brother is played by Mickey Rooney; in *Summer Holiday* it's Butch Jenkins.

† Huston had already proved himself a viable musical performer in the stage musical *Knickerbocker Holiday*, in which he sang/talked the lyrics of "September Song" way before Rex Harrison was cast in the "talk it, sing it" role of Henry Higgins in *My Fair Lady*. (*Summer Holiday* was the first time Huston sang onscreen, as he was replaced in the 1944 film version of *Knickerbocker Holiday* by Charles Coburn.)

and becomes empty. The diminishment of their relationship removes the heart of the film, and destroys any honesty about family and small-town life.

Comparing the two films reveals that each has fourteen story sequences; the musical is a very direct translation from the original. But there are fewer scenes with music in the musical than in the nonmusical! The characters in *Ah, Wilderness!* do not perform musically; they just live in a world where some musical performance naturally happens, such as at a school dance, a graduation ceremony, a band concert, etc. What music there is happens naturally; it's organic. *Summer Holiday* is required to give us a full musical performance as natural behavior and find justification for it. This illustrates the problem musicals have: the need to justify music—which, oddly enough, the *Ah, Wilderness!* movie has no problem doing. When a movie *becomes* a musical, it must justify its musical performance; it has to create a reason for full-scale singing and dancing, because it is asking the audience to assume musical performance is natural.

The "musicalization" of *Summer Holiday* makes several successful changes to accommodate musical performances, the biggest being the addition of a Fourth of July picnic scene. It is the only true production number in the film. The musical also has changed Richard and Muriel's nighttime walk home from the school dance into a daytime drugstore scene that moves into a major song-and-dance number as they romp home together through a park. The original graduation sequence (which contains a song) is extended to include a drive home afterwards in the family car—the "Stanley Steamer" number, no doubt influenced by and inspired by "The Trolley Song" from *Meet Me in St. Louis*. The number celebrates the era, the family unit, and the small-town world; it's a musical joy ride despite the somewhat unimaginative lyrics.* This scene is one of the highlights of the musical version. *Summer Holiday* has also turned a scene in a bar (in which Richard gets drunk and is lured by a barfly) into a musical number that uses color imaginatively: the drunker he gets, the redder (and more elaborate) the woman's (Marilyn Maxwell) dress becomes. Not only is it

---

* Songwriters Harry Warren and Ralph Blane collaborated on the song, which repeats the word: "Honk, honk. Honk, honk, honk." Warren had done the music for both "Chattanooga Choo Choo" and "On the Atchison, Topeka and the Santa Fe," and Blane had created the lyrics for "The Trolley Song." People jokingly called them "the transportation fellas," and "Stanley Steamer," one of the best, peppiest songs in the film—the only one with potential hit quality—nevertheless is not as good as earlier work from either of them and has too much honking!

redder and redder; her hat gets bigger and bigger, her neckline lower and lower, and her bling brighter and brighter. ("You're one of the sweetest kids I've ever met," she sings.) *Summer Holiday* opens with Walter Huston singing/talking "Our Home Town," which sets up the nostalgic mood the movie wishes to capture and establishes a musical universe. He performs it well, and introduces all the main characters with it, getting the film off to a good start.

But *Summer Holiday* missed musical opportunities. *Ah, Wilderness!* has a scene at a band concert which could have been translated. A lonely walk through town by Richard cries out for a beautiful, melancholy song, but Rooney was not the performer for such a number. Primarily, there is no final love song for Richard and Muriel. No grand-finale number, again celebrating the family and the town. No high-school dance. No amusing song for Sid and Lily, such as "I'll Never Be Jealous Again" from *The Pajama Game*, and no love song.* Why these two were not given a comedy duet or a great and sad love song is one of the great questions of *Summer Holiday*. And there's no musical interaction between father and son to express the inherent respect and tenderness they feel for each other. *Summer Holiday* definitely needs more music than it has, but there were numbers cut prior to release. There was to have been another number for Rooney and DeHaven, a lavish Persian dream, which was actually shot but cut from the film before release. The number was designed to grow out of a scene in which the couple's attempts to express their innocent love was laid out in the dialogue. Rooney's mind was to move away, hearing the poetry of Omar Khayyám as he looked at DeHaven and tried to express himself. The song that would accompany this transition was "Omar and the Princess,"

---

* Morgan and Moorehead were not really singers. A planned song for Morgan ("Never Again") was cut, as was a song for Gloria DeHaven ("Wish I Had a Braver Heart"). A first offering of Huston singing "Spring Isn't Everything" was also eliminated, although his reprise remained. The extravagance of shooting musical numbers and then cutting them was, of course, entirely unintentional, but, as stated earlier, not uncommon. Even *Singin' in the Rain*, thought of as a "perfect" musical, had two big numbers cut, both specifically designed for stars Reynolds and Kelly. Debbie Reynolds, after she dances with Kelly on the soundstage to "You Were Meant for Me," had a fully shot and recorded number in which she walked around the lot, posing by a billboard with Kelly's image, singing and dancing to "You Are My Lucky Star." It was a singular showcase for a young woman the studio felt would become a hot property, but it came too soon after the romantic duet and slowed the action down, even though she's lovely and a star in the making. Kelly's number was an extension of his delighted feelings about Reynolds after she jumps out of the cake. He leaves the party, wanders around town, singing and dancing in an extension of her "cake" song, "All I Do Is Dream of You." Stardom protected no one from a cut song that was out of whack in the overall picture.

with lyrics paraphrased from the *Rubaiyat*. According to Hugh Fordin's *The World of Entertainment*, "The set was raked; there were jade trees, a tiny brook, arched over by a dainty inlaid bridge, and exquisite birds. The fantasy was heightened by bathing the set in an opalescent, greenish light." Existing photos show Rooney and DeHaven attired in turbans and Hollywood-kitsch Persian costumes.

Summer Holiday didn't play well with its original audiences, but today it has its enthusiasts, who praise it for its experimental quality. Placed in historical context, it looks like a musical that is striving to move forward and define the genre in ways that would emerge in years ahead. It demonstrates basic issues, and credit for that has to go to its director, Rouben Mamoulian, a man who's become too forgotten for what he accomplished both on the stage and in movies regarding musicals. Mamoulian knew what he wanted to do with *Ah, Wilderness!* when he (and a talented team at MGM) turned it into *Summer Holiday*. He wrote to Arthur Freed about the translation: "It is obvious that to turn a dramatic play into a musical you have to make drastic cuts in it in order to allow time for music, songs and dancing. It is equally obvious that you cannot drastically cut a good dramatic play without spoiling it, crippling its subject and emaciating its characters. A tenuous story filled out with elaborate and overblown 'musical numbers,' unrelated specialties of dance and song, comedy routines, etc. has for long been the standard stuff that musicals were made of. . . . However, this is not the kind of musical we want to make."

Mamoulian had summed up the history of musicals and proposed a new direction: "What we want to do is, for lack of a better and newer definition, a 'musical play'—meaning by that a story which will be told through the medium of integrated dialogue, songs, dance and music, with each of these elements taking an organic and vital part in the telling of the story." *Summer Holiday* may have been a failure, and it may or may not be a crowd pleaser today, but it represented a marking point for the Freed unit in terms of thinking about original movie musicals. It's important in the historical progression of the musical film.

Studio Styles

As the musical genre moved forward, the phenomenon of studio style began to have an impact on its development. The seven major studios—Columbia,

MGM, Paramount, RKO, 20th Century–Fox, Universal, and Warner Bros.—each developed a particular type of musical, which amounted to a house brand. Although they would always imitate each other's successes, studios built movies for the stars they had under contract, which dictated which genres they'd emphasize. They all made musicals, because musicals made money, but the types of musicals—and the way they made them—became their corporate style. They decided on their own business strategies, fueled by competition for ticket sales, and thus contributed differently to the advancement of the genre. Studio style was, of course, also influenced by changes outside the system, such as technological advances (sound, color, widescreen), national crises (the Depression), and international events (World War II). Musicals—as is true for all movies—can be seen to transition from black-and-white to color, from pre-Code sexuality to restrictive censorship, and from a concern with job loss and financial crisis to the pressures of war and then the expansive luxury of peacetime prosperity. These changes were across the board for all studios.

The giant among studios for the creation of the musical was always MGM. (See chapter V.) Most attempts to analyze musicals are about MGM—particularly the Freed unit—with the notable exceptions (which are legion) devoted to the RKO years of Astaire and Rogers. After the 1930s and the Fred-and-Ginger collaboration, however, RKO created very few significant musicals. The studio made B films, switched its emphasis toward film noir, became confused about its own image under the leadership of Howard Hughes, and ultimately collapsed. It did find success in distributing the Walt Disney animated musicals, beginning with *Snow White and the Seven Dwarfs* in 1937. Universal had a major success with the 1936 *Show Boat*, made money with Deanna Durbin, and moved into low-budget teenage romps starring a roster of talented youngsters (the Donald O'Connor/Peggy Ryan collaboration, singer Gloria Jean). In the early years, Paramount made sophisticated musicals that contributed to both artistic growth and popularity through the work of Lubitsch and Mamoulian, and rode Bing Crosby's star vehicles to the bank. Toward the end of the 1930s, the experimental Lubitsch/Mamoulian tradition fizzled out, morphing into college musicals, a *Big Broadcast* series, and some weak, but still entertaining, fare. One oddball film kept the Paramount experimental tradition alive: *You and Me* (1938), directed by the unlikely Fritz Lang, known more for crime and noirish stories of femme fatales and desperate men. *You and Me* qualifies as a genuine genre mix: gangsters and jailbirds, department-store settings, labor issues, romance, comedy . . . and music by

Kurt Weill. The opening number sums up the mélange. Set to a song about the power of money, it shows the audience a bundle of unrelated goods: guns, wine bottles, marble statues. The musical numbers (including one in which women dance out of martini glasses and one set in a prison done entirely with whispers and contrived codes made by knocking on walls) are shot with creative camera movements and imaginative editing. Stars Sylvia Sidney and George Raft are caught up in a sometimes rhythmic dialogue presentation, and make the best of it. *You and Me is* experimental in nature, but for the most part Paramount, a studio of early musical innovation, stuck with Bing Crosby—a smart business decision—and later developed Betty Hutton and Martin and Lewis in a series of show-business musicals. (Paramount did release the very sophisticated and charming 1957 *Funny Face*, directed by Stanley Donen, costarring Astaire and Audrey Hepburn, with Kay Thompson thrown in, which did much to keep the musical form alive toward the end of the studio system.) Warner Bros. brought success to Busby Berkeley and Dick Powell, featured James Cagney in *Yankee Doodle Dandy* and a couple of lesser vehicles; and cleverly developed Dennis Morgan and Jack Carson as a duo. Above all, they were the studio that turned Doris Day into a triumph of enduring stardom. In the 1940s, they made biopics and patriotic musicals but were not a major force in the genre. Columbia, officially known as a "Poverty Row" studio, is seldom given credit for its contributions to musicals, because its output was small, mostly due to financial restrictions. However, this was the studio that made two Astaire/Hayworth movies, *You'll Never Get Rich* and *You Were Never Lovelier*, and was responsible for the revival of Al Jolson's career with *The Jolson Story* and *Jolson Sings Again*. Columbia is also the studio that presented the talents of Gene Kelly as a choreographer for the first time; and the movie designed to showcase Rita Hayworth with Kelly as her costar is one of the most important musicals of the 1940s: the well-remembered and well-loved *Cover Girl* from 1944.

Each studio, in its turn, had something to contribute—RKO with Astaire/Rogers, Warners with Busby Berkeley, Universal with *Show Boat* '36, Paramount with transition-to-sound innovation, Columbia with the support of Kelly—but the two dominant studios for the genre were MGM and 20th Century–Fox. Everyone knows about MGM, but many overlook Fox, its real rival, which many people feel made better musicals than MGM during the 1940s. Twentieth Century–Fox was always famous for its excellent recording studio, which put movies on the screen with crystal-clear sound, a key element in musicals. That, of course, was an appreciation for the insider or connoisseur. What the average person liked about Fox musicals in the 1940s were two things: eye-popping Technicolor and equally eye-popping female movie stars. The studio lineup of female box-office champions who starred in brightly colored musicals were Alice Faye, Betty Grable, June Haver, and later Marilyn Monroe, roughly in that order of progression. All were blondes, and known in retrospect as "the 20th Century–Fox blondes." Each had musicals tailored especially for her and whatever level of talent she had, and that talent varied from star to star. Two of them, Grable and Monroe, became superstars.

A discussion of Fox blondes, from Faye to Monroe, defines the Fox musical factory system, but it has to begin with a blonde who started the trend but is seldom included in the pack. She's a very little blonde: Shirley Temple. All the famous musical Fox blondes overlapped in films, proving how shrewd the studio was in keeping its business running and moving forward with a series of connected star vehicles. Not all the "connective" movies were musicals, but the relay race "handoff" was in place at Fox for nearly three decades. Little Temple, the first, made films with the next, Alice Faye (*Poor Little Rich Girl* and *Stowaway*, both 1936). Faye then starred in *Tin Pan Alley* (1940) with Grable; Grable costarred with Haver in *The Dolly Sisters* (1945); Haver appeared with Monroe in *Love Nest* (1951) and Grable, the biggest musical star of them all, gave a boost to Monroe in *How to Marry a Millionaire* (1953).* The Fox blondes were powerhouses: Temple, Faye, Grable, and Monroe were all top-ten box office draws.

The first cash cow in the blonde lineup was the smallest, the child star Shirley Temple, who was spotted for stardom by a cheesy independent production house that exploited children. Educational Films, as the company was cleverly known, was a Poverty Row studio that made a series of shorts known as *Baby Burlesks*. When a talent scout from Educational arrived at Shirley's dancing school, she was about three years old, but she had the good sense to hide under the piano when she saw him. The scout was not deterred. After looking over the beribboned and decked-out children, he shrewdly said, "I'll take the one under the piano."

Shirley Jane Temple was born April 23, 1928, although the world would be told it was 1929 so she would appear younger than she was. Shirley didn't

---

* Sheree North was considered the next blonde in line after Haver, but her career was short-circuited when Monroe appeared out of nowhere.

need the lie; she was phenomenal without it. When she came to the attention of the bigger studios and began making movies, first for Paramount and then for Fox, she was barely four years old, but she had the stamina for stardom, the talent, and the emotional balance never to let it eat her alive. Nobody ever qualified more for the real-life title of Dickens's "Infant Phenomenon" than Shirley Temple. She was one of a kind, and most of her movies were musicals. Little Shirley could sing and dance, but her skill lay fundamentally in imitation. She was too young to really understand acting, but she could mimic, and if someone told her how to say something, she could do it; if someone asked her to speak in a foreign accent, she could do it; if someone told her to be scared like this, be happy like this, be sad like this, she could do it. And she did do it at the highest level. She took her fame in stride, once giving an interviewer the jaw-dropping remark (she was eight at the time): "When I was three and unknown . . ." She didn't know she was a phenomenon. She thought she was an ordinary person, just probably a grown-up and not a kid.

Shirley Temple became the greatest child star in movie history. She was a top-ten box-office draw in 1934, 1935, 1936, 1937, 1938, and 1939, ranking in the number-one position from 1935 to 1938.* Later in life, when she was happily married to Charles Black, she explained her success by saying, "I class myself with Rin Tin Tin. People were looking for something to cheer them up. They fell in love with a dog and a little girl." Her modesty is not unwarranted. Her movies were seldom great, and usually followed a standard format.

The films were the story of a small child on her own, dependent on the kindness of adults, having to endure and persevere with good old American gumption. She had to cope. There was always a crisis, but when it came she was ready for it. Shirley Temple's onscreen life was more often than not Dickensian—but in the very cleanest, best-mannered, and most all-American way possible. Although adults let her down—getting run over by cars, dying of unexplained illnesses, wandering off, proudly sign-

---

* There was also a "male Shirley Temple," a boy soprano named Bobby Breen, born in 1927, who was a popular musical star for about four years, from 1936 to 1939. Breen sang on Eddie Cantor's radio show, and made his first movie, *Let's Sing Again*, with costar Henry Armetta, in 1936. His films had titles like *Rainbow on the River* (1936), *Hawaii Calls* (1938), and *Escape to Paradise* (1939). He had a wonderful voice, and not much acting ability, but his fans adored him (his films are available on DVD today). His movie career ended more or less when his voice changed, but his movies are good examples of star vehicles. His vehicle may have been a kid's bicycle, but when he rode it, he rode it.

ing up for foreign wars, and even leaving her as a gambling marker shortly before committing suicide—Shirley soldiered on. She would become an orphaned child adopted by a rich father, or a rich mother, or perhaps a rich grandfather or grandmother or just a couple of guys or a bunch of airmen who had flown with her father or whatever. The appeal of Shirley Temple was not just that she was a child—she was the all-American child who personified our ideal concept of ourselves. And she was reassuring. If a child could endure these setbacks of all types, why couldn't the rest of us suck it up a little? Thus, Temple marched bravely through graveyards alone at night and raced on foot to bring help when it was needed. Nothing stopped

The infant phenom, a true box-office champion, little Shirley Temple, who could sing and dance and flash her dimples with the best of 'em

her. Nannies were run over, leaving her stranded. Fathers put bullets in their brains. Ships sank under her tap-dancing feet. The orphan asylum was always just around the corner or already a painful reality. Shirley handled it with an "Oh, my goodness" and a crunch on her animal crackers. "I'm very self-reliant, you know," she said in *Rebecca of Sunnybrook Farm*, and so she was. It wasn't escape from reality that she provided for her Depression audiences. It was the reassurance that they, too, could survive it.

Were we a nation of idiots? How could a child become our guiding light? Why did we look to a tiny creature with fifty-seven (count 'em) bouncing curls, chipmunk cheeks, and little Mary Jane tap shoes? There's an answer, and it's a very simple one. As a child, Shirley Temple was terrific. Not saccharine sweet, but spicy and feisty. Not obedient and docile, but argumentative and strongly independent. Not even entirely innocent—there was a sex appeal darkly ominous in her lap-sitting, daddy-hugging presence (as pointed out in a notorious review by none other than Graham Greene, who compared her seductiveness to Marlene Dietrich's). And there's something else: Shirley Temple was musical, and that gave her an outlet through which to connect directly to audiences of all ages. With most child actors, audiences would watch them and perhaps sympathize, but with Shirley they could watch and empathize. She was *us*, back when we were short and also now when we weren't. Sing it, Shirley, and tap it out. All of America was with her.

The Little Colonel (1935) is an example of a Temple movie that is not really a musical but contains natural musical performance in it to find a way to give Temple an opportunity to both sing and dance. It's also an example of a perfectly terrible plotline: sentimental, old-fashioned, racist, and predictable. Based on a novel by Annie Fellows Johnston written in 1895, it's the old melodramatic story of a young woman who is disowned by her father because she chooses to run away with a man of whom he doesn't approve. In this case, the old father (Lionel Barrymore) disapproves of his daughter (Evelyn Venable) wedding a Yankee (John Lodge). As usual, she does it anyway. The setting is in Kentucky in the 1870s, after the Civil War has been lost by the South. Barrymore, the big colonel, apparently sat out the conflict in the twilight zone, since his plantation is intact, with no apparent damage. He stands around under oil paintings, wearing a snow-white suit, and giving orders to his African American servants. It's an antebellum world in a postbellum setting, and totally clichéd. Shirley, his granddaughter, charms the old devil out of his Yankee hatred . . . along with plenty of other nonsense. The musical aspect is slender—mostly just an old song sung at different times by both the mother and the child, or a spiritual at a baptism. But—the reason for talking about the movie in a book about the musical is there are also two tap numbers by Temple and Bill Robinson. These two routines are their first pairing in the movies, and so successful were they that they appeared together three more times.

Shirley Temple and Bill Robinson are a wonderful pair to watch. He's great and she's cute. He dances for her, up and down the stairs, demonstrating every possible type of tap routine: side to side on the steps, incorporating the bottoms of the steps, using sand to soft-shoe at the top of the steps. His dancing is effortless yet strong. His taps are sharply delineated, not only in sound but in physical execution. He has so much control that we can *see* each one. In their dance up the steps together (as he makes her go upstairs to bed), Robinson is teaching Temple about tap dancing and she follows, holding his hand. It's a copycat routine. This "dance cute" up the stairs in *The Little Colonel* became one of the most iconic musical moments of 1930s cinema. An audience is shown a close-up of two sets of dancing feet, side by side on the stairs: his big shoes, her little ones. They are in perfect sync. Later, in a scene inside the barn, he dances to the sound of a harmonica, and it's another "mentor/pupil" sequence. He does a little routine. She watches intently, then repeats it. When the format changes, so he can do his more elaborate work, it's like a conversation between an adult and a child in which the adult is patient but uncompromising in the lesson, and the child is precocious and dedicated to showing what she can do. *The Little Colonel* is full of casual, unapologetic racism that is appalling today, but when Robinson and Temple dance, there's something eternally accepting about it. They are so right together. Temple is the star, but the success of the routine is due to the remarkable talent of Robinson.

Bill "Bojangles" Robinson (1878–1949) had a long career as both a stage and film performer and also as a choreographer. He began by dancing for coins on the streets in Richmond, Virginia, where he was born. A headliner in vaudeville, he moved into Broadway musicals such as *Blackbirds of 1928* and *Brown Buddies* (1930). He made his feature film debut in the Bert Wheeler and Robert Woolsey hit *Dixiana* in 1930, which featured a two-strip Technicolor Mardi Gras finale in which he did a fabulous tap solo. He would return to the Broadway stage in *The Hot Mikado* in 1939, *All in Fun* in 1940, and *Memphis Bound* in 1945.

Robinson appeared in eight important musical features, four of them with Shirley Temple. Besides his debut in *Dixiana*, the other non-Temple films

were *Hooray for Love* (1935), *The Big Broadcast of 1936* (1935), and *Stormy Weather* (1943). He appeared as himself, doing a specialty number in all but the last of these three. His one number in *Hooray for Love* shows how audiences missed out by having only these limited appearances from Robinson. He does a number supposedly set "on the streets of Harlem," and it tells a little story of a young woman (Jeni Le Gon) being evicted from her apartment until the "mayor" (Robinson) comes along to help her, aided by one of the movers (Fats Waller). The level of singing and dancing and personality on display by these three superb performers is enough to drive any musical, but they are afforded only the one bit. (The filmmakers had the grace to stage this as a dress rehearsal, so that when it concludes, all the cast leap to their feet crying out "Great! Great!"—which it is.)

The very talented Le Gon sings "I'm Livin' in a Great Big Way" and dances. Robinson reprises the song, shares it with her, and dances with her. He then does a spectacular tap solo and—as if anything could top what had already happened—he and Waller sing the song together. Robinson does one of his shticks—makes a singing noise as if he's blowing into a trumpet without a mouthpiece—and Waller does what he does: scats along, interposing his perfect little musical comments on the song lyrics. In *Hooray for Love*, Robinson's dancing is not limited by the need to adapt to another star presence like that of the little Temple. When they're together, she does a great job, and the two are utterly charming; but Robinson was a genius, and seeing him able to show his inventive and utterly magical tapping without the need for any plot excuse or adjusting to someone else is a great moment in musical viewing. Robinson is a revelation because he is so light-footed. Although every tap he put down was clearly heard and delineated, he was not a heavy-footed, bang-that-floor tap dancer. His feet seem to be barely touching the ground sometimes, his shoes hovering over the floor, flying up and down with an ease that appeared to require no strength. His entire body language was one of a relaxed dancer who could just glide along over a floor, despite the fact that his feet were beating out a crystal-clear staccato sound. He was an amazing tapper, and holds the reputation as the best ever.* Tap dancing caused him no grief. His feet flew.

* Both Fred Astaire and Eleanor Powell danced—in blackface—tributes to Robinson: Astaire with "Bojangles of Harlem" in *Swing Time* (1936) and Powell with a Robinson-inspired medley in *Honolulu* (1939). These numbers are questionable today, but were originally done with sincerity and respect for his talent. Powell's dance was introduced as a definite "impersonation"; Astaire's was more a tribute.

OPPOSITE A great pair of dancers, a little girl and an old man: Temple and Bill "Bojangles" Robinson snap it out in *The Littlest Rebel*.

Robinson and Temple would also dance together in *Rebecca of Sunnybrook Farm, Just Around the Corner,* and *The Littlest Rebel.* In the first, they do a military number to "Parade of the Wooden Soldiers." Their dancing is varied, snappy and jazzy, martial, and then bluesy. Temple always seemed to be more comfortable dancing with Robinson than with anyone else, and he brings out the best of her abilities. (Robinson also did the choreography for Temple's 1936 film *Dimples.*)

It is obvious how much confidence the studio has in Shirley Temple in *The Little Colonel.* The sets are lavish, the costumes beautiful, and Temple is surrounded by reliable talent. The studio went all out, including an expensive Technicolor sequence for the grand finale. Throughout the movie, Temple asks for stories, designating them by color: "I want a green story" or ". . . a yellow story." This brings a little risqué quality forward when she asks her grandfather if he knows any blue stories. "Not any I can tell you," he says. In the end, the color sequence is designed to showcase her "pink" story, and the predominant color is indeed pink, including Temple in a hoop-skirted pink dress adorned by blue ribbons and a blue sash. When she pops up behind a bush in medium close-up, her golden curls, peachy skin, and lovely pink-and-blue dress must have startled—and enchanted—audiences.

One of Temple's best *musical* films—as opposed to her literary adaptations (such as *Heidi*) or her films that have musical numbers but are dramatic in nature (such as *The Little Colonel*)—is *Captain January* (1936). Based on the Laura E. Richards story ("The Lighthouse at Cape Tempest"), the plot is the usual Temple fare—i.e., she's an orphan who was rescued from a shipwreck as a tot by a curmudgeonly old lighthouse keeper (Guy Kibbee). In its storyline, it's typical Temple: everybody loves her; there's trouble afoot when a mean truant officer tries to take her away from Kibbee; rich relatives appear and rescue her; everybody ends up happy. Where it isn't typical is its musical presentation.

Captain January opens up in a musical number in which Temple, asleep in her bed, is awakened by music from a Victrola Kibbee has quietly snuck into her little room. In these opening minutes, *Captain January* is an innovative musical. Temple sits up in bed and starts singing "Early Bird" to the camera. As she gets out of bed, tidies her room, washes her face, and puts on her clothes, she sings and tap-dances. It's a pure musical number, with a character whose world is a musical one. She's not talking or singing to anyone, and there's no motivation other than music. Shirley Temple sings and dances as she lives, not for a living! What's more, within a few short minutes she does a full, flat-out choreographed routine down the wooden sidewalk of her little town. When she saunters out of the general store, wearing a little sailor cap and outfit, dancer Buddy Ebsen (who plays one of the locals) says, "Here comes Star!" She greets a group of townsmen standing around, and after "Here's your music, Star, let's get going" from Ebsen, he lifts her up on top of the barrel and she belts out "At the Codfish Ball." After she finishes the first chorus, Ebsen lifts her down onto the wooden sidewalk and she continues singing and dancing to the music. Ebsen then joins in, and the two of them truck down the steps and set off down the sidewalk in a fully choreographed dance routine. When the singing is finished, they dig into a real travelling dance down the sidewalk, up and down steps, incorporating different levels and objects. Ebsen, a rubber-legged ragdoll of a dancer—what was called a "personality dancer"—provides a great counterpoint to Temple. Their dance across time and space incorporates barrels and kegs of different sizes and shapes, various boxes, the side of a shingled building, some planks, and sets of stairs they tap up and down.

Temple is photographed in medium close-up for her song, which is in one take, with a cut just as Ebsen lifts her down and joins her; they roll out, down the steps and off onto the sidewalk, singing together. They do an energetic "moving" dance number, a real movie dance, staged by Jack Donohue. The choreography has been carefully created to use five judicious cuts that conceal transitions, and to maintain fluidity and a sense of speed and unstoppable motion. The dance has no real explained purpose other than that they are doing it for friends. They're not portraying performers, and musical motivation is not anything other than "This is how they both act in daily life." He's a fisherman. She's an orphan.

Captain January was shot in 1936. Nearly a decade later, when Gene Kelly, Rita Hayworth, and Phil Silvers dance down the street to "Make Way for Tomorrow" in *Cover Girl*, they are actually all three playing professional performers, yet their dance is considered innovative and an example of an unjustified musical performance. *Captain January* is in its opening much more like a movie of the 1940s and presented Temple at the height of her dancing ability. In certain ways, the routine is even better than her dances with Bill Robinson. With her first Robinson dances, she was younger, and there's the sense that he's leading her, protecting her in the tapping, and that she's imitating his moves. The dances are charming and very well done, and Robinson is incomparable. But in "At the Codfish

Ball," Temple is old enough and experienced enough to have no need to look at her partner for direction. She dances alongside Ebsen as an equal, and the repertoire of moves she can make has been seriously expanded since *The Little Colonel*. At this point in her career, she is at the peak of her powers, just that much older, and her understanding of the plot, her role in it, her dialogue, is stronger than ever, and she delivers well. She no longer has to imitate behavior; she can *comprehend* it. She's confident; she swings out on her own.

Temple could keep up with anyone in a dance number: here with Buddy Ebsen "at the codfish ball" in *Captain January* . . .

Temple movies always have one musical number that can only be labeled "the love song." The fact she sings it to a father figure—or even a grandfather figure—is somewhat unsettling. In *Captain January* she sings "The Right Somebody to Love" to Guy Kibbee; in *The Littlest Rebel* she sings "Believe Me, If All Those Endearing Young Charms" to John Boles; "When I'm with You" to Michael Whalen in *Poor Little Rich Girl*; "Picture Me Without You" to Frank Morgan in *Dimples*; etc. Since she's a child, it's logical she'd sing to a father or some elderly male benefactor, but the overt love songs in these movies are close to hair-raising for a modern audience.

It's interesting to note that as an adult performer in movies, Shirley Temple didn't sing and dance. The two final films of her childhood career, *Kathleen* (for MGM in 1941) and *Miss Annie Rooney* (for Edward Small Productions in 1942), more or less mark the end of her musical years. In the former, she imagines herself as a famous stage performer and a dubbed operatic voice is used, and she does a little dancing in the latter; but for the most part she was already being eased out of the musical arena. (She was thirteen when she made *Kathleen* and fourteen for *Rooney*.)

The next Fox blonde was the lovely Alice Faye, who was a real singer and also a dancer. She could lay down some serious steps if asked to, but at a relatively early point in her career she was seldom asked to. It was her singing audiences wanted. Faye had a lovely contralto voice, superb for ballads, and a low, almost husky speaking voice that was seductive. Her bosomy figure, her large blue eyes, and her gentle demeanor endeared her to audiences. She officially became a big-name star when she headlined *Lillian Russell* in 1940, a biopic about the famous nineteenth-century stage

. . . and sing with anyone, too: with Jack Haley and Alice Faye in *Poor Little Rich Girl.*

performer, which was designed to be a Faye musical vehicle. Faye was the perfect mannequin for the turn-of-the-century clothes that Fox liked to design and that were synonymous with Russell. In the corseted dresses, big hats, and soft pompadours of the day, Faye looked completely at home and utterly natural. With her profile framed against a big hat brim, or her curves enclosed in a wasp-waisted traveling suit, she was appealing to both male and female fans.

Faye started singing and dancing as a teenager. After appearing onstage in New York in *George White's Scandals* in 1931, she was invited by Rudy Vallee to be his band singer. Her lovely voice, curvaceous body, and sweet personality attracted attention on the Vallee bandstand, and in 1934 she was invited to Hollywood, making her movie debut in *George White's Scandals* that same year. Signed by Fox, she began a steady appearance in 1930s black-and-white musicals, one after another, from 1935 onward, almost all of which gave her good opportunities to sing. Some of these films are forgettable (except for *Every Night at Eight* in 1935 and *Sing, Baby, Sing* in 1936) and some were top box-office draws, such as her two 1936 Shirley Temple vehicles, *Poor Little Rich Girl* and *Stowaway*. (In the latter, she sang one of her loveliest hits, "Goodnight, My Love," and in the former she made famous "You've Gotta Eat Your Spinach, Baby.") Faye projected an almost passive quality, and this allowed Fox to build stories for her that were often dramatic vehicles that could costar her with actors who didn't sing or dance. She was paired with the nonmusical Henry Fonda and Tyrone Power, among others, in stories that were about how she suffered at the hands of caddish and selfish men (which allowed for a torch song). In 1938, Faye rose to significant co-stardom with her appearance in the all-star *Alexander's Ragtime Band*. Using all Irving Berlin hits, *Alexander's* (sold in the trailer as "two years in the making . . . at a cost of over two million dollars! . . . truly the proudest achievement of Twentieth Century–Fox") was one of the most successful movies of the decade. She made her first movie in color in 1939 (*Hollywood Cavalcade*), and then costarred in 1940 with Grable in the song-filled black-and-white *Tin Pan Alley*. (Grable had only the second lead, but made a mark for herself.) The next year, Faye began a run of four highly entertaining Technicolor films: *That Night in Rio* and *Week-End in Havana* in 1941, and *Hello, Frisco, Hello* and *The Gang's All Here* in 1943. (She also made two black-and-white films during this period.) But two things affected her career and her sense of what she wanted for her own future: Betty Grable

and marriage. The huge stardom of Grable really began in 1940 when Faye bowed out of *Down Argentine Way* due to illness. Grable replaced her, and the film was the start of her own remarkable list of colorful musicals. Faye's marriage to bandleader Phil Harris in 1941 changed her personal life. She joined him in his hit radio show, gave birth to two daughters (one in 1942 and the other in 1944), and felt less interested in her career. Faye had been worked hard by Fox; she was not only exhausted, but used up, and had disagreed with boss Darryl F. Zanuck more than once about her career. After her appearance in the black-and-white film noir *Fallen Angel* in 1945,* she felt she had not been treated fairly. In her opinion, she had done her best work in the acting department, and yet the studio didn't

Alice Faye became a major 20th Century–Fox star with her own persona, a softly appealing leading lady with a great singing voice.

* The film was not a musical, but Faye did sing one song in a scene when she and costar Dana Andrews were on a nighttime picnic—she sang along to the radio.

Faye was paired with all of Fox's top-ranked leading men, such as Tyrone Power, Don Ameche, and, here, John Payne in *Tin Pan Alley*.

want to recognize her skills. She retired from movies, leaving the field to Grable.*

In musicals, Faye was a beautiful, softly feminine woman even when she was playing a tough babe who could tell a man off. There was about her a sense of decency, and of a woman made for loving others. As her career advanced, this vulnerability became more strongly attached to her characters; in her earlier years, with her hair a more white-blond of the Harlow type, she was often cast in lower-class roles. When her major stardom emerged, she was, even when playing a successful woman like Lillian

---

* The two women remained good friends for life. Each always spoke well of the other. Grable said, "Everybody loves Alice," and Faye said Grable was "lots of fun, and certainly loved life." In later years, Faye was famous for her wonderful sense of wry humor about her years in Fox musicals. "I made six films with Don Ameche," she said, "and in every one of them my voice was deeper than the plot." In describing the callousness of the studio she toiled for, she commented that when she finally retired, after making millions for the studio, there was no thank-you note, gift, or recognition given to her—"not even a pickle dish." She dubbed her home studio "Penitentiary Fox."

Russell, often presented as a woman made to suffer because of her deep love and loyalty to a man unworthy of her. This quality allowed songwriters to compose beautiful ballads for Faye to introduce.* The evolution of Alice Faye into stardom can be traced by comparing *King of Burlesque* (1935) and *Hello, Frisco, Hello*, made eight years later. If they seem to be similar, it's because they are: they tell exactly the same story, and *Frisco* is literally a color remake of the former. Faye is very good in both films, but she has been changed as she has evolved to the height of her fame. In the first film, in which the story has a much harder edge, she's brassy, openly sexy, and has her hair dyed into the platinum look of Jean Harlow. By the time of *Frisco*, she is softer, more elegant, and has a classier look and a gentler characterization. It's as if she's undergone one of her own plot reforms: from brassy singer in the Bowery to high-class Broadway star.

Faye's two best and most typical films illustrate who she was in her years as "the Fox blonde": *Alexander's Ragtime Band* and *Hello, Frisco, Hello*. One is from the 1930s and the other the 1940s; and one is black-and-white and one in color. Both costar her with handsome leading men (Tyrone Power and Don Ameche in *Ragtime*, John Payne in *Frisco*). Both give her hit songs that were nominated for an Academy Award ("Now It Can Be Told" in *Ragtime* and her signature song, "You'll Never Know," in *Frisco*, that year's winner).

Almost forgotten today, *Alexander's Ragtime Band* (already discussed regarding its importance in Ethel Merman's career) might be thought of as a sort of marking place for musical development. On the one hand, you can say that musicals can't get any better than this, so why try? There's a star-studded cast, vintage Irving Berlin tunes, two new ones, a rapid pace, and a plot small enough not to get in the way but epic enough to make room for tons of music. (The storyline moves from 1911 to 1938, which is twenty-seven years in the lives of the characters, who never age, never change, and nobody cares.) On the other hand, despite how entertaining the movie is, it's a form of musical stagnation. Musical performances are given no explanation or introduction. People sing because they're professionals. Characters just come out and sing and dance, and most of the songs have no relationship to the drama.

---

* Faye introduced nearly twice as many top *Hit Parade* songs in her movies as her closest competition: Judy Garland had thirteen and both Grable and Doris Day had twelve each. Faye introduced a whopping twenty-three.

Alexander's Ragtime Band is a musicals crossroad. Sound has been around for a decade, and experimentation with the form has taken place (*One Hour with You*; *High, Wide and Handsome*); cinematic adaptations have been made of Broadway shows (*Show Boat*); startling original musicals have been created (*You and Me*); and legendary stars have solidified their careers (Astaire, Crosby, Jolson). Artists have shown what movie musicals could be (Berkeley, Astaire, Lubitsch). The thirties have defined the genre as entertainment and also as to what they could become as cinematic art. Would things stop here and settle for making money and repeating success, or would they move forward?

In *Alexander's Ragtime Band* can be seen both the old and, briefly, the new possibilities. A lovely new song was written for Faye, "Now It Can Be Told." She comes out to stand in front of "Alexander's band" so she can sing it to an elegant supper-club audience. Tyrone Power (Alexander), young and gorgeous, leads the band (which is mostly what he's given to do in the movie—stand there and wave his arms until it's time to kiss Faye). Power's "best friend," Don Ameche, will play the piano; Power will conduct; and Faye will sing. Lovely song. Beautiful movie stars. Lavish set. Music. In the plot, however, Faye has resented and disliked Power from the beginning, and Ameche has fallen in love with her, whereas Power finds her difficult. As Faye sings "Now It Can Be Told," she sings her heart out, looking toward Power with her beautiful big eyes, her body tense with meaning. Power looks, doesn't see, looks again, and realizes she's telling him she loves him despite everything. He then looks again and responds. He feels the same! Their looks are intercut with shots of Ameche, seeing it himself, and knowing he has lost the woman he loves to his best friend. Suddenly, *Alexander's Ragtime Band* becomes what musicals can be. Using cutting, a dialogueless exchange clearly demonstrated through song and music, three people come to an understanding of how they feel, and all three understand what this means to their lives. No one says "Eureka!" and an audience doesn't have to be told—except, of course, it *has* been told, because "now it can be told"—told through the medium of cinema, using cutting and lyrics. The drama need be no bigger than the music. The acting need go no farther than the waving of arms, the pounding of piano keys, and the singing. Because of the musical subtext, no audience could possibly misunderstand what was happening in this scene.

Alice Faye is beautifully contrasted in *Alexander* with costar Merman, who plays another woman in Power's life—not the "other woman," but just another woman. Merman never wins his love, but she does take Faye's place as the band's lead singer. As the band rises to fame in Europe and then comes to New York, Merman is presented singing tunes in her bombastic and very physical style. She sings, dances, and struts in nightclubs in front of packed crowds who love her. Faye, who has gone into hiding after realizing she still loves Power even though she married Ameche, is seen singing for her supper in a series of low-class bars and dives. All her songs are sad, romantic, or torchy, and she's showcased in the frame as a lonely woman who has lost her love. The film cuts back and forth between the two women and their music. As Merman and a dancing troupe knock out big, loud songs, Faye is seen in contrast singing (with just a piano accompaniment) songs like "All Alone" and "What'll I Do?" How good Alice Faye really was becomes clear. Against the strength of Merman, with all the energy and costuming and dancing feet, Faye can hold her own all by herself in the frame. *Alexander's Ragtime Band* is the peak of her 1930s black-and-white career.

Hello, Frisco, Hello is a typical Fox musical of the 1940s, but ramped up to the highest level of production. Alice Faye had been offscreen since the release of *Week-End in Havana* in 1941, the last film she made before bowing out of *Down Argentine Way*. Grable had caused a sensation and was herself being put in Fox musical after Fox musical. *Hello, Frisco, Hello* would be Faye's return to her home studio and the movie business. Faye is supported by a strong cast: the handsome John Payne for her leading man, comic Jack Oakie in support, along with June Havoc, Lynn Bari, and Laird Cregar. Faye wears beautiful costumes; the sets are detailed and attractive; the songs are tuneful, and the dances well staged by Val Raset; the cinematography, by a balanced duo of Charles Clarke and Allen Davey (one a careful lighter and the other an efficient man for a setup), was so perfectly in sync that they won the Oscar that year for Best Color Cinematography. The music was one of the film's best assets, consisting of old, well-known tunes carefully arranged for the modern ear, and one spectacular new hit by Harry Warren and Mack Gordon: "You'll Never Know."

Hello, Frisco, Hello is studded with songs. It opens right up onto a floor show after a little drive through the Barbary Coast, which allows an audience to go past a cornucopia of different musical performances: a barbershop quartet, a lyrical and sentimental soprano, a low-class girl trio, etc., all intercut with barkers and spielers. When the tracking camera arrives at "Shakey's Colosseum," the floor show presents the four stars (Faye, Payne,

Oakie, and Havoc) in a little song and dance to "Lindy Lou." With the plot ploy of Payne insisting the group then do "the new material" without the owner's permission, there's no time wasted. The film holds nothing back from its paying customers. Faye and Payne sing "Hello, Frisco, Hello" and then she segues into "You'll Never Know." All this in the opening minutes! This is a movie that puts its cards on the table, aces up and out.

Faye changes her clothes in almost every scene, wearing spectacularly designed dresses in mauve, yellow, pink, green, black-and-white with vivid red touches, and pale blue that matches her beautiful eyes. She sings song after song, from her Oscar-winning signature ballad to "Ragtime Cowboy Joe," "They Always Pick on Me," "Has Anybody Here Seen Kelly?," "Sweet Cider Time," "By the Light of the Silvery Moon," etc. And there's more. Oakie and Havoc do a comedy number, and a roller-skating group performs to "It's Tulip Time in Holland."*

Everything about *Hello, Frisco, Hello* worked, but its true asset was the leading lady, the beautiful and sympathetic Alice Faye. There's something indescribable about her. She's utterly natural, an easy and confident singer with no angst. She not only respects the songs she sings—she makes them personal. She doesn't pump a song out, blasting it; she lets it roll out, seemingly wrapped in velvet. The magic of Alice Faye is that, seen in her traditional medium close-up as she sings, she becomes irresistible. Her appeal is universal.

Faye gave up her movie career by her own choice.† (She continued working alongside her husband on radio in *The Phil Harris–Alice Faye Show*.) If she had remained at Fox making musicals, what might have happened, with Grable on the top and Haver in the wings, is anyone's guess. She and Grable were actually very different. Faye is closer in looks to Marilyn Monroe—the big, wide-set eyes, the lush mouth, and the vulnerable look combined with a zaftig body. (Grable was smaller, leaner, and zippier—she gave off the energetic zeitgeist of the war years.) What Faye brought to the musicals was important, however. She sang her songs as if they had mean-

---

* For a time, 20th Century–Fox thought roller skating might be the new ice-skating box-office concept. Roller skaters were also brought out for a big number in Grable's hit film *Pin Up Girl* in 1944. Roller skating, however, was something every kid in America could do, and it had produced no Sonja Henie or Esther Williams to headline some plots. The roller-skating number soon disappeared.

† Faye returned to movies much later in life, appearing in a remake of *State Fair* in 1962 and *The Magic of Lassie* in 1978; both were mother roles.

ing in the plot—the lyrics were a form of very specific dialogue that told of her feelings. Yet she didn't emote them the way such later singers as Streisand would do. She shared the song; she laid it out simply as the beautiful thing many of her best tunes were, and nowhere is that more apparent than in her rendition of "You'll Never Know" in *Frisco*. "You'll never know just how much I care," Alice Faye sings to John Payne, and for a long time in the film he doesn't seem to know. If Oscars were given for knowing how to make a song mean something, Alice Faye would have been 1943's Best Actress of the Year.

Sitting around the dressing room, having a cigarette, two Fox blondes worth their weight in box-office gold. Never rivals, always friends: Betty Grable and Alice Faye

The Queen of the Fox Blondes—and of the 20th Century–Fox lot for a decade or more—was the remarkable Betty Grable. Everyone who was there in a movie house from 1941 to the early fifties loved her, because there was no reason not to. She was pretty, perky, sexy, unpretentious, talented, and looked fantastic in Technicolor. Her films delivered everything they promised, and she introduced some of the big hit numbers of the decade: "My Heart Tells Me," "Kokomo, Indiana," "The More I See You" (with Dick Haymes), and "You Do," among others.

Betty Grable was no overnight success. She hit it big with *Down Argentine Way* in 1940, when she was twenty-five, but she had started working in the business when she was just fourteen. She had been under contract to Samuel Goldwyn, RKO, and Paramount and had spent nearly a decade going up and down the ladder of success. She was in Paramount's "college" movies (*Pigskin Parade*, 1936, and *College Swing*, 1938); played in some of the Wheeler and Woolsey comedies (*The Nitwits*, 1935); traipsed around as a Goldwyn Girl when far too young; and had sung with the Ted Weems band. She felt she had tried it all and was ready to give up when, in 1939, she received an offer to play a secondary role in Cole Porter's new show, *Du Barry Was a Lady*, starring Bert Lahr and Merman. Her specialty

The box-office queen of the 1940s, Betty Grable, turns "My Heart Tells Me" into a hit with nothing but an upsweep, a bathtub, and a radiant smile. (*Sweet Rosie O'Grady*)

number with Charles Walters, "Well, Did You Evah!," brought down the house, landed her on the cover of *Life* magazine, and gave her a whole new shine in the eyes of Hollywood.

With Alice Faye out ill, and *Down Argentine Way* ready to shoot, Darryl Zanuck capitalized on Grable's Broadway success and rushed her in as Faye's replacement. The trailer for the movie referred to the female star as "bewitching Betty Grable, the sensational stage star of *Du Barry Was a Lady*." Grable was given a handsome leading man, Don Ameche, comic support from Charlotte Greenwood and Leonid Kinskey, specialty numbers by Carmen Miranda, some location shooting as backup, colorful dresses and sets, a big dance number entitled "Down Argentina Way," and a romantic love duet with Don Ameche, "Two Dreams Met."

Whereas Faye's basic movie persona represented the thirties, a decade of Depression, social ills, and anxieties, Grable became the star for the forties—a time of war and a need for energy, optimism, and patriotism. Movie stars have to reflect the times, and musical-movie stars have to be able to put across the type of songs that work for the audiences of their day. The shift from Faye to Grable took place partly due to Faye's marriage and motherhood and to her own choice, but it nevertheless reflects the movement out of the upheaval of America that took place in the 1930s to the pulling together of the American people during World War II. Faye's characters underwent rejection and pain, however temporary in the plot, but Grable's could walk away from it more easily. The plots of their films were markedly different in terms of how seriously the audience was supposed to take things, of how deeply the leading lady was to suffer and for how long. Not every plot was the same in this manner, but the general difference between Faye and Grable is that Grable's films were usually lighter in tone and she had a triumphant quality.

By the time Grable's career was in high gear, she was the central force in the frame and almost the entire show. *Coney Island* (1943) displays the set Grable pattern. It's colorful, tuneful, peppy, and fast-moving, and it features her in musical number after musical number. Like Faye's *Hello, Frisco, Hello*, the movie opens up in music: a quick run down a street in old Coney Island, with an amusement-park montage, followed quickly by a brief beginning to set up the leading man (George Montgomery) and the comic relief (Phil Silvers). Betty Grable then comes out onstage to romp around, singing "Put Your Arms Around Me, Honey." The studio knows who Grable is and what she can do that is her own. The song and dance are a throwaway—a joke characterization that sets up Grable's character as flashy and cheap. This was something of a Fox ploy: Alice Faye was presented as unfashionably dressed and cheap in *Alexander's Ragtime Band*, and Tyrone Power had to shape her up. But Grable does her musical intro as a real comedy number, pushing the loud singing, the unattractive voice, and the jumping around stage like a demented pogo stick. Watching, Phil Silvers ogles her rear end when she turns her back to the audience and bends over, wiggling her butt: "Nice voice," he says. (Montgomery replies, "Yeah, loud too.") Grable loved to do comedy like this. The audience loved it, too, knowing that soon enough, they'd have their real Grable, thus buying into one of the prime characteristics that was sold as her persona: she's a good sport. She's unpretentious, not worried about glamour, and just one of the gang, good for a joke. As she hops around the stage, Grable is, of course, wearing a short costume to reveal her beautiful legs, and she's got a mountain of hair, red lips, a bright smile, and a creamy complexion. She also has a tiny mirror attached to a garter at her knee, and she "flashes" the audience—both the one inside the frame and the one in the audience—with it, reminding everyone to just get a look at those legs! Grable's feisty comedy, her ability to do a low comic turn, added to her charm. She wasn't just a romantic lead who sang. She was an all-American gal with that noble quality we all prize: spunk. *Coney Island* has no lengthy plot interruptions despite the movie being about the shenanigans that take place as two rivals (Cesar Romero and Montgomery) cross and double-cross each other.

Grable does it all in *Coney Island*. She comes out in green and white, sporting a large hat in the shape of a shamrock, and sings "When Irish Eyes Are Smiling." She dances with a stage horse (two men inside) in blue and white to "Winter, Winter" and "Pretty Baby." She puts on a black wig and mulatto makeup to become a "Dixie gal," "Miss Lulu from Louisville." She sings the title song. She wears a Lillian Russell hat, with a diamond ring, earrings, a necklace, and a bracelet on each wrist to croon the movie's big love song, "Take It from There." She sings and dances in the grand finale to "Danger in a Dance," allegedly a number from her hit musical *Lovely Ladies*—a practically epic showcase during which she changes her costume three times, dances in three different styles, sings her head off, and comes out for a big bow in time to reprise the love song and reconcile with Montgomery. She was paired with Hermes Pan (in white tie and tails), and in the spectacular finish he lifts her off the floor in six continuous spins as they traverse the floor à la Fred and Ginger.*

There is almost no music in *Coney Island* that isn't performed by Grable. Phil Silvers has one brief comedy number ("In My Harem"), in which he's followed by a gyrating harem girl in a 20th Century Fox–style kootch number, and character actor Charles Winninger sings "Who Threw the Overalls in Mrs. Murphy's Chowder?" A group of young people on the beach play harmonicas to "The Darktown Strutters' Ball" and Silvers does a comedy warning about danger to Montgomery by singing some brief comedy lyrics ("get the money, get the money"). But *Coney Island* is about

---

* The dances were staged by Fred Astaire's working partner in the 1930s, Hermes Pan, who told me he enjoyed being Grable's dancing partner in this grand finale. Pan's dancing was graceful and elegant, and he partnered well with Grable. He was used to fading back, giving maximum support and never competing. He knew their dances weren't about him.

Betty Grable. She's what the audience came to see, paid to see, and wanted to see. The movie sets her up in various ways—comic, beautiful, ethnic, glamorous, sweet, all in different colors and settings and rhythms. *Coney Island* illustrates the Grable musical because it demonstrates that with a star of her popularity and various talents across a wide range (depth isn't needed), a musical has no need to *explain* with musical performance or to *narratize* or to provide subtext. The film is free to provide any sort of setting

or costume in a musical number for Grable because all that matters is that she perform it. This gave songwriters license, as well as costumers and decorators. Her musicals could indeed be colorful, tuneful, and set anywhere, anyplace, anytime. The only requirement was the star's musical presence. Grable didn't need characterization or justification. She was her own genre.

America's World War II pin-up girl, Betty Grable, showing off her assets in one of her biggest hits of the era, *Coney Island*

The superstardom of Betty Grable was originally designed to last for a short time: the dark days of World War II, in which a Technicolor musical was especially welcomed by moviegoers. By all logic, she should have been a brief star of the second tier; she became instead the all-time female box-office champion, reigning a full ten consecutive years in the top ten and rated number one in 1943 (and number two in both 1947 and 1948, just behind Bing Crosby). She was also number two in 1951, her last year on the list. Grable herself was matter-of-fact about her success: "There are two things that made me a star, and I'm standing on them" was one of her great quotes, referring to her beautiful legs, which were insured for a million dollars by the studio. She also said, "I can sing a little, dance a little . . . I'm just lucky, I guess."

Through the years she was a star, and in retrospect, some have questioned Grable's popularity. What was it, anyway? Those who were there at the time know the answer: she's pure fun. She exuded positive energy. She wore a smile on her face that lit up the screen, and nothing got her down. She was literally the spirit of World War II America—and not just because of her famous over-the-shoulder pinup, but also because of her Fox musicals, which are filled with music, comedy, bizarre clothes, and gob-smacking colors. Fox as a studio was well aware of how her ordinariness translated into extraordinariness, and what a miracle that really was. In *Moon Over Miami*, a film that confirmed the stardom she had claimed in *Down Argentine Way*, there's a telling conversation between the characters played by Don Ameche and Grable. She has arrived on a party scene, sung and danced up a storm, and blown away the crowd both in the frame and in the movie audience with her energy and glamour. When she sits down at a table with Ameche, meeting him for the first time, he talks to her about what he sees:

Ameche: "You know, you're not very pretty . . . No, it's not a beautiful face by a long ways—cute, maybe, for people who like cuteness . . . And I noticed your figure . . . that's practically perfect. But it has no poetry. It's built on architectural principles like the sculptures on radiator caps." Grable listens in a bit of a shock, but takes it well, interjecting with wry amusement: "You want this chair back pretty badly, don't you?"

"Your voice isn't pitched very nicely either—suits your personality, but that doesn't make it good," he continues.

"Anything else?" Grable inquires.

Ameche then leans toward her and gives his summation: "I think you're wonderful—and I hope I fall in love with you."

This conversation is the essential analysis of Grable. She's okay, or as she says in the movie, "just a girl." But she was okay in a sensational, crowd-pleasing way, and she never failed her audience. Her movies are today exactly what they were when she made them: happy entertainment, dependent on music and dependent on Grable to put the music across. They are reminders of the point of a musical: to provide an uplifting entertainment through musical performance. Grable, no matter what she's asked to do or whom she's asked to sing and dance with, delivers a solid, cheerful—and reliable—performance. With Grable onscreen, a single song could go a long way. In *Moon Over Miami*, at the aforementioned party sequence, a musical marathon begins when Robert Cummings sits down at the piano and sings "You Started Something" to Grable. When he finishes, she sings it back. Then the tap-dancing Condos Brothers start tapping to it, and are joined by Grable for a full-out tap routine. Within minutes, Ameche asks Grable to dance with him, and he sings it to her on the dance floor. It was like some kind of wartime rationing situation: make whatever you have stretch into more—as long as you had Grable to help out. For those who want to grasp why Betty Grable was a star, watch her sitting in a bathtub in *Sweet Rosie O'Grady*, shown in an extended Technicolor close-up, singing the Harry Warren/Mack Gordon song "My Heart Tells Me." She holds the viewer completely, doing well by the song despite a rather ordinary voice, but keeping the eye engaged with her bright smile and slight turns of her head. There is nothing in the frame but her, and she comfortably fills the huge screen. Grable could hold her own no matter what. She understood that the movies she made were about music, and if nothing else made much sense or needed to be taken seriously, the songs and dances did matter and had to be taken seriously by the people doing them. She's always light on her feet; always looks terrific; and always makes it all seem easy. She might have been "just a girl," but that was what made her special: just a girl, but what a girl! Or, as the wartime variation of an old song said, "I want a girl just like the girl who married Harry James." (Grable wed James in 1943.)

Grable's career continued to be strong after the war ended. Her roles grew past the "pinup girl." Whereas she began by always playing show-girls or entertainers, in movies such as *Coney Island*, *Sweet Rosie O'Grady*, and *Billy Rose's Diamond Horseshoe*, her postwar career incorporated a new maturity. One of her greatest hits was *Mother Wore Tights* (1947), in which she plays . . . Mother. She still sings and dances, but the bulk of the story has her married to costar Dan Dailey and concerned with the happiness and security of her two daughters. Grable also played the wife of an alco-

Grable's dream was to be cast opposite Fred Astaire, but she accepted the lesser-known Dan Dailey for *Mother Wore Tights*, and he became her most popular dancing partner.

holic (Dailey again), in *When My Baby Smiles at Me* (1948) and a woman eager to give up her career and adopt a child in *My Blue Heaven* (1950). These roles were not great dramatic turns, but she was no longer cast only as a performer. (When offered a nonsinging supporting role in the serious *The Razor's Edge* (1946)—a dipsomaniac who's murdered and tossed in the river—Grable turned it down, saying, "The audience would expect me to rise out of the water with lily pads in my hair, singing a hit song.") In *How to Marry a Millionaire* (1953), she had a nonmusical role, a comedic gem alongside Lauren Bacall and Marilyn Monroe, which she played well; the movie, an early CinemaScope feature, was a big box-office draw anchored by Grable's name and wide appeal. In *Meet Me After the Show* (1951), she danced with Gwen Verdon in two numbers choreographed by Jack Cole, a Bob Fosse influencer: "No Talent Joe" and "I Feel Like Dancing." Grable didn't have the polish and controlled physical delineation of Verdon, but she worked hard and could keep up. When given something special, she always rose to the occasion, and she loved her work with Verdon. *Meet Me After the Show* also presented her differently in costuming. She was tastefully dressed, looking elegant, something that hadn't always been true for her earlier films. (The costumes were by Travilla.) As if to make the point that this was a more mature Grable, who had moved beyond pinup but was still sexy, *Meet Me* gave her a cheap and trashy number, "It's a Hot Night in Alaska," performed when her character fakes amnesia and "thinks" she's a showgirl rather than the Broadway name she's become. Grable loved doing "low-down" dances where her comic skills could be put to use. She was unafraid to grind it out. She was terrific doing "I Wish I Could Shimmy Like My Sister Kate" and "Honey Man" in 1950's remake of *Coney Island* called *Wabash Avenue*. These movies all worked. Grable was a crowd pleaser. Audiences just plain liked her, no matter what she played. Her fans never deserted her.

The most overlooked of the Fox blondes was June Haver. She was a singer/dancer that Fox really focused on for a time, as they consciously, in a real business plan, groomed her to take Betty Grable's place. From 1943 to 1953, Haver was real competition for Grable, or at least as much competition as Grable ever had. She was similar to Grable in looks, a small woman with blond hair, blue eyes, a peachy complexion, and a bright and beautiful smile. She had a low speaking voice that recorded well, and was a very competent musical performer. Haver was dainty, with a delicate grace. Her demeanor was inherently more ladylike than Grable's; she could do lightly comic dance routines, but she didn't take on the cheap, wiggly dances that Grable could do with so much tongue-in-cheek panache.

A remarkably pretty Illinois girl, Haver began her career early, singing on radio with various bands. Her first feature movie appearance was as a hatcheck girl in *The Gang's All Here* in 1943. Spotted by Fox personnel, she was immediately given a leading role in a nonmusical, *Home in Indiana* (1944), and also appeared in two musicals, *Irish Eyes Are Smiling* (1944) and the unusual *Where Do We Go from Here?* (1945). The decision to set her up to take over in the typical Fox musical when and if Grable retired or became unpopular prompted the studio to costar the two just as they had costarred Grable and Alice Faye in the black-and-white success *Tin Pan Alley*. The resulting film, *The Dolly Sisters* (1945), is still a Betty Grable vehicle, but Haver is front and center alongside her in big numbers. This chance to grab the spotlight put her in a difficult position: costar to Betty Grable. Side by side and dressed in matching costumes, Grable and Haver looked a great

deal alike. Fox shrewdly decided to capitalize on that, seizing the opportunity to create a potential new star (Haver) and to send a subtle warning to the one they had (Grable). After Grable married band leader James and had two daughters, like Alice Faye before her she grew less interested in her career. She was always reliable and professional, but she had been working all her life and was eager to stay home and relax a little. Fox imagined she'd shape up when she saw the younger and very perky Haver dancing right alongside her. They were wrong: Grable was never a driven careerist, although she was rumored not to love Haver.

The Dolly Sisters definitely put Grable in the starring role, with billing above both Haver and leading man John Payne, but it managed to showcase Haver successfully. It was a movie that reflected the Fox understanding of musicals; it presented both musical intimacy (Grable and Payne singing during romantic clinches such as "I Can't Begin to Tell You" and "I'm Always Chasing Rainbows") as well as the thing many wartime audiences came to see: spectacle. (Intimacy and spectacle were the bread and butter of musicals, and *The Dolly Sisters* had both.)

The spectacles in *The Dolly Sisters* were jaw-dropping. In a number known as "Don't Be Too Old Fashioned," the sisters lead off (with matching ermine muffs) singing lyrics that admonish women to be bold ("Light a cigarette, be a suffragette") and to "wake up to the magic of the makeup kit." The number segues into a sequence called "Powder, Lipstick and Rouge." When this Ziegfeld-type part of the number begins, the curtains open to reveal a giant makeup kit, which opens outward so the traditional beautiful girls in ostentatious costumes can parade out, each singing a little

Two Fox blondes cast as *The Dolly Sisters*: June Haver (left) being developed as competition for Grable (right) in case she got uppity with the studio. All they could do about it was smile.

dialogue about who she is. There's Lady Lipstick who wears a giant lipstick tube on her head ("use the indelible kind"), Patricia Powder ("Ooooh, what I do to a blue serge suit"), Patsy Powder Puff (who complains Patricia couldn't do her job without her help), Rosie Rouge ("You won't be called a hussy"), and Mascara ("I can do for you what I did for Theda Bara"). The costumes have a 1940s Daliesque look, with enlarged eyelashes all over Mascara's dress, and Rouge shot under hot red lights. After all this, Grable and Haver return in matching red outfits to sing and dance and make the point: "Beautiful faces come out of vanity cases." They conclude by bringing the number full circle, back to a few bars of "Old-Fashioned Girl."

In a second spectacle, Grable and Haver sing a version of "The Darktown Strutters' Ball" in French (because they're in Paris), with a chorus of girls parading around in darkish makeup (known in the trade as "light Egyptian"). One has supersized dice on her head, and another a large deck of cards. One, unfortunately, is wearing a watermelon. After the parade, Haver and Grable reappear in their own "light Egyptian," dressed in rags and dark wigs as little Topsys to do an energetic and snappy tap dance. (These demonstrations of racial insensitivity are all over Hollywood musicals, and never fail to shock when they turn up.)

Grable's box-office power carried the movie easily into the hit category, and also carried June Haver forward in her career. After *The Dolly Sisters*, she was immediately given a starring vehicle of her own: *Three Little Girls in Blue* (1946), a remake of one of Grable's own movies, *Moon Over Miami*, redesigned especially for her. The difference between Haver and Grable is well illustrated by this film, which has remained a favorite among musical fans; it's a colorful piece with a score by Josef Myrow (music) and Mack Gordon (lyrics), and shows clearly how Fox planned out its "blonde" musicals. It is, in fact, a *direct* remake of *Moon Over Miami*. The studio was clever. To create a potential replacement for a musical movie star, it just took a successful one made by the person they wanted to replace, changed its time frame (from the modern era back to 1902), its setting (from Miami to Atlantic City), and its score (from Ralph Rainger and Leo Robin, to Myrow and Gordon). The story remained exactly the same: an old plot about three women who want different things from life (as in *Three Blind Mice*, a Fox movie from 1938). Only the casting would shift. *Moon Over Miami* starred Grable along with Carol Landis and Charlotte Greenwood; those three became Haver, Vivian Blaine, and Vera-Ellen, respectively. The three women in each film take a small amount of money and go looking for

Three Little Girls in Blue, an example of Fox's star-development process: June Haver (right) had her own competitors lined up in Vera-Ellen (far left), who left for MGM, and Vivian Blaine (middle), who left for Broadway.

just one rich husband to float the whole family. Grable finds Ameche (the guy she really loves) and Robert Cummings (the actual rich guy, who'll end up with Landis). Haver finds George Montgomery, and Blaine ends up with Frank Latimore.*

Moon Over Miami opens with a scene in which Grable and Landis, as carhops, sing and dance their dialogue as they wait on customers. The setting is a Texas drive-in hamburger joint. This is changed to a New Jersey chicken farm for *Three Little Girls*, with the girls performing as they do their chores. Landis and Grable and their Aunt Susan (Greenwood) inherit $55,000, which is reduced to $4,287.96 "after taxes." (For *Three Little Girls*, the inheritance becomes a little over two thousand dollars, period.) There are only two sisters in *Moon Over Miami*, but in the remake the aunt is

---

* The comic leads are Greenwood and Jack Haley (*Moon*) and Vera-Ellen and Charles Smith (*Three Little Girls*), with the latter two having a big musical dance number of their own to showcase Vera-Ellen's skills. The music was "You Make Me Feel So Young." Vera-Ellen was dubbed by Carol Stewart, and the Fox studio brass apparently felt they had quite enough musical talent under contract. Vera-Ellen would move to MGM, where she would become a major dancing star for over a decade, appearing with both Gene Kelly (*On the Town*) and Fred Astaire (*Three Little Words*). Fox was concentrating on creating stardom for Haver and had no problem with dubbing George Montgomery (by Ben Gage) or Charles Smith (by Del Porter). But Vera-Ellen was given her own small showcase, an innovative dance number presented as a "dream ballet."

changed into a third sister, played by Vera-Ellen, who adds serious dancing into the mix.* The Miami location shifts to Atlantic City, so the "arrival to search for the rich man" number changes from "Oh Me, Oh Mi-ami" to "On the Boardwalk in Atlantic City." Both movies present the females as people who are not professional performers, and thus they either "just sing" in romantic numbers or "just dance" in dance numbers. One major difference is that the male leads of *Three Little Girls*, Montgomery and Latimore, do not sing or dance. (Montgomery "hums" a few bars, and both steer the women around dance floors, but they don't appear in performed numbers.) In *Moon*, both Robert Cummings and Don Ameche sing.

Both films maintain the basic storyline of the three women going to a luxury hotel to look for a millionaire husband, posing as heiress, secretary, and maid. Both films are used to support stardom: Betty Grable's and then June Haver's. (*Three Little Girls* also introduces Broadway success Celeste Holm to moviegoers, and she steals the show in her role as Frank Latimore's slightly wacky, down-to-earth sister. If you scrunch your eyes up tight, Celeste Holm and the *Miami* comedy lead, Charlotte Greenwood, look like the same person.) Both films were successful, and the studio strategy brought stardom to June Haver, although never at the level of the other Fox blondes. After *Three Little Girls in Blue*, she went on to make more successful movies until she retired in 1953, after *The Girl Next Door*. Haver is another example of a woman who could walk away from it, like Alice Faye and Deanna Durbin. After a brief, unhappy marriage (to musician Jimmy Zito), and the sudden death of the new man she planned to marry, she felt unhappy in show business. In 1953 she entered a convent, and after leaving, met and married actor Fred MacMurray in 1954. The two were one of Hollywood's happiest couples until his death, and Haver—except for brief TV appearances—never returned to show business. She died in 2005.

The next Fox blonde would become a legend. Marilyn Monroe was neither a great singer nor a great dancer, but she was good enough. Everyone accepted her breathy vocals as part of who she was, and her dancing was made into far more than it was by the great choreographer Jack Cole. Cole gave her hand gestures, hip movements, and head turns that had rhythm and attracted an audience's eye. The fact that her feet weren't doing much didn't matter when her bottom was waving from side to side or her hands were pointing at her bosom. (He utilized the former in her "Heat Wave"

* Grable, however, had one of her fans' favorite dances in *Moon Over Miami*, "Kindergarten Conga."

number in *There's No Business Like Show Business* and the latter in her "Diamonds Are a Girl's Best Friend" number in *Gentlemen Prefer Blondes*.) Monroe's career is not defined by musicals but by her offscreen life, her vulnerability, and her arresting presence inside the frame. Many books and articles have been written about her, but not much is ever said about her musical performances.

Monroe was something of a challenge for 20th Century–Fox. The studio apparently didn't originally see her as a musical star. (She did appear in a bit part in the Dan Dailey programmer *A Ticket to Tomahawk*, as one of four girls who backed him in musical numbers.) She was put into film noir, romantic comedies, dramas and melodramas, and murder plots; but when she suddenly, out of almost nowhere, became a household name, it was decided that, after all, she *was* a Fox blonde, and what Fox did best with its blondes was always musical. (She had appeared in a B musical for Columbia entitled *Ladies of the Chorus* in 1949, before she was well-known, and had sung two numbers and executed a minor dance.) Monroe made only two pure musicals for Fox, *Gentlemen Prefer Blondes* (1953) and *There's No Business Like Show Business* (1954). She also sang in *Niagara* (1953), *River of No Return* (1954), *Some Like It Hot* (1959), and *Let's Make Love* (1960), usually doing some dancing in connection. Monroe was a Fox blonde by showbiz accident more than anything else, because she was on her way to a legendary status as the epitome of the exploited sex symbol.

Monroe as a musical star in a typical Fox musical was not the Monroe who is usually defined as vulnerable, with a sad and wistful quality, a soul yearning for love and understanding while suffering the cruelties of an uncaring world. Musicals are different, and the Fox blondes—with the possible exception of some of Alice Faye's work—were never going to be walked over. Shirley Temple started the trend, and Grable and Haver carried it forward. In both *Blondes* and *Show Business*, Monroe was self-confident, playing a woman who knew how to use men if she had to in order to achieve her career goals. Monroe has one enduring solo (with a chorus of men): her immortal "Diamonds Are a Girl's Best Friend." Pink and orange, black and red, diamonds glittering everywhere on large trays and all over her arms, Monroe manages to put the number across as a satiric send-up of everything about women wanting a sugar daddy, rich men being willing to play the role, and the whole insane joke of it all, just as beneath the surface of the culture, the women's movement was getting ready to rumble.

The best movie by which to evaluate Monroe as a musical performer is

OPPOSITE A new blonde and the last of the tribe, prophetically singing "After you get what you want you don't want it" in *There's No Business Like Show Business*: Marilyn Monroe

There's No Business Like Show Business. She's surrounded by top-drawer names who've each spent a lifetime in the song-and-dance game: Dan Dailey, Donald O'Connor, Mitzi Gaynor, and Ethel Merman at the peak of her self-confidence, her powerful pipes still on key at full blast. (And there's also newcomer Johnnie Ray, a singer at the high point of his popularity with teenagers.) Monroe doesn't have the musical chops of a single one of these players. She is, however, Marilyn Monroe. What she's got doesn't necessarily need musical chops, and she's not a *terrible* singer/dancer, just not a highly skilled one. *Show Business* has dance numbers created by Robert Alton, but an uncredited Jack Cole designed Monroe's dances: lots of arm movement, swinging hips, a careful enunciation of the lyrics, and a sashaying "walk-dance." Cole's choreography is constructed to show off Monroe's body and to use the audience's established sense of her as a sex object, but without being offensive about it. Monroe has three numbers: "After You Get What You Want You Don't Want It," "Heat Wave," and "Lazy."

"After You Get What You Want" has a bold lyric that feigns innocence. "What you want" could be an ice cream cone, but with Monroe singing it, it's clearly sex: the male attitude toward it. (Once it's done, "Here's some taxi money and see you later.") It's the first song and dance performed by Monroe in the film, and she wears a tight, flesh-colored gown with blue and white sequins and spangles covering crucial areas. She looks nude, and she's in the best shape of her life. (She's also got a big feathered headdress that helps an audience keep its eyes off her lame dancing . . . at least a little bit.) Monroe performs in front of a nightclub audience, dancing around the tables, pouting, flirting, and complaining about not wanting what she gets, but owning the complaint for herself in the Mae West tradition of usurping the male prerogative. In her dance, she leans across tables, thrusting her bosom forward toward male customers. She sits backwards, spreading her legs and kicking one up in the air. She twists to the side, so her breasts are seen in profile. She's beautiful and young and lush, all pure sex, and yet despite all this, there's a strange sense of innocence about her. That was the thing that Monroe had that made her famous. It wasn't *just* sexiness, although she had that in abundance; it was the odd sense of childlike arrested development that people later labeled vulnerability. Monroe seemed to have an undernourished understanding of emotion that rendered her innocent. Watching her sing "after you get what you want you don't want it at all," as she sashays about, the only other star she evokes is Shirley Temple.

Monroe's second song is a full-out production number with elaborate costumes and a chorus of dancers—a Cuban thing with costumes, bongo drums, and palm trees. There's a full choreography for the ensemble, and it's too much for Monroe. She mostly prances around, swishing the ruffles on her skirt. She executes adequately, but she's swamped by the competition: color, decor, hairless chests, and real dancers. She loses her opportu-

Monroe and brunette Jane Russell in *Gentlemen Prefer Blondes*. They're just two little girls from Little Rock.

nity to own what she's singing and give it her personal vibe. Nevertheless, she has her moments. She sings, "I started this heat wave by" . . . and then takes hold of a palm tree's trunk and waves her bottom back and forth, singing no lyric at all. The audience can fill in "letting my seat wave" for itself. Monroe handles "Heat Wave," but she didn't need all the clutter around her.

"Lazy" is a PhD thesis. It's played as a rehearsal for a number to be done by Monroe, O'Connor, and Gaynor. Monroe is dressed in tight Capri pants, a low-cut V-neck top, and a brightly colored cummerbund. She lolls on a chaise longue, singing the song in a languid style. While she sings, draping herself around the sofa and hugging the pillow and rolling onto her back with her breasts thrust upward, the other two dance around her with slam-bang tapping and a high-energy pace. The slower she goes, the faster they go. The less she does, just showing off her body, the more they do, showing off their superb dancing. It's a musical contrast: sex vs. talent. And it's devilishly clever from a business point of view, because it can be watched two ways: "Wow, all Monroe has to do is roll on a couch and she upstages O'Connor and Gaynor!" or "Wow, look at how O'Connor and Gaynor's dancing upstages Monroe, who can only roll on a couch!" (The studio system always had something for everyone.) A character watching this performance actually says, "That boy and girl are just what Vicki needed. They made her look great."

Marilyn Monroe ended the Fox-blonde cycle. She became too big for its limiting label, and the time for the concept was over, as the studio era moved toward its death.* She was never defined by her musical performances, and her career didn't impact musical history much, but it did impact the career of the woman originally put under contract to become the next Fox blonde: the talented Sheree North, who is practically unknown today.

North made her Broadway debut as Whitey in the 1953 musical *Hazel Flagg*, which starred Helen Gallagher. She was spotted by Fox executives (who signed her to a four-year contract in 1954, hoping to develop her as an alternative to Marilyn Monroe). To launch her Fox musical career, North was costarred with the ever-reliable Betty Grable in a truly awful musical in 1955: *How to Be Very, Very Popular*. Grable was no longer interested in

---

* Sonja Henie was a blonde and she was under contract to 20th Century–Fox, but she was never really a "Fox blonde" in that she did not sing, she did not dance . . . she just ice-skated and counted her money.

her film career, but she suited up to give a helping hand to North. (It was her last film role.) Grable and North play two showgirls hiding out from gangsters, and North is accidentally hypnotized by Tommy Noonan and spends most of the film in a trance. (She does manage to do a wild routine to "Shake, Rattle and Roll," however.) *Life* magazine put her on the cover of their March 21st issue that year, with the label, "Sheree North Takes Over from Monroe." Despite the movie's terrible reviews and general audience ennui toward her, Fox did give North another try. And in 1956, she played the female lead in *The Best Things in Life Are Free*, a biopic about the successful songwriting trio of Ray Henderson, Buddy DeSylva, and Lew Brown. They were a blockbuster success on Broadway during the 1920s, writing such hits as the title song, "Button Up Your Overcoat," "Sunny Side Up," and "Good News," among others. They also found success in Hollywood, writing "Sonny Boy" for Al Jolson, and DeSylva ultimately became the head of Paramount Pictures. Gordon MacRae played DeSylva, Dan Dailey was Henderson, and Ernest Borgnine (not an obvious choice for a musical) was Brown.

The Best Things in Life Are Free is not a great musical. North played a dancer who was the alleged love of DeSylva's life. In routines staged by Rod Alexander, she had two big moments to shine. With the ballet star Jacques d'Amboise (billed as "Specialty Dancer"), she danced to "Black Bottom" and "Birth of the Blues," with Gordon MacRae singing the lyrics. In both numbers, she was a standout, but there were problems. First, her singing had to be dubbed (by Eileen Wilson), and the movie was a scattered plot intercut with musical numbers clearly designed only to showcase the famous hit parade of songs the trio had written. The direction was by the highly skilled and experienced Michael Curtiz, who had made silk purses before, but this time he seemed unable to do more than make the movie an entertainment at the entry level. Although the dances had a lively, 1920s Jazz Age sass to them, they were not enough to make the movie into anything special. Marilyn Monroe left movie musicals behind soon enough, but North left them very soon and for good. She returned to the stage, appeared often on television (she guested as Lou Grant's girlfriend on *The Mary Tyler Moore Show* and as Kramer's mother on *Seinfeld*). She also played in movies that were not musicals, such as *Charley Varrick*. She might have officially become the last of the red hot Fox blondes, but the times decreed otherwise. It was the end of an era, and of the concept of "the blonde," a Hollywood fantasy.

The Brazilian
Bombshell, Carmen
Miranda, wearing one
of her trademark outfits:
skyscraper hat, bare-
midriff blouse, yards of
jewelry, and whatever
else was available

Fox developed one other unique female musical performer, but she wasn't a blonde: Maria do Carmo Miranda da Cunha, better known as Carmen Miranda, the Brazilian Bombshell. She was tiny in height (barely five feet two), but big in every other way: big eyes, big mouth, big voice, big personality, big shoes, and very, very big hats. She made her Hollywood film debut in 1940 in *Down Argentine Way*. Although it was a movie designed to make a star out of Betty Grable, the very first image after the credits is a medium close-up of Miranda, singing "South American Way" (or, as she does it, "Souse Am-ur-it-kan way"). Fox knew the audience had never seen anything like her, and she'd be a great kickoff for a fun and colorful movie. Miranda floats in time and space for almost two minutes, with no cuts interrupting her song. She's an unlocated presence for the viewer, not yet a character because no story has been established. Miranda exists in the frame on her own terms, which are musical. She's simply there to define the genre and the location (and never mind that she's Brazilian, not Argentinian). She establishes the musical universe of South America (that place where they samba), the World War II "Good Neighbor" Latin American policy connection, Technicolor, performance space, and the attitude to be taken for what is going to follow: Enjoy!

Miranda was designed to be a supporting player, not a star, but she added real flavor and punch to Fox musicals during the war years. An audience simply *had* to let go of credibility to accept her presence. Inside an already escapist musical universe, she pushed the boundaries: a woman whose English was so bad she could barely be understood and whose outfits lay outside all fashion rules. She wore bananas on her head, wedgies on her feet, and bowling-ball baubles around her neck. She boom-chicka-boom-chicked around a dance floor, babbling incomprehensibly, grinning, wiggling her eyebrows, waving her hands, feet, and rear end, and removing an audience not only from the plot but also from any sense of reality. Miranda was fun. She couldn't have made it in anything other than the musical genre,* and Fox understood that letting her do what she did was a great idea, because she was what musicals were all about, a kind of crazy release, a travel to the *other*. Fox made Carmen Miranda a household name, still recognizable today; sadly, she died at age forty-six in 1955.

Fox was a studio that was more experimental than some of the others. When Busby Berkeley arrived there after his unhappy time at MGM, his major work, *The Gang's All Here* (1943), reflects that openness. He's even crazier than at Warner Bros. in the thirties! What a movie! It just doesn't care. It's got Carmen Miranda, Charlotte Greenwood, Edward Everett Horton, and Eugene Pallette, Benny Goodman and His Orchestra, Phil Baker . . . and these are not the stars. These are the zany supporting actors of the time coupled with one of the greatest big bands in pop-music history; and the star is the beautiful and softly glamorous Alice Faye. Her leading man is James Ellison, the sort of man who had to step up to be a lead during World War II when so many actors were called into active service in the military. *The Gang's All Here* has Fox's usual impeccable sound recording, as well as its usual neon-electric Technicolor, and a fast-paced plot with

---

* In 1953's *Scared Stiff*, a Martin and Lewis musical remake of Bob Hope's 1940 comic horror film *The Ghost Breakers*, Miranda stayed within the "nightclub performer" role. Seeing her playing opposite Jerry Lewis is worth the price of admission.

a great deal of comedy relief. It's a totally bizarro movie, or as one sober scholar decorously described it, "an eccentric creation." It was released in the depths of World War II and would be called "1940s escapism" (which meant from the terrors of war) as opposed to "1930s escapism" (which meant from the Depression).

The opening of *The Gang's All Here* is key to the success of the film and to Berkeley's particular musical presentation. The first thing seen is a very small, disembodied head, singing away to the audience, surrounded by an all-black screen. The circle around the head will widen and open up, finally to reveal a ship at dockside, with coffee from Brazil being unloaded. There's a taxicab, people in daytime clothes, and everyone is singing and talking. This opening establishes two important things for an audience: it locates them in a musical universe and it makes them accept it—they have nothing else to hold on to onscreen. Within a short time, the camera moves back and away from the busy wharf to find a logical explanation for the singing: this is *not* really taking place at a wharf but on a nightclub stage. During World War II, when films had government restrictions as to what they could spend on new materials, the audience of the day would have easily at first accepted the "fake" look of the ship, the wharf, etc., as real, especially with the taxicab present. The film has cleverly prepared an audience for a nonrestricted staged musical world. Even a modern viewer thinks, "Okay, it's a fake musical like they used to make"—and then, "Oh, no! It's okay, we're in a nightclub!" The fake nightclub then suddenly seems to be a real place, as opposed to the "wharf" and the "ship."

All the musical numbers in the film are grounded in this cleverness. The next one is Benny Goodman and His Orchestra playing at the Stage Door Canteen for soldiers. There really was such a place during the war, and orchestras like Goodman's did play there. The number is thus "realistic." The next number, however, is "A Journey to a Star," sung by Alice Faye as Ellison takes her home They ride the Staten Island ferry, and the movie overtly breaks the fourth wall. Ellison beseeches her to sing for him. She says, "All right, soldier," and begins to "conduct" as music swells up. "Hear the orchestra?" she asks him. "Yeah," he replies, "where's it coming from?" "Where's your imagination?" she says, and then, accompanied by a full musical arrangement, sings her song on a ferry boat where there is no orchestra. The audience has been told the truth. It's all fake, and there's no reason to care. We're here for the music. The audiences of the 1940s were completely used to musical presentations, and could and would accept all kinds of them (which didn't mean that filmmakers didn't have to present them carefully to be successful).

The next number in *The Gang's All Here* tests the audience's mettle. It is the very famous "The Lady in the Tutti Frutti Hat," an epic production number featuring Carmen Miranda, some monkeys, bevies of beautiful girls, and a ton of very, very large bananas. This crazy number, which lifts off from the nightclub and goes into that dilated place Berkeley always created, becomes kaleidoscopic in bright, vivid Technicolor. Before the film ends, there will be a second large production number of this sort, "The Polka Dot Ballet." These two songs are both rhythmically structured and reinforced by Berkeley's use of repetition. Since Berkeley is now working with three-strip Technicolor, a viewer can see what his musical presentations are really all about: visual hysteria—brought under a militaristic control. Perfect for World War II.

Twentieth Century–Fox made other innovative musicals: *State Fair* (1945), *Where Do We Go from Here?* (1945), *Centennial Summer* (1946), and *The I Don't Care Girl* (1953) were all movies with imaginative material. The last three are rarely discussed, and yet they are examples of how special the Fox musicals really were. *Where Do We Go from Here?* (with June Haver, Joan Leslie, and Fred MacMurray) had music and lyrics by Kurt Weill and Ira Gershwin.* It also had an unrealistic story line involving a wartime 4-F (MacMurray) whose only wish was to find a way to get into the army and serve his country. When he finds an ancient lamp in a pile of scrap collected to help the war effort, out of it comes a genie who grants him his wish. MacMurray enters the army instantly, only it happens to be the army of George Washington at Valley Forge. He then makes it into the navy, but it's that of Christopher Columbus; and in the modern world, finally, into the US Marines. The movie involves cartoonlike behavior (a deer crossing what will become Fifth Avenue with a stop-and-go light in the middle of the forest). The songs are sung dialogue. The Columbus sequence is a mini-opera. The movie presents an excuse for musical performance inside a dream world, after establishing itself first as a traditional movie musical set within a USO canteen.

The I Don't Care Girl is a pretty terrible movie starring Mitzi Gaynor as the vaudeville queen Eva Tanguay, but it has some of the most imagina-

---

* Although Haver was prominently featured in *Where Do We Go from Here?*, it wasn't a Haver vehicle, created *for* her. She was on her way upward, but not yet the star.

tive choreography in musicals of the era.* Choreographer Jack Cole was ahead of his time, and the visual presentations have a mid-century-modern look, with strong color palettes of orange and red, blue and purple, and stylized settings. In one particularly striking presentation, "The Johnson Rag," Gaynor (a good dancer) cavorts with Oscar Levant and two young males in a dance that predates the architectural and pseudo-robotic movements that will be seen popularized later by choreographers such as

A minor musical, *The I Don't Care Girl* showcases Fox's imaginative approach to choreography as Mitzi Gaynor and Matt Mattox dance Jack Cole's modern routine in spectacular costumes: "The Johnson Rag."

Michael Kidd and Bob Fosse. The setting is Italian Renaissance in look, with mandolins and harpsichords, and bold colors of yellow, black, and white. Gwen Verdon, Cole's dance assistant, introduces the "Beale Street Blues" number, sashaying sexily around a colorful set, swinging her hips and shaking her ruffled petticoats. *Centennial Summer* (Fox's answer to *Meet Me in St. Louis*) has music by Jerome Kern; and it's a lovely score that produced two major hit songs, "All Through the Day" (with lyrics by Oscar Hammerstein II) and "In Love in Vain" (lyrics by Leo Robin). The 1945 *State Fair* starred Jeanne Crain (dubbed by Louanne Hogan); it was a com-

pletely original movie musical, predating the big MGM original movie successes of the Freed unit, with songs by Rodgers and Hammerstein, the only film score they ever wrote together.† Their great hit *Oklahoma!* had already opened on Broadway, and Hollywood was eager to capture their talents

* Cole choreographed and staged "I Don't Care," "The Johnson Rag," and "Beale Street Blues"; the other numbers were done by Seymour Felix, including the first version of "I Don't Care." He also acted in the Minnelli comedy *Designing Woman* (starring Gregory Peck and Lauren Bacall), even though he'd never acted before. Cole played a temperamental choreographer (no stretch!) and also staged fight scenes and special material for singer/dancer Dolores Gray, who was cast as a TV star.

† "It Might as Well Be Spring" won the Oscar for that year.

for a movie. Twentieth Century–Fox shrewdly offered them an *Oklahoma!* kind of project, set in Iowa, but with a modern setting rather than a period piece, yet with a similar mixture of homespun characters and issues that come up against the test of a harsher reality. In this case, a sister (Jeanne Crain) and a brother (Dick Haymes) travel to the annual state fair with their parents (Charles Winninger and Fay Bainter), where they find more sophisticated partners (Dana Andrews and Vivian Blaine). As was true in *Oklahoma!*, *State Fair* offered a picture-perfect look at rural life, colorful characters, comedy and drama intermingled, love encountered and challenged, and a beautiful score. (What the movie lacked was dancing: no Agnes de Mille to challenge conventions.)

State Fair earned four million dollars at the box office, a large sum for 1945 (having cost two million, it was highly profitable). *State Fair* was a "sing as they live" kind of musical in some sequences. People attending the midway section of the fair burst into "It's a Grand Night for Singing," and the farm family sing "Our State Fair" together. Jeanne Crain, sitting alone in her room, tells an audience how she feels, wanting some excitement, something more in her life, when she "sings" "It Might as Well Be Spring." But a professional singer in front of a band (Vivian Blaine) sings "That's for Me," reprised by Dick Haymes, who plays a young man who wants to be a songwriter. It's a clever mix of explained and unexplained musical performance—a movie pointing to the future.

Fox was a studio that understood that musicals were different things for different people. Some customers didn't want art, originality, or weird variations. They wanted nothing more than to see a Broadway hit on film—either because they loved Broadway hits or because they lived where none were available. If a movie musical did nothing but re-create a successful stage show, Fox was willing to take a chance on it at the box office, and that's why the studio purchased the rights to *Call Me Madam*, one of Ethel Merman's personal triumphs. The story was inspired by President Harry Truman's appointment of the famous Washington hostess Perle Mesta to the ambassadorship of Luxembourg. The character of Sally Adams was created for Merman: the rich widow of a Texas oil tycoon who becomes ambassadress to "Lichtenburg." The original show opened on Broadway in 1950, directed by George Abbott and choreographed by Jerome Robbins. It had terrific music by Irving Berlin, a book by Howard Lindsay and Russel Crouse, and La Merman, supported by Paul Lukas, Russell Nype, and Galina Talva. Merman was given plenty of comedy, lots of glamorous clothes to wear, and a lineup of Berlin's best 1950s songs written especially for her, including "The Hostess with the Mostes' on the Ball." *Call Me Madam* had everything . . . but it really wasn't a very good show. It was special, however, because it had Merman (and Berlin), and that was enough for Fox. The studio wasn't worried. Merman had made *Call Me Madam* work on Broadway, and she'd make the movie work, too. *Call Me Madam* was turned into a 1953 hit movie starring Merman, supported this time by George Sanders, Donald O'Connor, and Vera-Ellen. Nothing much was changed, and Merman had a hit movie in the film that probably comes the closest of all her movies to presenting her as she really was onstage.*

Twentieth Century–Fox made its own brand of innovative musicals, among them *State Fair*: Fay Bainter, Dick Haymes, Jeanne Crain, and Charles Winninger—the Fraike family having a musical adventure in Iowa.

* Fox *did* expand the choreography to accommodate the talents and stardom of Donald O'Connor. A song from the 1940 Broadway show *Louisiana Purchase*—"What Chance Have I with Love?"—was added for him, and the dances (by Robert Alton) were adapted and expanded for O'Connor and Vera-Ellen.

Call Me Madam was almost a return to the transition-to-sound practice of transferring a hit Broadway show directly onto film. Two other Broadway musicals that were turned into unpretentious and honest representations of the originals managed at the same time to become very stylish and cinematic movies: *The Pajama Game* (1957) and *A Funny Thing Happened on the Way to the Forum* (1966). *The Pajama Game* is a faithful re-creation that offers a clear sense of the original show, although the action was opened up for some dance numbers. For instance, Bob Fosse's choreography for the final number, "7 1/2 Cents," had a pajama fashion show included, and "Once-a-Year Day" was turned into a sensational outdoor picnic dance extravaganza, shot on location. (*The Pajama Game* was directed by Stanley Donen and George Abbott.) *A Funny Thing* (a United Artists release) kept its original leads, Zero Mostel and Jack Gilford, as well as the raunchiness, the political incorrectness, and the breakneck pace; but does not directly recreate the stage show: it eliminates five songs. However, the director,

A Broadway show that became a lively and energetic Warner Bros. movie: *The Pajama Game*, featuring Carol Haney doing justice to Bob Fosse's choreography for "Once-a-Year Day"

Richard Lester, was currently a highly respected talent for his imaginative use of cinema, which was about bringing back slapstick conventions from silent comedy and using rapid cutting and overdubbing to be 1960s hip. He had successfully introduced the Beatles to movie audiences with that style in *A Hard Day's Night* (1964) and *Help!* (1965) and was a critics' darling. His version of *A Funny Thing* is an unusual example of transferring a stage musical to film, because he respects the essence of the original but presents it through a clever and masterful wielding of cinema techniques. (There's more than one kind of fidelity in adaptations.)

Despite such hits as *The Pajama Game* and *A Funny Thing*, Warners and other studios were never strong musical rivals to MGM—only Fox offered a serious and consistent competition. Fox could be sly inside a musical number in a way that would never happen at MGM. Jane Russell cavorted with an "Olympic team" on shipboard in *Gentlemen Prefer Blondes*, ironically singing "Anyone Here for Love?" as the men—all Greek Adonises—ignore her while doing their athletic routines. The implication about their sexuality was not lost on audiences. Grable's "No Talent Joe" in *Meet Me After the Show* was similar. Grable dances among a group of big, heavily muscled bodybuilder types, singing about her lover ("He's a slow Romeo"). In both numbers the men, who seem brainless and sexless, ignore the women, and the message is subversive and sophisticated. Fox had a style all its own. It was in sum much more than a studio for "blonde" musicals. And its musicals had an Americanness that audiences embraced. When it came to song and dance, Paramount had Europe, MGM had Paris, Warners had Broadway, but Fox had Coney Island, Wabash Avenue, Miami, and Iowa.

The big studios dominated the musical field, but one independent producer, Samuel Goldwyn, had an excellent track record. A producer of many types of movies, among them prestige classics such as *Dodsworth* (1936) and *The Best Years of Our Lives* (1946), Goldwyn's company made seventeen significant musicals. In addition to the 1930s Eddie Cantor films that featured the early choreography of Busby Berkeley, Goldwyn moved forward in 1938 with an ambitious musical called *The Goldwyn Follies* (released by United Artists). Its plot was lame—a short-order cook, played by singer Kenny Baker, tries to become famous in Hollywood. Shot in three-strip Technicolor, *Follies* was a combination of an old-fashioned revue (hence, the title) and a plot-driven musical. It was a mishmash designed to have "something for everyone": blues singer Ella Logan, opera star Helen Jepson, comedian Bobby Clark, ventriloquist Edgar Bergen and his dummy,

Charlie McCarthy, and the insane antics of the singing, dancing, clowning Ritz Brothers—the Marx Brothers on steroids, if such a thing were possible. The topper was dancer Vera Zorina appearing in a ballet choreographed by George Balanchine. The original songs were to be composed entirely by George and Ira Gershwin, but George died (at age thirty-nine) before the score was completed, and Vernon Duke took over to complete the score, although the Gershwins had managed to write four songs before George's death: "Love Walked In," "I Was Doing All Right," "I Love to Rhyme," and "Love Is Here to Stay."*

After Cantor, Goldwyn made a popular star out of Danny Kaye, a musical success on Broadway who went on to further success in film, television, and theater over nearly five decades. Kaye began performing as a teenager on the borscht belt and in vaudeville, and appeared in a few short films. After making his stage debut in 1939 in *The Straw Hat Revue*, he jumped to fame in the highly theatrical and expressionistic hit *Lady in the Dark*, by Moss Hart, Kurt Weill, and Ira Gershwin. The story was about a successful magazine editor (British star Gertrude Lawrence) who is under analysis because, as one song says, "She would make up her mind." The premise allowed for an experimental production, with action flowing in and out of reality through dream sequences. The show took Broadway by storm, getting rave reviews and creating a stir because of its seemingly avant-garde presentation of abstracted sets, psychiatric concepts, and imaginative theatrical techniques. *Lady* was designed to showcase the famous and beloved Lawrence and to present her on Broadway like the theatrical icon she was. That worked all right except for one thing—Danny Kaye, neé David Daniel Kaminski, who stole the show right out from under her high heels every night when he presented what would become his signature accomplishment: rattling a hilarious song/recitation, a kind of "Peter Piper picked a peck of pickled peppers" number entitled "Tschaikowsky." In it, Kaye fired off the names of multiple Russian composers at high speed. Audiences loved it; critics called it "sophisticated."†

---

* Duke composed the music for the ballets *Romeo and Juliet* and *Water Nymph*, cowrote "Spring Again" with Ira, and claimed in his autobiography to have contributed to "Love Is Here to Stay." The major numbers for the antic Ritz Brothers ("Here Pussy Pussy" and "Serenade to a Fish") were written by Sid Kuller and Ray Golden.

† The movie version of *Lady in the Dark* (1944) featured Ginger Rogers in the Lawrence role. Despite his success and his ownership of his role, Kaye was not offered it, since he had already been put under contract by Goldwyn. (The movie was a Paramount release.) Comic Mischa Auer played

Danny Kaye surrounded by the "Goldwyn Girls," who appeared in Goldwyn musicals to provide glamour and sex appeal while Kaye handled the comedy and the singing and dancing

After appearing in another hit show (*Let's Face It!*) in 1941, Kaye was lured to Hollywood by Goldwyn, who saw in him another Eddie Cantor and decided to follow the Hollywood Golden Rule of Success: if it worked once, do it again. Kaye was to be starred in films that were designed around his specific talents, looks, and personality, and which would feature him doing tongue-twisting lyrics. Kaye was a performer in the right place at the right time. The war years brought on a category of musical entertainment that can be labeled by one of the World War era's favorite adjectives: zany. "Zany" meant utterly irrational or even mildly insane, and the undercurrent of stress and worry of the war years was apparently relieved by the sight (and sound) of a performer who was willing to go bananas for the duration. (In addition to Kaye's rise to film stardom, there were the continuation of Martha Raye's; the addition of performers like singer/contortionist, Cass Daley; the strange deadpan of Virginia O'Brien; and, of course, the Queen of the Crazies, the bouncing Betty Hutton.)

The first of these Goldwyn films to star Kaye was *Up in Arms*, a 1944

the part, but did *not* perform "Tschaikowsky," which was omitted. The movie did not do well at the box office but is a cult favorite today because of its surrealistic images.

RKO picture release that, in addition to Kaye, starred Dana Andrews, Constance Dowling, and the popular radio and recording star Dinah Shore. Appearing in theaters in the depths of war, *Up in Arms* was about love, combat, singing and dancing, patriotism, and hypochondria—not necessarily in that order. It's a classic example of the frenzied World War II musical comedy. Kaye's character is an elevator operator who works in a medical building to be close to doctors. When he and his pal (Andrews) are drafted, Shore and Dowling also enlist.

Up in Arms cares nothing for integration of tone, merely designing songs and dances for the two major musical talents it's striving to promote. There are two types of musical numbers: verbal-comedy patter songs for Kaye and ballads for Shore. They go together like pickles and ice cream, with Kaye emoting all over the frame and Shore patiently waiting her turn to get a word in. Their music isn't even written by the same composers. Shore sings songs by Harold Arlen (music) and Ted Koehler (lyrics): a low-key "Now I Know" and a bluesy "Tess's Torch Song," which she does to perfection. Kaye's two lengthy numbers were specifically written for him by Sylvia Fine (Kaye's wife) and Max Liebman.* The first is a satire about movies. (It's sometimes listed by its official title, "Manic Depressive Pictures Presents," and other times called "Theater Lobby Number.") It's the first real number of the film, although the plot has been operating for several minutes. While the four leads are standing in line at Radio City, Kaye sings the credits for an imaginary movie, right down to the gaffer, and then, in a somewhat Cantorish eyeball-rolling and highly energetic recounting of the plot, he goes on and on about such things as "Carmelita Pepita the Bolivian Bombshell," who is living where it's "Conga!" all the time, or "when it's cherry blossom time in Orange, New Jersey." His other solo is "Melody in 4-F," a "git-gat-gittle" mélange about the fate of a draftee, the sort of thing that audiences of the era loved, understood, and roared at, but seems demented today. "Melody in 4-F" is pure Danny Kaye.† Sung on shipboard as the troops head to the Pacific, it's a scat song, rapidly paced and loaded with weird sounds, invented words, facial tics, and slapstick gestures. It's punctuated with Kaye pretending to shoot a machine gun, and it's a relief when it's over.

* Kaye also lip-syncs to a recording with female voices.

† It was originally written for the stage version of *Let's Face It!*

While Kaye is capering about spreading tension and capturing Japanese soldiers like a hot-wired Sergeant York, Shore gracefully does what she's expected to do. She sings *her* first song ("Now I Know") quite far into the running time, suddenly saying, "Would anybody be surprised if I sang a song at this point?" Someone answers by saying, "Well, it's about time," and it certainly was. It's one of Hollywood's oddities that Shore never became a real movie star. She's lovely, low-key, and natural, and she can really sing.

Shore and Kaye do one big number together. It's Kaye's fantasy after he's hospitalized, and an audience is taken "into his head" for a gigantic wedding scene involving the Goldwyn Girls (with Virginia Mayo, not yet a star, prominent among them). It's lavishly produced with tons of costumes, flowers, dancers and singers prancing about, a rooty-tooty-all-rooty number from the war years in which everyone sings phrases such as "hep, hep, hep" and "Solid, Jack, pitch me some woo." In one section of their extended choreography, Kaye and Shore sing the blues together well, but the unity of their costarring never really gels. They both give it everything they've got, but he upstages her, sticking out his tongue, herking and jerking about, while she wisely acts as if none of it is really happening, never losing her dignity. Shore, a successful woman whose career lasted for decades, had inner strength under her southern graciousness. She had surprising gifts. When Kaye does one of his spitting, contorted, verbal attacks, she's asked to repeat it after him. She not only can, she does, syllable to syllable, padiddle to padiddle. Kaye's an alleged genius at reciting complex sounds rapidly, but Shore can do it, too. Nevertheless, the bottom line is that *Up in Arms* made Danny Kaye a movie star and didn't do the same for Dinah Shore. She did, however, later become a huge television star, her easy manner perfectly suiting the venue that was a piece of household furniture.

Besides *Up in Arms*, Kaye's other movies for Goldwyn were *Wonder Man* (1945), *The Kid from Brooklyn* (1946), *The Secret Life of Walter Mitty* (1947), *A Song Is Born* (1948), and *Hans Christian Andersen* (1952). *Wonder Man*—only his second film—clearly illustrates that the Danny Kaye musical pattern is already established. It's a mixture of crime and comedy and song and dance. The good news is that the movie is colorful and tuneful and gives Kaye two costars, Virginia Mayo and Vera-Ellen. The bad news is that the movie also gives the audience two Danny Kayes—he plays twins! One Kaye is a nightclub performer, Buzzy Bellew, an extrovert, and the other Kaye is a meek scholar (Edwin Dingle) with a photographic mind who is writing a book. (He writes with both hands simultaneously because "it saves time.") After Bellew is shot—an event that comes right out of nowhere, showing once again that murder is no stranger to musical movie plots—his ghost possesses the body of his intellectual twin to urge him to find the killer. (This can happen, the film explains, because the two men are "superidentical twins—a rarity.")

Kaye is exhausting, an ego allowed to run wild. His numbers are bizarre, "wacka wacka" things, such as the "Bali Boogie" he and Vera-Ellen do early in the film. Vera-Ellen does backflips, Kaye uses his hands to imitate snakes, and they prance about in Hollywood-Balinese costumes. Kaye is shot (because he's going to testify against a criminal), after which he knows no shame. He barks like a dog, crows like a rooster, hoots like an owl, and mews like a kitten. He also recites "The Village Blacksmith," sings "Ochi Chornye" in a Russian accent, sneezes repeatedly (he has allergies), and ultimately has to disguise himself as an extra in an opera and go onstage, as in the Marx Brothers' *A Night at the Opera* (and also Milton Berle's *Always Leave Them Laughing*, although Berle's show is an operetta). The shy brother saves the day by singing out the plot from the crowded stage, explaining who the killer is and revealing hidden identities ("Choo

Comedian Danny Kaye became a successful musicals star for Samuel Goldwyn, daydreaming with Virginia Mayo (right) in *Wonder Man*.

Choo Laverne is Minnie Smith," etc.). Goldwyn found gold in Danny Kaye.*

All the studios worked hard to create successful musicals, and spent a great deal of money doing so. Musicals were expensive, and not just because of costumes, sets, and rehearsals. The studios had to have highly trained personnel under contract, readily available to "turn out" musicals for their factory system. Stars who could sing and dance were, of course, necessary, along with cinematographers, directors, and editors; but making musicals also required composers, arrangers, lyricists, recording technicians, choreographers, dance rehearsal leaders, and a full orchestra—an army of specialized and expensive talents. These musical hires had to be compatible with (and help create) studio style. In addition, studios employed workers whose jobs were so esoteric that most people today don't even realize they existed. MGM had special seamstresses who worked only to create different versions of the same dress for a dance number (e.g., one with a heavily beaded hemline to keep the dress from swinging in the wrong place, a second version without the beads for when it needed to swing, and a third version that was only partially beaded for the plot scene that leads into the number). In an oral-history interview given to Donald Knox for the American Film Institute, Gene Kelly discussed this issue in regard to *An American in Paris*: "We might have three dresses made for Leslie . . . and the audience would never know they were three different skirts. One would be for the dance, one for the scene, and one for a section of the dance where we'd want her leg extended. This is an item unto itself, just knowing what costumes will move well on dancers." MGM had a staff of seamstresses who knew.

Studios also employed people known as "script timers." A timed script was used to determine where any movie might be taking too long to make a point—an expensive waste—and in the case of musicals, where there were too many numbers or overly long choreography. Shooting a conversation scene and later cutting it was wasteful, but actually filming an elaborate musical number and having to drop it could be disastrous to a budget. Script timers were capable of reading aloud a shooting script to provide the budget department with an estimated pre-production running time for the

---

* Kaye's most popular films with today's audiences are two he made for Paramount, not Goldwyn: *White Christmas*, in which his talent is under control and well used, and *Court Jester*, a likable Robin Hood–ish spoof in which his antics are at their funniest.

movie. This was a difficult and specialized job that required timers to know the speech rate of certain stars, to estimate how much time would pass as an actor moved around a couch, and in the case of a musical, to predict how long it would actually take to go "dancing in the dark"—very difficult to accomplish with no sound or choreography.

Walter Strohm, an MGM budget man, said that script timing was "an infallible and invaluable tool." One of the most famous timers in the business was MGM employee Nora Janney, who described her job: "You have to make your mind a screen and you see the characters and read their dialogue and react as you think they would react according to the story . . . You use a stopwatch. The people you are working with are artists acting and they are going to make as much out of their parts as possible . . . you have to allow for it." Janney described how each genre established its own tempo. "Drawing room comedies run pretty fast, and westerns are pretty fast. Musicals are very heavy."

Of all the specialized behind-the-scenes talents, none were more significant and important to success than the songwriters who made the music. Hollywood had the money to attract almost any working composer or lyricist. After the transition to sound, songwriters were lured to Hollywood for the opportunity to create in a supportive environment, the potential to sell records and sheet music—and, of course, for the money, the glamour, the prestige, and the sunny weather. The "American songbook" luminaries—Irving Berlin, Cole Porter, George and Ira Gershwin, Jerome Kern, Rodgers and Hart, Rodgers and Hammerstein, Harold Arlen, et al.—came to Hollywood to write songs. Many of the best songwriters took up residence to write original scores for films. (The names that preceded them—men like Rudolf Friml, Victor Herbert, Sigmund Romberg—also had their songs and stories transposed into movies.) These songwriters, who were musical cultural forces, had their Broadway shows made into films, their hit songs bought and featured, and had contracts offered for new tunes specifically written for particular stars and films.* A few composers

---

* To show respect for the importance of songs in movies, in 1934 the Motion Picture Academy created the category of Best Original Song, acknowledging tunes created for and introduced in movies. The awards have been given to such standards as "The Way You Look Tonight" (Irving Berlin), from *Swing Time*, "Over the Rainbow" (Harold Arlen and Yip Harburg) from *The Wizard of Oz*, and "Secret Love" (Sammy Fain and Paul Webster) in *Calamity Jane*. There've been zingy specialty winners ("Baby, It's Cold Outside" from *Neptune's Daughter* and "Zip-a-Dee-Doo-Dah" from *Song of the South*), tunes immortalized as theme songs (Bob Hope's "Thanks for the Memory" from *The*

and lyricists, however, did most of their work in Hollywood, not on Broadway. Becoming permanent residents in California, either under contract or readily available to the studios: Johnny Mercer, Hoagy Carmichael, Ralph Rainger, Mack Gordon, Ralph Blane, Sammy Cahn, and Hugh Martin, who were all mostly known for their songs in Hollywood musicals. After they had settled into California, Mercer, Carmichael, (and Harold Arlen) all tried to match their Hollywood successes by doing Broadway shows, but none really triumphed. One exception was the talented Frank Loesser, who reversed the usual pattern of a Broadway success hired to go to Hollywood. He was a Hollywood success who went to Broadway and found his greatest fame. He had headed to Hollywood as a young man around 1936, and teamed up with successful movie composers like Burton Lane, Jule Styne, and others, writing lyrics for musicals such as the Jack Benny vehicle *Man About Town* (1939), *Happy Go Lucky* (1943), and *Thank Your Lucky Stars* (1943). Loesser was more or less a working professional until he decided to write both music and lyrics himself and turned out one of World War II's biggest hits, the immortal "Praise the Lord and Pass the Ammunition ("All aboard, we ain't a-goin' fishin')." He created two scores for Paramount (*The Perils of Pauline* and *Variety Girl* in 1947) and then decamped for Broadway, where he became a legendary figure with hits like *Where's Charley* in 1948, *Guys and Dolls* in 1950, and *The Most Happy Fella* in 1956. He did maintain ties with Hollywood, including writing songs for Esther Williams in *Neptune's Daughter* and for Betty Hutton and Fred Astaire in *Let's Dance*. Loesser was versatile, and could write clever character songs, folk songs, operatic songs, whatever-you-need songs. He was also a generous mentor to young composers such as Meredith Willson and Jerry Ross.

A major example of a typical Hollywood songwriter was the prolific Harry Warren, who was always defined as "a Hollywood movie songwriter." Warren lived from 1893 to 1981, and thus he was born right alongside movies and died about the time the musical genre lost steam. Although he did work on Broadway and Tin Pan Alley, the majority of his composing was done in Hollywood. The job of a Hollywood studio composer involved musical collaboration. Warren worked with more lyricists than any other songwriter: Al Dubin, Johnny Mercer, Mack Gordon, Dorothy Fields, Ira

---

Big Broadcast of 1938), relative obscurities ("Sweet Leilani" from *Waikiki Wedding*), and a modern attempts at a classic ("You'll Be in My Heart" from *Tarzan* in 1999).

Gershwin, Gus Kahn, Arthur Freed, Ralph Blane, and Leo Robin among them. Warren's career solidified into a steady run of lifetime employment after he teamed with Dubin in 1933 for *42nd Street*. Dubin was already an established lyricist, having written such hits as "Tiptoe Through the Tulips" and "Painting the Clouds with Sunshine" (both with composer Joe Burke). (He had also written one of my favorite lyrics for a Sammy Fain song: "Nobody Knows What a Red-Headed Mama Can Do.") Warren and Dubin were well suited to each other, and they were responsible for four hits from *42nd Street*: "You're Getting to Be a Habit with Me," "Young and Healthy," "Shuffle Off to Buffalo," and the title song. After *42nd Street*, Warren and Dubin were a Warner Bros. team, and Warren took up permanent residence in California despite his dislike of Hollywood. ("It looked like a small town in South Dakota.")*

Harry Warren's work defines what movie songs could and should do. In his formative years, he had played drums in a traveling carnival show, where he learned how to write a rat-a-tat rhythm with a staccato sound that worked well for tap-dancing numbers. His music was a film editor's dream because his rhythms could be matched by cutting on the beat, songs like "Chattanooga Choo Choo" or "I Got a Gal in Kalamazoo" (both with lyrics by Mack Gordon). His music didn't sound like the Ruritanian world of crinolines and cavaliers; it evoked images of modern America, with its zing and sass and slang, perfect for movies. Although his music is often described with such words as "melodious" and "harmonious," what he really put forth was a forward-moving line, much like the narrative of a good movie story. Warren's tunes could be set to lyrics that sounded like dialogue coming out of the mouths of real people, and audiences responded to the immediacy generated by his songs. From 1932 to 1957—over two and a half decades—Warren wrote Hollywood musicals, moving from studio to studio: Warners in the 1930s, Fox in the 1940s, MGM in the fifties, and Paramount in his last five years of active work. He wrote over 250 songs in his lifetime, and fifty of them became standards. The American Society of Composers, Authors, and Publishers (ASCAP) lists Harry Warren as the seventh-highest-ranking originator of American songs in the earnings category. The famous radio show *Your Hit Parade* (which ran from 1935 to 1953 on radio) ranked forty-two of Warren's songs in its top-ten list—Irving Berlin had just thirty-three. And yet Harry Warren is not a well-known

* Al Dubin died in 1945 of alcoholism at the age of fifty-three.

name like Berlin, Cole Porter, or George Gershwin. (He once said, "Even my best friends don't know who I am.") Because he was mostly a studio employee, his music was an assignment.* His job might need him to write for someone who was not a great singer . . . or someone who couldn't sing at all but would need to look believable when lip-syncing in close-up . . . or who would be acting the song as part of the plot and characterization needed at that moment in the film . . . or who was a famous star with a persona that had to be served. Movie composing was in service of a system. One of Warren's most successful songs, "You'll Never Know," was specially written for Alice Faye's style and voice, but since it was a World War II release, also for the mood of the audience. However, the film in which it would appear, *Hello, Frisco, Hello,* was set in 1908, so Warren had to write music that could be modern, with a wartime sense of loss and yearning, and still seem appropriate to 1908. He had to juggle narrative meaning, star power, time period, and the need to sell sheet music to the audience.

When Warren arrived at Fox, he was assigned the task of writing for Carmen Miranda, who sang in Portuguese. His understanding of rhythm was perfect for Miranda because the construction of her music required a different beat, one from a Brazilian/Portuguese musical tradition. Miranda was fussy about her music and knew what she could do and what would work for her. She had her own backup group (her Bando da Lua, musicians who had accompanied her from Brazil). Warren cooperated with her, accepting her ideas and loving her band. "It was a joy to listen to them," he said. "They had such humor and gusto. They played with such vitality." Warren understood that Miranda, her music, and her band were about having fun; they were visually exciting, energetic, and empathic. His job was not to interfere with that but to accept it—a decision a Hollywood composer had to make to succeed.

Harry Warren is only one example of the high-level Hollywood composer/lyricist. Hollywood hired many first-rate people; the studios knew good songwriters and how to deploy them. All the composers and lyricists who wrote for movies were writing for one of three things: a star, a plot situation, or a spectacle. (And possibly all three at the same time!) Their job was not fundamentally different from writing music for the stage or for Tin

---

* He was featured in a 1933 Vitaphone short under the grand title *Harry Warren, America's Foremost Composer*. In a brief nine minutes, he was seen performing some of his own compositions, among them "Forty-Second Street" and "You're My Everything."

Pan Alley or for a big band, but Hollywood was working on a budget under a time constraint, driven by a star system, and beholden to the box office. Movie music had to connect audiences to the characters and their situations, and that meant a conversational quality in the lyrics and a swingy little rhythm in the music. "Isn't this a lovely day to be caught in the rain?" Astaire asks Rogers in *Top Hat*, but he asks her through the music of Irving Berlin. "So set 'em up, Joe, / I've got a little story you oughta know," Astaire says to a bartender in *The Sky's the Limit*, and "Have yourself a merry little Christmas," Judy Garland tells her distraught younger sister, Margaret O'Brien, in *Meet Me in St. Louis*, ". . . Next year all our troubles will be out of sight." These words are musical dialogue; they elevate the ordinary question, the self-pitying dumped love, and the big-sister reassurance into something an audience *experiences*. Sometimes the words are no more than ordinary conversation, low-key date-night talk. "Moonlight becomes you," Bing Crosby tells Dorothy Lamour, in *Road to Morocco*, "it goes with your hair." As dialogue it's pretty dumb. As a song it's a hit.

Movie songs could be soliloquies—rueful, passionate, humorous, secret conversations with the audience. Astaire, speaking through the Gershwins, strolls a country lane in his tuxedo and tells us—only us—"I was a stranger in the city / Out of town were the people I knew / I had that feeling of self-pity / What to do, what to do, what to do?" Judy Garland in *Meet Me in St. Louis* secretly confides in us: "I just adore the boy next door," and in *Wizard of Oz* lets us know her secret dream about a world "somewhere over the rainbow" where "bluebirds fly."

Lyrics—and the accompanying music—provide the soliloquy that proves the musical is not trivial, the aside that solidifies the identification between audience live in the house and actor unreal on the screen. A shy Frank Sinatra sings "What's Wrong with Me?" asking himself (and viewers) in *The Kissing Bandit*, "Why didn't I kiss her?" Gene Kelly told Donald Knox how important Hollywood musical stars felt the lyrics were: "If you are . . . talking about a girl and you're saying that she's wonderful, you sing 's'wonderful, s'marvelous, that she should care for me. . . .' You're telling the other fellow about it. You say, 'Singin' in the rain, just singin' in the rain. What a marvelous [sic] feeling, I'm happy again.' You state it, then you prove it. You further your thesis by dancing it . . . it bridges the gap between the spoken word and the dance." Movie songs usually had a preconceived purpose. Some were to provide subtext when needed, helping elude the censors, a perfect dodge for a mass-market medium that presented a socially acceptable surface with an underlying ambiguity about sex. Lyrics could be witty dialogue—or ruminations about lost love, passionate desires for romance, and sophisticated acceptance that something that once seemed wonderful was in fact "just one of those things." Some songs were best used for production numbers unrelated to plot and character. Their sense of place and setting and feeling was overwhelming, evoking images of a fantasized world that didn't fit easily into any plot. Cole Porter's "Begin the Beguine" was such a song; it was used as performance music for Astaire and Eleanor Powell in *Broadway Melody of 1940* as well as for a large production number in *Night and Day*. "I'm with you once more under the stars / And down by the shore an orchestra's playing . . . / To live it again is past all endeavor . . ." The music has an exotic quality, with a Latin beat, and it expresses an unfulfilled desire. Songs were helpful in plot movement, especially with what were known as "traveling" songs ("We're Off to See the Wizard"), or crazy characterizations (anything written for Betty Hutton, such as the one about her boyfriend, "Murder, he says . . . Is that the language of love?" or her wartime sex life, "I'm Doin' It for Defense"). And there were always the fun numbers that just cried out for dance interpretation ("Diga Diga Do") or female pulchritude ("You Stepped Out of a Dream").

A perfect use of a song in a movie is "That Old Black Magic," sung by Johnnie Johnston (while Vera Zorina danced) in *Star Spangled Rhythm*. The number has no narrative context; the movie is a series of numbers in a revuelike format with a weak little plot to hold them together. "That Old Black Magic" thus is almost a modern music video. The lyrics are a kind of speech, a soliloquy to self that's sung by a GI looking at a photograph and thinking, remembering his girl, asking himself why he loves her. He sings and the audience is then taken inside the photo. Zorina comes to life and dances—as if what he's thinking is actually happening. The lyric simply asks, "I should stay away, but what can I do?" He explains to himself why he knows he won't stay away: "You're the lover I have waited for / The mate that fate had me created for," and finally the definition of that fate: "And every time your lips meet mine, / Darling, down and down I go, / Round and round I go, / In a spin, loving the spin I'm in, / under that old black magic called love." It's a musical "To be or not to be."

The composers and lyricists who wrote the music for Hollywood movies are the ghost figures of movie culture. They are never mentioned as the screenwriters they really are, and many of their names are not familiar to the average movie viewer. The ability to write a song as a form of dialogue or a revelation of character, or to set a mood, explain a situation, or define the subtext of the movie—not to mention providing the fun and the pleasure of good music—was a specialized talent . . . and key to the history of movie musicals. It was useful as business strategy.

V

The Musical as an
Art Form

S O FAR, HISTORY HAS SHOWN US that when sound came in, the rush to create musicals was mostly motivated by straightforward thinking: let's get some songs and dances up there on the screen. Why do people sing? Because they do. How should we transition into song and dance? By having someone start playing the intro music. The practical business found practical solutions to questions they felt didn't need to be asked; but as film artists began to think more and more about musicals, and innovators stepped up to make them, the original Hollywood musical and its experimental variations came along, arrived, had success or no success, and then disappeared and reappeared while the rank-and-file musical film in which people sang and danced with no apparent concern about it rolled on. Inevitably, after a decade of all-singing, all-dancing movies, the desire to create a musical that was about being musical emerged and took hold. In other words, at first people in Hollywood made musicals without thinking about it and then they started thinking about it. One of the places where they started thinking about it was the Arthur Freed unit at MGM.*

MGM had three major production "units" during the golden era of the studio system, each under the leadership of one individual and thus loosely identified by his name: Jack Cummings (the nephew of Louis B. Mayer), Joe Pasternak (who had helped turn Deanna Durbin into a star at Universal), and Arthur Freed. Cummings had started at MGM as an office boy and worked his way up, learning every aspect of movie production by toiling in

OPPOSITE Arthur Freed found his first success (uncredited) as assistant producer on the legendary musical fantasy *The Wizard of Oz*, the story of Dorothy Gale from Kansas, who dreams of a world over the rainbow.

* There was nothing officially labeled "the Arthur Freed unit." It exists in retrospect as observers note that Freed built trust and respect with a group he used repeatedly. He worked with these same people all during his years at MGM; thus, they became the famous "Freed unit." Other producers did the same, but Freed's were exceptionally talented.

different departments, and by 1935 he had begun producing feature films. He had a long and prolific career. He was responsible for many successful MGM musicals, among them Eleanor Powell's *Born to Dance* (1936); the *Broadway Melody* of both 1938 and 1940; Esther Williams's debut as a leading lady in *Bathing Beauty* (1944); *Three Little Words* (1950), in which Fred Astaire and Red Skelton played songwriters Bert Kalmar and Harry Ruby; the remake of *Roberta*, *Lovely to Look At* (1952); the 3-D *Kiss Me, Kate* (1953); the much-respected *Seven Brides for Seven Brothers* (1954); and the Elvis Presley musical *Viva Las Vegas* (1964). The films he produced were unpretentious, star-driven, and always competently directed and performed.

Joe Pasternak was born in Hungary in 1901 but immigrated to America in his late teens. He started out working as a busboy in the Paramount commissary and worked his way forward, ultimately moving into management. An obvious hard worker and up-and-comer, in the late 1920s he was hired by Universal Pictures to oversee their office in Berlin. He returned to America when the Nazis became a problem and when Universal began having financial troubles. Pasternak was the producer of the vehicles that made Deanna Durbin a star: *Three Smart Girls* (1937), *One Hundred Men and a Girl* (1937), *Mad About Music* and *That Certain Age* (both 1938), et al. His success with her labeled him as a producer of movies that starred female singers, preferably young, and that featured a happy, somewhat sentimental family story—the sort of musical that was labeled schmaltz. His MGM musicals with "schmaltz" include two wartime hits, *Two Girls and a Sailor* (1944) and *Anchors Aweigh* (1945), as well as Jane Powell's *Luxury Liner* (1948) and *A Date with Judy* (1948), and Mario Lanza's highly successful biopic *The Great Caruso* (1951). He was the producer of an early Judy Garland success, *Presenting Lily Mars* (1943), and oversaw her final MGM movie, *Summer Stock* (1950). Pasternak made over sixty musicals and became strongly identified with them. He also produced the provocative Ruth Etting biopic *Love Me or Leave Me* (1955) and the beautiful and underrated *Billy Rose's Jumbo* (1962), two musicals with a melancholy strain. Pasternak's work had straightforward charm, great pacing, and top-level production values.

Pasternak and Cummings are usually compared unfavorably with the man who ran the Rolls-Royce of the MGM production units, Arthur Freed. However, they were both important business and creative forces behind the large output of MGM musicals. They worked efficiently and economically to create quality product that audiences were happy to consume. They knew how to handle a star vehicle, and since MGM was the "studio of stars," they were key figures in the MGM musical success. For an audience at the time, the Cummings and Pasternak musicals were not only welcome, but perhaps *more* welcome than some of Freed's artier work. Freed's unit pushed the musical format forward artistically, but it also created famous flops such as *Yolanda and the Thief* (1945) and *The Belle of New York* (1952). It's also important to remember that not all the Freed productions were films like *An American in Paris*, with lofty artistic goals. The Freed unit also produced *The Harvey Girls* (1946), *Easter Parade* (1948), and *Take Me Out to the Ball Game* (1949), all of which were excellent, but which provided the same unpretentious kind of musical entertainment that the Cummings and Pasternak units featured.

In turn, Pasternak and Cummings films often reveal the same sort of thinking about the definitions of musical films that the Freed unit developed. What goes around comes around. Pasternak's *Easy to Love*, an Esther Williams vehicle, shows his unit thinking about musical performance. No matter how peculiar the time or place, an audience will accept it because they've already seen the actor do it in an established professional context. Thus all three MGM units knew that it was expedient to establish a character first in any film *as* a professional musical performer. This is done with Tony Martin, one of Williams's costars in *Easy to Love*. He is first established as a singing star through dialogue and plot and by having him sing in his nightclub act. In a later scene, when Martin is wooing Williams, he turns up at the door of her room in Cypress Gardens, where she works, and coaxes her to "come down for dinner." The preliminary for their date becomes a "natural performance" musical number in an ordinary resort lobby.

After leaving her room, Martin starts downstairs to wait for Williams, and on the stairs he begins to sing "That's What a Rainy Day Is For," as it has begun (conveniently) to rain outside. As he crosses the lobby, a brace of elderly ladies staying at the resort perk up when they see him (he's handsome!) and hear him (and he can sing!). The old ladies gather around him, so he, like the gracious star he is, accommodates them by moving to the piano. He sits down to play, and continues singing while they join him in the song. He gets up and dances with one, while the musical accompaniment, without him, continues. The choreography includes his picking flowers out of the vases in the lobby to distribute one blossom to each lady. As he is doing this, and the music continues, the film cuts to Esther Williams as she comes downstairs. She joins in, also singing and dancing. This is natural and believable—the establishment of the "real" world as a musical performance space, because both Williams and Martin have previously been established as musical performers. It's their job to entertain the old ladies with music . . . literally.

The number illustrates the MGM musical attitude, which was not that of the Freed unit alone. A story has emerged—Martin invites Williams to dinner, goes downstairs to wait, encounters old ladies, entertains them until she comes. But it's a story done through music and, significantly, *only* because the film is a musical and Tony Martin has a number to do. The musical evolved this way everywhere in Hollywood, but the Freed unit took it to a different, more self-conscious level.

MGM supported the three different units with equal enthusiasm for all, and credit for that has to go to the studio head, Louis B. Mayer, who is seldom acknowledged for his interest in musicals (and often not for anything at all). Yet had he not been willing to support the high costs of musical production . . . had he not believed in the genre and its variety . . . had he not been willing to sign contracts for all those musicians and specialized talents . . . the history of the genre would be very different. Songwriter Harry Warren said of Mayer, "Of all the moguls I had any dealings with, Mayer was the most courteous and considerate. He loved music, and the people he seemed to like best were composers, musicians, and singers. When he hired Johnny Green as the director of the music department, he told him he wanted the greatest orchestra and arrangers in the business. Johnny pointed out that it would cost a lot of money, and Mayer said, 'We've got a lot of money.' Working for Mayer was a pleasure."

The history of the musical film, however, has to focus on the Freed unit and its spectacular array of talent in all categories and its desire to move the musical forward, defining its conventions and solving its challenges at a high level. It's been said that everyone in Hollywood thought of the Freed unit as Hollywood's Royal Family, and that it thought of itself that way, too. Freed came to MGM during the transition-to-sound period, hired to write songs. To Nacio Herb Brown's music, Freed penned lyrics for *The Broadway Melody* (the 1929 Oscar winner), *The Hollywood Revue of 1929*, and *Going Hollywood*, among others, and the two men had many hits together, not the least of them being "Singin' in the Rain."

Freed was a surprising amalgam of influences and experiences: he attended the Phillips Exeter Academy; he was a song plugger; he was a vaudeville performer; he served in World War I, etc. At MGM, he studied everything that was happening on the lot, watching while the songs he created were rehearsed, performed before the camera, and photographed. He was a studio gadfly, always around, always learning, and in particular, always helping find and develop musical talent. In 1938, Mayer gave him an opportunity to become an uncredited associate producer if he could find a suitable property and make it into a movie.* Arthur Freed found a suitable property. It was called *The Wizard of Oz*.

The Wizard of Oz became one of the most famous movies of all time, and made an iconic figure out of the young Judy Garland. It is usually described as a "fantasy" rather than as a musical, despite it being forever identified with Garland, her signature song ("Over the Rainbow"), and musical instructions to "Follow the Yellow Brick Road." It *is* a musical, but one which has no need to explain itself as such. Even though in the beginning a small girl sits by a haystack and sings her heart out for no reason, once she's gone over the rainbow and into fantasy land, it's a world where lions sing and dance, tin men live, scarecrows talk, and there are horses of different colors. Singing and dancing is as normal as anything else. It's important to note, however, that Arthur Freed began his work as a producer in the year 1939 with two very different musicals: his first, *The Wizard of Oz*, a fantasy in which musical performance need not be explained, and his second, *Babes in Arms*, a backstage story in which every musical performance *was* explained. Freed began by mastering the opposites of musical presentation: the unreal and the real.

Over time, the practical business of moviemaking had settled into these two opposites to make musicals work: (1) stories that gave an audience a setting in which performing music was logical—that is, the backstage musical or some form of rehearsal or puttin'-on-a-show story or a biopic; and (2) a story that renounced reality by saying directly to the audience "This is not real." The latter presented a setting that was not in a real place geographically, or created a time and place or a world that was obviously a fantasy. Real and unreal. Backstage and fantasy. Ultimately, musicals

---

* The producer was Mervyn LeRoy. Freed received his first producer credit on his next film, *Babes in Arms*, but was a key player on *Oz*. In his book on *Oz* director Victor Fleming, Michael Sragow says Freed had been pushing Mayer to make *Oz* as a musical for Garland before LeRoy came to the studio.

OPPOSITE, TOP Glinda, the
Good Witch (Billie Burke),
reassures the new arrival
in Oz (Garland) that she's
done a good deed by
dropping a house on the
Wicked Witch of the East.
The Munchkins agree.

OPPOSITE, BOTTOM The
Fabulous Four in Oz: the
Scarecrow, the Tin Man,
Dorothy, and the Cowardly
Lion, take a run through the
poppies.

ABOVE Dorothy and her
pals are on the Yellow
Brick Road just outside the
Emerald City.

RIGHT The Wicked Witch
(Margaret Hamilton,
left) and one of her
henchmonkeys look into
the crystal ball to locate
Dorothy (Garland).

would become more than just those two polar opposites and find ways to be both.

Freed's career was secured by his contribution to *Oz*. The casting of the four musical leads—Judy Garland, Ray Bolger, Bert Lahr, and

Dorothy prepares to go home with the help of her team (clockwise), Frank Morgan, Bert Lahr, Garland, Jack Haley, and Ray Bolger. (Toto's asleep in his basket.)

Jack Haley—was perfection. Garland, one of the most iconic figures in musical-film history, was at the beginning of her real stardom, supported by a trio of highly individualistic performers. Lahr was a distinctive comic who could sing and dance, and Haley, although not as distinctive, was nevertheless a highly successful musical performer. (He was a last-minute replacement for Buddy Ebsen, who was forced to withdraw because of an allergy to the silver powder in the Tin Man makeup.) Bolger was a comic actor who appeared in stage, film, and TV productions; he was the one of the three best known as a dancer. (He was the original Hoofer in Balanchine's *Slaughter on Tenth Avenue* ballet.) Over time he would appear in musicals that placed him alongside such stars as Garland (*The Harvey Girls*), Doris Day (*April in Paris*), June Haver (*Look for the Silver Lining*), and Eleanor Powell (*Rosalie*). He returned to the stage for hit shows *By Jupiter* (1942) and *Where's Charley?* (1948), in a role he also played in the 1952 movie version.

Bolger was a unique dancer. He wasn't just "rubber-legged" à la the lesser Ebsen. Bolger was elastic. He was capable of moving more than his legs; his entire body was loose and flexible. He could bend himself in all directions, but always without it looking difficult or tormented. Holding his back ramrod straight, he could descend to the floor in a split that had both legs sticking straight out from his hips—and then go right back up again, and back down and back up yet again. He could bounce, up and down, higher and higher. He flew high when he danced, and he also possessed a distinctive voice and a charming personality that could make broad comedy work in a low-key manner. Bolger was a true musical personality. In *Where's Charley?* (Frank Loesser's first book musical on Broadway), he found his greatest stage hit, with songs like "Once in Love with Amy," which he turned into a sing-along for the audience every night. For the movie version, which was not a big hit, Michael Kidd did the choreography and Bolger was given more dancing. (He also asked the movie audience to join in on "Amy" in the same way as on Broadway, but with less success. Most audiences in the movie house did not cooperate.)

From *The Wizard of Oz* onward, Freed became a top MGM producer,

Back home again, safe and sound, but maybe a little less colorful: Garland, with (above and to the left) Frank Morgan, Charley Grapewin, Bert Lahr, Ray Bolger, Jack Haley, and Clara Blandick

and he remained in that job for over twenty years. (He died in 1973.) Not all of the Freed unit movies were musicals—he and his group also made nonmusicals, like *Any Number Can Play* (1949), with Clark Gable as a gambling-hall owner, and *Crisis* (1950), with Cary Grant as a doctor on vacation in a Latin American country, forced to perform brain surgery on a dictator. His most memorable movies, however, *were* musicals. For his production unit, Freed assembled around him some of the greatest talents of the era—songwriters, composers, arrangers, lyricists, choreographers, designers: Roger Edens, Conrad Salinger, Robert Alton, Ralph Blane, Hugh Martin, André Previn, Saul Chaplin, Johnny Green, Preston Ames, Lennie Hayton, Kay Thompson, Adolph Deutsch, Irene Sharaff, Lela Simone, John Alton, Betty Comden and Adolph Green, and others. Of course, as a top of the line MGM producer, Freed had access to all the star and directorial talent the studio had available. He was in a position to make influential musicals with plenty of money and talent to back him up. Over his years as a producer, Arthur Freed and his collaborators created an astonishing list of major musical films that are well-remembered and loved by moviegoers today: *Babes in Arms, Strike Up the Band, For Me and My Gal, Cabin in the Sky, Meet Me in St. Louis, On the Town, Annie Get Your Gun, Show Boat* (1951), *An American in Paris, Singin' in the Rain, The Band Wagon, Brigadoon, Silk Stockings, Gigi,* and more.

Chief among those who wanted to create at a high level were directors Vincente Minnelli and Stanley Donen and dancers Gene Kelly and Fred Astaire. Minnelli and Kelly worked together to elevate musicals into a consciously American art form, and they are the two most commonly credited with the success of the Freed musical productions, but Astaire and Donen can never be overlooked. Astaire is Astaire, and although he had announced his retirement in 1946, he returned to replace Kelly in *Easter Parade* (1948) after Kelly broke his ankle. Astaire then found he was happy to go on working, and since he never seemed to age or lose energy, he did some of his best work for Freed. After *Easter Parade*, he went on to do *Royal Wedding, The Band Wagon, Silk Stockings,* and others.

Fred Astaire and Gene Kelly are the two great dancer/choreographers of motion picture musical history. That they were both unquestionably movie stars is a curiosity, since innovators and creators usually remained behind the scenes on Hollywood films. Both men had strong personalities offscreen (although Astaire was shyer than Kelly) and could dominate their working situations. For many years, it was fashionable to compare them and choose which one was the "best," but as the decades have passed, this increasingly seems a useless effort. What's the point? They are very different, and as I wrote in 1976 their styles were really very personal. Both were small men, but Kelly was a muscular type and Astaire was lean and lithe. There were broad similarities in the characters they created—they were, after all, both dancers—but both played brash Americans who joked and often conned their way toward their true moment of deep expression: the dance. Astaire used the joy and tenderness of his routines to save his characters from the brink of banality, and Kelly tried to make the personality of his dance and that of his character exactly the same. In the beginning, Astaire was thought of as a romantic, and Kelly as sexy. The simplified idea was one I wrote: "A woman might give her heart and soul to Fred Astaire—but she saved her body for Gene Kelly."

Such distinctions have become irrelevant as the two men no longer are contrasted as living stars doing their work. In retrospect, it can be seen that Kelly was always striving for perfection, and Astaire was always achieving it. As Liza Minnelli put it in an interview for TCM: "When Gene danced, you knew it was a great dance number. When Fred danced, you thought he was making it up on the spot."

Over their long lives, Kelly and Astaire maintained a gentlemanly distance, full of dignified mutual respect. Except for a late-in-life small routine to introduce clips in 1976's *That's Entertainment, Part II*, they danced together only once: in one of the numbers in the revuelike *Ziegfeld Follies*. It should be an immortal moment, or the summit of movie dance, or something other than what it actually is: just another routine in a fairly dull movie. *Ziegfeld Follies* is a colorful, star-studded showcase for MGM's roster, and a lumpen parade of largely unsuccessful musical numbers and painful comedy skits. The Astaire/Kelly number is brief, set to a song called "The Babbitt and the Bromide" from the 1927 Broadway show *Funny Face* (in which Astaire performed it with his sister, Adele). Its choice was a compromise.

Astaire and Kelly were determined to make their routine work—both were perfectionists—but also determined not to be disagreeable or disrespectful to each other. Kelly said, "We were so nice and polite and generous to each other that it was almost boring," and Arthur Freed commented that "it was a real Alphonse and Gaston routine." To work with the audience's idea of the two men as potential rivals, the dance was set up by a little (very little) insider comedy, some banter. Kelly tells Astaire that he is a dancer in the movies and asks him, "Did you see a picture called *Cover Girl*? . . . Well, who did all the dancing in that?" Astaire innocently replies, "You're not Rita Hayworth?" "No," Kelly fires back, "I'm not, *Ginger*!" And then, mercifully, they dance.

"The Babbitt and the Bromide" is a story dance in which two men meet on an almost bare stage at three different times: youth, middle age, and the

Looking a bit uncertain about it, Fred Astaire and Gene Kelly, the two musical legends of film history, appear in their only prime-time dance number together: "The Babbitt and the Bromide" from *Ziegfeld Follies*.

afterlife. Each time, they ask each other the same vocalized questions, and then dance. Since their styles are different, they compensate by essentially showing not much style at all, but they do put on a show. Their first set is a hard-hitting romp with fast-paced tapping, and as they progress in age, they knock each other's hats off, bump rears, stomp toes, waltz around with harps, and execute leaps and turns and flourishes, but none of it has personality. The highlight is a splendid moment in which Astaire kicks Kelly right in the nose, an unexpected shenanigan. Only Astaire could get his foot high enough to engage the nose of the rapidly moving Gene Kelly! When the song is over, the two men shake hands and grin, and that's all we get from a pairing of the two legendary male dancers of the silver screen.*

* When Astaire and Kelly appeared together as hosts for *That's Entertainment, Part II* in 1976, Kelly directed the opening, closing, and interior sequences in which the two of them sang and danced the credits and introductory material for MGM musical numbers from the past. They were both trim,

Stanley Donen seldom gets the full credit he deserves as a witty, skilled director of comedies and musicals, most likely because his early years were spent in collaboration with Kelly. The importance of Donen in Kelly's success is a topic of debate, and much has been written about their working relationship. Who did what, and who was the real talent? After splitting with Kelly, Donen went on to a highly successful career in musicals, whereas Kelly's directorial efforts, such as *Invitation to the Dance* (1956) and *Hello, Dolly!* (starring Barbra Streisand, 1969), were failures. Donen made two important original musicals on his own: the MGM hit *Seven Brides for Seven Brothers* (1954) and Paramount's *Funny Face* (1957, one of Astaire's best in his later years). Michael Kidd's choreography for *Seven Brides* was groundbreaking in its day. In the "House-Raising Dance," seven of the era's most dynamic male dancers (Jacques d'Amboise, Marc Platt, Matt Mattox, Tommy Rall, and Russ Tamblyn among them) bring an energy onscreen that's infectious, full of acrobatic leaps, gymnastic skills, high kicks, and jumps as the brothers execute a "challenge dance" with another set of seven male dancers. In an opposite mood, the seven men dance in slow motion (physically real, not camera-created) to a bluesy, sexy song called "Lonesome Polecat" as they dream of the women they're denied. The dance takes place in snow (on a set, not location) and involves chopping wood, swinging an axe, and moving about in a trancelike state while moaning in what is obviously their sexual frustration. In 1954, to see strong men mixing the swing of an axe and ballet moves while dressed like lumberjacks was a first. Kidd choreographed, but Donen knew exactly how to shoot and cut (in widescreen) to give the number a maximum effect. "Lonesome Polecat" took 1954 audiences by surprise.

Donen's *Funny Face* was an excellent Astaire vehicle, and a fabulous visual experience. The plot involved fashion photography, and Astaire's character was allegedly based on Richard Avedon, the celebrated photographer, who acted as a consultant. Donen shot on locations in New York City and Paris and proved he could do a *Singin' in the Rain*–type musical on his own, without Gene Kelly, and not at MGM but at Paramount. He claimed his space. Donen had always called Astaire his inspiration, and his idea in *Funny Face* was to re-create the Astaire/Rogers kind of numbers, to once

cheerful, looking years younger than their ages, and on top of their game. They seemed happy to be together and even happier to be dancing. No signs of age were visible in their routine. They might be rehearsing for "The Babbitt and the Bromide," as if it were still the 1940s.

again use music to express character emotions. Astaire sings and dances in a darkroom, in an apartment plaza, and outdoors on grass. Donen was inventive, and particularly adept at facilitating the beginning of a number, letting characters move directly into a song or dance and then allowing the music to join the process. When there is no pause as the music begins to rise up so the dance can begin, the movie onscreen has real pace, never loses energy, and takes on a sense of natural movement. The idea that characters who aren't professional musical performers still sing and dance every day is helped by this style, and Donen was a master of it. At the very least, his codirectorial credit on *Singin' in the Rain* qualifies him as an important name in musicals history.

Matt Mattox leaps high in the barn-raising dance by Michael Kidd for Stanley Donen's hit *Seven Brides for Seven Brothers.*

The first movie to carry the codirecting credit of Gene Kelly and Stanley Donen was *On the Town,* based on the now-legendary 1944 show that brought the Broadway debuts of Leonard Bernstein, Betty Comden and Adolph Green, and (as a choreographer) Jerome Robbins. A story about three sailors on shore leave in Manhattan, the movie starred Kelly, Frank Sinatra, and Jules Munshin, and the women they meet and romp around town with were Vera-Ellen, Betty Garrett, and Ann Miller. It was a true dance musical, a fully developed story loosely based on the Bernstein/ Robbins ballet *Fancy Free*. The movie, not made until 1949, is controversial. Most of the original songs, among them the lovely, bluesy "Lonely Town," were dropped, and new ones ("Prehistoric Man") were added. The ballet, however, was retained, although rechoreographed, and those who love the movie appreciate its exuberant dancing.* Others find the movie a little cold around the heart, and don't appreciate its enforced masculinity. Extravagant claims about its having been shot *entirely* on location (it wasn't) or being the first musical to be shot on location (it wasn't) made it significant in its own day but are no longer of interest to audiences. Many complain about its songs (except for "New York, New York"), its unattractive costumes, and its lack of production polish. Once a movie that took pride of place as a true dance film, a groundbreaking musical innovation, *On the Town* becomes less and less popular while other original Hollywood musicals become more respected. *On the Town* stands, however, as the first feature-film directorial Kelly/Donen collaboration, a glimpse into their ambitions for dance on film, and a representation of their desire to make "the art of dance" accessible to the general moviegoing public. *On the Town*'s importance in the Kelly/Donen collaboration and vision for dance on film was summed up by Kelly in an interview for the BBC in 1974: "We made better pictures than that, but that was the apex of our talent. That was it. I think it was maybe my biggest contribution to the film musical."

The personnel in the Freed unit were ambitious, and thus inspired to bring the musical under a benign scrutiny. They wanted to make the best product possible, and they wanted to push the boundaries of the musical genre, test the form, take it apart and find out what made it work best. They were practical—the bottom line was always box-office success— but they were also experimental and imaginative. Many of them—Freed himself—were well aware of the different types of musicals that had already been made, and they knew there had already been attempts at creating films with a fully integrated presentation of music and performance. They wanted to add to what had been done before, emulate the best of it, and take it even farther. As a result, the Freed unit musicals, good or bad, are as a group a textbook on musicals, because the unit was a graduate

---

* In the major ballet, "A Day in New York," Kelly and Donen replaced Sinatra, Munshin, Garrett, and Miller with other dancers, one of whom was a young Carol Haney. Kelly felt only he and Vera-Ellen could do the planned balletic routine.

Margaret O'Brien and Judy Garland as sisters, doing an impromptu song and dance in the story of a family, *Meet Me in St. Louis*

school in film study. The era of the unit's work is the era in which the musical became conscious of itself *as* a musical—and thus not a world of natural behavior but a world of *musical* behavior. Studying Freed unit musicals reveal three important questions that apply to the structure of musical films, and musical films are all about structure: (1) Musical Establishment: When does a viewer first become aware that the world of the movie is one in which people will sing and dance for some reason? (2) Musical Integration: How closely integrated are the musical numbers and the plot? (3) Musical Intervals: How often do musical numbers occur, and with what intervals in between them? The Freed unit movies are those in which these questions are asked and answered by successful resolutions. A set of guidelines emerges from watching them.

Since an audience starts living in a film's universe as soon as the opening credits are rolling, the establishment of that universe as musical needs to be almost immediate. A perfect positive example of how to open a musical film is Vincente Minnelli's classic *Meet Me in St. Louis* (1944), a Freed unit hit, which starts by showing the audience a picture postcard of a lovely family home in St. Louis in summertime. This house—will the family leave it and move to New York or stay in it forever?—is the main plot point of the film. The first scene takes place in its kitchen. After a brief discussion about the homemade ketchup being brewed on the stove ("Too sweet?" "Too sour?"), one of the children easily, naturally, starts singing "Meet Me in St. Louis" as she moves upstairs. The song was not written for the film but was a tune familiar to the audience. The little girl (Joan Carroll) is not a musical performer. Her vocal is untrained, naturalistic. As she moves through the house, the song is picked up by her grandfather, also a nonsinger, and then passed to her sisters as they arrive home, singing with the friends who drop them off. The movie is firmly located in a world in which everyone sings. This *Meet Me in St. Louis* opening is ideal for a musical film. It quickly moves an audience into the theme of the movie (the St. Louis World's fair), the style of the film (musical), the importance of the house (a family home), the period setting (costumes and art direction), and the special joy of living in St. Louis. It moves from amateur nonsingers easily bringing music into the universe, over to two professional performers, Judy Garland and Lucille Bremer, one of whom was already famous as a musical star. Action fluidly flows forward, from nonmusic to acceptable music to professional music. One single opening number accomplishes this: the audience knows right away where they are, and what will be the terms on which to receive the rest of the movie.

If the story, or forward movement of the plot, is disrupted too completely in order to accommodate a musical number, even if it's a good number and the audience enjoys it, the performance tends to detach viewers from their story experience. Even a backstage musical needs to consider this issue. The more poorly a musical number is integrated into the film, the less it has to do with anything going on with the characters and the farther away an audience is driven. There are exceptions to this, primarily the astonishing kaleidoscopic formations by Busby Berkeley, but also certain numbers built especially for a single performer's talent. If a dance by Astaire or a song by Crosby doesn't relate closely to plot, their star presence provides a kind of integration, as the audience knows they are there to sing and dance in places where the plot will allow it. *Meet Me in St. Louis* demonstrates well-integrated musical numbers: the family sings around the piano; two sisters perform as "amateurs" at a party in their home; a girl

sings about the boy next door; a group of young people taking a trolley ride sing together; an older sister comforts a younger one with a Christmas song, etc. The numbers are about the family living in its house in St. Louis, and they're natural to the life they're living in that house in that city. (The Freed musicals almost always provide close integration between the music and the plot.)

Musical films *must* present musical performances at necessary intervals, but the film can't lose the audience's acceptance of that necessity. The right number of musical presentations set into a story at the right time—the spacing of numbers inside the plot—is crucial to success. If there's forty minutes between numbers, the audience forgets they're watching a movie in which people sing and dance. However, back-to-back numbers can spoil the fun. Watching a musical, a viewer can often just *feel* how wrong it is to have a number come so soon after a previous one, and can certainly tell when too much time has passed since the last musical performance. Audiences who went to a lot of musicals during the 1930s and 1940s would often respond to back-to-back numbers with catcalls; they were sensitive to musical spacing. Too much music was too much music, which is why so many musical numbers were designed, scored, performed, photographed, edited, and then later dropped from the released film. The Freed unit movies are rigorous in this regard. Gene Kelly's singing "I've Got a Crush on You" for *An American in Paris* and a fully staged presentation of "You Are My Lucky Star" for *Singin' in the Rain*—among others—were ruthlessly dropped prior to release.

These three structural issues are successfully addressed and resolved in *Singin' in the Rain*, the musical for people who don't like musicals. Love it or hate it (and few hate it), overrate it or underrate it, *Singin' in the Rain* makes a perfect musical yardstick. For people who don't like musicals, it's still a very funny comedy. For people who don't want comedy, there's a charming romance. For people who think romance is sappy, there's the history of the transition to sound in film treated with great humor. And for everyone who wants a musical, there are all kinds of different numbers, old tunes and new tunes and great performers to present them. It's also a good way to see why Freed productions were hits.

On May 20, 1950, the Broadway team of Betty Comden and Adolph Green arrived at MGM, hired by Freed to write an original movie musical, including both book and lyrics. They had a clause inserted into their contract that said if existing songs were used (instead of their own com-

OPPOSITE Gene Kelly, an umbrella, a lamppost, and some heavy California dew in the musical for people who hate musicals: *Singin' in the Rain*

positions) they could only be by Irving Berlin, Cole Porter, or Rodgers and Hammerstein. (Freed later brushed this aside, saying to them, "Kids, I never heard of any such clause!") Howard Keel was to be the lead—Gene Kelly was far too deeply involved in finishing *An American in Paris* to be considered—but when he read the script Comden and Green presented, he wanted to be part of it. He took the starring role, and MGM added Donald O'Connor and newcomer Debbie Reynolds (who was not yet an accomplished tap dancer). Thus, the film showcases three stars who, in retrospect, all had amazing career longevity and a high level of accomplishment. Rehearsals started on April 12, 1951, and Reynolds worked separately with Ernie Flatt to get her dancing up to speed. The production closed on November 21, 1951; the movie was previewed in late December and early March and went into general release on April 10, 1952. *Singin' in the Rain* cost MGM $2,540,000 to make, over budget by $620,996. It opened to great reviews and ended up grossing $7,665,000 in its first run—a huge hit by the standards of the day. It was both a critical and a commercial success.

Singin' in the Rain does what musicals are supposed to do. This doesn't make it the best musical ever made, although many would argue that it is. It just makes it a successful one in all areas of production. To solve the problem of letting the audience know it's in for a show where people will sing and dance, it first shows Debbie Reynolds, Gene Kelly, and Donald O'Connor (attired in yellow rain slickers, rubber boots, and carrying big black umbrellas) singing the title song cheerfully as they walk toward the audience. Only then does the film's title appear onscreen: *Singin' in the Rain*. You're hearing it, you're seeing it, and it's all about musical performance. The audience was told in advance.

The integration between the story and the music is exemplary. *Singin' in the Rain* is a satire in which musical numbers are not only wedded smoothly into the plot but also further the theme: the mishaps of the transition to sound for both actors and technicians. It's a film about film history, and its musical numbers comply. "Make 'Em Laugh," with Donald O'Connor doing an amazing tour de force of slapstick dancing, is about the violence of American silent comedy. "Moses Supposes" is like a Marx Brothers routine set to music. "You Were Meant for Me" is a gentle, loving self-parody of typical love duets in movies, showing all the props used and how audiences are manipulated by them. "Beautiful Girl" is a tribute to a Busby Berkeley 1930s number, and "Good Morning" uses an old song as a setting for an imaginatively choreographed tap number that displays several different

types of movie dancing (including a little musical shout-out to *An American in Paris*, the previous Freed unit hit). "Broadway Melody" (which contains "Broadway Rhythm" and a Kelly-Charisse surreal pas de deux) is itself a miniature movie musical, a film within a film. "Would You" takes place in a dubbing booth, showing how Reynolds's voice will replace Jean Hagen's on film. All the numbers are about movies except "All I Do Is Dream of You" (when Reynolds jumps out of a cake) and the title tune.

The art of the movie musical—the demonstration that the genre must be lifted off the page of the screenplay—can be illustrated by *Singin' in the Rain*'s title number. It's possible that Gene Kelly's puddle splash may be the most widely recognized of any Hollywood musical performance. Everyone knows the "Singin' in the Rain" dance. All you have to do is hum a little

Three stars havin' a good mornin': Donald O'Connor, Debbie Reynolds, and Gene Kelly in *Singin' in the Rain*

"doo do do do, do do do do do" and everyone smiles, recognizing the familiar intro refrain. The script for this scene says:

> *Don brings Kathy home in a taxi, they kiss, she tells him to be careful not to get too wet, he's a big star now.*
>
> KATHY: This California dew is a little heavier than usual tonight.
> DON: Really? From where I stand the sun is shining all over the place.
>
> *They kiss again, Don holding his umbrella over them. As Kathy goes in Don looks up at the rain, motions the cab to drive off, closes his umbrella, starts strolling and singing. Don dances in the wet street. Then he notices a policeman eyeing him with suspicion, collects himself and strolls off.*

The key words in the script are: "Don dances in the wet street." Six words: Don-dances-in-the-wet-street. Onscreen, these six words become four minutes of song and dance that define Gene Kelly and are often used to define the entire Hollywood original musical. The rain dance: so easy, so relaxed, so happy and emotional, so simple. Just a little "Don dances in the wet street" moment on film.

But what did it take to put it up there? Experts in many areas had to work together to design, plan, compose, shoot, edit, perform, sew, light, choreograph, and make rain. And in the end, what might seem to be just a little dance is cleverly created to present a man in love, acting silly because he's happy, playing in puddles like a kid, rushing out into the street, a great coordination of performance and technology in sync. What is supposed to take place at night, in a chilly rain, is grounded in gray and black, but the frame is also filled with warm touches of color that speak to what Don feels: his reddish shoes, the red fire hydrant, the shop windows, lit with yellow lights, the red alarm box. It's a cold, gray street in the rain and a guy with an umbrella, but the detailed decor in each carefully designed store window is colorful, suggesting warmth and happiness, his inner state. The camera moves with him, around him, toward him, away from him, and the viewer finds Kelly's exhilaration in that movement and shares in it. When he turns a corner and jumps up onto a lamppost, it's just a little leap—we've seen Kelly go higher—but with the music lifting and the camera watching, it's as if he soared into the air. The movie, with all its technology, but especially with its music, lifts a viewer up there, too. That's what musicals do, and that's why they're hard to make.

In the most unpretentious way possible, *Singin' in the Rain* gives an audience the playing levels necessary for a good musical: carefully established reality and unreality. It tells a story about people who are in the business of moviemaking, opening up on a glamorous Hollywood movie premiere in the mid-to-late 1920s, where a great star (Kelly) tells an interviewer his "life story." He narrates the tale of his world of music lessons, culture, serious dramatic goals, and "dignity, always dignity." As he talks, the audience is shown something totally different. He was a tough little poor kid. He and his pal (O'Connor) snuck into movies and bars, grew up to play cheap vaudeville theaters, started in movies by doing slapstick and western stunts. This combination of pompous narration and undercutting visuals is a big joke in the very first sequence. It's a truth-revealing flashback that includes a musical number showing O'Connor and Kelly doing a fabulous tap routine to "Fit as a Fiddle," wearing cheap green plaid suits. The scene presents two levels, an outer truth that is revealed to be false by the inner

Gene Kelly and Cyd Charisse heat up the screen in the "Broadway Melody" finale number in *Singin' in the Rain.*

one, but while taking something away, at the same time giving back something: musical performance.

The opening accomplishes the goal of setting an audience up for a musical in a sly and subtle manner, but it's also very funny as it shows how people who make movies create false publicity about themselves. Don Lockwood (Kelly) is a low-class scrambler, not a legit actor, and Lina Lamont (Jean Hagen) can't even talk—and she's stupid and venal. An audience meets these characters in full regalia as the fakes they are, lying to their fans openly at a premiere. This is their working world. The opening sets the comedy tone, establishes sympathy for the lead, reveals his leading lady as a phony, shows the audience that the hero is trapped in a world in which he also needs to be a phony to endure, and still makes audiences laugh. Most importantly, it continues the musical universe already shown in the credits. It's a guidebook for how the movie will work. When Kelly and O'Connor do the fast-paced, comedic "Fit as a Fiddle," they own the screen and the story and the music. An audience forgives Kelly for his hypocrisy—and it's the dance that makes them do it.

As the film progresses, real and unreal are clearly defined, with an easy transition between them: first, there's the real world in which people make movies for a living and create false publicity about themselves and pretend they can talk when they can't; second, there's the world they work in, where they're creating those fantasies and photographing them, so the audience can watch the unreal getting made; third: there's a movie within a movie, in which the made thing is projected on the screen as part of the movie. The movie lays it out: this is where these people are real people; this is where they manufacture unreality for a living; this is the unreality they manufacture and create. It's a real road map for musicals, with plenty of time for the transitions and plenty of reassurance about why people might be singing and dancing. No wonder people who don't like musicals like *Singin' in the Rain*. It's safe. And it's simple.

Vincente Minnelli and Gene Kelly

The business men of Hollywood—and the creative artists—finally and fully arrived at the understanding that the challenge of the musical, as it evolved and grew and deepened and varied itself, was for a film (under the leadership of a director, working with all the collaborators) to find a way to resolve its apparent violation of realistic conventions. This put the director of a musical in a difficult position. Musicals, not unlike horror films and sci-fi movies, have to make people accept as real something they know isn't real: zombies are outside on our lawn, and they're hungry, or we're stuck on Mars because the spaceship just broke down. The zombies and the spaceship are easier for audiences to live with than people singing and dancing because an audience sees people facing zombies and broken equipment exactly the way they themselves would: in horror and with an urge to go home. There's emotional verification: viewers know they get scared and they know their equipment breaks down. What they also know is they don't sing and dance about it.

Directors of musical films had to find a way to aid an audience in accepting musical performance as a natural and welcome part of the whole. And they had to find a way to smoothly move an audience out of a nonmusical world into a musical one. Where is real space, and where is musical space, and how do you get from one to the other? And why does it matter? These are decisions a director must make, and there's no formula for doing it the same way every time. There are script-related ways to move in and out (a line of dialogue, a line of the song spoken to start) and sound ways (bringing the up-and-coming music in under a conversation) and purely cinematic ways (a cut, a dissolve, a camera movement). A director has to find the right one so an audience accepts, and then enjoys. A successful musical has to establish musical spaces, create and use performance arenas, transform a story into a musical universe, and provide an audience with suitable transitions from one to another.

Vincente Minnelli became one of the great innovators in musicals regarding these issues. Nobody ever understood them any better than he did. (He was also a master director of melodramas and comedies.) Minnelli was a visual artist. His films have wit and charm and beauty, but they also have cinematic style. His ability just to *decorate*, make everything in the frame look right, look beautiful, look appropriate and complementary to other things inside it, was unparalleled. He was one of the few directors who could develop his own personal vision in musicals, a difficult genre for a director because there is no more collaborative genre, none more dependent on the talents of so many others to succeed. (If ever there was an anti-auteur genre, it's the musical.)

Minnelli was born into show business, his father a violinist and his mother a French-Canadian actress. He toured with them until he was eight years old. By the time he was sixteen he was designing costumes and scenery for burlesque, and eventually he became an art director at Radio City Music Hall. He worked on Broadway, and arrived in Hollywood in 1937. This original trip to Hollywood took him to Paramount Pictures, where he'd been hired to become a producer of musicals. Nothing he tried to do panned out, and he's credited with only one major musical moment from this period—the bizarro "Public Melody No. 1" number featuring Martha Raye and Louis Armstrong in a movie directed by Raoul Walsh, 1937's *Artists and Models*. (When I once asked Walsh about how he approached directing the musical performances in his musicals, he told me, "I went outside and smoked a cigarette until they were over with.") After a fruitful return to Broadway, Minnelli came back to Hollywood for good and began directing movies in early 1940 at MGM; his name is synonymous not only with MGM, but also with the Freed unit. His movies, whether comic, dramatic, or musical, share common characteristics. His filmed universe was one of fantasy and reality mixed, of dreams and deceptions, and of a decor that is always carefully researched, designed, and executed with the purpose not only of being rewarding in and of itself, but also of defining character and setting. Minnelli's sensitivity and background were made for musicals, since he had no qualms about making movies set in an unreal world. As he grew in experience, he became a director who gave substance to artistic dreams through color, design, camera movement, and cutting. He is a major force in the advancement of the musical genre who worked well with both Gene Kelly and Fred Astaire—and worked equally well without either of them to bolster his musical-performance vision (as in *Gigi*, which won nine Oscars).

Minnelli, much like Orson Welles at RKO, had the run of the studio to poke around and learn about filmmaking. His talents were often used without his receiving credit in those early days—it was he who supposedly suggested the "all fruit orchestra" in which pears, apples, etc. become musicians who play "Our Love Affair" in the Rooney/Garland *Strike Up the Band*. Minnelli also directed musical numbers for the adaptation of Cole Porter's *Panama Hattie* (1942), particularly Lena Horne's rendering of "Just One of Those Things," and did Horne's "Honeysuckle Rose" in *Thousands Cheer*. In 1943, however, he finally directed his first feature musical, *Cabin in the Sky* starring Horne, Ethel Waters, Eddie "Rochester" Anderson, Rex Ingram, Louis Armstrong, the Duke Ellington Orchestra, and John W. Bubbles (John Sublett). He took over direction of *I Dood It* (1943), with Red Skelton, but was not responsible for all the numbers. No one paid much attention anyway, because his next film was the guarantee

that he would become a major force in the Freed unit: *Meet Me in St. Louis* in 1944.

Meet Me in St. Louis, as we have seen, showed that Minnelli could create a world in which music was natural, a world in which characters flowed easily from singing or dancing to not singing or dancing without any rupture in the audience's sense of honesty. The film was a lovely mixture of musical expression, nostalgic family life, and comic interludes. It also contained a subjective presentation in which child actress Margaret O'Brien experienced the terror—delicious terror—of Halloween. This episode is somewhat like a musical number—it's a few moments in which one character (O'Brien's Tootie) leaves an established reality and experiences a different level, which is that of a horror film. The skill to direct such a transition is the same one that Minnelli would use for musical performances in future films.

Only about one third of Minnelli's MGM films were musicals, but those films are the ones most closely associated with him. Before he directed Gene Kelly in a full narrative movie he made two musicals with Fred

Vincente Minnelli's first solo credit as director for a complete musical feature, *Cabin in the Sky*, with Ethel Waters, Eddie "Rochester" Anderson, John W. Bubbles, and Lena Horne

Astaire: *Yolanda and the Thief* in 1945 and *Ziegfeld Follies*, which was shot in 1944 and not released until 1946. Both are of importance to the history of musicals because even before he worked with Kelly, Minnelli had created significant and lengthy film ballets.

In working at the Freed unit, Minnelli learned to master the two basics of musical presentation: the backstage or "real" (*The Band Wagon*, 1953) and in *Yolanda* the "fantasy." *The Band Wagon* opens with an auction scene, but before that auction takes place a viewer sees a familiar image: the top hat and cane universally associated with Astaire's years with Ginger Rogers. An audience can easily absorb this clever visual establishment of a layered concept: Astaire the actor/dancer, familiarly associated with his trademark props, will be placed *inside* a story in which Astaire will play actor/dancer "Tony Hunter," who is not Fred Astaire but *is* Fred Astaire. Astaire will be playing a character based on the audience's knowledge of his movie past, but since that character's career has collapsed, and since Astaire's career has very definitely not collapsed (he's the star of the movie), the character is based only on his image.

The musical has suddenly become arty! Intuition and instinct are replaced by "self-reflexivity." *The Band Wagon*, an entertainment, opens with a subtle statement that asks the audience to participate in a shared conspiracy, an agreement that we're all going to sit down and watch Fred Astaire be Fred Astaire, and to accept that the movie will have levels of role playing and theatricality. The opening says directly that we should accept what we see as conveniently not realistic, and it'll be okay, because it has a relationship to something we *do* know as real—old Fred Astaire movies, which, of course, were not real in the first place, only they *were* because they were on the screen. Now we can all feel very sophisticated. The good news is that no one has to analyze *The Band Wagon* this way—it can just be enjoyed for Fred Astaire, always a genius no matter what else is happening.

The Band Wagon will, in the end, be a musical about how entertainment (popular art) can triumph over the pretentious—always welcome news—but it's also a justification for the Hollywood musical. It neatly disposes of the problem of why people are singing and dancing by providing a logical context for all its numbers: they're being rehearsed or performed for a live audience within the plot . . . or they're being performed by people we know (and accept) as competent musical performers who do it for a living. Whenever a character (or characters) performs music outside the theater context, that number is given a very logical narrative explanation. For instance, Astaire and Cyd Charisse aren't sure if they can reconcile their two dance styles (Broadway and ballet). They go to Central Park to try it out, finding a little dance pavilion with live music, and they dance privately, alone in the park, to the beautiful "Dancing in the Dark." The music is explained, the space is explained, their motivation is explained—and it's all directly linked to their jobs as dancers. In addition to "Dancing in the Dark," there are three other dances that lie outside this explanation: Astaire's "By Myself," his dance to "A Shine on Your Shoes" in an arcade, and "That's Entertainment," featuring Astaire, Jack Buchanan, Oscar Levant, and Nanette Fabray.

Jack Buchanan, Fred Astaire, Nanette Fabray, and Oscar Levant define "That's Entertainment" in *The Band Wagon*.

"By Myself" is the first full musical performance of the film, done by Fred Astaire after his arrival on the train to New York from Hollywood. He declares his need to walk and just see the world in which he first found success, the Forty-Second Street theater district. As he moves off from the train, walking along its length, smoking a cigarette, he goes into musical-performance mode. For no reason—except, of course, that he's Fred Astaire pretending to be Tony Hunter, which has already been clearly established. Astaire does not dance this number; he walks it. It is, in addition, almost not sung, he semi-talks it. Astaire walks and talks about himself, explains himself, shows an audience himself. The film has barely begun and

Cyd Charisse shows Fred Astaire who's boss as they dance to Michael Kidd's choreography for the satiric ballet "The Girl Hunt" in *The Band Wagon*.

we have a full characterization presented through musical performance. Why does an audience accept this? Tony Hunter is a singer/dancer, and Fred Astaire is a singer/dancer. We know this is Astaire's natural behavior. He always sings and dances on film, so why not this time? Why not now? His character is isolated from the "reality" of the film. He walks and talks and sings and explains that he has no relation to the rest of the world as he moves forward. He's alone, by himself; and if there's one thing a musical audience knows, it's that Fred Astaire is in a class by himself.

After Astaire finishes "By Myself," he enters a penny arcade and does a complicated dance routine that completely violates the backstage idea ("A Shine on Your Shoes"). However, the movie has just brought an audience through natural musical performance successfully, and will now cleverly flow the acceptance that's been earned into a new arena. The arcade is a staged area, like a performance space. It will never be seen in the movie again. It's an unreality defined by its artful design and its purpose. It is a place to play, and thus, why not a place to sing and dance? Viewer psychology accepts this arena as a staged area for musical performance and accepts Fred Astaire performing within its artificiality.

After this double-number opening, *The Band Wagon* can pretty much get away with anything. It tells a story about a group of people who have a *need* to put on a show—i.e. to do musical numbers. They need to find places to perform music. The story sets up the problem of the musical film as its own problem, and resolves it through the cooperation of the audience, who buy into it. The movie will culminate with the amusingly original "The Girl Hunt" ballet. It is a miniature movie, as much a piece of cinema as it is a ballet. It achieves itself through cutting, camera movement, traveling through time and space, and genre reference. It is a *movie* ballet, incapable of being done on a Broadway stage, where it is allegedly taking place. Shades of Busby Berkeley!

The Band Wagon was not a musical thrown together swiftly to meet a deadline. It had a long rehearsal period, six weeks, and there was nothing improvisational or accidental about it. It cost $2,169,120 to film (with $314,475 going to the "Girl Hunt" ballet alone) but grossed $5,655,505. It has three very strong and separate musical influences: Minnelli, Astaire, and choreographer Michael Kidd. (And there is a fourth: British music-hall and theater star Jack Buchanan, a very compelling figure onscreen.) There is no stylistic chaos, however. All have equal opportunity. Minnelli's influence is felt in "A Shine on Your Shoes," with its complex decor and noise and crowds. The setting is one of Minnelli's design triumphs: the penny arcade of our dreams, full of unusual toys and selling hot dogs! The dance grows organically out of Astaire's response to the overwhelming sensory input of Forty-Second Street. Astaire's own insistence on keeping the camera tight on his dancing and respectful of the emotional feeling of any dance is evident in "By Myself" and especially in "Dancing in the Dark" and the elegant "I Guess I'll Have to Change My Plan," which he and Buchanan perform with great charm. Kidd's choreography, with its rambunctiousness and high energy, is well represented by "The Girl Hunt." This combination of different, very defined and individualistic talents could have caused tension, but it didn't. Astaire had never danced in the style of Kidd previously, but he was open and willing, and allegedly very fond of this "Girl Hunt" ballet. *The Band Wagon* illustrates the Freed unit's ability to turn out a hit musical with top-notch talent, and do it harmoniously.

Yolanda and the Thief is a different matter. It's marred by a silly story: naive Lucille Bremer believes Fred Astaire is her guardian angel (for real), and he uses that belief to try to con her out of her considerable fortune. Bremer looks too mature and too sophisticated to believe anything so nonsensical, and Astaire looks dubious about the premise. The movie is set in a fictitious South American country (with llamas) called Patria, and there isn't enough music that works to make anyone want to forgive the writers. The songs are not outstanding (written by Freed and Harry Warren), and Astaire doesn't dance enough. On the positive side, the Technicolor is beautiful, the sets and costumes are original and imaginative, and Mildred Natwick is funny as Bremer's comic aunt. *Yolanda and the Thief* has its fans, but almost everyone is aware that the film, which was a huge flop, is an experiment gone wrong. What it does have are two significant musical numbers featuring Astaire and Bremer, one of which is historically important.

Lucille Bremer was a "protégée" of Arthur Freed's. A blue-eyed redhead, she looked good in Technicolor, and Freed believed she could be a star. He gave her every opportunity and all the support anyone could need. She was launched in Freed unit musicals in a key role as Judy Garland's older sister in *Meet Me in St. Louis*, but other than a duet with Garland, she had no musical numbers to perform. (She had to be dubbed, anyway.) This was followed by an impressive showcase in *Ziegfeld Follies*. She was paired with Astaire in two extended dances: a stunningly produced and costumed story ballet to "Limehouse Blues," in which the dance takes place in Astaire's mind, and a romantic tale of a jewel thief at a lavish ball, set to the lovely song "This Heart of Mine." Bremer is not one of Astaire's best partners, but these duets are relevant in film history because they are both "ballet" numbers which predate *On the Town* and *An American in Paris*. Since Bremer had already danced with Astaire and survived, *Yolanda and the Thief*, her next musical, was planned as her elevation to stardom. The trailer released with the movie clearly states that "Bremer rises to stardom" in the movie. She didn't, and after a few more nonmusical films, not at MGM, she retired from show business.

Bremer's dancing isn't sharply delineated like Astaire's, and she's not flexible like Rogers or sensuous like Hayworth. She stays with him, however, and he looks happy to be whirling her about. Bremer has a slight sense of reserve about her, and the mark of the Astaire duet with a female dancer is that his partner gives in to him completely. Astaire was the choreographic seducer; his partners had to enter his world of dance-floor magic and surrender . . . at which point they would become far better dancers than they

had ever imagined possible: Astaire lifted them into his realm. But Bremer doesn't quite go there—even if her costumes do.

Yolanda and the Thief's importance lies in its two main dances: one is the happy "Coffee Time," done to an unusual 5/4 rhythmic Latin beat, with a spectacular setting on an optically undulating floor (designed to emulate sidewalks in Rio). The other is a surrealistic ballet that runs between ten and twelve minutes and uses cinema to deceive. In the plot, Astaire has begun to worry about what he's doing to heiress Bremer, and as he prepares for bed (in fetching silk pajamas), he looks concerned and distracted. He puts out his light, and his face remains worried in the semidarkness. The camera moves from him, rising up and away in a graceful arc, then turning toward an open window. Without a cut, the camera moves past the window and begins to turn down, moving toward a water glass Astaire left on a table. The glass contains a red carnation Bremer gave him when he was convincing her he was the embodiment of her guardian angel. Suddenly, Astaire's

Lucille Bremer, as a naive convent girl by way of the Freed unit, meets her "guardian angel," Fred Astaire, in one of MGM's musical failures (which featured an extended ballet by Eugene Loring), *Yolanda and the Thief.*

hand enters the frame and plucks the carnation out of the glass. He then turns and walks to the other window in the room, the one that looks out on the crowded streets. Clearly restless, he goes to his closet and takes out clothes, beginning to dress. A dissolve shows him fully dressed and exiting the small hotel. As he moves into the street, he puts the carnation in the lapel of his white suit, then moves through the crowded marketplace in which, earlier in the film, a bum called out to him, asking for a cigarette. As Astaire moves into this space, which was clearly established earlier in the film, the same derelict calls out, "Have you got an American cigarette?" Astaire goes to him. The man takes the cigarette and holds it up to be lit, but a third arm reaches out from under the armpit of his second arm, repeating the action . . . and then comes a fourth arm, a fifth arm, a sixth. Increasingly surprised, Astaire lights them all. The appearance of the third arm is the first moment an audience is allowed to understand that all the action since Astaire reached for the carnation has been a dream. It's a startling revelation, and a subtle one. Everything up until the multi-armed smoker is totally "realistic" as previously established in the movie. A viewer has been tricked into accepting a relocation into a musical dream world.

Astaire moves into a dance. Surrounded by children as he tries to leave the square, he throws a coin into their group to distract them. As he moves off, a shower of gold coins falls on him—the coins will define the world he enters, a mark of separation, but also a mark of his greed: a visual metaphor. As he moves forward from the children, he also moves up a small incline. The lighting changes, more gold coins rain down on him, and all the people in the busy square disappear. A slow, rhythmic beat begins, and a *misterioso* quality emerges. Astaire was always a master of the mysterious mood in dance; his body control made it possible for him to convey tension to an audience without becoming stiff or rigid. His is the tension of anticipation, but also of mystery: What lies ahead? Where am I? Why? The subtle rhythmic beat suggests "the other" is somewhere in this world, and suddenly it appears: a yellow-and-brown brick road which he can dance/follow farther into a surrealistic landscape.

As Astaire dances into this world, a chorus of washerwomen appears. These washerwomen are obviously the night crew from *Vogue* magazine. They're wearing the goosed-up Latin peasant design that appealed to Minnelli during this period—the costumes for *The Pirate* have a similar quality. The "otherness" of this opening part of the dance is reflected in the soundtrack; there's percussion—a ratchet-and-wood-sticks beat—that creates anticipation, enticement, and excitement. The dance draws a viewer into an unexpectedness. The women capture Astaire in fabric, trapping him, and eventually he sees a large pool of water. Out of the pool rises an apparition that a viewer knows is Bremer, although she's wrapped head to toe, face covered, with golden cloth that's blowing in the wind, rising above and around her. She walks from the pool, passing Astaire, who, of course, follows. She stands awaiting him, and he comes to her, slowly unwrapping each layer of fabric, taking a little time between each long swath. Underneath, Bremer is clad in a flowing dress enhanced by the ballet's motif: gold coins. (This dress is said to have cost $1,500 to make, a lot of money in those days, and worth every penny.) When Astaire moves Bremer away from the water and to a private space, and slowly, beautifully unwraps her, they dance to the beat of Latin music. It's utterly entrancing, highly visual, full of gold coins and gold images, and both literally meaningful (she's rich) and beautiful (he wants her now for more than her money). Then it all falls apart. Lucille Bremer (dubbed) begins to sing "Will You Marry Me?" The mood and tone of the piece fall to earth with a resounding thud. To put it bluntly, the song is seriously dumb, and changes the possibility of the dance from something mysterious and rather beautiful to something downright foolish and pretentious. The presentation never recovers its original haunting, dreamlike aura. It goes berserk, involving jockeys, binoculars, derby hats, and a literal interpretation (Astaire losing his money at the racetrack) that a third-grader could understand. A group of Furies take hold of Astaire. (These are the Furies who have green, yellow, and blue hats, elbow-length satin gloves, and high-heeled shoes.) The choreography for Astaire and Bremer becomes more about steps than about mood, and takes on a Broadway-show quality. As the ballet descends into failure, no dust falls on Fred Astaire. As always, he maintains his own standard of detached elegance. In the end, the Furies drag him away, capturing him again in long pieces of fabric, and a dissolve takes viewers back to "reality" as Astaire, tangled in his bedclothes, wakes up. This dream ballet was a nightmare (in more ways than intended).*

---

* The choreography is by Eugene Loring. In the 1940s, movies often used a Daliesque design to present "dream sequences" that were a pseudo-Freudian visualization. There were whole movies, such as *The 5,000 Fingers of Dr. T,* that used the conceit, and spectacular sequences such as Hitchcock's Dali-designed dreams in his thriller *Spellbound. Yolanda* was released three years prior to Britain's *The Red Shoes* (a Powell-Pressburger film), which is often cited as a landmark in its integration of ballet dancing into a movie story.

Dance sequences that used the "It's all a dream" idea appeared in many movies, including *Her Highness and the Bellboy*, with Hedy Lamar and June Allyson, and *Diamond Horseshoe*, with Betty Grable. Audiences did not take to the idea and seldom responded well, but filmmakers loved the freedom to create outside any established reality, and *Yolanda and the Thief*'s dream-sequence ballet was a major effort in that direction. Having a movie character dream of singing and dancing made an easy connection to viewers for whom sitting in the dark imagining themselves doing the same thing was neither unfamiliar nor uncomfortable. And the Freudian dream (going "into the head" of a sleeping character) was not the only musical way of going into "unreality." It was also fairly common to picture the thoughts and imaginings of a character who was awake, taking the audience "into the head" of an alert person who was "thinking." For instance, an awake Marion Davies pictures herself performing with Bing Crosby in *Going Hollywood*, and Eleanor Powell sits in an empty theater in *Broadway Melody of 1936*, as her "ghost" self leaves her body and goes up on stage, singing "You Are My Lucky Star." She then becomes a real person, not a ghost figure, and is joined by a full orchestra in the pit and a costumed line of chorus boys on stage. They perform to "Lucky Star" in a designed universe of crystal, cellophane, and twinkling lights. The extended number ends with the sight of an applauding audience—all of whom disappear, leaving Powell once again sitting alone in the theater.*

The "idea" dances and songs were the first stirrings of the business trying to become artistic, trying to release the musical performance from the need for explanation and plot justification. They reveal the desire for integration, and for a world in which it was acceptable for men and women to sing and dance as they lived. They are yearning for a true musical world. Ironically, the business was worried about having to apologize or explain to an audience *why* humans were tapping and twirling and singing when that was what the audience had come to the musical for in the first place. Soon enough, it would become commonplace for sailors and librarians and fashion photographers and farm girls to just do it—just sing and dance. A leading proponent of "just do it," no matter who the character might be, was Gene Kelly.

* An amusing variation of the idea occurs in *Singin' in the Rain*. Donald O'Connor and Gene Kelly tell Millard Mitchell their idea for what appears onscreen as the "Broadway Melody" number. In a reflexive joke, when the number finishes and the audience is returned to Mitchell, listening, he says, "I can't quite visualize it. I'll have to see it on film first."

Eugene Curran Kelly was a Pittsburgh boy born into an Irish-American family in 1912. Ambitious, bright, and talented, he arrived in New York City at the age of twenty-six, a college graduate, an experienced performer, and the owner of a successful dance school. Within a rapid three years, he had made theater history in three ways: as an actor in William Saroyan's

The Time of Your Life (playing Harry the hoofer); as the musical lead in the groundbreaking musical adaptation of John O'Hara's *Pal Joey,* in which he played the antiheroic title role; and as a choreographer for the Broadway hit *Best Foot Forward.* This tripart talent made him a perfect candidate for Hollywood stardom, and in 1940 he arrived, under contract at first to David O. Selznick, who would soon enough sell him to MGM, the studio Kelly was born to thrive in. Kelly was a driving force in the idea of bringing respect for American dance and dancers through the motion picture. He took dance seriously, and he wanted to lift the musical form upward into art, or at least to push it as far as possible in terms of incorporating new ideas.

Gene Kelly's MGM musical debut, with partner and megastar Judy Garland—a good way to begin—in *For Me and My Gal*

Kelly's first MGM musical was for the Freed unit. *For Me and My Gal* was a starring vehicle for the newly mature and established talent of Judy Garland. Her main costar was to be the reliable George Murphy, under contract to MGM and a handsome, easygoing hoofer who could also sing a little. Murphy was well liked both on- and offscreen, and his relaxed charm was perfect for the role of leading man who wasn't supposed to interfere with the focus on Garland. Murphy had already supported other new stars, such as Lana Turner in the 1940 musical *Two Girls on Broadway,* and played the rejected-suitor role in the Fred Astaire/Eleanor Powell hit *Broadway Melody of 1940.* The role of the heartless (and ruthlessly ambitious) man who would marry Garland out from under Murphy was a plum given to Kelly, whose musical ability combined with Garland's charisma to make a strong onscreen team. When they do their first number—the title tune—in a little café, they are allegedly doing an improv. The naturalness with which they sing and dance is the sort of magic that can't be predicted, but that's immediately obvious to an audience. Kelly moves Garland around the space of the restaurant, in among the tables and alongside the countertop, with great style and grace. She falls in beside him as if she's found herself a home. Understanding what a major opportunity he'd been given, Kelly gave everything he could to the film. MGM saw his hard work and his potential and upped the ante on his role. Kelly's character ends up getting back the girl he's married after losing her—even though original test audiences still felt Murphy should get her in the end. MGM always knew star material when they saw it, and Murphy's ease was trumped by Kelly's ease. Kelly also had bite; Murphy only had ease.

MGM did not overlook Kelly in its advertising. A full-page ad selling *For Me and My Gal* in the December 1942 *Hollywood* magazine has a photograph of Judy Garland inside a big red star, wearing her costume from the "Ballin' the Jack" number from the movie. The copy says, "MGM's own Ziegfeld Girl Goes To Town in a musical . . . Blazing With Bigness." In small type below are the names of Garland's costars: George Murphy, Gene Kelly, Marta Eggerth, and Ben Blue, all treated equally. The monthly column allegedly written by "Leo the Lion" says Kelly is "a find." He's "a heel with a heart." A short review in another section of the magazine says that "it's not necessary to predict a future for Gene Kelly. His future is here."

Kelly's really lofty dance ambitions were seen early in his career, and not at MGM. Loaned to Columbia Pictures for a film to showcase the studio's hot property Rita Hayworth, Kelly found himself singing and dancing in

Cover Girl (1944). It says a lot about him that he could quietly and competently get himself noticed—and on his own terms—in this vehicle built to deify the gorgeous Hayworth. Kelly moves about confidently, however, no doubt knowing offscreen that this was his best chance to get noticed not only as an actor/singer/dancer, but also in the way he really wanted to be noticed, as a choreographer.

Cover Girl was a Rita Hayworth movie. It also starred Gene Kelly. What no one anticipated is that as the years went by, it would become a Gene Kelly movie that also starred Rita Hayworth. Hayworth's glamour and stardom were huge, and the movie was all about her, her looks, her personality, and her dancing. She officially became a household name with *Cover Girl,* inspiring *Life* to put her on its cover four times, and her studio to allow paper dolls and coloring books bearing her image to be created and sold. She was all over the movie magazines—on covers, in stories about her private life, in fashion photos, in ads for cigarettes, sodas, and facial cream. A photo of her in a seductive nightgown, sitting pertly on a bed, became a GI pinup favorite. *Cover Girl,* as a title, meant Rita Hayworth; it was a musical designed to let moviegoers watch her character (named Rusty) be turned into a supermodel, with a little musical fun thrown in, all of it linked directly to her, the home-studio contract player at Columbia Pictures. And yet, there *was* Gene Kelly. MGM had not yet figured out exactly what to do with him, so Kelly brought with him his dance assistant, Stanley Donen, and with everyone concentrating on Hayworth, the two of them began to develop *Cover Girl* into the kind of musical presentation that interested *them.* The result was Hayworth and Kelly costarring effectively in what became one of the most commercially and critically successful of wartime musical movies.

Cover Girl has a Jerome Kern score (with lyrics by Ira Gershwin, although one song, "Make Way for Tomorrow," also had the help of Yip Harburg). When Kelly and Hayworth sing and dance to the beautiful "Long Ago and Far Away" (with Hayworth dubbed by Martha Mears), it's the beginning of an audience understanding that Kelly's dances with his leading ladies would consciously suggest a sexier relationship than Astaire's. Kelly's eyes reflect desire when he looks at Hayworth, and when the two come together physically, swaying slightly so that their bodies can touch, the heat—particularly considering Hayworth's sensuous quality—is observable. Hayworth was promoted as a sex object in Hollywood, but she could really dance, and no one ever thought otherwise. Hayworth keeps up with no trouble. Her famous run down a seemingly five-mile ramp, a strapless golden dress blowing out behind her, while her "Cover Girl" music plays, became iconic.

Two numbers showcase Kelly's choreography. The first is "Make Way for Tomorrow," which he dances with Hayworth and the comedy relief, Phil Silvers, and the second is when he partners himself in a spectacular four-minute routine, the "Alter Ego" dance. Kelly, Hayworth, and Silvers dance out of a waterfront diner together and do an exuberant romp through the streets, singing "Make Way for Tomorrow" with an infectious energy. Their pep zings an audience awake. Kelly dances as if he's been unleashed. The trio's routine involved interaction with props (faking rowing a boat) as well as with character actors (Jack Norton, playing his usual shtick as a drunk). Their dance is one of the hallmarks of how musicals would mature and change in the 1940s. Both audiences and critics loved the dance, and comedian Silvers was proud of his participation in it, since he wasn't a trained dancer. (Tom Santopietro's *Sinatra in Hollywood* reports that a

Cover Girl, the movie that made a true star out of Kelly, was not made at MGM, but at Columbia Pictures with Kelly (left), Phil Silvers (center), and Rita Hayworth (right). The three romp the streets demanding everyone "Make Way for Tomorrow."

friend remarked to Silvers that he didn't know Phil was a dancer. "I'm not," Silvers replied. "Kelly hypnotized me." Sinatra, similarly complimented on his dancing with Kelly, said, "It was Gene who saw me through it." Kelly could will people to dance or browbeat them into it, but he had also been a dance teacher and knew how to guide his "pupils.")

As delightful as "Make Way for Tomorrow" was—and Kelly and Hayworth also tear it up in Kelly's fast-paced "Put Me to the Test"—the high point of *Cover Girl* for Kelly's career and reputation was the "Alter Ego Dance." "It was the most difficult thing I've ever done," Kelly said later, "and I wouldn't want to have to do it again." The dance is set up by the lonely and dejected Kelly, having lost Hayworth, walking in the streets, stopping to talk to his reflection in a plate-glass window, and then beginning to dance with himself when "he" comes down out of the window into the street. This was a technically difficult task. Kelly would do the dance, be photographed, and then have to do it a second time, carefully matching his first take. He had to be sure to put his foot on the sound stage exactly where it needed to be in relation to his other self, using spots marked with chalk and tape. The soundtrack of dubbed dancing steps also had to match, so that the two images could be optically joined in editing. For rehearsals, Donen danced with Kelly, so the look and feel of the routine could be worked out. Each man would later claim the dance was his creation, but most likely it was a working collaboration to which each contributed. (We'll never know which one dominated.) Kelly was the higher-ranking person by virtue not only of his stardom, but by the fact he was the one doing the dance and the one who actually did the choreography.* Donen was Kelly's assistant, but he had technical expertise that Kelly didn't have. Whoever is responsible, the dance was a success, and a milestone in both careers. It ended with Kelly heaving a garbage pail into a plate-glass window, destroying the alter ego who had danced in the streets with him so effectively. By supporting Kelly's interests in choreography and his collaboration with Donen, Columbia Pictures made an important contribution to musical history.

Kelly's "Alter Ego Dance" says who he was: a man who wanted to do original choreography *on film*. It is a completely cinematic dance, and couldn't be achieved by a single individual in any other medium. His historical importance is related to his desire to incorporate cinema into his

---

* *Cover Girl*'s credits list "Dance Numbers Staged By Val Raset and Seymour Felix" but Kelly, with Donen as his dance assistant, created the alter-ego number completely separately and on their own off in a corner. Kelly also was allowed to do all his numbers.

work, and to his sense of dance, a three-dimensional art form, having to flatten itself to enter the two-dimensional frame of the motion picture. All his life Kelly worked to reconcile dance and film, and his achievements lie there. As a choreographer, he was a true cinematic innovator. He worked to capture the kinetic force of a flesh-and-blood dancer inside the image, planning the dance so that it could be cut and edited without disturbing a viewer's sense of motion and involvement. He was carrying forward the work of Fred Astaire, whom he deeply admired, Astaire also having cared about dance and the way it was photographed for film. Astaire created dance interludes that exist for all time as pure and beautiful parts of films that are sometimes banal. Kelly wanted to go one step farther, caring about the *total* film and dance's place in it. His approach was more consciously intellectual, and he discussed his thinking about the relationship of the dance and the camera in many interviews. "If the camera is to make any contribution to dance, the focal point must be the pure background, giving the spectator an undistorted and all-encompassing view of dancer and background. To accomplish this, the camera must be made to move with the dancer so the lens becomes the eye of the spectator, your eye." He wanted to do with his body what the actor did with words. He wanted to devise a cinematic language of dance that replaced dialogue and told the audience as they watched what a character thought, felt, was. He strove for perfection, and sometimes the striving showed.

At first, MGM wasn't sure Kelly should *be* a musical star. This seems insane today, but his success onstage in *Pal Joey* was in a role that suggested dramatic ability. He could play a not-so-nice guy, which indicated he might do nonmusical roles. Whether a star with musical ability would actually become a musical star is a topic rarely addressed in musical history. Claudette Colbert could sing, and did so in *The Smiling Lieutenant* and *Zaza*, among other films, but audiences liked her better in comedy or drama. George Raft was a highly skilled dancer of the tango, and even though he became famous with gangster films like *Scarface* (1932), his early years found him appearing in musicals like *Night After Night* with Mae West and *Bolero* (1934) and *Rumba* (1935), two movies that costarred him with Carole Lombard.* In the latter film, most of their dancing was done by

---

* A very young Raft can be seen—unbilled—as Cagney's rival in a dance contest in *Taxi!* (1932). Cagney whirls a fast-stepping Loretta Young around the floor at top speed, while Raft steers his partner with oily confidence. Raft wins.

Veloz and Yolanda, but that was because Lombard was not a trained dancer. In both films, close-ups of their feet were "dubbed," but Raft could actually dance. (He was well known in Hollywood for squiring around women who were great dancers, and when he and Betty Grable were an item in the early 1940s, nightclub audiences loved it when they took to the floor. They were said to be so sensational together that the other dancers would take their seats to watch.) Raft's image as a tough guy eliminated his dancing potential, but he did end up onscreen teaching Jerry Lewis how to do a mean tango (in *The Ladies Man*, 1961). Raft had the deadpan look down flat, and his tiny feet could really move across a dance floor. It's just that audiences didn't want to see him that way.

Audiences *did* want to see Gene Kelly that way. *Cover Girl* changed his fate. The studio understood it not only had a star; it had a *musical* star, and a search was conducted for a story that could become a big Technicolor wartime hit shaped for him. The result was the box-office hit *Anchors Aweigh* (1944) costarring him with the heartthrob of the era, Frank Sinatra, as well as young Dean Stockwell, Kathryn Grayson, Pamela Britton, and José Iturbi.* Kelly was given free rein in planning his musical numbers, and among them is one of his most famous, "The Worry Song," in which he danced with the cartoon figure of Jerry the Mouse. Kelly was aware of Disney's experimentations with mixing live dancers and cartoon figures, and he worked with MGM's own cartoon-department personnel, William Hanna and Joseph Barbera (and Irving G. Reis of optical effects) to create a four-minute routine that moviegoers loved.

Kelly's dance with Jerry reflects his innovative and imaginative approach to dance—most specifically, it marks his understanding that dance on film is a whole new world of physicality. Following a carefully prepared storyboard, Kelly did his own dance, was photographed, and the dance of the cartoon mouse was animated to match him frame by frame. The two figures were then optically linked. The final sequence required over ten thousand painted frames and nearly two months to complete. The dance looks natu-

* Pianist José Iturbi was part of MGM's donation to uplifting America's cultural IQ during the war years. In the early forties, there was a general love affair with the idea of casting classical musicians in movies, and Iturbi glided through a successful Hollywood career with ease. He always wore a look of incredible happiness on his face, combined with a "What's actually going on here, anyway?" quality that kept him slightly detached from the proceedings. He was pretty much plot-proof, acting as if all he knew was that he'd been asked to sit down and play the piano—and he was getting paid for it. Any plot silliness wasn't *his* fault.

Gene Kelly liked to dance with unexpected partners: the animated Jerry the Mouse in *Anchors Aweigh* . . .

ral, real, and it's fun to watch. (Referring to his partner Donen, Kelly said the number "would have been impossible for me without Stanley.") *Anchors Aweigh* earned Kelly a Best Actor nomination—a rarity for a dancer—and became not only a hit, but a fondly remembered one.

Despite his artistic ambitions, there's a bit of recycling going on in Gene Kelly's work. In *Anchors Aweigh,* he and Kathryn Grayson have a private moment of romance on a sound stage. As they stand together near an inactive Spanish hacienda set, he wants to tell her how he feels about her but says the right words only "go with *that* world. If you lived in *that* house, then I could do it." She tells him, "But I *do* live in that house." Kelly goes into a speech about how if she really lived in the world of escapism, she'd be a princess and he'd be a royal bandit and he would come to her and sweep her away. He asks her to look into the empty set, a large, dark space with no lighting. They turn their backs to the audience, and the camera moves from them toward the darkness, so that when the lights come up on the set a romantic dance number takes place, with Grayson on a balcony in white lace, and Kelly in cape, Spanish hat, and a black mask.

It's not Kelly's best routine, as it looks today somewhat like a cheesy dancing school recital effort full of body tension, but it nevertheless has panache. Stardom is written all over it. Kelly was good at Spanish-style dancing, having been taught by Angel Cansino, Rita Hayworth's uncle. Kelly's asking a girl he loves to envision a film he is talking about is later put onscreen literally in the "You Were Meant for Me" number with Debbie Reynolds in *Singin' in the Rain*. Kelly repeated in that film what he had learned: have the man ask his girl to envision something, and put it on the screen for the audience as a musical number. His innovation is to make the creation of the effect the enticement, rather than just show the effect. "You Were Meant for Me" reveals the wind machine and the colored lights. (At the end of the *Anchors Aweigh* dance, he picks up a single rose, thrown down to the dance floor, and as he picks it up, the camera moves to it as a final punctuation. This idea is reused at the end of the *American in Paris* ballet.)

. . . and Frank Sinatra, who became a lifelong friend . . .

Some people will always believe there's more meaning in a leotard than a top hat, but many people do not appreciate Kelly's lofty goals, feeling that his was a misguided attempt to bring art to the masses. His work is labeled as pretentious, and his screen image dismissed as sexist. Close observation shows that there's almost an element of apology in Kelly's work, a sort of "I'm sorry I'm a man and I'm dancing instead of playing football" quality. It's true that Kelly has an off-putting masculinity that seems forced to many

... and himself, in his famous "Alter Ego" duet in *Cover Girl*.

modern moviegoers. His flamboyant, optimistic characters—sailors, guys in loafers, nightclub owners—fit well in their own era, but now seem alien. Kelly's work may appear to people today to be a mockery of masculinity, but in its own day it brought athleticism and a down-to-earth quality to dance. He seemed breezy and ordinary, a self-proclaimed "Brando of dance."* But his particular brand of masculinity was a part of his times. He was trying to gain respect for dance, and his insistent masculinity was part of that attempt.† But in a piece such as his *Slaughter on Tenth Avenue* (from *Words and Music*), his dancing is posturing and his partner, Vera-Ellen, lacks the sexuality or eroticism to

* In the chic and sophisticated 1957 *Les Girls*, Kelly succumbed fully to the idea of himself as Brando, dancing a satire number, "Why Am I So Gone About That Gal?" His partner was Mitzi Gaynor, portraying a roadside restaurant waitress while Kelly enacted the *Wild One* Brando, arriving in leather jacket and boots, accompanied by his motorcycle gang. The movie, directed by George Cukor, was a sort of musical *Rashomon:* three ex-showgirls give three different versions of their experiences with Kelly as they tour together in a troupe called Les Girls.

† In 1958, he wrote, directed, and produced an episode for television's *Omnibus* called "Dancing: A Man's Game," in which he illustrated the link between dancing and other sports. He did a tap dance with boxer Sugar Ray Robinson and danced with skater Dick Button. Baseball's Mickey Mantle and football's Johnny Unitas joined in, and Kelly revealed his deep passion for dancing as well as his natural inclination toward teaching.

humanize the Kelly presence. Together they're almost a satire on sex, despite the superb Richard Rodgers music. And the Kelly choreography is an example of dance narratizing the music. It's a literal interpretation of the sounds and rhythms, creating a story that can be heard as well as seen. Watching some of Kelly's routines reveals his tendency to caricature. He liked doing flashy dances in a Douglas Fairbanks swashbuckling mode. (His ballet in *The Pirate* is admittedly an exception: it's supposed to be a subjective vision of his character from the point of view of the naive Garland.) He liked to dance with children and animated characters. He had the ability to be childlike: jumping and splashing in rainy puddles with the obvious joy of a youngster uninhibited by the need to maintain dignity. His routines were often comic and mocking ("By Strauss" in *An American in Paris*). His characters could be surly, à la Pal Joey, or wolfish and girl-chasing, which was considered charming in World War II. In the end, however, the bottom line of Gene Kelly is that he contributed to the history of dance in a most significant way, mostly through the Arthur Freed production system at MGM.

Arthur Freed is the creative business force that united Vincente Minnelli with Gene Kelly, two very different men. Kelly was wary at first, even though Minnelli was an experienced director and the husband, at the time, of his dear friend Judy Garland. But wariness of anyone else's ability and full confidence in his own was the mark of the work of Gene Kelly. Ultimately, the two very different men forged a productive partnership. Minnelli said in his autobiography that it was "the most intense professional association I've ever had with an actor."

The most important collaboration between Vincente Minnelli and Gene Kelly is undoubtedly *An American in Paris*. In 1951 the five films nominated for the Best Picture Oscar included, besides *American*, four dramas: *A Streetcar Named Desire*, *A Place in the Sun*, *Quo Vadis*, and *Decision Before Dawn*, all of which had distinguished literary antecedents. When *American* won, it was the first musical to become Best Picture since *The Great Ziegfeld* in 1936. It won a total of six awards, and Gene Kelly was given a special statuette in recognition of "his versatility as an actor, singer, director, and dancer, and specifically for his brilliant achievement in the art of choreography on film." These wins were not greeted with huzzahs in all quarters; many were very grumpy indeed that what was considered lightweight fare had triumphed over serious stuff like *Streetcar* and *A Place in the Sun*. Most film historians today, however, see *An American in Paris*, with its box-office

The Oscar-winning landmark musical *An American in Paris* paired Leslie Caron and Gene Kelly in a tender love story that was "here to stay."

success, excellent critical reviews, and official recognition by the Motion Picture Academy, as the true birth of what is called the "art musical." It's definitely an *arty* musical, partly because it's about artists—musicians and painters—but mostly because it has a seventeen-minute ballet. However, it isn't so arty that it isn't fun. It has humor, color, and charm, and at the time of its release it lured Americans to want to visit Paris, and to believe that perhaps they could . . . and certainly they *should*.

An American in Paris came about because Arthur Freed had a simple premise he wanted for a musical, and he told it to writer Alan Jay Lerner: make a movie about an American artist living in Paris, and make sure it uses the music of George Gershwin, especially his tone poem *An American in Paris*. When the finished script reached director Minnelli, he conceived the idea of designing scenes around famous paintings by artists like Utrillo, Dufy, Renoir, and Toulouse-Lautrec. The result was a beautiful-looking musical that captured the imaginations of moviegoers. It lifted Kelly to a new status, and made a star out of its first-time leading lady, Leslie Caron.

An American in Paris is a prime example of the Arthur Freed unit's approach to the integrated movie musical. It opens up in a view of Paris that can be seen as a tribute to the opening of Mamoulian's *Love Me Tonight*. Gene Kelly narrates a discussion of how beautiful the "star called Paris" is and when the camera "hears" his voice, it moves up toward his window, first going to the wrong one, and then finding him. An element of unreality has been immediately established—the leading man is talking directly to the audience, not to others inside the film—and after viewers enter his small room, his dialogue will be accompanied by a sort of pseudo dance as he goes about his morning routine. His narration is a little song and his movements in his tiny space are a little dance. He appears to be musical, and yet he's neither singing nor dancing. But the opening has established the prior musical influence of *Love Me Tonight* (and if an audience doesn't know that, it doesn't matter), and as soon as we join him in his daily life, we will find musical performance after musical performance. It's a perfect setup.

The characters in *An American in Paris* are not all supposed to be professional performers. Georges Guétary plays a music-hall singer/dancer à la Maurice Chevalier (who was originally supposed to play the role), and Oscar Levant is a professional concert pianist who gets gigs only in his own head. Kelly, however, and his leading lady, Caron, are not professionals. Yet they dance, and Kelly also sings. There are two other important characters: Nina Foch as the heiress who is Kelly's patron (and would-be romance) and the city of Paris; neither sings and dances, but Paris is made into a musical space. You can sing in it. You can dance in it. You can fall in love in it. Paris is the character that steals the show in *An American in Paris*.

The Freed unit's accomplishment is on full display in *An American in Paris*. All songs and dances are integrated into the storyline; the spacing of music is appropriate; the execution of each number is highly professional; and the music is Gershwin, which means the best there is. Every number gives its own joy, but has a plot meaning. Leslie Caron is explained by Guétary to Levant through a series of costumes, songs, and dances that reveal his adoration of her, but also reveal the fact that he really doesn't know who she is. What is happening onscreen is supposed to be a little conversation between friends Levant and Guétary. The latter will tell the former about the girl he loves (Caron). They are sitting in front of a framed mirror, and inside the mirror, as the two men disappear, represented by their voices on the soundtrack, Caron dances to the music of Gershwin's "Embraceable You," a song that is flexible in that it can be sweet, sexy, romantic, or jazzy.

The visual presentation in the frame is monochromatic and used to show different sides of Caron's personality, as Guétary describes her through different colors laid over the whole frame. As Guétary talks, Levant says what he thinks, which is a misunderstanding of Guétary's enthusiastic (but blind) oversimplification of her as all things at once. She's sexy, says Levant; no, demure, says Guétary. She's studious; no, fun. She's this and she's that; she's everything . . . but what? As each man makes a decision, Caron dances in the style of that definition, and in a costume that fits it, overlaid with an appropriate and matching color. Thus, through music, three characters are defined, relationships are outlined, and the basis for why Caron and Guétary will not end up together is presented. Plot and character and emotions are all presented through music, with the pleasure of the music and the dance standing on their own at the same time.

Kelly's character is defined as kind, fun-loving, good with children—through music ("By Strauss," "I Got Rhythm"). Levant is presented as comic relief who's an egomaniac by having him play all the instruments in a fantasy of himself performing the Concerto in F—he's even in the audience. (It was funnier when Buster Keaton did it in *The Playhouse*.) Kelly and Levant's friendship is presented through "Tra-la-la," and Guétary is shown as being from another era—and thus, although talented, wrong for Caron—when he does a Ziegfeld number, "I'll Build a Stairway to Paradise," with a chorus of women in feathers and pearls. And, of course, Kelly and Caron fall in love to the music of "Our Love Is Here to Stay."

An American in Paris is the epitome of a musical that knows how to present precise meaning with all its numbers, but the reason it is best remembered today is the seventeen-minute *American in Paris* ballet, which speaks to viewers in terms they can easily understand: it tells a story and reveals inner emotions already established. It confirms prior information, which doesn't diminish its visual impact. The ballet, taking place inside Kelly's head immediately after he believes he's lost Caron, the girl he loves, retells the story of his life in Paris. He is seen to love the stimulation of Paris, with its colors, art, freedom, and European ambience. He is seen to find Leslie Caron, lose her, rediscover her in a flower market, and lose her again. He is seen to be among his GI buddies, doing a Jimmy Cagney / George M. Cohan strut that marks them as American, and they enjoy all that Paris has to offer—and when he finds Caron to dance with again, the two of them dance with joy and then enter a private, bluesy world of sexuality. *Entertainment Weekly* quoted Patricia Ward Kelly, the actor's widow, as saying,

"The sequence is pure lovemaking. Several countries figured it out and that piece was cut because it was considered too risqué." This love scene turns into yet another loss, putting Kelly back where he started. The ballet is much written about, with its influences of art, its Gershwin music, and its choreography, but its narrative is just as important. The power of the colorful ballet arises partly from what precedes it: a black-and-white ball in which color is taken away from a viewer's eye for a period of time, so that when the ballet unfolds, the restoration of color, especially its vivid hues, seems even more powerful and meaningful. It's a visual cleansing of the palate.

The *American in Paris* ballet is not only considered to be the beginning of the musical as an art form; it is also commonly referred to as "the first" bal-

The "hope you guys know what you're doing" seventeen-minute ballet set to Gershwin's "An American in Paris," with Kelly and Caron and troupe

let in a mass-market Hollywood film. As we've seen, ballets *did* occur earlier. The ballets from *The Goldwyn Follies* (by Balanchine), *Ziegfeld Follies*, *Yolanda*, et al., are discounted because movie-goers didn't fully embrace them.* This is typical of film history, in which so much has been lost or forgotten and the need for simplification forgets innovation to settle for "the beginning," which often means popular recognition coupled with financial success. What gave *An American in Paris* the ownership of movie ballet, however, was not just the Oscar for Best Picture, not just the overwhelming critical and commercial success, but also the way the ballet was presented by Kelly and Minnelli. It gave an average American audience, whether familiar with ballet or not, a ballet it could understand. It was a story ballet, although covertly so. An audience could follow it, get inside it, and feel its emotion without lyrics to guide them. They could see it was somehow a retelling of what they had just witnessed about the musical relationship of Leslie Caron and Gene Kelly. It was love, and it was sex, and it was the movies—three things they knew. They didn't have to decide it was also Cinema. It was entertainment as art and art as entertainment. It worked. The success of the *American in Paris* ballet was also due to the insistence of Gene Kelly on presenting dance on film in ways Americans could not only enjoy but respect. Deciding to create a seventeen-minute ballet as a finale to a mass-market musical was a gutsy thing to do, and Kelly's importance to the achievement of the Freed unit cannot be denied.

Although *An American in Paris* is the most famous Minnelli/Kelly collaboration, *The Pirate*, which preceded it, is perhaps the one that best unites their individual talents. Minnelli and Kelly are both at full throttle. Minnelli presents a world of color, camera movement, costumes, crowds, and chaos, all under masterful control in a seaport landscape that is full of movement and character. Kelly is allowed full license to be who he is most comfortable being onscreen: a rogue, a seducer, a con artist. *The Pirate* is a movie that announces itself as "unreal" from the very beginning, with a set of storybook drawings behind the credits, followed by a narration from leading lady Judy Garland as she tells her friends her own lurid imaginary con-

---

* There was also the 1948 British success, Michael Powell and Emeric Pressburger's beautiful *The Red Shoes*, which was actually a story about the world of ballet that incorporated dances fully into its story. The British film business did not fear ballet. It brought moviegoers the balletic Powell-and-Pressburger *Tales of Hoffmann* in 1951; and a 1949 bonbon starring Anna Neagle, *Maytime in Mayfair*, openly labeled one of her numbers a ballet and referred to "choreography" and "choreographer."

ception of the pirate Macoco, the notorious "Mack the Black." Garland's Manuela is introduced as a repressed young woman, about to be married to a man she doesn't love, but dreaming of freedom, of the sea, and of a sexy pirate. (Little does she know that the pirate is really the overweight, prissy old guy she's going to marry.)

Minnelli helped to create a role for Garland that would allow her to be both her naive and uncertain movie self (the one audiences knew and loved) and a newer, more sophisticated Garland (as he had presented her in *Till the Clouds Roll By*). She has costumes that are haute cinema, beautiful songs to sing ("Love of My Life"), and her gloriously wild dance ("Mack the Black") in which she reveals a vibrant and sensual woman. Manuela is a virgin who's dying not to be one, and when she imagines Kelly to be Mack the Black, she watches him from her window, and her fantasy turns into the "Pirate Ballet." Minnelli and Kelly work in perfect harmony to create a fevered maiden's fantasy pirate. The dance is a frenzy of explosions, flashing blades, pistol shots, torches, treasure chests, captured women, dead bodies, and actions worthy of Douglas Fairbanks, a childhood favorite of Kelly's. The dance is set against a blood-red sky, with Kelly dressed in black, and for the first (and last) time in a movie dance, showing off his naked thunder thighs. The ballet becomes a mini action film, a little pirate-movie dance that is witty and outrageous.

A marriage of talents: Vincente Minnelli and Gene Kelly in the "Nina" number from *The Pirate*

The arrival of Gene Kelly into the movie is developed through a musical number ("Nina," one of Cole Porter's most imaginatively rhymed lyrics, wedding "seen ya," "neurasthenia," and "schizophrenia"). When Kelly's Serafin arrives in Port Sebastian, music arrives as well. He comes in off the sea, out of an open world, and from the world of entertainment—he's a traveling performer with a troupe of actors. He enters Minnelli's whirling world of cinema and brings it under his own control, because he treats it as if it's a stage designed for his performance—which, after all, it is.

Kelly's most famous dance is the somewhat simple (but highly effective) dance in the rain that everyone knows; for most moviegoers, it defines him. However, it may be that a more insightful and revealing definition of Kelly and his personality and style can be found in this complex "Nina" dance. It's a movie dance, layered and alive, and it reveals all his strengths and weaknesses, but most of all it reveals his ambitions for dance on film and his dedication to making dance cinematic. The choreography credit for *The Pirate* is shared by Robert Alton and Kelly, and the direction by Minnelli is certainly an important factor; but the "Nina" number is pure Gene Kelly. He dances a piece of choreography that conquers cinematic space and transforms all of Port Sebastian into a dance venue. The dance is presented as a solo, because his chorus of "Ninas" (the women he can't resist) appear and disappear. Perhaps the most accurate thing to be said is that the choreography is a duet between the camera and Gene Kelly—or, that is, between Vincente Minnelli and Gene Kelly. They dance together. It's a dance in which Serafin dominates, entertains and enthralls his audience *inside* the movie. It's also a dance that defines borders as it goes forward. Kelly moves around the town square, up onto verandas, down drainpipes, etc., like Fairbanks in a silent movie. Kelly meets and lures his "Ninas" by not only involving them in his dance, but by bringing them into his performance and thus into his fantasy of himself. Minnelli and Kelly have united to present an audience with a dance number that says music liberates, music is sexy, and the person who lives out his musical fantasy has all the fun.

As Kelly dances around the town square of Port Sebastian, dressed as a strolling player in colorful clothes, he is mobile through space and uses camera movement through and across that space. The song has a slightly Latin beat, to go with the Caribbean setting, and Kelly displays his athleticism as he moves. He's comic, mocking, wolfish—all traits associated with the typical characters he plays. He's acting his role of Serafin, the ham actor, as he dances, and this is significant. Most dancers abandon their character when they begin to dance: Kelly does not. He integrates his character and the dance. He presents a strutting sexuality that's designed for fun—he's selling—but it will turn out to be showmanship, not smarm.

He's a dancing ad for his troupe and their show. The worst aspect of the dance lies in his posturing, wiggling his butt, and being overly conscious of his body. The best aspect is his mastery of cinematic space, dancing up onto a little artificial stage created in the square that has tiny barber poles placed around it. These poles delineate layers in the frame for the viewer, and the dance has an impressive depth, an almost 3-D effect enhanced by Minnelli's keeping a colorfully dressed crowd around Kelly, some of whom are moving past him from one side of the screen to the other as he dances, as if they were just passing by. Kelly uses props as he goes, going up and down on the set, showing his athletic skill. He ends the number by arriving at the open-air theater he will perform in later, triumphantly leaping up onstage in front of a giant poster advertising himself: Serafin! It's a movie dance. It could not be done onstage.

The "Nina" dance in *The Pirate* represents what the Freed unit always wanted to do, what Kelly hoped to achieve, and what Minnelli knew how to deliver. It's a sophisticated wedding of music, image, dance, and cinema. Minnelli said it was "a fantasy, highly colored, theatrical as possible, flamboyant, swirling and larger than life." Film historian Joel Siegel wrote in *Film Heritage,* "*The Pirate* is, above all, an exuberant parody of operetta conventions, with diffident winks at Victorian melodrama and swashbuckling romance. It's a glorious and sophisticated entertainment, an immense, lavish production yet as enchantingly weightless as a daydream." And it was also a flop. Audiences didn't respond to its sophistication—they liked more of a *Me and My Gal* Kelly-and-Garland pairing. *The Pirate* violated their sense of stardom, and that was always a no-no. The costumes seemed weird and unattractive, and Garland didn't look well. (News of her attempted suicide had broken during the filming.) There wasn't enough music or any "singable" songs; but there was too much plot, too much comic tension, and not enough joy. When Minnelli and Kelly later found a tender love story between an ex-GI and a young Parisienne (in *An American in Paris*), audiences settled down and embraced the experimentation and the balletic dancing. Kelly was both surprised and crushed by the failure of *The Pirate*. Clive Hirschhorn's book on Kelly reports him as saying, "Vincente and I honestly believed we were being so dazzlingly brilliant and clever that everybody would fall at our feet and swoon clean away in delight and ecstasy—as they kissed each of our toes in appreciation for this wondrous new musical we'd given them. Well, we were wrong. About five and a half people seemed to get the gist of what we set out to do."

Minnelli, Kelly, Donen, Astaire—the talent at the Freed unit was prodigious, but the driving forces toward making the genre genuinely artistic were largely Minnelli and Kelly. With the Oscar wins for *An American in Paris,* they achieved their goal of creating something that contained art, ballet, and the best of American music, all taking Americans outside their own world in the postwar era. In Minnelli's case, it was always the lament he put into his version of *Madame Bovary:* "Is it wrong to want things to be beautiful?" In Kelly's case, it was the driving ambition to gain respect for dance and to prove musicals could be important art. These goals may seem middlebrow today, but they brought something special to the world of the majority of moviegoers, who loved them for it. The average people in the movie house didn't realize they were getting a lesson in sophistication; they just thought they were having fun.

As the end of the 1950s arrived, the musical hit its peak with the Freed unit innovations through another spectacular triumph: Minnelli's musical *Gigi* won Best Picture of 1958,* repeating the unexpected accomplishment of *An American in Paris.* The future of the musical seemed unlimited. At last respect was verified. At last the definition of the genre with all its challenges had been made. At last everyone knew how to make a musical. At last there would be serious, artistic work featuring real ideas and serious choreography. None of that turned out to happen, however. Lying ahead was . . . not much. A lot of stuff . . . but really, not much.

* The other films nominated were *Auntie Mame, Cat on a Hot Tin Roof, The Defiant Ones,* and *Separate Tables.*

VI

The Death of the Musical?

THINGS LOOKED ROSY AT THE END OF THE 1950S. The business had fully endorsed the musical as an American art form: in one single decade, there had been bookend Best Picture Oscars for two original Freed unit creations: *An American in Paris* in 1952 and *Gigi* in 1959. There *were* some clouds on the horizon, of course. The studio system seemed shaky, television was threatening, lawsuits were pending, and stars defecting . . . but for musicals it seemed as if things could just wait until the clouds rolled by.

The peak of 1950s musical success was the creation of *Gigi*. The high-riding duo of Alan Jay Lerner and Frederick Loewe (fresh from the stupendous Broadway success of *My Fair Lady*) did the score. Cecil Beaton designed the sets and the overall production. The story was based on a Colette novel and play. Leslie Caron, at her peak of confidence, played the title role, and the supporting cast was divine: handsome Louis Jourdan, reliable Hermione Gingold, beautiful Eva Gabor, and effervescent, though older, Maurice Chevalier.* Inspired by "Sem" (Georges Goursat) caricatures and paintings by Constantin Guys and Eugène Boudin, director Vincente Minnelli insisted the production go to Paris, producer Freed said yes, and the beautiful city became a perfect location. The legendary restaurant Maxim's unexpectedly agreed to let the crew shoot there. The Palais de Glace was used for an elaborate skating scene. An auberge about an hour's drive from Paris made a romantic place for a lovers' tryst. The Tuileries, the Avenue Rapp, and the Cours de Rohan were used, and the Bois de Boulogne became a location. The dresses were made by Karinska, the hats by Paulette, the gloves and hose by Repetto, the accessories by

---

* Chevalier celebrated his seventy-fifth birthday on set.

Leslie Caron, in the title role of *Gigi,* before, all girlish and open to life . . .

Jacques Fath, the hairstyles by Guillaume, the men's suits by Breslave, and their hats by Gilot. All of this finery was supervised and coordinated and dictated by Beaton, with Minnelli's input and final approval. No detail was too small to ignore. An archived note from the production files listed some items Minnelli requested: "Six swans to attack Gaston; one white horse to tread delicately among the diners at the Pré Cataelan and subsequently eat a diamond bracelet." It was all beautiful and sumptuous and sophisticated and carefully designed and brilliantly executed.

The shooting in Paris was chaotic, however. Paris had one of its worst heat waves in decades, and the ice in the Palais de Glace melted under the hot lights. Gabor insisted that a talented young French actor be replaced with her personal choice, Jacques Bergerac, who turned out not to be able to skate, although his big scene took place on the ice. Dust, horse manure, and bad weather plagued the shoots in the Bois. Everyone became nervous when Janet Flanner (the famous Genêt of *The New Yorker*) came to Maxim's to cover the shoot. (They needn't have worried: she thought everything looked great.) To top all the problems off with an appropriately esoteric event, Minnelli was bitten by one of the swans.

The shoot left Paris to film beach scenes in Venice, California, and do necessary reshoots, including close-ups of Jourdan that had been neglected in France. Minnelli had to move on to his next film (*The Reluctant Debutante,* not a musical), and quarrels broke out, confusion abounded, and the first preview of the movie (on January 20, 1958, in Santa Barbara) was twenty minutes too long. Nevertheless, the preview cards were favorable, and all challenges had been met. *Gigi*'s music was full of high spirits ("The Night They Invented Champagne"), wry comedy ("She's Not Thinking of Me"), rueful reflection ("I'm Glad I'm Not Young Anymore"), and unsentimental sentiment ("I Remember It Well"). It culminated in the lovely title song, and delivered a romantic happy ending that was a relief to preview audiences. *Gigi* reminded everyone of what MGM and Hollywood could do with its money, its talent, and its determination to entertain. *Gigi* was the triumphant decade finale, the whiz-bang eleven o'clock number, and the fulfilling goodnight song all rolled into one.

In its initial release, *Gigi* grossed over thirteen million dollars. Why should anyone making musicals be worried? *Gigi* looked like good news. As the calendar turned over to the 1960s, the musical appeared to be as popular as it had ever been. The first half of the 1960s brought *Can-Can* (1960), *Flower Drum Song* (1961), *The Music Man* and *Gypsy* (both 1962), *Bye Bye Birdie* (1963), *The Unsinkable Molly Brown* and *My Fair Lady* (both 1964)—all the traditional Broadway adaptations Hollywood had been able to rely on for decades. There were many positives in hand: the young stars developed in the late fifties (Elvis Presley in *Blue Hawaii* and *Viva Las Vegas*, Pat Boone in *Bernadine* and *April Love*); old stars still working the

. . . and after, all seductive and aware

street (Crosby and Hope in *Road to Hong Kong* and Sinatra, Dean Martin, and Crosby in *Robin and the 7 Hoods*); new stars with an unprecedented musical fame and a new kind of sound (the Beatles appeared in *A Hard Day's Night* in 1964 and *Help!* in 1965, buoyed up by a jaunty cinematic style from Richard Lester); and the reliable Disney musical successes (*Gay Purr-ee*, 1962). There was Technology with a capital T that had been developed by the studio system: CinemaScope, VistaVision, Todd-AO, 3-D, and stereophonic sound. There were the *Beach Blanket* musicals, the emergence of the B rock-and-roll musicals—there was music all over the screen. In particular, there were two blockbuster hits, one an original movie musical, *Mary Poppins* (1964), and one a Broadway adaptation, *The Sound of Music* (1965). Both of them starred a fresh young newcomer to the movie screen, Julie Andrews.

Andrews became the first genuine musical star to emerge in the 1960s, and except for Barbra Streisand the only legendary one. The "star singer" who danced and entranced was a staple of the studio system's musical business, and here was yet another to make cash registers ring. Andrews triumphed. She became a star of the sort that would inspire the business to think "star vehicle" and assume things would proceed as usual. She photographed well; she was fresh, talented, versatile; and she could sing, possessing a glorious, crystal-clear, soprano voice that was loud and resonant without being brassy or harsh. Her background had given her a strong work ethic and a no-nonsense approach that appealed to American audiences. Andrews had been a child star in the British music halls, and her success in the London production of *The Boy Friend* brought her to America's attention. She was hired in 1954 to re-create her leading role in the Broadway version.* In 1956, she appeared on American TV in the musical *High Tor* opposite Bing Crosby—a great showcase, since Crosby's fame guaranteed she would be noticed. Her lasting fame as a stage performer was secured when she opened that same year in the triumphantly successful *My Fair Lady* as Eliza Doolittle. In 1957, while appearing in *My Fair Lady* in New York (she also did the London production), she gave a memorable performance in the Rodgers and Hammerstein TV musical, *Cinderella*, a live broadcast that allegedly was seen by more people than had ever watched a musical. In 1960, she opened in another smash-hit show on Broadway, *Camelot*, which also featured music by Lerner and Loewe, and which costarred her with the

---

* Andrews did not appear in the 1971 movie version. Twiggy replaced her.

nonsinging actor Richard Burton as King Arthur. At first, *Camelot* suffered from comparisons to the earlier *My Fair Lady*, and the loss of its director, Moss Hart, who died shortly after the show opened. But its beautiful score, combined with the singing of Andrews and Robert Goulet as Lancelot, lifted it to musical heights. Burton managed to illuminate the role of King Arthur, and eventually, *Camelot* became a legendary motif for the administration of John F. Kennedy. If Andrews had never gone to Hollywood, she would still be one of the biggest names in Broadway history because of her early stage work in *My Fair Lady* and *Camelot*.

In 1964, however, Julie Andrews had one gigantic setback—she lost the leading role in the movie *My Fair Lady* to Audrey Hepburn—and one gigantic step forward: she secured the lead in Disney's *Mary Poppins*. *Mary Poppins* and *My Fair Lady*, as movies, ran a road race in 1964, and the outcome has to be seen as a tie. The movies are very different in subject matter—the first is based on a children's book, the second on a George Bernard Shaw play—but both have highly successful scores, strong casts of secondary characters, accomplished stars, experienced directors, and legions of skilled craftsmen and women at work to make them look and sound exactly right. The main difference between them is that one has Julie Andrews and the other does not. Inexplicably, Audrey Hepburn, a nonsinger, was cast in the plum role of Eliza Doolittle that had been owned and defined by the British Julie Andrews. Hepburn is lovely, and her individualistic look and timeless chic—not to mention her considerable acting ability—do justice to the role. The problem is simple: Eliza Doolittle, the singing version, belonged to Julie Andrews, and everyone knew it. Hepburn had to be dubbed by the ever-reliable Marni Nixon. Rex Harrison reprised his stage role (which was offered first to Cary Grant), and George Cukor directed so well that he received the Best Director Oscar for 1964. *My Fair Lady* is a competent musical film, but it breaks no ground and has nothing particularly distinguished about it other than that it is a movie version of a very important Broadway show and gives history the opportunity to see Rex Harrison make talking a song into an art form.

Mary Poppins, on the other hand, is one of the most effective mixes of animation and live action the Disney studio ever released. Richard M. and Robert B. Sherman wrote a memorable score packed with songs that became hits. When the decision was made to turn P. L. Travers's crabby and mysterious Mary Poppins (who in the books is an Edna May Oliver type) into a young and beautiful woman to be played by Andrews, they lost

me in the process. (I was a childhood devotee of the cranky old governess, whom I thought of as a great role model.) The movie, however, apparently lost almost no one else, becoming a gigantic hit and winning the Best Actress Oscar for its star, who snatched it neatly out of the waiting hands of Audrey Hepburn, who had been given the role everyone assumed would land the prize. It was high drama at the Oscars, with Harrison tactfully thanking his "two fair ladies" when he won his own award.

British efficiency was what Mary Poppins was all about, and Andrews was perfect. The songs themselves have a crisp, brisk pace, although some of them contain a somewhat brooding, or almost mysteriously sad, undertone. "Feed the Birds" drove children out of the theater where I first saw it, all wailing in terror. (My own daughter cried out, "Take me home!") Even "Chim-Chim-Cheree," the Oscar-winning Best Song of the year, has a sense of melancholy in it. But it was Andrews's ability to deliver the rousing "Supercalifragilisticexpialidocious" that showed her off to perfection. Her "A Spoonful of Sugar" made the song much more than it was; as her lifelong friend Carol Burnett remarked, "She can sing 'Spoonful of Sugar' and you don't get diabetes." In the long tradition of the studio system—when trying out a new star, be careful and surround her with a strong cast—the Disney company costarred Andrews with the proven talent Dick Van Dyke, the comic Ed Wynn (in his final screen appearance), and reliable performers like Glynis Johns, Hermione Baddeley, Reta Shaw, David Tomlinson, and Jane Darwell.

My Fair Lady and *Mary Poppins* are showcases of musical strengths: great music, performances, stories, and production values—but neither is a landmark movie musical. The significance they have lies in that one of them did not star Andrews, though it had made her a star on Broadway, and the other *did* star her and made her a movie star. And both films, highly successful, greatly reviewed and appreciated by audiences, made big money at the box office. This inspired Hollywood to believe that musicals would indeed be popular forever, and no matter what they cost, they'd win the Oscar and draw in the cash. This turned out to be a very, very wrong assumption; but making Andrews a star was not a bad idea. Although no longer singing for a living, Andrews is still a star, over fifty-five years later.

Julie Andrews was in many ways an unpredictable actress for Americans to embrace. She has about her a let's-get-this-done quality that doesn't exude warmth. She can be chilly. Her singing style is efficient. She *does* get the job done and does not slobber a song's lyrics, nor does she beat

OPPOSITE Julie Andrews, aka Mary Poppins, drifts in on just the right wind over London . . .

the emotions of the words to death. Her greatest asset is the clarity of her diction. No matter what she sings, every word is perfectly enunciated, and that draws an audience to her. She really cares that they know what she's "saying" in her song. There is a careful perfection to her work, a precision to both her songs and her dances that says "I am a professional." Andrews could make it look effortless. She skimmed through whatever she was given to do, but without making it trivial; she made it easy, but real. Her main asset, of course, is a fabulous voice, but it's combined with acting ability, intelligence, and an understanding of what is needed from her that never fails. She seems honest, and that is a characteristic that Americans always value.

When the dust settled, Andrews had triumphed over one of the greatest role losses in any actress's lifetime, made history in a Disney film that would last forever, and proved she was not someone who could be shoved aside. That was enough for any movie career, but ahead of her, in 1965, was the greatest musical role she would play in films: Maria in *The Sound of Music*. As if Eliza Doolittle and Mary Poppins were not enough—not to mention her stage role as Queen Guenevere—Andrews stepped up and nailed the big one. She played the lead in the greatest-all-time-grossing musical in the history of the genre.

The Sound of Music was only Andrews's third film, and as it was being prepared and cast, she was not yet an Oscar winner or a surefire choice for the role.* But she had a quality that would work for a nun—she seemed straightforward, honest, even innocent. She could look as if she really were a young woman who wore no makeup, never had her hair done, but was still attractive. The fact that audiences didn't associate her with sophisticated movie roles meant that she could *be* a nun—she wasn't familiar as other characters, other types. She wasn't quintessentially American, so that the Austrian angle worked. She was a good actress, who would help lower the cholesterol level of the material; in short, she was perfect, especially because she could really, really sing. The reason studio backers hesitated about Andrews was simple: she was not well-known, and a very expensive movie was going to be carried by her. By the time the movie came out, of course, Andrews had become a star, and that problem was no longer anyone's worry.

The Sound of Music arrived onscreen exactly in the middle of the 1960s. It was the summation of a studio-system movie musical: three decades of

OPPOSITE . . . and Maria von Trapp expresses her love of life in the most successful box-office musical of all time, *The Sound of Music:* two legendary Julie Andrews roles, both grads of the school for governesses.

* She did the nonmusical *The Americanization of Emily* between *Poppins* and *Music*.

superb entertainment. It was an adaptation of a hit Broadway show, but it also represented a musical in which nonprofessionals sang and danced because they sang and danced. It was a half-and-half, a transition. Its success blinded moviemakers to an impending problem for the musical's popularity, but its critical reception should have alerted them that something negative might be going to happen.

The Sound of Music opened slowly, received some terrible reviews, and went on to become a blockbuster hit. It is the epitome of the

Broadway-to-Hollywood musical adaptations. Under the direction of veteran Robert Wise, who had already proved himself by turning *West Side Story* into a smash, the movie was "opened up" in a truly cinematic fashion. It begins by shutting an audience up with a breathtaking helicopter shot of Julie Andrews standing in a green meadow, the magnificent Alps all around her. As the camera circles in and around, she sings, "The hills are alive with the sound of music." A viewer knows at once that this will not be a horizontal recreation of a stage play. The movie *uses* the outdoors, the gorgeous European locations, and the superior sense of editing that Robert Wise possessed to create a movie that masses and masses of people adored and would see again and again and again. And again.

It's a great movie for debate. *The Sound of Music* is either beloved or hated. Those who love it appreciate its music, its true story, its real-life drama, its fabulous location setting, and its list of hit songs that have endured. Those who hate it find it middlebrow, schmaltzy, and fake. But love it or leave it alone, it climbed every mountain and became a social yardstick: if you liked it, you were a sentimental nerd. If you hated it, you were cool. And soon enough, if you overrode the cool and embraced it as pop culture, you were supercool. Most people who went, taking their children, were simply thrilled to have a family movie that worked. The critics divided along a professional line. The trade papers, representing those who made movies, raved about *The Sound of Music* and predicted big box office. The chic magazines, representing an "informed readership," went after it with a vengeance. Stanley Kauffmann in *The New Republic*, Brendan Gill in *The New Yorker*, and Bosley Crowther in *The New York Times* killed it. Kauffmann said the movie was "sickening" and labeled Julie Andrews "the most revolting refreshing actress in films." Gill said it was "hokey" and the acting "well under ordinary high school level." The *Times* labeled it "operetta kitsch," called the acting "horrendous," and panned Christopher Plummer for being "as . . . phony as a store-window Alpine guide." These somewhat elitist magazines and newspapers might have been predicted to react this way, but two other reviewers whose sources were more directly connected to mass moviegoers also weighed in negative: Judith Crist of the *Today* show and Pauline Kael of *McCall's*, a now defunct women's magazine. Crist denounced the movie from her television pulpit, but had also really torn it to shreds in her column for the *New York Herald Tribune*. She wrote her review under a now famous headline: "If You Have Diabetes, Stay Away from This Movie." She dubbed it "The Sound of Marshmallows" and spent a lot of time later in her life ruefully remembering the "hate mail from all over the world" she had received as a result. Kael's approach was one of righteous indignation: the movie's popularity was the lowering of all standards and the destruction of the true art of cinema, because *The Sound of Music* was "probably going to be the single most repressive influence on artistic freedom in the movies for the next few years." It was "the sugar-coated lie that people seem to want to eat." Kael's approach was so resoundingly negative and angry that she was fired from her job as a film critic.

With *The Sound of Music*, the cultural divide that occurred in the 1960s was underway for the musical. Popular was bad; emotion was uncool; and musicals became a suspect genre because songs and dances were about feelings and plots were often oversimplified to accommodate the need for emotions to emerge through music.* *The Sound of Music* itself was scorned, but not destroyed by the disdain of its perceived middlebrow appeal. It rolled on—it still rolls on—and Kauffmann, Crowther, Gill, and Crist are used as classroom examples of critics who were wrong on specific films that have endured despite their pans.†

Andrews hit the high point of her commercial musical success with *The Sound of Music*. Her back-to-back musical blockbusters, *Poppins* and *Music*, seemed to mean that she was the equivalent of the Grables, Doris Days, and Deanna Durbins of the past. All that needed to be done to make more millions with her was to create a string of star vehicles—the Julie Andrews musical. However, the unpredictable happened. Her next three musicals were all failures: *Thoroughly Modern Millie* (1967), *Star!* (1968), and *Darling Lili* (1970), although the latter has become a cult favorite today. Of these three, *Star!* is undoubtedly her worst.

Star! is a real musical disaster. The title should be punctuated not with an exclamation point but with a question mark. Back in 1968, it seemed

---

* Tom Santopietro writes in his book on *The Sound of Music* that he believes the published starting point of the intellectual war against the American middle-class popular culture was launched in July of 1964 in *Esquire* magazine with an article written by David Newman and Robert Benton entitled "The New Sentimentality." They provided a convenient check list for what was in (Antonioni and Malcolm X) and what was out (John Wayne, Gene Kelly, and *The Sound of Music*). The musical was an obvious target for this point of view, but time has not supported their list well. What the list did do was reveal that America was about to divide itself, turn on itself, and bite itself in the rear over culture wars.

† *The Sound of Music* still ranks as the highest-grossing musical of all time.

like a guaranteed hit, what with its award-winning director, Robert Wise, its lineup of beautiful songs by Cole Porter, the Gershwins, Noël Coward, et al., its biopic genre, its choreography by Michael Kidd, its gorgeous clothes designed by Donald Brooks, and above all, its Flavor of the Decade superstar leading lady, Julie Andrews, riding the wave of an international popularity. *Star!* surely would be great entertainment, all 175 minutes of it, but it bombed. Cut by nearly a full hour by its studio, 20th Century–Fox, it was released under a new title, perhaps hoping to fool people, but no, it bombed again.* *Star!* was a failure, a costly one, and a warning sign of things to come.

Julie Andrews was the only thing that made *Star!* worth watching, but she was unfortunately saddled with a trite script and a main character with no viewer empathy (a star no longer well-known to audiences). No one cared much about Gertrude Lawrence in 1968. Once a famous West End diva who found fame in the 1920s, Lawrence was warmly welcomed by Broadway when she first came to America, and her last great triumph had been playing the role of Anna in the original production of *The King and I* onstage with Yul Brynner. Instead of starting with her death during the run on Broadway of this hit show, *Star!* inexplicably started with a framing story linked to a mysterious conquering of her fears about doing *Lady in the Dark* in the 1940s. The Gertrude Lawrence movie story was set up as a 1920s/1930s tale, but one that was not told in American genre terms of flappers, stock market crashes, and the Depression. There's no familiar story door for an audience to enter, and also no emotions in the personal story for them to take hold of—Lawrence flits off from one husband, insults a second so much that he of course adores her (a movie cliché), ignores her daughter, drinks, and worries about her career. There is no reason to love her or even like her, and certainly no reason to care when her big crisis in life becomes overspending. (Wow! How tragic! Unpaid mink bills!) As always in a musical, however, it's the music that counts, and *Star!* didn't even manage to come alive in that category, although it *does* have a great deal of music. The songs and dances are presented as if they're onstage—again a cinematic setback to 1929—but with lavish costuming and stylized décor. These carefully presented numbers appear to be reproductions of the originals, though with cleverly modernized looks and attitudes. The costumes are outstanding, including a fashion show of stunning 1920s gowns. The

---

* The new title was *Those Were the Happy Times*, a prophetic "were."

runway parade isn't a musical number, but time is taken for it (the excuse being that Lawrence had to model for a living for a while). Andrews is the last model in line, wrapped in a black velvet coat studded with silver, underneath which is a showstopping silver-and-black dress—the best thing in the movie.

Andrews re-creates Lawrence's hit songs with her usual careful diction and performance charm. The film has an almost reverent attitude, and for the audience the viewing experience is somewhat like being in a mausoleum. Lawrence is laid out for viewers to revere, but when Andrews sings "Burlington Bertie from Bow" in a tramp's version of top hat and tails, American audiences thought Betty Grable and Dan Dailey owned that song; they'd first heard it in *Mother Wore Tights*. For them, the tragedy of "Limehouse Blues" was not Andrews in a clown suit, but Fred Astaire being accidentally shot while dreaming of an exotic dance with Lucille Bremer in *Ziegfeld Follies*. And when Andrews does "Parisian Pierrot," "The Physician," and "Dear Little Boy," they had no nostalgia or cinematic connections for those songs at all. Nothing links the numbers together emotionally, and nothing draws a viewer into them. *Star!* is a waxworks musical, and as a tribute to Gertrude Lawrence, it makes her look trivial, inconsistent, and unlikable—a selfish woman who's getting between the audience and the Julie Andrews everyone likes. Get off, Gertie! Give us Julie! (In the beginning the film seemed to think Gertrude Lawrence was Fanny Brice, as she comes out and ineptly messes up a chorus line, a parallel to an early scene in *Funny Girl*. After that she becomes tragic, only not so much.)

Although her "star vehicle" musicals failed, Andrews's dramatic career was solid. She got good personal reviews in an underappreciated Alfred Hitchcock film, *Torn Curtain*, in 1966, and working with her husband, director Blake Edwards, she appeared to good reviews in comedies such as *S.O.B.* (1981). Her final musical success was in *Victor/Victoria* (1982), one of the few genuine hit musicals of the eighties. *Victor/Victoria* was a sly social commentary with excellent comedy scenes directed by Edwards. Its stellar cast included the superb Robert Preston, who had never been given enough movie musicals, as well as James Garner, Lesley Ann Warren, and Alex Karras. The mature Julie Andrews is perfectly presented in her musical mode in *Victor/Victoria*.* Edwards understood her, and knew the sophistication she was capable of, and he built the film especially for

---

* Andrews began to do fewer and fewer musicals and more and more dramatic parts as she matured.

her. Although the score is not especially good, the film was fun, and it drew audiences not just for its music, but also for its wit and open attitude toward gay life.

Victor/Victoria is a movie in which Julie Andrews's chilly efficiency works because her job is to hide her sexuality in the music. She's a female who pretends to be a male who pretends to be a female. It was perfect for her somewhat ambivalent and neutered sexual persona. She was not about being sexual, which didn't mean she couldn't enact passion. Her essence, however, is not warm and is not outreaching; it's the crisp nanny presence, all starched and available for rescue or instructions but not necessarily for messing about and being passionate. Americans liked her. We had enough hot-pants female stars in our lives over the years. She was a breath of fresh air.

The enormous early-sixties success of Julie Andrews—and especially of *The Sound of Music* at the box office—encouraged Hollywood studios to believe erroneously that the survival of their entire system lay in lavish musical production. Besides the Andrews flops, the business created other mammoth titles almost entirely based on the idea that if *The Sound of Music* was big, and if *The Sound of Music* was musical, all they had to do was make a big musical to make big money. In 1967 there appeared *Doctor Dolittle;* in 1968 *Chitty Chitty Bang Bang;* in 1971 *The Boy Friend* (a British-American production); and in 1969 and 1971, respectively, two famous James Hilton novels (previously turned into beloved and highly successful movies)—*Goodbye, Mr. Chips* and *Lost Horizon*. All were made into dreadful musicals. *Chips* had a nonsinger in the title role (Peter O'Toole), and songs were thus often presented only as "thoughts" on the soundtrack while an audience heard but didn't see singing. These big movie musicals were all expensive studio failures.

At the midpoint of the decade, however, there was enough good news with *Poppins* and *Sound of Music* to keep the business optimistic. And there was something else. Another female singing-and-dancing star emerged: Barbra Streisand. Following the tradition of the business, moviemakers again naturally assumed—as they had with Andrews—that a strong female musical star meant that star vehicles could be created for her that would guarantee the genre's box-office future.

Barbra Streisand was a Broadway star who made the transition from stage fame to movie fame—she and Julie Andrews, but not Merman, Martin, and others. There's no easy answer to the why of that. Would you say that a movie star had to be extremely pretty, like Andrews? Streisand wasn't. Would you say that singers needed to reprise the Broadway roles that made them famous on film to make it? Andrews lost both *Camelot* and *My Fair Lady* and still made it. When it comes to movie stardom of any kind—but most particularly musical fame—it's an unpredictable mélange of elusive answers and accidents of fate.

Streisand, like Julie Andrews in *Mary Poppins* (and Marlee Matlin in *Children of a Lesser God*), made her film debut and won the Oscar as Best Actress for it. Streisand had to share hers with Katharine Hepburn (for *A Lion in Winter*), but still, her film debut made Streisand a movie star. Previously, it had made her a Broadway star, but being a Broadway star for her was temporary. After a long and successful run in *Funny Girl* in both New York City and London, Streisand decamped for Hollywood and never appeared again on the Broadway stage. When she first undertook the role of Fanny Brice in the theater, the musical was all about Brice. It was *her* story, *her* world, *her* songs. The "funny girl" *was* Brice, and the job of the producers was to try to find a young talent who could fill her shoes. Streisand could and did, but by the time the movie was made, the "funny girl" had become Barbra Streisand.*

Funny Girl, the movie, was directed by the legendary William Wyler, who had behind him such films as *Jezebel* and *The Letter*, with Bette Davis, *The Best Years of Our Lives*, with Myrna Loy and Fredric March, and *The Heiress*, with Olivia de Havilland, among others. *Funny Girl*, however, was the first musical in his then forty-three-year career, and he brought to it everything his lifetime as a first-rate director of great intelligence and sensitivity had taught him. He presented Streisand impeccably as Fanny Brice, a character she fully understood. The production was lavish (you know that when the credits say "Furs by . . ."). Some of the original songs from the show were cut, but three new ones were written, designed especially for Streisand, songs not associated with Brice but that could be associated instead with *her:* "Funny Girl," "Roller Skate Rag," and "The Swan." (Two standards were also chosen specifically for what Streisand could do with them, "I'd Rather Be Blue" and Brice's signature "My Man.") Everything about the production looked expensive, carefully calculated, and pleasing to the eye. Great care was taken—it took nine days to shoot the dramatic

---

* The stage show had debuted on March 26, 1964. The movie had its world premiere on September 18, 1968.

Barbra Streisand in the role that made her a movie superstar and won her an Oscar, Fanny Brice in *Funny Girl*

pre-intermission number that traveled over time and space, "Don't Rain on My Parade." The finished movie received eight Oscar nominations, including one for Streisand for Best Actress (the movie's only win).

The movie begins with a classic "Here is a star, but wait for her" presentation. The camera follows (from behind) a woman in a leopard skin coat and matching hat as she walks up to a theater marquee that says FLORENZ ZIEGFELD/FANNY BRICE in neon lights. She stops to look, enters the lobby, walks past the doorman, goes into the theater itself, walks up to an onstage mirror, looks into it, turns the high collar of the coat down so an audience can see her face for the first time . . . and says to her own image, "Hello, gorgeous!" After that, the movie is all about confirming her entrance: the clothes, the drama, the star worship, and the attitude that says "We all know why we're here."

As "Fanny Brice" sits in the empty theater and thinks back across her life (cue flashback), the movie lays out the question that was part of Brice's life and that was the question the movies were asking about Streisand's potential as a movie star. Brice's mother (Kay Medford) sings, "Is a nose with deviation such a crime against the nation?" Throughout the movie this concept will be repeated in dialogue or lyrics: "You don't look like the other girls." "You're no chorus girl, you're a singer and a comic." "I can't sing these lyrics about being beautiful . . . I'd feel silly." Song titles include "If a Girl Isn't Pretty" and "His Love Makes Me Beautiful." Somewhere along the adaptation process, the story of Brice became more one of offering a unique physical presence, Barbra Streisand, up to the public as a potential movie star, and less about Fanny Brice. And yet the basic property is the story of Fanny Brice, a role given originally to a young actress as a challenge: Could she reach that height? She surpassed it. Audiences embraced Streisand as herself. Brice was a terrific comedienne and a great singer. Streisand is a terrific singer and a good enough comedienne. Fanny Brice didn't need to be movie-star beautiful, because movie stardom was never her goal. For Streisand, it *was* a goal, and her debut movie had to prove to the public that they would want to look at her on the big screen even though she was not conventionally beautiful. When I was growing up, a girl who had style, dressed attractively, and had made herself look good without beauty was tactfully said to have "personality." That's what society awarded to the not-so-pretty. In *Funny Girl*, Streisand, we are told, has personality. (Later, in *On a Clear Day You Can See Forever*, she would become beautiful and even define the term for her era, and finally even go beyond that and teach that a woman's beauty could be defined by talent, independence, intelligence, and self-confidence.) In *Funny Girl*, Streisand wears stunning clothes, all designed to show off her bosom and lovely shoulders; she has great hairstyles, long polished fingernails, perfect makeup; and she stands amidst expensive settings: everything is designed around her, to support her, to incorporate her into the concept of successful movie star. By the time she gets to *On a Clear Day*, everything is outrageously BIG and she can compete easily with it and hold her own. She can handle it, and no one even thinks for a second that she can't. She belongs.

Funny Girl is a well-directed, well-produced, well-conceived movie, but as a musical it's not much. It's not really about music: it's about Fanny Brice, a great showbiz biopic. Its best musical moments are those that isolate Streisand as a singer and let her be herself: "People," when she moves away from her costar, Omar Sharif, in an alley; "Don't Rain on My Parade," which she sings in continuity as the film is edited to travel across time and space (the difference between theater and film); and in her grand finale, "My Man." In the latter, Streisand, who brought Fanny Brice wonderfully to life and who owed her career to her, nevertheless deals with Brice once and for all. Wearing a deep V-necked black dress, singing against a black background, she delivers "My Man" the way Barbra Streisand would sing it, not the way Brice herself ever did it. Streisand powers it down to the floor, showing it who's boss. Funny girl? Tough girl. Herself and no one else.

In 1975, a sequel to *Funny Girl* was released: *Funny Lady.* In the nearly seven years that had passed, Streisand had changed. She had become a show-business legend, mature, confident, and professional. The musical was a showcase for *Barbra Streisand,* although it told the story of Brice's second marriage (to showman Billy Rose) and how she learned she had finally rid herself of the ghost of Nicky Arnstein, whose seven toothbrushes (one for each day) had been the most impressive thing she had ever seen. ("In all these years I've been in love with nothing but those goddamned toothbrushes.") What the plot reveals, without making a big deal out of it, was that Fanny Brice fell for con men. Nicky Arnstein was the "ruffled shirt" version and Billy Rose the cheap-suit version. Clotheshorse or rag bag, Arnstein and Rose were the same guy: gamblers who knew a good bet when they saw it, and Fanny Brice was that bet. The only difference between the two men is that Arnstein is wounded when called Mr. Brice, and Rose immediately cuts the offender off with "Rose. Rose. Mr. Rose." He asserts himself and shoves it in the speaker's face where Arnstein was too much a gentleman to call attention to the error. However, Fanny Brice is now Barbra Streisand, because Barbra Streisand isn't ever going to be anyone but herself. Although the plot gives us Brice, the movie gives us Streisand, who in the modern media is the bigger star. Brice has been subsumed.

In many ways, *Funny Lady* is more of a musical than *Funny Girl* was; it's just not a good one. It's stuffed with music—eighteen songs in all—and except for Ben Vereen's messy-looking "Clap Hands" number, each one is perfectly presented to showcase Streisand. James Caan, as Rose, smartly matches up to Streisand by being wryly low-key when she's raging, hanging in with the anger when they're supposed to be fighting, and creating his own separate portrait of a showbiz character. Omar Sharif reappears as Arnstein, which was imperative for the film to work, and although he has only two really big scenes, he plays both exactly right. Sharif was an excellent Arnstein, presenting him as appreciating Brice's quirks and humor—and her peculiar beauty—with gentlemanly amusement, always good-mannered, and quietly exuding a powerful sexuality, but only in the very best of taste.

Funny Lady does not have the good luck to have a brilliant director like William Wyler. Herbert Ross directs, and there's no firm hand setting the tone; rather, there's someone who appears to be catering to Streisand's stardom. There's an imitation "Don't Rain on My Parade" travel across time and space—to the tune of "Let's Hear It for Me"—but without the rhythm and clarity of the earlier effort. Streisand is showcased, alone onstage, or in a lavish production number for extended songs. She sings the Billy Rose tune "More Than You Know" (allegedly at a recording session) with great power and emotion. She tries to do "I Found a Million Dollar Baby (in a Five and Ten Cent Store)" in a messy dress-rehearsal comedy sequence (like the one in *The Band Wagon*), where she's stranded in a white tuxedo, standing on a gigantic cigarette holder, trying to sing and dance as smoke envelops her. When she appears in the overchoreographed "It's Gonna Be a Great Day," it's pretentious, designed to allow her to work the song over and show off her voice, her perfect body, her dramatic styling. It's a real "Look at me, Ma" tour de force. After she sees Arnstein for the first time since the end of *Funny Girl* and learns he's married (for wealth, to an older woman), she goes on a bare stage to belt out "How Lucky Can You Get" with irony that changes to belief—it's her "Rose's Turn" number. "Do you want to know what it's really like?" she asks an imaginary audience. "*Fan . . . tas . . . tic!*" Then she stalks out. Barbra Streisand in this phase of her career does a song as if it's a Shakespearean soliloquy. She's just got to be the one to interpret it for eternity.

Like Merman, Streisand was an outsized talent with an outsized personality (and a voice to match) built for the Broadway stage. She was exaggerated, almost cartoonish, and certainly not a conventional beauty. As such, she was built for comedy, and her breakthrough stage-musical role, as Miss Marmelstein in *I Can Get It for You Wholesale*, had reflected the conventional mentality that would inevitably cast her that way, as a second lead. But Streisand was no second banana, and even if she had been one, would never have stood for it. The perfect star-making role in the theater came along, crafted just for her: that of Fanny Brice, her counterpart in comic skill, self-generated glamour, and powerful singing interpretation. *Funny Girl* was the definitive Barbra Streisand role. Everything that followed was some kind of variation on Fanny Brice—except for one. Streisand showed everyone her originality, her mastery of style, and her out-of-this-world glamorous sexuality in Vincente Minnelli's *On a Clear Day You Can See Forever*. Unfortunately, the movie was not a success. Audiences never saw the equivalent Streisand onscreen again.

Yves Montand checks out the success of his hypnotic spell on Barbra Streisand in the Minnelli-directed musical *On a Clear Day You Can See Forever*, a star vehicle of the old school.

On a Clear Day was a theatrical musical comedy with book and lyrics by Alan Jay Lerner and music by Burton Lane that had starred Barbara Harris. Although it opened in 1965 to mixed reviews, it managed to run for a respectable 272 performances. In 1970, Paramount Pictures bought it as a showcase for Streisand, who requested Minnelli as her director. The movie was designed as a star vehicle: everything was adjusted to put Streisand at the very center of the film. Characters were eliminated to give her more screen time; songs were eliminated to give her more performance time. New songs were written especially for her—"Go to Sleep" and "Love with All the Trimmings" were tailor-made for her voice and her style. Even before the credits, Streisand sings across images of flowers that are being planted by her hands and observed to be growing in splendid, dramatic color, presumably because of her voice and her touch. She is then seen to be dancing/walking through riotously beautiful bushes of flowers as she finishes her song. Only then do the credits (inside visually stunning rectangular shapes that move and change colors) appear. In this precredit musical number, Streisand's voice soars, and when she appears, she's dressed in the haute-couture child-woman style of the era, with white stockings and shoes, a big hat, and a supershort skirt. As the credits roll, she sings the title song gloriously. Even the moving rectangles, changing colors with a chameleon's skill, dare not compete. They move and they change all right, but the effect is that of a sedate psychedelic that wants to listen and not distract. The plot destination is a college class taught by Yves Montand, playing a French psychiatrist who uses hypnosis. Suddenly everything falls flat for a few minutes (until Streisand reappears), and that's pretty much the story of what goes wrong in *On a Clear Day*. It's designed for Streisand to shine, and when she's not present, it's a dud. She's cast in a dual role—not twins, but one woman who's two people. First she's the Miss Marmelstein/Fanny Brice Brooklynese flibbertigibbet (who dresses in couture, makes flowers grow, and consults a hypnotist because she wants to quit smoking—it won't fit into her fiancé's plans for a perfect corporate wife). That character—Daisy—gets on a viewer's nerves pretty fast. (And also on those of Montand's character, who later says, "Why must you turn into a caterpillar?" when Daisy comes out from under hypnosis and her real self appears.) Streisand isn't successful at pretending to be naive, overwhelmed, and insecure. It's just not who she is. Her other half is named Melinda, who lives in Regency England. It is in this role, touched with the visual enchantment Vincente Minnelli can conjure up, that Barbra Streisand really becomes the most glamorous and emblematic creature of 1970s America. Whereas in *Funny Girl*, Streisand as Brice finds glamour and style, and she sings beautifully, both comic songs and serious songs, her role needs her to maintain a certain level of insecurity and self-doubt until the end. *Funny Girl* made her a movie star, but kept her in an impersonation of Brice's talent and glamour. *On a Clear Day* released her *own* personal glamour, and with it came a sexuality that only the 1970s could showcase. As Melinda, Streisand was like a 1930s exotic Greta Garbo, only this time Garbo was hot.

Vincente Minnelli's direction, production values, and oversight of costuming turned Melinda into a unique beauty. She was mysterious (as opposed to the kooky Daisy), alluring, visually stunning, and extraordinary. Whereas before only Streisand's voice removed her from the ordinary, as Melinda everything about her was something that can only be described as *other*. When Daisy is put under hypnosis and the film goes into the past, it's a world of astonishing color and detailed decoration, in which Melinda, a kitchen maid's daughter, is elevated to a lady by her own cleverness. She's seen walking gracefully toward a man who cannot resist her. As the two of them fondle their wineglasses and eye each other in a crowded room (she rubs her glass between her breasts and runs her tongue

THE DEATH OF THE MUSICAL? 499

around its rim), her song, with its lyrics, tells of secret emotions that are being demonstrated onscreen. Minnelli and Streisand together embrace a beauty that is abstracted, yet tangibly present in the images, a beauty that is beyond what can be found in real life. It's possible to see that Streisand is a true actress capable of more than kookiness.

Unfortunately, the overall film doesn't really work. Montand has to stand around, being allowed to sing, but only briefly: "Melinda," "Come Back to Me" (his biggest number), and finally a piece of the title song. Montand's task is to admire Streisand as Melinda, and he does this very well when she finally appears in present tense in front of him, strumming a harp, stunning in Regency dress, and singing "He Wasn't You" to him. Previously, Melinda appeared only in flashbacks that represented someone inside Daisy's head, but when it's made clear that Montand has fallen in love with this character, she wipes Daisy off the screen and appears before him. The song is about the yearning that can come with unfulfilled love, the dream of someone you want but cannot have. It's a great moment, but never enough. The return of the caterpillar Daisy begins to shred the mood and the plot: she flails; she overacts; she's a caricature, not a person. As Daisy, Streisand, hampered by clothes that were the height of style but look ridiculous and infantilize her today, has one excellent moment: a duet with herself entitled "Go to Sleep." One Daisy is in bed, one sits in a chair—and both can sing.

On a Clear Day cannot be a first-rate musical because it doesn't have enough music. A basic tenet of the genre is violated. The first song after the credit sequence appears more than half an hour into the film, and the second nearly fifty minutes after the beginning. Secondary characters—Jack Nicholson as a stepbrother out of nowhere and Larry Blyden as Daisy's hapless fiancé—are relegated to short scenes. Daisy is apparently a millionaire if her wardrobe (with matching hats and shoes) and living spaces are any indication, and it's never clear whether she's a real college student or a drop-in, and she has no apparent occupation. Her job is to sit in a chair and be hypnotized so the intoxicating Melinda can emerge. The movie also employs a popular musical conceit of the day: a song is sung on the soundtrack over images in which no one is singing. Minnelli seems to have his little joke on this when, as Montand sings "Come Back to Me" from atop the Pan Am Building and from inside his office, Daisy hears him (she has powers!) and tries to run away. As she roves the city, everyone and everything she comes in contact with is singing with Yves Montand's voice: a dog, a small child, an elderly couple, people around a fountain.

Everywhere she goes, he's singing, but it's never him. *On a Clear Day* has many problems, but it also has an exquisite visual presentation of Barbra Streisand's unusual beauty, which she always knew was there and which Vincente Minnelli puts on the screen for everyone to see. And it's hers and no one else's. As Melinda, she's a masterpiece.

As her fame grew, Streisand essentially stopped making musicals.* Her career as a singer did not, of course, stop, as her concerts and recordings continued. But the idea of her as a star willing to be in weak vehicles designed for her to carry died a quiet enough death. She made one final example of the genre—her magnum opus, in which she was producer, director, cowriter, and star. The movie was *Yentl*, released in 1983 and based on Isaac Bashevis Singer's story "Yentl, the Yeshiva Boy." It was a beautiful film, and for a directorial debut, a remarkable effort. It wasn't a bad musical, either, but it had one problem: it was directed by a woman and that woman was a seriously big movie star, and critics, both professional and nonprofessional, went after her. Streisand attracted fans, but also detractors.

Yentl would be Streisand's final movie musical. She worked on it for five years before she put it into production. The finished film reflects that careful consideration in both positive and negative ways. On the plus side, it's a beautiful and original work that has been presented with great intelligence and care; but it also has a didactic quality in certain scenes that reflects the determination of the creator to make her points and make them overly clear. *Yentl* is a film about a woman made by a woman and starring a woman which has been unjustly criticized and neglected. As a musical, it's presented by someone with a complete understanding of the parameters of the form. The music—sung only by Streisand—belongs to Yentl, her character. Music is the expression of her repressed (and hidden) self. If she's alone in the frame, she can sing, and she does. If she's among others, in a social situation, she sings on the track "inside her head." When the movie ends, and she's on her way to America, she sings—finally—inside the frame but among groups of people who ignore the fact that she's singing. Yentl is going where her voice can not only be heard, but be accepted. It's a simple concept of musical definition, but it is an accurate usage of the form, and it's beautifully done.

---

* After *Funny Girl* in 1968, she made *Hello, Dolly* in 1969, *On a Clear Day* in 1970, and *Funny Lady* in 1975. She would make only two more: a remake of *A Star Is Born* in 1976 and *Yentl* in 1983.

Yentl has fluid camerawork and soft, golden lighting inside a world of earthy brown. It's set in Eastern Europe in 1904, and the costumes and settings have great visual beauty. Streisand sings in a sincere style, less bombastic than usual, and her voice has never been lovelier. She doesn't kill the songs; she presents them as the inner heart and soul of a thinking and feeling woman. The songs themselves (music by Michel Legrand, lyrics by Alan and Marilyn Bergman) are ruminations, the articulations of a woman who is thinking outside the restrictions of society: "Where is it written?" . . . "Papa, can you hear me?" . . . "No wonder he loves her" (as she meets Hadass, the beautiful and traditionally Jewish young woman played by Amy Irving) . . . "The way he makes me feel." These are more lines of dialogue than song lyrics. They are her thoughts in a nonmusical musical way. *Yentl* is a modern musical, and the problem of how to update the form is solved by Streisand's intelligence and skill. Everything she does musically is consistent and appropriate for the parameters of her characterization of Yentl. Although once or twice a slight touch of the modern (or a touch of Fanny Brice) pops up, it's quickly put back down. *Yentl* is a beautiful movie and also a beautiful musical. Streisand deserves recognition as a *director*, not just as a female director, but at the very least *Yentl* should have brought her far better rewards than it did. If Streisand had not been thought of as "a female director," given negative reviews, and been blocked in her progress, could she have done more innovative musicals? Who knows?

It can be seen in retrospect that the 1960s and 1970s were transitional years for musicals, the yes-and-no period of lavish films trying to duplicate past successes alongside "modern" movies trying to make the form fresh by denying the form. There was good news (*The Sound of Music*, Julie Andrews, and Streisand) and there was bad (*Goodbye, Mr. Chips* and Peter O'Toole, despite his obvious talents, and a load of other musical failures). The two decades became an arena in which moviemakers split into two camps: those trying to do what had always worked (create stars, make Broadway adaptations and biopics) and those trying to be innovative and modern (create musicals that addressed harsh realities in order to be current with the times). There was a lot of flailing around, and musicals—the tried-and-true great American reliable genre—became unreliable.

During the 1960s and 1970s, despite Andrews and Streisand and *The Sound of Music,* the "happy musical" began to seem trivial and old-fashioned; but as is always the case, history is complex. There was one last hurrah for the old warhorse Broadway adaptation that could win an Oscar, *Oliver!* in

1968, but it wasn't exactly a happy musical. Lots of people were jumping around and romping up and down the streets of Dickens's London, but there was abandonment, death, robbery, fear, child exploitation, and even murder to contend with. Based on a hit show from the London theater, the film had choreography by Onna White to go with music by Lionel Bart. *Oliver!* was a musicalization of Dickens's *Oliver Twist,* and had the luck to be directed by Sir Carol Reed, one of Britain's most experienced and capable talents. Most people remember him as the man who put the legendary *The Third Man* on the screen to great success, but Reed had also directed many other types of stories, including a musical for Jessie Matthews early in his career (*Climbing High,* 1938).

Oliver! has energy, and it has great art direction. It even has some good songs, "Consider Yourself," "As Long as He Needs Me," and "I'd Do Anything" among them. What it doesn't have is star power, and whereas a Broadway (or London) show can get by on voices, a movie needs personalities. Oliver Reed is excellent as Bill Sykes, but the other leads are not names and are not presented as surrogates to a viewing audience, who

Streisand directed and starred in an underrated musical about a young woman posing as a male in order to become educated and independent: *Yentl.*

Oliver!, a throwback to an earlier era of big-time Broadway adaptations: boys work (and sing and dance) . . .

thus have no identifying figure. Ron Moody plays Fagin—he did the role in London—and the key role of Nancy was given to a singer named Shani Wallis, who was unknown to American audiences. Oliver was played by Mark Lester and the Artful Dodger by Jack Wild. The former was ordinary and the latter solid, but none of these players could connect to an audience the way moviegoers wanted them to in musical films. *Oliver!* rounded out the 1960s as the imitation of a happy, polished, exuberant Hollywood movie, but its dark and depressing world, its nonstar universe, and its designer gloom don't inspire much joy today. *Oliver!* is not on many people's best-musical lists.

Outside the musical genre, films were becoming smaller, grittier, dirtier, and more violent. The musical faced the need to become more realistic, but not in a pretend way. The way to make a good one had become understood, but what to make one *about* became a problem. If the form was supposed to be entertaining, lighthearted, and escapist—if that was its goal—what was it going to do with the challenges of changing morals, the Vietnam War, and the new movie realism? Who could have predicted that to deal with this pressure, the musical would try to commit suicide? Who knew that in order to keep step with the times, the musical form, perhaps inspired by the success of the arty Freed unit, would try to become importantly serious?

From the beginning there was always a "serious" form of the entertainment musical film—the 1936 *Show Boat*, for instance—and it's possible to look back to three key films of the 1950s and early 1960s and see them as harbingers of change that pointed forward to a deeper darkness that would infuse the form during the 1970s and onward: Judy Garland's version of *A Star Is Born* (1954), the final Stanley Donen/Gene Kelly opus *It's Always Fair Weather* (1955), and the Broadway adaptation *West Side Story* (1961).

A Star Is Born is an openly tragic musical. The basic story has a long history: its origins are found in a movie called *What Price Hollywood?* (1932), which was reconstituted as the nonmusical 1937 *A Star Is Born*, starring Janet Gaynor, and remade in 1976 with Barbra Streisand and Kris Kristofferson and in 2018 with Lady Gaga and Bradley Cooper. *A Star Is Born* is about alcoholism, suicide, failed marriage, career disappointment, the cruelty of show business, and the rapacity of the press and of fans—not exactly a romp through Paris. *A Star Is Born* features the older Judy Garland (that is, the older-looking Garland; she was only thirty-four at the time). Her costar is the nonmusical James Mason, an elegant actor who in every way manages to embody what his character represents: a man too sensitive and refined to survive the crass world of show business.

. . . and girls work (and sing and dance)

A Star Is Born is Garland's magnum opus. She is in her final glory in a film released not by MGM, but by Warner Bros., and produced by the man who was her husband at the time, Sid Luft. The story is about a girl from the sticks named Esther Blodgett who, because she's loaded with outrageous talent, will be turned into a top-of-the-line movie star named Vicki Lester. Where this plot once would have been a tale of triumph, rising to a crescendo of positive achievement, sending everyone home with a happy ending, *A Star Is Born* offers the bad news that no one really wants: success is a bummer.

A Star Is Born is a pseudo biopic, a form of musical in which the audience is used to finding disappointment and tragedy. It tells a familiar tale of the disappointment of fame, but it also finds success in presenting a leading lady who not only can sing but also can act. Garland is not outclassed by Mason, and thus their screen romance doesn't seem like some kind of casting mismatch. The film's main success lies in its ability to run parallel universes: the joyous rise to success while falling in love on the one hand, and on the other, exploitation, removal of personality (Blodgett's name is changed without her knowledge), hucksterism, and the slavery of a studio contract. The world of artifice is revealed realistically when, like the happier *Singin' in the Rain* before it, *A Star Is Born* shows an audience how movies are made.

The musical numbers are—an important decision—designed to be successful as songs and dances, but also to contain a subtext that reveals tragedy and disappointment. (This was an indicator of what the future of the musical would be.) The film opens with a fabulous re-creation of a big-time Hollywood charity show at which Norman Maine (Mason) is to appear. The scene is chaotic, kaleidoscopic, full of all the noise and excitement and congestion such an event really has.*

When Mason shows up drunk, he is rescued from public embarrassment by Garland and her singing group. When he wanders onstage, she weaves him into their lively song and dance, to the delight of the audience. The song being performed is "Gotta Have Me Go with You," an obvious lyric for the situation, but also for what will become their relationship. The number has two levels: one is a successful musical performance that's bouncy and fun; the other is the tragedy of angry, drunken, and irresponsible

---

* The director is George Cukor, and it was his first movie made in color. He did not direct the "Born in a Trunk" number, however. That director was Richard Barstow.

behavior that must be controlled and camouflaged. When Mason goes looking for Garland later, she's at a small nightclub after hours, sitting around and singing with the band. It's a glorious moment. Her song became one of her signatures, right up there after "Over the Rainbow": "The Man That Got Away." Her performance is shot in one take, and Garland is on display as herself as well as Esther Blodgett. Mason, watching her, is incorporated into the presentation with bookended reaction shots that show him in a kind of glow as he realizes her talent. He will, tragically, become her man that gets away.

More than in any other aspect of *A Star Is Born*, it's the performance of "The Man That Got Away" that reveals the seriousness of the film's musical purpose. The scene wasn't easily achieved. Four different versions were shot and recorded before the final was chosen. The song had to be right—the entire film leaned on it—because it's the song, its meaning, Mason's reaction to it, and Garland's rendering of it that are the foundation for everything that follows. Why should deciding how to costume, edit, record, and shoot this classic moment be so difficult? Mason was a great actor. Cukor was a great director. Harold Arlen and Ira Gershwin were great songwriters. And as all serious modern moviegoers know, Judy Garland was a great singer. But the four different versions reveal the great

A Star Is Born, the story of Esther Blodgett/ Vicki Lester, has been a durable movie property, but no version is more famous than the one with Judy Garland and her costar James Mason.

challenge of how to indicate impending sadness in the subtextual usage of music. The three rejected versions have superb music, orchestration, and singing, but they don't look the same and thus they don't mean the same. In the rejected versions, Garland is dressed in two different outfits and has three different hairdos. In one version, she wears a pink, short-sleeved shirt-waist blouse and a straight gray skirt, and looks all right, but her makeup is the overglamorized look of a *star* . . . and she's still Esther Blodgett at this point in the plot. In the other two versions, she wears a tannish shirtwaist dress with short sleeves and a straight skirt, and the color and the fit are unflattering. She looks middle-aged and frumpy. In one of these two similar presentations, she is shot in intense close-ups, and her delivery of the song is over the top. She appears neurotic and increasingly joyless as she sings. In the version that made it into the movie, Garland wears a simple dark-blue dress with a white collar. The effect is youthful; the collar frames her face and sheds a flattering light on her. Her hair is drawn back into a less matronly style, and she looks like a girl, not yet famous, eager and optimistic. Her pleasure in the song itself—and her chance to sing it with a group of musicians she loves and who clearly love and appreciate her—is apparent. Garland moves among the group in the one take, but they recede, their faces disappear, and she becomes the focus.

All four versions of "The Man That Got Away" are trying for something: expressing through music a specific place (an after-hours gathering of musicians), a lost and lonely man who's looking for a woman he can't forget, and an innocent girl who has stardom written all over her. The moviemaking team worked hard to provide a loose, casual feeling in the room, while still allowing for an electric current to begin to sizzle when Garland moves into play, casually taking the sheet music and beginning to sing. In earlier versions, this casualness was overworked. Garland was laughing, chatting; she playfully tossed a mute to a trombone player. The "naturalness" was forced, and distracted a viewer from the importance of the action. The scene is supposed to be low-key but revealing. Happy but with a foreboding of tragedy. It's in the lyrics, it's in Mason's character, and it's in Garland's voice. With "The Man That Got Away," *A Star Is Born* announces that it will be a tragedy. There will be no happy ending ("The road gets rougher/It's lonelier and tougher . . ."). As Garland picks up the sheet music, considering joining in, piano player Tommy Noonan lightly says, "Take it, honey." And take it she does—right over the rainbow toward sadness, in a darkened room, after hours, with friends around her but also with the man who'll leave her alone and heartbroken. Other movies had been serious musicals, but *A Star Is Born* embraced tragedy through a single musical number.

Every song in the film is performed by Garland, all with a purposeful (and tragic) undertone: "Here's What I'm Here For" shows how the press intrude into their lives; "It's a New World," which she sings a cappella as a personal favor to Mason, reflects the optimism in their new life together; in "Someone at Last," she comes home from work to find him lonely and despondent and—using things around their house—creates a comedy number about moviemaking, mocking her career and Hollywood to make him laugh, denying the importance of her fame and his loss of stardom; and "Lose That Long Face" is a devastating portrait of the pain of stardom. As Garland performs this silly, cheerful number for her latest film, the photography is interrupted to reset for close-ups. Garland goes to her dressing room and has a breakdown. The song, for which she wears a clownish costume, is all about being happy. While having to perform it, she's under the worst pressure of her life, because her husband has sunk deeply into alcoholism.

Between takes, in her dressing room, Garland begs Charles Bickford (head of the studio and Mason's old friend and champion) to tell her why her husband drinks, and then confesses in sobs, "I hate him for failing . . . I hate me, too." As she chokes and wipes her face, a knock on the door is heard, summoning her back to filming. She hastily pulls herself together, repairs her makeup, and is soon seen in medium close-up, smiling brightly and pumping out the lyrics: "Don't give in to a frown/Turn that frown upside down . . ." The difference between what is seen as she's filmed (and what will be seen by her audiences later) and what is happening behind the scenes as she creates the entertainment is text and subtext.

There is another musical number in *A Star Is Born*, an extended movie within a movie that runs for fifteen minutes of screen time: the famous "Born in a Trunk." It's Warner Bros. proving to MGM the old "Anything you can do we can do better." It is a miniature musical movie of the kind MGM used to make, including some fairly overt references to the "Broadway Melody" finale in *Singin' in the Rain*. It could also be thought of as Judy Garland's life story, especially when she sits on the edge of the stage to sing about being "born in a trunk . . . in Pocatello, Idaho" and having to perform as a child. It's Judy Garland as Esther Blodgett becoming Vicki Lester because she's Judy Garland. Proof of the modernist viewpoint

A Star Is Born: Judy Garland with the Oscar she won *in* the movie but not *for* the movie . . . She was robbed.

of *A Star Is Born* as a musical is that it contains within itself what the musical genre has always been: this little "story" of success, with music. In this case, says the musical under scrutiny, we're giving you a revisionist version. Garland will not have a happy ending. Mason will die by suicide, and she'll be left with her fame but without the love of her life.

A Star Is Born announced itself in its advertising as a serious musical, so it was no surprise for audiences that things were tragic. But *It's Always Fair Weather* was more deceptive. It was a musical with an already defined pedigree: the Freed unit, Gene Kelly, Cyd Charisse, Michael Kidd (as both performer and choreographer), and two other successful stars associated with musicals: dancer Dan Dailey and singer/dancer Dolores Gray. And its story echoes back to another successful musical, *On the Town*, which also starred Kelly and was a Freed unit success. (*On the Town* was about three sailors; *It's Always Fair Weather* is about three ex-army buddies.) Whereas *On the Town* was a celebration, a joyous, energetic romp for three guys let loose from their shipboard duty for an anything-may-happen weekend in the big city, *It's Always Fair Weather* has an opposite trajectory. As the film begins, the three guys (Kelly, Kidd, and Dailey) celebrate survival. World War II is over, and they're going home. Excitement is behind them—it's an ending, not a beginning. Their friendship, forged in fire, will endure—or so they believe—even though they are saying goodbye and going their separate ways. Each has his American dream of success: an elegant gourmet restaurant for Kidd; becoming a famous painter for Dailey; and getting rich for Kelly. The dance they do as they prepare to separate—in which, among other things, they dance with garbage-pail lids on their feet—is terrific, but has more of an air of drunken departure than *On the Town*'s sober, shared anticipation. The three veterans promise to meet again at the same bar in ten years . . . and so they do. Most of the film takes place in that later time frame, and therein lies the problem: when they reconvene, the three are all unhappy with their lives. Kidd owns and operates a low-class diner; Dailey is a stressed-out advertising executive; and Kelly is a con artist and gambler trying to avoid his creditors. As soon as they meet, they discover they can't stand one another. It's a recipe for a bitter and sour story rather than a peppy musical, and why didn't anyone see that coming? Behind the scenes, Donen and Kelly were no longer compatible. Kelly was coming off a disappointing experience with *Invitation to the Dance,* the movie he hoped would present ballet to the masses.* He and Kidd clashed over choreography, with Kelly rumored to be so jealous of Kidd that he cut his big solo. MGM was beginning to feel the postwar problems that would ultimately end the studio system, and Arthur Freed himself was losing his optimistic belief that his type of musical would last forever. Everyone was grumpy, disillusioned, and uncooperative.

Where *Singin' in the Rain* had been a funny and charming satire of the movies, *It's Always Fair Weather* was designed as a mockery of television, with its ads, its sentimentality, and its exploitation of ordinary people as guinea pigs for shows such as *This Is Your Life.* (The script by Comden and Green was a sort of recycling of their earlier version of the three servicemen concept from *On the Town.)* The difference between the two movies is key. *Singin'* has a nostalgic, loving sense of Hollywood's past and a tolerance for its foibles. *Fair Weather* is angry at the competition from TV, openly scorning its goals and its audiences. Running underneath the story of friendship gained, friendship lost, and friendship regained is a depressing sense of something good that America had lost, and the something mean and small that had grown in its place.

It's Always Fair Weather can't deny what's under the surface *or* what was going on with those who made it. It *is* an example of people who were once happy with each other and happy to be doing what they're doing and happily trying to make it become art, now suddenly losing faith. Audiences smelled the rot and saw the negative. The film lost money, but it's significant for two reasons: (1) it's a genuine example of a Freed unit product, made at the midpoint of the decade (1955), that points to the reason musi-

---

* *Invitation to the Dance* was made in Europe (to help MGM use frozen funds) during 1952. MGM disliked it, shelving it until it was finally released in 1956.

THE DEATH OF THE MUSICAL? 511

cals like this aren't going to keep going forever, and (2) despite all that, the dances are delightful.

In addition to the wonderful split-screen presentation of three dancers wearing garbage-can lids, it contains two delightful numbers by the female costars of the film. Cyd Charisse has her own flat-out showcase, dancing with a group of "boxers" to "Baby, You Knock Me Out," and Dolores Gray does a show-stopping "Thanks a Lot, but No Thanks." Both women are attired for their dances in high-fifties fashion: Charisse in a split skirt and turtleneck and Gray in a fishtailed strapless gown. Both women are talented and beautiful. Gray has a face built for CinemaScope: her mouth is a mile wide—she's a sort of sexy Carol Channing. She's an excellent comedienne, and her portrait of a smarmy TV hostess is perfect ("I want millions of people to sit at home and cry—and love me "). Charisse never missed a step in anything she was given to do, and this film was no exception. One other musical presentation was designed to be the highlight of the film: Gene Kelly on roller skates, flying around Manhattan's sidewalks and streets and stores, happily singing "I Like Myself." The number was designed to be another "Singin' in the Rain" dance: Kelly out in the streets, bringing music to the whole world, inspired by his emotions and singing all about it while coping with a problem (instead of rain, roller skates). Comden and Green's work was often derivative of itself, and the idea of repeating the "street" success for Kelly is an example of it. This time, however, despite the delicious trill in his voice, the lyrics made the number unappealing to many. The self-love seemed all too true.

It's Always Fair Weather, seen today, is something of a minor classic. Its desperation and disappointment are acceptable—no one any longer expects total joy from the Freed musical format. When the three stars get roaring drunk and dance up and down the streets together in widescreen, with the screen marked off in thirds so each has a space all to himself, yet in co-ownership with the other two, it's spectacular. The sight of all three guys rushing toward the camera, and the camera itself rushing alongside them as they leap wildly down the street, gives any viewer a lift. The trio dances with humor and skill, and each man manages to make the dance into an individual characterization without losing the trio concept. It's one of the Freed unit's best ensemble male dances. All three men are real dancers. Kelly was Kelly, and Kidd was Kidd (one of the most successful choreographers of the era), and Dan Dailey was an underrated hoofer with a strong screen personality. Dailey was a tall man, and towered over both Kelly and

Michael Kidd, Gene Kelly, and Dan Dailey celebrate "We're Civilians Now" with garbage-can lids on their feet in *It's Always Fair Weather*.

Kidd, but he was a real tapper, a light stepper with a dapper air. He not only could act, but he could also put on a lampshade and clown around (which he does in this film). (He costarred with Betty Grable in four films, all successes at Fox, and was Oscar-nominated for his performance in one of them, *When My Baby Smiles at Me*.) A specialty number was created just for him as the pressured advertising executive: "Situation-Wise," a rip-off of the "Moses Supposes" number from *Singin' in the Rain*, a wordplay song. Dailey did it well.

As for Kelly's "I Like Myself," it, too, has gained over time. Kelly is relaxed, easy, and the Kelly/Donen relationship—in its death throes—has one last hurrah. Kelly is followed on skates by a fast tracking camera, moving as if it's on skates itself, giving the routine a lightness and buoyancy that's the characteristic of the Kelly/Donen collaboration. Racing and sweeping, the camera moves. Racing and skating, Kelly moves. For one last time, Kelly in front of the camera and Donen behind the camera are perfectly united. But it led nowhere—it was their final collaboration.

There are four landmark Broadway musical productions: Kern and Hammerstein's *Show Boat* in 1927; Rodgers and Hammerstein's *Oklahoma!* in 1943; *West Side Story* in 1957, with music by Leonard Bernstein and lyrics by Stephen Sondheim; and Lin-Manuel Miranda's 2015 *Hamilton*. Each was a groundbreaking theatrical event, and the first three have been made into movies, with the fourth awaiting its transformation. The biggest movie success of all—*West Side Story*—was released in 1961, to critical acclaim and a box-office bonanza, but there were some glitches in the filmed version: The leading lady was the beautiful actress Natalie Wood, who was neither Hispanic nor a singer (she was dubbed by Marni Nixon); and the leading man, Richard Beymer, was also not a singer (he was dubbed by Jimmy Bryant). The story is about a passionate young Romeo-and-Juliet love, and Wood and Beymer generated no chemistry. Nevertheless, the 1960s opened with this blockbuster musical winning ten Academy Awards, including Best Picture and Best Director, and again confirming the audience's love of the genre and suggesting a successful future. *West Side Story* seemed to provide the kind of modernization of musicals that audiences could be comfortable with—mixing sets and real streets, transferring original material from Broadway to the movie house without losing its newness, and moving into ethnicity in a comfortable way. The music was fresh; the dancing was athletic and amazing; and the story was a classic one, young love doomed to failure in a way that made death acceptable to the musical format. It seemed like progress of a sort that the mass market could embrace.

West Side Story provided a possible way to resolve the tension between the real and the unreal linked to musical performance: act as if there's no difference between them on a daily basis. Present a world in which people sing and dance as if that *is* what reality *is*. Music and plot were seamlessly integrated in *West Side Story*. Music is what matters, and it provides everything: characterization, delineation of emotions, and direct communication among people. But it also reveals the way the genre is heading: to self-consciously making viewers aware of its devices as devices. When Tony and Maria (Beymer and Wood) first meet in a crowded gym at a dance, they see each other and slowly everyone else disappears, and they begin to dance alone in an abstracted space. It's a visualization of how they feel, how they are drawn at once to each other, and how they will express their emotions. So very new, so very theatrical and innovative. And yet, moviegoers had seen this back in 1934 in *Dames*, when Dick Powell sang "I Only Have Eyes for You" to Ruby Keeler and everyone in the movie disappeared but her. It's the same thing. The difference is in the attitude taken toward it. It's no longer intuitive, or just done by instinct as a good idea for something cinema can do that the stage can't. In *West Side Story*, well directed by Robert Wise and Jerome Robbins, it's put forward in a way that asks an audience to understand cinema rather than just enjoy a number.

West Side Story's mixture of designed sets and real locations meshed well with its treatment of the story, which fused the musical performance and the plot into one entity. After the overture, a series of aerial shots of New York City ultimately locates the real streets of Manhattan . . . only they're now the *musical* streets of Manhattan. Dance is filling the streets, and it's

serious dance. It's a world in which young men express themselves through it—musical performance is their way to let off steam, show who they are, and bond with one another. *West Side Story* is about a place where conflict is resolved through music, primarily dance, and where lovers find a space of their own through color and song. It's a movie that literally confirms the world as a stage.

As the 1960s moved forward, the threatened collapse of the studio system actually occurred, brought on by competition from TV and increased foreign film distribution; legal decrees that stopped the studio practices of block booking and theater ownership; changing audience tastes; the letting go of censorship restrictions, etc. By 1970, *everything* in the Hollywood working world was different, and the sour taste that had been detected in

An explosion of testosterone in the streets of New York from *West Side Story,* in which the real world becomes a dance floor

It's Always Fair Weather and the tragedy that drove *A Star Is Born* were becoming the norm in movies. *Bonnie and Clyde* was released in 1967 and *Easy Rider* in 1969, and the movie world that followed was a different place. It was time for a new kind of musical, and the 1970s began to bring it: the tragic musical, or the musical with some kind of very realistic problem (Nazis, for instance), or the musical that couldn't be about anything except itself.

Four musicals from the 1970s illustrate what *A Star Is Born*, *It's Always Fair Weather*, and *West Side Story* were pointing toward: *Darling Lili* (1970), *Cabaret* (1972), *New York, New York* (1977), and *All That Jazz* (1979). The earliest example, lavishly produced, gorgeously costumed, and containing a great deal of genuine humor, is Blake Edwards's *Darling Lili*, starring his wife, Julie Andrews, the proven musical box-office champion. It didn't work—at least it didn't work at the box office, and it still has a general reputation as a failure, despite being a favorite of certain connoisseurs. *Darling Lili* puts self-reflexivity in musicals to rest once and for all by being so totally about role playing and performances designed to deceive (both on- and offstage) that there's not much left to develop. The movie mixes moods (it's both satiric and serious, comic and tragic) and mixes genres (war, music, comedy, romance, slapstick, woman's film, et al.). An audience doesn't know what to expect, since they are denied consistency. For instance, as Andrews sings the hauntingly beautiful lyric of "Whistling Away the Dark" as the film opens ("Tell me dreams really come true"), a cut shows a blimp flying over London and a submarine rising up, two instruments of death outside her theater that intercut into her song. Two genres (war and musicals) clash and interact. Similarly, Andrews will do a sweet number ("I'll Give You Three Guesses") wearing a yellow daisy-studded dress. She swings out over the audience, singing in her lovely voice, demurely playing to them. Later, when she believes Rock Hudson (her lover) has cheated on her with a French stripper, she does the number differently, as a boom-boom striptease with a hard beat. Two versions of the same thing. Everything in *Lili* has a duality, or another possible interpretation, and who knows who anyone is, and why does it matter? Everybody sing! Lili is a German spy, but also an English music-hall favorite. Hudson is an American air ace, but also a man with a secret mission. Two—not one—inept Inspector Clouseau types try to figure it all out; and two—not one—evil Germans try to figure it out for different reasons. And there's a mysterious man in the middle who could be anyone or anything (Jeremy Kemp). Everybody sing again.

Darling Lili's opening and closing numbers are actually, self-consciously, about the purpose of the musical film. The first version—the opening scene—shows Andrews (as Lili) singing during an air raid in World War I. She's pinpointed in the dark on the widescreen, and is slowly revealed in full in her English theater setting as the song progresses. Her music takes away darkness, and she dances around the stage, singing her "Whistling Away the Dark" lyrics that address why music is necessary, especially in the darkest of times. At the end of the movie, after much plot complication, events in different moods, and multiple genres have passed, Lili, the German spy, is welcomed back to England. She repeats her song, and out of the darkness in the wings appear the men who have fought in the war, as if her music can regenerate life. *Darling Lili* was a failure because it was about itself: a musical about musicals, and also about genre. It shows what a dilemma the form was facing by 1970—what was its purpose now that times had changed, and would anyone still want it?

Cabaret and *New York, New York* show the two possible answers to the question. The first is the tried-and-true staple of musical success, the adaptation of a hit Broadway show, based on a respected play, John Van Druten's *I Am a Camera*, which itself had been based on a distinguished book,

Julie Andrews and her "dawn patrol" admirers in *Darling Lili*

Christopher Isherwood's *Goodbye to Berlin*. These credentials seemed foolproof: book, theater, hit New York musical—how could anything go wrong? And it didn't. The second film, directed by Martin Scorsese, is an original motion-picture musical that linked itself to earlier movies—in particular, Judy Garland's *A Star Is Born* and since the references were the very best of MGM's Freed unit successes, how could anything go wrong? But everything did.

Cabaret, the film, starred Judy Garland and Vincente Minnelli's talented daughter, Liza, as Sally Bowles, with Michael York as the hero and Joel Grey as the cabaret's Master of Ceremonies (re-creating his award-winning performance from Broadway). Three new songs were written for the movie, Minnelli's "Mein Herr," "Money Money," for her and Grey, and Minnelli's very personal solo, "Maybe This Time." (Several songs in the stage production were not included, among them "Don't Tell Mama," "Telephone Song," "It Couldn't Please Me More," "Married," and "What Would You Do?")* The movie lived up to its pedigree, winning eight Academy Awards, including Best Actress (Minnelli), Best Supporting Actor (Grey), and Best Director (Bob Fosse).

Cabaret was filmed on location in Berlin and various parts of Germany, and this move out of the soundstages that were home to more traditional musicals is significant. Bob Fosse, the dynamic choreographer/director, removed almost all the songs and dances that didn't take place in the primary cabaret setting of the Kit Kat Klub. In fact, the movie has only one number outside Berlin in a wider world, "Tomorrow Belongs to Me." The world of the movie is seen through a reflection in the Klub's warped mirror. Musical numbers are used to explain parallel events taking place *outside* the cabaret. (And the musical performers perform *only* onstage, not out in the streets in real life. They *are* performers. That's their only musical reality.) "Life is a cabaret," sings Minnelli, and director Fosse links onstage musical performance to real-life Berlin through cinema. They mirror each other, and converge in the end. Through it all, Grey, as emcee, is the audience's guide. The cabaret exists independent of time and space. Inside it, there's no sense of whether it's day or night.

Bob Fosse had proved himself as both a dancer and a choreographer for films as early as his appearance in 1953's *Kiss Me, Kate*. Working with three sets of paired dancers in the "From This Moment On" number (Ann

* The songs were by John Kander and Fred Ebb.

Miller/Tommy Rall, Bobby Van/Jeanne Coyne, and Fosse/Carol Haney), the movie's choreographer, Hermes Pan, noted that Fosse and Haney had a way of dancing that was distinctive. He invited them to choreograph their own section of the dance, which was staged to look as if it was taking place under the proscenium arch. The forward-driving song was meant to allow the dancers to run and race and explode with energy across the width of the frame.

Fosse eagerly took charge. Writing in his definitive biography, *Fosse*, Sam Wasson says, "Fosse's section was short, only forty-five seconds, but it showed, for the first time, what happened when Bob Fosse danced on

Judy Garland's daughter, Liza Minnelli, proves she's a star in her own right, as Sally Bowles in *Cabaret*.

film in what would become known as the Fosse style." Fosse had come close to almost accomplishing that goal in the rarely seen *The Affairs of Dobie Gillis* earlier in the same year, but his herky-jerky movements and weirdly twisted body positions were overshadowed by the emerging stardom of perky Debbie Reynolds and the hot-tapping Bobby Van, the film's two headliners. Fosse was Fosse in *Dobie,* but as Wasson points out, he really broke through and was seen in "From This Moment On" in *Kiss Me, Kate:* "he leaps and lands in a baseball slide . . . Fosse and Haney . . . spin forward together and freeze . . . slither in syncopation, shoulders hunched and knees bent, boy and girl Fosses. . . . The Fosse influence is unmistakable to the modern viewer." There's a historical statement being made that's almost anticinema: "Broadway Melody" could have looked like this if the dancers had been allowed to feel it, express it, and move back and forth across a widescreen proscenium-arch stage with youthful abandon. Fosse's work reclaims dance for the dancers, allowing their bodies to contort, twist, and be accompanied by expressive hand movements. Even later in his career, after he incorporated cinema, putting rhythm and energy into the dance through cutting, camera movement, and framing, Fosse remained an innovator who saw dance as attitude and social commentary.

In making *Cabaret* his own, Fosse created a musical that was a synthesis of elements. He turned the stage success into a modern musical on his own terms, an original and innovative example of the genre. The numbers became commentary rather than the whole reason for the musical. He goes back to the beginning of movie-musical interpretation and just says boldly: "There are two different worlds here, one in which people sing and dance for a living and one in which there are Nazis, and if *they're* singing, it's going to turn into 'Tomorrow Belongs to Me.'" And there's no spatial denial: the cabaret is a real place, a cabaret, and thus it must reflect inside what is going on in the outside world. One number is intercut with a dog being killed, and one with a man being beaten in the streets. Fosse's presentation is anti-Astaire: he'll cut a song and dance forty-seven times to be effective if it suits his goal, which is always larger than any single number.

Cabaret reconstitutes the musical format. It maintains the need for a strong singing star (Minnelli), but it introduces politics, reality, and ugly forces (fascism, anti-Semitism) as motivation for music and tells a story that involves abortion, sexuality, and death. The music is used for a purpose other than lightening our hearts—it's there to teach us something and make us aware of what reality is. If musicals could have found a way to continue the *Cabaret* musical premise on a regular basis, they might not have lost power at the box office. As it was, Fosse made one other significant "realistic" musical that was also successful: *All That Jazz* in 1979. It was an autobiographical film about his desire to make a Felliniesque *8½*, only his was a musical. It begins with an audition scene, and since those auditioning are singers and dancers trying out for musical roles, it's a musical number: "On Broadway." It has an almost documentary-like effect, as Roy Scheider (playing Fosse as a character named Joe Gideon) goes among the candidates, keeping some and eliminating others. *All That Jazz* is the opposite of most biopics, in that it traces the decline of a musical performer rather than the rise of one. Where the Freed unit talents of Minnelli/Kelly/Donen brought the moving camera into the choreography, Fosse in his musicals brings in the editing table, cutting with a rhythm and making the beats of the dance the cuts of the film. The dances are designed to be cut in specific ways that are linked to the choreography. The attitude toward the human body dancing has shifted radically. Fosse contributed to a sense of abstraction in musical presentation: the talent of the individual dancer didn't matter as much as what the dancer evoked. *All That Jazz* is, let's hope, the only musical that incorporated open heart surgery into its world (with an actual beating heart revealed), and also the only one that ends up with the protagonist in a body bag.*

Bob Fosse modernized the musical, whether anyone wanted it modernized or not. He upgraded it to contain sex, sin, and disaster. None of those elements were ever really absent in earlier musicals, but they were offstage, or briefly apparent, or buried in musical numbers. Fosse brought them on front and center. He also changed the idea that the dancer, in particular, had to be respected by the camera. On the contrary, his movies said,

---

* The Bob Fosse stage hit *Chicago*, with music by Kander and Ebb, was also made into a movie musical (in 2002). Based on the Roxie Hart character (Ginger Rogers) from a 20th Century–Fox film of the same name (1942), the story is a cynical and hard-hearted look at 1920s yellow journalism. A woman shoots her husband and hires a slick lawyer to get her off by manipulating her image in the press. The film was directed by Rob Marshall, and although it won awards and has excellent numbers, the presentation doesn't take the genre anywhere new. The musical numbers are imaginary, dreamed by Roxie (Renée Zellweger, who's not a good singer/dancer) as an escape from her grim reality. The movie is cut in the hip style of certain types of music video—wham, wham, wham, lest we get bored by music. Two terrific performers do shine: Queen Latifah (as a warden) and Catherine Zeta-Jones, who won Best Supporting Actress for her portrait of Velma Kelly, a nightclub performer who's Roxie's idol and role model.

Liza Minnelli and Robert De Niro as a mismatched pair of lovers who can make beautiful music: *New York, New York*

the camera can sit still and let the cutter do the dancing or at least be the partner of the dance. The result changed the dynamic of the musical for a viewer. No longer was the audience lifted up into a vicarious participation, a release into freedom of movement. Now the audience was a watcher of a rhythmic assault, in which the dancer paired with his or her own destruction.

As the 1970s moved toward a close, Scorsese presided over a musical set in post–World War II America and destined to be a failure but perhaps linked to a line of dialogue that is heard up front in the film: "The war was over and the world was falling in love again."* That may or may not have been true, but certainly the world didn't fall in love with *New York, New York*. I first saw it on a hot summer night, and I was the only person in the theater. The projectionist came out and tried to con me into going home so he could close down. (There were still projectionists in those days.) When I refused, he yelled at me, "You're gonna hate this, lady, and don't try to blame me!" He didn't know I was a musicals fan, and that not only would I not hate it, I would actually love it. I respected what it was trying to do, and the music was wonderful.

The hero of *New York, New York*, if you can call him a hero, is the egotistical, unfaithful, angry and jealous Jimmy Doyle, played by Robert De Niro, an unmusical actor. He talks a lot in the film about something he calls "a major chord," which he defines as "when you have everything you could ever possibly want . . . everything . . . the woman you want, the music you want, and enough money to live comfortably." Scorsese was clearly going after a musical movie version of a major chord with *New York, New York*, giving us all the music we'd want, the story we'd want, the stars we'd want, the 1940s musical era we'd like to see again. It was a nostalgia trip back to the wartime musicals, clothes, attitudes, and sounds, but being Scorsese, he couldn't let it alone. He had to tell the cinematic truth, and personalize the use of cinema, because that's who he is as a film director.

New York, New York is a variation of the musical genre, made at a time when almost everyone who tried to make a musical was experimenting in some way with the form. Scorsese's premise is clearly seen onscreen: realistic events and passions and disappointments are combined with an artificial old-Hollywood production design and look. The idea was to counterpoint elements for a meaningful commentary. The result was that audiences were distracted by the artifice and distanced from the story and the characters.

Whenever I've told Scorsese that I like this film—and I've told him that more than once—a brief look of gratitude, followed by an almost imperceptible but definite shudder, is his reaction. "It was a difficult time," he always says. Shooting the movie took twenty-two weeks. It doubled its original budget, costing about $14 million, and the first cut ran four and a half hours. The final cut released ran 153 minutes, and reviews were not positive. Four years later, in 1981, a version that ran 163 minutes and included some crucial restored material, was released to positive reviews,

---

* The Vietnam War had ended two years earlier, and it was a period of cultural transition in America.

but the film remains problematic. No one wants to own it. When *La La Land* was released in 2016, its writer and director, Damien Chazelle, happily admitted to influences like *The Umbrellas of Cherbourg*, a French homage to American musicals, but didn't mention that his film's ending was similar to that of *New York, New York*. (*La La Land*'s basic plot is about two people, both looking for success, who fall in love, with one making it big and the other ending up owning a nightclub.)

Scorsese is a first-rate film historian, and he understands the musicals he's referencing in his movie, which he called "a fantasy fused with reality." He sets up the movie clearly: it will be a world defined by the 1940s Hollywood musical. It's a musical about musicals, and the songs are directly linked to narrative event: "You Brought a New Kind of Love to Me," "The Man I Love," etc. Scorsese made a form of backstage musical in which two characters have different musical styles, one popular (Minnelli's) and one esoteric (De Niro's). De Niro is given a sort of harsh "Gene Kelly" personality, and Liza Minnelli is modeled on her mother, but both are too strong as actors to be swamped by these powerful personae.

The movie finds its raison d'être in its eleven-minute presentation "Happy Endings," the movie within a movie that stars Minnelli and that De Niro, her ex-husband, goes to see in a movie house. "Happy Endings" is directly linked to *A Star Is Born*'s "Born in a Trunk" with Minnelli performing her version of her mother's original (which was itself a reference to the "Broadway Melody" finale in *Singin' in the Rain*). The little "movie" charts the story of its own heroine and her rise to stardom. It includes an homage to earlier musicals and a stylized microcosm of the entire real story it's inside of. The movie embraces the conflict between real and unreal worlds of the kind that exist in musicals, and both celebrates and criticizes the format.

Both *Cabaret* and *New York, New York* embrace the idea of being movies about movies. They welcome modernism, because what else is a movie to do in the world of the 1970s? The dilemma this presents for any audience's response in terms of affirmation is represented in a melancholy way in *New York, New York*, a movie made by a man who understands musicals and Hollywood's history. Early in the film, De Niro stands on a train platform looking down to a lower subway level where a sailor and his girl dance under a streetlight. Are they a sailor and a girl from *On the Town*? Is De Niro watching an imaginary movie? The dance is clearly a tribute to musicals of the past, but there's no joy on either side, neither in the dancers nor in the watcher—and for that matter, not in the audience either. It's an academic exercise. And it represents the truth: when it comes to old musicals, we can only watch them, we can't get into them—nor, apparently, can we now make them. Is it too late? Is the time for them gone with the wind? Is the musical dead?

Looking at these key musicals (including *It's Always Fair Weather*, a production of the Freed unit, the place where trying to become "serious" had first become really important), we can see how the genre was trying to both deny itself and replicate itself. *A Star Is Born* is an antimusical. It contrasts what musical films provide an audience—a beautiful, cheerful, happy ending facilitated by musical performance—with a different world or even the actual act of producing musical performance. The film is shot partially on location at a time when most musicals were being shot indoors on sets. It strips away viewer complacency regarding musicals, and shows how someone (the musical star) has to suffer to create the joy of a musical performance: the price an entertainer pays. The implication is that *A Star Is Born* is a musical that's the truth about musicals. Behind the façade of happiness is a world of misery—a musical misery, of course, but still a misery.

West Side Story gives an audience three layers. It uses the very real streets of Manhattan, but shows how alienated teens create on these real streets an unreal world of their own—their private world of music and dance. Even further inside itself appears an even deeper world: the shared fantasy of the doomed lovers. *New York, New York* contrasts two different musical styles (pop music and jazz) and essentially does what *A Star Is Born*, its parent film, does: it tells the story of a female musical performer and what she suffers for fame and success. But it's different from *A Star Is Born* in that it's a film historian's musical: this is what musicals *used* to be, it's saying, and consciously makes that point by shooting on sets and soundstages at a time in film history in which every effort was being made to shoot in real locations and avoid that look. *New York, New York* creates a musical by re-creating the artifice of the Freed unit.

Darling Lili works with an audience's knowledge of previous movies, not just musicals but also nonmusicals. It is one of those movies of its era that self-consciously uses formal cinematic devices such as rack focus. Musical performance is often removed from the screen itself and heard only on the soundtrack, so that there's a separation of the visual and the aural. The effect of this is enormous—it changes everything. Instead of participating vicariously in a song or a dance, the viewer is pushed back, out of

it, more conscious of *being* a viewer rather than a dancer/singer. The main issue is that such fancy-shmancy techniques block an audience's emotional participation in the music. (*Darling Lili* opens and closes with a more traditional approach.)

Cabaret is an interesting variation because it doesn't actually break with any real tradition of the musical. It keeps to a usual format audiences understand—it's a form of backstage musical. However, it shifts the idea—reverses it—so that it becomes a "frontstage" musical. All the numbers (except "Tomorrow Belongs to Me") take place inside the cabaret, and they are the audience's explanation of what is going on in Nazi Germany. They aren't the escape; they are the commentary and the explanation. *All That Jazz* sets itself up as a total musical, a sort of drugged-out version of an earlier love story. (*Chicago* plays its music as occurring inside Roxie Hart's head, as she hides from her ugly reality.)

All of this stuff—and it *is* stuff—was a way to try to make the musical, the tried-and-true old-fashioned musical, into a modern treatise about politics, bad experiences, sex, death, the end of Hollywood, and all sorts of things that were heavy burdens for the format to carry. No one ever thought musical presentation couldn't be serious—opera and ballet had proved that long ago. The problem was that the movies had established a genre, and had defined it clearly for viewers as something else, and viewers either didn't like it or didn't want some of these new experiments.

The popular motion picture entered into a period of satire, inversion, and destruction of generic form. Comedies became black comedies; crime started to pay, and the cavalry destroyed instead of rescued. To be "current," movies increased violence; decreased faith in America; had no happy endings; spread despair and cynicism; eliminated escapism, fantasy, and joy in performance. What could the musical do? Misery wasn't its top motivation, and it couldn't invert itself; that would mean removing all music and thus making a nonmusical.

The musicals being discussed understood that if the genre was to go forward and be original, the task would be to deny musical performance while still maintaining it in some other form. The solutions found were ingenious:

1. Ignore the problem and return the musical to its original place, the stage or film, and have one character be a musical performer who could experience misery (in other words, do a biopic or a fake biopic).

OPPOSITE Roy Scheider and dancers in Bob Fosse's very personal musical, *All That Jazz*

2. Remove all the characters who sing and dance except for one person who is not a professional performer but who magically has music inside.

3. Set the music in some unreal place, in a movie within the movie, in fantasy, or in a dream or in a second universe or in a woman's imagination or a frustrated man's head.

4. Increase self-referential elements—make the movie musical about movie musicals.

When Hollywood began moving the musical toward a cerebral experience rather than its former, more visceral or participatory one, it essentially killed the musical at its core. In addition, its expensive production needs became a deterrent to an American film industry greatly reduced in quantity (and quality). By the end of the 1970s, Hollywood had become wary of musicals, seeing them as potential financial risks. Many people began to think musicals were passé, and not only passé, but outré. "Is the musical dead?" asked some, and "The musical is dead," pronounced others. While attempts to make "grown-up" variations that could address serious issues continued, MTV (launched on August 1, 1981) began satisfying the need for song, dance, story, and image to be wedded. But MTV gave it out in small doses so no one had to commit to it very seriously. All that was needed was a little touch of it. A "musical" could be nothing more than a Campbell's soup ad for television as in the much celebrated sixty seconds of Ann Miller tapping out a great campy joke. By the time Hollywood had wobbled into the 1980s, musicals were in jeopardy and yet still alive. Still alive and in various ways, still kicking. They might be only pastiche, or a nostalgic reference to old musicals, but musicals *were* being made.

VII

Epitaph

AFTER THE TRANSITION YEARS OF THE 1960S AND 1970S that were just discussed, the history of the musical film becomes a bit of a jumble. Everything had changed: no more studio system; no more day-laboring songwriters knocking out hit tunes; no more sheet-music sales; and no more easy access to singers and dancers eager to be made into movie stars. The moviemakers' lament (possibly the title for a Frank Loesser hit song) became "Woe is me, the musical is dead." As always, it seems, film history says something slightly different.

The musicals made from 1980 to 2010 *do* reveal the diminishment of the form as a reliable commercial venture, but they also show that filmmakers never fully gave up on them, making sometimes desperate—and often ill-guided—attempts to "innovate" or "create" them without regard for any historical knowledge of what had gone before. Two formats continued to be made: Broadway adaptations and biopics. And two others which had always been around emerged as strong forces in the genre: the animated film and the performance documentary, which had mostly existed in a short form designed to precede a feature film. The "original" Hollywood musical format, on the other hand, became an area of struggle: what to do without the tradition of musical movie stars; what to do about the expense of musical recording and production; what to do without composers to write original show tunes; what to do, what to do, what to do.

The two formats that emerged strongly—animation and the performance documentary—were unequal in influence. Animation became a creative force and documentaries were relatively unimaginative, with some exceptions, and the form more or less went nowhere. Animation kept the past alive. It became the dominant area for original music composers as well as for singing actors. Never mind that they might be dubbing pandas or mermaids or lions and were never themselves seen onscreen. They were singin'—and they were making movies. Since animated films were aimed mostly at children, that meant young moviegoers were being exposed to the concept of the musical film as if it were a natural and delightful thing. As a child, I might have been watching Astaire and Kelly, whereas as a child my daughter might have been watching Tinker Bell, but we both learned to love musical performance in the movies.

"Some Day My Prince Will Come," sings Snow White, and through the magic of Walt Disney, he actually shows up.

The dominant force in the history of the animated musical was, of course, Walt Disney. Disney was always an innovator. His influence has never waned, being as alive today as it ever was. He is well remembered for his entrepreneurship with theme parks, and he also made successful shorts, television shows, live-action movies, documentaries, and nature films, but in movie history he's a major musical player, not only because he made so many successful examples, both live-action and animated, but also because he was a creative thinker regarding the relationship of music and sound to the moving image. Many of his earliest cartoons were musicals, such as "Who's Afraid of the Big Bad Wolf?" (Cartoons in the sound era were often musicals, such as "I Love to Singa" and Betty Boop's "Minnie the

Moocher." Warners even called its cartoons "Merrie Melodies and Looney Tunes.")

The pre-1980s work of Disney is relevant. With his first full-length-feature animated film, *Snow White and the Seven Dwarfs* in 1937, Walt Disney became a significant musical creator. *Snow White* is a work of genius. Disney (and his enormous staff of creators) took an old once-upon-a-time story, added comedy and music, and brought it to life with animation that

used cutting, camera movement, and viewer perspectives to make it seem real. In *Snow White*, there's a point at which a viewer simply forgets the drawings are not real people—the unity of animation, cinema, music, and story blends into something acceptable as a movie about human beings, including the squirrels. The story had everything: an evil queen, a beautiful princess, a handsome prince, and no less than seven little comedians (plus a forest full of concerned birds and animals). The universe of *Snow White* is idealized, made up of line drawings and color paints, but it's about things people want to believe in and dream about. Nowhere is that made clearer—or achieved more successfully—than in the music.

Snow White contains hit songs that have become standards: "Some Day

In the meantime, she's got these little guys to take care of. (*Snow White and the Seven Dwarfs*)

My Prince Will Come," "I'm Wishing," "Whistle While You Work," and "Heigh-Ho." The script skillfully blends these tunes—all new—into familiar conventions of dialogue from fairy tales: "Mirror, mirror, on the wall, who's the fairest of them all?"; a poisoned apple; a huntsman who can't bear to kill the lovely young girl; etc.

Disney knew how to create "lovable" characters. The seven dwarfs are a master class in what's needed for a sitcom: seven individuals, each with a clearly defined comic purpose, which is no secret to the audience. It's right there in their names: Doc (the straight man and leader), Sleepy, Happy, Bashful, Dopey, Grumpy, and (the perfect scene punch line) Sneezy. The seven little men are all alike and yet brilliantly differentiated.*

Disney's seven characters appear onscreen in just the right amount of the running time. (Two planned scenes were deleted before completion: a soup-eating dinner, with "There's music in your soup, slurp, slurp," and a scene in which the little men work together to build a bed for Snow White.) The dwarfs are a visual treat—a weird chorus line—as they walk home from work, jauntily singing . . . or as they run to the rescue of their princess, driving the wicked queen over a cliff . . . but especially, when, after dinner, they simply "sit around" their cottage making music together to entertain their royal guest. The seven dwarfs sing, dance, and play musical instruments while giving out with a yodeling song. All seven bounce around the cottage while the ever-present rhythm of the song keeps the frame alive. Dopey is on drums and Grumpy is at the pipe organ, appropriately keeping his back to the merriment because, after all, he's grumpy about it. The carefully edited and timed turning of Grumpy's head to secretly participate in the joy is part of what becomes a true choreography, a miniature story inside the "dance." Two dwarfs get together, one standing on top of the other inside a big coat, to create a "tall man" who can twirl Snow White around the floor. Doc tap-dances, Sleepy plays the oboe, and all sway back and forth, watched by an audience of little forest animals—squirrels, bunnies, and birds—sitting on the open windowsill. Everyone has a heck of a good time, including the audience. Although there's not a single real dancer inside the frame, this scene is a model of how to cut, photograph,

---

* The idea of seven male oddballs living alone and needing a woman's touch would be effectively used later in 1941's *Ball of Fire*, with seven intellectuals researching an encyclopedia, disrupted by nightclub singer/dancer Sugarpuss O'Shea (Barbara Stanwyck), as well as in *Seven Brides for Seven Brothers*, in which seven lonely backwoods bachelors are shaped up by the oldest brother's bride, Jane Powell.

and shape a narrative song and dance for the maximum pleasure of an audience, partly by placing a "reaction shot" group of animals inside to trigger the response desired from the viewer. The extended number is ended by the character designed to do it: Sneezy sneezes. And then there comes a quiet moment in which the little men ask Snow White to tell them "a true story about love." She sings "Some Day My Prince Will Come." Disney's first musical feature was a winner in all categories.

Disney's talented staff were brilliant at creating movement within the frame that matched the rhythm of a song, and from *Snow White* onward, the Disney studio turned out successful animated musicals that are legendary: *Pinocchio* (1940), *Fantasia* (1940), *Dumbo* (1941), *Peter Pan* (1953), and many others. He experimented with live action and animation (*Song of the South,* 1946), and created movies that were anthologies of various musical numbers, such as *The Three Caballeros* (1945).*

The Three Caballeros is a masterpiece of cartoons, music, live-action dancers and singers, colorful comedy, and eye-popping visuals. It was psychedelic before anyone had heard the term. Designed to comply with the government's desire to promote good relationships with Latin America during World War II (our "Good Neighbor policy"), *The Three Caballeros* is absolutely an experimental film, although because of its Disney parentage and its commercial release, it's seldom defined that way. The voices used are those of Aurora Miranda (Carmen's sister), who appears live singing and dancing, Sterling Holloway, José Oliveira, Dora Luz, and Carmen Molina. The Latin-beat music became popular, and songs like "Baia," "You Belong to My Heart," and the title tune became hits. A series of separate stories unfolds in *Caballeros* after Donald Duck unwraps an exploding birthday present that brings him into the world of José Carioca and Panchito.

A very simple lesson in the wedding of music and image is demonstrated in *Caballeros* by the brief presentation of "Baia," with the lyrics being sung after a rhythmic beat introduces an orchid-pink overlay on an animated scene involving flowers, dripping water, a large pool, and a river with a sailboat drifting down it. "Oh, Baia," sings a dreamy, yearning voice, and the animation, the beat of the song, the movement of the camera, and the emphasis of the lyrics combine in perfect synchronization. A viewer who has any kind of innate rhythm can immediately feel the eye being carried

---

* Disney also made fantasy comedies with live actors such as *Bedknobs and Broomsticks,* which was musical, and *The Absent-Minded Professor,* which was not.

forward in time matched to the editing, the viewed events, and the internal thump of the music as drops of water fall off flowers and hit the pool, all perfectly wedded. It's an exercise in musical performance, only there are no people, there is no strong narrative pull (other than a boat moving forward), and there's no point other than the understanding of how to match film and music through editing, color, camera movement, and song. It's almost a classroom exercise.

The Three Caballeros experimented with combining live dancers and animated characters during the same period that Gene Kelly was working on his dance with Jerry the Mouse at MGM for *Anchors Aweigh*. Kelly always paid tribute to the help he received from the Disney studios, and the two films were released in a similar time frame, with the Disney being the more ambitious of the two since it was a full-length feature. Aurora Miranda dances with cartoon characters against an unreal background, and a chorus of female dancers cavorts among cartoon cacti. The overwhelming finale of the film begins with Donald Duck, Panchito, and José Carioca doing a dance to "The Three Caballeros" that has really never been equaled for its freewheeling use of music and visuals that look like someone's drug-induced nightmare. "We're three caballeros, three gay caballeros"—and *boom!* their heads expand and explode, turn into guitar strings, and pop around the frame, poking out of stars that explode across an animated sky. It has to be seen (and heard) to be believed. This experimentation with what musicals were at the core is nearly forgotten, yet it's an important advancement from Disney.

Fantasia was released by Disney through RKO in 1940, just after the outbreak of World War II in Europe. It was an ambitious project designed as a mass-market experiment about the relationship of music and image. It was presented as "tasteful" entertainment, but, most importantly, as an educational moment for Americans to pull up their lowbrow socks and improve themselves. As such, *Fantasia* was in a perfect position to lead the advance troops that would appear after America entered World War II: musical numbers featuring classical ("highbrow") performers with the implication that democracy was inclusive. Even highbrows were welcome at the party! Having José Iturbi play jazz and flirt with Jeanette MacDonald (in *Three Daring Daughters*) and Risë Stevens play Bing Crosby's ex-girlfriend (in *Going My Way*) assured the public that classical musicians were okay, which meant classical music was okay, too. *Fantasia*'s goals were not about inclusiveness, however; they were about music. And film.

Fantasia was an avant-garde experiment, but it was presented as Disney having fun with culture. Deems Taylor, a public intellectual of his day, put on a tuxedo to act as the audience's guide through the eight pieces of popular classical music interpreted with animated images. Taylor introduces *Fantasia* as "this new form of entertainment." What we'll see, he tells us, are interpretations from the heads of artists, not trained musicians. He explains to viewers the "three kinds of music" the film will present: "the kind that tells a definite story . . . the kind that, while it has no specific plot, does paint a series of more or less definite pictures. And then there's a third kind, music that exists simply for its own sake." He calls the latter "absolute music" and says the film will open with that.

The first piece in *Fantasia* is Bach's Toccata and Fugue in D Minor, played by the Philadelphia Orchestra and directed by Leopold Stokowski. What is onscreen represents a beautiful bursting of color, light, rhythm, and sound that is very literal in its representation of the striking of timpani

Walt Disney's *Fantasia*, an experimental feature that fully explored the relationship of music and the moving image. Mickey Mouse does duty as the Sorcerer's Apprentice.

or the strumming of a harp. The visuals are beautiful (Taylor defines them as "a picture of the various abstract images that might pass through your mind" as you listen). It's a basic idea, often described as "simple" today, but historically important in its brief lesson for average filmgoers about sound and image.

The remaining seven pieces presented in *Fantasia* are a remarkable blending of comedy, established cartoons (Mickey Mouse), sophistication, weird ideas, and terrifying images. I saw *Fantasia* as a small child, and it scared me witless. Unanchored onscreen as it was, without characters, movie stars, or plot definitions, it seemed to hover over me as a very real menace that could actually come down and get me. It was worse than any horror film. (I sat through *Fantasia* like the moviegoing trouper I already was, but I still want to run away from it.)

Fantasia interprets Tchaikovsky's *Nutcracker* Suite (which Taylor says "nobody much performs today") as a ballet for fish, flowers, mushrooms (politically incorrect Chinese coolies), dragonflies, snowflakes, and lily pads, led off by a Tinker Bell prototype who flies amidst sparkling blossoms and flowers, fronds, and cobwebs. Two more pieces appear before a "fifteen-minute intermission": Dukas's *The Sorcerer's Apprentice*, whose title role is played by Mickey Mouse, and Stravinsky's *The Rite of Spring*, which is presented as "a pageant" representing the story of the growth of life: "Science, not art, wrote the scenario." With hot lava bubbles and arid deserts, life advances from a blob into fish and amphibians and on to a plethora of hideous dinosaurs who fly, swim, run, and walk around until they all die. For me as a first-time viewer, the popcorn counter was a welcome oasis.

After intermission, one of the most interesting and timeless parts of the film is presented, treating it as a bit of a joke. A special guest is introduced: the soundtrack. An audience is shown that when a track produces a sound, it also produces an image. Different instruments are played—harp, violin, flute, trumpet, bassoon, bass drum, cymbals, snare drums, and even a tiny triangle. Each time the sound is made, the audience can *see* an abstraction of color and sharply delineated lines moving unpredictably and unexpectedly in front of their eyes in different ways. This is the best part of *Fantasia*.

The movie concludes with three more numbers, the first of which is Beethoven's Sixth Symphony, the *Pastoral*, presented as a Mount Olympus world of centaurs and unicorns, featuring Bacchus, Vulcan, Diana, Apollo, Pegasus, Morpheus, et al. Taylor says that Beethoven's work was "a musical picture of a day in the country" but that Walt Disney had decided to give it a Mount Olympus setting. (The centaurs have girlfriends—Taylor calls them "centaurettes"—who strut around like burlesque girls showing their stuff.) The "Dance of the Hours" is a comedy ballet, featuring dancing ostriches, hippos, crocodiles, and elephants. Taylor explains that it progresses from dawn to noonday to early evening to night and back to dawn again. The lead ostrich is Fanny Brice with feathers; the hippos spin and twirl; the elephants blow water bubbles; and the crocodiles (or are those alligators?) provide menace. The final number, which begins with Mussorgsky's *Night on Bald Mountain* and evolves into Schubert's "Ave Maria," is Walpurgis Night. The demons are out, yellow-eyed and skeletal—and there's darkness, ghosts, graveyards, and grotesques. Purple! Red! Orange! Yellow! Gigantic yellow eyes, gyrating forms, orgiastic dances, an alleged depiction of Satan's "infernal army" out on the prowl . . . but wait! Church bells peal, and vocals arise to sing "Ave Maria," and a restoration of trees and water appears, enhanced by the sight of golden clouds. Hellfire is gone. The piece was conceived as a depiction of "the struggle between the profane and the sacred" represented by the juxtaposition of two very different pieces of music—*Bald Mountain* and "Ave Maria." It's a mess, but scary. Significantly, I always forget that there's the "Ave Maria" section. I only remember the demons.

Fantasia is important historically, but it was not a financial success for Disney. It was, however, a critical success, as the recognition of the experimental possibilities of film—particularly when combined with music—was clearly delineated. If World War II had not sent Disney's animators into military service and converted much of the studio to government projects, Disney might have done more with these concepts, and the influence might have been felt more directly and quickly on other musical products from Hollywood.

Fantasia finally found its audience in the 1960s, when colleges began showing it for its psychedelic appeal. It has become a cult classic, receiving a full restoration with a new soundtrack in 1982. It even inspired a sequel, the seldom discussed *Fantasia 2000* (released in that millennial year), with James Levine conducting the Chicago Symphony Orchestra. The format of the newer version is identical to the old, but instead of one culturally acceptable highbrow narrator (Deems Taylor), *Fantasia 2000* opts for popular faces of film and television to do joke intros (Steve Martin, Penn and Teller, Bette Midler, James Earl Jones, Angela Lansbury, and for musical seriousness, Quincy Jones). The new images interpret Beethoven's Fifth,

Respighi's *Pines of Rome* (inexplicably presented as a ballet with whales), Gershwin's *Rhapsody in Blue,* the Allegro from Shostakovich's Piano Concerto no. 2 (used to illustrate Hans Christian Andersen's story "The Steadfast Tin Soldier"), Saint-Saëns's *Carnival of the Animals,* Elgar's *Pomp and Circumstance* marches (with Donald and Daisy Duck to lead the animals into Noah's Ark), and Stravinsky's *Firebird* Suite (about "death and renewal"). One piece from the original is included: Mickey Mouse's appearance as the Sorcerer's Apprentice. The highlights were the Al Hirschfeld drawings used to illustrate the Gershwin music and the flock of dancing birds in the Saint-Saëns, who provide the answer to what would happen if you gave a yo-yo to a bunch of dancing flamingoes.

The power of Disney to combine music, story and character, and animation never diminished. The Disney studio continues to make musicals today, remaining a powerful creative force. *Frozen* (from 2013) was one of the biggest hits of the new century. The animated characters were mostly humans, with a talking reindeer, a comic snowman, and a bunch of trolls thrown in. Based loosely on the "Snow Queen" fairy tale, the plot tells a tale of two sisters, Elsa and Anna, who enact a metaphor about female power. The movie is otherwise an old-fashioned musical, and it produced one big hit song, "Let It Go." The emotional premise is that "the heart is not so easily changed, but the head can be persuaded" (troll wisdom) and also that "love" will empower and provide the reassurance and courage needed to be persuaded. As has always been true of the Disney animated musicals, the pace is excellent, the story is strongly told without wasted moments, the visuals are both beautiful and frightening, and the comedy has charms. *Frozen* had an additional asset: its story of sisters who must learn to love and understand both themselves and each other presented a feminist point of view without rhetoric.

The Walt Disney studio did much to keep the Hollywood American musical creatively and commercially alive from 1980 to the present day. Disney became a mainstay of musical presentation, and without it the form would have been in an even weaker position historically than it was in the years from 1980 onward. In addition to the films discussed, Disney released other successes, like *The Little Mermaid* (1989), *Beauty and the Beast* (1991), *Aladdin* (1992), *The Lion King* (1994), *Pocahontas* (1995), *Hercules* (1997), and *Mulan* (1998). These movies contained an effective wedding of song and story, and often produced Oscar-winning popular songs, but because they're animated, which freed creators from the restrictions of explaining

musical performance, they didn't change or influence the historical development of the musical in a significant way.

The Disney success in keeping the musical alive and fresh was not quite matched by that of the performance documentary. Its history is largely forgotten, but it was the original musical movie format when sound first came in: Vitaphone and Movietone shorts recording great musical performers of the era. From the very beginning of musicals, the short performance film—a kind of documentary—was a staple of movie production. Sometimes these

Walt Disney's animation studios maintained musical success over time with films such as *Peter Pan* (1953) . . .

shorts were literally photographs of a singer singing, a band playing, or a dancer dancing, but sometimes they were little short-story films with plots that incorporated musical performances. Ruth Etting became a star in this form, and Bing Crosby rose to his first fame when Mack Sennett put him in a series of two-reelers that led him to feature films. There are all kinds of these performance shorts: sing-alongs, composers singing their own material, big bands banging out their hits, cowboys twanging around campfires, and abstracted "art" films such as *An Optical Poem* by Oskar Fischinger, which interpreted Liszt's Second Hungarian Rhapsody with geometrical figures. One of the most famous of these short-form musical documentaries is *Jammin' the Blues,* made by Warner Bros. in 1944, directed by Gjon Mili and photographed by Robert Burks. A solemn voice tells a viewer, "This is a jam session," where great artists "play hot ad-lib music. It could be called a 'Midnight Symphony.'" A viewer is treated to seeing Lester Young, Sidney Catlett, Jo Jones, Barney Kessel, Red Callender, Harry Edison, Marlowe Morris, John Simmons, and Illinois Jacquet at their peak. Seen against a stark black background, surrounded with slowly rising cigarette smoke, they improvise the blues and accompany singer Marie Bryant, reflected in a shiny piano top, as she sings "On the Sunny Side of the Street." (Bryant, against a white background, then does an authentic jitterbug with Archie Savage.) These original "concert films" or musical documentaries are amazing, and they are not unlike their latter-day counterparts in that they record live performances of fabulous musicians of the era:

. . . The Lion King (1994) . . .

... and *Frozen* (2013).

Bessie Smith, Cab Calloway, Gene Austin, Woody Herman, Fats Waller, Artie Shaw, Ethel Merman, Duke Ellington, Louis Armstrong, and many others.

In the transitional 1960s and 1970s, new developments in light-weight cameras, digital equipment, and filming and recording capacities inspired on-site live-performance documentaries in all categories, and the musical-performance variation came alive again. A major event was the first rock concert film, *Monterey Pop* (1969), shot live at the 1967 Monterey Pop Festival and featuring, among many greats, Janis Joplin doing "Ball and Chain" and Jimi Hendrix's immortal "Wild Thing." *Woodstock* (1970) and *The Last Waltz* (1978) from the transition years are two differing examples of the form in that the latter more or less ignores the audience at the event of its recording, and the former makes the audience and its response to the music into characters/players in the story. Movie audiences responded well to both types—lost themselves in *The Last Waltz* and in its excellent cinematic presentation (it was directed by Martin Scorsese) and also lost themselves in the cultural phenomenon of *Woodstock*, being able to participate in an event that defined the times.

The Last Waltz achieved film immortality with its celebrated opening title. In sharp white letters jumping out from a deep black background, the words blazed out even before the credits: THIS FILM SHOULD BE PLAYED LOUD. Amen to that, as the documentary announced it was cutting loose and would pump up the volume to the skies and still never be loud enough. *The Last Waltz* captures the end of an era: The final night of the Band's farewell tour occurred at San Francisco's Winterland Ballroom on Thanksgiving Day, 1976. (The movie was released in April of 1978.) Director Scorsese shot the movie with seven 35mm cameras operated by such talents as Michael Chapman, Vilmos Zsigmond, and László Kovács, using sets from the San Francisco Opera company's *La Traviata*, and with stage and lighting design by Boris Leven. (The crystal chandeliers that hung overhead were said to have been used in *Gone with the Wind*.)

The beauty of *The Last Waltz* was that it was cinema as well as music, with head photographer Chapman working from a carefully prepared chart that indicated where a camera needed to be specifically for the beat of each number. The movie has been called "a time capsule," and much has been written about how it captures the bombed-out quality of a rock-and-roll band that had toured and toured and finally couldn't tour anymore, so a big feastday party was thrown and, with a little help from their friends, they made a big movie about their big burnout. It brings onscreen the Band, Eric Clapton, Muddy Waters, Neil Young, Bob Dylan, Joni Mitchell, Van Morrison, Ronnie Wood, Neil Diamond, Emmylou Harris—guests who some feel hijacked the show. Live songs are cut into the interviews and studio editing and recording sessions that were conducted by Scorsese.

There are varying opinions on *The Last Waltz*. Its rerelease poster announced, "It Started as a Concert. It Became a Celebration. Now It's a Legend." *Rolling Stone* dubbed it "the greatest concert movie of all time," but Roger Ebert felt differently, writing that "the overall sense of the film is of good riddance to a bad time . . . The viewer with mercy will be content to allow the musicians to embrace closure, and will not demand an encore." (Ebert also pointed out that despite this, he gave the film three stars because "it is a revealing document of a time.")

The most important thing regarding the history of *The Last Waltz* is that Martin Scorsese, an eclectic lover of all types of music, understands what cinema is and instinctively knows how to cut to rhythm, and, even more significantly, how to film a rhythmic performance. He uses his cameras the way Astaire, Berkeley, and Kelly and Minnelli used theirs: to wed image, sound, editing, lyrics, performers' movements, and everything onscreen into *one* "musical" performance. The camera moves forward, backward, swoops around an instrumentalist, and glides behind someone, framing up musicians, switching from player to player.

Scorsese understood what he'd filmed. He deliberately chose to begin his documentary with the final encore number, so viewers can never forget they're watching something that is over and done with and will never come again. The cinema is great and the music is great, but there's a mood and a narrative, too. It's a goodbye to all that, a very loud one, directed by a man who could understand what it all meant. The music becomes the movie and the movie becomes the music, and it's impossible to separate them. When it's over, Robbie Robertson simply says, "Good night. Goodbye." It's a fabulous last line, an unfunny "Nobody's perfect," a satisfied "Frankly, my dear, I don't give a damn," and a weary, slightly cynical "I think this is the beginning of a beautiful friendship." Scorsese knew *The Last Waltz* was not a movie to be made about an audience, but a movie to stay inside the performance onstage. It's as close as anyone can come to being part of a live musical stage performance. Its important lesson for feature musicals of any type was the eternal reminder: cinema is an art form unto itself, so use it.

The earlier *Woodstock*, shot on 16mm film and later blown up to 35mm for theatrical release, was a Warner Bros. film. (Warner Bros. was always a pioneer.) It was a filmed record of the Woodstock Music and Art Fair, which took place on an upstate New York farm for three days, from August 15 to 17, 1969. Assembled by a team of six editors, among them Scorsese and his legendary editor Thelma Schoonmaker, the finished film* shows singers and cavorters on stage and singers and cavorters in the fields, and its success inspired more live-performance documentaries.

Concert footage of Richie Havens, Jimi Hendrix, Joan Baez, Joe Cocker, Country Joe and the Fish, Arlo Guthrie, Crosby, Stills and Nash, the Who, and Sha Na Na are all seen in the movie. (Some artists who were there do not appear, big names like Ravi Shankar, the Grateful Dead, Blood, Sweat & Tears, Jefferson Airplane, Creedence Clearwater Revival, and Janis Joplin.) What *Woodstock* brings to the musical is the excitement of live

---

* In 1994, a director's cut was released, entitled *Woodstock: 3 Days of Peace and Music*, which added forty minutes of footage to the original. Footage shot at the festival was also used in two other documentaries made by the original director, Michael Wadleigh: *The Last Performance* (1990) and *Jimi Hendrix: Live at Woodstock* (1999).

performance that can turn into a narrative of its own while still recording a true-life event. Audiences extended their participatory desires through such films, and the format thus teeters on the brink of being truly a breakthrough. There *is* a kind of story, there *is* a kind of character; song order matters; and both dancing and singing appear. However, the fundamental issue that plagues successful musicals is always the basic question—*why* are these people singing and dancing?—and *Woodstock* has a simple and easy answer: it's their job. No explanation is needed, no establishment of motive is needed, and no layers of reality need to be manipulated . . . so no real progress in genre history is made.

These documentaries are important to the musical's history, however, and many began to appear, keeping alive the idea of music and performance onscreen. As MTV continued to attract young viewers, the musical documentary became a solid box-office draw, especially for high-school and college students, who sometimes couldn't afford concert tickets, were too young to be allowed to attend, or couldn't travel to where the concert was taking place. First-rate film directors were often attracted to making them, turning them into something very special as reflections of American culture, the power of live performance, and the social situation in which concerts took place. There were Rolling Stones documentaries, concert films by Rod Stewart, the Temptations in their prime, the fabulous 1982 Gospel celebration *Say Amen, Somebody,* and the exuberant *Chuck Berry Hail! Hail! Rock 'n' Roll* (1987), with the terrific back-and-forth of Berry and Etta James in a happy challenge: ". . . if you want to dance with me." Jonathan Demme made art with *Stop Making Sense* (1984), and 2009's *When You're Strange* (about the Doors, narrated by Johnny Depp) valiantly set out to tell the group's true story and refute what many felt was the inaccuracy of the 1991 Oliver Stone biopic, *The Doors. The Doors* captured moments in history in ways a nonmusical documentary could never have achieved. There are a great many of these "concert" movies, but they are photographic records of live performances, and technically not the sort of musical this book is about.* However, they *are* musicals. Individuals are performing music for audiences. And they keep alive the idea that music and image can be wedded in different ways.

The other two formats of the musical genre that endured past the transition years into the 1980s—the biopic and the Broadway adaptation—had

---

* Two fake versions of these performance documentaries—the "mockumentaries" *This Is Spinal Tap* (1984) and *Waiting for Guffman* (1997)—are real musicals.

The documentary musical rose to an art form in Jonathan Demme's *Stop Making Sense,* featuring David Byrne and the Talking Heads.

varying success, although neither disappeared. The musical biopic endured largely because it became topical, embracing stories of diversity (*La Bamba,* 1987, and *Ray,* 2004), drug addiction (*Bird,* 1988), untimely death (*Sweet Dreams,* 1985), and specific areas of music, such as country (*Walk the Line,* 2005). These films became serious dramas with music, and they succeeded as much for their stories and their superb performances by stars like Jamie Foxx as Ray Charles and Reese Witherspoon as June Carter as much as anything else.

The lack of confidence in the financial success of the musical film *did* affect the biopic, however. The reliable old form sometimes failed. In 2004, the second attempt to tell the story of Cole Porter's life through a "musical" film, *De-Lovely,* starring Ashley Judd as Linda Porter and Kevin Kline as the composer, fell flat. Since *Night and Day* (the 1946 biopic with Cary Grant) had become a test case for how *not* to tell someone's life story, *De-Lovely* was structured to be the dead Porter's own point of view of his life and his work. It was a tale told from the grave. The story shifts from a real biographical mode (giving facts about Porter's life) to a fantastical mode that incorporates meaningful performances by unrelated characters, but with the lyrics commenting on what was happening in Porter's life as he remembers it just after his death. Shifts into musical-performance mode thus have no need for justification. The songs are often not presented in their entirety, and they're performed by latter-day interpreters like Elvis Costello, Sheryl Crow, and Diana Krall. Clearly the filmmakers felt today's audiences would come to see and hear these performers, because they knew who they were, not because they knew Porter's music or even knew who Porter was. The movie separates the songs from their original shows and original performers, so there's no "And then I wrote . . ." cliché, but the shifts move the music to an emotional context related to Porter's life story, which isn't that well-known, either. There's a loose, drifting quality to the plot, and in the end, despite Kline and Judd both doing an excellent job, the movie manages not to tell the real tale of Porter's world or give the real flavor of his music in its era any more than *Night and Day* does. In fact, in terms of Cole Porter's music, *Night and Day* put it in better context, with performers who gave it out the way it had been written, in the world of hypocrisy that Cole Porter inhabited.

The biopic was ripped from its safe moorings by the 2015 gangsta rap release *Straight Outta Compton,* the story of N.W.A, a revolutionary hip-hop group from southern Los Angeles. In one sense, it was a typical biopic—an underdog situation for audiences to support—but its music removed it totally from the typical. Telling several stories simultaneously, it was shot on location in the actual settings. The movie injected energy into the biopic, containing excellent performances by O'Shea Jackson Jr. as Ice Cube (Jackson is Ice Cube's son) and Paul Giamatti as N.W.A's manager Jerry Heller.

Straight Outta Compton had headliner credentials. Members of N.W.A were involved: Ice Cube and Dr. Dre were producers, along with Eazy-E's widow (Tomica Woods-Wright), and MC Ren and DJ Yella were both creative consultants. The film took audiences by storm, becoming both a commercial and a critical success, even though it was a depiction of a group that the average moviegoer may not have known much about. Despite a lawsuit from Heller, claiming his depiction was inaccurate and that a great deal of the movie had been ripped off from his autobiography, and despite claims that the story had too many omissions and too much female abuse, the biopic proved that there was a wide audience for a no-holds-barred story with hip-hop music. *Straight Outta Compton* was good filmmaking (directed by F. Gary Gray) that went nationwide with a story that only a few decades earlier either would have not been filmed at all or would have been relegated to niche B film programming.

As we've seen, the movie business *never* gave up on adapting Broadway shows to film. But few created in the transition years made real money and even fewer were innovative. In the 1970s, in addition to those already discussed, there were such movies as *Fiddler on the Roof, Man of La Mancha, Oh! Calcutta!, A Little Night Music, Jesus Christ Superstar, Hair, Godspell, Mame*—none of which was truly successful. Only *Grease* in 1978 found big success. *Grease* had the asset of two big musical stars of the era, John Travolta (who can really dance) and Olivia Newton-John. *Grease* was satiric, a little joke about teenagers in the good old days of high-school hops. It made $100 million at the box office, was rereleased to great success in 1998, and spawned a less successful sequel, *Grease 2,* which was an original Hollywood effort. However, *Grease* was something of a one-off. (It was paying tribute to the audience's memories of their high-school years more than to musical movies.) *Grease* was not unique in any way regarding presenting musical performance, but it was smart because it read 1978 audiences correctly. Moviegoers *would* accept a musical format *if: if* it embraced teen age culture; *if* it paraded a lineup of old stars that mature audiences had loved in the golden era of the studio system (Eve Arden, Joan Blondell) and a lineup of beloved TV stars (Dody Goodman, Sid Caesar) and showcased a former rock-and-roll teen idol (Frankie Avalon); *if* it paraded a loving sense of nostalgia with a twist of lemon.

Nostalgia—and pastiche—had been embraced as an acceptable way to do musicals in earlier years. It reassured audiences that they weren't being old-fashioned or out of step or uncool by watching a genre that perhaps wasn't cynical enough for the modern world. This form of hiding was thought to be a way to keep the genre afloat. (Nostalgia could be the musical's excuse for itself.) Gene Kelly, still young enough and nimble enough to be onscreen without embarrassment, participated in this yearning for old musicals. As early as 1964, he appeared in *What a Way to Go!,* in which Shirley MacLaine played a woman who just wants a simple life with a husband who's lazy enough to hang around the house and make her happy, but who keeps accidentally inspiring the men she marries to become superrich and famous—and then, suddenly very, very dead. Each of the marriages is a fantasy of an old Hollywood genre: "I see our life together as a wonderful old silent movie," she says, then "as a wickedly romantic French comedy," and "as all about love and what will she wear next?" Inevitably, Kelly arrives for "one of those big Hollywood musicals." Kelly is charming as no-talent Pinky Benson, a small-time nightclub clown who takes off his makeup and becomes a star ("Benson Boffo Balladeer"). MacLaine could really dance, and she and Kelly do a terrific routine on the deck of a battleship, singing with Nelson Eddy and Jeanette MacDonald–type voices. The number delivers an old-fashioned musical performance—it was choreographed by Kelly—and sends up old musicals at the same time.

In 1967 Kelly went to France to appear in Jacques Demy's *The Young Girls of Rochefort,* which was intended as an affectionate homage, not a spoof, but which despite the presence of the beautiful sisters Françoise Dorléac and Catherine Deneuve, fell flat. Kelly plays an American concert pianist who comes to a small town and joins a theatrical troupe. Everyone sings and dances and falls in love, but the audience is left to fend for itself. The movie ends up reminding everyone how hard it really is to make a musical work. As Kelly said, "They all made the mistake of assuming that it's easy to learn to dance for a film because it looks so easy. It isn't." Not only Kelly but also Stanley Donen tried to join the nostalgia musicals brigade. In 1978 he directed *Movie Movie,* a pseudo "double feature" of two alleged 1930s movies: a boxing film and a musical called *Baxter's Beauties of 1933,* about a dying Broadway producer puttin' on one last great show (after apparently watching *42nd Street* too many times). Despite Donen's directorial ability, Larry Gelbart's clever script, dances by Michael Kidd, and an imitation of a 1930s tune ("It Just Shows to Go Ya"), the fun didn't really work all that well. Whether these attempts at pastiche were satiric or honestly respectful, they didn't generate the old feelings in audiences.

Besides the Kelly and Donen attempt to re-create the form, both Ken Russell's *The Boy Friend* (1971) and Peter Bogdanovich's *At Long Last Love* (1975) were also failures. The former worked hard to create an acceptable spoof of musicals while still creating a homage to their presumed escapism. The movie played on two levels: a cheap production done by a second-rate troupe, which was paralleled with a fantasized, lavish version that could be what Hollywood might have done with it in the old days, with all the money and talent the studios seemed to have to burn. Christopher Gable choreographed the fantasy numbers in a Berkeley-like manner, and well done though they were, the music failed to lift an audience into the joy of singing and dancing; *The Boy Friend* became a cerebral exercise. *At Long Last Love*—an original, not an adaptation—had a director who really knew what old Hollywood musicals were all about, and he was given enough money to re-create the glamour. The result is a gorgeous-looking film with sets, costumes, props, and art-deco flourishes that is a treat for the eyes but, alas, an assault on the ears. The two main stars—Burt Reynolds and Cybill Shepherd—do not sing and dance well enough to attempt to be Astaire

and Rogers, and their "sidekicks," played by John Hillerman and Eileen Brennan, can't cover for them. Even Madeline Kahn, who *can* sing and dance, and the music of Cole Porter (whose fabulous songs are featured) can't plug the holes. (It should be noted, however, that times change and opinions shift. Writing in the October 1, 2018, issue of *The New Yorker*, Richard Brody hailed *At Long Last Love* as "an overlooked masterwork" with "giddy and daring long takes" and "joyfully strutting and swinging production numbers.")

Movies like *The Boy Friend* and *At Long Last Love* and others show that the people working in the business still wanted to make musicals, and the audience wanted to see them—only they wanted to see good ones. There was a disconnect. How to resolve what was happening to the musical? Re-creating an old western was different: you could update it by making it bloody, a Vietnam metaphor, a serious questioning of policies and changing times—and besides, actors could still ride horses. It was harder to do that same sort of update with musicals, and apparently not enough actors could still sing and dance.

One of the most successful Broadway adaptations of the 1970s was the hit musical *Grease,* nostalgic but sharp, with John Travolta pointing the way.

In the 1980s, the decade of musical desperation that followed the transitional 1960s and 1970s, movies presented Broadway adaptations *Annie* (1982) and *A Chorus Line* (1985), and in the 1990s, the lavishly produced *Evita* (1996), starring Madonna, but again, there was no groundbreaking musical definition. After the millennium, the Broadway adaptations continued with unpredictable results.* *Chicago* (2002) was a box-office success; *Phantom of the Opera* (2004) and *Sweeney Todd* (2007) were not. *The Producers* (2005) was a disaster, even though a Broadway smash. *Dreamgirls* (2006) did well; *Mamma Mia!* (2008) made money, but only because of Meryl Streep, whose stardom also drove *Into the Woods* (2015) to some recognition. Original Hollywood musicals like *Xanadu* (1980), which remade an old Rita Hayworth hit (*Down to Earth*), were disasters. And *Xanadu* cast Gene Kelly, giving his character the same name as the one he played in *Cover Girl* (Danny Maguire). The clever *Little Shop of Horrors* (1986) was a delightful horror/sci-fi musical based on a stage adaptation of a low-budget Roger Corman movie. *Little Shop* stressed comedy and was fun, but it didn't get the musical anywhere. It broke no new ground.

To really understand the history of the musical in the more modern era, it's necessary to ask a basic question: what happened to innovation? Some of it was found, oddly enough, in Broadway adaptations, particularly in the unexpected emergence of the "cult film musical" which could have its origins rooted in cultural weirdness. Two really significant ones began in the 1960s/70s transition period and had varying levels of success and longevity: *The Rocky Horror Picture Show* and *Tommy*, both of which were made into movies in 1975 and both of which had unusual assets. These adaptations worked because they appealed to young people, who made them into cult favorites. *The Rocky Horror Picture Show* smartly changed the genre emphasis from musicals to comic horror and became the all-time number-one cult hit movie. It influenced moviegoing habits by inspiring midnight screenings, dress-up masquerades, and all kinds of audience-participatory bizarro behavior. It was based on a 1973 British stage spoof, *The Rocky Horror Show*—a huge hit in London but a flop in New York, even though the Belasco Theatre was turned into a cabaret to accommodate it. The film version made sure to disassociate itself from this disaster—by adding "Picture" to the title. The movie had an excellent cast: Tim Curry repeating

* The longest-running off-Broadway musical in history, *The Fantasticks* was released as a movie in 2000 after sitting on the shelf for five years. It went nowhere.

his original role as Dr. Frank N. Furter and newcomers Susan Sarandon and Barry Bostwick. Cleverly directed by Jim Sharman, *Rocky Horror* represented what the new decades were beginning to reflect when it came to musicals: it made fun of the genre, and combined it with horror, rock and roll, science fiction, and even a touch of porn. *Rocky Horror* was one of the smarter efforts in that it did at least provide one new twist: it turned the audience into musical performers. Dressed up, often boozed up, patrons sat in their seats and sang their heads off, a trend that has yet to really go anywhere in musical history despite sing-along events for *The Sound of Music*, *High School Musical*, and some other cult movies.*

The movie version of the Who's rock opera *Tommy* was directed by Ken Russell and starred Ann-Margret as Tommy's mother, the band's Roger Daltrey as the grown Tommy, Elton John as the Pinball Wizard, and Tina Turner as the Acid Queen, along with Eric Clapton, Jack Nicholson, and the other members of the Who. Director Russell, famous for his visual excess, brought that excess right onto the screen and shoved it into the audience's faces—the old idea of *spectacle*, a musical staple, turned into a world of skulls and serpents and sex. *Tommy* presents a temple for a cult that worships Marilyn Monroe, and the priests wear Monroe masks. Ann-Margret's orgasm overflows her apartment with colorful liquid, and Elton John wears big glasses and a pair of platform wedgies that look taller than the Empire State Building. *Tommy*, had it been successful, might have defined the new musical: horror, excess, and visual extravagance—with music. (The songs in *Tommy* were memorable: "Tommy Can You Hear Me?," "Pinball Wizard," and "See Me, Feel Me" among them.)

The idea that young people would buy musicals if they were cult films prevailed. Another was unleashed in 2001, a screen adaptation of *Hedwig and the Angry Inch*, an off-Broadway musical about an East German transsexual who marries an American GI and winds up deserted in Kansas. It had original music by Stephen Trask and an ahead-of-its-time story and should have become a hit as a movie, but it found lasting success as a cult hit on

---

* *The Phantom of the Paradise* (1974), stylishly directed by Brian de Palma, updated the *Phantom of the Opera* story by locating it in the Paradise discotheque, with a Phantom whose face was destroyed by a record press! He busies himself by composing a rock opera based on the Faust legend, and the movie has a cuckoo quality that is very satisfying, with songs by Paul Williams such as "Old Souls," "Upholstery," and "The Phantom's Theme." It flopped in its initial release, but has become another example of a 1970s cult favorite. A smart satire of the 1970s music business, it's the movie the "I know more than you do" people namedrop when *The Rocky Horror Picture Show* is mentioned.

college campuses. The movie presented the scriptwriter, John Cameron Mitchell, as its star and director, and kept the fabulous score. The movie is full of cinematic dazzle, and reaches out into an opened-up world in a way the stage musical could not achieve. (The "angry inch" of the title is all Hedwig has left after his sex-change operation to qualify as an American wife.)

The bizarre or sexually adventurous cult movies *Tommy*, *Rocky Horror*, and *Hedwig* are musicals adapting to the changes of the moviemaking process and audience desires, but they didn't do well enough to make expensive musical production viable. The influence they might have had was diminished by the lack of box office. An exception was *Hairspray*, based on the John Waters cult classic. The property was originally a movie with music that was turned into a successful Broadway musical that was turned into a fairly successful movie musical in 2002.

The most significant area for discussion of the history of the genre lies in the category of original Hollywood musicals, and a number of those *were* made from 1970 through 2015, some of which have already been described.* "Original" doesn't always mean original music composed and used for the first time in the motion picture. "Original" means an idea that was generated for the movies; it means innovation (or failed innovation) for the format. Alas, from 1970 onward, most of these films were failures. The musical film, a truly American art form, once rich with innovation and invention and full of great talents that became legends, began to falter, often trying to deny itself to survive. Over the decades being discussed, there were a great many films that told audiences not to worry, no one was *really* singing or dancing onscreen, and things were going to turn out rotten, rotten, rotten. Everything would be okay! An unhappy ending! The attempts to be successful were varied.

Because of the success of MTV and music videos with the youth market, story musicals began to be made to court teenagers and college students. Three movies about being on the brink of maturity, or not being certain what you wanted from life—or what you could get if you knew what you wanted—were successful original musical pictures: *Saturday Night Fever* (1977), *Fame* (1980), and *Dirty Dancing* (1987). Each had its own subtext, and all three emphasized dancing, which made them undeniably musical movies. *Dirty Dancing* was an unexpected smash hit that made a star out of

---

* In India, the famous "Bollywood" musicals began to thrive, but that is not the subject of this book.

Patrick Swayze. It's a curious musical because it has barely any singing. It's a "soundtrack" musical, but loaded with sexy dancing choreographed by Kenny Ortega and executed by Swayze and his main partner, Jennifer Grey (Joel Grey's daughter), with great style and passion.

Dirty Dancing concerns a young girl who, unnoticed and unappreciated by her parents, finds herself at the family's summer vacation in the Catskills. In that sense, it's an old-fashioned musical. The music mixes favorites from the past ("Be My Baby") with some new numbers by artists who were featured on the best-selling soundtrack, including the biggie hit song, "(I've Had) The Time of My Life." The success of the movie lay in the dancing, which was hot and uninhibited, but the strength of the supporting cast helped: Jack Weston, Jerry Orbach, Lonny Price, and Charles "Honi" Coles among them. Many refer to *Dirty Dancing* as a "redefinition" of the musical, the first of many movies to be so labeled. However, there's no real "redefinition," in that musical performance is fully explained and understood: professional dancers at a summer resort teach a young girl how to dance, which involves rehearsing, dancing after work, and dancing onstage. What *Dirty Dancing* did was to make an overt statement about what everyone had always known: dancing, for the movie audience, was about sex.

Fame was the forerunner of TV's *High School Musical,* but without the light heart. It told the story of a high school for the performing arts, tracing a four-year period in the lives of students who were desperate for . . . FAME. The movie was a big hit, inspiring a popular television series in 1982 and a later Broadway adaptation. It's historically significant in that it was one of the first movies to be recorded directly onto a compact disc (digital audio was used on the soundtrack), more than two years before the first CDs appeared on the market. *Fame* is an attempt to resolve the musical's problem regarding the joy of musical performance—it shows high-school students full of energy, life, and optimism when they perform music, but trapped in a world of teenage angst. There's a plot full of sexual insecurity and threats from everywhere. The cast, however, sings and dances all over the place: in rehearsals, in classes, out in the streets, back in the cafeteria, up on the roofs. The students dance everywhere because they are learning and want to practice—and because they're young and just gotta dance. The movie was a sensible solution to the problem of the musical genre's need to be full of energy and a positive urge to sing and dance, yet also to be modern and downbeat and "realistic," even gritty. Again, however, *Fame* doesn't break new ground; but it does deserve credit for maintaining traditions in a viable manner.

Saturday Night Fever took the musical into a lower-class milieu, telling the story of a high-school graduate who works in a dull job in a paint store, but who comes alive at night, wearing a white suit and dancing to the Bee Gees in a discotheque.* Since the guy was John Travolta, who became a star as a result of this role, the movie works. It's a limited form of musical, however, in that dance is done in a disco, but nowhere else. Otherwise, it's all about dead ends in life, street gangs, rape, disappointment, and having to grow up and realize that finding ecstasy in a dance once a week may not work over a lifetime. (The sequel to this movie, 1983's *Staying Alive,* also with Travolta, was a failure. Everybody had gotten over it.)

What *Saturday Night Fever* reminds us—besides the fact that there was once a disco craze and the Bee Gees were danceable—is that musicals are strongly linked to star musical performers. It was a star vehicle for someone not yet a star. Travolta made the movie into more than it actually was with his amazing dancing and his dark good looks. Like Fred Astaire before him, Travolta knew how to walk down the street and make it as good as a choreographed dance. He swings along, walking to work, and nothing like him had been seen since Astaire walked down the streets of New York. (Astaire, in fact, thought Travolta was a fabulous dancer.)

No matter what he does, Travolta is believable as a dancer. When he plays an angel in Nora Ephron's nonmusical *Michael,* he goes to the dance floor in a roadside joint and begins to weave and bob in his own peculiar form of physical movement. (Travolta makes all his routines look improvised.) Out onto the floor, one by one, all the women—customers, waitresses, anyone who is female—come out toward him. They fall into rhythm with him, until he's leading them in a step-dance line that's an ecstasy of dance performance, yet relaxed and easy. Travolta revealed his truth as a movie dancer in *Michael.* If Travolta had been born earlier, he would be a movie-musical legend. As it is, he's a phenomenon, and the legend issue hangs in the balance. Travolta has given audiences some of the best and most astonishing dancing moments of the last forty years. It's riveting to watch him walk down the street, dance to "Staying Alive" in *Saturday Night Fever,* or take the floor to do an intensely focused improvised routine with Uma Thurman in *Pulp Fiction.* He's a hit man babysitting the boss's girlfriend, which includes buying her a burger, driving her around, getting

OPPOSITE John Travolta makes a white suit legendary in his first starring role (and the Bee Gees' disco music on the soundtrack hits the charts at the top).

* The Bee Gees' soundtrack album was ranked number one for twenty-four weeks on the charts.

her drugs, jamming a needle into her heart to prevent overdose . . . and sticking a cigarette in his mouth, taking her to the floor to out-Watusi everyone and win a dance competition.

Flashdance (1983) was almost exclusively about dance performance, and piled its music onto the soundtrack, while its leading lady "expressed" herself, dancing in a fetching sweatshirt. Her story was supposed to be gritty: steel welder by day, go-go girl by night, and secret prima ballerina in her dreams.

In 1984 two opposite original musical types were released: *The Cotton Club* and *Footloose*. The former was a gangster film featuring the celebrated Harlem nightclub, and there was musical talent aplenty. Unfortunately, the spectacular numbers, set to old tunes like "Crazy Rhythm" and "Doin' the New Low Down," were seldom shown complete, always being intercut with the dramatic scenes of the story. *The Cotton Club* was designed to be a highly modern musical, with all performances organic to action. *Footloose*, on the other hand, was as old-fashioned as could be gotten away with. It told the story of a town where dancing had been outlawed, and the kids had to break free and—*dance!* (It was fun, but it was a musical in which the cast didn't sing. The soundtrack was presold, however, so audiences often did the singing to familiar songs for themselves. At least they were participating.)

There were always musicals somewhere, popping up unexpectedly, having a brief success or a quick failure, never entirely disappearing but not thriving the way they once did. Retro stories such as *For the Boys* (1991), about a USO entertainer in World War II and her life of fame, and *That Thing You Do!* (1996) about a boy band in the 1960s, came and went. In 1985, Barry Manilow was approached by Dick Clark, who talked him into developing a made-for-television musical film built around the popular song "Copacabana," cowritten by Manilow with Bruce Sussman and Jack Feldman. The result was a success on TV, as an album, and later as a stage show and nightclub act. *Copacabana* inspired musicals to continue appearing on TV. Later television delivered a real musical with singers and dancers and plenty of the old Mickey/Judy success included *High School Musical* (in 2006). Before *High School Musical*, *Cop Rock* surfaced on television on ABC in the 1990–91 season.* In it, everyone sang, and sometimes they even

* ABC had presented a thirty-minute musical-comedy series in 1968–69 called *That's Life*, starring Robert Morse, E. J. Peaker, Shelley Berman, and Kay Medford. If it had not been musicalized, it would have been a typical family sitcom of the era.

danced. It was the story of the Los Angeles criminal system—cops and detectives, judges and social workers, criminals and juries—all of whom were living in a musical universe. The music was eclectic—any type would do, from rock to folk, from pop to classical, from gospel to rap. It was a daring idea, and it counted on audiences accepting musical performance. When the world of L.A. suddenly became a dance arena, and everyone got up and started moving, the show really had something going for it. Alas, it cost a fortune to make a single episode—the old bugaboo of the musical—and it lasted only half a season, a total of eleven episodes. It was not received with wholehearted love, but it did have loyal followers who wanted more.

It's useless just to make lists, but it's important to remember that musicals, often presumed dead, were always hanging around. Some were seen and remembered. Some were ignored and forgotten. *Newsies* (1992) with Christian Bale, Ann-Margret, Robert Duvall, and Bill Pullman, is an ambitious example. It was based on an 1899 strike by the boys in the streets of New York who sold newspapers for a living. It failed in its day, but was later made into a Broadway musical, and it has its own devoted following. Its main claim to fame was that it was the directing debut of choreographer Kenny Ortega, who would become an important figure in musical dance creation. The very next year came *Swing Kids* (1993), also starring Bale, along with Barbara Hershey, Robert Sean Leonard, and Noah Wyle. It's a weird story about the Nazi persecution of teenagers who were enthusiastic swing dancers, having responded to American music. (I would have liked to be at the pitch session for this movie: "It's about jitterbuggers and swing dancers and . . . *Nazis!*") Kenneth Branagh was the main Nazi. Although not exactly a musical, Warren Beatty's imaginative and colorful *Dick Tracy* (1990) had everything it took to be one, including Madonna as a night-club singer doing several Stephen Sondheim songs. The movie deserves to be seen, as its recreation of a comic book world of Chester Gould's square-jawed detective is an art-direction triumph. The cast includes Al Pacino, Glenne Headly, Mandy Patinkin, Charles Durning, Paul Sorvino, Seymour Cassel, Dustin Hoffman, Dick Van Dyke, Catherine O'Hara, James Caan, and more. With an impeccable eye, Beatty put together a feast of costumes, sets, makeup, and glamour—a comic book that popped off the page and started moving at top speed on the screen. And with music! Unfortunately, its originality was largely unappreciated, and it flopped.

Occasionally something ethnic emerged. In 1984, Prince made a dynamic film debut with *Purple Rain,* as a young music artist fighting convention with his very personal style of sexy and futuristic rock, a semiautobiographical movie that introduced one of his biggest hit songs, "When Doves Cry." The movie was a minor hit; in 1986 he directed himself in *Under the Cherry Moon,* shot stylishly in black-and-white but condemned by critics. In 1988, the talented Spike Lee created *his* high school musical (set in college), *School Daze,* and in 1990 he made the jazz-centered *Mo Better Blues.* In 1981, there was *Zoot Suit,* directed by Luis Valdez, starring Daniel Valdez, Edward James Olmos, and Tyne Daly. It was an extremely stylized musical presentation about a serious subject: the 1942 railroading of a Chicano gang to San Quentin on a murder rap. The story is about efforts to set them free. The gang's leader comments on the situation, and so does his zoot-suited alter ego. In an unusual presentation, the musical was filmed onstage, as if it were taking place in a theater. It was being performed in front of an audience who are playing, ironically and inevitably, the role of the watching audience inside the movie itself. *Zoot Suit* was a resounding failure, but at least it was an experiment and gave audiences a look at a Latino world.

Many originators of hit television shows were fans of musicals and created musical versions of their shows successfully (and smartly). *Moonlighting* with Cybill Shepherd and Bruce Willis did a musical episode called "Atomic Shakespeare." *Buffy the Vampire Slayer* had the best one in "Once More, with Feeling"; the underrated (and hilarious) *Psych* had a two-hour special, "Psych: The Musical." *Bob's Burgers* did "Flu-oise"; *South Park* did a parody of *High School Musical* called "Elementary School Musical" (in season 12), in which a dad wanted his kid to be in musicals and not play basketball. One of my favorites was the animated comedy musical from *The Simpsons:* "Oh, Streetcar!" with the immortal lyric "Stella! Stella! You're puttin' me through hell-a!" And there were more TV musical series, among them the recent *Crazy Ex-Girlfriend.* In spring of 2018, *The New York Times* reported the arrival of an NBC TV show, *Rise,* whose main plot points would be "the uproar over a high school musical production" in a dead Pennsylvania steel town. (Critic James Poniewozik said, "Bring it on, *Friday Night Footlights.*")

As the decades passed, original musicals continued the struggle to find new ways for musical performance to be explained: the characters didn't really sing or dance, they just did it in their heads; the characters were not people, but animated figures; the "characters" weren't characters, but real people in a documentary performing live onstage for a paid audience; or the characters appeared to sing but a recording of someone else was played, and that someone else might be of the opposite sex, or a trio, or a duet, or whatever. In other words, a form of denial of musical performance became the norm. These denials tried to change, redefine, and make the musical new and "modern." Two of these musicals (which can only be described as "experimental," or to put it in fan terms, "a couple of doozies") were *Pennies from Heaven* in 1981 and *One from the Heart* in 1982. These were movies that did not succeed at the box office, nor did they fully succeed artistically; but they were films that took the musical seriously and were attempts to find a place for originality in the genre in the changing times. The first, *Pennies*, was about the very concept of musicals, about performance onscreen of musical numbers, and the second, *One from the Heart*, was about technological experimentation.

Pennies from Heaven was based on a successful British TV show created by Dennis Potter. It was designed as a sophisticated presentation of artistic modes, about the musical's effect on an audience in its heyday, and about the differences between the actual world and the one a musical would depict to entertain a mass audience. It wasn't a hit. Since it was born on British television, and its music is all old recordings, technically it's not "original." But it's original in that it confronts very directly the issues that govern the musical format, and that also brought on its problems as it developed historically. In that, it's a success. It's a failure in that it offers a "solution" to those problems by directly discussing the issue of "reality and unreality" that's linked to presenting musical performance inside a plot. That problem becomes the subject of the film itself. The story is set in Chicago in 1934, but the characters are really living in two different artistic modes: a movie one (based on Busby Berkeley and Astaire/Rogers numbers) and a second one (based on paintings by Hopper, photos by Walker Evans, etc.). A moviegoing audience understands it's in a movie-designed world of old movie designs.

Pennies from Heaven stars Steve Martin and Bernadette Peters as a traveling sheet music salesman and a grade-school music teacher. Neither is a professional performer. They live in a 1930s movie-set world, and they exist inside two contrasting universes: the realistic one of the 1930s American Depression, and a fake one inside their heads which has been gleaned from their constant moviegoing. And in case any viewer doesn't understand that, there's an extended musical performance in which Martin and Peters go to the movies—*Follow the Fleet* with Astaire and Rogers—and as they sit in the audience watching "Let's Face the Music and Dance," they are seen to

Everybody wants to be Fred and Ginger, including Steve Martin and Bernadette Peters, who imagine themselves dancing to "Let's Face the Music and Dance" in *Pennies from Heaven*.

enter the movie to become Fred and Ginger, replacing the film's stars and taking over the choreography. Martin and Peters perform the number with great skill, accurate almost to a fault—and thereby illustrating that it really did take Fred and Ginger to make it work emotionally.

The story of the movie concerns prostitution, murder, rape, abortion, hanging—all great musical topics, of course. In this case, these horrible issues are used as an explanation and justification for the type of escapist musical Hollywood created during the era. The goal is not to invalidate the art of the musical, but also not to shirk any responsibility such escapism has in deluding the masses. Thus, exactly what the goal is never emerges in a coherent form. Martin's world disappoints him, lets him down, and closes in around him, so his escape, quite literally, becomes the musical reality that takes place in his head—in his head and nowhere else. Martin is not playing a man who *can* sing or dance, or who even imagines himself as a singer/dancer in a change of profession. He imagines himself remembering what he's heard and seen at the movies. What he's imagining is the empathy of moviegoing, the vicarious experience. And thus, out of his mouth can come a woman's voice or a famous singer's voice or the sound of a group singing or whatever. The viewing audience is never asked to accept that the people in *Pennies from Heaven* sing and dance, because they don't. They only imagine (or dream) that they do. What an audience is asked to accept is that female voices can come out of men, or that we can continue to hear a song being performed and see Martin in the frame with his mouth closed as the song goes on. The idea of considering why people sing and dance or whether they should or why they should is obliterated. Those people up there doing it? It's not them. No need to worry.

Pennies from Heaven should be a disaster, but Martin and Peters are talented and the design elements are superb. It's different, and thus intriguing, and the music is satisfying. The story is dreary and depressing, but there are fabulous moments. At one point, Christopher Walken jumps up onto a bar counter and proceeds to do a wonderful strip as he tap dances, and he is a terrific dancer. Vernel Bagneris performs the title song outside a diner in a shower of golden coins as Martin watches him from inside the eatery. A grade-school classroom filled with children all in white, seated behind little white pianos, à la Busby Berkeley, bang out a number. The whole movie turns into a PhD thesis with lip-syncing, and how many musicals could be made in that mode? It was an idea that had no room to grow.

Pennies has thirteen musical numbers plus one across the opening credits and another for the closing credits. It contains a total of thirty-three minutes of music out of its one hundred and seven minute running time, which means that just about a third of the movie is music. The longest plot gap between numbers is twelve minutes, but the average gap is only five minutes. It should be *more* fun, but it has a killjoy attitude. The movie presents a denial of the musical performance that asks a viewer to note that it is happening for cerebral reasons, and thus not participate in it but only observe it. The film also allows its main characters to speak directly to the audience about the unreality of movies. The possibility of musical happiness is questioned and overtly refused. (Martin is arrested for murder and hanged in the end, and Peters becomes a prostitute.) Although the movie loves the idea of musical escape, it clearly says it doesn't work.

One from the Heart was described by its creators as "a fantasy about romantic love, jealousy, and sex." Sounded good to an 1980s audience! It starred Frederic Forrest, Harry Dean Stanton, Teri Garr, Nastassja Kinski, Raul Julia, and Lainie Kazan, not all of whom were singers and dancers, but all of whom were part of the repertory company of Zoetrope, the studio headed by its cofounder Francis Ford Coppola; this ambitious project was his brainchild. Coppola is a true movie visionary, and he sensed that the time had come for "electronic cinema," something he had announced on the Academy Awards telecast of April 9, 1979, when he said, "we're on the eve of something that's going to make the Industrial Revolution look like a small tryout out-of-town . . . a communications revolution about movies and art and music and digital electronics and computers and satellites and, above all, human talent—and it's going to make things that the masters of the cinema, from whom we've inherited this business, wouldn't believe possible . . . all these things that are going to be possible." Coppola was right, but like most visionaries, he was pretty much ignored. Nevertheless, he made *One from the Heart*.

It was a concept movie musical. In his commentary on the soundtrack of the 2003 restored version, Coppola explains his idea of embracing the theatricality of the musical, returning it to overt stagecraft and using multiple cameras to create the kind of nonstop performance mode audiences sitting in a Broadway show could find. Coppola loves musicals and had directed them while a student—and furthermore, as he says, "music is my life." His lofty goal was to return the musical film to its theatrical roots, but in cinematic terms. To the extent to which he actually achieves this, *One from the Heart* is the musical that should have earned the excitement that would, twenty-five years later, be given to the lesser *La La Land*.

Fluidity was Coppola's goal—never stopping his camera. With necessary compromises forced on him, he found himself using one camera instead of multiples, and thus his "musical fairy tale" could do only part of what he wanted. Without multiple cameras, so that he could shoot like live television, he fell back on the plan Alfred Hitchcock used in *Rope:* move and mask until the ten minutes of film the older cameras held had run out. When Coppola achieves his goals, a viewer experiences the sense of being inside a musical, up close, and surrounded by music at all levels. A clear example of what he wanted appears in two parallel scenes, one between hero Frederic Forrest and Harry Dean Stanton (as his best friend), in the latter's apartment, and the other with heroine Teri Garr and Lainie Kazan (*her* best friend, Maggie) in the latter's apartment. In a ten-minute take, the camera moves to follow Forrest and Stanton in their conversation, until they sit down on a couch. Over their heads, behind a theatrical scrim, can be seen Garr and Kazan in their scene. There's no cut, no stopping of the flow of music or story, and their performance continues until the ten minutes run out and a dissolve removes an audience from the settings. Coppola says that he wanted to "let the lyrics tell the story."

The idea of making musicals that would be "live cinema"—that is, movies made in real time the way old television shows were shot in New York in the early years—was a revolutionary one that could have updated the genre and freed it from its old-fashioned traps. To have the songs on the soundtrack—in this case, sung by Tom Waits and Crystal Gayle—could have worked as a symbolic character expression of an internal state, the way the dance had done for Astaire and Rogers. Gayle singing "I'm sick and tired of pickin' up after you" is perfectly in harmony with story and character.

A re-created Las Vegas, a sad and lonely Teri Garr, in an unusual musical directed by Francis Ford Coppola, *One from the Heart*

One from the Heart re-created real locations on Hollywood sound stages, which was not a common practice in 1982. The city of Las Vegas was built: streets, motels, apartment houses, an entire department store, the McCarran Airport terminal—all to scale—plus a miniature replica of the Vegas strip, neon lights and all. *American Cinematographer* magazine reported that Coppola wanted a particular look—"not unreal, but not quite real either—a look that was impressionistic and sometimes even surreal." The project's cinematographer, Vittorio Storaro, added a statement regarding his work for the movie and his own ambitions: "It is an attempt of reunification between two different energetic poles, two natures that are equivalent even though they belong to opposite signs, both being part of what we call the visible light: the life. Male and female, positive and negative; nature and technology; night and day; heat and cold; light and shadow." Any way you think about it, it was a lot to hang a few songs on.

Coppola consulted Gene Kelly for advice on the dancing sequence involving Teri Garr and Raul Julia. They disagreed on how the story of the dance should play out, with Coppola ultimately going with his own preference for the initial release (which was very brief, said to be not much more than a week in theaters). When time came for the restoration in 2003, Coppola changed his mind and restored the movie to Kelly's original idea. The difference illustrates the strength of the old musicals and the role that dance played in both narrative and characterization in those years. Garr and Julia execute a tango that is at first just the two of them in a large space, but which extends outward into two different sections: a large, exuberant street dance, and a smaller, romantic interlude in which their relationship becomes more involved. Coppola's plan was to present these three pieces in this order: original acquaintance dance; smaller, more intimate and involved dance; and finale out in the streets. (This was the original release.) Kelly disagreed strongly, feeling that the order should be: original acquaintance dance; big burst out into the streets with the crowd; and then the finale which would show them in a more intimate relationship. (This is the 2003 release.) Kelly also felt that the big dance in the streets should involve only trained dancers and be a large, specifically choreographed piece. Coppola felt it should have *some* trained dancers, but also ordinary people who were not dancers just walking around and keeping the sense of Las Vegas alive. This part was never changed.

Kelly's role in the production, and his suggestions, reveal how utterly the former Hollywood system embraced and understood the parameters of musical films. Since the dance was an expression of the growth and change of a character relationship—it was a narrative device as much as a musical number—it had to tell the story of what happened to the two characters during their night of fun in natural development order. Therefore, their intimacy dance had to appear last.

The story of *One from the Heart* is a musical story. Two people have been living together for five years, but they are not on the same page. She wants travel, excitement, and "to dance." He wants security, marriage, and perhaps a family. When they each have an affair on the night of the Fourth of July, she's exhilarated (but a bit guilty), and he's depressed and clear that he wants her back. When she leaves him, and he asks why that other guy, she explains by saying, "He sings to me." He says sadly that he would sing to her, but "I can't sing, honey." Nevertheless, he chases her to the airport as she's flying off to Bora Bora with her new lover (a young and beautiful Raul Julia) and tries desperately to win her back by croaking out "You Are My Sunshine." (In the end, she returns to him. Who could believe she wouldn't, after that?)

Coppola created characters for whom music had specific meaning and character logic, set them in a musical world (with Waits and Gayle on the soundtrack), and separated them by giving them participation in separate magical musical events. (Garr does her tango with Julia; Forrest watches Kinski dance.) It was a good idea. Unfortunately, the world wasn't ready for it, and it was flawed in its overall presentation. It loses its musical focus from time to time; Coppola could not sustain his "live cinema" plan with only one camera and conventional editing techniques; and it was too experimental for general audiences. But in it was buried the future of a genre that needed the imagination of a forward thinker like Coppola.

Pennies from Heaven and *One from the Heart* were honest failures, but pretentious attempts to "comment" on the musical were also created, as if an audience needed to be taught that musical performance was unnatural and could be indulged on film only in ways this particular movie could explain. Some of these movies, like Woody Allen's *Everyone Says I Love You* (1997), just flopped; but another, Baz Luhrmann's *Moulin Rouge!* (2001), was taken very seriously by many. It was a high-speed, chopped-up mishmash of songs from many eras and sources, with the idea behind it that if everyone moved fast enough, no one would notice it was a musical in which there was no talent. If Michael Bay had made this movie, he would have been run out of town on a rail, but it also would have been cut better.

With some of its casting, *Moulin Rouge!* also endorsed the concept that an actor in a musical didn't need to be able to sing or even talk/sing lyrics.*

Everyone Says I Love You presents itself as a love song to the great music of the past. Unfortunately, it's also about a bunch of snarky New Yorkers banging around the city (as well as Paris and Venice) looking for whatever it is they don't have, although they appear to have everything. It was supposed to be a homage to old musicals, but it also satirized them to a point of concealed ridicule. The film has an apology built into it, a kind of "We all know this is a guilty pleasure" quality, but there *is* love of the old songs. The fact that half the stars can't sing them properly was supposed to be okay, and audience members are asked to accept that it's okay because, after all, these people are movie stars. Allen's movies always have a lineup of currently recognizable names, a kind of insurance against failure, and *Everyone Says* has real singers in Goldie Hawn, Edward Norton, and Alan Alda, but tuneless duds in Julia Roberts, Tim Roth, and Allen himself. There's no logic to the presentation of music, and entry into a number—not to mention song integration—is sadly lacking. Everyone is oh so clever, and disjointed events are created to accommodate songs—such as a party in Paris at which all the guests are dressed like Groucho Marx and dance around the Ritz hotel singing "Hooray for Captain Spaulding"—in French. It wasn't all that clever, although the choreography was by Graciela Daniele. Many people oohed over a scene in which Goldie Hawn floated on air as she duetted with Allen on "I'm Through with Love," but her floating had no real meaning or joy. Fred Astaire had floated on air in *The Belle of New York* (and danced on the ceiling in *Royal Wedding*), and Marge and Gower Champion had floated across a starred heaven in *Lovely to Look At,* and somehow the emotion behind the action was made tangible. In *Everyone Says,* it's a concept, nothing more—but one that would influence a later film, *La La Land.*

Movies trying to be original often ignored what had been done in the movies of the past. The musicals of the Hollywood studio system experimented, played with ideas, but not in a consciously intellectualized way. *Shine on Harvest Moon* (a 1944 movie from Warner Bros.) starred two contract players who did all kinds of movies and thus were functional, econom-

---

* Nonsinging star personalities, of course, had always been dubbed in Hollywood, with some notable exceptions like Jimmy Stewart in *Born to Dance* (inept but charming) and Marlon Brando in *Guys and Dolls* (inept and calamitous).

ical, and useful all year round: Dennis Morgan and Ann Sheridan. Morgan had a beautiful tenor voice, and Sheridan could sing and dance. Both were good-looking, and Sheridan was celebrated for her sex appeal (she was known as the "Oomph Girl"). They were successfully starred together in *Harvest Moon,* which became a very big hit for the studio. It was a biopic about two vaudeville stars, Jack Norworth (who wrote the title song as well as the famous "Take Me Out to the Ball Game") and his wife, the star singer Nora Bayes. Costarring Jack Carson, S. Z. Sakall, Irene Manning, and Marie Wilson, *Harvest Moon* was literally stuffed with musical numbers, and Morgan, Sheridan, Carson, Manning, and Wilson all performed. It was a dramatic biopic, stressing the troubles Bayes and Norworth had getting bookings due to being blacklisted during a period of their working lives. It was meant to be entertainment and nothing else, and it moved along from dramatic event to dramatic event, weaving its songs and dances easily into the story. Most of the musical performances were presented logically as happening onstage or at rehearsals, but others branched out easily into "We're at a happy dinner-party celebration, and we're all professionals so let's perform for each other." It also managed to fully integrate a song into the nonperformance space in a police station. Having been arrested for starting a fight, Morgan, Sheridan, and Carson are recognized by a policeman at the station, who says, "I heard you sing that song"—and he, as an amateur, begins the number; they chime in. This unconscious introduction of a number that is not being performed onstage but in the real world is fully justified, an example of how Hollywood movies didn't always maintain their own barriers and *could* think outside the box.

Two musical presentations in *Shine on Harvest Moon* are more significant. When Bayes and Norworth believe they have finally obtained a booking after a long dry spell, they show up at the theater only to find it dark and no one there. Once again, they're told, their enemies have blocked them. Bayes (Sheridan) says, "Let's leave, this empty theater is depressing," but Norworth (Morgan) says, "Oh, no, it's not depressing. I see a full house—look at all those people." The house is magically filled, she's suddenly standing there in a white satin gown, and the audience is taken into his head in a literal interpretation of his dream sequence—no psychiatry about it, just his "I picture this" and the audience pictures it. Moments like this in ordinary musicals show that the "great breakthrough" of more arty musicals was the overt suggestion to an audience that the self-reflexivity involved was about cinema itself. It was the attitude toward "seeing it in the head" that was different, not the execution of it. *Shine on Harvest Moon* also plays with technology. Its giant final number, in which Bayes and Norworth are restored to fame and are appearing in the *Ziegfeld Follies,* is presented in Technicolor. (The rest of the movie is in black-and-white.) Two spotlight operators up in the fly gallery say "It's time" and turn colored filters on. It's another self-conscious calling attention to the artifice of film, and it's done only for a grand musical finale. Presumably no one will wonder why the film turns to color: the color change *represents*. It represents the stars' restoration to fame and success; it represents the transference of an audience to a musical world; and it represents "This is the movies and we can do it." (It also represents stinginess. Warners didn't want to spend the money it would take in 1944 to have shot the whole film in color.) The number uses color beautifully. Morgan and Sheridan are set against a blue sky, with her in bold yellow and white and him in a blue-gray top hat and tuxedo. The number wanders through various songs, especially the new one written specially for the film, and allows Carson and Wilson to perform. Carson does a "magic" act in which he goes *poof!* and instigates the appearance of *Follies*-type girls, all dressed as various vegetables since the scene takes place on a farm. Viewers are treated to women dressed as corn, carrots, lima beans, peas in a pod, tomatoes, cabbage, cauliflower—my favorite is a beautiful girl with her head inside a watermelon. (This sequence also has the Four Step Brothers dressed as whiteface clowns, tapping out one of their acrobatic routines.) This final number could not have easily been done onstage, although it's not one of Berkeley's extravaganzas. (LeRoy Prinz staged the dances.) But again, the ideas that were to become the hallmarks of the more "artistic" musical are present in this simple entertainment biopic.

Despite the fact that when musical films appeared after 1980 they were often pretending to be something else (cartoons, biographies) or masquerading as think pieces, it seems more or less true that audiences always had a hunger for musical performances. They were, after all, watching MTV regularly.* The link between musical films and what MTV provided—songs by famous recording artists set to fantastic images of all types—is revealed by a movie like *Across the Universe* (2007), which proves that audiences not only wanted musicals, but people in show business wanted to make

---

* MTV was a training ground for many new young film directors, and a creative outlet for many who were already established: David Lynch, Michael Bay, David Fincher, Martin Scorsese, et al.

them. Thirty-three songs written by the Beatles are sucked up and used by a group of shaky singers who enact a trite story about a Liverpool shipyard worker who comes to America and—hold for the surprise—falls in love. As the music rings out, a whole lot of disaster, representing the chaos of America during the Vietnam War, rolls out: race riots, drugs, protests, and class snobbery. It's a perfect example of the problem the musical had: no composers to create original film scores, no strong singing and dancing talent, but a big need to be *significant*. The movie has a cult following, but not many are true movie fans. Directed by Julie Taymor, the movie illustrates the difference between what is visual theatrically and what is visual cinematically. It has visuals that are spectacle, but that don't utilize what cinema has to offer through manipulation of time and space.

After the millennium arrived, it became increasingly fashionable to pronounce musicals a dead genre. And yet they would still pop up. In 2001 there was the über failure of *Glitter,* starring Mariah Carey, a movie that tried to recycle the kind of plot that had once worked. In 2005, John Turturro directed an unusual example, *Romance + Cigarettes,* a highly personal effort about the marital crisis of a blue-collar couple (James Gandolfini and Susan Sarandon). A great cast (including Kate Winslet, Steve Buscemi, and Christopher Walken) do everything karaoke-style; it's a crazy mess that needs to be seen and given a place on the list of original efforts. In 2008 *High School Musical 3: Senior Year* appeared in movie houses, a musical that decided that if *High School Musical* and *High School Musical 2* could succeed on TV's Disney Channel, why couldn't a third one work in movie theaters? It reteamed director Kenny Ortega (the original director and choreographer) with the popular original stars Zac Efron, Vanessa Hudgens, and Ashley Tisdale. It was full of basketball, college decisions, breakups and hookups, but most of all, it was full of the same energetic and exuberant dancing and singing that had made the TV shows a success. Most people dubbed it (and its predecessors) "Archie and Veronica," but the truth is that these musicals were fun, and superbly executed. In *High School Musical 2,* when the teenagers burst out through the doors of the school to leave for summer vacation, singing and dancing with an unbridled energy (and a very high level of talent), it puts the opening number of *La La Land* to shame. And does anyone remember *Step Up* (2006), *Step Up 2: The Streets* (2008), *Step Up 3D* (2010), and *Step Up Revolution* (2012)? No? Well, they were all musicals, with dance numbers that combined everything from hip-hop to ballet to tango to an imitation Fred and Ginger on a Manhattan block. Cher's star power drove *Burlesque* in 2010, casting her with Christina Aguilera, Stanley Tucci, Kristen Bell, and Peter Gallagher and proving the old "star vehicle" concept could still work. *Pitch Perfect* appeared in 2012 with Anna Kendrick and Rebel Wilson—a story about an a capella singing group—and would generate such popularity that it inspired *Pitch Perfect 2* (2015) and *Pitch Perfect 3* (2017). The "innovations" that these movies provided were mostly through different types of music, such as gospel: in 2012, a minor and generally overlooked movie called *Joyful Noise* nevertheless did solid business, largely due to gospel and its stars, Dolly Parton and Queen Latifah. It seemed strange to think that a movie like *Joyful Noise* could even be made: a trite story pitting Parton (a wise-old-philosopher type with big money, big wig, big ideas, and of course, big boobs) against an angry rival (Latifah). The two women fight over who will run the church choir, what type of music the choir should sing, and end up in a public brawl. The thing that makes *Joyful Noise* is, of course, the music (with two songs newly penned by Parton). The movie is a musical, and it knows enough how to be one, but the critical establishment ignored the low-budget story about a Georgia church choir.

All these releases, however distinguished or undistinguished, prove that the musical wasn't really dead. It wasn't chic, perhaps, but it wasn't dead. What it didn't have was critical endorsement, the stamp of approval, the "We never had this before" or "Now it's serious" cachet that would make it okay for all of us to go see it—and not only go, but claim we liked it. The musical needed to be told it was smart by somebody.

There *was* one other innovation after the 1970s. Changes in the culture brought changes onscreen. After the civil rights movement made serious headway, movies starring African American musical performers became more prevalent, and access to that incredible musical talent pool was, at least to a degree, unlocked for the general moviegoer. The all-black musical had, in fact, existed since the transition to sound: *Hallelujah* and *Hearts in Dixie* were both successful in 1929. In the 1940s there were *Cabin in the Sky, Stormy Weather, New Orleans,* and Disney's *Song of the South,* as well as *Carmen Jones, Porgy and Bess,* and *St. Louis Blues* (a biopic about W. C. Handy starring Nat "King" Cole and Eartha Kitt) in the 1950s. Most of the enormously talented African American musical performers of the studio-system years were relegated to specialty numbers, such as Lena Horne in *Words and Music* or *Till the Clouds Roll By,* or the Nicholas Brothers in *Orchestra Wives, Sun Valley Serenade,* and *The Pirate.* Bill

"Bojangles" Robinson had his roles in Shirley Temple films, and musical performers such as Fats Waller, Dooley Wilson, Cab Calloway, and Duke Ellington appeared from time to time.

The vibrant Ethel Waters, whose voice flowed lazily out of her like a velvet river, was never given the opportunities she should have had in movies. There was a warmth in her performance personality that, combined with her bright smile, made her a true audience winner. As the star of *Cabin in the Sky*, she is at her radiant best singing "Taking a Chance on Love" while Eddie "Rochester" Anderson plays a guitar and John W. Bubbles looks on. She lays it out easy, as if the lyrics are a personal observation just noticed on the spot. Waters began by singing jazz and blues in clubs and appearing on Broadway in revues such as the 1930 *Lew Leslie's Blackbirds*, finally opening in *As Thousands Cheer* in 1933 as the first African American performer to get equal billing with white performers. (She was also the first African American to have her own national radio show.) Although she starred in *Cabin in the Sky*, she was usually seen only in a solo number (*Stage Door Canteen*, 1943), given a supporting role (as Jeanette MacDonald's companion in *Cairo*, 1942), or showcased for her dramatic ability (*The Member of the Wedding*, 1952, and *Pinky*, 1949, for which she was nominated as Best Supporting Actress). In the end, her remarkable, but erratic career in movies left her remembered more as an actress than as a musical performer.

When I think of all the great African American performers who are casually inserted into movies, I realize how much entertainment was lost to audiences over the years. Just consider the moment in Nicholas Ray's beautifully tragic film about young lovers, *They Live by Night*, released in 1949. As newlyweds on the run, Farley Granger and Cathy O'Donnell visit a nightclub, and the fabulous Marie Bryant, a singer/dancer who toured with Duke Ellington, moves around the club singing "Your Red Wagon." A Cotton Club star, Bryant had a great voice and a wonderful way with a song. She's only in this one scene in the movie, but her glamorous attire combined with her warning lyrics ("Just keep draggin' your red wagon") are meant to be typical nightclub entertainment, but also a song sounding the ring of doom for the lovers. Bryant permeates the atmosphere, claims the club space, delivers vocal purity, and more than anything else that's happening defines the noir ambience of a world in which the young lovers have no chance. Couldn't she have done an encore? Couldn't she have had more to do in other movies? And Marie Bryant is only one example. What, for instance, if the world had been a place where Josephine Baker could have become a big name in Hollywood? After leaving America and becoming a nightclub star in France, Baker made two good musicals there: *Zou-Zou* (1934) and *Princess Tam Tam* (1935). The former starred her with the famous "Spencer Tracy of France," Jean Gabin, and it had a backstage plot about a Creole laundress who unexpectedly "goes on" in a *42nd Street* plot ploy and becomes a great star. Baker is awesome in feathers, swinging on a swing, and she's equally spectacular as an African girl who's transformed into an Indian princess in *Tam Tam*. Baker became famous in 1931 for her signature song, "J'ai Deux Amours," and for her erotic "Danse Sauvage" in which she wore nothing but a skirt decorated with some aroused-looking bananas. What a loss to film history!

In the 1933 black circuit film *Slow Poke*, starring Stepin Fetchit (real name Lincoln Theodore Monroe Andrew Perry), the fabulous young Bunny Briggs is featured. He's one of the world's tap-dancing legends, and watching him makes a viewer realize again what was lost. Briggs went on to tour with big bands such as the Dorsey Brothers, Charlie Barnet, and Count Basie, getting a chance to create his own unique style of bebop tapping. Later known as "the Duke's dancer" because of his appearance with Ellington at the 1960 Monterey Jazz Festival, he remained a top-level tapper for decades, finally getting a notable appearance in the 1989 movie *Tap*, starring Gregory Hines.*

The Nicholas Brothers, Fayard and Harold, were showstoppers no matter what musical extravaganza they were dropped into for a dancing "bit." They danced from head to toe, using their whole bodies, and gracefully involving the waving of their delicate hands into their routines. They could jump high into the air, come down onto the floor in splits, and pull themselves back up to full height without using a hand for help. And they could jump, split, jump, split, jump, split, over and over again without any "ouch!" in it. They were classy, at ease with each other and the audience, and seemingly happy, just happy, to be dancing. They were the best!

The three Berry Brothers—all amazing dancers—had body control that allowed them to literally do a number in slow motion without camera

---

* Briggs received a Tony nomination for *Black and Blue* on stage in 1989 and became a member of the American Tap Dancing Hall of Fame in 2006. Hines became a major force in bringing respect for tap dancing and for an older set of African American tappers. Hines himself was a phenomenal tapper, and danced in *The Cotton Club*, *White Nights* (1985), and *The Preacher's Wife* (1996), the latter a musical remake of *The Bishop's Wife* (1947). I saw Gregory Hines, with his brother, Maurice, and his father (also Maurice) in late 1968, when they were billed as Hines, Hines, and Dad and opened for Judy Garland on a road tour. Their tapping was nothing short of amazing.

assistance. They could *hold*, but with no wobbles and no tricks. They were three blood brothers who worked with Duke Ellington at the Cotton Club, engaging in a legendary "dance fight" with the Nicholas Brothers in 1938. (There seems to have been no declared winner, but what would anyone give to have been there for that?) The Berry Brothers appeared in a few movies, the two best-known being *Lady Be Good* (1941) and *Panama Hattie* (1942). In their *Lady Be Good* number, they sing "You'll Never Know" and demonstrate their unique style, a form of tap dancing, although they didn't wear taps on their shoes. They were acrobats, incorporating somersaults, cartwheels, spins, and splits into their routines, and using canes they tossed back and forth in the air. In top hats and tails, they combined the cakewalk and the prancing strut in a "freeze and melt" dance in which they twirl, stop dead—hold—and then suddenly go at high speed again. In one jaw-dropping routine they performed onstage, they would jump from an elevated balcony directly into full splits. The early death at age thirty-eight (of heart failure) of one of the members of this "flash tap" acrobatic team has kept them from the fame they deserve.

There were so many great African American singers and dancers whom movie audiences saw nothing of in musicals, or saw very little of: Waters, Sarah Vaughan, Hamtree Harrington. Even Lena Horne, who was the first African American signed to a long-term contract with a major studio (MGM), wasn't given enough to do. Eddie "Rochester" Anderson could dance, and his moonwalk was fabulous. Just to look at Dorothy Dandridge's musical strut in her small part in the "Chattanooga Choo Choo" number in *Sun Valley Serenade* is to feel the loss of her musical talent. Fats Waller could have made me believe anything from Don Corleone to Hamlet to Mr. Micawber; he was a great misbehavin' personality.

Three musicals of the poststudio era show how the traditional forms of the musical were slowly transformed to star African American talent: *The Wiz* (1978) and *Dreamgirls* (2006) are Broadway shows adapted for the movies; and *Idlewild* (2006) is an original movie musical. *The Wiz* came first. It was based on a 1975 hit with Motown-inflected songs by Charlie Smalls, direction by Geoffrey Holder, hot-dancing choreography by George Faison. The movie, however, was a resounding failure.

In fact, *The Wiz* is a musical tragedy. It was shot at the Astoria Studios in Queens and on various New York locations, and it had talent to burn. But its characters get lost in spectacle, and most of the talent is wasted. It was an example of excess and financial waste—it was one of the most expensive musicals ever made—and both critics and audiences rejected it.

A new take on the land of Oz. Nipsey Russell as Tinman, Diana Ross as a modern-day Dorothy, Michael Jackson as Scarecrow, and Ted Ross as the Lion ease on down the road in *The Wiz*.

Tony Walton designed sets that ate up the dancers, leaving them lost in long shot or overshadowed by the sets surrounding them. Sidney Lumet was a New York director, but the New York of gritty realism, not the abandoned amusement park New York of fantasy. Actors, too, were lost in over-costuming, and the luminously beautiful (and supertalented) Diana Ross had her glamour tamped down to accommodate the revised Dorothy, a twenty-four-year-old Harlem schoolteacher (a rewrite to help explain the thirty-four-year-old Ross playing her, even though in real life Ross could have passed for twenty and had the energy of a sixteen-year-old). *The Wiz* was an example of how confused people who made musicals often were at this point. *The Wiz* assumes that photographing a Broadway show as an even bigger spectacle would be all that was needed, and that shifting from realism into fantasy called for no explanations, no coherence, and no common sense. A movie that can kill a successful stage musical as well as a beloved children's book as well as memories of a hit movie (the original *Wizard of Oz*) is a real death bomb. *The Wiz* set back musicals, set back all-black films—and set back the studio that made it (Universal) financially. It had all the talent in the world: Diana Ross, a superstar; Michael Jackson, a legend in the making; two real talents from the Broadway show, Ted Ross as Lion and Mabel King as Evilline, the Wicked Witch; the comic Nipsey Russell; and the iconic Richard Pryor. As if all that weren't enough, there was Lena Horne—truly in a class by herself.

Think of the talent wasted in *The Wiz*. Diana Ross is not only a stunning beauty and style setter, but also an amazing singer and a deep, feeling actress with natural ability. Her appearance in the 1972 Billie Holiday biopic, *Lady Sings the Blues* was outstanding, both in acting and singing. She should have had a decades-long career playing all sorts of roles, only some of which needed to be musical. Lena Horne was at least given a dramatic finale in *The Wiz*, but it's only a moment. When Glinda the Good Witch comes down from her star, Horne is radiant in sparkling blue, with dozens of stars on her gown and headpiece. She looks younger than anyone else in the entire movie, even though she's sixty-one at the time. She sings "Believe in Yourself" as if she means it, and gives it something it never had before—sass and sex appeal and genuine conviction. She's one of the most beautiful women ever, a real Glinda and a real musical power. She should have had more.

Michael Jackson could be one of the greatest movie losses of all. In *The Wiz*, as Scarecrow, he's covered with costume and makeup and can hardly be found inside the trappings, but when he dances, even in long shot, any eye can see he's something extraordinary. Watching him when he can be identified as himself, in his music videos, especially *Thriller*, his unique style marks him out as being in the tradition of Astaire, Kelly, and others who didn't just dance but made it a form of personal expression. Jackson spins as fast as any dancer has ever spun, and his precise steps, his sharp and separate delineation of each foot movement, are still able to flow together to look as if he's a well-oiled machine. He's a human robot, making the mechanical smooth and meaningful, a truly modern dancer. He may have redefined the term, if only for updating the moonwalk of old minstrel shows into a flashy, slap-down-the-floor statement that says, "I'm not your usual moonwalker." Lumet called Jackson "the purest talent I've ever seen." There's a poignant moment at the end of *The Wiz*, almost lost among the junk, in which Scarecrow/Jackson says sadly, thoughtfully, "Fame . . . fortune . . . success . . . all there is that's real is friendship." Jackson's career, despite all the videos and TV and concert appearances, was still largely lost to the history of narrative musicals in which he could have been so memorable.

Dreamgirls appeared on Broadway in 1981, to great critical and commercial success, but it was 2006 before it was finally made into a movie. No one, apparently, felt it was a safe bet for a mass audience, even though Motown-style music had long since swept America. Direction of the movie was taken over by Bill Condon, whose prior success writing the movie version of *Chicago* (2002) gave backers confidence in the possibilities of the story, loosely based on the Supremes. The original show (directed by Michael Bennett) moved an audience from watching the performances as an audience to being inside the story as the participants experienced it. Switching points of view is a cinematic tradition, and Condon attempted to turn the play into cinema by embracing the technique, but with results that audiences didn't fully understand. *Dreamgirls* has pace, energy, and an ambitious integration of plot and music, but what it really puts onscreen is a blazing lineup of talent: the beautiful and musically dominant Beyoncé, the excellent singer/actress Jennifer Hudson, and two leading men, Jamie Foxx and Eddie Murphy, who both did their own singing and who were dynamite.

One of the craziest, most innovative musicals made since the millennium is *Idlewild*, written and directed by music-video veteran Bryan Barber. It starred André 3000 and Big Boi of OutKast, along with Terrence Howard, Ving Rhames, Cicely Tyson, Ben Vereen, Malinda Williams, Paula Patton, Patti LaBelle, and Paula Jai Parker. As a viewer of hundreds of musicals, I would say about *Idlewild:* Attention Should Be Paid. It's provocative, inventive, and full of cinematic ideas and imagination. Musical lovers should see this movie, because it *is* a movie. It's also a bit of a mess, but at least a viewer is rewarded for patience by an outlandish abandonment of the sort that scares many moviegoers and drives them out of the theater and back to their TV sets. *Idlewild* is what the genre needs more of, although many viewers labeled it a "long music video."

Idlewild is set in 1935 Idlewild, Georgia, and it tells a story of two young men, Percival (André 3000) and Rooster (Big Boi), who were childhood friends but grow up to make different choices in life. That puts the film in familiar gangster genre territory—the world of *Angels with Dirty Faces* (1938), for instance—but the script becomes a problem, and not because it mixes genres. Musical numbers and gangster movies are old friends, from the story of Ruth Etting (*Love Me or Leave Me*); Priscilla Lane's numbers in

The Roaring Twenties, with James Cagney; the spoof with children shooting cream pies at each other, *Bugsy Malone* (1976); or Nicholas Ray's *Party Girl* (1958), with Cyd Charisse as a nightclub performer being threatened with acid in her face. The problem is that *Idlewild*'s script doesn't wed them successfully, and the movie ends up in a divided universe: two different movies, two different genres, and more than two styles of music. In the

latter category, the wedding is well achieved. The hip-hop of the leading duo is mixed with blues, jazz, and soul, and it becomes a blend that excites and energizes. For a movie lover, there's a fearless use of cinematic tricks: singing cuckoo clocks, a talking rooster on a flask, animated notes dancing across a musical page, and time modulations that are beautifully edited. There's an astonishing modernized "Stormy Weather"–type finale with white pianos, and great dancing (choreographed by Hinton Battle) that is an eclectic mix of swing dancing, jitterbugging, tapping, and modern style.

Big Boi throws it down with a high-stepping chorus line of beauties in an original musical from 2006 that combined gangsters and music, *Idlewild*.

A common complaint about *Idlewild* is that it juxtaposes beautiful 1930s clothes, sets, and ambience with modern music. Why not? Another common complaint is that its gangster movie is too brutal and violent to go with musical performance. The movie defines itself as a modern musical-performance world, perhaps going back in time to own a 1930s mainstream Hollywood genre movie, since African American performers hadn't been allowed to make many of them at the time. The numbers take place onstage, with music always in the plot background and turning up in odd places, such as a cuckoo clock. What comes out of *Idlewild* is what the musical needed in 2006: an unpretentious letting go of the fear to just try things. Play with the form. Mix it up a little or even a lot. With its wonderful music, exuberant dancing, and crazy use of cinema, *Idlewild* fearlessly made one of the most interesting movies of the millennium, even though it doesn't work. It dared to break rules but knew it was breaking them.

As I have said, musicals didn't really die: audiences still wanted them and filmmakers still wanted to make them. The musical hung around, and it hangs around. Solutions to its challenges were found by creative forces decade after decade, but the need to find actors/performers/stars and creative directors to execute those solutions seemed to grow over time. The bottom line is: if you're going to make a musical, shouldn't the people in it be able to sing and dance? This brings us to 2016 and a movie called *La La Land*.

VIII

Final Number

N 2016, TWO MUSICALS OPENED IN THEATERS. The first was a mockumentary called *Pop Star: Never Stop Never Stopping*, with Maya Rudolph, Andy Samberg, and the Lonely Island group. It was satiric but still a true musical with good songs and performances, plus funny comedy. This movie sank without a trace. In the fall of 2016, a second musical called *La La Land* appeared. Critics nationwide swooned, dropped to their knees, and proclaimed the American movie musical had been revolutionized. Audiences immediately followed their leaders, turning out in happy droves, proclaiming the rebirth of an old form in new terms—and sending box-office figures to the skies. Even detractors—a small group—bent over backwards to say that "after all, we've got to remember that director/writer Damien Chazelle loves musicals." *La La Land* soared upward on an Oscar-bound trajectory, and then, with its creators, cast, and crew tuxedoed and tiaraed and ready for their victory lap, an ending right out of a Hollywood musical script occurred: The front-runners were unseated by a low-budget underdog, *Moonlight,* and the Best Picture Oscar was snatched from the hands of the anointed ones. *La La Land* lost in a wild-ass finish never seen before in Oscar history. After that, a lot of people stepped up to say they'd never liked *La La Land* anyway, and what was all the fuss about? *Moonlight* was new and original, they said. *La La Land* was pastiche. Not since Harry Truman upset Thomas Dewey had so many previously uncounted voters appeared to say they knew it all along.

The musical genre was left standing at the altar. Uncertainty reigned. Based on the *La La Land* success, new musicals were already in the works, and since they cost a lot of money, no one wanted to talk about the success of *La La Land* being a fluke, or even possibly a mistake. What had happened to the revolution of the musical it had supposedly brought, to its

Emma Stone and Ryan Gosling dance a little bit in *La La Land*.

originality, to its "new take" on an old genre, to its swooning critics? What, after all, was *La La Land* to the history of the musical?

La La Land opens up directly into a precredit musical number of the old-school MGM variety: a one-take cinematic phenomenon in which ordinary people (although dressed in color-coordinated outfits) are stuck in an L.A. freeway jam on a bright, sunny day. They emerge from their cars and dance in CinemaScope, and when they finish, the credits roll.

This is about as good an establishment of a musical universe as can be planned. The choreography may not be great, the song may not be a hummer, but the idea is impeccable: ordinary people on their way to work sing and dance, which means an audience hasn't had to transition out and into, but just ease themselves into a musical world. The film continues with a little plot for the "meet brute" of the leading lady and leading man, insulting each other with appropriate digits as he honks and she doesn't respond fast enough, so he speeds by her in disgust. The heroine (Emma Stone) goes home to her apartment, and her three roommates (soon to disappear from the plot) try to convince her to accompany them to a party—again done as a musical number. An audience has sat down, found a musical world, found the movie's title, found its lead characters, and moved onward into a continued musical universe in which all the characters sing and dance as they live. And then that's over with. No more of that stuff. The world doesn't ever sing and dance again, although musicians play in jazz clubs, at parties by the pool, and in concerts. The two leads, in their private world together, become the location of musical expression: they become the people who sing and dance, even though neither of them can really do either very well. The tradition of the American musicals the film sets out to emulate—a place where everyone and everything is musical—is gone.

La La Land isn't worried about any of that. Why? Because its "an homage." It's about nostalgia, although the filmmakers are nostalgic for something they didn't experience when it was new. Their nostalgia is about nostalgia, and it's also about superiority: "We love old musicals and we've seen them—have you?" There are references (admitted proudly by the filmmakers) to *Singin' in the Rain* and *The Umbrellas of Cherbourg;* and critics hopped on others, such as Goldie Hawn's floating upward in *Everyone Says I Love You*, backdrops similar to *An American in Paris*, or Astaire and Eleanor Powell tapping across a sparkling floor in *Broadway Melody of 1940*. Few mentioned Marge and Gower Champion dancing across a blue sky with stars in *Lovely to Look At*, because that remake of the Astaire/Rogers *Roberta* isn't considered chic. It's not on the list of movies you need to have seen—it's got Red Skelton, for heaven's sake, and Kathryn Grayson and Howard Keel, not cool people.

Director/writer Damien Chazelle talked often in interviews about his love of old musicals, listing Jacques Demy's poetic *Umbrellas of Cherbourg* as "the greatest movie ever made." This explains everything, because it isn't, but it *is* stylish, romantic, dreamy, melancholy, and sadly, sweetly nostalgic about a young love in which the two leads end up with others. And it's also something else: quintessentially French. *La La Land* is not like an MGM musical. It's not energetic, optimistic, or determined to pin down joy for its characters. It's not American. And despite the leaping about on cars in its opening number and all the camera movement it beautifully spools out in key scenes, it's not kinetic. The screen is dead around its protagonists, and one of its main stylistic devices (used at least three times) is to drop lighting out of the frame around one of its two stars, leaving him/her in a lone and empty spotlight, to share isolation, to illustrate the need for something that isn't there, and to project the idea of a dream . . . and the feeling of sadness.

Great musicals turn a location into a dream itself—the postwar Paris of *An American in Paris,* the sizzling glitz of Las Vegas in *One from the Heart,* the turn-of-the-century family home in *Meet Me in St. Louis.* Since making space into a musical world is a primary challenge of the genre, the essence of any setting, real or unreal, has to be interpreted and designed as the "persona" of itself. Paris becomes "that star" where all Americans want to go to find their more artistic, freer selves, with better food to eat. Las Vegas upgrades personal escape, gambling on one-night relationships, taking risks, on the movie set of our dreams; and St. Louis gives us the idea of America we were promised as children: safe, familial, and guaranteed to have a happy ending. The Los Angeles of *La La Land* has none of that. It used forty-eight locations in forty-two days of shooting but never captured the fabulous sleaze and utterly American personality of Los Angeles. Production designer David Wasco turned the real L.A. into a fantasia of a city—and it looks fine—but it doesn't interpret either the real place or its movie essence. There is a movie L.A., but it's film noir—potent, dark, sexy, with light streaking out from the shadows to reveal nothing good. But those are not the visuals seen onscreen in *La La Land.* Its world is neither Los Angeles itself nor an interpretation of it. It's more an interpretation of Scorsese's Manhattan world in *New York, New York,* or perhaps even the world of New York beautifully set up in *On the Town.*

Director Chazelle loves music and understands that cinema should move and use the tools available. His finest achievement is filming dance numbers with a minimum of cuts—in long takes or single takes—and to photograph a dancer Fred Astaire–style: showing the full body, including the dancing feet. But Fred Astaire's dancing perfection is not present in Chazelle's stars. The movie says that's okay: they're just two little people, à la Capra, who have a dream, and they're gonna try like heck.

Trying isn't enough. Successful musicals have to find a way for the song and dance numbers to express the meaning of each character (and their relationships) through lyrics, dance movements, and the sound of music. Since the principals aren't great singers or dancers, *La La Land* doesn't count on that. It talks instead. Stone explains everything, and Gosling *really* explains everything. (Perhaps this is wise, since the numbers actually explain little.) Gosling is a jazz man who wants to keep the pure art of improvisatory and collaborative jazz alive, but when he's playing the way the film says he should, he plays alone. Emma Stone is an actress who dreams of stardom, but her high point is a monologue that grows out of her one-woman show—no other actors. She's a sad sack, uncertain, insecure, fearful, and willing to give up rather than keep trying. The plot becomes confused and confusing as the movie travels forward to its *New York, New York* ending in which she's a star, he's got his nightclub, and he sits down at the piano to "play" the plot of the movie they might have had if they hadn't wanted careers. The story becomes "You can't have it all." They chose career over love.

After the first flood of loony claims that *La La Land* had brought the modern musical to life as the golden maiden it could be if it had lesser music, nonmusical stars, and plenty of hotcha stuff to decorate the frame (not to mention twirling cameras, which I admit I loved), detractors began to complain about its social issues: feminists labeled Emma Stone's character a weak woman who marries the jerk she ran away from, and cultural critics noted Gosling was a white man who saves jazz. (There are only a few African American musicians seen in silhouette or backgrounds, until John Legend is allowed to be the villain who stands in the way of pure jazz. Legend's character actually asks the most important plot question of the film, saying to Gosling, "How can you be revolutionary when you're a traditionalist?")

For film purists, the problem of *La La Land* lies in a question that's not asked, but that can be observed. When Emma Stone goes into her bedroom, a fragment of a movie poster with Ingrid Bergman's face has been enlarged on the wall. When Stone and her friends talk in front of it, Bergman steals the scene away from them. One look at her and it's clear why *La La Land*, an academic exercise, doesn't own your heart. Bergman, even on a poster, shines with the radiant light of a great film star. She was not a professional singer, but when she gave out with "See Me Dance the Polka" as a barmaid in the 1941 *Dr. Jekyll and Mr. Hyde*, she was everything a musical star should be. The song revealed her sexuality, her joie de vivre, and her openness to life. When Spencer Tracy spotted her behind the bar, bouncing up and down as she hummed along, his Hyde was cooked. Nothing like Ingrid Bergman or her sheer aliveness happens in *La La Land*. There isn't even any authenticity to Emma Stone's stated love of the old movies her aunt introduced her to, such as *Casablanca*. (Her aunt, a great movie fan, apparently never saw *Rebel Without a Cause*.)

And here lies a problem regarding the musical over time and history. Once the studio system—the old Hollywood—disappeared, changing into an international system that no longer kept superb musicians, composers, and arrangers under contract, that no longer nurtured real singers and dancers, and that no longer worked hard to locate and create stories that could be musicalized—it became much harder to make a musical. Fewer and fewer were made, and most of the ones that were kept to a simple tradition of Broadway adaptation, documentary, animation, or biopic. The original musical struggled to be original: to find young composers, relevant plots, and musical-performance stars.

It's an ironic truth that in 2016 one of the best musical numbers appeared in a spoof about old Hollywood, *Hail, Caesar!*, by Ethan and Joel Coen. In a full six-minute routine, the Coens managed to put on a fabulous re-creation of a 1950s dance number à la Gene Kelly, choreographed by Christopher Gattelli, who fully understood the style of the era. He created a hot tap that is more fun (and more authentic) than anything in *La La Land*. The setting is a bar called the Swingin' Dinghy, and the tappers are a bunch of sailors on leave, led by Channing Tatum. (The song is hilarious: "No Dames!") Tatum looks athletic, like Kelly, and the extended dance number includes sand dancing (using peanut shells), a broom for a partner (like Kelly with his mop in *Thousands Cheer*), swing dancing from the 1940s, and dancing on tables. The best part is that the creators had obviously seen *That's Entertainment!*, which showed how MGM shot one of Eleanor Powell's dance numbers. Powell was seen dancing on one part of the screen with the camera moving backwards, the stage being split apart and moved into place to accommodate her changes in direction. "No Dames!" is presented through this format: here's the dance, here's the dance being shot. Unlike the later *La La Land*, *Hail, Caesar!* pays homage to earlier movies and famous movie dancers without making it look like stealing or a weak imitation. The Coens and Gattelli make a number that is itself fresh and original, utterly humorous and satiric, and yet lovingly respectful. The difference seems to lie in the fact that, unlike the stars of *La La Land*, Tatum and company can really dance.*

Musicals are strange beasts, seemingly so predictable and yet so unexpected. In the summer of 2017, a violent crime movie about a getaway driver with wrecked eardrums appeared. It was called *Baby Driver*. The kid who drove could only do so if he wore an earpiece to control his tinnitus. He could listen to wild music and time his driving moves to the beat of the song. He shifts, he steers, he stomps on the brake. It's choreography. As a

---

* Tatum danced well in both *Step Up* and *Magic Mike*.

result, he and his car were the best dance team anyone had seen onscreen since Fred and Ginger, and the film turned out to be a musical of sorts—of sorts, I admit, but a musical. To sit in a movie seat and hear rhythm, watch editing and movement onscreen, all perfectly timed to the beats of the song—to see moves all coordinated like a perfectly mechanized dance movement—was a musical experience. *Baby Driver* was an original riff on the musical, an *action* musical, and a new way to go about showing people living to music in a real, cruel world with things stuck in their ears.

By the end of 2017, it was clear that both moviemakers and moviegoers still wanted musical performance. Some wanted nostalgia, as in *The Shape of Water,* when a mute woman and the fish she loves re-create "Let's Face the Music and Dance" from *Follow the Fleet* to express their commitment, and let's hope that's the last time someone decides it's a good idea to try to be Fred and Ginger. Others wanted a full-out, real, shakin' new musical with people who could tear it up singin' and dancing', as in *The Greatest Showman,* starring Hugh Jackman, Zendaya, Zac Efron, and Michelle Williams. Panned by most critics, *Showman* soared at the box office through word of mouth, proving audiences would think for themselves and embrace a film that had heart and a high level of musical skill.

In late 2018, a new musical with a great pedigree arrived in theaters: Hollywood's fourth version of *A Star Is Born,* and the third to be presented as a musical. Directed by Bradley Cooper and costarring him with the fabulous Lady Gaga, the movie received mixed reviews but took hold of the box office and held on, confidently expecting a slew of Oscar nominations in the style of its ancestors.* The new *Star* retells the familiar story of the famous guy heading downward, awash in booze and pills, who meets a blazingly talented young woman he mentors as she rises upward. They fall deeply in love but are on doomed reverse trajectories. Theirs is an intense, insular world of concert tours hermetically sealed off from natural behavior—a life of fans, arenas, airplanes, and hotel rooms. They represent the isolation of modern fame and talent, and one of them is going to have to die.

Cooper directed expertly in his debut at the helm. He created a film universe that sets up what moviegoers have seen in documentary-style concert films, but he takes them into its emotional interior. He upsets the male/female ratio of the story, giving himself more to do, including a "tough guy

---

* It did indeed receive eight nominations, but had only one win: Best Original Song, "Shallow," by Lady Gaga, Mark Ronson, Andrew Wyatt, and Anthony Rossomando.

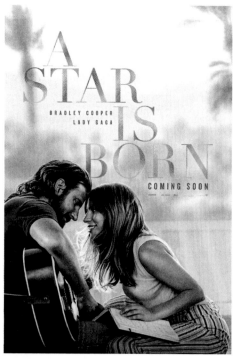

A Star Is Born . . . and born . . . and born . . . and born . . .

. . . with Janet Gaynor and Fredric March in 1937 . . .

. . . Judy Garland and James Mason in 1954 . . .

. . . Barbra Streisand and Kris Kristofferson in 1976 . . .

. . . and Bradley Cooper and Lady Gaga in 2018.

can weep" scene (the film is something of a male weepie, in fact). Cooper's good, but Gaga is terrific. She can really sing, and she lives up to the challenge of her predecessors, Garland and Streisand. As a singer, she's the real McCoy, and as an actress, she has no fear of emotion. She's both wildly erotic and glamorous (singing "La Vie en rose" in a drag club) as well as waiflike and insecure (in her love scenes).

Today's audiences are familiar with the star-making process, so *Star* had to be updated for a world in which a cheap form of instant stardom is available to anyone through the internet. (In the earlier films, the rise to stardom provided excitement and the trappings of renaming, selling, and redesigning were revealed.) *Star* 2018 shows that Lady Gaga, right up front in her first big number, knows how to transform herself to "star" on a Saturday night after she's done working. She goes to a drag club to play a role, and to appropriate a local form of stardom for herself.

A Star Is Born 2018 reminds an audience how really emotional and dramatic a good musical can be. It has honest-to-goodness stars who deliver what stars are supposed to deliver; and its music soars to depict two people whose love is born in music and lives through music. When Lady Gaga begins to commercialize her musical style, they fall apart.

And the beat goes on. Rami Malek wins the 2018 Oscar for Best Actor for portraying Freddie Mercury in the musical biopic, *Bohemian Rhapsody*.

The success of *A Star Is Born* indicated, at the end of 2018, that musicals were not just hanging around on the periphery to be tried out occasionally as a revival stunt. They might be back in all sorts of new ways. By Christmas, and the end of the year, *Mary Poppins Returns* was also in theaters, starring Lin-Manuel Miranda and Emily Blunt, and families were taking children to musicals, just like in the old days. All of a sudden, the genre was

part of everyday culture again—and critics like John Jurgensen, writing in *The Wall Street Journal*, were referring casually to "the recent rebirth of musicals in Hollywood." *Bohemian Rhapsody*, a biopic about Queen's Freddie Mercury, was winning awards, and the Coen brothers had begun their episodic (and underrated) *Ballad of Buster Scruggs* with Tim Blake Nelson singing to people and shooting at them as equally entertaining—and appropriate—acts. Early 2019 brought out a weird quasi-musical, *Climax*, from experimentalist Gaspar Noé, full of sex, violence, LSD, and young dancers executing some exciting choreography. The Elton John biopic, *Rocketman*, opened, soon followed by a live-action remake of *The Lion King;* the Aretha Franklin documentary, *Amazing Grace;* Danny Boyle's *Yesterday;* and Martin Scorsese's stunning mix of fact and fiction, *Rolling Thunder Review: A Bob Dylan Story by Martin Scorsese. Judy,* with Renée Zellweger as Garland, and a film version of *Cats* was underway. An experimental musical concept movie, *Waves*, was to be released in 2019. *Waves* would tell a story constructed around music, with the rhythm of editing dictating the rhythm of the story. A zombie musical was in the works, and a zombie version of any genre was a certain endorsement of box office potential. Who knew what the future might hold?

After watching ninety years of musical films, what do we know? In our everyday worlds, we don't sing to each other, nor do we dance down the streets. Okay, set aside couples dancing in the living room, old alums back for reunion week, families singing their favorite songs on car trips, drunken frat boys out in the streets. On a day-to-day basis, living our normal lives, going about our business, we do not sing to each other to express our feelings—"I love this cheese, Mr. Waiter, may I have more please?"—nor do we twirl along the streets in the rain. We are not living in a musical universe—a real piece of good luck for most of us.

Protagonists in the movie form known as "the musical," however, *are* living in a musical universe. They express their thoughts and feelings by singing and dancing. This means musicals as a movie story form have to be designated "unrealistic," or what my friend film historian Bob Smith dubbed "inherently anti-naturalistic." There are different types of musical stories (backstage, biography, Broadway adaptation, operetta, etc.), but no matter what type is on the screen, there always comes that moment: there's a sudden shift out of what we in the audience recognize as our behavior over to what we can recognize as musical-movie behavior. For some reason or no reason, a character starts to sing and/or dance. This is the difference between movies that are not musicals (or even movies that just have some musical moments in them) and the musical genre. We go from what we accepted as real to something we know is unreal, even though we knew when we sat down in our seats that the very first moment of the movie's "real" wasn't real, either. A movie may have dinosaurs, spaceships, talking dogs, cavemen, hair extensions, and even Bruce Willis, but we know how to accept the "real" that's defined. Musicals are different. They have to establish this first movie "real," and then they have to take us out of it to another "real," the world of musical performance. In the 1935 movie *Broadway Hostess*, Phil Regan tells Allen Jenkins he's been singing his love to Wini Shaw for years but she doesn't hear him. "Try talkin' instead of singing," Jenkins advises him. Musicals do the opposite: they try singing instead of talking. Audiences are asked to reverse their own daily reality.

Musicals have two layers: an established story world and an established musical-performance world. The first layer is constructed from what we know and have experienced either as our own behavior or as behavior we have seen in other movies: our regular moviegoing experience. Even in the most far-fetched, exploding-fireball, alien-creatures movies, we have ourselves felt the experiences generated by the story in our lives: getting scared, falling in love, visiting strange places. This first layer of movie magic is usually more than enough to entertain us. And it contains its own "release" or "escape"—two words often associated with movie watching. We can connect outside ourselves. We can be flown to the moon, kiss Grace Kelly, be miniaturized, go into the past, walk the streets of Paris, ride wagons west . . . But when in any of these experiences or places we find people singing and dancing, the movie has introduced us to a second layer. That second layer is constructed for us out of experience we don't have, can't have—or aren't having. This is the gift of the musical: the second layer, the inner reality, the musical world within the first layer of the movie world. Musical characters are living in a world of musical performance, and the viewer is transported accordingly from a "real" world to that world, whether there's a logical explanation for it or not. This "layering" is not restricted to the so-called "artistic" musicals: All musicals transition from dialogue to song, or movement to dance, in some way, even if it's just "And now Fred Astaire, who plays a dancer, is going to do a number for his audience in his new Broadway show, and we'll watch him do it." An excuse is given for why he will sing and dance—it's his job—and we'll move into that job performance with him. The history of the movie musical reveals how this process evolved to include not only the ordinary (a backstage musical) but also a specifically delineated world of inner feelings, including a dream sequence or a "thinking" or imagining process.*

Because of this moving in and out of narrative space—layering—musicals are all about structure. They have to accomplish a story presentation that combines musical and nonmusical elements in a seamless way. They are constantly challenged not only by the need for plot, believable characters, motivations, etc., but also by the need to find a reason for someone singing and dancing. They need to justify musical performance and find a way to transition in and out of the performance mode. Over time, audiences became conditioned to the transitions, and often accepted some very sophisticated variations of it without wondering where they were or what was happening.

In the end, we can see that the issues driving the musical never change; only the attitude taken toward them by filmmakers changes. There's never been anything more closely integrated regarding music, plot, and characters than *Love Me Tonight* or *One Hour with You*. There's never been music that surpasses Gershwin, Berlin, Kern, Rodgers, Porter, et al. There have never been better performers than Garland, Astaire, Kelly, and never better directors than Minnelli, Donen, Walters, Lubitsch, and Mamoulian. Nobody creates more innovative choreography than Jack Cole, Hermes Pan, Bob Fosse, and Busby Berkeley. No musical movie is more straightforwardly unpretentious and entertaining than *Easter Parade, Royal Wedding,* or *Summer Stock*. None is more successfully arty for a mass market than *An American in Paris*. None has a more original premise than *Les Girls* (the *Rashomon* of musicals), etc., etc. The musical remains what it became: a stylized representation of life, where "reality" is presented not through the actions normally associated with everyday life but through musical numbers, the act of singing and dancing. A different mode of reality is established, a reality of music, where feelings, emotions, ideas are given to an audience through song and dance. The old musicals were smart enough to know that.

Who today can outsmart the old musical? Who wants to try?

Someone, I hope.

---

* On an episode of his TV show in 1964, Jack Benny presented a comedy "hillbilly musical." When a character asks him why Connie Francis is suddenly singing, Benny gives the appropriate answer: "When you're doing a musical, you've gotta put a song in it someplace."

Acknowledgments

I must begin by thanking all the talented people in Hollywood, both behind the scenes and in front of the camera, who filled my life with the joy of musical films from my earliest movie-going days onward. I regret there were so many fabulous musical moments I had no space to discuss: Astaire dancing on the ceiling, Kelly making music with his loafers and a newspaper, Bobby Van jump-dancing across a small-town terrain, Judy Garland urging me to "get happy," etc., etc. I had no room for details on *Royal Wedding*, *Easter Parade*, *Lady in the Dark*, *Take Me Out to the Ball Game*, *Two Weeks with Love*, *Good News* (1947), or *Excuse My Dust*, not to mention deranged oddities such as *A Matter of Time* (1976), directed by Vincente Minnelli, starring his Liza alongside Ingrid Bergman and her daughter, Isabella Rossellini . . . or *Bugsy Malone* (also from 1976, prime-time for weird musicals), a creepy satire on gangster films populated with kid stars, toy cars, guns filled with whipped cream instead of bullets . . . and perhaps the craziest musical of them all, a short from MGM's unbelievable *Dogville* series in which canines are seen plonking on pianos with paws, getting up on hind legs to prance around in top hats and little spats, strutting in spangles and dangling earrings, and, because it *is* from MGM, executing a perfect chorus line in rain coats and hats for a "Singin' in the Rain" grand finale. (Well, it hurts to ignore stuff like that!)

I have many people to thank:

—Lea Carlson, who has worked with me for nearly twenty years and has become a dear friend as well as a supportive colleague. Nothing I do could ever get finished—or be any good at all—without her wise counsel.

—The colleagues I have at Wesleyan University, who make the daily task of dissecting movies a joy: Steve Collins, Scott Higgins, Marc Longenecker, Leo Lensing, Sadia Shepard, and Michael Slowik, whose book on the transition to sound was the best I read on the topic, and the piano-playing President of Wesleyan, Michael Roth, who not only teaches film but is a Fred Astaire fan, two key requirements for a good college president.

—Archivists Joan Miller of the Wesleyan Cinema Archives, Mary Huelsbeck of the Wisconsin Center for Film and Theatre Research, and the ever-reliable and generous Howard Mandelbaum and his wonderful team at Photofest, who helped me on the weekends when I was working from South Dakota.

—The team of professional and supportive people at Alfred A. Knopf, who worked hard to produce a beautiful book, including Marc Jaffee, Kevin Bourke, Maggie Hinders, Carol Devine Carson, and Roméo Enriquez.

—Logan Ludwig and my son-in-law Robert Jahrling, who transferred my crude typing to computers with accuracy and skill, and who, along with my daughter, Savannah, helped with basic research.

—Jay Fishback, who took my book jacket photo, and Barb and Van and all the Fishback family (including Nadine), who are dear friends and neighbors who have given us so much fun, good food, good times, and good conversation, and who helped me on this book more than they know.

—Earl Hess and Pratibha Dabholkar, who may be surprised to be thanked, but the cover of their book on *Singin' in the Rain* inspired me to use it myself!

I have been lucky in life to have made literally hundreds of loyal and delightful friends. Those who shared ideas and kept me laughing and moving forward for this particular book include Sam Wasson (author of the definitive *Fosse* and the source of much inspiration), David Laub of A24, Ed Decter, Larry Mark, Jeffrey Lane, Jeremy Arnold, Domenica Cameron-Scorsese, Owen Renfroe, Conor and Tyler Byrne, Bob Smith (who is a genius about musicals), Michael Geragatelis, Teresa Weaver, Richard Teller (the best real-life dancer), and David Kendall (Czar of Obscure Recorded Music), and ever so many more. I am also grateful to good critics like David Thomson, A. O. Scott, the late Richard Schickel, Leonard, Alice, and Jessie Maltin; movie directors who love old films, like Alexander Payne, Marty

Scorsese, and Clint Eastwood; colleagues from the American Film Institute (Bob Gazzale, who owes me the world's largest hamburger), Jean Firstenberg, Bob Daly, Tom Pollack, George Stevens Jr., Jon Avnet, and more; and Annie Schuloff of the National Board of Review. My good fortune includes having had the chance to meet and talk about their movies with many of the stars I loved over the years, among them Betty Grable, June Haver, Fred Astaire, Gene Kelly, and Hermes Pan. Thanks also go to Ava Astaire McKenzie and Patricia Ward Kelly for their amazing insights.

To have been able to work with the brilliant Bob Gottlieb for over thirty-five years has been my privilege and my very, very good fortune. No one has ever made me laugh any harder, and no one has ever taught me more. He knows everything about everything, and he puts up with me. I am grateful.

I have dedicated this book to my daughter and granddaughter and thanked my son-in-law for his help, so my final family thanks go to my husband, John. I first saw him on a bright and sunny fall day. I was coming up a hill and he was coming down, but I was plodding along, and he was . . . well . . . he was singing and dancing, oblivious to the dubious (and even slightly terrified) looks he was getting from passers-by. He was happy in his music and in his own definition of reality, which just happened to be the one I had thought could exist only in the movies. As I stood and watched, he sailed by, crossing the street to leap over a fire hydrant, take three twirls, and then roll on, never missing a beat. In my head I heard a song title from the 1945 *State Fair*, the only musical ever written directly for the screen by Rodgers and Hammerstein: "That's for Me." I was right.

Bibliography

American Cinematographer. Vol. 63, no. 1. January 1982. Issue on *One from the Heart*.

The American Film Institute Catalog: Feature Films, 1931–1940. Patricia King Hanson, executive editor. 3 vols. Berkeley, Los Angeles, Oxford: University of California Press, 1993.

Anderson, John Murray. *Out Without My Rubbers: The Memoirs of John Murray Anderson, as Told to and Written by Hugh Abercrombie Anderson*. New York: Library Publishers, 1954.

Astaire, Fred. *Steps in Time*. New York: Harper, 1959; Da Capo Press, 1961.

Barrios, Richard. *A Song in the Dark: The Birth of the Musical Film*. New York: Oxford University Press, 1995.

Basinger, Jeanine. *Gene Kelly*. New York: Pyramid, 1976.

———. *Shirley Temple*. New York: Pyramid, 1975.

Brideson, Cynthia and Sara. *He's Got Rhythm: The Life and Career of Gene Kelly*. Lexington: University of Kentucky Press, 2017.

Brown, Peter Harry, and Pat H. Broeske. *Down at the End of Lonely Street: The Life and Death of Elvis Presley*. Harmondsworth, UK: Dutton, 1997.

Carey, Gary. *All the Stars in Heaven: Louis B. Mayer's MGM*. New York: Dutton, 1981.

Connor, Jim. *Ann Miller: Tops in Taps*. New York: Franklin Watts, 1971.

Croce, Arlene. *The Fred Astaire and Ginger Rogers Book*. New York: Vintage, 1972.

Delamater, Jerome. *Dance in the Hollywood Musical*. Studies in Photography and Cinematography, no. 4. Ann Arbor: University of Michigan Press, 1981.

Eyman, Scott. *Ernst Lubitsch: Laughter in Paradise*. New York: Simon & Schuster, 1993.

Feuer, Jane. *The Hollywood Musical*. Bloomington: Indiana University Press, 1972.

Finler, Joel W. *The Hollywood Story*. New York: Crown, 1988.

Fordin, Hugh. *The World of Entertainment!: Hollywood's Greatest Musicals*. Garden City, NY: Doubleday, 1975.

Freedland, Michael. *Al Jolson*. New York: Stein and Day, 1972.

Fricke, John. *Judy Garland: A Portrait in Art and Anecdote*. New York: Bulfinch Press, 2003.

Friedwald, Will. *A Biographical Guide to the Great Jazz and Pop Singers*. New York: Pantheon Books, 2010.

———. *The Great Jazz and Pop Vocal Albums*. New York: Pantheon Books, 2017.

———. *Sinatra! The Song Is You: A Singer's Art*. New York: Scribner, 1995.

Fumento, Rocco, ed. *42nd Street*. Wisconsin/Warner Bros. Screenplays. Madison: University of Wisconsin Press, 1980.

Furia, Philip, and Laurie Patterson. *The Songs of Hollywood*. Oxford and New York: Oxford University Press, 2010.

Gallafent, Edward. *Astaire and Rogers*. Film and Culture series, ed. John Belton. New York: Columbia University Press, 2002.

Garrett, Betty, with Ron Rapoport. *Betty Garrett and Other Songs; A Life on Stage and Screen*. Lanham, NY: Madison Books, 1998.

Giddins, Gary. *Bing Crosby: A Pocketful of Dreams—The Early Years, 1903–1940*. Boston: Little, Brown, 2001.

———. *Bing Crosby: Swinging on a Star—The War Years, 1940–1946*. Boston: Little, Brown, 2018.

Gilvey, John Anthony. *Before the Parade Passes By: Gower Champion and the Glorious American Musical*. New York: St. Martin's Press, 2005.

Goldman, Herbert G. *Banjo Eyes: Eddie Cantor and the Birth of Modern Stardom*. New York: Oxford University Press, 1997.

———. *Jolson: The Legend Comes to Life*. New York: Oxford University Press, 1988.

Grant, Barry Keith. *The Hollywood Film Musical*. West Sussex: Wiley-Blackwell, 2012.

Green, Stanley, and Burt Goldblatt. *Starring Fred Astaire*. New York: Dodd, Mead, 1973.

Guralnick, Peter. *Last Train to Memphis: The Rise of Elvis Presley*. New York: Little, Brown, 1994.

Harvey, Stephen. *Directed by Vincente Minnelli*. New York: Museum of Modern Art/Harper & Row, 1989.

Henie, Sonja. *Wings on My Feet*. New York: Prentice Hall, 1940.

Hess, Earl J., and Pratibha A. Dabholkar. *The Cinematic Voyage of "The Pirate": Kelly, Garland, and Minnelli at Work*. Columbia: University of Missouri Press, 2014.

———. *"Singin' in the Rain": The Making of an American Masterpiece*. Lawrence: University Press of Kansas, 2009.

Hirschhorn, Clive. *Gene Kelly*. Chicago: Henry Regnery, 1974.

Hoberman, J. "Wisecracks in Drag and Blackface in Eddie Cantor 4-Film Collection." *New York Times*, July 9, 2015.

Hotchner, A. E. *Doris Day: Her Own Story*. New York: William Morrow, 1987.

Hudson, Scott. "David Bowie and Bing Crosby." *Argus Leader (Sioux Falls, SD) Entertainment Guide*, July 23, 2015.

Jenkins, Henry. *What Made Pistachio Nuts? Early Sound Comedy and the Vaudeville Aesthetic*. New York: Columbia University Press, 1992.

Kaplan, James. *Sinatra: The Chairman*. New York: Doubleday, 2008.

Kaufman, David. *Doris Day: The Untold Story of the Girl Next Door*. New York: Random House, 2008.

Kellow, Brian. *Ethel Merman*. New York: Viking, 2007.

Kelly, Gene. "Dialogue on Film," recorded at the American Film Institute, published in vol. 4, no. 4 (February 1979): 33–44. AFI Archives.

Knox, Donald. *The Magic Factory: How MGM Made "An American in Paris."* New York: Praeger, 1973.

Kreuger, Miles, ed. *The Movie Musical: From Vitaphone to 42nd Street, as Reported in a Great Fan Magazine*. New York: Dover, 1975.

Kreuger, Miles. *"Show Boat": The Story of a Classic American Musical*. Oxford University Press, 1977.

Layton, James, and David Pierce. *King of Jazz: Paul Whiteman's Technicolor Revue*. Severn, MD: Media History Press, 2016.

Lertzman, Richard A., and William J. Birnes. *The Life and Times of Mickey Rooney*. New York: Gallery Books, 2015.

Lev, Peter. *Twentieth Century–Fox: The Zanuck-Skouras Years, 1935–1965*. Austin: University of Texas Press, 2013.

Levinson, Peter J. *Puttin' on the Ritz: Fred Astaire and the Fine Art of Panache—A Biography*. New York: St. Martin's Press, 2009.

Levy, Emanuel. *Vincente Minnelli: Hollywood's Dark Dreamer*. New York: St. Martin's Press, 2009.

Maltin, Leonard. *The Great Movie Shorts: Those Wonderful One- and Two-Reelers of the Thirties and Forties*. New York: Bonanza Books, 1972.

———. "On Gold Diggers of 1933." *Movie Crazy* no. 21 (summer 2007), 1–15.

———. *Hooked on Hollywood: Discoveries from a Lifetime of Film Fandom*. Pittsburgh, PA: Good-Knight Books, 2018.

Mann, William J. *Hello, Gorgeous: Becoming Barbra Streisand*. New York: Houghton Mifflin Harcourt, 2012.

Martin, Tony, and Cyd Charisse, as told to Dick Kleiner. *The Two of Us*. New York: Mason/Charter, 1976.

Marx, Harpo, with Rowland Barber. *Harpo Speaks*! New York: Proscenium Publishers, 1985; originally published by Bernard Geis, 1962.

Mast, Gerald. *Can't Help Singin': The American Musical on Stage and Screen*. Woodstock, NY: Overlook Press, 1987.

McBride, Joseph. *How Did Lubitsch Do It?* New York: Columbia University Press, 2018.

Milne, Tom. *Mamoulian*. Bloomington: Indiana University Press, 1969.

Minnelli, Vincente, with Hector Arce. *I Remember It Well*. Garden City, NY: Doubleday, 1974.

Morley, Sheridan, and Ruth Leon. *Gene Kelly: A Celebration*. London: Pavilion Books, 1996.

Mueller, John. *Astaire Dancing: The Musical Films*. New York: Knopf, 1985.

Naremore, James. *The Films of Vincente Minnelli*. New York: Cambridge University Press, 1993.

O'Brien, Daniel. *The Frank Sinatra Film Guide*. London: B. T. Batsford, 1998.

Pasternak, Joe. *Easy the Hard Way: The Autobiography of Joe Pasternak*. New York: Putnam, 1956.

Phillips, Brent. *Charles Walters: The Director Who Made Hollywood Dance*. Lexington: University Press of Kentucky, 2014.

Pike, Bob, and Dave Martin. *The Genius of Busby Berkeley*. Reseda, CA: EFA Books/Creative Film Society, 1973.

Powell, Jane. *The Girl Next Door . . . And How She Grew*. New York: William Morrow, 1987.

Prigozy, Ruth. *The Life of Dick Haymes: No More Little White Lies*. Jackson: University Press of Mississippi, 2006.

Riley, Kathleen. *The Astaires: Fred & Adele*. New York: Oxford University Press, 2012.

Rubin, Martin. *Showstoppers: Busby Berkeley and the Tradition of Spectacle*. New York: Columbia University Press, 1993.

Santopietro, Tom. *Considering Doris Day: A Biography*. New York: Thomas Dunne Books, St. Martin's Press, 2007.

———. *The Importance of Being Barbra*. New York: Thomas Dunne Books, St. Martin's Press, 2006.

———. *Sinatra in Hollywood*. New York: Thomas Dunne Books, St. Martin's Press, 2008.

———. *The "Sound of Music" Story*. New York: Thomas Dunne Books, St. Martin's Press, 2015.

Schickel, Richard. *The Disney Version: The Life, Times, Art and Commerce of Walt Disney*. Chicago: Ivan R. Dee, 1997.

Sennett, Ted. *Hollywood Musicals*. New York: Harry N. Abrams, 1981.

Siegel, Joel. "The Pirate." *Film Heritage*, vol. 7, no. 1 (fall 1971), 21–32.

Silverman, Stephen M. *Dancing on the Ceiling: Stanley Donen and His Movies*. New York: Knopf, 1996.

Slowik, Michael. *After the Silents: Hollywood Film Music in the Early Sound Era, 1926–1934*. Film and Culture Series, John Belton, ed. New York: Columbia University Press, 2014.

Strait, Raymond, with Leif Henie. *Queen of Ice, Queen of Shadows: The Unsuspected Life of Sonja Henie*. New York: Stein & Day, 1985.

Tannenbaum, Rob, and Craig Marks. *I Want My MTV: The Uncensored Story of the Music Video Revolution*. New York: Plume, 2011.

Taylor, John Russell, and Arthur Jackson. *The Hollywood Musical*. New York: McGraw-Hill, 1971.

Thomas, Tony. *Harry Warren and the Hollywood Musical*. New York: Citadel Press, 1975.

Tormé, Mel. *The Other Side of the Rainbow with Judy Garland on the Dawn Patrol*. New York: Morrow, 1970.

Warren, Doug. *Betty Grable: The Reluctant Movie Queen*. New York: St. Martin's Press, 1974.

Wasson, Sam. *Fosse*. New York: An Eamon Dolan Book, Houghton Mifflin Harcourt, 2013.

Whitburn, Joel. *The Billboard Book of Top 40 Hits*, 9th edition. New York: Billboard Books, 2010.

Williams, Esther, with Digby Diehl. *The Million Dollar Mermaid: An Autobiography*. New York: Simon & Schuster, 1999.

Zimmerman, Paul D., and Burt Goldblatt. *The Marx Brothers at the Movies*. New York: G. P. Putnam's Sons, 1968.

Index

Page numbers in *italics* refer to illustrations.

Buck Privates, 306
Buffy the Vampire Slayer (TV show), 560
Bugsy Malone, 579
Bundle of Joy, 332
Burke, Billie, 427
Burke, Joe, 413
Burke, Johnny, 154
Burks, Robert, 542
Burlesque, 572
Burlesque (Hopkins and Watters), 53
Burnett, Carol, 183–84, 240, 485
Burns, George, 29, 130–31, 141, 188, 255
Burton, Richard, 483
Buscemi, Steve, 571
Busse, Henry, 302
Butler, David, 44n
"But Not for Me," 266, 272
Butterfield, Billy, 165
Button, Dick, 466n
"By a Waterfall," 41, 100
Bye Bye Birdie, 176
Byington, Spring, 353
"By Myself," 449–51
Byrne, David, 547
By the Light of the Silvery Moon, 200

Caan, James, 496
Cabaret, 114n, 516–21, 519, 524, 527
Cabaret (Broadway show), 517–18, 520
Cabin in the Sky, 14, 338n, 430, 446, 447, 572–73
Cabot, Bruce, 324
Café Metropole, 231
Cagney, James, 11, 40–41, 101, 200, 204, 205, 278–81, 280, 282, 284–86, 289–90, 358, 462n, 579
Cahn, Sammy, 156, 161, 199, 412
Calamity Jane, 6, 200, 203, 206, 411n
Calendar Girl, 306
Callender, Red, 542
Call Me Lucky (Crosby), 169
Call Me Madam, 192, 401–3
Calloway, Cab, 15, 17, 120n, 124, 318, 543, 573
Camelot, 482–83, 493
camera: Astaire and, 71–73, 76, 79; Berkeley and, 51–52, 71–73, 87, 92, 94, 95–96; close-ups, 38–39, 42; dance and, 48–49; early, 37–38; faked close-ups, 20; hand-held, 114–15; Henie's ice skating

and, 232–34; innovations in Sunny Side Up, 41–42; Jolson and, 119; kaleidoscopic overhead shot, 38, 52; Kelly and, 462, 474; liberation of, 65–66; Love Parade and new meanings, 49; multiple, 71; overhead shots, 87, 89–91, 94, 95, 122; zoom shots, 69n
Camille, 238
Can-Can, 159, 161, 481
Cancel My Reservation, 167n
Cannonball Run II, 161n
Canova, Judy, 309–11
Cansino, Angel, 465
Cansino, Eduardo, 256
Cantor, Eddie, 51, 56–57, 86–87, 89–92, 96, 131–36, 131–33, 135, 140, 163, 189, 192, 311, 360n, 404–5
Capra, Frank, 33–34, 65, 69n, 144, 151–53, 218n
Captain January, 366–68, 368
Captains Courageous, 3
Career Girl, 308
Carefree, 251, 253
Carey, Mariah, 571
Carlisle, Kitty, 137
Carmen, 146, 315, 317
Carmen Jones, 315, 572
Carmichael, Hoagy, 153, 412
Carminati, Tullio, 243, 316–17
Carnegie Hall, 316
Carnera, Primo, 13–14
Caron, Leslie, 81, 85, 255, 332, 410, 468–72, 468, 471, 479, 480–81
Carousel, 160, 343–44, 346–48, 347
Carousel (Broadway show), 65n, 343, 346–47
Carradine, John, 191
Carroll, Earl, 19n
Carroll, Joan, 437
Carroll, John, 183
Carroll, Nancy, 52–54, 53
Carson, Jack, 156, 196, 202–3, 322, 358, 569–70
Carter, June, 296, 547
Casablanca, 12, 196, 587
Castle, Nick, 229
Cat and the Fiddle, The, 240
Catlett, Sidney, 542
Cats, 593
Caulfield, Joan, 154, 256
Cavanaugh, Page, 196

ILLUSTRATION CREDITS

The images on the following pages courtesy of Wisconsin Center for Film and Theater Research: 82, top right; 156; 158; 159; 281; 320, top and bottom; 321; 340; 372; 402; 436; 460; 498.

The images on the following pages courtesy of Wesleyan University Center for Film Studies, collection of Jeanine Basinger: 53; 93; 285, bottom; 361; 429; 453; 519; 541; 542; 547.

All other images courtesy of Photofest.

A NOTE ON THE TYPE

This book was set in Fournier, a typeface named for Pierre Simon Fournier *le jeune* (1712–1768), a celebrated French type designer. Coming from a family of typefounders, Fournier was an extraordinarily prolific designer of typefaces and of typographic ornaments. He was also the author of the important Manuel typographique (1764–1766), in which he attempted to work out a system standardizing type measurement in points, a system that is still in use internationally.

Fournier's type is considered transitional in that it drew its inspiration from the old style, yet was ingeniously innovational, providing for an elegant, legible appearance. In 1925 his type was revived by the Monotype Corporation of London.

Composed by North Market Street Graphics, Lancaster, Pennsylvania
Printed and bound by LSC Communications, Crawfordsville, Indiana
Designed by Maggie Hinders